D0938688

PSYCHIATRY AND THE CULTS

SECTS AND CULTS IN AMERICA
BIBLIOGRAPHICAL GUIDES
(General Editor: J. Gordon Melton)
(Vol. 10)

GARLAND REFERENCE LIBRARY
OF SOCIAL SCIENCE
(Vol. 349)

BIBLIOGRAPHIES ON SECTS AND CULTS IN AMERICA
(General Editor: J. Gordon Melton)

PSYCHIATRY AND THE CULTS
An Annotated Bibliography

John A. Saliba

GARLAND PUBLISHING, INC. • NEW YORK & LONDON
1987

Library of Congress Cataloging-in-Publication Data

Saliba, John A.
Psychiatry and the Cults.

(Sects and Cults in America. Bibliographical guides;
vol. 10) (Garland Reference Library of Social Science;
vol. 349)
Bibliography: p.
Includes indexes.
1. Cults–United States–Indexes.   2. Sects—United
States–Indexes.   3. Psychiatry and religion–Indexes.
I. Title.   II. Series: Sects and Cults in America.
Bibliographical guides; v. 10.   III. Series: Garland
Reference Library of Social Science; v. 349.

Z7834.U6S24   1987   [BL2525]   016.291   87-19668
ISBN 0-8240-8586-8

Printed on acid-free, 250-year-life paper
Manufactured in the United States of America

To my sister, Marlene

CONTENTS

ACKNOWLEDGMENTS

Many people deserve and have my appreciation for their aid in making this book possible. I am indebted, in particular, to Sue and John Ditsky who made invaluable editorial suggestions and undertook the unrewarding task of proofreading the manuscript through its many stages; to William Ghesquiere who not only helped with the correction of typing mistakes, but also provided many insightful comments which improved the text considerably; to Violette H. Geiger for proofreading the manuscript in its later stages; and to Janice Grey for her professional reading of the final draft. Special thanks are due to the reference librarians at the University of Detroit, particularly Joyce Kordyban, for their patient assistance in tracing many of the books and articles quoted in this bibliography, and to the University of Detroit for a year's Sabbatical leave, during which most of the research was completed.

PREFACE

THE NATURE AND SCOPE OF THIS STUDY

The presence of new religious movements in the West in the second
half of the twentieth century has become a cause for concern in many
segments of society. The dangers of cultism have made the headlines
in popular magazines and newspapers, been vehemently debated in public conferences, academic meetings, and professional journals, and
been argued convincingly in the courtrooms. The discussion in psychological and psychiatric literature has had an impact that goes far
beyond its academic boundaries. It occupies, in fact, an influential role in the public forum and has figured prominently in many
litigations throughout the country.

One of the universal questions about the cults has been a psychological one: are they a sign that those who join them suffer from
intellectual, mental, and/or emotional disorders, or do they actually
cause such abnormalities? Is membership in a cult socially detrimental, making its members unable to relate to their parents and
peers? The searching question, which is being addressed in professional literature, is whether the new religious movements, cults,
or spiritual revivals are a sign of serious pathology. Does participation in them lead to personality problems? Does membership
aggravate any previous psychological weaknesses? Or are they just
different, although somewhat unusual, expressions of religious fervor
and behavior, which are common to all religions and which have made
an appearance in diverse cultures throughout the history of the human
race? Or do these new movements have, on the contrary, some therapeutic value? Are they a form of alternate therapy in an age marked
by rapid social change and cross-cultural contacts? Do they, in the
long run, contribute to the growing-up processes, the life-transi-
tions, the solution of crises, and the sociocultural adaptation of
some people? Do they cater to the many needs, religious and otherwise, of their committed members?

These fundamental questions have been operative in the accumula-
tion of this annotated bibliography, which is intended primarily as
a reference guide for psychiatrists and counselors who advise cult
members, ex-cult members and their bewildered parents, and lawyers
who use psychiatric arguments in the courts. The opposing viewpoints, expressed in the books and articles quoted in the following
pages, convey the message to psychiatrists and lawyers alike that,
contrary to public opinion and to some statements made in courts of
law, decisions about cults and cult members are not easily reached
nor universally accepted.

Assumptions of This Study.

Several assumptions have guided the compilation of this bibliography and its arrangement. The first postulate deals with the
definition of a cult. We have opted for a sociologically-oriented
view of a cult which is free from religious evaluation of its theological orthodoxy, and from psychological judgments on the nature
and effects of cultism. A cult is simply a religious and/or spiritual
group which is marginal in a society and which is considered out of
the mainstream by the majority of people. This definition avoids
arguments about the religious or pseudo-religious nature of the
cults, an issue which may be theological rather than psychological.
Cults are religious when they either 1) stem from spiritual traditions, Eastern or Western, which have been generally recognized as
"religious" by most scholars in the academic field of religious
studies; and/or 2) adhere to beliefs and rituals which are, as a rule,
listed as religious in the academic field. Thus, to give a few representative examples, the Hare Krishna Movement and Yoga institutes
or ashrams are examples of religious groups because they have their
roots in Hinduism. Those cults or sects which center around the
belief in the so-called Ascended Masters, like the Church Universal
and Triumphant, can be considered religious because many of their
beliefs (for instance, in the afterlife) are integral to most
religious systems. In like manner, those groups which believe that
flying saucers will be coming to save humankind from its present
state of affairs are religious because of their millennial dreams
and their conviction that spiritual beings will soon be coming to
our rescue. Consequently, those cultic groups whose focus has been
political or social have not been included in this volume unless
they have been judged to contribute directly to the questions under
investigation.

Another assumption is that the psychiatric examination of the
cults should take seriously into account the cultural and historical settings in which they flourish. The new movements, even if
they possess unique features which have never been recorded in the
history of religions, are not isolated incidents in the latter half
of the twentieth century. They have to be understood in relation
to similar phenomena both in Western history and in other cultures.
The diachronic and synchronic perspectives of the new movements
throw light not only on the nature of "cultism," but also on the kind
of religious, social, or psychological response one might adopt towards cults and their individual members and, consequently, on the
type of advice given to those who have recourse to counseling
professionals.

One final assumption behind this bibliography is that the problems which the cults have allegedly brought into being should be
put into the context of the psychology of religion. Many psychologists and psychiatrists writing on the new movements have been
working, to a large degree, from a traditionally Western, often
Freudian, approach to religious beliefs and practices. One can,
therefore, compare their psychological evaluation of cults with that
of traditional churches and religious communities. Other scholars,
who have pursued the relatively new field of cross-cultural psychology

and psychotherapy, are in the process of developing quite a different
approach to the psychology of religion, an approach which might lead
them to a very different appraisal of the new movements.

Divisions of the Bibliography.

With these conditions in mind, the task of selecting and ordering the material becomes more manageable. Apart from Chapter One,
which lists the sources used in compiling this bibliography, three
major chapters covering the historical, cross-cultural, and contemporary dimensions, comprise the bulk of cited works. Chapter Two
annotates those works on the cults and related topics before 1973,
when the current controversy arose. Here the material will be
divided into four parts. The first will deal with religion, psychology, and psychiatry, and will list major works on the psychology of
religion and studies on conversion, religious experience, and mysticism. Part Two will take up the problem of the relationship between
religion and mental health, one of the foremost concerns in psychology and theology for over half a century. Part Three will comprise
generic studies on sects and cults. Part Four will concentrate on
studies of individual cultic movements. The first two parts give
the necessary background material and include some works on Christianity and Judaism; the third and fourth parts contain studies on
cults, sects, and other religious groups. The material sometimes
overlaps, since an essay on religion and mental health might contain
references to both traditional churches and to sects and cults.

Chapter Three deals with cults or new religious movements in
non-Western societies. The material is divided, for easy reference,
into three parts. The first part consists of introductory material
on cross-cultural psychiatry and psychotherapy as well as general
works and specific studies on folk psychiatry in different parts of
the world. The second is dedicated to studies of individual religious movements. And the third contains material on shamanism and
related phenomena. As in the previous sections, it is not always
possible to divide the material into tight compartments. In spite
of their somewhat arbitrary nature, the divisions of this chapter
correspond roughly to three areas of cultic interest found in current
psychology and psychiatry in the West, namely: 1) theoretical assessment of the psychological significance of the new movements and of
the psychiatric issues they have brought to the fore; 2) investigation into the psychodynamic processes which operate in individual
groups; and 3) psychological evaluation of cult leaders.

Chapter Four deals with contemporary writings and takes into
account those essays and books published since 1973. This year
seems to mark the blossoming of the psychiatric controversy about
the relationship between cultic involvement and mental health.
PSYCHOLOGICAL ABSTRACTS began including an index reference to
"cultism" for the first time in 1973, an innovation that indicates,
if nothing else, the growing awareness of the erupting debate in
the psychological disciplines. As in the previous chapters, this
one will also be subdivided into several topical parts for easy reference and consultation. Part One will embrace research on religion

and psychology, religious experience and mysticism, and the relationship between religion and mental health. Part Two will list comprehensive studies on the cultic phenomenon, which include overviews of
cults, professional advice on how to counsel those involved, works
on Eastern psychologies which provide background information on the
main theme of this study, and material on New Age healings which
have been frequently linked with cultic attitudes and behavior.
Part Three will deal with specific cults, including the various
forms of meditation and Yoga, charismatic groups, and Eastern and
other cultic movements. Finally, Part Four will focus on the brain-
washing/deprogramming controversy and the related subject of religious conversion.

Areas Left Out.

    Many factors, particularly those of space, impose limitations on
the works cited. One vast area left out is the voluminous publications on the relationship between religion and theology and the
psychological disciplines, an area which has occupied an important
place in the academic world ever since the rise of psychology as an
independent academic subject. The interest in this relation has not
subsided, but has rather increased, as witnessed by the emergence of
journals like the JOURNAL OF RELIGION AND HEALTH and, more recently,
the JOURNAL OF PSYCHOLOGY AND JUDAISM, the JOURNAL OF PSYCHOLOGY AND
THEOLOGY, and the JOURNAL OF PSYCHOLOGY AND CHRISTIANITY. Topics
like the development of adolescent religion, drugs and religious experience, the parapsychological effects, real or putative, of certain
spiritual or religious exercises often advanced as ways of improving
one's psychic ability, and the purely physiological effects of certain religious techniques (like meditation) have been omitted, even
though they may at times be linked with the principal theme of this
bibliography.

Works Cited.

    The selection of works in this bibliography has been confined
to books and articles in professional journals. Dissertations and
newspaper and magazine articles are therefore omitted. Besides
considerations of space, we discovered that a healthy rationale
favored such limitations. The best dissertations usually end up
published either in book or in article form, while newspaper and
magazine articles, more often than not, reflect scholarly theories
and research already made public in scientific journals. We have
also tended to concentrate on materials in academic journals because
this is where the exchange of views on the psychological effects of
the cults is best represented and where the bulk of the research
results has been published. Consequently, we have largely omitted
material which has appeared in the so-called alternative periodicals
and which has been published by the cults themselves. Exceptions to
this rule have been made when the works in question have been deemed
valuable for understanding the topic under discussion. Thus, from
an anthropological point of view, this bibliography leans towards
the etic rather than the emic approach to the psychology and
psychiatry of the new religious movements.

The material in this bibliography has further been restricted
to publications in the English language which are available in the
United States. The time span covered begins with the late nineteenth
century and ends with the year 1985.

Type of Annotations.

The annotations are largely descriptive of the works cited, but
are deliberately written to provide information about the authors'
views relevant to this study. Where necessary, for instance in the
Sources, an attempt has been made to evaluate the usefulness of the
materials for research purposes. All the books and articles listed
have been read or consulted. An attempt has been made to present a
comprehensive coverage of available literature. When this has not
been possible, special attention has been taken to include differing
perspectives, views, and positions on the phenomenon of cults.

In the Introduction, we have presented an overall evaluative
survey of the psychiatric discussion on the cults, while at the
beginning of the various sections we have endeavored to summarize
the major trends of the works cited and to offer occasional comments
on their contribution to the study of cultism.

There is one major practical problem which psychiatrists and
psychologists face in the wake of the cults, namely, that the majority
of them have not been given sufficient training in religious matters
to help those involved in these new movements. This problem is even
further aggravated by the fact the cults have raised such an impas-
sioned upheaval in some quarters that a balanced psychiatric evaluation of them has been rendered very difficult, if not altogether
impossible. This bibliography aims at remedying this situation by
providing a broad spectrum of psychological and psychiatric studies
of the new movements and a much wider and more objective platform for
evaluating their impact both on society at large and on individuals.

INTRODUCTION

THE DEBATE ON THE CULTS IN CURRENT PSYCHIATRIC AND PSYCHOLOGICAL LITERATURE: AN ASSESSMENT

Two major theories on contemporary cultism have emerged in psychological and psychiatric literature. The first looks on the cults as dangerous, often pseudo-religious, organizations that create mental and emotional problems for those who join them. The second proposes the theory that the new religious movements offer young adults alternate therapies which help them in the many crises of life, especially those linked with adolescence. In this introduction we will describe each position as typified, respectively, by one of its most well-known proponents. An evaluation will follow each outline of the two theories mentioned above. Finally, several more fundamental issues in the study and understanding of cultism and in the application of therapy will be explored.

Margaret Thaler Singer's Theory

Probably more than any writer on the new movements, Dr. Singer represents the first theory which looks at the cults as a social plague and a psychological menace. Because of her active involvement in counseling ex-cult members and their families and in testifying in favor of distraught parents in many trials throughout the United States, her name has become a household word, especially among those who have been personally affected by the presence of the cults, and who follow the reports of their activities in anti-cult literature and various national news magazines and local newspapers.

The Cult and Its Features

The definition of a "cult" has long been a topic of debate in the social sciences, particularly in sociology. Although it is difficult to find a clear, well-studied definition of a cult in any of Singer's few publications, there is an implied one in most of her writings and public statements. A cult is a spurious, pseudo-religious group headed by a powerful leader who offers illusionary cures and gives simplistic answers to all of life's problems and riddles (West and Singer, item 1355, p. 3246; Singer, item 1324, p. 72).

Several distinctive features appear in most cults. First, cults
are led by authoritative, domineering, ruthless leaders who aim at
controlling the public and private lives of their followers. Singer
calls these leaders "venal quacks" (item 1355, p. 3245). Secondly,
the cults are distinguishable by their double standard of ethics.
While they openly promise spiritual advancement and social and
intellectual benefits for those who join them, in point of fact,
avarice, personal convenience, and desire for power are the underlying motives of their founders and/or leaders. Cult members are encouraged to deceive and manipulate outsiders, especially when they
are recruiting or soliciting funds for questionable charitable or
educational goals (item 1323, p. 18). And finally, the cults bring
about a major disruptive change in the life-styles of those who
join them. It is the view of Singer (item 1355, p. 2349) and several
other scholars, like Conway and Siegelman (item 1188), that such a
drastic alteration in values, ideology, and life-style is the direct
cause of physical, intellectual, and emotional harm to the vast
majority of members.

In order to understand the impact of cults on our society, one
must begin by identifying them and estimating their prevalence.
Singer thinks that there are some three million Americans involved
in about 2,500 to 3,000 new cults, which vary in size from two dozen
members to thousands of ardent followers. The majority of those
committed to cult belief and practice are young adults between the
ages of 18 and 25. Most of them are well-educated, often with
college degrees, or at least some college experience, and come from
middle-class and upper middle-class families (cf., for example, item
1355, pp. 3248-50).

The majority of the new religious movements can be classified,
according to Singer, into ten types. These are, in her own words,
as follows:

> 1) neo-Christian religious cults; 2) Hindu Eastern
> religious cults; 3) occult, witchcraft and satanism
> cults; 4) spiritualist cults; 5) Zen and other Sino-
> Japanese philosophical cults; 6) race cults; 7) fly-
> ing saucers and outer space cults; 8) psychological
> cults; 9) political cults; 10) certain communal and
> self-help or self-improvement groups that, over time,
> become transformed into cults (item 1355, p. 3249).

Singer herself has studied members of groups where an intense
relationship between the leader and the devotee is one of the major
features. Among those specifically mentioned by her are Jim Jones's
People's Temple, the Church of Scientology, the Divine Light Mission,
the Unification Church, Synanon, the Worldwide Church of God, the
Hare Krishna Movement, and Transcendental Meditation. Seventy-five
percent of those ex-members she has counseled had left the cults
through legal conservatorship, and most of them had seen, at times
by coercive means, deprogrammers. Although she assures us that none
had been through deprogramming in its extreme form (item 1323, p. 75),
their condition was clearly pathological. These ex-members were
spacey, programmed individuals who had been reduced to zombie-like

creatures (item 1355, p. 3429). This view of what cult membership
does to an individual has been endorsed by several psychiatrists
and has become widespread in popular religious literature.

One of the methods Singer used to study her clients who had been
cult members has been to compare their present condition to what
they were like before they suddenly abandoned their families and
educational pursuits and after they got involved in one of the movements. This she achieved by interviewing at least two relatives
and/or friends of each ex-cult member in order to obtain a pre-
cult psychological profile. Their intellectual interests, academic
accomplishments, and emotional behavior in the pre- and post-cult
stages were contrasted. Singer appears to have been overwhelmed by
the drastic transformation that membership in a cult is capable of
inducing in young adults.

Many practices which most of the cults endorse and encourage are,
according to Singer, a cause for alarm. After being recruited under
false pretenses, cult members are exploited and practically enslaved.
They are subjected to long training sessions during which they are
indoctrinated into cult belief and behavior. Their subservience to
the cultic leaders and total obedience to the rules of cult-life are
maintained by programs of "coercive persuasion" or "brainwashing"
(item 1325, p.16). Retaliation against defectors, antagonism against
parents, seculsion from outside contact, and rigid control of one's
personal life are among the techniques shared by many of the new
cults. The chief model Singer uses to understand what happens when
a person joins a cult is the Chinese indoctrination or brainwashing
of prisoners-of-war (item 1355, pp. 3248 ff.). Jonestown is indirectly taken as a paradigm of what might happen to many contemporary
cultic groups.

The negative features of the cults are brought into focus when
these new religious groups are compared to other apparently similar
institutions in our society. Cults are distinguishable from communes
in many important aspects. Communes have no rigid structures headed
by a powerful leader who holds absolute, divine authority. They are
not reinforced by the religious concept of revelation. They have no
rigid boundaries--people are allowed to join or leave the community
freely, without fear or restraint. Unlike cults, communes pose no
threat to society (item 1355, pp. 3247-48).

In like manner, when comparing cults to other religious groups,
like religious orders, or to other strict organizations, like army
training camps, Singer found the similarities somewhat superficial.
Trainees in religious orders are indeed sequestered, but only for a
short period of time. Ritual fasting and mortification are also
present, but they are not imposed on all by force as an essential
part of religious life. Applicants to religious orders often go
through psychiatric screening and are informed of the duties and
obligations that come with membership. Members of religious orders
start their new way of life with a trial, an experimental period,
prior to full commitment. They are not tricked or manipulated into
joining by empty promises and misrepresentations. Their commitment
is free and deliberate.

There is, Singer points out (item 1355, pp. 3251-52), a marked
difference between members of the new cults and those of established
religious orders. The former behave like programmed robots: intensive smiling, repetitive monologues of cult jargon, and a preachy
conversational style, rather than dialogue, are commonly shared behavioral patterns. The latter, on the other hand, exhibit an average
variety in their speech and behavior and are, moreover, outgoing in
their relationships with outsiders, making a real contribution to
social life (item 1323, p. 18).

Why People Join Cults

If cults are such unpleasant organizations, why is it that so
many young, intelligent adults are attracted to them? Singer gives
two answers to this question. She first explains that the general
cultural condition of our times encourages the rise and spread of
new religious movements. She accepts the common sociological view
that cults come into being during "periods of unusual turbulences
in human history" (item 1355, p. 3247). Modern young adults, she
further observes, have adopted a romantic, anti-intellectual posture.
They are skeptical of the benefits of an educational system that
doesn't guarantee them a secure job in the future. Moreover, they
are concerned with the possibility of nuclear war. They have lost
faith in the large, often impersonal, institutions of our society.
Our age is experiencing a period of philosophical materialism and
of rapid culture change. It is not surprising that modern youth
has become vulnerable to the lure of the cults.

Secondly, Singer stresses the individual psychological make-up
of the people who actually join these movements. Those who become
cult members are vulnerable individuals--a view shared by many
psychiatrists who do not agree with Singer's theory of cultism (cf.
Levine, item 1266, p. 80). Shyness, homesickness, uncertainty of
purpose, alienation, loneliness, depression, and unchannelled
idealism are the characteristics she observes in those attracted to
the cults (item 1355, p. 3252). People who are drawn to the cults
are often between jobs and/or commitments. They are in conflict
with their families or are struggling with serious life problems,
such as sex, marriage, and the need to earn a livelihood. In a
state of boredom, restlessness, uncertainty, and confusion, people
find it hard to see any meaning or purpose in life (item 1324, p.
72). Drifting young adults are easily deceived by the promise of
peace, security, and happiness so readily assured by already committed, enthusiastic cult members.

This vulnerability of modern youth does not mean, according to
Singer, that the majority of those who become cult members are
mentally ill or psychologically weak. Rather, they are average
individuals who share similar problems with the majority of young
adults in our society. Singer insists that the family situation
should not be held responsible for driving people to join the cults
(item 1323, p. 19). The blame is placed on the cultic recruitment
methods which successfully entice and dupe young adults "seeking
relief from many age-appropriate developmental crises" (item 1325,
p. 16).

Effects of Cult Membership

Singer is alarmed at the alleged effects of cultism on those who
have been recruited. When one joins a cult, a sudden, catastrophic
change takes place. The new members abandon their academic and
intellectual pursuits, as well as their recreational activities.
They break contact with their friends and acquaintances. Their cognitive flexibility and adaptability are reduced. They become almost
incapable of thinking rationally or of making their own decisions.
In general, their psychological and physical conditions deteriorate.
They regress, becoming extremely passive, suggestible, and dependent. Cults induce "empty mind" states and trance-like conditions,
and render their members unrealistic in the face of life's problems
and challenges (items 1324, pp. 75-76; 1325, pp. 17-18). The cults
are, in Singer's opinion, dangerous groups which not only disrupt
families, but also create both physical and psychological upheavals
in the lives of those who have been manipulated to join them.

It is not surprising, therefore, that Singer thinks that cult
members are in need of therapy. The cults make them sick--so sick,
in fact, that cult members who want to return to their former states
of life are faced with many re-entry problems and require professional assistance. Singer's main work has been with ex-cult members,
helping them overcome their dependency on the cult and directing
them in their attempts to regain control of their lives. This is
not an easy task, because the damage done by the cults takes a long
time to heal, and therapists are not trained to deal with the problem (item 1325, p. 15).

Evaluation of Singer's Views

The position on cults espoused by Singer is widespread not only
among counselors and psychiatrists, but especially among anti-cult
groups who take her assumptions and conclusions for granted. But
the careful researcher who examines her views is bound to raise a
host of questions in connection with both her method and theory,
and with many of the major statements she makes about the cults.

Singer's Methodology

One of the major problems with Singer's methodology is that she
neglects to supply any statistical breakdown of her clients. From
her brief remarks on the subject, one can distinguish several different types of clients who were brought to her office for professional consultation and/or treatment: 1) a majority who had left
the cults, mainly through some kind of pressure or force exerted by
their parents, and who had been deprogrammed; 2) several who had
left the cults on their own and needed help to readjust themselves to
their previous life-styles; and 3) a few individuals who eventually
returned to the cults. Apparently, most of her clients came from
groups which stress an intense relationship between the followers
and a powerful idea or leader. Again, we are supplied with no
statistical information in this area which is important, if for no

other reason, because of Singer's own views on authority in the
cults. She maintains that many cult leaders who claim divine revelation assume a dictatorial attitude towards their followers. But
where a powerful idea—and not a living, charismatic figure—is the
motivating force of the movement, the authority system must differ
significantly.

Three hundred cult members interviewed by Singer are a small percentage of the three million people allegedly involved in the new
cults. Reliable statistical figures on cult members just do not
exist. We have no idea how many people have been partly or wholly
committed to the cults over the last two decades. In like manner,
we lack statistical information on what percentage of those who ever
come in contact with the cults are actually turned off without ever
seriously considering the prospects of becoming members. Neither do
we possess any hard evidence on the number of cult members who leave
the cults of their own free will without any re-entry problems that
need psychiatric intervention. Reports by scholars and ex-cult members alike agree that the vast majority of people who come in contact
with a cult belong to one of the above mentioned categories (Gordon,
item 1220, p. 609).

In like manner, our data linking cult membership with mental illness, psychological immaturity, and intellectual weakness is minimal
and unreliable because the impartiality and objectivity of the method
used is questionable. Singer seems to assume that the problems,
which her clients no doubt had, were caused by the cults themselves.
She makes no effort to report how many of the ex-cult members she
counseled had a history of psychological problems before they joined
the cults. It is conceivable that the psychopathology she noticed
in her clients antedated their cultic involvement, and that membership in the cult either brought their illness to the fore or even
aggravated it. Several psychological abnormalities, which Singer
deduced from her tests and interviews, could have been the result of
deprogramming which, no matter how mild and gentle it might be, is
always a traumatic experience.

The first major obstacle to the plausibility of Singer's theory
is her method. Her research is not carefully documented. She fails
to avail herself of a standard procedure in psychological research,
namely, the use of "control groups" against which one can compare
the psychological state of ex-cult members. Further, some of her
assumptions seem to be completely gratuitous and her conclusions
leave the impression that they have been hastily reached.

Other difficulties beset the scholar who looks into Singer's
method. She seems to have relied on two sources for information on
the cults. First, she took what the majority of her deprogrammed
clients said about cult life as documented factual reports. According to her own observations, these people exhibited a lot of anger
against the cults they belonged to and tended to view their past
involvement as a waste of time in a movement which had used them
(item 1325, p. 18). We are not suggesting that these cult members
were untruthful or dishonest in their depiction of cult life. But
the trained researcher will be on guard against any partiality or

lack of objectivity which might influence his/her reports and conclusions. Accounts of ex-members are accounts of people who have
given up their commitment and who are likely to regret their past
involvement, results which deprogramming techniques are, in fact,
geared to produce.

The second source of information on which Singer relied was the
parents, relatives, and friends of her clients. She tried to reconstruct the history of her clients, attempting to sketch a picture
of what the cult members were like before they joined the cults and
comparing it with the psychological profile of the persons she was
counseling. Singer was specifically endeavoring to analyze several
intellectual abilities and emotional aspects to determine how these
had apparently changed during her clients' relatively short period
within the cults. But she doesn't tell us the criteria by which she
evaluates these changes. And she seems to assume that all the changes
actually occurred during, and because of, cult involvement. We are
led to believe that all the changes that can take place when someone
joins a cult are negative and harmful. Had she examined some cult
members who are happy in their commitment, she might have arrived at
some startling conclusions. Further, the reliability of her informants is not self-evident. Young adults do not always confide in
their relatives and friends when they are going through a crisis.
Before joining a cult, a person often undergoes subtle changes over
a period of time, changes of which the individual may not be fully
aware. Besides, those individuals who are deliberating whether they
should join a cult do not usually consult their parents and friends
because the response is likely to be unsympathetic. Relatives and
friends, no matter how well-intentioned, are unlikely to approve of
their offspring's abandonment of traditional, cultural, and religious
values. Many parents have been influenced by anti-cult campaigns
and are not impartial observers of the new religious movements.

One is led to conclude that Singer's method is hampered by a
second major problem, namely, that the information she collects about
the cults does not stand the test of impartiality and objectivity.
Had she used some well-tested sociological and anthropological
methods, such as participant-observation, and had she explored at
some depth religious beliefs and values outside the Judeo-Christian
tradition, she would certainly have been able to see some of the
beliefs and practices of the new cults in an altogether different
light.

Singer's Therapy

Another area of Singer's work which requires scrutiny is her
therapy. She states that her clients are given individual psychotherapy to help them re-enter mainstream culture and to readjust
themselves to "normal" life (item 1325, p. 16). She also conducts
group sessions, which are not a form of group psychotherapy or encounter groups but rather meetings aimed at providing a setting for
mutual support. Discussion and education are the goals of these
sessions, during which ex-cult members learn how they were decep-
tively recruited and cunningly indoctrinated, and how logically

inconsistent cult beliefs and practices are. Singer concludes that
it might take between eight and eighteen months for ex-cult members
to return to their previous psychological and mental condition and
to their former belief systems and life-styles.

There is no doubt that many of the re-entry problems experienced
by cult members are real. What Singer fails to realize is that re-
entry problems, like indecision, often follow whenever a person
makes a major shift in life-style and commitment. These problems,
therefore, cannot be viewed as being unique to ex-cult members or
as being caused by the cults. They are life problems and not cultic
ones. They are frequently experienced by divorced people and by ex-
members of Catholic religious orders. Singer considers the cults
to be the sole source of the troubles her clients are experiencing
and her therapy is, consequently, narrowly directed toward those
harmful conditions judged to be brought about by the cults. The
problems which the individuals were facing before they joined a cult
are never discussed. The past vulnerability of her clients and
their search for meaning are bypassed, and a considerable amount of
time is spent in group meetings, attacking the belief systems of the
new religious movements and berating those cultic practices which
led them to be unwillingly snared into the cult's treacherous webs.
Such therapy sessions have the flavor of anti-cult propaganda, which
includes learning how to interpret the individual's past involvement.
In such group meetings a lot of time is apparently assigned to induce a sense of guilt and inadequacy in ex-cult members (who were
so easily duped by smiling faces), and then to find good reasons
for exonerating them from any responsibility they might have had in
deciding to join a cult. All the blame is placed on the cults.
The power-hungry, charismatic leader, the deceitful ploys of the
"brainwashed" members, and the evil methods of recruitment and
indoctrination undermined the free will of those who joined a cult
when they were unable to make their own decisions.

Another difficulty with Singer's therapy is that she does not consider the possibility that family therapy may be needed both before
and after cult involvement, even though she states that "certain
family backgrounds may render some young people more vulnerable than
others to the lures of the cults" (item 1355, p. 3250). Surely, it
is reasonable to assume that when a young person abandons one's
religious upbringing, if any, and rejects one's family roots, the
family situation may, sometimes, require analysis (cf. Melton and
Moore, item 1279, pp. 65-69).

Singer's Theory of Cults

Singer's major theory, that the cults are the cause of mental
illness, stands or falls on the viability of her method which, as
has been pointed out, leaves much to be desired. Further, it
succumbs to the fallacy of the circular argument. The cults are
are taken to be the cause of mental and emotional illness, which
itself proves that the cults are institutions responsible for the
illness.

Finally, Singer's approach doesn't conform to the basic principles of academic research. To understand the cults and their effects, one doesn't study solely the small percentage of those members who have been brought to the psychotherapist's office, often through family pressure, if not coercion.

Cults and Religious Orders

The attempt to draw comparisons between the cults and other groups in our society, notably communes and religious orders, is a useful methodological approach that might help us understand the new religious movements and the reasons why people join them. We think that the comparison between religious cults and Christian religious orders is a perfectly legitimate and appropriate one, provided it is carried out on an academic basis and not used as a tool to denounce the cults and their life-styles. For a meaningful comparison, one must explore both the similarities and the differences. It is unfortunate that Singer has neglected to point out not only the similarities, but also some of the more important differences.

The first major difference between the new cults and traditional religious/monastic orders or congregations is that the latter are established options within a faith community. Religious orders thus recruit members (and solicit funds) from the larger community to which they belong. Among Catholics, membership in a religious order is generally looked upon favorably, even though there are exceptions. Family members usually understand what religious life is about and share in some of its ideology. The conflict of values, interests, and ideology between families and cult members has, therefore, little parallel in Roman Catholic experience. It is possible that much of the anti-cult rhethoric and accusations are based on a few, simple cultural facts: namely, that the cults recruit members from outside their religious faith, and that those who join adopt an altogether different religious viewpoint and cultural perspective from that of their parents. People who join cults are, therefore, abandoning both their religious and cultural heritage. They are passing a negative judgment on the traditions of their family. The resultant family debates and conflicts are what one would normally expect.

Another important difference is that Christian religious orders are not millennial. Many cults, on the other hand, believe that the end of the world is near at hand. This gives their work a certain urgency. The "overzealous" activity of many cult members, though disconcerting to outsiders, can be better understood within the framework of their ideology. Because religious orders do not preach that the end of the world is around the corner, the commitment of their members is more likely to express itself in social work, charitable endeavors, and educational pursuits than in preparing for the coming new age or final catastrophe.

Besides, contemporary religious orders are not led by charismatic figures who claim divine revelation. Their founders, who have long since passed away, may still be revered as saints, but they never held the same kind of position that some gurus hold with their devotees.

While both religious orders and cults encourage commitment to an
ideology, their mission to spread that ideology is differently conceived. The commitment in Christian religious orders is directed
to Jesus Christ and, therefore, differs considerably from the adula-
tion which many cult members seem to bestow on their living founders
and leaders, whose behavior may not always be exemplary.

Lastly, religious orders are selective in accepting members.
Singer is aware of this difference but does not explore it. Though
the use of psychiatric testing and evaluation of prospective candidates is a relatively recent procedure adopted by several religious
orders, some examination of candidates has always preceded entry
into religious life. Moreover, the first year or so in religious
life is conceived as a trial period during which both the novices
and their instructors test the genuineness of the vocation. A weed-
ing out process takes place which, though not foolproof, helps
eliminate serious problems before they develop. Members of religious orders do not usually undergo a traumatic conversion experience
which leads them to enter religious life. There are obvious reasons
for this. Those who join a religious order do not have to change
their faith perspective, and thus the realization that they are
called to a more intensive form of Christian living often comes
gradually and almost imperceptively. In the case of the cults, the
general impression is that joining one of them is relatively easy,
with no careful prior screening and much less testing. The entry
into a religious movement always has drastic consequences because
the neophytes adopt a new religious and social identity that is
bound to create family conflict. Although the decision to commit
oneself to a cult may not have been taken suddenly or on the spur
of the moment, as we are sometimes led to believe, the person who
joins is more likely to experience a mental and psychological
disturbance. Singer seems, moreover, unaware of the fact that some
cults have become more selective in accepting members and others
have asked well-established ones to leave. One must admit that
these are exceptional cases, but they may indicate a trend towards
some kind of evaluation of aspirants to the ranks of cult membership.

The similarities between religious and/or monastic orders and
the new cults are equally impressive. Like cults, religious orders
train their novices into a new way of life and provide ways of
reinforcing this education during membership. To what degree this
training is heavy indoctrination, mild enculturation, or simply a
form of religious education very often depends on the point of view
one decides to adopt. While most members of religious orders are
not, as Singer correctly observes, sequestered for life, there are
several monastic institutions where a life of total isolation from
mainstream culture and society is more rigidly followed than in the
majority of the cults. The accusation that religious life can be
oppressive has at times been made by both members and ex-members
of religious orders.

Like cults, religious orders teach their members to think and
behave differently and to adopt priorities and values which are
ignored and repudiated by society at large. The commitment in
religious orders, usually expressed by the vows of poverty, chastity,

and obedience, and by the acceptance of a common rule, goes against
most of the cultural values in Western society and sets apart those
who have taken vows. One could easily see this commitment as a form
of "deviant" behavior. The life-style of religious and monastic
orders has also several features of a sub-culture, such as wearing
distinctive clothing and adopting a life-style in which most domes-
tic duties are shared. As in the majority of the cults, religious
life can be highly structured and demanding, with specific times
allotted for many common activities, including long sessions of
prayer, instruction, and meditation. Members of religious orders
often work for long hours with little pay, which is handed in to
the common fund, over which only the appointed leaders have full
control. Singer's scant comments on religious life indicate that
her knowledge of the subject is superficial. The reader who is
familiar with religious life and who accepts some of its ideology
is left with the impression that Singer doesn't quite understand it.

We are not suggesting that religious orders and cults ascribe to
a smilar ideology or follow an identical life-style. We maintain
that several ideological and practical aspects are similar enough
to enable us to understand some aspects of the life-style of some
of the cults and to assess their significance. A case in point is
the adoption by several cults of the celibate life, which Singer
doesn't quite understand. She writes:

> With many of the cults, sexuality is suppressed
> because the leaders don't want lateral coalitions;
> they don't want members to get too personally
> involved and tie allegiances with one another, as
> this distracts from the sense of purpose, dedica-
> tion to the cause, the work, the fundraising, and
> the recruiting (item 1323, p. 19).

This interpretation of celibacy should also be logically applicable
to religious and monastic institutions. Singer would have arrived
at a better understanding of the attitudes toward sex of some cults
if she had explored the nature of religious dedication and commitment
as expressed in Christian and Buddhist monastic institutions. But
her Freudian training precludes any positive evaluation of chastity
and celibacy, neither of which have to be explained as a selfish ploy
in the hands of some misguided, manipulative despot.

Fact and Folklore About Cults

Singer's view of the cults suffers from several factual flaws.
We restrict comments to some of the more flagrant ones:

1) Singer's description of the features of a cult is by far too
negative. Scholars in other academic disciplines, notably sociology,
have attempted to define cults and describe their characteristics
without including a blanket denunciation of their religious and
spiritual beliefs, values, and intentions. Others have discovered
that some cult members perform normally on regular psychological
tests (cf. Ross, item 1792). Singer leaves no room for discerning

genuine religious groups from harmful fads, even though there are a
few groups she doesn't think are very harmful. Her classification
of cults into ten types covers practically all religious groups with
the exception of Judaism and the major Christian churches. She
seems reluctant to admit that Eastern religions have a place in the
religious life of humankind and that their relevance might go beyond
their geographic boundaries. Genuine religious conversion to Eastern
traditions lies within the realm of human possibility. Admittedly,
some Buddhist and Hindu groups in the United States are faddish and
many of those who join them may not be religiously motivated. These
groups and people are subject to the criticism Singer levels at them.
But any person familiar with the literature on Eastern religions,
both in Asia and in the West, would find Singer's comments factually
mistaken.

2) The attack on cult leaders has been a prominent feature in the
anti-cult establishment. It must be acknowledged that there is some
foundation for the accusations directed against several of the gurus
and self-made prophets of our age. But "venal quacks" are found in
all professions, religious or secular (see, for example, Temerlim
and Temerlim, item 1339). They are exceptions rather than the rule.
They do not discredit professions, religious or otherwise, as a whole.
Further, religious leaders may be misguided in their claims to prophetic calling and quite wrong in teachings, but they could still
be sincere (Hargrove, item 1228, p. 34). The fact that some of them
appear to have adopted a life-style of luxury, especially when compared to that of their devotees, should not be generalized and used
to justify a total denouncement of cults. The image of a religious
leader living in wanton luxury and preying on ardent followers is
foreign not only to the Judeo-Christian tradition, but also to the
Buddhist and Hindu notion of the spiritual life.

3) The accusation that the cults are deceptive cannot be applied
indiscriminately to all the new religious movements. While several
groups have recruited members and solicited funds on false pretenses
or without clearly explaining the nature of their mission and programs, the majority of the groups advertise themselves unmistakenly
as Hindu or Buddhist, or whatever the case might be. It would be
practically impossible for any young adult to join, for example,
the Hare Krishna movement without knowing that one is joining an
Eastern religious group.

4) Finally, we find Singer's position a little confusing, if not
contradictory. We are told, for instance, that those people who
join cults are normal, yet vulnerable, individuals. Their vulnerability explains why they end up in a cult. But if they are just
as vulnerable as the average person, then why is it that they alone
are successfully recruited? If they are more vulnerable than the
average young adult, as Singer seems to state at one point (item
1324, p. 80), then they must have some additional problem or weakness which makes them prime targets for successful cult recruitment.
One is left with the impression that every young adult is liable to
be trapped by the advances of members of new religious movements.
But this position borders on the ludicrous. The majority of those
who actually come in contact with a cult are repulsed, rather than

attracted, to its belief-system and life-style. Besides, the large
percentage who actually join a cult do not persist in their commitment. Singer seems to have forgotten a major factor in what is
essentially a market economy, even in the religious realm. The new
religious movements are definitely seeking new members. Those who
become members, however, are themselves on the streets looking for
a cult to join. Many cults have been short-lived for the simple
reason that they failed to attract a following.

In like manner, the position that those who join a cult are
brainwashed or coercively persuaded is not very convincing. The
model of the American prisoners-of-war in China, taken mainly
from Lifton (item 1865), is highly deficient since 1) members to the
new religious movements are not physically abducted or detained, and
2) prisoners-of-war are not recruited. There is no doubt that once
a person joins a cult, social and psychological pressures to stay
come into play. But any serious commitment entails such pressures.
Besides, if one were to accept the theory of brainwashing, one has
to conclude that brainwashing in the cults is not very effective,
since the turnover rate of new members is rather high. An ineffec-
tual brainwashing is simply not brainwashing at all. Admittedly,
those ex-cult members who were brought to Singer for treatment were
psychologically sick people in need of therapy and counseling; but
her position that the cults are the root of their emotional and
intellectual problems is based on unwarranted generalizations and
belongs more to the realm of popular folklore than to scientific
fact buttressed by impartial and objective evidence.

Marc Galanter and Charismatic Sects

This totally negative picture of the cultic phenomenon, proposed
by Margaret Singer and other counseling psychologists and psychiatrists, is balanced by a different interpretation that sees the
cults as ways of assisting young adults in their efforts to cope
with the many social and religious problems they have to face in
today's changing world. The studies of Marc Galanter and his associates (see items 1209; 1210; 1722; 1743-1747) offer an alternative
approach to the analysis of the cult phenomenon and to the understanding of its significance with a corresponding program for
therapeutic help and professional counseling.

The Cult and Its Features

Galanter's studies do not start with a clear-cut definition of a
cult. He seems to identify cults with sects and other religious
movements which do not fit into mainstream religion. He considers
both as somewhat large charismatic and/or evangelical religious
groups. He describes them as organizations whose members 1) adhere
to a consensual belief system, 2) maintain a high level of social
cohesiveness, 3) are strongly influenced by group behavioral norms,
and 4) impute divine or charismatic powers to their leaders. Two

added features are typically cultic: 5) religious deviance, and
6) rejection of the majority culture (items 1209, p. 1539; 1743,
p. 987). None of the above characteristics are necessarily negative
or harmful. Two fairly common, although not universal, traits of
cultic life-style, namely communal living and abstinence from sex,
are certainly not new in the history of religions and can interpreted
positively (item 1209, p. 1542).

Galanter makes no assessment of the prevalence of cults in contemporary Western society. He does observe, however, that most of
their members are college-educated, as were most of their parents.
Cult members are generally white, single, and more often male (items
1745, p. 1577; 1209, p. 1529). Galanter appears to include all new
religious movements under the label "charismatic religious sects."
He classifies them into five major groups: 1) neo-charismatic sects;
2) Eastern religions; 3) psychological cults; 4) politically-oriented
cults; and 5) satanism, witchcraft, and similar groups (item 1209,
pp. 1542-43). His main area of research covered current members of
the Unification Church ("Moonies") and of the Divine Light Mission
("Premies"). His subjects included several hundred young adults,
most of whom were studied on the scene while they were committed
members (see items 1464; 1722; 1747). In order to conduct such a
study, Galanter obtained full cooperation from the respective group
leaders. One study followed a whole group of prospective Unification
Church members through their initial training period (item 1745),
while another solicited participation of ex-members of the same
church to join in a well-planned research project (item 1743). All
these studies were conducted under strict control, using a sample from
the general population as a comparative base. Other studies carried
out by various psychiatrists were taken into account and are frequently referred to in his writings. We find in Galanter's works
not only careful documentation and statistical records, but also an
outline of his methodological procedures. He is wisely cautious
about overgeneralization (item 1209, p. 1546), and aware that studying those members of religious cults who volunteer to participate
in research programs may not reach the "more dysfunctional minority"
nor "tap the more severe symptoms" (item 1209, p. 1540). He concedes
that some tests may be unintentionally distorted due to cognitive
dissonance (see, for example, item 1747, p. 168), and also admits
that the researchers' attitudes may influence the subjects they are
studying as well as the conclusions they reach (item 1209, p. 1546).

In their research on the members of new religious movements,
Galanter and his associates explored the religious qualities of their
subjects and correlated them with their psychological states. Their
questionnaires were designed to measure attitudinal, mental, and
emotional responses. Neurotic distress, religiosity, general well-
being, level of belief, sense of purpose, and the feelings of being
coerced were the main areas of information solicited from the
subjects.

The results of these studies did not lead Galanter to be alarmed
at the phenomenon of the cults, even though he maintains that some
members of modern religious sects might need psychiatric intervention

(item 1209, p. 1543). His main concern is to understand, rather than
condemn, these "deviant" religious movements and their enthusiastic
members. When he followed in the tracks of one group of aspirants
to the Unification Church as they went through the sequential training workshops, he discovered that over 90 percent of these neophytes
dropped out of the training program. He concluded that the brainwashing model could not explain why people joined this highly controversial religious movement. Lifton's theory of brainwashing (item
1865) was inapplicable because the prospective "Moonies" were not,
like the American prisoners-of-war in China, "abused or coerced into
compliance" (item 1747, p. 169). The recruitment and teaching techniques were a form of "psychological engagement rather then coercion"
(item 1209, p. 1541). He also points out that the tragic events at
Jonestown and the disruption of the nuclear family, though often
associated directly and causally with the new religious movements,
do not help us understand this new phenomenon nor unveil the central
features of cultic life and involvement. Jonestown is such a unique
event that it cannot be taken as a example of cultic life and behavior, while the breakup of the nuclear family can be traced to
several social and cultural forces which came into being well before
the advent of the recent cults.

Galanter, therefore, looks for other models to explain why cults
come into being and why some of them achieve success. He suggests
that the answer to the riddle of the cults may be found, in part at
least, in the psychology of religious experience and/or conversion
(see, for example, item 1464, p. 691). Consequently, he finds it more
useful to compare the new religious movements with such groups as
Alcoholics Anonymous (item 1745, p. 1578), some drug-free therapeutic
communities (item 1209, p. 1541), activist political groups (item
1743, p. 987), several Protestant sects, like the Moravians and the
Anabaptists (item 1745, p. 1578), and other "enthusiastic religions,"
such as Quakerism, Voodoo, and Pentecostalism (item 1722, pp. 281,
288).

Moreover, his research led him to the conclusion that it is more
rewarding to seek understanding of the beliefs and practices of the
new movements in terms of the psychology of the group rather than
from the perspective of a member's individual psychosis (item 1209,
p. 1547). He consequently turns to different disciplines for theoretical frameworks through which he can interpret the belief systems
and behavioral patterns of the cults. From social psychology, he
applies attribution theory to grasp the decision-making process of
joining a cult (item 1749, p. 169) and to explain how new attitudes
are adopted (item 1744, p. 75). He links this theory with cognitive
dissonance to understand how and why people come to accept belief
systems without critical analysis or assessment. From anthropology,
he borrows several sociobiological ideas to interpret cults as providing adaptive mechanisms to distress symptoms, and finds support-
ing evidence in evolution and ethology (see items 1210; 1743-44).
And from sociology, he applies the systems theory where the relationship between components of the cult, rather than the effects which
cult membership has on the individual, are stressed (item 1209, pp.
1545 ff.).

Why People Join Cults

In order to understand the rise and spread of the new religious
movements, Galanter asks the central psychological question: What
motives and forces, conscious or unconscious, lead an individual to
profess one's allegiance to a cult? Galanter points to several
social reasons or conditions. Our society is characterized by a
"decline in the integrity of traditional community networks" (item
1209, p. 1547). Rapid communication may have expanded loose ties
with many people but has also weakened close, intimate, family
relationships. Our society is also noted for its demand for personal autonomy, which creates many unresolved problems.

Those young adults who join the cults are, therefore, likely to
come from troubled families where there are relatively weak ties
between parents and their offspring, relatives, and peers. Hence,
young adults have limited social bonds and are likely to be lonely
and alienated and more open to break completely with their life-
style and establish new bonds and relationships. Men and women who
join cults are also preoccupied with traditional religious issues,
such as the meaning of life, personal incompleteness, and destiny.
In general the person attracted to a cult is undergoing some psychological distress, accompanied by severe anxiety and disorganization
of life (items 1464, p. 689; 1209, 1539-40). Because prospective
cult members are facing an important transition in commitment and
values, they encounter greater emotional stress. Galanter concluded
that over 30 percent of cult members had sought psychiatric help
before they joined a cult. While there is no evidence of prior
insanity or mental illness, there are cases where people suffering
from severe psychopathology sought and received admission into one of
the new religious groups, a fact confirmed by other researchers (see,
for example, Lofland, item 1868; Bainbridge, item 1716). The people
who are attracted to or join a cult are typically experiencing
psychological and mental problems more intensely than their peers.
They are looking for ways to come to grips with their personal
deficiencies, emotional difficulties, and intellectual problems. It
is precisely because of these conditions that participation in a
cult becomes a distinct possibility.

The Effects of Cult Membership

Seen from the above perspective, the results of entering cultic
life and of accepting cultic ideology can be dramatic. The cults
become comfort systems (item 1747, p. 169), offering relief from
the tensions of life (item 1209, p. 1542). Galanter concludes from
several studies that through participation in a cult the psychological well-being of individuals improved, often leading to the
abandonment of drugs and alcohol, improvements which have been
recorded by other researchers (such as Robbins and Anthony, item
1890). Cult members reported that they felt much better and attributed their improvements to their new way of life. This personal
testimony is supported, according to Galanter, by the fact that
"there is a positive relationship between the psychological well-
being and cohesiveness in a large group" (item 1744, p. 71). Con-

version to cultism has, in Galanter's view, a much more positive role. It has a "potential restitutive function" (item 1209, p. 1540), resolving conflicts, enhancing one's sense of purpose and meaning, and improving communal relationships. The claim so frequently made by converts to the new movements, that they have become more integrated as persons, is, to some degree, also corroborated by Galanter's research. Galanter suggests that we should, therefore, look on the charismatic religious experience not as a form of mental illness, but rather as a normal experience leading to social adaptation (items 1209, p. 1544; 1464, p. 689). These experiences, which might also be called mystical or transcendental, have positive effects, even if they are ultimately judged to be purely subjective.

The cults are, therefore, for many people, alternate therapies. They supply answers and offer solutions to problems that no other form of traditional counseling or therapy could provide. This does not mean that traditional therapists and counselors have no role to play in the field of religious cults. Rather, Galanter foresees that "psychiatry will ultimately be expected to develop approaches to assist in the psychological adjustment of persons who have joined charismatic cults" (item 1209, p. 1534). Since he observes several parallels between religious cults and psychiatric treatment (item 1646, p. 689), he thinks that the psychotherapist can learn from what happens to the individual when he/she joins a cult. In particular, the therapist will become conscious of how important belief systems and moral values are in the treatment of patients (item 1746, p. 498). Galanter envisages cooperation between therapists and cult leaders in helping cult members adjust to their new lives and overcome their emotional and intellectual problems. This approach is not new in psychotherapy (items 725; 726) and its theoretical basis finds support in medical anthropology (see, for instance, items 641; 754).

The cults, in Galanter's view, are not a panacea for the psychological difficulties of young adults. Both cult and ex-cult members may require psychiatric counseling tailored to their specific needs. In dealing with cult members the therapist is expected to take an empathetic view of the patients' beliefs and to keep in mind that his or her allegiance is with the client, no matter what the parental pressures might be. Galanter is cautious on the controversial issues of conservatorship and deprogramming because he thinks that further research on the matter is needed. For those who have left the cults and are experiencing some difficulties in readjusting to a new way of life, he favors Singer's group approach, although he doesn't give many details of what should take place in the therapy sessions (item 1209, p. 1544).

Evaluation of Galanter's Research

Galanter's approach to the new religious movements is in sharp contrast to Singer's methodological procedures and theoretical assumptions. He avoids a rigid, negative definition of a cult, and this leaves him the option of relating it more positively to other

religious and secular groupings in our society, and applying diverse
models to understand the effects which cults might have on those
who join them. He assumes a much more neutral stance towards the
cults and their leaders than many other psychiatrists who have been
counseling ex-cult members. Consequently, he is less judgmental
and even less inclined to make sweeping generalizations on cult life.
His writings do not exhibit the qualities of an anti-cult diatribe.

The methodology applied by Galanter is also significantly different from Singer's in that his main efforts have been to study people
who are current members of new religious movements. This provides
us with an insider's view and helps us examine the effects cults
might have on at least some of their members. Galanter is aware
that his approach is not immune from difficulties, but he has
grasped the methodological significance of the need to draw a picture of cult life as seen from the point of view of the active
participants who appear to have found their new commitment meaningful and rewarding. The conclusion that the effects of the cults
could be similar, in some respects, to those of traditional therapy
leads the researcher to analyze the new religions from a much more
constructive perspective.

The above observations do not imply that Galanter's research on
the cults is flawless. On the contrary, his studies raise several
methodological and theoretical difficulties.

Methodological Problems

Granted that the examination and interviewing of cult members
are legitimate and profitable pursuits, one can still ask what steps
should the research take to overcome some of the difficulties which
Galanter himself acknowledges. If ex-cult members are not impartial
in their depiction of cult life, the same can be said of active cult
members, whose positive response to questionnaires might be little
more than self-justification and rationalization of a belief system
and life-style in which they have invested their future. What is at
stake is the very content of the questionnaire that Galanter and
his associates used in their study of the members of the Unification
Church and the Divine Life Mission. The fact that a substantial
majority indicated that their "general well-being" had improved
considerably after they joined the cult may tell us more about their
present religious attitudes than about their psychological and mental
conditions. Truly enough, a positive state of mind is part of the
general well-being of the individual who reports it. But we still
need more objective criteria to help us evaluate the effects of
cults on their members on a long-term basis. In like manner, we
are not surprised to find that many cult members scored well on
the religiosity scale. We cannot, however, interpret this result
unless we specify the content of true religiosity as distinct from
sheer faddishness. The sense-of-purpose scale, used by Galanter,
is, in itself, not very revealing. Members of the People's Temple,
a political activist group, a scientific expedition, and a Christian
fundamentalist church could all have performed well on this test.
Galanter is also fully aware that the relationship between the

researchers and their subjects is one of the factors which must be taken into account in the study of the new movements and the mental health of their members. If this is correct, then one must look carefully at research sponsored, approved, and partly supervised by the leaders of the movements. While we agree with Galanter that the need to study the active members of cults should be given priority, we think that there still are many issues in the relationship between researchers and cult leaders which have to be worked out.

Another difficulty in Galanter's method is that, although he suggests that the new cults can be compared with other religious and other organizations (religious or otherwise), he never makes any detailed comparisons. For instance, he chooses Alcoholics Anonymous as a model for understanding the cults, but he does not draw any schematic outline of their similarities and differences.

Theoretical Problems

The new cults present a challenge not only to scientific method-ology, but also to theoretical formulation. Scholars studying these movements constantly look for a general framework or model to under-stand their rise and to gauge their impact on society at large and on the individual. Galanter offers several theoretical alternatives to the monolothic view of Singer, the most original of which is sociobiology, a theory which is hotly debated in anthropology. The main interpretation, which seems to underlie the different theories Galanter uses, is that the cults provide a "relief effect" from stress. This view is similar, if not identical, to the deprivation theories so commonly found in sociological (e.g., Glock, item 384) and anthropological literature (e.g., Aberle, item 756) to explain the rise of various religious movements. Such theories are appealing because they offer an underlying purpose or intent to human behavior. They make sense because they suggest that human beings try to satisfy their desires. They tend to be functional explanations which are usually reductionistic, taking an intense religious involvement as a form of political action or as a substitute for therapy. Social scientists appear to be more at ease with studying an individual's quest for power or desire for physical and emotional well-being than they are with genuinely religious aspirations.

While deficient as an overall theoretical explanation of cult formation, theories of need have the advantage of directing us to some of the problems of our culture. They urge us to question the sociocultural conditions which make the emergence of cults feasible or more opportune. But they do not lead to an in-depth understanding of the cult phenomenon, nor do they enable us to discern accurately the positive and negative features of cult life. While there is no doubt that some kind of therapy may be required by those who have left the cults willingly or by pressure, a better theory of cult formation has to be devised before a workable program of therapy can be developed and put into action. Galanter has laid the foundation of a more constructive approach to the problem of cults. His work will, no doubt, be the subject of future research and discussion.

His more cautious viewpoint on the cults brings the balance needed
in both public and academic spheres where the negative and often
melodramatic picture of the cults presented by Singer holds sway.

Issues in the Study of Cults

The debate in psychiatric literature on the mental health of cult
members has raised several issues about the cultic phenomenon of our
age and the ways one can respond to some of the problems it has
brought in its wake. One of the most outstanding questions is the
method and theory one should adopt in the study of religious beliefs
and experiences. The difficulties which many parents of cult members
are going through, the pains of re-adaptation which those who leave
a cult are faced with, and the actual conditions of cult life which
may be deemed harmful cannot be understood, and much less solved
or dealt with, unless a workable, objective method and an impartial,
balanced theory have been developed and applied to the study of
cults.

Theory and Method

The different theoretical assumptions and methodological procedures of diverse scholars are responsible, in part at least, for the
irreconcilable views on the significance of the new religious movements and on the possible need or urgency of psychiatric intervention. We suggest that the following considerations, often neglected
in psychological and psychiatric literature, are requisites for
understanding the emergence and persistence of the cults as well
as for counseling and administering therapeutic care when these are
legitimately called for.

1. Any study of cults or cult members must be of long duration.
It is a fallacy to think that one can even begin to fathom the
phenomenon simply by administering brief questionnaires over a short
period of time, or by applying several standardized psychological
tests, or by conducting relatively short therapeutic sessions. It
must be stressed that longer, more intensive studies of individual
cults must precede psychiatric evaluation. There are several sociological monographs on the new religious movements (e.g., items 1844,
1868) which could serve as models for the type of intensive study of
cults which must precede any evaluation.

2. The study of the psychology of cult members must follow the
study of the cult itself. One cannot pass accurate judgment on the
effect of a cult on its members without knowledge of the ideology
and life-style of the cult. Since many of the new religious movements have a foundation in Eastern philosophy and religion, one
must first begin with a study of Eastern traditions. Failure to
abide by this simple and reasonable procedure could lead to a
distortion of the facts and to some untenable conclusions. Singer
provides an example of such distortion when she lists Zen Buddhism

with the rest of the "destructive" cults (item 1355, p. 3249). Even
the most rudimentary knowledge of Zen will show that her position
cannot be maintained (see, for example, item 517).

3. Active cult members must be included as a primary source of
information on the cults. While researchers should be aware of the
fact that their information may be selective, they must realize that
believing participants in a religious group have the right to express
and interpret their own attitudes, values, and life-styles, no matter
how strange, or "deviant," these might appear to be. Furthermore,
the sincerity of cult members has to be taken for granted unless, of
course, there is clear proof to the contrary.

4. To offset the one-sided views which both cult and ex-cult
members are likely to impart, the academic method of participant-
observation seems necessary for any in-depth study of the new cults.
A first-hand, objective observation of the cultic life-style is, in
our opinion, a preliminary requirement for any understanding of the
cult phenomenon.

5. The comparative method can be used with profit when both the
similarities and the differences are drawn between the cults and a)
similar institutions and organizations in Western culture, and b)
parallel religious movements in different societies. Looking at
religious movements in different historical periods and in diverse
cultures might provide methodological guidance and theoretical
insight to the study of new religions in the West.

6. The primary goal of research on the new cults must be a
further understanding of the phenomenon and then to help those who
have experienced problems in their contact with the cults. The
social sciences are not a tool of debunking "strange" religious
beliefs, nor a form of apologetics for traditional family life, nor
avenues for conducting diatribes against people who have abandoned
the faith of their upbringing. Objectivity and impartiality, on
which the social sciences so often insist, are applicable in the
study of the cults. General conclusions on cults, drawn from therapeutic sessions with dissatisfied and/or deprogrammed ex-cult members, and/or with irate parents, violate these basic principles and
reduce research to religious harangues or social diatribes.

7. The theoretical assumptions of any research project must be
flexible and open to the possibility that there might be a genuine
religious and spiritual dimension in many of the cults. Any psychological and/or psychiatric approach which starts with the implicit
assumption that religious commitment is an expression of serious
pathology is bound to be reductionistic and will not contribute to
our understanding of the cults. Such an approach would also be an
example of faulty logic, in that the negative assumptions on cultic
life-style and the alleged pathological state of cult members are
adduced to prove each other.

8. It is also important to explore the attitudes, values, and
religious assumptions of the researchers studying the new movements
and of the psychiatrists counseling cult and/or ex-cult members and

their families. Because cults might have some therapeutic effect on
their members, they could be conceived as competitors with more traditional forms of treatment. The accusation that some psychiatrists
and counselors are wrongfully imputing mental illness to cult members
for motives which are far from professional may not be completely
without foundation (see Richardson, item 1297, and Robbins and
Anthony, item 1890).

9. The study of new religious movements must take seriously into
account the social and cultural conditions in which they emerge and
flourish. Although most psychiatrists writing on the subject acknowl-
edge this principle, they frequently fail to give it anything but
lip service. The new movements cannot be understood solely as an
expression of a person's psychology or pathology. They are social
movements which come into being at certain crucial periods in human
history. The problems which the cults have allegedly brought to
many people will not be eradicated by deprogramming, forceful counseling of ex-members, or an all-out attack on the cults themselves.
Such actions might in fact make matters worse because they direct
our attention away from the reasons why the cults appeared in the
first place.

10. One must be very wary of sweeping generalizations and all-
inclusive judgments. The variety of cults makes generalization
virtually impossible. Similarly, a blanket judgment that holds the
cults responsible for inducing mental illness and creating emotional
upheavals is neither justified nor supported by current sociological
research on the subject. In the words of one psychiatrist, "as in
other areas of psychiatric work, a priori judgments and absolute
generalizations seldom, if ever, apply" (Levine, item 1265, p. 596).

11. The principles and methods which are used in general counseling are also applicable to cult members. The listening skills
which have been developed during the training of psychiatrists,
counseling psychologists, and other mental health professionals
should be used in all cases when cultic issues are under discussion.
Empathy has its place not only when parents of cult or ex-cult members are being counseled, but also when cult members are expressing
their beliefs, feelings, concerns, and attitudes.

12. Finally, research on the new religious movements must direct
itself to one of the more important questions, namely, that of religious experience, conversion, and commitment. With few exceptions,
psychological and psychiatric studies on the cults have tended to
eschew this topic. This leads to the important issue of the relationship between religion and/or theology and the psychological
disciplines.

Religion, Psychology, and Psychiatry

One of the major difficulties in the psychiatric study of the
new cults is that the researchers have little, if any, academic
background in the study of religion and even less interest in the
spiritual dimension of a person's life. A student who graduates

with a doctorate in psychology or psychiatry may never have taken one course in religion. In spite of the more balanced approach to religion in humanistic and transpersonal psychologies, the influence of Freud is still the dominant factor in the study of religion and cults (items 1098, pp. 3197 ff.; 1279, pp. 70-71). Not only has religion been largely ignored in psychological research, but the traditional bias against religion and religious experience persists. And although attempts have been made to bridge the gap, the fact is that "mental health professionals are admittedly religiously tone deaf" (Hargrove, item 1228, p. 32).

This insensitivity and lack of empathy are more clearly manifest when religious conversion to the cults is under study. Most psychiatrists either ignore it completely or assume, in typical Freudian manner, that any kind of religious experience, mystical or otherwise, is a regression to childhood and hence pathological (see item 1058). This negative, a priori judgment on religion has direct links with the view that the cults are the direct cause of mental illness. It is not surprising that some (item 1228, pp. 31-32) have seen the attack against the cults as a threat against religion in general.

This anti-religion and anti-conversion stance does not, however, have to be the underlying assumption in the psychological and/or psychiatric study of the cults. It is precisely in the area of religious experience, conversion, and commitment that the psychological disciplines can contribute to our understanding of the rise and success of new religious movements. Our opinion is that a more balanced approach (see item 1345) is indispensable not only for evaluating the significance of the cultic phenomenon, but also for providing basic guidelines for the counseling of those who have recourse to mental health professionals.

Psychiatry and the Cults

CHAPTER I

SOURCES FOR THE STUDY OF PSYCHIATRY AND THE CULTS

The study of psychiatry and the cults has been increasing steadily over the last decade. This interest is manifested in several new encyclopedias of psychiatry and psychology which have begun to include essays on the new movements and Asian psychologies. In this chapter we include those publications which we used to trace most of the items annotated. The relationship between religion and mental health has long been a subject of investigation in the psychological disciplines and many bibliographies are available. Besides the regular psychological or psychiatric journals, like the AMERICAN JOURNAL OF PSYCHIATRY, PSYCHOLOGIA, PERCEPTUAL AND MOTOR SKILLS, and the JOURNAL OF TRANSPERSONAL PSYCHOLOGY, periodicals dedicated to the fields of sociology, theology, philosophy, and the history of religion have published occasional essays on the cults that discuss or refer to the psychological issues raised by involvement in cultic groups.

The following sources include: A) general bibliographies on religion and mental health and on the new religious movements as well as several encyclopedias of psychology and/or psychiatry which contain material relevant to the main topic of this volume; and B) a comprehensive list of journals where the articles cited in this bibliography have been published.

A. BIBLIOGRAPHIES AND ENCYCLOPEDIAS

1.   ABSTRACTS IN ANTHROPOLOGY. Farmingdale, NY: Baywood Publishing Co., 1970-1985. Vol. 1-12.

Contains abstracts of scholarly articles published in over 200 journals, mostly in English. The focus is on anthropological studies which are to a large degree concerned with non-literate societies and cross-cultural comparisons. Four major areas are covered: 1) archaeology; 2) physical anthropology; 3) linguistics; and 4) cultural anthropology (ethnology). The essays on religion, religious movements, and shamanism are included under the sub-section "Symbol Systems." In recent years a sub-section on medical anthropology lists materials on folk medicine and therapy.

3

2.   Adams, Charles J., editor. A READER'S GUIDE TO THE GREAT RE-
       LIGIONS. New York: Free Press, second edition, 1977. xvii,
       521 pp.

       Contains excellent bibliographic essays on world religions,
       including primitive religions, Hinduism, Buddhism, the reli-
       gions of China and Japan, Judaism, Christianity, and Islam.
       Though there is little reference to new religious movements
       in the West, this guide provides the basic material for the
       study of diverse religious ideologies. Given the influx of
       Eastern traditions in Western culture, this book offers the
       necessary background for understanding many of the new reli-
       gious movements (especially those of Eastern origin). If one
       accepts the hypothesis that the new cults must be seen in a
       broader religious context, then this book contains the pre-
       requisite information for any psychological and/or psychiat-
       ric evaluation of the cults and those who join them.

3.   Arieti, Silvano, editor. AMERICAN HANDBOOK OF PSYCHIATRY.
       New York: Basic Books, 1959. 2 vols.

       Volume Two contains several essays on religion that focus
       on the psychiatric and psychotherapeutic aspects of both
       Christianity and Eastern religions. Also included is a
       chapter on the role of immediate experience for dynamic
       psychiatry. Zen Buddhism is given as an example of this
       kind of intense experience.

       Contains items 198, 244, 288, 328, 478.

4.   Berkowitz, Morris, and J. Edmund Jones. SOCIAL SCIENTIFIC
       STUDIES ON RELIGION: A BIBLIOGRAPHY. Pittsburgh: Univer-
       sity of Pittsburgh Press, 1967. xvii, 258 pp.

       Has sections on: 1) religion, psychiatry, medicine, and psy-
       chology; 2) religion and health; and 3) the impact of reli-
       gious beliefs on behavior. There are no annotations and no
       subject index. Some interesting material is included but is
       difficult to locate.

5.   Blood, Linda Osborne. COMPREHENSIVE BIBLIOGRAPHY ON THE NEW
       CULT PHENOMENON. Weston, MA: American Family Foundation,
       n.d. 111 pp.

       Compiles an exhaustive bibliography, catalogued by author-
       ship, on all aspects of modern cults. The works cited are
       divided into two sections, "Books and Scholarly Literature"
       and "Popular Literature," the latter part comprising about
       one fourth of the volume. There are well over 2,000 refer-
       ences to sociological, theological, psychological, psychi-
       atric, and legal studies on the new movements. Since the
       material is not annotated or arranged in any categories for
       easy consultation, and since there are no indices, this book
       is certainly not intended or suitable for easy reference.

6.   Bowman, Mary Anne. WESTERN MYSTICISM: A GUIDE TO BASIC WORKS.
     Chicago: American Library Association, 1978. vi, 113 pp.

     A selected bibliography on Western mysticism intended for
     the use of librarians, undergraduate students, and the general
     public. The following areas are covered: the philosophy,
     history, practice and experience of mysticism; oriental mysti-
     cism in Western contexts; mystical experience in literature;
     and mystical and contemplative writings. Short annotations
     to most of the works cited are added, though the last section
     mentioned above is largely a book list. There is no section
     dedicated to psychological and/or psychiatric studies, but the
     subject index refers to some of these studies, which are quoted
     under diverse headings. A useful bibliography, though rather
     narrow and limited in scope.

7.   Brunkow, Robert de V., editor. RELIGION AND SOCIETY IN NORTH
     AMERICA. Santa Barbara, CA: American Bibliographical Center-
     Clio Press Inc., 1983. xi, 515 pp.

     Includes a short bibliography on cults of the twentieth
     century and of Eastern religions, with some references to the
     psychology of religion. A lengthy list of relevant periodicals
     is added.

8.   Burr, Nelson R. A CRITICAL BIBLIOGRAPHY OF RELIGION IN
     AMERICA. Vol. 4, parts 1 and 2, of RELIGION IN AMERICAN
     LIFE. Edited by James Ward Smith and A. Leland Jamison.
     Princeton: Princeton University Press, 1961. xx, 541 pp.

     Contains references to standard historical works on many
     sects and cults of the nineteenth and early twentieth centu-
     ries. A short section (pp. 176-77) deals with "psychological
     studies of revival movements."

9.   Campbell, Robert J. PSYCHIATRIC DICTIONARY. New York: Ox-
     ford University Press, 5th edition, 1981. 693 pp.

     Describes briefly "brainwashing" (also called menticide) and
     sensory deprivation, experienced by many explorers and ship-
     wrecked persons who, under severe stress, develop mental and
     psychological abnormalities. Since the essay contains no
     reference to, nor makes a connection with, the cults, the
     reader is presented with an objective view of brainwashing
     without the emotional slant so often found in both scientific
     and popular writings.

10. Capps, Donald, Lewis Rambo, and Raul Ramshoff. PSYCHOLOGY OF
     RELIGION: A GUIDE TO INFORMATION RESOURCES. Detroit: Gale
     Research Co., 1977. xii, 352 pp.

     A good collection of partly annotated psychological and
     psychiatric studies. The material is arranged in several
     sections, including the social and experiential dimensions of
     religion. One area covered is religion and mental health.
     There are also several basic studies on Yoga and Zen.

11.   Choquette, Diane. NEW RELIGIOUS MOVEMENTS IN THE UNITED
       STATES AND CANADA: A CRITICAL ASSESSMENT AND ANNOTATED
       BIBLIOBRAPHY. Westport, CT: Greenwood Press, 1985. xi,
       235 pp.

       A carefully annotated bibliography surveying literature in
       the English language on the new religious movements since the
       middle 1960s. Materials are arranged by discipline: history;
       sociology; anthropology; psychology; psychiatry; theology;
       religion; and law. The volume includes a section on selected
       publications of personal accounts, popular studies, and the
       new religious movements and the spiritualization of knowledge.
       Contains author, title, and subject indices.

12.   Corsini, Raymond J., editor. ENCYCLOPEDIA OF PSYCHOLOGY. New
       York: Wiley and Sons, 1984. 4 vols.

       Contains, besides entries on religion and psychology and
       religious behavior, one short essay on deprogramming and
       religious cults. The author subscribes to the brainwashing
       theory of cult formation. In an article comparing different
       views of psychological health (vol. 3, pp. 99-101) and in an
       essay on Zen Buddhism (item 1490), Zen is treated as a school
       of psychotherapy.

13.   Cronbach, Abraham. "The Psychology of Religion: A Biblio-
       graphical Survey." PSYCHOLOGICAL BULLETIN 25 (1928): 701-19.

       Reviews and evaluates early English, German, and French
       literature on the psychology of religion published between
       1926 and 1928. The author divides the material of 140 books
       and articles as follows: 1) descriptive; 2) controversial;
       and 3) practical, the latter being further subdivided into
       a) therapeutic and b) clerical and pedagogical. He further
       comments that "on the whole the caliber of this literature
       is not high" (p. 713).

14.   Cronbach, Abraham. "Religion and Psychoanalysis: A Biblio-
       graphical Survey." PSYCHOLOGICAL BULLETIN 23 (1926): 701-
       13.

       Surveys 76 titles in English, German, and French on the psy-
       choanalytic study of religion prior to 1926. The material
       is divided into three sections: 1) libidinous, including the
       infantile; 2) pathological; and 3) therapeutic. The author
       points out that religion is commonly treated as the result
       of pathology, though sometimes it is said to be the cause of
       neurosis. Occasionally, however, religion can play a part
       in the therapeutic process.

15.   Donahue, Michael J. NEW RELIGIOUS MOVEMENTS: A BIBLIOGRAPHY.
       Washington, DC: American Psychological Association, 1984.
       Psychological Documents, MS 2600. 49 pp.

       Compiles more than 600 books and essays on new religious
       movements in the USA written over a period of 30 years. The

material encompasses various approaches to the new movements, such as social and psychological theory and research, personal accounts, descriptive reports, legal analyses, polemics, and apologetics. Besides chapters including bibliographies and general resources and legal issues, there are sections dealing with specific groups like the Unification Church, Jim Jones's People's Temple, Eastern Religions, Scientology, and the Occult. This is an ordered and balanced selection. Because it is devoid of annotations, the reader will find it impossible to distinguish between scholarly works and popular literature.

16.   Driver, E. D. THE SOCIOLOGY AND ANTHROPOLOGY OF MENTAL ILL-
       NESS: A REFERENCE GUIDE. Cambridge: University of Massa-
       chusetts Press, 1972. x, 487 pp.

       Lists 5910 items without annotation, and divides them into
       a few major topics including: 1) attitudes towards mental ill-
       ness; 2) characteristics of the mentally ill; and 3) etiology
       of mental illness. There is also a short section on religion
       and mental illness. A detailed index is provided.

17.   Eysenek, H. J., W. Arnold, and R. Meili. ENCYCLOPEDIA OF
       PSYCHOLOGY. New York: Herder and Herder, 1972. 3 vols.

       Contains a description of brainwashing (menticide, coercive
       persuasion) and its methods. The word "cult" is still used
       to refer to "rite" or "worship" as distinct from belief--a
       meaning more commonly ascribed to it before the rise of the
       new religious movements. A lengthy essay on religion and
       psychology is also included.

18.   Favazza, Armando R., and Ahmed D. Faheem. THEMES IN CULTURAL
       PSYCHIATRY: AN ANNOTATED BIBLIOGRAPHY, 1975-1980. Columbia:
       University of Missouri Press, 1982. 194 pp.

       A bibliography which reflects the interest among anthro-
       pologists and psychiatrists alike in cross-cultural research
       and therapy. The materials, mostly in English with some
       French and German titles, are briefly annotated and listed in
       alphabetical order by author. There are 29 references to
       cults. References to healing, possession, glossolalia, and
       to individual cults or movements are also found. A list of
       118 journals, from which the articles are taken, is included.
       This bibliography updates Favazza and Oman's earlier work
       (item 19).

19.   Favazza, Armando R., and Mary Oman. ANTHROPOLOGICAL AND CROSS-
       CULTURAL THEMES IN MENTAL HEALTH: AN ANNOTATED BIBLIOGRAPHY,
       1925-1974. Columbia: University of Missouri Press, 1977.
       386 pp.

       Lists over 3500 items arranged in order of their year of
       publication. A lengthy introduction explains the author's
       use of sources and means of identifying articles. Various
       tables show the number of essays written in each journal per

year. There are also lists of countries and cultures which
are the subject of the research conducted in mental health.
Author and subject indices are appended.

20. Franck, Loren, Monty L. Lynn, Mark Mendenhall, and Gary R.
     Oddous. SEVEN YEARS OF RELIGIOUS CONVERSION: A SELECTED
     ANNOTATED BIBLIOGRAPHY. Washington, DC: American Psycho-
     logical Association, 1982. Psychological Documents,
     MS 2479. 6 pp.

     Covers thirty articles published in sociological and psy-
     chological journals from 1975 to 1981. The authors claim
     that, though not exhaustive, the list provides a thorough
     summary of the limited amount of empirical and theoretical
     literature on conversion. Several studies on the new reli-
     gious movements are included.

21. Freeman, Ruth St. John, and H. A. Freeman. COUNSELING: A
     BIBLIOGRAPHY WITH ANNOTATIONS. Metuchen, NJ: Scarecrow
     Press, 1964. 986 pp.

     Contains a long section (pp. 71-283) on religion, listing
     many items, published mainly between 1950 and 1964, on reli-
     gion and mental health and therapy. This volume has no
     indices, but its coding system somewhat facilitates the search
     for relevant material.

22. Goldenson, Robert M. THE ENCYCLOPEDIA OF HUMAN BEHAVIOR.
     New York: Doubleday, 1970. 2 vols.

     Discusses brainwashing (coercive persuasion) primarily
     within the context of the Korean prisoners of war. Phases
     of brainwashing are threefold: isolation, thought control,
     and political conditioning. After release from prison the
     ex-prisoners showed a "zombie reaction," a condition which
     has in more recent literature been applied to cult members.
     There are several references to cults or sects but no entries
     on religion in general or on any particular religion.

23. Harré, Rom, and Roger Lamb. THE ENCYCLOPEDIC DICTIONARY OF
     PSYCHOLOGY. Cambridge, MA: MIT Press, 1983. 718 pp.

     Has several short articles on Christian, Buddhist, Tantric
     and Yoga psychology and on unofficial and alternative psychol-
     ogies. This work reflects one current trend in psychological
     literature that maintains that meditation and similar methods
     of Eastern and Western origin can be therapeutic.

24. Jarrell, Howard R. INTERNATIONAL MEDITATION BIBLIOGRAPHY.
     Metuchen, NJ: Scarecrow Press, 1985. x, 432 pp.

     A comprehensive, partially annotated bibliography covering
     titles in six languages. The material is organized in the
     following sections: 1) articles; 2) books; 3) doctoral disser-
     tations and master's theses; 4) motion pictures; 5) recordings;
     and 6) societies and associations. Christian meditation, Zen,

Yoga meditation, and Transcendental Meditation are included. Several approaches, theological, sociological and psychological, are represented. There are no author, title or subject indices.

25. Jarrell, Howard R. INTERNATIONAL YOGA BIBLIOGRAPHY, 1950-1980. Metuchen, NJ: Scarecrow Press, 1981. ix, 221 pp.

Divides the publications on Yoga into 1) books; 2) journal articles; and 3) magazine articles. A list of Yoga periodicals, together with author, title, and subject indices, are appended. There is a section on the therapeutic use of Yoga. Published material in seven European languages is included. There are no annotations.

26. Jones, Charles Edwin. A GUIDE TO THE STUDY OF THE PENTECOSTAL MOVEMENT. Metuchen, NJ: Scarecrow Press, 1983. 2 vols, xlv, 1199 pp.

A partially annotated bibliography of works, mainly in English, on the Pentecostal/charismatic movement. The items listed are divided into four sections: 1) literature on the movement without references to the doctrinal tradition; 2) Wesleyan and Baptist works classified by doctrinal emphasis; 3) schools; and 4) biography, which includes material on members of these movements and some critical publications. The author's interest is largely theological, but some references to the psychology of the movements are included.

27. Jones, Charles Edwin. A GUIDE TO THE STUDY OF THE HOLINESS MOVEMENT. Metuchen, NJ: Scarecrow Press, 1974. xxviii, 981 pp.

Gives an extensive list of over 7000 items dealing with the holiness movement, particularly those groups which trace their origin to the Wesleyan tradition. The material is divided into three major groupings: 1) Christian Holiness Association; 2) the Keswick Movement; and 3) the Holiness-Pentecostal Movement. Short historical notes on each religious group are provided, but there are few annotations to the works cited. Though mainly a theological book showing interest in history, doctrine, evangelistic work, mission, sermon, and pastoral theology, there is some material pertinent to the theme of psychiatry and the cults.

28. Kanellakos, Demetri P., and Jerome S. Lukas. THE PSYCHO-BIOLOGY OF TRANSCENDENTAL MEDITATION: A LITERATURE REVIEW. Menlo Park, CA: Stanford Research Institute, 1973. xiii, 103 pp.

Reviews published and unpublished literature on meditation, particularly Transcendental Meditation, up to 1972. The volume includes a specific section on the psychological effects of meditation. This annotated bibliography, though limited in scope and partial to TM, includes several interesting

studies on TM in its early stages in the United States. It
is argued that research shows that a consistent set of physiological and psychological effects is correlated with the
practice of TM. The authors suggest that the possibility of
long-term deleterious effects from the practice of TM by
unstable people should be investigated.

29.   Kaplan, Harold, Alfred H. Freedman, and Benjamin J. Sadock.
       COMPREHENSIVE TEXTBOOK OF PSYCHIATRY III. Baltimore:
       Williams and Wilkins, 3rd. edition, 1980. 3 vols.

       Carries two major essays, one on Religion and Psychiatry
       (item 1098) and one on the cults (item 1355). The former de-
       fines cults as healing techniques, the latter as harmful
       institutions causing pathological conditions in those who
       join them.

30.   Karpinski, Leszek M. THE RELIGIOUS LIFE OF MAN: GUIDE TO
       BASIC LITERATURE. Metuchen, NJ: Scarecrow Press, 1978.
       xx, 399 pp.

       A selected and annotated bibliography, mainly of works in
       English, designed for use by undergraduate college students
       and the general public. The material is divided into six
       parts: 1) religions of mankind; 2) religions of the past;
       3) Judaism, Christianity, and Islam; 4) Asian religions; 5)
       the beliefs of native peoples; and 6) the occult. There are
       sections on the psychology of religion, on sects in various
       religious traditions, and on contemporary trends in North
       America. The material cited includes reference works, scrip-
       tural texts, handbooks and surveys, critical works and studies,
       and lists of journals.

31.   La Barre, Weston. "Materials For a History of Crisis Cults."
       CURRENT ANTHROPOLOGY 12 (1971): 3-45.

       Overviews mainly anthropological material on new religious
       movements. The main divisions include: 1) empirical studies
       in different parts of the world; 2) synoptic surveys, classi-
       fication, terminology, and non-primitive crisis cults; 3)
       psychological, economic, political and military theories of
       causality. The author's view is that no particular explanation
       can exclusively and exhaustively account for any single cult,
       and that a holistic approach is required to understand the
       causes of these movements. Comments by various scholars and
       the author's response contribute to a lively discussion. About
       450 references are cited.

32.   Lesh, Terry V. "Zen and Psychotherapy: A Partially Annotated
       Bibliography." JOURNAL OF HUMANISTIC PSYCHOLOGY 10.1 (1970):
       75-83.

       Divides the material into the following sections: 1) history
       of Zen; 2) Eastern and Western modes of thinking (compared and
       contrasted); 3) Zen and psychotherapy; 4) Zen and identity

(self and mind); 5) Zen and mind; and 6) practices and techniques of "Zazen" and other methods of meditation. Although
dated, this is an important and useful bibliography showing
the interest in the psychotherapeutic use of Zen before it
was labeled a destructive cult in some quarters.

33.   Martin, Ira Jay. GLOSSOLALIA, THE GIFT OF TONGUES: A BIB-
       LIOGRAPHY. Cleveland, TN: Pathway Press, 1970. 72 pp.

       Lists: 1) primary and secondary books and periodical arti-
       cles on glossolalia; 2) journals which frequently publish
       material on the subject; 3) formal and informal statements
       made by different denominations; 4) theses and dissertations;
       5) commentaries, encyclopedias, and dictionaries; and 6) tapes
       and microfilms. Most of the titles are in English. There are
       no annotations or indices and, though the stress is heavily
       on theological literature, several standard psychological
       studies on speaking in tongues are mentioned.

34.   Meissner, W. W. ANNOTATED BIBLIOGRAPHY IN RELIGION AND PSY-
       CHOLOGY. New York: Academy of Religion and Mental Health,
       1961. 235 pp.

       A comprehensive, well-annotated bibliography of books and
       articles, in English, German, or French, published before 1961.
       Besides sections on the psychology of conversion, religious
       experience and religion and mental health, there are several
       entries on oriental religions, primitive religions, and other
       religious movements. An index of authors is given.

35.   Menges, Robert J., and James E. Dittes. PSYCHOLOGICAL STUD-
       IES OF CLERGYMEN: ABSTRACTS OF RESEARCH. New York: Thomas
       Nelson and Sons, 1965. 292 pp.

       An exhaustive coverage of the literature on the psychology
       of the clergy, aimed at providing a broad perspective of the
       field and pointing to areas in need of further research. The
       material is divided into several categories, including the
       personality characteristics of clergymen, their effectiveness,
       and their state of mental health or illness. The research
       abstracts are ordered to include a sample, the procedure
       pursued, and some of the main results. The vast majority of
       the works cited are in English but there are French, Spanish,
       Italian, German, and Latin titles. About 700 entries published
       within a two-year period prior to publication of this volume
       are mentioned. This book provides material for comparing
       the psychological characteristics of those people who have
       dedicated their time and energy to religious pursuits.

36.   Menninger, Karl. A GUIDE TO PSYCHIATRIC BOOKS IN ENGLISH.
       New York: Grune and Stratton, 1972. xvi, 157 pp.

       Provides a list of books dealing with such topics as social
       pathology, the relationship of religion to psychiatry, and the
       psychology of new religious movements in non-Western cultures.
       Special reading lists for physicians and clergy are drawn up.

12   PSYCHIATRY AND THE CULTS

37.   Mills, Watson Early, editor. CHARISMATIC RELIGION IN MODERN
       RESEARCH: A BIBLIOGRAPHY. NABPR Bibliographic Series I.
       Macon, GA: Mercer University Press, 1985. 178 pp.

       Contains 2105 items on charismatic groups which the author
       classifies in three types: 1) Pentecostal; 2) neo-Pentecostal;
       and 3) the Jesus movement. Several works on the psychology
       of glossolalia are included. Author and subject indices are
       appended.

38.   Murphy, Michael, and Steven Donovan. "A Bibliography of
       Meditation Theory and Research, 1931-1983." JOURNAL OF
       TRANSPERSONAL PSYCHOLOGY 15 (1983): 181-228.

       Lists over 750 entries, mainly articles in English scienti-
       fic journals and some books and doctoral and master's theses.
       Religious, philosophical, and metaphysical literature on medi-
       tation is omitted. There are no annotations and the works
       are listed simply in the authors' alphabetical order.

39.   Pattison, E. Mansell. "A Contemporary Bibliography on
       Psychiatry and Religion." CLINICAL PSYCHIATRY AND RELI-
       GION (item 294), pp. 305-11.

       Comprises a short, useful (though dated) list of books
       dealing with topics such as psychoanalysis and religion,
       existential psychotherapy and religion, psychopathology and
       religion, mental health and religious vocations and psycho-
       logy and religious experiences.

40.   Popemore, Cris. WELLNESS. Washington, DC: Yes! Inc., 1977.
       443 pp.

       An annotated bibliography of many topics centered around
       the new age movement. Nutrition, natural childbirth, herbs,
       healing, and oriental medicine are included. Sections on
       mental health (pp. 182-201), reflexology (pp. 398-400), and
       shiatsu and acupuncture (pp. 400-8) describe several books
       which give treatments for relieving stress.

41.   PSYCHOLOGICAL ABSTRACTS. Arlington, VA: The American Psycho-
       logical Association, 1929-1985.

       A major source for information on published materials on the
       psychology and psychiatry of religion and of new religious
       movements. Since 1973, relevant material on the new movements
       is indexed under the label "cultism." Of special value are
       the references to studies on religion and mental health. The
       short annotations contained in these volumes are descriptive
       in character.

42.   Rambo, Lewis R. "Current Research on Religious Conversion,"
       RELIGIOUS STUDIES REVIEW 8 (1982): 146-59.

       A good summary of anthropological, sociological, historical,
       psychological, psychoanalytic, and theological perspectives

of religious conversion. A section on conversion to the new
religious movements is included. The implicit suggestion is
that conversion to the cults should be studied as a process
of religious conversion, similar to conversion to any religion
or belief system. The author thinks that a lot of research
still has to be done in the psychology of conversion. He
asserts that a psychology of religion "can never be adequate
without the explicit and systematic enrichment provided by
other disciplines" (p. 153). Each section has a short, select
bibliography of the major works in the field.

43.   Schaub, Edward L. "The Psychology of Religion." PSYCHOLO-
        GICAL BULLETIN 23 (1926): 681-700.

        Reviews over 70 books and articles in English, German,
        and French published in the early 1920s.

44.   Schermerhorn, Richard A., editor. PSYCHIATRIC INDEX FOR
        INTERDISCIPLINARY RESEARCH: A GUIDE TO LITERATURE, 1950-
        1961. Washington, DC: Department of Health, Education,
        and Welfare, Vocational Rehabilitation Administration,
        1964. xvii, 1249 pp.

        Contains a short section (pp. 873-78) covering the relation-
        ship between religious beliefs and practices and mental health,
        mental disorder, and therapy. The material shows that the
        problem of the relationship between religion and mental health
        antedates the current debate about the cults. There are no
        annotations and no indices.

45.   Shapiro, Deane H., and Roger N. Walsh, editors. MEDITATION:
        CLASSIC AND CONTEMPORARY APPROACHES. Hawthorne, NY:
        Aldine, 1984. xxii, 722 pp.

        Presents a large selection of essays on Transcendental
        Meditation, most of which had been previously published.
        This large volume covers both the theory and practice of TM.
        The physiological and psychological effects of TM are dealt
        with at length in several of the articles. The editors have
        brought together some of the best material on TM. Because
        of the many bibliographies included in the essays, this
        collection is a standard reference guide to the student of
        Transcendental Meditation.

        Contains items 1369, 1394, 1434, 1450, 1555, 1598, 1634, 1636.

46.   Sharma, Umesh, and John Arndt. MYSTICISM: A SELECT BIBLI-
        OGRAPHY. Waterloo, Canada: Waterloo Lutheran University,
        1973. 109 pp.

        Contains over 1500 selected entries on mysticism in various
        religious traditions. The books and articles cited are not
        annotated and are restricted to publications in English since
        1900. A subject index is appended.

47.   Smith, Jonathan C. "Meditation as Psychotherapy: A Review of
       the Literature." PSYCHOLOGICAL BULLETIN 82 (1975): 558-64.

       Reviews 30 books and articles from 1926 to 1973 and exam-
       ines three sets of findings on the psychotherapeutic effects
       of meditation, namely: 1) that those experienced meditators
       who particiapted in meditation research appear happier than
       non-meditators; 2) that beginning meditators show improvement
       on a variety of tests after four to ten weeks of meditation;
       and 3) that those persons who are randomly chosen to learn
       and practice meditation show more improvement over four to
       ten weeks than those who follow an alternate treatment. The
       author disputes the common conclusion that the various forms
       of meditation have therapeutic effects. The alleged bene-
       ficial results, he argues, could be due to the expectation
       of relief (the placebo effect) or of simply sitting or rest-
       ing on a regular basis.

48.   Steggles, Shawn, Cornelius Holland, and Robert Fehr. "Gestalt
       Therapy and Eastern Philosophies: A Partially Annotated
       Bibliography." JOURNAL OF HUMANISTIC PSYCHOLOGY 23 (1983):
       119-28.

       Lists 52 items published in English between 1947 and 1979.
       The material is classified into three categories: primary,
       secondary, and tertiary references, the last of which is not
       annotated. Yoga, Tantric Buddhism, Zen, and Transcendental
       Meditation are among the Eastern philosophies included. The
       view that Eastern traditions suggest an alternative psycho-
       logical understanding of the human person is strongly repre-
       sented. This is a good bibliography for the incipient reader.

49.   Summerlin, Florence A. RELIGION AND MENTAL HEALTH: A BIBLI-
       OGRAPHY. Rockville, MD: National Institutes of Mental
       Health, 1980. 401 pp.

       An annotated bibliography covering various aspects of the
       relationship between religion and mental health and illness.
       Besides a section on the influential role religion can play
       in both health and illness, this volume has sections on re-
       ligious experience, sects and cults, and Eastern religious
       traditions.

50.   Timmons, Beverly, and Joe Kamiya. "The Psychology and Physi-
       ology of Meditation and Related Phenomena: A Bibliography."
       JOURNAL OF TRANSPERSONAL PSYCHOLOGY 1 (1970): 41-59.

       Contains over 300 references, mainly to articles written
       in several languages and published in professional journals.
       Besides the effects various kinds of meditation techniques
       have on mental health, the physiological benefits of medita-
       tion as well as the relationship between meditation and para-
       psychology are covered. This could well be the earliest
       bibliography on the subject since the rise of the new reli-
       gious movements.

51.   Timmons, Beverly, and Demetri P. Kanellakos. "The Psychology
        and Physiology of Meditation and Related Phenomena: Bibli-
        ography II." JOURNAL OF TRANSPERSONAL PSYCHOLOGY 1 (1974):
        32-38.

        Updates an earlier bibliography (item 50).

52.   Turner, Harold W. BIBLIOGRAPHY OF NEW RELIGIOUS MOVEMENTS
        IN PRIMAL SOCIETIES. Boston: G. K. Hall, 1977-78. Vol. 1:
        Black Africa. x, 277 pp. Vol. 2: North America. x, 286 pp.

        An extensive bibliography in many languages on new reli-
        gious movements in non-literate societies. The first volume
        divides the material by country. The second, largely dedi-
        cated to references to the American Indians of the United
        States, lists many millennial movements in these tribal
        societies. The annotations, where given, are rather brief.
        A very short subject index is provided. This is a useful,
        comprehensive collection, though it is not easy to locate
        specific material.

53.   Walker, Benjamin. ENCYCLOPEDIA OF METAPHYSICAL MEDICINE.
        London: Routledge and Kegan Paul, 1978. x, 323 pp.

        Describes non-orthodox medical treatments which have been
        applied to heal various physical and psychological disorders.
        Sections on acupuncture, exorcism, spiritual healing, and
        religious therapy are included. A short basic bibliographic
        guide is provided after each chapter. These forms of therapy
        are classified as occult, spiritual, fringe, out-of-the-way,
        and offbeat. The author holds, however, that they cannot be
        dismissed as useless or dangerous superstitions since they
        have helped human beings through many centuries. Those people
        who in our time use them or experiment with them cannot be
        called credulous.

54.   Weiman, Mark. YOGA: A BIBLIOGRAPHY. Berkeley, CA: The Move-
        able Foundation Workshop Press, 1980. 135 pp.

        A list of English books, films, filmstrips, and recordings
        on Yoga, some of which are briefly annotated or described.
        Since most of the works cited are by Indian gurus in the
        West, this collection provides an inside view of Yoga and
        and the claims that it has physical and psychological
        effects on those who practice it. Lack of indices makes it
        somewhat hard to locate specific material. The references
        to audiovisual materials make this bibiliography particularly
        useful for teaching purposes.

55.   Wilson, John F., and Thomas P. Slavens. RESEARCH GUIDE TO
        RELIGIOUS STUDIES. Chicago: American Library Association,
        1982. viii, 192 pp.

        Consists of annotated references to many religions, includ-
        ing new religious movements in the USA. Though the question

of the new cults and mental health is not explicitly treated,
there are many relevant sources on topics like meditation and
mysticism.

56.   Wolman, Benjamin B., editor. INTERNATIONAL ENCYCLOPEDIA OF
        PSYCHIATRY, PSYCHOLOGY, PSYCHOANALYSIS, AND NEUROLOGY. New
        York: Van Nostrand Publishing Co., 1977. 12 vols.

        Contains two short articles on Adler's and Jung's views on
        religion (vol. 9, pp. 427-32) and a longer essay on religion
        and psychoanalysis (pp. 432-45). The latter essay discusses
        primitive religions, Eastern religions (the Great Mother God-
        dess Religions and Hinduism), and Western Religions (Judaism
        and Christianity). Typical psychoanalytic interpretations
        are given. The shaman, for example, dramatizes the expulsion
        of those psychological elements which cause anxiety, depres-
        sion, resentment, jealousy, and anger. He is the repository
        for his people's narcissistic desire and terror. A short
        bibliography on psychoanalysis and religion is added. Sur-
        prisingly, little is said about Buddhism, Japanese religions,
        or Islam. Buddhism and Japanese religions are briefly men-
        tioned in articles on mental health and psychiatry in Asia
        and psychology in Asia (vol. 2, pp. 144-52), while Islam
        receives minor attention in an essay on psychiatry in Turkey
        (vol. 9, p. 289).

57.   Wolman, Benjamin B., compiler and editor. DICTIONARY OF BEHAV-
        IORAL SCIENCE. New York: Van Nostrand Publishing Co., 1972.
        ix, 478 pp.

        Lists no entries on cults or sects, but has brief refer-
        ences on religious mania and the therapeutic practices of some
        religions like, for instance, the confessional and pastoral
        counseling.

58.   Zaretsky, Irving I. BIBLIOGRAPHY ON SPIRIT POSSESSION AND
        SPIRIT MEDIUMSHIP. Evanston, IL: Northwestern University
        Press, 1966. xvi, 106 pp.

        Makes a preliminary attempt to compile a list of ethno-
        graphic sources on the subject. The areas covered are mainly
        societies in sub-Saharan Africa. The subject matter includes
        new religious movements which incorporate both indigenous and
        Christian religious elements. The limited material surveyed,
        written in English and French, is largely descriptive. There
        are no indices.

59.   Zaretsky, Irving I., and Cynthia Shambaugh. SPIRIT POSSES-
        SION AND SPIRIT MEDIUMSHIP IN AFRICA AND AFRO-AMERICA: AN
        ANNOTATED BIBLIOGRAPHY. New York: Garland, 1978. xxiii,
        443 pp.

        Greatly expands Zaretsky's previous bibliography (item 58)
        and provides the researcher with ethnographic and interpre-
        tative material on a much-explored religious phenomenon. The

titles included, in English, German, and French, are briefly
annotated and a shorter list of Portuguese writings about the
phenomenon in Brazil is added. The bibliography is organized
alphabetically by author. There is a short index which includes material under such headings as: Theoretical Sources
of Spirit Possession, Altered States of Consciousness Research, Glossolalia, and Religious Movements. Lists of
journals, newsletters, and periodicals are also appended.

B. PERIODICALS CITED

ACADEMIC PSYCHOLOGY BULLETIN
ACADEMIC THERAPY
ACTA PSYCHIATRICA ET NEUROLOGICA
ACTA PSYCHIATRICA SCANDINAVICA
ADDICTIVE BEHAVIORS
ADOLESCENCE
ADOLESCENT PSYCHIATRY
ADVANCEMENT OF SCIENCE
ALCOHOL HEALTH AND RESEARCH WORLD
ALIENIST AND NEUROLOGIST
AMERICAN ANTHROPOLOGIST
AMERICAN BEHAVIORAL SCIENTIST
AMERICAN CORRECTIVE THERAPY JOURNAL
AMERICAN ETHNOLOGIST
AMERICAN IMAGO
AMERICAN JOURNAL OF CLINICAL HYPNOSIS
AMERICAN JOURNAL OF INSANITY
AMERICAN JOURNAL OF NURSING
AMERICAN JOURNAL OF ORTHOPSYCHIATRY
AMERICAN JOURNAL OF PSYCHIATRY
AMERICAN JOURNAL OF PSYCHOANALYSIS
AMERICAN JOURNAL OF PSYCHOLOGY
AMERICAN JOURNAL OF PSYCHOTHERAPY
AMERICAN JOURNAL OF SOCIOLOGY
AMERICAN MERCURY
AMERICAN PSYCHOLOGIST
AMERICAN QUARTERLY
AMERICAN SOCIOLOGICAL REVIEW
ANNALS OF THE AMERICAN SOCIETY OF ADOLESCENT PSYCHIATRY
ANNALS OF THE NEW YORK ACADEMY OF SCIENCES
ANNALS OF PSYCHOANALYSIS
ANNUAL REVIEW OF ANTHROPOLOGY
ANNUAL REVIEW OF NUTRITION
ANNUAL REVIEW OF PSYCHOLOGY
ANTHROPOLOGICAL QUARTERLY
ARCHIVES OF GENERAL PSYCHIATRY
ART PSYCHOTHERAPY
ASIAN MEDICAL JOURNAL
AUSTRALIAN AND NEW ZEALAND JOURNAL OF PSYCHIATRY
AUSTRALIAN JOURNAL OF PSYCHOLOGY

AUSTRALIAN JOURNAL OF SOCIAL ISSUES
AUSTRALIAN PSYCHOLOGIST
BEHAVIOR RESEARCH AND THERAPY
BEHAVIOR THERAPIST
BEHAVIOR THERAPY
BEHAVIORAL NEUROPSYCHIATRY
BEHAVIORAL SCIENCE
BEHAVIORISM
BIBLICAL WORLD
BIOSCIENCE COMMUNICATIONS
BRITISH JOURNAL OF CLINICAL PSYCHOLOGY
BRITISH JOURNAL OF HOSPITAL MEDICINE
BRITISH JOURNAL OF MEDICAL PSYCHOLOGY
BRITISH JOURNAL OF PSYCHIATRY
BRITISH JOURNAL OF SOCIAL AND CLINICAL PSYCHOLOGY
BULLETIN OF THE MENNINGER CLINIC
BULLETIN OF THE SOCIETY OF PSYCHOLOGISTS IN ADDICTIVE BEHAVIOR
CANADIAN JOURNAL OF PSYCHIATRY
CANADIAN JOURNAL OF PSYCHOLOGY
CANADIAN JOURNAL OF THEOLOGY
CANADIAN MEDICAL ASSOCIATION JOURNAL
CANADIAN PSYCHIATRIC ASSOCIATION JOURNAL
CANADIAN PSYCHOLOGIST
CANADIAN REVIEW OF SOCIOLOGY AND ANTHROPOLOGY
CENTRAL ISSUES IN ANTHROPOLOGY
CHICAGO REVIEW
CHICAGO THEOLOGICAL SEMINARY REGISTER
CHILD PSYCHIATRY QUARTERLY
CLINICAL PSYCHOLOGY REVIEW
COGNITIVE THERAPY AND RESEARCH
COMPARATIVE PSYCHIATRY
COMPREHENSIVE PSYCHIATRY
COMPREHENSIVE PSYCHOTHERAPY
CONFINIA PSYCHIATRICA
CONTEMPORARY PSYCHOANALYSIS
CORNELL JOURNAL OF SOCIAL STUDIES
COUNSELING AND VALUES
CREATIVE CHILD AND ADULT QUARTERLY
CRIMINAL JUSTICE AND BEHAVIOR
CULTIC STUDIES JOURNAL
CULTURE, MEDICINE, AND PSYCHIATRY
CURRENT ANTHROPOLOGY
CURRENT PSYCHIATRIC THERAPIES
DISEASES OF THE NERVOUS SYSTEM
ECCLESIASTICAL REVIEW
ETC: A REVIEW OF GENERAL SEMANTICS
ETHNOHISTORY
ETHNOLOGY
ETHOS
EXPERIMENTAL AND CLINICAL PSYCHIATRY
EXPOSITORY TIMES
FAMILY COORDINATOR
FAMILY PHYSICIAN

GENETIC PSYCHOLOGY MONOGRAPHS
GESTALT JOURNAL
GREGORIANUM
GROUP
GROUP PSYCHOTHERAPY
HARTFORD QUARTERLY
HILLSIDE JOURNAL OF CLINICAL PSYCHIATRY
HISTORY OF CHILDHOOD QUARTERLY: THE JOURNAL OF PSYCHOHISTORY
HISTORY OF RELIGIONS
HORIZONS: JOURNAL OF THE COLLEGE THEOLOGY SOCIETY
HOSPITAL AND COMMUNITY PSYCHIATRY
HUMAN CONTEXT
HUMAN ORGANIZATION
HUMAN RELATIONS
ILIFF REVIEW
INDIAN JOURNAL OF CLINICAL PSYCHOLOGY
INDIAN JOURNAL OF PSYCHIATRY
INDIAN JOURNAL OF PSYCHOLOGY
INSIGHT: INTERDISCIPLINARY STUDIES OF MAN
INSIGHT: QUARTERLY REVIEW OF RELIGION AND MENTAL HEALTH
INTERACTION
INTERNATIONAL JOURNAL OF CLINICAL AND EXPERIMENTAL HYPNOSIS
INTERNATIONAL JOURNAL OF FAMILY THERAPY
INTERNATIONAL JOURNAL OF GROUP PSYCHOTHERAPY
INTERNATIONAL JOURNAL OF GROUP TENSIONS
INTERNATIONAL JOURNAL OF PSYCHIATRY
INTERNATIONAL JOURNAL OF PSYCHOANALYSIS
INTERNATIONAL JOURNAL OF PSYCHOANALYTIC PSYCHOTHERAPY
INTERNATIONAL JOURNAL OF PSYCHOSOMATICS
INTERNATIONAL JOURNAL OF SOCIAL PSYCHIATRY
INTERNATIONAL MENTAL HEALTH REVIEW NEWSLETTER
INTERNATIONAL REVIEW OF APPLIED PSYCHOLOGY
INTERNATIONAL REVIEW OF PSYCHO-ANALYSIS
INTERPERSONAL DEVELOPMENT
ISRAELI ANNALS OF PSYCHIATRY AND RELATED DISCIPLINES
ISRAELI HORIZONS
JOURNAL FOR THE SCIENTIFIC STUDY OF RELIGION
JOURNAL OF ABNORMAL PSYCHOLOGY
JOURNAL OF ABNORMAL AND SOCIAL PSYCHOLOGY
JOURNAL OF ALTERED STATES OF CONSCIOUSNESS
JOURNAL OF AMERICAN FOLKLORE
JOURNAL OF ANALYTICAL PSYCHOLOGY
JOURNAL OF APPLIED PSYCHOLOGY
JOURNAL OF BEHAVIORAL MEDICINE
JOURNAL OF BEHAVIOR THERAPY AND EXPERIMENTAL PSYCHIATRY
JOURNAL OF BIBLICAL LITERATURE
JOURNAL OF CHRONIC DISEASES
JOURNAL OF CHRONIC DISEASES AND THERAPEUTIC RESEARCH
JOURNAL OF CLINICAL PSYCHIATRY
JOURNAL OF CLINICAL PSYCHOLOGY
JOURNAL OF CLINICAL PSYCHOLOGY AND THERAPEUTIC RESEARCH
JOURNAL OF CONSULTING AND CLINICAL PSYCHOLOGY
JOURNAL OF CONSULTING PSYCHOLOGY

JOURNAL OF CONTEMPORARY PSYCHOLOGY
JOURNAL OF CONTEMPORARY PSYCHOTHERAPY
JOURNAL OF COUNSELING AND DEVELOPMENT
JOURNAL OF COUNSELING PSYCHOLOGY
JOURNAL OF CREATIVE BEHAVIOR
JOURNAL OF CROSS-CULTURAL PSYCHOLOGY
JOURNAL OF FAMILY THERAPY
JOURNAL OF GENERAL PSYCHOLOGY
JOURNAL OF GERIATRIC PSYCHIATRY
JOURNAL OF HILLSIDE HOSPITAL
JOURNAL OF HUMANISTIC PSYCHOLOGY
JOURNAL OF INDIAN PSYCHOLOGY
JOURNAL OF INDIVIDUAL PSYCHOLOGY
JOURNAL OF INSTRUCTIONAL PSYCHOLOGY
JOURNAL OF JEWISH COMMUNAL SERVICE
JOURNAL OF MARITAL AND FAMILY THERAPY
JOURNAL OF MARRIAGE AND FAMILY COUNSELING
JOURNAL OF MEDICAL ETHICS
JOURNAL OF MENTAL SCIENCE
JOURNAL OF MIND AND BEHAVIOR
JOURNAL OF MORMON HISTORY
JOURNAL OF NERVOUS AND MENTAL DISEASE
JOURNAL OF NEUROPSYCHIATRY
JOURNAL OF OCCUPATIONAL MEDICINE
JOURNAL OF OPERATIONAL PSYCHIATRY
JOURNAL OF PASTORAL CARE
JOURNAL OF PASTORAL COUNSELING
JOURNAL OF PASTORAL PRACTICE
JOURNAL OF PERSONALITY
JOURNAL OF PERSONALITY AND SOCIAL PSYCHOLOGY
JOURNAL OF PROJECTIVE TECHNIQUES
JOURNAL OF PSYCHIATRIC NURSING AND MENTAL HEALTH SERVICES
JOURNAL OF PSYCHOANALYSIS IN GROUPS
JOURNAL OF PSYCHOANALYTIC ANTHROPOLOGY
JOURNAL OF PSYCHOHISTORY
JOURNAL OF PSYCHOLINGUISTIC RESEARCH
JOURNAL OF PSYCHOLOGICAL ANTHROPOLOGY
JOURNAL OF PSYCHOLOGICAL RESEARCH
JOURNAL OF PSYCHOLOGICAL STUDIES
JOURNAL OF PSYCHOLOGY
JOURNAL OF PSYCHOLOGY AND CHRISTIANITY
JOURNAL OF PSYCHOLOGY AND JUDAISM
JOURNAL OF PSYCHOLOGY AND THEOLOGY
JOURNAL OF PSYCHOSOMATIC RESEARCH
JOURNAL OF RATIONAL-EMOTIVE THERAPY
JOURNAL OF RELIGION
JOURNAL OF RELIGION AND HEALTH
JOURNAL OF SOCIAL PSYCHOLOGY
JOURNAL OF SOCIOLOGY AND SOCIAL WELFARE
JOURNAL OF STUDIES ON ALCOHOL
JOURNAL OF THE AMERICAN ACADEMY OF PSYCHOANALYSIS
JOURNAL OF THE AMERICAN ACADEMY OF RELIGION
JOURNAL OF THE AMERICAN ACADEMY OF RELIGION AND PSYCHICAL RESEARCH
JOURNAL OF THE AMERICAN MEDICAL ASSOCIATION

JOURNAL OF THE AMERICAN PSYCHOANALYTIC ASSOCIATION
JOURNAL OF THE AMERICAN SOCIETY FOR PSYCHICAL RESEARCH
JOURNAL OF THE AMERICAN SCIENTIFIC AFFILIATION
JOURNAL OF THE AMERICAN SOCIETY FOR PREVENTIVE DENTISTRY
JOURNAL OF THE AMERICAN SOCIETY OF PSYCHOSOMATIC DENTISTRY AND
  MEDICINE
JOURNAL OF THE HISTORY OF BEHAVIOR SCIENCE
JOURNAL OF THE NATIONAL MEDICAL ASSOCIATION
JOURNAL OF TRANSPERSONAL PSYCHOLOGY
KEYSTONE FOLKLORE QUARTERLY
LANGUAGE AND SPEECH
LANGUAGE IN SOCIETY
LISTENER
LISTENING: A JOURNAL OF RELIGION AND CULTURE
MAIN CURRENTS IN MODERN THOUGHT
MAN: JOURNAL OF THE ROYAL ANTHROPOLOGICAL INSTITUTE
MEDICAL ANTHROPOLOGY
MEDICAL JOURNAL OF AUSTRALIA
MEDICAL OPINION
MENNONITE QUARTERLY REVIEW
MENTAL HYGIENE
MODERN SCHOOLMAN
NAROPA INSTITUTE JOURNAL OF PSYCHOLOGY
NATIONAL ASSOCIATION OF PRIVATE PSYCHIATRIC HOSPITALS JOURNAL
NEW BLACKFRIARS
NEW ENGLAND JOURNAL OF MEDICINE
OCEANIA
PACIFIC SOCIOLOGICAL REVIEW
PASTORAL COUNSELOR
PASTORAL PSYCHOLOGY
PERCEPTUAL AND MOTOR SKILLS
PERSONALITY AND INDIVIDUAL DIFFERENCES
PERSONNEL AND GUIDANCE JOURNAL
PERSPECTIVES IN PSYCHIATRIC CARE
POLITICAL PSYCHOLOGY
PRACTICAL ANTHROPOLOGY
PROCEEDINGS OF THE ANNUAL CONVENTION OF THE AMERICAN PSYCHOLOGICAL
  ASSOCIATION
PROCEEDINGS OF THE ROYAL SOCIETY OF MEDICINE
PROFESSIONAL PSYCHOLOGY: RESEARCH AND PRACTICE
PSYCHEDELIC REVIEW
PSYCHIATRIA CLINICA
PSYCHIATRIC ANNALS
PSYCHIATRIC JOURNAL OF THE UNIVERSITY OF OTTAWA
PSYCHIATRIC QUARTERLY
PSYCHIATRY: JOURNAL FOR THE STUDY OF INTERPERSONAL PROCESSES
PSYCHOANALYSIS AND THE PSYCHOANALYTIC REVIEW
PSYCHOANALYTIC QUARTERLY
PSYCHOANALYTIC REVIEW
PSYCHOANALYTIC STUDY OF SOCIETY
PSYCHOENERGETIC SYSTEMS
PSYCHOHISTORY REVIEW
PSYCHOLOGIA: AN INTERNATIONAL JOURNAL OF PSYCHOLOGY IN THE ORIENT
PSYCHOLOGICAL BULLETIN

PSYCHOLOGICAL MEDICINE
PSYCHOLOGICAL MONOGRAPHS
PSYCHOLOGICAL RECORD
PSYCHOLOGICAL REPORTS
PSYCHOLOGICAL REVIEW
PSYCHOLOGY: A JOURNAL OF HUMAN BEHAVIOR
PSYCHOLOGY TODAY
PSYCHOSOMATIC MEDICINE
PSYCHOTHERAPY AND PSYCHOSOMATICS
PSYCHOTHERAPY IN PRIVATE PRACTICE
PSYCHOTHERAPY: THEORY, RESEARCH, AND PRACTICE
PUBLIC OPINION QUARTERLY
PUBLICATIONS OF THE AMERICAN SOCIOLOGICAL SOCIETY
RELIGION IN LIFE
RELIGIOUS EDUCATION
RELIGIOUS STUDIES
RELIGIOUS STUDIES REVIEW
RESEARCH JOURNAL OF PHILOSOPHY AND THE SOCIAL SCIENCES
REVIEW FOR RELIGIOUS
REVIEW OF RELIGIOUS RESEARCH
REVISION: A JOURNAL OF CONSCIOUSNESS AND CHANGE
R. M. BUCKE MEMORIAL SOCIETY: NEWSLETTER-REVIEW
SAMISKA: JOURNAL OF THE INDIAN PSYCHOANALYTIC SOCIETY
SCHIZOPHRENIA BULLETIN
SCIENTIFIC AMERICAN
SEMIOTICA
SMALL GROUP BEHAVIOR
SOCIAL ACTION
SOCIAL BEHAVIOR AND PERSONALITY
SOCIAL CASEWORK
SOCIAL COMPASS
SOCIAL FORCES
SOCIAL PROBLEMS
SOCIAL PSYCHIATRY
SOCIAL SCIENCE AND MEDICINE
SOCIAL WORK
SOCIOLOGICAL ANALYSIS
SOCIOLOGICAL INQUIRY
SOCIOLOGICAL QUARTERLY
SOCIOLOGY AND SOCIAL RESEARCH
SOCIOMETRY
SOUTH AFRICAN JOURNAL OF PSYCHOLOGY
SOUTHWESTERN JOURNAL OF ANTHROPOLOGY
SPIRITUAL LIFE
STUDIES IN FORMATIVE SPIRITUALITY
STUDIES: AN IRISH QUARTERLY REVIEW
SUICIDE AND LIFE-THREATENING BEHAVIOR
THEOLOGY
THEORIA TO THEORY
TRANS-ACTION
TRANSACTIONAL ANALYSIS JOURNAL
TRANSACTIONS OF THE ALL-INDIA INSTITUTE OF MENTAL HEALTH
TRANSACTIONS OF THE NEW YORK ACADEMY OF SCIENCES

TRANSNATIONAL MENTAL HEALTH RESEARCH NEWSLETTER
TRANSCULTURAL PSYCHIATRIC RESEARCH REVIEW
UPDATE: A QUARTERLY JOURNAL ON THE NEW RELIGIOUS MOVEMENTS
VOCATIONAL GUIDANCE QUARTERLY
VOICES: THE ART AND SCIENCE OF PSYCHOTHERAPY
WESTERN PSYCHOLOGIST
YOGA RESEARCH
ZYGON: A JOURNAL OF RELIGION AND SCIENCE

CHAPTER II

PSYCHIATRY AND THE CULTS IN HISTORICAL PERSPECTIVE

The current debate on the psychological effects of cult involvement is not new in the history of the relationship between psychiatry
and religion. The literature since the beginning of this century
testifies to a continuous exchange of views on the negative or positive effects of adherence to belief systems and participation in
religious rituals. There is a definite tendency among psychologists
and psychiatrists to evaluate new religious movements or sects as
more harmful to the individual's mental health than traditional
Judeo-Christian religious beliefs. Sects and cults have often been
cited as examples of unhealthy religion or judged more harshly as
signs of serious pathology. It should be borne in mind that the
contemporary debate on cultic groups emerges out of a psychological
approach to religious beliefs and practices, particularly to intense
religious or mystical experiences and sudden conversions, which not
only questions their contribution to mental health but also links
them with mental illness.

One major issue in psychological literature until the early 1970s
centered around the relationship between religion and mental health.
The Freudian view that religion is at the root of neurotic and
psychotic illness elicited a response from the religious community.
For Freud was not talking about cults or bizarre religious groups but
of the Judeo-Christian tradition as he knew it. The reaction to his
position, taken up by many of those scholars who accepted, at least
in part, his psychoanalytic viewpoint, was to point out that religion can be therapeutic. Societies like the Academy of Religion and
Mental Health were established to explore the relationship between
religion and mental health and to bridge the gap between professional
psychiatry and religious counseling. Several journals, notably the
JOURNAL OF RELIGION AND HEALTH, THE REVIEW OF RELIGIOUS RESEARCH,
PASTORAL PSYCHOLOGY, and the JOURNAL OF PASTORAL CARE, were started
to encourage research by scholars and clerics on the issue of how
religion could have an impact on a person's mental health or illness and to explore ways in which ministers of religion could
effectively help those who came to them for advice.

The literature prior to the contemporary debate on psychiatry
and the new cults is therefore relevant to the theme of this book.
For most of this century the academic discipline of psychology was
largely dominated by behaviorists and psychoanalysts. The former
simply ignored religion; the latter treated it almost like a disease.
This rather negative view of religion is still reflected in academic

25

psychology and counseling programs which either ignore the subject
completely or else refer to it casually when dealing with mental
illness. Most introductory textbooks in psychology, unlike their
counterparts in sociology and cultural anthropology, hardly mention
religion at all. On the other hand, there is a vast literature
explaining how religion can in fact be a source of help to believing
individuals in their struggles to cope with life and in the development of their personalities. The pro-cult/anti-cult controversy is
prefigured in the pro-religion/anti-religion debate which left its
mark on both religious and psychological literature. One major
difference is that the contemporary debate has reached the news
media and the general public and is not restricted to scholarly
literature.

Other areas of the psychology of religion, specifically religious
conversion, religious experience, and mysticism, are surely indispensable in any examination of the psychological effects of involvement
in cults. Further, the psychological attempts to relate religious
development to age groups and to outline the psychological features
of a religious stage peculiar to adolescence are important when one
considers the fact that the majority of recruits to the new religions
are young adults. Psychologists have also discussed authoritarianism
in religion and the characteristics of religious leaders and prophets.
These two areas are in fact central to the contemporary anti-cult
literature which accuses cult leaders of creating undemocratic and
totalitarian societies in which they play the part of absolute dic-
tators. All these topics, discussed outside the current polemic,
contribute to our understanding of the religious processes leading
to conversion, to our evaluation of ecstatic and mystical states
which have been part of traditional religions in many cultures, and
to our assessment of dogmatic and authoritarian cult leaders whose
honesty and authenticity have been frequently doubted.

A. RELIGION, PSYCHOLOGY, AND PSYCHIATRY

This first section deals with the psychology of religion and is
divided into two parts. The first part includes general introductory
texts, most of which dedicate several chapters to the areas mentioned
above. They further refer to many sects, like Quakerism, Christian
Science, and revivalist movements. Examples are given from the mainline Christian churches and, less frequently, from Eastern religions.
The works of Freud and Jung, which are representative of two major
approaches to religion, are mentioned in this section. The second
part lists specific studies on religious conversion, religious
experience, and mysticism.

The psychology of religion has always encouraged a special interest in the study of religious experience, conversion, and mysticism.
These seemed to stand out in the life of those individuals who,
before their new experience, practiced their religion simply as part
of a culture. One notable effect of the experience was the change
in the person's ideology, life-style, and personality. Clinical

psychologists and psychiatrists began to observe similarities between the behavior and attitudes of some of their patients and those
of people claiming to have been transformed by a new perception of
reality and by a special sense of the holy that was previously
missing in their lives.

Religious experience was thus discussed in the context of pathology, specifically as a psychotic-like experience. It was commonly
held that religious experience was a type of loss of reality. Its
effects were seen as largely negative, as constricting the ego and
curtailing judgment and perception. The symptoms of hysteria, hypnosis, or psychosis seemed so similar to those of religious experience that even moderate researchers, like Boisen, conceded that
religious experience and mental disorder were closely related. The
person who reported such an experience was said to have regressed in
the psychoanalytic sense that he or she had been forced, under the
pressure of stress or anxiety, to flee from reality into a more infantile and secure state. One common opinion held that the changes
which often took place in one's personality following a religious
experience were indicative of dissociation, which means that the
individual's set of activities, thoughts, emotions, or attitudes had
became separated from the rest of one's personality and functioned
independently.

Some attempts were made to see religious experience in a more
positive light. Several writers have insisted that hysteria and
dissociation are not always linked with it and that apparent regression was temporary and might even prove beneficial. The question
was also raised whether religious experience should be understood
more in terms of the social conditions which brought it into being
than in terms of one's mental state.

Much of the focus of psychological research and reflection was
directed towards religious conversion. A common approach, first
proposed by William James, was to distinguish between sudden and
gradual conversions. Three theories seem to dominate the literature.
The most popular one was that sudden conversion in particular was
pathological and had disintegrating effects on one's personality.
Sudden conversion was connected with revivals where mass hysteria
and emotionalism were evident and where suggestion played a key role.
Several disposing factors to the experience, especially unconscious
conflicts, low self-esteem, psychosexual problems, and fundamentalist
religious beliefs, were also signs of existing pathology or incipient
psychological disorder. Because sudden conversion was related to
acute anxiety, some argued that its occurrence was not based on religious grounds and could, therefore, be explained as a psychological
phenomenon that occurred during adolescence.

A second opinion, however, tended to give a much more positive
evaluation of conversion, sudden or otherwise. In spite of the
presence of some suggestibility and emotionalism, conversion leads
a person from childhood to adulthood and is thus similar to a rite
of passage. It is integrative and wholesome and helps the individual
resolve harmoniously many conscious and unconscious problems. Without denying its origin in psychological conflicts, its expression in

neurotic forms, and its possible results in hallucinations and serious
delusions, these scholars tended to see conversion as a phase in personality development. The convert is likely to have less friction
and to cope better with crises. His or her transformation leads to
optimism and to the sublimation of animal instincts.

A third approach, similar to the second, maintained that conversion was a form of regression in the service of the ego. This view,
formulated by Boisen, admits that conversion is a step backward to
an infantile and primitive form of thinking and feeling, but it benefits the person, who emerges more integrated and more secure in his/
her individuality. The neurotic conditions existed before the experience, which performed the same function as a psychotherapeutic
treatment. It was conceded that a conversion experience is not
always advantageous; it might, in fact, be a sign of pathology and,
in the long run, make the patient's condition worse.

Mysticism was treated as an intense form of religious experience
that often accompanied conversion. On its negative side, mysticism
was explained as a form of pathology found in conjunction with hyper-
suggestibility, hysteria, schizophrenia, manic depressive psychosis,
and epilepsy. The mystic, probably because of the tendency to withdraw from the world, is inclined to disintegration and dissociation
and is prone to hallucinatory visions. Repressed desires and neurotic tendencies are the main pre-conditions for the mystical experience which leads to abnormal phenomena like glossolalia, visions,
and stigmata. Some went so far as to link mysticism with sadism and
masochism.

On the positive side, mysticism was seen as a creative method of
dispelling frustration. It is a state of self-reliance, self-confidence, and freedom from anxiety and hence a sign of maturity. It
enhances one's personality by developing compassion and sympathy.
One's character could emerge stronger as a result of the experience.
Some maintained that mysticism arose out of persecution and suffering, or out of affluence and degeneration, and was a mechanism for
coping with, and in some instances remedying, otherwise unbearable
human conditions. When explained in terms of neurophysiological
changes, mystical methods (like Yoga and Zen) were ways of releasing
psychosomatic tension, and contributed to the well-being of the
individual. Boisen's theory of regression in the service of the ego
was also applied to the mystical experience. Deikman, in terms taken
from cognitive psychology, describes it as a "de-automatization,"
that is, a process whereby the individual becomes aware of and
reflective on those well-learned processes that normally take place
without consciousness. This process is in fact regressive, but it
finally steers the person to a richer and different kind of awareness. Several attempts were made to show how the mystic differs
from a schizophrenic (Wapnick, item 186) or a psychotic (Aaronson,
item 98).

Most of the discussion of religious experience, conversion, and
mysticism took place within the context of the Judeo-Christian
tradition, though some scholars incorporated material from Eastern
religions. When comparisons are made between Western and Eastern
religious beliefs and practices, two trends of thought are apparent.

The first treats both religious phenomena as similar psychologically. The second prefers the Christian conversion experience because it is judged to be religiously and psychologically healthier and less prone to problems. Since the mid-sixties, however, one can detect a growing interest in Eastern psychologies and practices, an interest that accompanied the growth of the academic study of religions in many colleges and universities throughout the Western world.

The discussions of these various types or levels of religious experiences were, at times, intense and acrimonious. The problems raised concerning their pathological qualities remained unsolved. The reductionist tendencies of psychologists and psychiatrists collided head-on with the attempts of theologians and ministers of religion to rebut them. The former relied mostly on studies of sick patients, and it is difficult to determine whether the latter's pathological symptoms were actually caused by religion or whether some of the doubtlessly extreme and harmful religious ideas and practices can be interpreted as expressions of, or outlets for, deep personality problems which originated in a non-religious context. Boisen's solution that conversion represents a regression in the service of the ego leaves some unanswered questions. Why, for instance, does the individual regress at all? What is the precise mechanism which turns a regression into a step towards maturity? Why does the return to a psychologically immature state manifest itself in religious form? Is there a time limit to this regressive stage? What are the consequences if the individual persists in this condition?

The problem of conversion or religious and mystical experience remains central to the study of both traditional religions and new movements. Many of the questions which psychologists have in the past asked about these issues have reemerged with the advent of the new cults. Is conversion itself a result of an already existing pathology? Does it add to the problems of the individual and worsen his/her psychological state? Or is it an attempt by a sick person to overcome one's personal crisis? Or is conversion an ambivalent phenomenon which could contribute either to psychological betterment or to mental illness? Or are there some genuinely religious conversions which contribute to the maturity of the person? And if the latter is correct, what criteria should be used to evaluate religious experiences? The current debate about whether members of new cults have been brainwashed is actually one about religious conversion.

1. General Introductory Texts.

60.   Akhilananda, Swami. HINDU PSYCHOLOGY: ITS MEANING FOR THE
        WEST. New York: Harper and Brothers, 1946. xviii, 241 pp.

        Outlines Hindu psychology and compares it to its Western
        counterpart. The various functions of human personality,
        like cognition, will, and the various levels of conscious-

ness, are explored. To the Hindus, religion is not a barrier
to psychological development, but rather the basis for it.
Religion functions to help people overcome difficulties and
frustrations and is thus not antagonistic to psychology. To
the author, Hindu psychology is: 1) more dynamic than Western
psychology; 2) more concerned with the total mind; 3) more
interested in the superconscious and paranormal states of
mind; and 4) more positive since the basic urge in one's personality is happiness. The author might have unintentionally
offered some partial explanation of why Hindu religious groups
in the West have achieved some measure of popularity.

61.   Allport, Gordon W. THE INDIVIDUAL AND HIS RELIGION: A PSYCHO-
       LOGICAL INTERPRETATION. New York: Macmillan, 1950. 147 pp.

       Discusses, among many other topics, three common types of
       conversion, which: 1) occur in a definite crisis situation;
       2) are triggered by an emotional stimulus; and 3) take place
       gradually, over a period of time, without any major upheavals.
       All three are related to the religion of youth. None of these
       conversion types is said to be pathological. Whether a re-
       ligion is mature or not can be judged by a number of criteria,
       tolerance of the existence of diverse religious views being
       one sign of religious maturity.

62.   Argyle, Michael. RELIGIOUS BEHAVIOR. Glencoe, IL, Free Press:
       1959. xii, 196 pp.

       States that psychology is concerned only with the causes or
       empirical conditions of religious phenomena and that psycho-
       logical research can tell us nothing about the truth, validity,
       or usefulness of them. The author stresses that the results
       of scientific studies of religion can, however, be relevant
       to religious practices. Besides a brief survey of psycholog-
       ical theories of religious beliefs and practices, the book
       includes accounts of the environmental factors in the function
       of religious attitudes, the variation of religious beliefs
       and activities with age, and the correlation between person-
       ality traits and attitudes, such as racial prejudice and
       authoritarianism, and religious groups. Denying that one can
       start by assuming that religion is a mark of insanity, the
       author explores the empirical relations between religion and
       mental illness. He finds that young people who are religious
       are somewhat more neurotic, and that some minor religious
       leaders suffer from various problems like paranoia, hysteria,
       and schizophrenia. The evidence on mystics is rather mixed.
       The author concludes that there is little concrete evidence
       that religion either causes or prevents mental illness. A
       lengthy bibliography is included.

63.   Clark, Walter Houston. THE PSYCHOLOGY OF RELIGION. New York:
       Macmillan, 1958. 485 pp.

       Points out that although conversion may not seem to be
       mentally healthy, there is a close relationship between

psychotherapy and the conversion process. Religious experience and mysticism may be highly integrating for one's life,
yet there is always the danger of losing one's grip on
reality. Two features commonly found among religious persons, namely, 1) the tendency towards withdrawal and isolation
from others, and 2) the inclination to act impulsively with
less inhibition, are also present in psychotics. Sects are
more likely to build character, change lives, and sustain
individual morals. Besides incorporating in his analysis
revival movements and sects, like Christian Science, the
author also includes many references to the Eastern religious
traditions.

64.   Coe, George A. THE PSYCHOLOGY OF RELIGION. Chicago: Univer-
      sity of Chicago Press, 1916. xv, 365 pp.

      One of the early attempts to draw up a psychology of reli-
      gion. The author covers such areas as religious conscious-
      ness, the idea of God, conversion, prayer, mysticism, and the
      mental traits of religious leaders. Religious conversion is
      explained as "a particular instance of the differentiation of
      the individual consciousness, which is also social conscious-
      ness..." (p. 174). Religious leaders, shamans, priests,
      prophets, and some of the founders of the then-newer cults,
      including Joseph Smith and Mrs. Mary Baker Eddy, are said to
      exhibit shamanistic traits found in primitive societies. Some
      accounts of the mystical processes given by mystics themselves
      are examined and their functional aspects noted. Yoga is a
      deliberate attempt to achieve the mystical state of union
      with God.

65.   Coe, George A. THE SPIRITUAL LIFE: STUDIES IN THE SCIENCE OF
      RELIGION. New York: Eaton and Mains, 1900. 279 pp.

      Covers some basic psychological perspectives of religion,
      including religious development, adolescent difficulties,
      religious dynamics, and spirituality. In a chapter on
      religious healing, the author questions the technique used
      by Christian Science. Mental healing is related to hypnosis
      and miracles to the power of suggestion. It is insisted that
      there is a hygienic and therapeutic value to the Christian
      attitude toward life.

66.   Conklin, E. J. THE PSYCHOLOGY OF RELIGIOUS ADJUSTMENT. New
      York: Macmillan, 1929. 340 pp.

      Contains chapters on the psychology of religious experience,
      conversion, mysticism, and faith healing. Some criteria for
      evaluating whether religious experience is wholesome or not
      are given. False sanctification, speaking in tongues, apoca-
      lyptism, fanaticism, and aberrant militancy, often found in
      sects, indicate psychological abnormalities such as escapism,
      hysteria, and paranoia.

67.   Dittes, J. E. "Psychology of Religion." THE HANDBOOK OF
       SOCIAL PSYCHOLOGY. Edited by G. Lindzey and E. Aronson.
       Reading, MA: Addison-Wesley, second edition, 1969, vol. 5,
       pp. 602-59.

       Discusses the problems of defining and measuring religion
       and observes that easily accessible objective indices of re-
       ligion are distinguishable from, and possibly not correlated
       with, subjective personal orientations. The literature on
       the relationship between religion and social attitudes,
       particularly prejudice, and between religion and personality
       characteristics is reviewed. Religious experiences are inter-
       preted as a constriction of the ego. They curtail a person's
       usual patterns of perception, judgment, and behavior control.
       The author states that these experiences have frequently been
       linked with hypnosis, hysteria, psychosis, and regression in
       the service of the ego.

68.   Dresser, Horatio W. OUTLINES OF THE PSYCHOLOGY OF RELIGION.
       New York: Thomas Crowell, 1929. xiii, 451 pp.

       A textbook on the psychology of religion, covering prayer,
       faith, worship, belief, religious consciousness and its devel-
       opment, conversion, and mysticism. The role of sudden
       religious conversion is discussed. Some mystical phenomena
       are judged to be pathological. The author thinks that a
       rational kind of religion is natural and argues that the
       divine can be understood as the profound element in human
       experience, a principle which underlies most of his discus-
       sions.

69.   Fern, Virgilius. "The Psychology of Religion." PRESENT-DAY
       PSYCHOLOGY. Edited by A. A. Roback. New York: Philosoph-
       ical Library, 1955, pp. 961-72.

       Outlines some of the work done in the psychology of reli-
       gion and complains about its religious provincialism. It is
       asserted that religion is a response to the totality of life,
       giving ultimate meaning, and that it must be of vital signif-
       icance to both health and illness.

70.   Flower, J. Cyril. AN APPROACH TO THE PSYCHOLOGY OF RELIGION.
       New York: Harcourt, Brace and Co., 1927. xi, 248 pp.

       Discusses, besides the nature of religion and the mechanism
       of the religious response, several religious movements, in
       particular, John Rave and the Peyote cult of the Winnebago
       Indian tribe, and George Fox and the Quakers. Both are clear
       examples of frustration and the expansion of consciousness
       leading to a religious experience, the former in a simple
       level of culture, the latter in a more complex civilization.
       The religious experience of Fox occurred in the context of
       environmental shock and was precipitated by nervous and psy-
       chological changes which take place at puberty. Rave's
       experience can be explained by the fact that he was a sensi-

tive person with characteristics of mental instability. The psychopathology of religion is discussed at length. The author maintains that while religion can be an escape from reality, a consolation in times of disaster, and a refuge from infantile regression, it is not always so, nor can it be said that it came into existence for this purpose.

71. Freud, Sigmund. THE STANDARD EDITION OF THE COMPLETE WORKS OF SIGMUND FREUD. Translated from the German under the editorship of James Strachey. London: The Hogarth Press, 1966-74. 24 vols.

Contains all of Freud's works and a good general index that is invaluable, since Freud did not write a great deal specifically on religion. Particularly revealing are his two short essays, "Obsessive Acts and Religious Practices" (vol. 9, pp. 115-28), and "A Religious Experience" (vol. 21, pp. 167-72). Two books, TOTEM AND TABOO (vol. 13, pp. 1-161) and MOSES AND MONOTHEISM (vol. 23, pp. 1-138), though now rather outdated in both the ethnographic data they rely on and in their theoretical assumptions about non-literate cultures and ancient Middle-Eastern societies, nevertheless provide the general framework of the common link in psychoanalysis between religion and neurosis. The essay on "Dreams and Occultism" (vol. 22, pp. 31-56) gives a brief, somewhat negative view of occult beliefs and practices.

72. Grensted, L. W. THE PSYCHOLOGY OF RELIGION. New York: Oxford University Press, 1952. v, 181 pp.

A brief introduction to the psychology of religion, covering: 1) individual religion (including conversion and mysticism); 2) the development of religion (where cults are placed); and 3) corporate religion (in which context religious propaganda and evangelism are discussed). Those who have a religious experience are distinguished from those who are hysterical or dissociated by the fact that the former are aware of the conflict within themselves and are trying to solve it. The mystic's withdrawal from the world, however, could be a sign of psychosis. A religious community in its more stable and organized form not only reinforces and saves one's ego from insecurity, but also "involves the danger of encouraging a regression to a childish level of suggestion" (p. 146).

73. Hickman, Frank S. INTRODUCTION TO THE PSYCHOLOGY OF RELIGION. New York: Abingdon, 1926. 558 pp.

Discusses at some length the structure, roots, and development of religious experience and conversion. Common religious topics, like prayer, worship, belief in God, and divine inspiration are dealt with from a psychological point of view. Conversion, which implies a mental revolution or a change in religious integration, is distinguished from normal religious development. Among the features of sudden religious conversions are listed a number of antecedent causes which prepare

the individual for such an experience. Conversion energizes
and brings unity into a person's life "both through a reduction of mental friction and a release of new energy" (p. 265).
It is also an incentive to optimism, to social improvement,
and to the sublimation of animal instincts.

74. Jastrow, Joseph. THE PSYCHOLOGY OF CONVICTION: A STUDY OF
     BELIEFS AND ATTITUDES. Boston: Houghton Mifflin, 1918.
     xix, 387 pp.

     Deals with the interaction between the logical and psycho-
     logical aspects of human nature. After an introduction to
     the psychology of belief, the author examines several cases,
     including a then-contemporary New York medium, and Mrs. Mary
     Baker Eddy, the founder of Christian Science. Reflecting on
     the latter's theories of Malicious Animal Magnetism (MAM),
     he remarks that she is a typical example "of a nervous in-
     valid with a highly irritable constitution becoming a chronic
     victim to delusions of persecution" (p. 203).

75. Johnson, Paul E. PSYCHOLOGY OF RELIGION: A PSYCHOLOGICAL
     ANALYSIS OF WHAT IT MEANS TO BE RELIGIOUS. New York:
     Abingdon, 1959. 304 pp.

     Advances the position that the most authentic religious
     behavior is a "primary, first-person experience" and that a
     religious conversion is the outcome of crises and conflicts
     which may resemble mental illness. Revivals are necessary
     for the survival of religious beliefs and values. The phenom-
     enon of spiritual healing, which can lead to the neglect of
     medical services and endanger one's health, is discussed. It
     is maintained that religious behavior such as worship, con-
     fession, and forgiveness can have therapeutic effects.

76. Jordan, George J. A SHORT PSYCHOLOGY OF RELIGION. New York:
     Harper and Brothers, 1927. 160 pp.

     Covers some of the more common religious themes like sin,
     conversion, prayer, worship, and religious belief. Most of
     the recorded conversions, including St. Paul's and St.
     Augustine's, are said to be "involuntary" and can be seen
     as the result of "unconscious cerebration." Three stages
     of conversion, namely, a sense of unrest, a crisis and feel-
     ing of being in the grip of another power, and a sense of
     joy and abiding peace, are described. Psychology not only
     shows the inner need for a conversion and rebirth, but also
     warns us against spurious methods and forms it can take.

77. Josey, Charles Conant. THE PSYCHOLOGY OF RELIGION. New York:
     Macmillan, 1927. xi, 362 pp.

     Provides a general introduction to religion, which includes
     chapters on the subjects of asceticism and mysticism, both
     of which are frequently the expressions of the noblest side
     of personality, stimulating growth and development. But

these religious practices can also be pathological. Those
who indulge in exaggerated forms of self-deprivation and
penance are more likely to reap physically and psychologically harmful results. Repressed desires and neurotic
tendencies are among the favorable conditions for mystical
experiences. Suggestibility is considered to be one of the
psychological principles necessary for understanding religious behavior. It can explain many healing practices, such
as those found among Christian Scientists.

78.   Jung, Carl G. THE COLLECTED WORKS OF C. G. JUNG. Edited by
       Herbert Read, Michael Fordham, and Gerhard Adler. Translated
       by R. F. C. Hull. New York: Bollingen Series XX, Princeton
       University Press, 1957-79. 20 vols.

       Contains the many writings of Jung on religious topics
       covering both Eastern and Western traditions and including
       several occult subjects. Volume 11 is a collection of Jung's
       major religious works, including "A Psychological Approach to
       the Dogma of the Trinity" (pp. 107-200), "Psychotherapists or
       the Clergy" (pp. 327-54), "Yoga and the West" (pp. 529-57),
       "The Psychology of Eastern Meditation" (pp. 558-75), "The
       Holy Men of India" (pp. 576-88), and "Foreword to the I
       Ching" (pp. 589-608). Three volumes (12-14) are dedicated
       to his study of alchemy and its symbolism. His study of the
       occult, "On the Psychology and Pathology of So-Called Occult
       Phenomena" (vol. 6, pp. 3-88), is one of the earliest in-depth
       psychological studies on the occult. A general index (vol.
       20) is also available.

       See items 254, 546.

79.   Leuba, James H. A PSYCHOLOGICAL STUDY OF RELIGION: ITS
       ORIGIN, FUNCTION, AND FUTURE. New York: Macmillan, 1912.
       xiv, 371 pp.

       Though obviously dated in discussing issues like the
       origin of religion and magic, this volume adds a short sec-
       tion on "psychotherapeutic cults," which includes Christian
       Science, Mind Cure, and New Thought. The new religious groups
       are judged to be irrational in the views they propound. Their
       curative practices depend on the then-recent discoveries about
       suggestibility. However, the author states that an apologist
       for the psychotherapeutic sects would be able to make several
       claims in support of these teachings, particularly that the
       cults have proved their value by their results.

80.   Leuba, James H. "A Study of the Psychology of Religious
       Phenomena." AMERICAN JOURNAL OF PSYCHOLOGY 7 (1896): 309-85.

       Focuses on religious conversions, particularly sudden ones,
       which are central to religious life. The first part of this
       long paper presents a careful analysis of the conversion
       experience in six natural phases, namely, the sense of sin,
       self-surrender, faith, joy, appearance of newness, and the

role played by the will. The second part studies several
Christian doctrines, specifically those of justification,
faith, grace, and freedom of will, in the context of religious conversion.

81.   Olt, Russell. AN APPROACH TO THE PSYCHOLOGY OF RELIGION.
       Boston: Christopher Publishing House, 1956. 183 pp.

       Introduces the reader to the psychology of religion and
       discusses religious conversion, the psychology of temptation,
       sin, and religious healing. Mysticism leads to several ab-
       normal religious phenomena, like glossolalia, stigmatization,
       and visions. Witchcraft is explained as a type of mass
       hysteria. Healthy religion promotes mental health, but over-
       subjectivism in religion contributes to poor adjustment and
       is pathological.

82.   Ostow, Mortimer, and Ben-Ami Scharfstein. THE NEED TO BELIEVE:
       THE PSYCHOLOGY OF RELIGION. New York: International Univer-
       sities Press, 1954. 162 pp.

       Discusses the link between psychiatry and religion and
       applies the interpretative techniques of psychoanalysis to
       clarify religious phenomena. Religion is said to use guilt
       to encourage a passive acceptance of communal obligations and
       to maintain restrictions needed for a stable society. Several
       religious themes, like religious experience, conversion, and
       mysticism, are explored in the context of Augustine's life.
       Conversion is believed to bring an end, at least temporarily,
       to a powerful struggle within the human psyche. Sufi and Bud-
       dhist mystics are, like schizophrenics, estranged from their
       own personalities. The visions of prophets are interpreted
       as hallucinations and their belief that the end of the world
       is imminent is a case of schizophrenic paranoia. The author
       concedes that not all prophecy has neurotic or psychotic
       elements. But many occult phenomena, such as automatic
       writing, bear some resemblance to prophecy and are instances
       of hysteria.

83.   Pitts, John. PSYCHOLOGY OF RELIGION. London: Kingsgate
       Press, 1929. 112 pp.

       Discusses religious conversions, many of which are sudden
       and can be traced to the unconscious. The author's view is
       that conversion is psychologically beneficial because it
       unifies the divided self.

84.   Pratt, James Bissett. THE RELIGIOUS CONSCIOUSNESS: A PSYCHO-
       LOGICAL STUDY. New York: Macmillan, 1920. viii, 488 pp.

       Maintains that conversion, which can be gradual or sudden,
       aims at the unification of character and the achievement of
       a new self. Some Christian and Hindu conversion experiences
       are compared and they are found to contain the same steps of
       psychological development. Religious revivals are treated as

part of group psychology and are related to similar events in primitive society. These revivals break down the inhibitions to emotion, to action, and to belief, and can be the first step towards serious pathological problems. Mysticism, with the many Western and Eastern methods used to achieve it, is treated at length, and the author feels that at least some mystical experiences could be a sign of pathology, even though they seem to offer temporary relief from the chronic sense of unreality. Milder forms of mystical experiences are judged to be more healthy.

85.   Pratt, James Bissett. THE PSYCHOLOGY OF RELIGIOUS BELIEF. New York: Macmillan, 1907. xi, 327 pp.

Examines the psychological nature of religious belief systems in various cultures, including primitive peoples, Eastern societies, and Western civilization. The development of religious belief through adolescence and the types of belief found in mature life are outlined. Three types of religion are distinguished: 1) the religion of primitive mentality, which is naive and unsophisticated, and which corresponds to the religion of early human beings and of children; 2) the religion of feeling, which refers to a person's inner experiences and which satisfies emotional needs; and 3) the religion of thought or understanding, which is based on some reasoning.

86.   Pruyser, Paul W. A DYNAMIC PSYCHOLOGY OF RELIGION. New York: Harper and Row, 1968. x, 367 pp.

Attempts a novel introduction to the psychology of religion. Instead of focusing on the common topics of prayer, worship, conversion, mysticism, etc., the author orders the data in terms of psychological categories, uses normative and clinical observations with appropriate fluidity, assesses religious propositions as products of religious concept formation, and takes into account the inconspicuous, everyday features of religious life. It is maintained that the most significant contribution of psychoanalysis to the psychology of religion is "its insistence upon of the role of conflict in religion, and of religion in conflict, personal as well as social" (p. 8). Religion is then defined as "a way of problem solving."

87.   Schaub, Edward L. "The Psychology of Religion in America During the Past Quarter-Century." JOURNAL OF RELIGION 6 (1926): 113-34.

Reviews the development of, and contribution to, the psychology of religion by American scholars in the first quarter of the twentieth century. The various explanations of religion are briefly sketched. The author warns of the dangers of looking at all religious beliefs and practices as prelogical and pathological and of studying religious expressions without reference to their historical and environmental contexts.

88.   Selbie, William S. THE PSYCHOLOGY OF RELIGION. Oxford:
       Clarendon Press, 1924. xii, 310 pp.

       Introduces the reader to the psychology of religion. Some
       of the traditional areas in the field, like religious con-
       sciousness, worship, prayer, belief in God, immorality,
       conversion, and mysticism are dealt with. The author cautions
       that a highly emotional religious conversion may be a sign of
       pathology and may be brought into being by both suggestion
       and hypnotism. Mystical experiences are explained naturally
       by recourse to suggestion, imitation, association, and educa-
       tion, though it is admitted that they could be normal if they
       strengthen one's character and increase one's spiritual and
       moral powers. The same experiences are abnormal when they
       lead to dissociative states and when they hinder the develop-
       ment of higher values.

89.   Stolz, Karl R. THE PSYCHOLOGY OF RELIGIOUS LIVING. Nashville,
       TN: Cokesbury Press, 1937. 375 pp.

       A general introduction to the psychology of religion based
       on lectures delivered in several theological seminaries, uni-
       versities, and summer schools for ministers and laymen. Part
       One deals with the background of the religious quest, while
       Part Two dwells on religious experience and personality.
       There are chapters on occultism, religion and mental health,
       and religious maturity. While admitting that occult phenomena
       may be the product of fraud and deception, the author favors
       further research on the subject. He acknowledges that some
       religious practices, like confession, are therapeutic. The
       part played by religion in helping people adjust to reality
       and achieve independence, emotional stability, and socializa-
       tion is discussed.

90.   Stratton, G. M. PSYCHOLOGY OF RELIGIOUS LIFE. London: Allen
       and Co., 1911. xii, 376 pp.

       Approaches the psychological study of religion from the
       point of view that religious life is one of conflict and thus
       projects mental discord and unrest. Three areas of conflict
       are discussed: emotional, behavioral, and mental or intellec-
       tual. It is maintained that religion is an idealizing factor
       in human life.

91.   Strunk, Orlo. MATURE RELIGION: A PSYCHOLOGICAL STUDY. Nash-
       ville, TN: Abingdon, 1965. 154 pp.

       Outlines religious maturity according to: 1) to "Depth psy-
       chology" (Freud, Jung, and Fromm); and 2) "Height psychology"
       (James, Allport, Frankl). A synthesis is then attempted
       listing the chief features of a mature religion, among which
       are the belief in a creator or a being greater than oneself,
       and involvement in the world. Mature religious feelings are
       characterized by profound experiences of mystical oneness,
       while mature religious actions include elements of harmony,
       love, and commitment.

92.   Strunk, Orlo. RELIGION: A PSYCHOLOGICAL INTERPRETATION.
        Nashville, TN: Abingdon Press, 1962. 128 pp.

        Endeavors to introduce the psychological study of religion
        by raising several psychological questions one may ask about
        religious beliefs and practices. The cognitive, affective,
        and conative aspects of religion are discussed. Religion is
        seen as a problem-solving device, as an aid to the achievement
        of self-adequacy, and as a comprehensive and integrative force.
        It is argued that though the distinction between sudden and
        gradual religious conversion experiences is a useful one, the
        psychological process in both is the same. The neurotic per-
        son may achieve self-adequacy through religion.

93.   Strunk, Orlo, editor. READINGS IN THE PSYCHOLOGY OF RELIGION.
        New York: Abingdon, 1959. 288 pp.

        Provides a rich selection of readings on various aspects
        of the psychology of religion. The history of the subject,
        religious experience and conversion, and religion and psycho-
        therapy are among the areas covered.

94.   Swisher, Walter Samuel. RELIGION AND THE NEW PSYCHOLOGY: A
        PSYCHO-ANALYTIC STUDY. Boston: Marshall Jones and Co., 1920.
        261 pp.

        Includes chapters on mysticism and neurotic states, conver-
        sion, and healing methods like those followed in Christian
        Science. The author maintains that the mystic is a neurotic
        whose repressed sexual instinct plays an important role in
        his/her experiences and behavior. The view of conversion
        presented is somewhat ambivalent for it is held that, while
        the person who does not need to go through an emotional
        conversion experience is deemed to be a psychologically
        healthy person, religious conversion and psychoanalysis are
        said to have the same goal, namely, to resolve one's inner
        conflicts and to restore a person's balance.

95.   Thouless, Robert H. AN INTRODUCTION TO THE PSYCHOLOGY OF
        RELIGION. Cambridge: Cambridge University Press, third
        edition, 1971. viii, 152 pp.

        Discusses and evaluates Freud's position on religion and
        mental illness. He notes that even in Jung's view, though
        mental health results from the adoption of a religious
        attitude, the aim of religion is not to cure people of neu-
        rotic tendencies. Chapters on the psychology of meditation
        (including Zen, Yoga, and the Spiritual Exercises of St.
        Ignatius), conversion, and mysticism are included. The author
        rejects the view that all mysticism is related to hysteria.
        In spite of the attempts that have been made to explore medi-
        tation techniques as an aid to psychotherapy, he asserts that
        more remains to be done to assess the lasting effects of
        meditation on the development of personality.

96. Wieman, Henry N., and Regina Westcott-Wieman. NORMATIVE
     PSYCHOLOGY OF RELIGION. New York: Thomas Crowell, 1935.
     x, 564 pp.

     Includes a lengthy chapter on psychotherapy and religion,
     besides a section on conversion and mystical experiences.
     Religion can fulfill several psychotherapeutic functions,
     such as assistance in the resolution of inner conflicts,
     vocational guidance, confession of wrongdoing (psychopro-
     phylaxis) and preparation for the great crises of life. The
     author points out those areas where the religious worker can
     learn from psychotherapy. He warns that religion has to
     modernize itself in order to be therapeutically successful.

97. Zunni, Georgio. MAN AND HIS RELIGION: ASPECTS OF RELIGIOUS
     PSYCHOLOGY. London: Geoffrey Chapman, 1969. xiii, 365 pp.

     Summarizes and criticizes the many theories of religion
     advanced by psychologists, including James, Freud, and Jung.
     Genuine and spurious religion, the relation between religion
     and society, and the psychology of religious experience are
     among the topics discussed.

2. Studies on Conversion, Religious Experience, and Mysticism.

98. Aaronson, Bernard S. "Mysticism and Depth Perception."
     JOURNAL FOR THE SCIENTIFIC STUDY OF RELIGION 6 (1967):
     246-52.

     Sets out to show by experiments on two subjects whether
     the mystic's experience of expanded depth is related to the
     development of psychedelic experiences. The psychotic has
     a feeling of "ablated depth," in which alienation from the
     environment is central; the mystic, one of "expanded depth,"
     that is, one of involvement with the cosmos and the total
     environment. The psychotic sees space as an enclosing con-
     finement; the mystic, as an ever-growing area where interaction
     and growth are possible.

99. Allison, G. A. "Psychiatric Implication of Religious Conver-
     sion." CANADIAN PSYCHIATRIC ASSOCIATION JOURNAL 12 (1967):
     55-61.

     Discusses, with reference to major psychiatric works, reli-
     gious conversion as a clinical phenomenon, and reports on three
     adolescent patients who had a background of distorted inter-
     family relations, confused gender identification, and exposure
     to fundamentalist religious beliefs. The author holds that
     religious conversion leads to the resolution of many conscious
     and unconscious problems, including the oedipal conflict which
     is resolved through delayed identification with the parent of
     the opposite sex. In treating such patients, the therapist
     must help them realize that many of their instinctual drives
     need not be accompanied by strong feelings of guilt.

100.   Allison, Joel. "Religious Conversion: Regression and Pro-
        gression in Adolescence Experience." JOURNAL FOR THE
        SCIENTIFIC STUDY OF RELIGION 8 (1969): 23-28.

        Focuses on the more positive role of sudden and dramatic
        religious conversion experiences which lead the adolescent
        into adulthood and which are thus adaptive, integrative, and
        wholesome. Research carried out with a largely Methodist
        student body discovered several aggressive and oedipal themes.
        The author concludes that the conversion experience helps the
        individual achieve a new level of psychological organization.

101.   Allison, Joel. "Adaptive Regression and Intensive Religious
        Experience." JOURNAL OF NERVOUS AND MENTAL DISEASE 145
        (1968): 452-63.

        Concerns itself with the more intense and sudden religious
        conversions which are highly emotional, often accompanied by
        hallucinations, and which lead to behavioral changes. While
        admitting that the tendency has been to interpret these ex-
        periences as essentially pathological and psychotic with
        disruptive and disintegrating effects on the personality, the
        author leans towards the alternate view that such a conversion
        is a "phenomenon functioning to reintegrate the ego" and is,
        therefore, progressive and adaptive, giving the person a sense
        of well-being and self-esteem. For the author, sudden and
        dramatic conversion experiences are associated with greater
        amounts of primitive, non-rational thought-manifestations as
        well as with integrative results and do not occur of necessity
        within a rigid authoritarian and pathological context.

102.   Allison, Joel. "Recent Empirical Studies of Religious Conver-
        sion." PASTORAL PSYCHOLOGY 17 (August 1966): 21-27, 29-34.

        Reviews studies on sudden and dramatic religious conversions.
        Four major issues are covered: 1) the relationship of these
        experiences to psychotic phenomena, to mental health, and to
        personality growth; 2) the sensory experiences which facili-
        tate the hallucinatory aspect of the conversion experience;
        3) the importance of the cultural context; and 4) those atti-
        tudes which are conducive to, and affected by, conversion.
        The author concludes that these studies support the view that
        conversion is a means of promoting the integration of person-
        ality and may be a regression in the service of the ego. Its
        content can be better compared to mystical rather than schizo-
        phrenic manifestations. Areas of further research are listed.

103.   Ames, Edward E. THE PSYCHOLOGY OF RELIGIOUS EXPERIENCE.
        Boston: Houghton Mifflin, 1910. x, 428 pp.

        Provides a history of the psychology of religion and of the
        methods used to study religious phenomena, an outline of
        primitive religion and of religious development through
        adolescence, and a study of the place of religion in the
        experience of the individual and society. The normal process

of gradual religious growth is contrasted with the sudden
experience of conversion, which starts with a period of
personal dissatisfaction. Conversion is most commonly induced by revivals where suggestion plays a key role. Sudden
religious conversion is defective because it is not based on
intelligent and rational grounds for action. In a chapter
on the psychology of religious sects, the author asserts that
originally each of the Christian sects represented a type of
personality and a social stratification. While the communal
consciousness of the sects is their strength, it is also a
major flaw since it restricts their outlook.

104.   Arieti, Silvano. "The Loss of Reality." PSYCHOANALYSIS AND
       PSYCHOANALYTIC REVIEW 48.3 (1961): 3-24.

       Interprets the psychotic phenomena of loss of reality as
       based "on the process of active concretization." The process
       in various types of illusions, especially hallucinatory ex-
       periences, is examined. Some particular religious experiences,
       illustrated by a couple of historical examples, are seen as a
       type of this loss of reality.

105.   Asrani, U. S. "The Psychology of Mysticism." MAIN CURRENTS
       IN MODERN THOUGHT 25 (1989): 68-73.

       Sees mysticism as a universal, personal aspect of religion
       that has resulted in a method "of dispelling frustration,
       fear, and mental conflict, and of gaining peace, equanimity,
       and joy," and as "an inward search for unity whereby the
       narrow bonds of egotism are dissolved" (p. 69). Some Eastern
       techniques for mysticism are dealt with under the following
       headings: 1) Jnana Yoga; 2) Buddhist mysticism (mindfulness
       and attentiveness) and Pantajali's Astanga Yoga; 3) Bhakti
       Yoga, Christian mysticism, and Sufism; 4) Karma Yoga; and 5)
       other forms of Yoga. The state of mysticism known as the
       unitive life (or the Jivana Mukti state, the Sahaj state,
       etc.) is described as one characterized by self-confidence
       and self-reliance in action, non-attachment and relaxation
       after work, and freedom from anxiety and other mental ten-
       sions. It produces an environment wherein the integration of
       personality can take place.

106.   Bagwell, H. Roberts. "The Abrupt Religious Conversion Expe-
       rience." JOURNAL OF RELIGION AND HEALTH 8 (1969): 163-78.

       Explores the psychological conceptualizations of conversion
       from a historical perspective and from contemporary formula-
       tions. Sudden religious conversions occur in an instance of
       acute regression and are closely followed by either transient
       or long-lasting reintegration. In some cases, reintegration
       may be a state of better adaptation than the pre-conversion
       state. But such conversions could also be a sign of psycho-
       pathology.

107.   Beck, Robert N. "Hall's Genetic Psychology and Religious
       Conversion." PASTORAL PSYCHOLOGY 16 (September 1965): 45-51.

A critical evaluation of a commonly accepted view of religious conversion as a fundamental redirection or reorientation of self, necessary for the individual to mature and grow out of the earlier stages of one's life. This developmental cycle, in which the individual recapitulates the religious history of the human race from animism to ethical deism, turns one from egotism to altruism and from nature worship to transcendence. Hall, in spite of his Darwinian perspective, ignored the fact that the individual reacted creatively with his or her environment and denied objective reference to all religious experience. The author thinks that Hall's work was valuable, but too narrow in conception and scope.

108.   Bergman, Paul. "A Religious Conversion in the Course of
        Psychotherapy." AMERICAN JOURNAL OF PSYCHOTHERAPY 7 (1952):
        41-59.

        Describes the family background of a patient and his conversion experience during treatment. Several interpretations of this experience are discussed, including the view that it could be regarded as a psychotic-like episode or an expression of unconscious symbolism. The author thinks that such an experience does not point to any primary religious need or instinct. It is, however, an important dimension in one's life and should be taken seriously by psychotherapists.

109.   Bertocci, Peter A. "Psychological Interpretations of Religious Experience." RESEARCH ON RELIGIOUS DEVELOPMENT.
        Edited by Merton P. Strommen. New York: Hawthorn, 1971,
        pp. 3-41.

        Presents salient psychological interpretations of religious experiences and tries to reach some conclusions or generalizations. Several theories, including those of James, Freud, Jung, Fromm, Erikson, Allport, and Boisen, are outlined. The author concludes that any religious or peak experience is transformative, but that the transformation depends on one's belief system.

110.   Boisen, Anton T. OUT OF THE DEPTHS: AN AUTOBIOGRAPHICAL
        ACCOUNT OF MENTAL DISORDER. New York: Harper and Brothers,
        1960. 216 pp.

        An account of the author's own experience with mental illness and religious experience. He relates how, while suffering extreme stress, he had a valid religious experience which he describes as real madness. His central thesis is that mental disorders and religious experiences are closely related. He was led to believe that emotional illness could have a positive use, leading the individual to a deeper religious sense and to the integration of personality. A list of his own publications is included.

111.   Boisen, Anton T. "Religious Experience and Psychological
        Conflict." AMERICAN PSYCHOLOGIST 13 (1958): 568-70.

Relates the case of one of his patients with the aim of
exploring the interrelation between religious experience and
psychological conflict. Among his conclusions is the general
principle that "in order to understand mental disorder or
religious experience, one should be studied in the light of
the other" (p. 570). The case study presented in this paper
is an example of a person who goes through searching experiences which have definite schizophrenic features. Outstanding religious persons, like George Fox, Emanuel Swedenborg,
Paul of Tarsus, and the prophets Jeremiah and Ezekiel are
similar examples.

112.   Boisen, Anton T. "The Genesis and Significance of the Mysti-
        cal Identification in Cases of Mental Disorder." PSYCHIATRY
        15 (1952): 287-96.

        Presents the results of a study of the conditions under
        which a sense of mysticism arises in mental illness, of the
        forms it takes, of its significance, and of its relationship
        to recognized religious experience. It is concluded that
        mystical identification is present in some patients whose
        integrity is threatened and who are confronted with their
        own personal failure. Similarities between disturbed schizo-
        phrenics and important religious leaders (such as the Hebrew
        prophets and Saint Paul) are discussed.

113.   Boisen, Anton T. PROBLEMS IN RELIGION AND LIFE: A MANUAL FOR
        PASTORS. New York: Abingdon-Cokesbury, 1946. 158 pp.

        Presents a series of outlines and suggestions on religion
        and psychology intended to help pastors in their daily
        ministry. One chapter deals with the religious conversion
        experience, which is a phase of personal development. If
        eruptive or dramatic, it is likely to occur in times of
        increased personal problems and in crisis situations. It is
        maintained that those who haven't acquired a mature religion
        are apt to develop serious mental illness.

114.   Boisen, Anton T. "Concerning the Relationship Between Reli-
        gious Experience and Mental Disorder." MENTAL HYGIENE 7
        (1923): 307-11.

        Admits that the psychiatrist is correct when he compares
        the experiences of great religious figures, like Jesus, Paul,
        and Augustine, to mental patients, but he often fails to
        recognize the sharp contrast between them. Though voices and
        visions that may accompany conversion experiences are usually
        regarded as pathological, they result in an integration of
        one's personality, bringing the individual in harmony with
        himself or herself and with the environment. When the con-
        flicts cannot be resolved, then one develops psychopathology.
        The author gives some suggestions as regards the place of the
        religious counselor in the treatment of psychiatric problems.

115.   Brock, Timothy C. "Implications of Conversion and Magnitude
        of Cognitive Dissonance." JOURNAL FOR THE SCIENTIFIC
        STUDY OF RELIGION 1 (1962): 198-203.

Focuses on the favorable change in attitude toward another
religion, an attitude central to all conversions. Two factors
influencing this change are noted, namely, the implications
which the would-be converts see for themselves, and the pressures brought upon them to change their attitudes. It is
maintained that Festinger's theory of cognitive dissonance
(item 378) has implications for attitude changes under
conditions of forced compliance.

116. Bucke, Richard M. COSMIC CONSCIOUSNESS: A STUDY OF THE
      EVOLUTION OF THE HUMAN MIND. New Hyde Park, NY: Univer-
      sity Books, 1961. xvii, 326 pp. First published, 1901.

      One of the great classics of the study of mystical
      experiences. The author first describes cosmic conscious-
      ness as an awareness of the life and order of the universe.
      It is accompanied by enlightenment, a state of mental exul-
      tation and joy, and a sense of immortality. An outline of
      mental evolution is also sketched. Most of the book is given
      to describing instances of cosmic consciousness. Religious
      leaders, like the Buddha, Jesus Christ, Paul of Tarsus,
      Muhammed, Swendenborg, and Ramakrishna Paramahansa, as well
      as poets like Dante and Blake, are included. The psycho-
      logical factors which determine whether a person enters into
      a state of cosmic consciousness are given.

117. Christensen, C. W. "Religious Conversion in Adolescence."
      PASTORAL PSYCHOLOGY 16 (September 1965): 17-28.

      Presents a non-technical discussion of the psychodynamics
      of religious conversion as it usually occurs in adolescence.
      The following predetermining conditions are noted: 1) an
      unconscious conflict involving disturbed parental identifica-
      tion, an inferior self-image, or some form of sexual pathol-
      ogy; 2) an acute reaction occurring in late adolescence, a
      time of change; and 3) a fundamentalist church background
      in which the person had been raised. In order for the con-
      version to take place, there must also be a conscious conflict
      and an event which triggers the change. Religious conversion
      is, therefore, a process which, no matter how regressive it
      might be, functions towards reintegration which, admittedly,
      may be partial or, at times, never reached at all.

118. Christensen, C. W. "Religious Conversion." ARCHIVES OF
      GENERAL PSYCHIATRY 9 (1963): 207-16.

      Defines the religious conversion experience as an "acute
      hallucinatory episode" which is intense, sudden, brief in
      duration, accompanied by auditory or visual hallucinations,
      and effecting change in the convert's behavior. Several
      predisposing factors, such as unconscious conflicts, low
      self-esteem, adolescent age, psychosexual pathology, and
      fundamentalist religious belief, are examined and illustrat-
      ed by case histories. Revival meetings often precipitate
      religious conversion. Various components of this experience

are listed and the types of conflict resolution which it might
bring are examined. It is postulated that conversion is an
ego phenomenon which reintegrates the ego and is a special
instance of the "acute confusional state."

119.   Clark, Elmer T. THE PSYCHOLOGY OF RELIGIOUS AWAKENING. New
        York: Macmillan, 1929. 170 pp.

        A study of the religious experience of people in the 1920s
        and how this experience differed from that of an earlier
        generation. Three types of religious awakenings (or conver-
        sions) are distinguished: 1) definite crisis; 2) emotional
        stimulus; and 3) gradual. The first type is said to be the
        only one that can be compared with traditional conversions.
        The author finds no causal relationship between the physical
        facts of puberty and the phenomenon of conversion. The last-
        ing effects of religious training, the environment, and emo-
        tional life are examined. While it is noted that the sudden,
        emotional conversion experiences are being replaced by the
        more gradual type, it is stressed that the emotional factor
        is an essential part of religion.

120.   Clark, Walter Houston. "Intense Religious Experience."
        RESEARCH ON RELIGIOUS DEVELOPMENT. Edited by Merton P.
        Strommen. New York: Hawthorn, 1971, pp. 521-50.

        Presents three types of non-rational religious experiences:
        1) the mystical; 2) the esoteric; and 3) the one that leads
        to conversion. The main writings on the subject are also
        reviewed. The general features of mysticism and its effects
        on one's conduct are examined. The use of drugs to induce the
        mystical state is also explored. Theories on sudden conver-
        sion and on conversion to another faith are briefly mentioned.
        Faith healing, glossolalia, and possession are treated under
        esoteric experiences.

121.   Clark, Walter Houston. "The Psychology of Religious Experi-
        ence." PSYCHOLOGY TODAY 1.9 (February 1968): 47-49, 68-69.

        Points out the importance of religious experience for
        understanding religious life in general and suggests that
        psychedelic drugs are an "incomparable tool" for under-
        standing it. Experiments with such drugs led the author to
        conclude that, after psychedelic therapy, the subjects talked
        like religious people and became radically changed in their
        values and attitudes. Some theories of the psychology of
        religion are outlined and it is stated that religion, more
        than anything else, has the power to change human life and
        give it meaning.

122.   Clark, Walter Houston. "The Mystical Consciousness and World
        Understanding." JOURNAL FOR THE SCIENTIFIC STUDY OF RELIGION
        4 (1965): 152-61.

        Contrasts the rationality of the West with the mysticism of
        the East and discovers that Eastern religions have much to

teach us. Mysticism brings out the non-rational aspects in religious belief and behavior which should not be identified with superficiality. Mystical experience, which the author claims can also be obtained and controlled by drugs, does not make one a mental case, but rather helps develop one's compassion and sympathy.

123.   Clark, Walter Houston. "William James: Contributions to the Psychology of Religious Conversion." PASTORAL PSYCHOLOGY 16 (September 1965): 29-36.

Evaluates William James's work (item 144) on religious conversion under four headings: 1) the emphasis on experience and its consequences; 2) the focus on the individual; 3) the non-statistical use of extreme cases for his data and illustrations; and 4) a respect for the role of the unconscious. It is concluded that James's findings were not substantive but rather insightful and speculative. He is admired for his warmth and sympathy with his subject matter and for having stimulated others to study religious experiences of conversion.

124.   Deikman, Arthur J. "De-Automatization and the Mystic Experience." PSYCHIATRY 29 (1966): 324-38.

Puts forward a psychological model of the experience of mystics based on the assumption that meditation and renunciation are the main means employed to produce it, and that the process is one of "de-automatization." The main techniques to gain a mystical experience with its non-intellectual organization are described. The evidence, according to the author, points to a de-automatization, which is produced by meditation and enhanced by renunciation and which is a regressive process through which the individual moves to a different kind of awareness. The principal features of the mystic's experience are intense realism, unusual sensation, a sense of unity and ineffability, and an awareness of "transsensate" phenomena. The author warns, however, that "the mystic experience can be beatific, satanic, revelatory, or psychotic, dependent on the stimuli predominant in each case" (p. 217).

125.   De Sanctis, S. RELIGIOUS CONVERSION: A BIO-PSYCHOLOGICAL STUDY. New York: Harcourt, Brace and Co., 1927. 342 pp.

Outlines the scope and method of religious psychology and examines the types, causes, and processes of conversion. The pathological theory of conversion, which considers senility, infirmity, depression, conflict, neurosis, illusions, and hallucinations as responsible for the conversion experience, is discussed. The author concludes that while mysticism and conversion may be pathological, "true mystics and converts are extreme variations of the normal variation of human personality" (p. 243). Finally, the conditions which are favorable for the occurrence of religious conversion are listed.

126.   Dewhurst, Kenneth, and A. W. Beard. "Sudden Religious Con-
        versions in Temporal Lobe Epilepsy." BRITISH JOURNAL OF
        PSYCHIATRY 117 (1970): 497-507.

        Discusses six cases of religious conversion experiences
        in epileptics. The conversion experiences of various
        mystics and saints (like Saint Paul, St. Teresa of Avila,
        Joseph Smith, and St. Thérèse of Lisieux) who, the author
        thinks, were probably epileptic cases, are reviewed. The
        theological and psychiatric aspects of conversion are
        described.

127.   Douglas-Smith, Basil. "An Empirical Study of Religious
        Mysticism." BRITISH JOURNAL OF PSYCHIATRY 118 (1971):
        549-54.

        Examines over 200 mystics and compares them with psychotics
        and neurotics. The data, according to the author, support
        the view that mystical experiences are not connected with
        hyper-suggestibility, pathological lying, hysterical personal-
        ity, epilepsy, schizophrenia, paranoia, or manic-depressive
        psychosis. Religious experience seems to be a unique human
        experience which is not related to personality defect or
        abnormality, as are extrasensory perception and multiple
        personality.

128.   Dunlap, Knight. RELIGION: ITS FUNCTIONS IN HUMAN LIFE. New
        York: McGraw-Hill Book Co., 1940. xi, 362 pp.

        Includes a chapter on "initiation, proselytism, and con-
        version." The author holds that heavy proselytizing and
        conversion, motivated by the desire to save souls, could be
        signs of an egotistic trait or an expression of the ruthless-
        ness and egotism of an extrovert.

129.   Edward, Kenneth. RELIGIOUS EXPERIENCE: ITS NATURE AND TRUTH.
        Edinburgh: T. and T. Clark, 1926. x, 248 pp.

        Discusses the definition of religious experience and its
        development as well as the place of emotion in one's religious
        life. The influence of auto- and group suggestion in preach-
        ing, private devotion, and the church in general is examined.
        Highly emotional revivalist movements have all the features
        of mob hysteria and give rise to dissociation. The author
        observes that group suggestion takes place in several areas of
        life, and suggestion in religion is balanced by the creative
        and original nature of true spirituality.

130.   Fern, Robert O. THE PSYCHOLOGY OF CHRISTIAN CONVERSION.
        Westwood, NJ: Fleming H. Revell, 1959. 255 pp.

        Provides a historical overview of the psychological study
        of conversion and then deals with those conversions which
        are usually connected with a personal crisis. Two varieties
        of crisis conversion--the intellectual (as in the case of St.

Augustine) and the emotional (as in St. Francis of Assisi and
Ramakrishna) are discussed. The author argues that evangelical conversions, like those of such historical figures as St.
Paul, Martin Luther, and John Wesley, cannot be reduced to
an adolescent phase of one's life. The common denominator
of conversion is said to be "surrender," which has permanence
and a sense of sin as part of its distinguishing features.
Though maintaining the uniqueness of Christian conversion,
the author admits that conversion has similar psychological
elements in all religions.

131.   Fingarette, Herbert. "The Ego and Mystic Selflessness."
        PSYCHOANALYSIS AND THE PSYCHOANALYTIC REVIEW 45 (1958):
        5-40.

        Provides a broader theoretical analysis of mysticism from
        a psychoanalytic point of view and shows how the mystic way
        is at times parallel to psychoanalytic therapy and shares in
        some of the results. The language of a person undergoing
        therapy is similar in many ways to that of the mystic of both
        Eastern and Western traditions. The use of the term "self"
        in both psychoanalysis and in mysticism is compared and found
        in many respects to be the same. Both the experience of the
        subject undergoing therapy and of the mystic achieving enlight-
        enment are creative, rather than regressive, movements. The
        author then proposes ways of distinguishing between mystic
        experience and other kinds of human experiences.

132.   Furgeson, Earl H. "The Definition of Religious Conversion."
        PASTORAL PSYCHOLOGY 16 (September 1965): 8-16.

        Reviews the ambiguities in different definitions of reli-
        gious conversion and looks for some basis of agreement to
        construct a new descriptive definition. The distinction
        between a gradual and a sudden religious conversion, which
        originated with William James, is found to be faulty. The
        author regrets the tendency among some psychologists to limit
        conversion to the sudden type, making it akin to the process
        of self-abnegation and brainwashing. On the other hand, those
        who stress the gradual form of conversion end up by making it
        indistinguishable from other changes. The author provides
        his own definition, one which sees religious conversion as
        an abrupt, involuntary change in personality that, occurring
        in times of crisis, may have either a regressive or a regene-
        rative effect on the individual.

133.   Gallemore, J. L., William P. Wilson, and J. M. Rhodes. "The
        Religious Life of Patients with Affective Disorders."
        DISEASES OF THE NERVOUS SYSTEM 30 (1969): 483-87.

        A study of 62 patients suffering from affective disorders,
        who were found to have had an increased incidence of conver-
        sion and salvation experiences when compared to 40 normal
        controls. Those experiences that occurred when the subjects
        were in good health seemed to have resulted from an increased

capacity for emotional responsiveness. When ill, the subjects who had joy, love, and awe as primary affects tended to
have strong emotional experiences. Subjects with depression,
fear, confusion, and pain were more likely to doubt their
faith or to feel guilty about their lack of it. A surprising
number had no change in their religious feelings. A few
derived considerable benefit from their religion when ill.

134.   Gelhorn, Ernst, and William F. Kiely. "Mystical States of
        Consciousness: Neurophysiological and Clinical Aspects."
        JOURNAL OF NERVOUS AND MENTAL DISEASE 154 (1972): 399-405.

        Puts forth a theory to explain the underlying neurophysio-
        logical basis of altered states of awareness and reflects on
        the clinical implication of mysticism. The practice of Yoga
        and meditation (like Zen and TM) by many Americans has pro-
        vided examples of the relation between body relaxation and
        cognitive states and has led to the suggestion that these
        practices have some therapeutic value. TM, being an easily
        learned technique, could be used profitably in the treatment
        of psychosomatic tension states, such as anxiety and phobia,
        or of psychosomatic disorders, such as hypertension and
        diabetes mellitus.

135.   Gibbons, Don, and James De Jarnette. "Hypnotic Susceptibil-
        ity and Religious Experience." PROCEEDINGS OF THE ANNUAL
        CONVENTION OF THE AMERICAN PSYCHOLOGICAL ASSOCIATION 7.2
        (1972): 863-64.

        Endeavors to determine whether the emphasis on a personal
        experience among Christian fundamentalists is indicative of
        a relationship between the ability to be saved or to be a
        good communicant, and the tendency to be easily hypnotized.
        It is concluded that experiences of salvation are hypnotic
        phenomena "which occur without a formal induction in response
        to implicit or explicit suggestions conveyed by the speaker,
        the setting, and the attendant ceremony" (p. 863).

136.   Gilbert, Albin R. "Identifying the Mystical Variable."
        PSYCHOLOGIA 12 (1969): 139-46.

        Sets forth the characteristics of the mystic's mind and
        the way one attains the mystical experience. Phenomenology
        of this experience, drug revelation, psychology of the
        active way, and mysticism for the space age are discussed.
        The author believes that space exploration is conducive to
        mystical experience, which is not considered harmful to human
        personality.

137.   Gilbert, Albin R. "From Buddha to Pavlov--the Technique of
        Mysticism." PSYCHOLOGIA 10 (1967): 121-8.

        Deals with the mystical attitude which includes the dis-
        solution of the multiplicity of the personal ego and of the
        world itself. The contemplative and active techniques of

mysticism are described from the writings of the great mystics.
Mystical enlightenment results from a sudden insight and is
prepared for by protracted meditation and by continual conditioning. It is argued that this type of conditioning is
very similar to the conditioned reflexes developed by Pavlov.

138.   Glenn, Michael J. "Religious Conversion and the Mystical
       Experience." PSYCHIATRIC QUARTERLY 44 (1970): 636-51.

       Disagrees with the general trend in psychology to relegate
       religious conversion and mystical experience to the field of
       psychopathology and argues that these experiences, though
       sometimes pathological and regressive, can also be highly
       adaptive and creative. A short history of the concept of
       conversion is given and the work of several.psychologists,
       like James, Starbuck, and Leuba, is reviewed. It is pointed
       out that the trends in the 1960s indicate a shift to analyz-
       ing mystical and conversion experiences from an aesthetic and
       creative point of view. Because a conversion experience is
       frequently preceded by a period of turmoil or crisis, it can
       be an adaptive, conflict-resolving event. The author de-
       emphasizes the "passionate aspect of the conversion experi-
       ence" and stresses that only those well-thought-out changes
       are adaptive and thus healthy. Conversion points to creative
       potentialities of human life which can be either pathological
       or healthy.

139.   Goodenough, Erwin R. THE PSYCHOLOGY OF RELIGIOUS EXPERIENCE.
       New York: Basic Books, 1965. xii, 192 pp.

       Treats the psychology of religion as a crucial part of the
       study of human personality. The meaning of religion and the
       struggle for happiness and integrity within the human psyche
       are discussed. Nine types of religious experiences are
       described, namely, legalism, supralegalism, orthodoxy, supra-
       orthodoxy, aestheticism, symbolism and sacramentalism, the
       church, conversion, and mysticism. Religion, it is main-
       tained, has been the psychotherapy of all ages.

140.   Gordon, Albert I. THE NATURE OF CONVERSION: A STUDY OF FORTY-
       FIVE MEN AND WOMEN WHO CHANGED THEIR RELIGION. Boston:
       Beacon Press, 1967. xii, 333 pp.

       Primarily an attempt, through tape-recorded interviews, to
       understand the factors involved in formal converts to Judaism
       and Christianity, who were married or engaged. The author
       discusses the nature of conversion, its requirements, and
       its success or failure. These formal conversions are called
       ecclesiastical as opposed to the inner, twice-born, and
       heightened emotional experiences. They occur for well-
       thought-out reasons and are never sudden. They can also be
       influenced by crisis situations and can be triggered by
       nervous or mental disorders. They are related by the author
       to increased anxiety, restlessness, and indifference in our
       society. The general resentment and opposition of parents
       to conversion of their offspring is "clear and unequivocal."

141.   Guntrip, H. "Religion in Relation to Personal Integration."
       BRITISH JOURNAL OF MEDICAL PSYCHOLOGY 42 (1969): 323-33.

       Explores the nature of religious experience as a historic
       fact of human existence within the scope of modern psycho-
       analytic theory. Religious experience is considered to be
       the "culmination of the personal-relationship essence" of
       human living.

142.   Hill, William S. "The Psychology of Conversion." PASTORAL
       PSYCHOLOGY 6 (November 1955): 43-46.

       Reflects on two kinds of conversion, one which occurs
       gradually and slowly, the other suddenly and dramatically.
       What is important is not the speed by which the conversion
       takes place, but rather the change towards a new vitality that
       has occurred in the individual. The author regrets that some
       evangelists and revivalists have given to conversion overtones
       of emotionalism and mass hysteria.

143.   Hocking, William E. "The Meaning of Mysticism As Seen Through
       Its Psychology." UNDERSTANDING MYSTICISM (item 1154), pp.
       223-39.

       Discusses the various psychological theories of mysticism,
       particularly those of James (item 144) and Leuba (items 152
       and 153). The author argues that mysticism should not be
       linked with the state of dissociation and with other psycho-
       logical problems. Mysticism satisfies human needs and offers
       the possibility of a complete personality.

144.   James, William. THE VARIETIES OF RELIGIOUS EXPERIENCE: A
       STUDY IN HUMAN NATURE. New York: Collier, 1961. (First
       published in 1902.) 416 pp.

       Still the classic study of religious experience covering
       the topics of religion and health, conversion, mysticism, and
       saintliness. The author elaborates on various features of
       the religious life, which include "an assurance of safety and
       a temper of peace, and, in relation to others, a preponderance
       of loving affection" (p. 377). Conversion, sudden or gradual,
       is conceived of as a shifting of one's center of personal
       energies and of intensifying new emotional crises in which
       both explicitly conscious processes of thought and will, and
       subconscious motives, are at work. Pronounced emotional
       suggestibility and a tendency to automaticism are especially
       operative in sudden conversions.

145.   James, William. "A Suggestion About Mysticism." UNDERSTAND-
       ING MYSTICISM (item 1154), pp. 215-22.

       Proposes that the mystical state is but a sudden and great
       extension of the ordinary field of consciousness. In the
       mystical state diverse sensations coalesce into one. The
       mystical experience occurs when a mass of subconscious memo-

ries, conceptions, feelings, etc., come into view all at once. The author attempts to illustrate his theory by means of some of his own experiences.

146. Jones, E. Stanley. CONVERSION. New York: Abingdon, 1959. 253 pp.

Though mainly a theological study on Christian conversion, this book contains a chapter on the effect of conversion on one's health. The author believes that a religious conversion has a positive impact on both physical and psychological well-being. It "converts (a person) from fear and resentment, and therefore saves (one) from neurosis" (p. 158), and removes one's inner conflict and guilt. Conversion to Christianity subjects a person to the greatest therapeutic force in the universe, namely, the stimulus of Christ.

147. Jones, Rufus M. NEW STUDIES IN MYSTICAL RELIGION. New York: Macmillan, 1927. 205 pp.

Stating that "the time has come to stop using the word mysticism as an alias for what is uncanny and obscurantist" (p. 24), the author investigates the relationship between mysticism, asceticism, and the abnormal as well as the various effects mysticism has on religious organization and education. While confirming that the mystic has a constitution which by nature is in danger of disintegration and dissociation, he recognizes that these experiences tend to lend the mystic support and strength. Mysticism can be considered to be abnormal only in the sense that it does not have a utilitarian value.

148. Jones, W. Lawson. A PSYCHOLOGICAL STUDY OF RELIGIOUS CONVERSION. London: The Epworth Press, 1937. 397 pp.

Introduces the reader to the psychology of conversion. The criteria of religious experience and the general types of religious conversions are examined. The author distinguishes between gradual and non-gradual conversions and explores the age frequencies, the pre-conversion situations, the crises, and the psychological factors, manifestations, and results which accompany conversion. The sociological, psychological, and temperamental conditions for conversion are described. Various psychoanalytic interpretations are discussed. Finally, Christian and non-Christian conversion experiences are compared and it is concluded that the former are the highest kind, from the standpoint of both the individual's good and society's well-being. The author, rejecting psychoanalytic interpretations as inadequate, sees conversion as a highly successful mode of adaptation and a perfectly healthy type of human development. Religious conversion enriches and defines the self and tends to direct behavior to morally and socially valuable ends.

149. Kato, Katsuji. THE PSYCHOLOGY OF ORIENTAL RELIGIOUS EXPERIENCE. Menasha, WI: George Banta, 1915. 102 pp.

Investigates the typical conversion experiences of Japanese
Christians who gradually accepted the Christian faith. The
religious life of the Japanese, the psychology of conversion,
and several theoretical and practical deductions are considered.
The intellectual and social aspects of these conversions are
discussed. The author holds that conversion restores the
comfort of life, promotes welfare both in the individual and
in the family, and brings forth a new life, which alters the
person both physiologically and psychologically. He concludes
that Japanese converts find in Christianity a satisfaction for
the "increasing demands of their growing life" (p. 95).

150.   Kildahl, John P. "The Personality of Sudden Religious Con-
       versions." PASTORAL PSYCHOLOGY 16 (September 1965): 37-44.

Starts with William James's view about the two kinds of
conversion, gradual and sudden, representing respectively two
kinds of people, the once-born and healthy, and the twice-born
and sick person. Previous empirical research on the personalities of gradual or sudden converts is surveyed. It is concluded that sudden converts fall clearly into the hysteric
personality type and are less intelligent than those whose
conversion is gradual. The author is of the opinion that a
sudden and dramatic religious conversion does not promote
mental or emotional growth and maturity.

151.   Laski, Marghanita. ECSTASY: A STUDY OF SOME SECULAR AND
       RELIGIOUS EXPERIENCES. Bloomington: Indiana University
       Press, 1962. xii, 544 pp.

A comprehensive study of ecstatic experiences that includes:
1) a critical analysis of mystical texts; 2) a detailed examination of the experiences described in these texts; and 3) a
discussion of the results of the experiences with particular
reference to those beliefs that arise as a result of them.
The author focuses on what she calls "intensity experiences,"
which cannot be induced voluntarily and which are typically
rare. These experiences, she thinks, are "in themselves
delightful and have beneficial results" (p. 372). Lengthy
appendices include the questionnaire, the literary and religious texts, and the content analyses with examples.

152.   Leuba, James H. THE PSYCHOLOGY OF RELIGIOUS MYSTICISM. New
       York: Harcourt, 1929. xii, 336 pp.

A psychological study of those aspects of human nature
which are conspicuous in mystical religion. After discussing
the definition of mysticism and its induction by artificial
means, the author gives an account of Yoga and Christian
mysticism. Several distinguishing features of "supernatural"
mysticism are pointed out. The relation between mysticism,
hysteria, and neurasthenia is discussed. The author thinks
that some of the great mystics, like St. Catherine of Siena
and St. Teresa of Avila, suffered from hysterical attacks,
but that moderate mysticism common in many Christian saints

was entirely free of hysterical symptoms. Further, while
mystics suffered from periods of depression and ecstatic
trances leading to nervous instability and dissociation, they
cannot be identified with ordinary psychopaths whose moral
and intellectual faculties are impaired. Certain aspects of
the mystical methods used in healing cults are, according to
the author, similar to modern psychotherapy and can lead to
a more stable and synthesized mental life.

153. Leuba, James H. "Ecstatic Intoxication in Religion."
     AMERICAN JOURNAL OF PSYCHOLOGY 28 (1917): 578-84.

     Points out that intoxication and ecstasy hold the supreme
     place in religion and attempts to show that drug intoxication
     and higher mysticism are linked by certain psychological
     characteristics, by the purpose they serve, and by the mean-
     ing ascribed to them. It is contended that to maintain that
     mysticism is a divine, ineffable, and unutterable experience
     does nothing but encourage a romantic megalomania. Examples
     of the use of drugs in various religions are given. Intoxi-
     cation and ecstasy are sought for because they satisfy deeper
     needs and cravings, but they can also intensify the "sensa-
     tional and affective background of consciousness," and cause
     mental upheavals and hallucinations. Both intoxication and
     ecstasy "bring deliverance from the fatigues, the restraints
     and tensions of the daily struggle, and they create a sense
     of unlimited possibility and inexhaustible energy" (p. 584).

154. Linn, Louis, and Leo W. Schwartz. PSYCHIATRY AND RELIGIOUS
     EXPERIENCE. New York: Random House, 1958. 307 pp.

     Studies the relationship between psychiatry and religion
     in the different stages of human life. Religious conversion
     often offers satisfactory solutions to the problems of young
     people, but when it is associated with symptoms of emotional
     illness, such as a disorganized personal life, instability
     of character, and constantly changing goals, it calls for
     psychiatric treatment. The mystical state is said to contain
     certain universal features: 1) a retreat from reality; 2) a
     withdrawal from society; and 3) a sense of union with the
     absolute. Extreme forms of mysticism are indicative of mental
     illness. On some rare occasions the mystic may have insights
     beneficial both to the individual and to humanity.

155. Lloyd-Jones, D. Martyn. CONVERSIONS: PSYCHOLOGICAL AND
     SPIRITUAL. Chicago: InterVarsity, 1959. 40 pp.

     A criticism of Sargant's theory that conversion is simply
     a physiological process. His theory is described and some of
     his arguments dealing with Methodism, John Wesley, and St. Paul
     are refuted in some detail. It is argued that the events and
     experiences discussed by Sargant are theological rather than
     psychological issues, and that his analysis is rather shallow.
     The possibility of influencing the human mind is, however,
     admitted in some cults, like the snake-handling Christian

groups in the United States. Sargant's view is taken as a
warning to evangelicals not to condition converts and not to
produce the same kind of personality through well-planned
psychological techniques of influence. One should be wary
of the "temporary results" of evangelical conversions.

156. Maréschal, Joseph. "The Psychology of Mysticism." MODERN
      SCHOOLMAN 16.1 (November 1938): 3-8, 20-21.

      Addresses itself to two questions: 1) Does the phenomenon
      of mysticism transcend the province of psychology?, and 2)
      does it furnish data for psychological reflection? The author
      thinks that one cannot assume the fundamental identity of the
      mystical experience with ordinary psychological experience,
      but that even genuine supernatural mystical forms are subject
      to some degree of psychological investigation. Several dif-
      ficulties which the observation of mystical phenomena presents
      to the psychologist are discussed.

157. Maréschal, Joseph. STUDIES IN THE PSYCHOLOGY OF THE MYSTICS.
      Albany, NY: Magi Books, 1927. v, 344 pp.

      A theological, psychological, and comparative study of mys-
      tical phenomena. The author discusses, among other things,
      the feeling of divine presence in mystics and non-mystics,
      some distinctive features of Christian mysticism, and mystical
      grace in Islam. One chapter is dedicated to refuting Leuba's
      view (items 152) of mysticism as an illusionary phenomenon.

158. Maslow, Abraham H. RELIGION, VALUES, AND PEAK EXPERIENCES.
      New York: Viking Press, 1970. xx, 123 pp. First published
      in 1964.

      Discusses religious and trancendental experiences. The
      author, who maintains that human beings have a higher nature,
      covers different kinds of intense experiences, the organiza-
      tional dangers to transcendental experiences, and value-free
      education. Several appendices are dedicated to the religious
      aspects of peak experiences, the third psychology, and the
      validity of knowledge gained in peak experiences. The author
      claims that even one such experience might prevent a person
      from committing suicide and from becoming addicted to drugs
      and alcohol.

159. Masters, R. E. L., and Jean Houston. THE VARIETIES OF PSYCHE-
      DELIC EXPERIENCES. New York: Holt, Rinehart and Winston,
      1966. 326 pp.

      Presents various examples of psychedelic experiences and
      argues that while the use of drugs like LSD and peyote have
      negative elements, the experience they induce is of enormous
      potential value both for medicine and psychotherapy. The
      history of the debate about the use of such drugs is outlined
      and several of the main features of the drug experience, such
      as the body feelings, the experience of others, the role of

the guide, and the world of suprahuman phenomena, are de-
cribed at length. The authors hold that authentic religious
experiences can occur among drug subjects. The drug experience is seen as a voyage inward, which takes the individual
through sensory, recollective-analytic, symbolic, and integrative levels and which could, therefore, be therapeutic.

160.   Meyer, John C. "Two Types of Mystical Response." PSYCHOLOGY:
        A JOURNAL OF HUMAN BEHAVIOR 6.3 (1969): 53-60.

        Examines two types of mystical reaction arising out of two
        different conditions of existence. The first condition is one
        of persecution and deprivation, which gives rise to a messianic
        need for miraculous help from an outside source. The second
        is one of affluence and moral degeneration, producing a need
        for rigor and discipline that manifests itself in exercises
        of self-denial. This is a straightforward deprivation theory
        of mysticism.

161.   Moller, Herbert. "Affective Mysticism in Western Civiliza-
        tion." PSYCHOANALYTIC REVIEW 52 (1965): 115-30.

        Distinguishes between visionary or intellectual mysticism,
        which aims at the experience of understanding God or the
        universe, and affective mysticism, which strives for union
        with the divine. The latter type of mysticism in Western
        Christendom from the eleventh century onwards is discussed
        as a cultural complex. Sado-masochistic aspects dominated
        affective mystics as devotion to the physical suffering of
        Christ became more explicit and graphic. Oral-sadistic
        fascination is seen in the practice of tasting and eating the
        Eucharist to achieve union with God, while infantilism is
        expressed in the merger of the themes of God the lover and
        God the parent. Affective mysticism nurtures fantasies and
        feeling states and encourages a denial of reality. It is
        maintained that with the advent of modern utilitarianism
        and rationalism, affective mysticism has waned.

162.   Neugarten, H. "Psychotherapeutic Re-orientation and Religious
        Re-Birth." JOURNAL OF MENTAL SCIENCE 84 (1938): 1084-86.

        Maintains that in experiences of religious awakenings or
        rebirths, a primitive religious pattern erupts and subjugates
        the entire personality. The same experiences lead to a sense
        of support and, like psychotherapeutic orientation, result in
        a widening of the field of consciousness. Deep religious
        experiences can thus have a psychologically healthy outcome.

163.   Nicklin, George. "A Psychiatric View of the Mystical." R. M.
        BUCKE MEMORIAL SOCIETY: NEWSLETTER-REVIEW 2.1 (April 1967):
        11-13.

        Discusses mysticism particularly in the context of the
        beliefs and practices of the Society of Friends (Quakers).
        The normal mystical phenomenon, according to the author, is

a dissolution of the boundaries of the self without loss of
self-control. The mystical experience expands awareness and
does not endanger one's personal functioning. It can also be
a help in overcoming stressful conditions.

164.   O'Doherty, E. F. "Psychopathology and Mystical Phenomena."
       STUDIES: AN IRISH QUARTERLY REVIEW 40 (1951): 23-32.

       Maintains that psychology and psychopathology have nothing
       positive to contribute to the study of mysticism, but they
       do have an important role in the interpretations of visions
       and revelations which could result from the hallucinatory
       experiences of hysterical persons. Some mystical phenomena,
       like trance, catalepsy, loss of sensibility, and depersonal-
       ization, have been linked with hysteria.

165.   Overholser, Winfred. "Psychopathology in Religious Experi-
       ence." RESEARCH IN RELIGION AND HEALTH: SELECTED REPORTS
       AND METHODS (item 192), pp. 100-16.

       Reports on one of the discussion sessions held at the Fifth
       Academy Symposium. The topic focused on the relationship
       between emotional disturbances and religious functioning,
       especially in scrupulous persons who were either dominated by
       fear or compulsive doubts, or who were depressed because they
       were overwhelmed by the awareness of their own sinfulness.
       These people developed a feeling of guilt and a sense of
       disgust with themselves. Similar experiences were discovered
       among delinquents. Extreme anxiety, serious doubts, and un-
       resolved conflicts are, as a rule, signs of illness. Some
       criteria, like dedication to the service of others and high
       moral conduct, are given to determine whether a mystical
       experience was valid or not.

166.   Prince, Raymond, and Charles Savage. "Mystical States and
       the Concept of Regression." PSYCHEDELIC REVIEW 8 (1966):
       59-75.

       Agrees with the common hypothesis that mystical states are
       regressions in the service of the ego in opposition to Bucke's
       view (item 116) that they are the final step in the person's
       evolution to a higher state of consciousness. The author
       examines in sequence: 1) the concept of regression and its
       function in mental health; 2) neurophysiological data rele-
       vant to regression; 3) subjective experience of early infancy;
       and 4) several features of the mystical state. Mysticism is
       a regression to very early periods of infancy, a regression
       which leads to problem solving. It is a form of treatment
       for psychoneurosis and a step in the creative process.
       Mysticism (the ecstatic feeling which is related to the
       infant's nursing experience) is not, however, without its
       dangers because, instead of leading the individual to a
       healthy return to the real world, it can be a step towards
       psychosis.

167. Roberts, F. J. "Some Psychological Factors in Religious Con-
      version." BRITISH JOURNAL OF SOCIAL AND CLINICAL PSYCHOLOGY
      4 (1965): 185-87.

      Studies 43 theological students in order to determine what
      factors influenced their religious experiences. Several fac-
      tors, like age, parental belief, guilt, neuroticism, and ex-
      troversion were explored. The author concludes that sudden
      conversions were linked with a high neurotic scale.

168. Salisbury, W. Seward. "Faith, Ritualism, Charismatic Leader-
      ship, and Religious Behavior." SOCIAL FORCES 34 (1956):
      241-45.

      Concentrates on the relationship between motivation and
      common manifestation of religion as ritual, meditation, and
      leadership. The research was designed to investigate reli-
      gious motivation and the relationship that may exist between
      the feeling of faith and group experience. Based on question-
      naires sent to a select student body brought up in the Judeo-
      Christian tradition, the study concluded that, among other
      things: 1) there are social overtones to religious feeling;
      2) meditation is second in importance as a factor eliciting
      religious feeling; and 3) charismatic leaders rank third as a
      source of religious feeling. Studies like this tend to raise
      the question of whether religious experience can be better
      understood in terms of the social conditions, rather than as
      an expression of the mental condition of the individual.

169. Salzman, Leon. "Religious Conversion." CLINICAL PSYCHIATRY
      AND RELIGION (item 294), pp. 175-88.

      A slightly different version of item 172. The author points
      out that the regressive post-conversion character is marked
      by several of the following traits: 1) an exaggerated, irra-
      tional intensity of belief in the new doctrines; 2) a great
      concern with form and doctrine; 3) complete rejection of
      former beliefs; 4) intolerance of those who had diverse
      belief systems; 5) a crusading zeal; and 6) masochistic and
      sadistic activities.

170. Salzman, Leon. "Types of Religious Conversion." PASTORAL
      PSYCHOLOGY 17 (September 1966): 8-20, 66.

      Discusses two major types of conversion: 1) the progressive
      and maturational (e.g., the experience of Satori); and 2) the
      regressive and psychopathological (e.g., conversion to the
      Hare Krishna Movement). Several cases are presented to illus-
      trate how the former stands for the positive fulfillment of
      self-awareness, concern for others, and oneness with the world,
      while the latter typifies a destructive and disintegrating
      process. Religious conversion is "a specific instance of
      the general principle of change in the process of adaptation"
      (p. 10).

171.   Salzman, Leon. "Neurotic Religious Attitudes." JOURNAL OF
       RELIGION AND HEALTH 4 (1965): 322-27.

       Shows how the experience of a religious conversion can
       take place as an expedient or exploitive device that aims at
       reaching certain goals, or solving conflicts, or resolving a
       neurotic problem by a drastic change in one's life-style.
       It could also be a genuine response to spiritual demands
       resulting in greater psychological and religious maturity.
       Some excessive devotions as, for example, the scrupulous obser-
       vance of dietary laws in Judaism and in some Eastern religions
       and the evangelization methods of some Protestant fundamental-
       ist churches with their literal interpretation of the Bible,
       are pathological cases of obsessive-compulsive neurosis.
       Criteria for judging the claims of a person who states that
       he is the messiah, or of a convert who "sees the light" and
       rushes to become a monk, are given. Signs of pathological
       forms of conversion are provided.

172.   Salzman, Leon. "The Psychology of Religious and Ideological
       Conversion." PSYCHIATRY 16 (1953): 177-87.

       Argues that certain forms of religious behavior, like mysti-
       cism, fanaticism, stigmatization, flagellation, asceticism,
       and conversion, must be studied not only as spiritual acts
       but also in terms of their effects on the individual and on
       other people. Religious conversion is seen as an instance of
       change in the process of human adaptation. Major adjustments
       to fulfill one's needs can be either constructive or regres-
       sive. A conversion experience, which is always gradual in
       its development even though it is often perceived otherwise,
       can lead to maturity, but it can also be pathological. The
       literature on religious conversion is surveyed and several
       case studies are presented. The author's position is that
       conversion should also be studied in terms of the problems it
       has solved and the subsequent activities of the convert.

173.   Salzman, Leon. "The Psychology of Regressive Religious Con-
       version." JOURNAL OF PASTORAL CARE 8.2 (Summer 1954):
       61-75.

       A revised version of item 172.

174.   Schneiderman, Leo. "Psychological Notes on the Nature of
       Mystical Experience." JOURNAL FOR THE SCIENTIFIC STUDY OF
       RELIGION 6 (1967): 91-100.

       Elaborates on the claim that mysticism arises out of motives
       rooted in the human condition, but that the mystic ends up by
       losing himself/herself and departs from, or transcends, that
       condition. In mysticism, the layers of spiritual evaluation
       are stripped away and the individual returns to an original,
       mythical consciousness. Both the psychotic and the mystic
       transform their environment with this important difference:
       the former projects his/her feeling onto the external world,

while the latter takes the whole cosmos and makes it part of
his/her interior universe. Although the author does not
interpret mysticism as another form of psychological illness,
he still leans towards a psychoanalytic understanding of the
phenomenon. He stops short of making mysticism merely a
system for searching for a non-worldly father-figure.

175. Scroggs, James R., and William Douglas. "Issues in the
      Psychology of Religious Conversion." JOURNAL OF RELIGION
      AND HEALTH 6 (1967): 204-16.

      Reviews some of the basic literature on religious conversion
      and identifies several issues: 1) the problem of definition,
      which raises the question of the possible relationship between
      conversion, brainwashing, and psychotherapy; 2) the debate on
      whether conversion is a step in maturity, a psychopathological
      regression, or a regression in the service of the ego; 3) the
      possibility that there is a conversion that occurs in people
      who are prone to suggestion and/or hypnotism; 4) the typical
      age of the convert who is usually said to be an adolescent; 5)
      the part played respectively by both conscious decisions and
      unconscious motivations; 6) the tendency in scientifically-
      oriented studies towards reductionism; and 7) the use of
      appropriate conceptual schemes to understand the phenomenon
      of conversion.

176. Sedman, G., and G. Hopkinson. "The Psychopathology of Mys-
      tical and Religious Conversion Experiences in Psychotic
      Patients." CONFINIA PSYCHIATRICA 9 (1966): 1-19, 65-77.

      Considers the psychiatric aspects of mystical and conversion
      experiences which are encountered in clinical practice. Two
      types of religious experiences are distinguished: those which
      occur as part of psychiatric illness, and those which take
      place as abnormal psychogenic reactions and are indicative of
      personality problems. Individual symptoms (like delusions,
      hallucinations, and mood changes) are related to behavior
      accompanying conversion. Of the 12 patients who reported
      religious experiences, seven were diagnosed as schizophrenics,
      three as manic depressives, and two as suffering from person-
      ality disorders.

177. Seggar, John, and Phillip Kunz. "Conversion: Evaluation of a
      Step-Like Process for Problem-Solving." REVIEW OF RELIGIOUS
      RESEARCH 13 (1972): 178-84.

      Argues that the conversion model of Lofland and Stark (item
      1870), which sees conversion as a problem-solving device in
      stages, is not suitable for understanding conversion to a number
      of denominations and sects, specifically the Methodist Church,
      the Church of Christ, and the Mormon Church. While many con-
      verts had unresolved problems in life-crisis situations, a
      substantial number of others did not seem to have their con-
      version precipitated by any problem.

178.   Spellman, Charles M., Glen D. Baskett, and Donn Byrne.
        "Manifest Anxiety As a Contributing Factor in Religious
        Conversion." JOURNAL OF CONSULTING AND CLINICAL PSYCHOLOGY
        36 (1971): 345-7.

        Investigates the relationship between manifest anxiety and
        religious conversion. Three groups of 20 residents in a
        predominantly Protestant town were identified by the two
        community ministers as: 1) those having had a sudden religious
        conversion; 2) those who had had a more gradual religious
        development; and 3) those who were not religious at all. The
        MA scale was administered to the members of each group. The
        results show that the second and third groups did not differ
        significantly from each other in manifest anxiety, but the
        first group obtained higher scores on the same scale than the
        other two combined. The results seem to confirm the relation-
        ship between acute anxiety and sudden conversion.

179.   Stanley, Gordon. "Personality and Attitude Correlates of
        Religious Conversion." JOURNAL FOR THE SCIENTIFIC STUDY
        OF RELIGION 4 (1964): 60-63.

        Rejecting the view that religious conversion, sudden or
        otherwise, is a type of neurotic condition, the author con-
        cludes, from a battery of psychological tests administered to
        over 300 theological students, that people who report a reli-
        gious conversion are less neurotic, though more extroverted
        and fundamentalist, in their religious beliefs. Festinger's
        theory of cognitive dissonance (item 378) is used to explain
        the negative correlation "between the amount of parental
        belief and religious conversion" (p. 61).

180.   Starbuck, Edwin D. THE PSYCHOLOGY OF CONVERSION: AN EMPIRICAL
        STUDY OF THE GROWTH OF RELIGIOUS CONSCIOUSNESS. New York:
        Charles Scribner's Sons, 1901. xvii, 423 pp.

        One of the early classic studies of the psychology of re-
        ligious conversion. Three major areas are covered: conversion
        proper, religious growth that does not involve conversion,
        and a comparison between religious development with and with-
        out the conversion experience. The author holds that, though
        conversion is a normal human experience, it has its dangers,
        the most glaring of which is seen in "the emotionalism and
        excitement of religious revivals" (p. 165).

181.   Starbuck, Edwin D. "A Study of Conversion." AMERICAN JOURNAL
        OF PSYCHOLOGY 8 (1897): 268-308.

        Studies the mental and spiritual processes at work during
        conversion by a questionnaire which explores the features of
        sudden and gradual conversion and related circumstances. The
        motives leading to conversion, the experiences preceding it,
        the actual change, and the phenomena that followed it are
        analyzed. Other human experiences similar to conversion are
        recorded. Four views of conversion--sociological, psycholog-

ical, physiological, and pedagogical--are presented. From
a psychological point of view, conversion can be interpreted
as a sudden readjustment to a larger spiritual environment, a
harmonious solution to the conflicts and disturbances which
arise when the individual is faced with a new and better
course of action.

182. Sterba, Richard. "Remarks on Mystic States." AMERICAN IMAGO
      25 (1968): 77-85.

      Summarizes Freud's position on religious experience and
      argues that his observations cannot be generalized. The
      author thinks that every mystic experience of lasting effect
      is a conflict resolution. Mystics differ from psychotics in
      that they soon return to reality, while the latter remain
      deranged and disturbed. The basic element of mystical experi-
      ence is "the loss of the constructive frame of our Selves and
      the fusion with objects of the outside world" (p. 81). It is
      motivated by pressing needs for gratification and defense.

183. Strickland, Francis L. PSYCHOLOGY OF RELIGIOUS EXPERIENCE.
      New York: Abingdon Press, 1924. 320 pp.

      Discusses the nature of religious experience, its content,
      and its development. The sudden conversion, which occurs in
      a crisis situation, is said to be the real conversion. Many
      conversions to evangelical churches are explained as the
      result of crowd-feeling when the forces of suggestion are in
      full operation. Hallucination is evident in mystical experi-
      ences during which visions are seen and voices heard. Some
      forms of mysticism are not pathological.

184. Tiebout, Harry M. "Conversion as a Psychological Phenomenon
      (in the Treatment of Alcoholics)." PASTORAL PSYCHOLOGY 2
      (April 1951): 28-34.

      Draws a picture of the changes which occur in an alcoholic
      during a conversion experience. Several of the negative
      features of alcoholism, including depression, aggressiveness,
      egocentricity, and isolation, are listed. The changes that
      take place under the influence of Alcoholics Anonymous are
      described with specific reference to one patient. Two ques-
      tions are raised: 1) How is the conversion experience related
      to therapy?, and 2) what part does religion play in the con-
      version process? The author states that a conversion experi-
      ence brings with it positive attitudes which are necessary
      for psychological growth and maturity, and that religion
      provides the means for acquiring an affirmative outlook on
      life.

185. Walker, Kenneth. THE MYSTIC MIND. New York: Emerson Books,
      1962. 172 pp.

      Studies mysticism from the point of view of Gurdjieff's
      psychology. The author, basing his reflections on both
      Eastern and Western religious traditions, believes that the

human mind is slowly evolving toward a higher level of consciousness, which some mystics have already attained.

186.   Wapnick, Kenneth. "Mysticism and Schizophrenia." JOURNAL OF
        TRANSPERSONAL PSYCHOLOGY 1 (Fall, 1969): 49-67.

        Takes the experience of Teresa of Avila and that of a
        schizophrenic and draws similarities and differences of the
        processes both went through. While noting similarities in the
        anguish both suffered and in their return to the social world,
        the author stresses that they differ in their goals and out-
        comes. The mystic, unlike the schizophrenic, does not seek
        an escape from reality, but rather chooses a path that leads
        to psychological strength.

187.   White, John, editor. THE HIGHEST STATE OF CONSCIOUSNESS.
        New York: Doubleday, 1972. xxi, 484 pp.

        Mostly a collection of previously published essays and
        selections from books which deal with a wide variety of
        altered states of consciousness.

        Includes items 105, 166, 186, 566.

188.   Wolstein, Benjamin. "On the Limitations of Mysticism in
        Psychoanalysis." PSYCHOLOGIA 5 (1962): 140-45.

        Discusses the problem of the use of mystical experience in
        therapeutic situations. The theoretical and methodological
        differences between mysticism and psychoanalysis are discussed
        and the limitations of the former are stressed. The author
        holds that both can mutually support one another.

189.   Woollcott, Philip. "Pathological Processes in Religion."
        CLINICAL PSYCHIATRY AND RELIGION (item 294), pp. 61-76.

        A study of religious experience in three groups of subjects:
        1) famous saints or religious figures (like St. Augustine and
        Martin Luther); 2) Protestant and Roman Catholic clergy study-
        ing pastoral counseling; and 3) hospitalized psychiatric
        patients. Basing his work on Allport's distinction between
        extrinsic religion (which is essentially utilitarian, used to
        meet narcissistic, defensive, and infantile purposes of the
        personality), and intrinsic religion (which is a mature, self-
        less form of religion that aims at integration), the author
        thinks that the conversion experience of St. Ignatius of
        Loyola is an excellent example of religious regression being
        used to solve intrapsychic conflicts. In such a conversion
        the individual is transformed from an extrinsic to an intrin-
        sic religious orientation. A typical religious conversion
        in late adolescence is an important psychic event, but it
        should not be one on which the person bases his or her
        vocational commitment. Religion could also be used as a
        resource for improving adaptation in patients.

B. RELIGION AND MENTAL HEALTH

The literature which discusses the pathology of cult involvement
is related to the broader question of the effects of religion on a
person's mental health. In psychology, one can distinguish three
major viewpoints. The first holds that religion is deleterious to
psychological maturity and development, and that, consequently,
religiousness is a sign of pathology. The second position argues
that religion, on the contrary, not only helps one cope with the
problems of life, but also contributes to an individual's growth and
betterment. A third opinion maintains that religion can be healthy
or unhealthy, and then goes on to explore the ways in which one can
distinguish between the two.

The view that religion is a source of psychiatric trouble originated in clinical practice where the symptoms of pathology were
found to be similar in some respects to religious behavior, particularly of the intense type. Many psychiatrists still insist that a
great fear of God, a sense of sin, feelings of guilt, and superstitious behavior, which are often found in religion, do not contribute
to mental health. Religions are judged to be unhealthy because they
teach a somewhat negative theory of human nature, inculcate an authoritarian system of ethics, demand strict obedience and subjugation to
authority, and encourage infantile emotionalism. Other religious
practices, such as asceticism, seem at times to be masochistic or
sadistic. Religion fosters intolerant and belligerent attitudes,
which result in abnormal behavior. The uncompromising tenacity with
which religious beliefs are so often held has been linked, in
clinical practice, to a disturbed thinking process. The behavior
of some religious persons, especially in group meetings, amounts to
unbridled hysteria. Ritual behavior has been equated with obsessional neurosis, while prayer is likened to auto-suggestion or self-
hypnosis. Extreme forms of religious expression, like glossolalia,
are considered clear indices of one's pathology. In psychiatric
literature one encounters the common view that many, if not all, of
the revered Christian saints suffered from serious problems or from
sheer insanity. Even popular religious classics, like THE IMITATION
OF CHRIST, have been criticized for encouraging childish views of
God, excessive and morbid mortification, and pessimistic attitudes
which do not contribute to mental health.

In psychological literature individual religions or religious
groups are frequently dismissed as manifestations of a variety of
psychological problems. The main religions which are quoted in some
detail have been, until recently, Judaism and Christianity. Orthodox
religion is viewed as a manifestation of neurotic tendencies, while
fundamentalism is said to be a sign of immaturity. Sects and cults,
like the Holy Rollers, can foster mental illness. Spiritualist movements and claims of revelation appear to be magical in character and
hence unhealthy. Studies of clergymen and of the monastic life have
been brought forth to buttress the position that religion is a source
of many problems and creates many attitudes which do not contribute
to one's health.

Religion, therefore, contains potentially neurotic patterns of behavior. It not only lays bare one's psychological problems, but may play an important role in the initiation of psychosis. Religion can function as a defense against anxiety and as a security blanket which covers, rather than solves, one's life-problems. By insisting on a humility that thrives on a sense of inferiority, by demanding rigid and unchangeable behavior, and by making a person less self-dependent and self-reliant, religion is actually doing a disservice to the individual.

Opposing this attack against religion, many rose in its defense, contending that religion is not only a source of mental strength, but also a therapy that might be employed with profit by those suffering from a host of psychological problems. Religion is seen as a supportive factor in one's life, strengthening the ego and providing direction and meaning. Happiness, peace of mind, a sense of belonging, security and satisfaction, understanding of others, unity in a world filled with chaos, relief from anguish, and adjustment and adaptation to new conditions have all been listed as some of the positive consequences of a religious commitment that can result in sound mental and psychological well-being. Religious doctrines, specifically those concerning sin and the human condition, deal with the realistic conditions of human existence, and adherence to them must have therapeutic value. Religious values and attitudes are positively related to personal integration, a sense of personal worth and purpose in life, and altruistic behavior. Rituals of repentance and confession are judged, by their very nature, to be therapeutic because they free the individual from guilt and encourage him or her to move ahead, without the burden of past mistakes and the fear of punishment. Prayer, worship, and faith healing could be seen as therapy by suggestion. Apparently bizarre religious behavior, like asceticism, rather than being labeled masochistic, can break barriers against complexes and rid the individual of disruptive elements.

From this point of view, religion is a vital, health-creating experience. Christian evangelicals frequently have a deep and satisfying view of life, which is reflected both in their attitudes and relationships to other people. Deeply religious people have learned how to accept the frustrations of life and have been able to bear with the many disappointments and the suffering of their earthly condition by accepting religious answers to the ultimate questions about human existence. Pathology could be a sign that one's religious life is shallow and in need of rejuvenation. Religion, being a source of strength, can be an aid in promoting and restoring mental health. It can safeguard against suicidal tendencies and remove depression and fear.

Defenders of religion are also aware, however, that not all religion is good, and hence insist on the need to distinguish between healthy and unhealthy forms of religion. Religion is unhealthy if it doesn't grow emotionally and intellectually with other aspects of one's personality. If it degenerates into idolatry, adopts superstitions, or becomes compulsive and too legalistic, then religion is detrimental to psychological health. Sects are, at times, taken as

an example of unhealthy religion because they are divisive. Strict
discipline or tenacious and overbearing orthodoxy are likely to lead
to masochistic behavior. Though much disagreement remains on what
precisely are the healthy and unhealthy features of religion, this
approach proposes a more balanced opinion on the issue of the relationship between religion and health. It recognizes that religion
is ambivalent, in that it can both cause or solve personal problems,
produce or quell anxiety, stifle or promote one's personal growth.

The debate on religion and mental health is especially instructive
when one approaches the issues raised by the current cults. First
of all, it appears that it is impossible to reach a general and universal statement about the effects of religion on a person's mental
health. Religious maturity may, after all, depend on psychological
maturity, in which case one's religious behavior is an indication of
one's psychological state, rather than an expression of what religion
really is. Neurosis or schizophrenia can, for example, distort a
genuine and healthy religious experience. But on the other hand,
psychological illness can be precipitated by immature religious
beliefs and practices. Secondly, it is possible that the same
religious beliefs and practices could lead one person to mental
health and stability and another to insanity. In other words, to
take but a couple of examples, ascetical practices and the celibate
life are ambivalent; they could be indisputable signs of pathology
or simply expressions of one's self-control and dedication.

Finally, the real issue lies in the criteria for distinguishing
healthy from unhealthy religion. The sanity or insanity--of the
first Christian martyrs who, in the face of religious persecution,
opted for giving up their lives rather than renounce their faith;
the Buddhists priests who immolated themselves in protest during the
Viet Nam war; and the modern terrorists who are not afraid to die
for their cause because heaven awaits them--is subject to different
interpretations. It is certainly tempting to identify one's own
beliefs and behavior with psychological well-being, yet to denounce
similar beliefs and actions in different traditions as signs of
pathology. In the debate on religion and mental health, it is
difficult at times to determine whether the negative or positive
views, maintained and propounded so strongly, express more the religious or non-religious convictions of their proponents. Similarly,
in the arguments about the cults one doubts whether psychiatry is
being used, on the one hand, to defend one's religious roots, family
traditions, or secular ideology or, on the other, to support religious freedom at all costs and to justify and promote actual involvement in cultic groups.

190.   Academy of Religion and Mental Health. RELIGION, SCIENCE,
       AND MENTAL HEALTH. New York: New York University Press,
       1959. xvi, 107 pp.

       Contains the Proceedings of the First Academy Symposium on
       the Inter-Disciplinary Responsibility for Mental Health, 1957.
       The contributions and responsibilities of various disciplines,

including psychiatry, sociology, cultural anthropology, and
medicine are presented in position papers and in the ensuing
discussions. It is argued throughout that religion, the
behavioral sciences, and medicine can participate and collaborate in promoting mental health.

191. Academy of Religion and Mental Health. RELIGION, CULTURE,
      AND MENTAL HEALTH. New York: New York University Press,
      1961. xv, 157 pp.

      Contains the Proceedings of the Third Annual Symposium held
      by the Academy in 1959. Mental health is approached from
      sociological, anthropological, and religious perspectives.
      The exchanges between the scholars from different disciplines
      converge towards two major issues: 1) the question of the
      interdependence of religious commitment and scientific orien-
      tation; and 2) the problem of how to distinguish between the
      mentally healthy state of the individual and its relation
      to religious faith. Practical mental health implications are
      underscored and some research projects are proposed.

192. Academy of Religion and Mental Health. RESEARCH IN RELIGION
      AND HEALTH: SELECTED REPORTS AND METHODS. New York:
      Fordham University Press, 1963. x, 165 pp.

      A record of the Proceedings of the Academy's Third Sympo-
      sium, held in 1961. The summarized discussions deal with the
      following areas: 1) methods of collecting data; 2) the rela-
      tionshp between religion and social attitudes; 3) selection
      of personnel for the clergy; 4) psychopathology in religious
      experience; and 5) methodology and future plans. A useful
      bibliography, covering the decade 1950-1960 on questionnaires,
      field methods, current analysis, positive techniques, and
      statistical records, is provided.

      Contains item 165.

193. Akihilananda, Swami. MENTAL HEALTH AND HINDU PSYCHOLOGY.
      New York: Harper, 1951. 231 pp.

      Propounds the view that Indian psychology, which has its
      roots in Indian religion, has a therapeutic value. Because
      Indian psychology provides an understanding of the various
      states of human consciousness, it can make a definite con-
      tribution to Western psychology. The author illustrates
      how Indian psychology deals with the method of overcoming
      anxiety, the conquest of fear and frustration, and the means
      of integrating the personality. Meditation and Yoga prac-
      tices stabilize the emotions, unify one's will, and integrate
      the mind, leading to personality development.

194. Allport, Gordon W. "Behavioral Science, Religion, and Mental
      Health." JOURNAL OF RELIGION AND HEALTH 2 (1963): 83-95.

      Points out that even though the church and synagogue have
      been traditionally "therapeutic communities," religion has

many shortcomings. The large number of members in some
churches and the use of pathogenic appeals, like fear, guilt,
and superstition, do not contribute towards therapeutic help.
There is no firm evidence that religious persons are more mentally healthy than non-religious ones. The author discusses
whether some forms of religious sentiment are more therapeutic
than others, and then argues that intrinsic religion, where
intellectual and motivational commitment is central, is more
healthy than extrinsic religion, where religion is used as a
defense against anxiety and a means of security.

195. Anderson, George Christian. "Maturing Religion." PASTORAL
      PSYCHOLOGY 22 (April 1971): 17-20.

      Admits that many religious practices are masochistic,
sadistic, and hysterical, and that certain concepts of God
could be childish. But not all religion is neurotic. The
author attempts to find criteria for determining whether a
person claiming to have a religious experience is mature or
not. He concludes that the maturity of religion depends on
the psychological maturity of the individual. A person who
is still dependent will end up using religion as "a crutch
rather than as a creative experience," while another "who has
a neurotic need for power and authority will often be bigoted,
prejudiced, judgmental, and unforgiving" (p. 18). When mass
hysteria is used to induce conversion, when perfectionism is
preached, and when rigid performances of ceremonies are
insisted upon, then religion is not being practiced in a
mature way.

196. Anderson, George Christian. YOUR RELIGION: HEALTHY OR NEU-
      ROTIC? Garden City, NY: Doubleday and Co., 1970. 191 pp.

      Discusses the relationship between religion and mental
illness. Religion, according to the author, does not necessarily make a person ill; it could rather be a "vital, health-
creating experience." Psychological illness can, however,
bring about immature religious beliefs and practices. Sudden
religious conversions are unhealthy only if fear dominates
the experience and if no real spiritual growth takes place.
Glossolalia, masochistic practices, superstitions, and prejudice are also discussed. In his search for reliable
criteria of healthy religion the author rules out the example
of saints, most of whom, like St. Aloysius Gonzaga, were mad.

197. Apolito, Arnaldo. "Psychoanalysis and Religion." AMERICAN
      JOURNAL OF PSYCHOANALYSIS 30 (1970): 115-26.

      Examines the difficulties in dealing with religion in
psychoanalytic therapy and the conflict between religion and
psychoanalysis, a conflict which is on the decline. It is
argued that these problems stem from human nature, which is
neurotic, from the very nature of religion, and from the
psychoanalyst's professional yet negative attitude towards
religion. The author clings to a Freudian interpretation of

religion but maintains that no matter what his/her private
religious stance might be, the psychoanalyst must be aware of
the patients' views in order to help them with their religious
conflicts.

198.   Appel, Kenneth E. "Religion." AMERICAN HANDBOOK OF PSYCHI-
        ATRY (item 3), vol. 2, pp. 1777-82.

        Points out how psychotherapeutic concerns and methods have
        at times been similar to those found in religion. When reli-
        gion is supportive, wholesome, and courage-inspiring without
        making impossible demands, it contributes to one's health.
        Sympathetic understanding of a patient's belief is necessary.

199.   Argyal, Andras. "The Convergence of Psychotherapy and Reli-
        gion." JOURNAL OF PASTORAL CARE 5 (Winter, 1952): 4-14.

        Proposes the view that religion and psychotherapy converge
        in their orientations and are in agreement on essential issues.
        The major human ills with which psychotherapists normally deal
        are described. Two religious phenomena, repentance and con-
        fession, are then examined and found to be crucial for a
        religious and psychotherapeutic reconstruction of a person's
        life.

200.   Armstrong, Renate G., Gordon L. Larsen, and Stephen A. Mourer.
        "Religious Attitudes and Emotional Adjustment." JOURNAL OF
        PSYCHOLOGICAL STUDIES 13 (1962): 35-47.

        Attempts to determine whether there is a relationship be-
        tween a person's religious beliefs and his or her emotional
        adjustment, self-concept, interests, age, and education. A
        Religious Attitude Scale (RAS) was drawn up and administered
        to normal and hospitalized psychotic patients of three reli-
        gious groups: orthodox, conservative, and liberal Christians.
        No significant relationship was found between mental illness
        and the RAS score. With the exception of the liberal group,
        religious attitudes varied independently of, or were unrelated
        to, emotional adjustment, self-concept, and age.

201.   Bartmeier, Leo H. "Healthy and Unhealthy Patterns of Reli-
        gious Behavior." JOURNAL OF RELIGION AND HEALTH 4 (1965):
        309-14.

        Maintains that religion does not have the function of either
        creating or healing anxiety, even though religious beliefs and
        practices could produce healthy or unhealthy results in a
        person. Religion is neither a means to achieve peace of mind
        nor a method of solving one's psychological problems. Reli-
        gious practices, however, may be able to serve the needs of
        a person who suffers from neurosis or, on the other hand,
        could themselves also contain neurotic patterns of behavior.

202.   Becker, Russell, J. "Religion and Psychological Health."
        RESEARCH ON RELIGIOUS DEVELOPMENT. Edited by Merton P.
        Strommen. New York: Hawthorn, 1971, pp. 391-421.

Reviews the research on the relationship between religion and positive mental health. Studies on religious beliefs, practices, feeling, experience, and knowledge, and on how these might affect one's health, are included. People who have a strong religious identity and who practice their religion are more likely to be free of mental illness and neurotic symptoms. The author observes that detailed points of contact between positive psychological traits and religion are not easy to find, due perhaps to limitations in research procedures. Several directions for future research are suggested.

203. Belgum, David, editor. RELIGION AND MEDICINE: ESSAYS ON MEANING, VALUES, AND DEATH. Ames, IA: Iowa State University Press, 1967. xiii, 345 pp.

A collection of previously published essays on the relationship between religion and physical and psychological health. Five areas are covered: 1) the health of the whole person; 2) the psychological aspects of health; 3) the meaning of health; 4) values, guilt, and illness; and 5) the treatment of sickness.

Contains items 194, 235, 329.

204. Betts, George H., Fredrick C. Eiselen, and George A. Coe, editors. RELIGION AND CONDUCT. New York: Abingdon, 1930. 288 pp.

Comprises a report, written by several authors, on a conference held at Northwestern University in November, 1929. The papers cover several topics, including the therapeutic value of religion.

Contains items 215, 306, 315.

205. Blain, Daniel. "Organized Religion and Mental Health." JOURNAL OF RELIGION AND HEALTH 4.2 (1965): 164-72.

Comments on three areas of mental health: 1) the changes in psychiatry; 2) the greater contribution which religion can make to the mental welfare of the individual; and 3) the need of churches to participate in mental health programs. Organized religion is seen as a positive contributing factor to the mental health of a person.

206. Bloom, Jack H. "Who Become Clergymen." JOURNAL OF RELIGION AND HEALTH 10 (1971): 50-76.

Reviews the literature on the personality dimensions of "pulpit" clergy and seminarians. The interest focuses on the dynamics that allow an individual to maintain mental health in spite of being "a cultural deviant." One of the main conflicts of the clergy centers around an emotional life that is often deprived. The clergyman is angry because he

is respected not for what he is, but for what he does, and
not for what he does for himself, but for what he does for
others. He often sublimates this anger by setting himself
apart and by becoming an exception, a projection, and a
paradigm of an ideal person.

207.   Boisen, Anton T. "Religion and Personality Adjustment."
        PSYCHIATRY 5 (1942): 209-18.

Reviews a study of a Midwestern United States farming
village where the effects of religion on thought, conduct,
and organization of personalities were measured. The results
show that religion in this case was static rather than
creative. A nucleus of the faithful seem to contribute to
the well-being of the community.

208.   Boisen, Anton T. THE EXPLORATION OF THE INNER WORLD: A STUDY
        OF MENTAL DISORDER AND RELIGIOUS EXPERIENCE. New York:
        Willett, Clark and Co., 1936. xiii, 322 pp.

Starts with the hypothesis that there is an important
relationship between mental illness and sudden conversions
which have been common in Christianity since St. Paul's time.
Both may arise out of inner conflict and disharmony and both
may represent severe emotional upheaval or the healing forces
of nature. The book covers religious experiences, messianic
consciousness, and spiritual healing. Mystical experiences
provide an emotional reenforcement of traditional beliefs,
but they can also be pathological if accompanied by visions,
auditions, and morbid asceticism. Conversion may solve intra-
psychic conflicts and bring reorganization to the individual's
inner life, but it can also be related to serious mental
disorders.

209.   Boisen, Anton T. "Evangelism in the Light of Psychiatry."
        JOURNAL OF RELIGION 7 (1927): 76-80.

Defends evangelism against the criticism of psychiatry and
liberal theology. It is admitted that evangelicals adopt
attitudes which might have a negative impact on a believer's
mental health. The author maintains, however, that converts
to fundamentalist and conservative religious beliefs and
practices are led to a deeper meaning of human existence
and to a more abundant and healthy personal life.

210.   Bonnell, George Carruthers. "Salvation and Psychotherapy."
        JOURNAL OF RELIGION AND HEALTH 8 (1969): 382-98.

Starts with the assumption that to be human is to experience existential anxiety and that people sometimes develop
neurotic and psychotic anxieties. How one handles one's
anxiety is one's religion. When a person seeks to run away
from anxiety by reinforcing one's idols, by attacking one's
detractors, etc., one is more likely to become schizophrenic.
The author sees religion as a binding force that brings

meaning and direction to the psychotherapeutic process.
Redemption of the whole person is central to both religion
and psychotherapy. Common goals of pastoral counselor and
therapist are listed.

211.   Bornstedt, Theodore. "Religion as an Asset in a Psychiatric
       Patient: An Historical and Clinical Comment." JOURNAL OF
       PASTORAL CARE 22 (1968): 82-92.

       Argues that the psychiatric tendency to view religious
       convictions as a hindrance to mental health is not warranted.
       One example is given to show that a patient may reap great
       benefits if the therapist approaches religion as a source of
       strength, rather than of weakness and conflict.

212.   Bowman, Harold L. "Mental Hygiene in Relation to Religion."
       MENTAL HYGIENE 20 (1936): 177-86.

       Points out that, in spite of the fact that the rise of the
       psychological disciplines has put into question many claims
       of religious healing, psychiatry and religion could cooperate
       because their goals overlap. Some forms of religious belief
       and activity, which involve a distorted theory of human
       nature, an authoritarian ethic, and emotional behavior border-
       ing on infantilism, contribute to mental disease. Religion
       frequently creates tensions leading to guilt feelings, which
       are used to gain a hold over people. When religion keeps the
       mind subjugated and under strict obedience, then it is not
       contributing to mental health. But some forms of religion
       can help maintain a person's health by adhering to the goals
       of a mature personality.

213.   Bronner, Alfred. "Psychotherapy With Religious Patients."
       AMERICAN JOURNAL OF PSYCHOTHERAPY 18 (1964): 475-87.

       Reviews some of the literature on the relationship between
       psychiatry and religion since Freud and finds an increasing
       recognition of the role of religion in mental health. A
       number of case histories are presented to show the author's
       own approach and techniques in his work with religious
       patients who distort the benign aspects of religion. A
       positive acceptance of the patient's religious belief system
       is regarded as important, no matter what the therapist's own
       views might be.

214.   Casey, Robert P. "The Psychoanalytic Study of Religion."
       JOURNAL OF ABNORMAL AND SOCIAL PSYCHOLOGY 33 (1938): 437-52.

       Starts with an outline of Freud's works on religion and
       then goes on to the reaction to psychoanalysis and its devel-
       opment, particularly in Fromm. Some of the gains made and
       defects exhibited in psychoanalytic studies of religion are
       mentioned and several suggestions are put forward for future
       study. It is probable, the author states, that schizophrenics,
       manic depressives, and the feeble-minded find religion of some
       service to their needs.

215.   Charters, Jessie A. "Readjustments of Conduct Under the
       Stimulus of Religion." RELIGION AND CONDUCT (item 204),
       pp. 184-96.

       Raises the issue of whether religion can become a basis for
       a progressive, satisfying reconstruction of one's experience.
       Religious practices and sentiments like faith, prayer, and
       dependence on God can cure one's personality problems only
       when religion provides a meaning to life.

216.   Chesen, Eli. RELIGION MAY BE HAZARDOUS TO YOUR HEALTH.
       New York: Peter H. Wyden, 1972. ix, 145 pp.

       Puts forward the view, based on representative case
       histories, that religion is a consumer good which can affect
       one's mental health for better or worse. The relationship
       between religion and child development, emotional instability,
       and psychosis are among the topics dealt with. Tenacious
       religious beliefs are linked with disturbed thinking pro-
       cesses. The overzealousness of the Jesus freaks and other
       cults is a sign of a dissociation experience which provides
       an "incomplete escape from reality and is practically a
       threat to the person's mental well-being" (p. 90). Some
       religious beliefs, like the belief in God, can facilitate
       happiness and mental stability. Religion can also, by
       injecting meaning into one's life, be a safeguard against
       suicide. Some guidelines for helping parents develop in
       their children a healthy attitude towards religion are given.

217.   Chikes, Tibor. "Problems of Faith Healing." JOURNAL OF
       RELIGION AND HEALTH 4 (1965): 336-41.

       Argues that the very phrase "faith healing" creates an
       unreal dichotomy between medical and non-medical healing and
       that a unified view of healing should be developed. The
       author warns the church against using the gimmick of healing
       as a way of pleasing and attracting customers. Faith healing
       is unhealthy if it is sensational, commercialized, and over-
       emotional.

218.   Clineball, Howard J. "Mental Health Through Religious
       Community." PASTORAL PSYCHOLOGY 20 (May 1969): 33-42.

       Maintains that churches and synagogues should be involved
       in mental health because of the unique contribution they can
       make and also because mental and spiritual health are insepa-
       rable. Religious centers provide an opportunity for renewal
       of trust, a sense of belonging, support in times of crisis,
       satisfaction of one's spiritual needs, and an instrument for
       personal growth.

219.   Committee for Psychiatry and Religion. THE PSYCHIC FUNCTION
       OF RELIGION IN MENTAL HEALTH AND ILLNESS. New York: Group
       for the Advancement of Psychiatry, vol. vi, Report no. 67,
       1968. pp. 653-730.

After a brief account of the historical background, the uses of religion in mental illness are discussed. It is shown that elements of religion, like conversion and the belief that the end of the world is near, are commonly invoked and exploited in neurotic and schizophrenic subjects. The influences of religion on character are then explored. Finally, the place of religion in "normal" psychic functioning is considered.

220. Cortes, Juan B. "Religious Aspects of Mental Health." JOURNAL OF RELIGION AND HEALTH 4 (1965): 315-21.

Compares and contrasts the psychological views of Freud (see item 71) and Mowrer (see item 279) on religion. The presence of mental and emotional illness is, according to the author, a sign of frustration or distortion of our inner nature which has a deep religious dimension. The neurotic or mentally ill person has certain religious needs, the neglect of which can cause pathology.

221. Curran, Charles A. "Some Psychological Aspects of Vatican Council II." JOURNAL FOR THE SCIENTIFIC STUDY OF RELIGION 2 (1963): 190-94.

Looks on Vatican Council II as a revival movement and draws parallels between the Council and the individual's psychological counseling process. Both can lay the foundation for a dramatic and significant change in self-reorganization and reintegration resulting from a deeper self-knowledge.

222. Curran, Charles A. "The Concept of Sin and Guilt in Psychotherapy." JOURNAL OF COUNSELING PSYCHOLOGY 7 (1960): 192-97.

Explains the difference between theological sin and sin and guilt in general. The author contends that the former is linked with conscience. To do away with one's conscience and, consequently, with personal sin, would be to eliminate one of the main sources of therapy. The religious view of sin and guilt is seen as therapeutic.

223. Cutten, George B. THE PSYCHOLOGICAL PHENOMENON OF CHRISTIANITY. New York: Charles Scribner's Sons, 1908. xviii, 497 pp.

Examines the whole range of Christian phenomena from a psychological point of view and distinguishes between the abnormal and pathological on the one hand, and the normal and healthy on the other. In general, glossolalia, witchcraft, asceticism, and revivals are judged to be pathological, while prayer, worship, and faith healing (as practiced, for example, by Christian Scientists) are discussed as a form of therapeutics by suggestion.

224. Doniger, Simon, editor. HEALING: HUMAN AND DIVINE. MAN'S SEARCH FOR WHOLENESS THROUGH SCIENCE, FAITH, AND PRAYER. New York: Association Press, 1957. xix, 254 pp.

Contains the proceedings of a symposium on the various ways
in which science, faith, and prayer can work together to heal
the human body and mind. The topics covered include: 1) the
theories of several psychologists and psychiatrists on the
search for wholeness; 2) the opinions of theologians on the
relationship between religion and psychiatry; 3) the psychology of prayer; and 4) the effects of spiritual healing as
distinct from magic and psychotherapy.

225.   Dorsey, John M. "Religion and Medical Psychology." PASTORAL
        PSYCHOLOGY 19 (September 1968): 27-34.

        Stresses the fact that religion leads a person to realize
        one's wholeness of being and helps one achieve it. The author
        lists and describes several "sacred facts" which contribute
        to one's psychological development. Religion has a positive
        impact on one's personal growth by teaching the meaning of
        sin and guilt.

226.   Dreger, Ralph M. "Some Personality Correlates of Religious
        Attitudes as Determined by Projective Techniques."
        PSYCHOLOGICAL MONOGRAPHS 66, no. 3 (1952): 1-18.

        Aims at determining the emotional maturity of religious
        conservatives and liberals by means of projective methods.
        Out of several hypotheses, one which assumed that religious
        liberals are found to be more emotionally mature than con-
        servatives turned out to be correct. The people who took
        part in this test came from a variety of churches represent-
        ing conservative, liberal, and mixed congregations.

227.   Ducker, E. N. A CHRISTIAN THERAPY FOR A NEUROTIC WORLD.
        London: Allen and Unwin, 1961. 225 pp.

        Integrates Christian principles with modern psychothera-
        peutic treatments. The aim of Christian therapy is outlined
        and the ways of handling various human ills, like mental pain
        and hysteria, are described and illustrated by case examples.
        The author insists throughout on the power of the Christian
        faith to heal people from the stresses and strains of modern
        society.

228.   Duffey, Felix D. PSYCHIATRY AND ASCETICISM. St. Louis:
        Herder Book Co., 1950. 132 pp.

        Presents a Catholic psychological approach to ascetic
        practices. Seen in its Christian context as a way to self-
        discipline leading to perfection, asceticism is not, as so
        many psychiatrists claim, a perversion of nature but a
        spiritually and psychologically sound practice which leads to
        peace of mind. The author discusses also the psychology of
        mental prayer, self-knowledge and mortification. Asceticism,
        he asserts, has a preventive and curative value, setting up
        barriers against the formation of complexes and freeing one
        from disruptive elements.

229.   Ellis, Albert. "There is No Place For the Concept of Sin in
        Psychotherapy." JOURNAL OF COUNSELING PSYCHOLOGY 7 (1962):
        188-92.

        Refutes Mowrer's positive appraisal of the concept of sin
        (see item 279) and argues that it should play no part in any
        psychotherapeutic treatment. He vehemently asserts that to
        introduce it "in any manner, shape, or form is highly perni-
        cious and antitherapeutic" (p. 188). The therapist's main
        function is to help people rid themselves of the blame that
        is responsible for a negative self-image, the essence of
        psychological illness.

230.   Erikson, Erik H. YOUNG MAN LUTHER: A STUDY IN PSYCHOLOGY AND
        HISTORY. New York: Norton, 1958. 288 pp.

        A classic psychological study of Martin Luther. The author
        sees Luther's religious quest as conflict-ridden and his
        religious growth as a process of problem solving. Luther's
        whole range of feeling is assessed. Terms like "compulsion
        neurosis" and "compulsive rituals" are used to describe
        Luther's enduring tendencies. Crisis and emotional ill-
        health are associated with the development of extraordinary
        abilities, which are clearly manifest in Luther's achievements.

231.   Farr, Clifford B., and Reuel L. Howe. "The Influence of Reli-
        gious Ideas on the Etiology, Symptomatology, and the
        Prognosis of the Psychoses. With Special Reference to
        Social Factors." AMERICAN JOURNAL OF PSYCHIATRY 11 (1932):
        845-65.

        Studies religious expressions which were mere symptoms of
        delusional or emotional disturbances as distinct from those
        that were the cause or the aggravation of the problem.
        Various groups are examined: 1) people in whom religious
        factors were definitely the predisposing cause of illness;
        2) those who exhibited conflict about the moral and/or social
        aspects of religion; and 3) those whose religious beliefs and
        behavior were signs of existing psychic disorders. The author
        argues that in 70 percent of mental cases, religion played an
        important part in the initiation of the psychotic condition.
        Religious intolerance is said to be at the root of at least
        some psychological problems that people develop when they
        experience religious conflicts.

232.   Felix, Robert H. "Religion and Healthy Personality." PAS-
        TORAL PSYCHOLOGY 15 (November 1954): 9-16.

        Maintains that a strong religious belief and practice
        contribute to a healthy personality. The formation of the
        personality from childhood, through adolescence, and up to
        adulthood is outlined and related to religious development.
        Good religion is considered to be therapeutic.

233.   Galdston, Iago. "Psychiatry and Religion." JOURNAL OF
        NERVOUS AND MENTAL DISEASE 112 (1950): 46-57.

Argues that the corporate church and its dogma are valid, normal, and healthy components of the individual psyche. Freud's concept of superego is discussed. A weak superego is a very frequent source of pathology. Since religion tends to strengthen the superego, it has psychotherapeutic value.

234.   Gassert, Robert G., and Bernard H. Hall. PSYCHIATRY AND RELIGIOUS FAITH. New York: Viking Press, 1964. xx, 171 pp.

Discusses the relationship between psychiatry and religion, focusing on whether they are antagonistic to each other or whether each can contribute to the healing process. The problems of mental illness and the theory and practice of psychotherapy are among the topics dealt with. The authors believe that religion and psychiatry can cooperate and hope their work will be of assistance to those priests and nuns who encounter mental illness in their ministry. The psychological testing preparatory to the priesthood and religious life is also discussed.

235.   Godin, André. "Mental Health in Christian Life." JOURNAL OF RELIGION AND HEALTH 1 (1961): 41-54.

Discusses two basic questions, namely, whether the Christian religion can serve to strengthen and restore one's mental health and whether sound mental health can assist the Christian in daily life. Although the author gives an emphatic, affirmative reply to both questions, he thinks it is easier to demonstrate the second assumption than the first.

236.   Graff, Robert, and Clayton E. Ladd. "POI Correlates of a Religious Commitment Inventory." JOURNAL OF CLINICAL PSYCHOLOGY 27 (1971): 502-4.

Compares data on self-actualization and religiosity from the Personal Orientation Inventory (POI) and the Dimension of Religious Commitment (DRC). Less religious subjects tended to be more self-accepting, spontaneous, inner-directed, and less dependent than those with a high level of religiosity. The conclusion which can be drawn from this short study is that a less religious person is psychologically healthier.

237.   Groves, Ernest R. "Some Aspects of Mental Hygiene and Religion." SOCIAL FORCES 8 (1929): 187-9.

Argues that mental hygiene can at times find an ally in religion in the effort to help individuals with their problems. The emotional appeal of religion, with its conflicts and guilt feelings, can create mental problems. Faith and conversion can, however, work wonders in psychotherapy. Though mysticism is taken as evidence of mental unsoundness, the author argues that it can be a creative force that leads to the solution of personal problems.

238.   Guertin, Wilson H., and Arnold W. Schmidt. "Constellations of Religious Attitudes of Paranoid Schizophrenics." PSYCHOLOGICAL REPORTS 1 (1955): 319-22.

Investigates empirically Boisen's view that delusional thinking is either: 1) restitutional, when mystical elements are involved; or 2) unconstructive, when persecution is paramount. From the results of a questionnaire given to hospitalized paranoid schizophrenics, four types of religious people were drawn up: the faithful believer, the rational non-believer, the insecure independent type, and the emotional rejection and denial type. Boisen's views are generally confirmed.

239.   Guntrip, Henry. PSYCHOTHERAPY AND RELIGION. New York: Harper and Brothers, 1957. 206 pp.

Studies the nature and origin of mental pain and chronic anxiety and the natural and automatic defense set-up to ward off such psychological illnesses. The cure of anxiety through psychotherapy and the relationship between psycho-therapy, values, and religion are discussed. It is argued that spiritual values are of great importance "to healthy living, to full self-realization, and to a constructive contribution to our human environment" (p. 183). In some instances religious experience can stabilize a profoundly religious person, as was the case with John Bunyan, George Fox, the prophet Isaiah, and St. Paul. Severe psychoneurosis can, however, have a negative impact on religious experiences. Religion, when mature, leads to the highest goals of psycho-therapy.

240.   Hall, Charles E. "Contributions of the Clergy to Mental Health." PASTORAL PSYCHOLOGY 17 (June 1966): 19-24.

Discusses psychiatric treatment and contrasts it with some of the basic aspects of the structure of the church, which offers continuous help to people in their daily lives and when they face death. The church provides a theology which makes the vicissitudes of life meaningful, a community of believers which gives support, and significant rituals for the major events of one's life. The clergy play an important role as counselors in the context of the church which is complementary to, and not competitive with, psychiatric treatment.

241.   Hawthorne, Berkeley C. "Frontiers in Religion and Psycho-therapy." JOURNAL OF RELIGION AND HEALTH 5 (1966): 296-305.

Examines the relationship between religion and psychotherapy in three dimensions: 1) the shrinking distance between the two with the development of mutual understanding and cooperation; 2) the influence of psychotherapy on religion; and 3) the increasing interest of psychotherapists in religion as an important aspect of sound mental health.

242.   Haydon, A. Eustace. "Spiritual (Religious) Values and Mental Hygiene." MENTAL HYGIENE 14 (1930): 779-96.

Defines religion as a shared quest for satisfying spiritual values which contribute to the practical improvement in the

quality of life. These values, which include security and
creativity, are briefly described. In the wake of cultural
and social changes, which bring about physical, mental, and
psychological anguish, the author seems assured that new
techniques and methods in mental hygiene will help human
beings in their religious quests.

243.   Heath, Douglas H.   "Secularization and the Maturity of Reli-
        gious Beliefs." JOURNAL OF RELIGION AND HEALTH 8 (1969):
        335-58.

        Challenges the commonly held view that secularization leads
        to maturity. While admitting that research supports the
        thesis that religious orthodoxy is on the decline, the author
        disagrees with those who view secularization as a process of
        maturity and of assuming responsibility and, hence, as a sign
        of mental health. But he concedes that extreme interest or
        preoccupation with religious and philosophical issues in
        seventeen-year-old youngsters tends to be associated with
        immaturity. He contends that the secular attitude is rather
        ambivalent since it heightens the potential to become either
        mature or immature.

244.   Higgins, John W.   "Religion." AMERICAN HANDBOOK OF PSYCHI-
        ATRY (item 3), vol. 2, pp. 1783-88.

        Directs attention to some of the problems which are in-
        herent in a psychiatric situation where religious elements
        are present. The materialistic world-view often espoused by
        psychiatrists, together with their reductionist theories and
        preference for psychic determinism, has created an atmosphere
        of conflict which, one may add, is often still apparent in
        current psychiatric studies on cults. The author suggests
        some ways of reducing the conflict.

245.   Hiltner, Seward. "My Credo on Religion and Mental Health."
        PASTORAL PSYCHOLOGY 17 (June 1966): 49-51.

        Outlines his view of religion as an aid to mental health and
        encourages cooperation between the clergy and mental health
        therapists.

246.   Hiltner, Seward. "Freud, Psychoanalysis, and Religion."
        PASTORAL PSYCHOLOGY 7 (November 1956): 9-21.

        Admits that Freud's view of religion is largely negative,
        but argues that Freud was very aware of its importance in
        human life. Five propositions outlining Freud's "theology"
        are drawn up. It is argued that Freud's basic tenets must
        be incorporated into any relevant philosophy or theology.
        Psychoanalysis has made several important contributions to
        religious understanding. It has strengthened the argument
        for the legitimacy of the importance of the religious quest,
        provided insights for understanding religious distortions,

and made available tools for enriching religious doctrine
itself. Theology has also begun to make an impact on psychoanalysis.

247.   Hiltner, Seward. RELIGION AND HEALTH. New York: Macmillan,
        1943. xiii, 292 pp.

        Discusses 1) the relationship between religion and mental
        health, and 2) the practical implications for religious work-
        ers and counselors. Religion, according to the author, can
        influence one's personality both in healthy and unhealthy
        ways. If, however, religion does not grow intellectually
        and emotionally with other aspects of personality, or if it
        acts as a substitute for relaxation, work, etc., or if it
        makes the individual act in a compulsive manner, then it
        becomes repressive and harmful. The author believes that
        religion can contribute positively to mental health in
        several ways: it can lead to personal integration, diminish
        one's egocentricity and tendency to avoid responsibility,
        make a person less dependent on mere cultural standards, and
        help one face the mysteries of life.

248.   Hiltner, Seward. "The Contributions of Religion to Mental
        Health." MENTAL HYGIENE 24 (1940): 366-77.

        Reviews the then-current notion of health and the place of
        religion in a healthy personality. A healthy religion must
        be related to the personality as a whole and must grow both
        emotionally and intellectually. Any signs of compulsiveness
        are indications of pathology. Some of the healthy effects of
        religion are the integration of one's life, altruism, inde-
        pendence from mere cultural standards, and strength to face
        both physical and psychological difficulties.

249.   Hoffmann, Hans. RELIGION AND MENTAL HEALTH: A CASE WORK
        WITH COMMENTARY, AND AN ESSAY ON PERTINENT LITERATURE.
        New York: Harper and Brothers, 1961. xvi, 333 pp.

        Aims at providing the basis for discussing the relation-
        ship between religion and mental health. Thirty-eight case
        studies are presented under three headings: Personality and
        Chaos, Personality and Structure, and Personality and Love.
        The author brings to light certain aspects and problems of
        human experience in which religion plays a vital role in
        promoting or undermining an individual's mental health. A
        lengthy essay (pp. 273-329) critically surveys literature on
        the subject.

250.   Hulme, William E. "Sacramental Therapy." JOURNAL OF PASTO-
        RAL CARE 5.2 (Summer 1951): 23-29.

        Argues that both religious confession and communion have
        therapeutic value, but that they should not be used as an
        escape from the responsiblity of counseling.

251.   Johnson, Paul E. "Religious Psychology and Health." MENTAL
           HYGIENE 31 (1947): 556-66.

           Remarks that in spite of the advancement in medicine, the
           incidence of mental illness is on the rise and calls for
           cooperation between the different healing professions. The
           author outlines the particular expertise which the pastoral
           counselor, with his/her religious resources, can bring to the
           health team. To those who suffer from guilt, sorrow, anxiety,
           fear, and hostility, religion can provide healing of confession
           and forgiveness, comfort in time of grief, the increase of
           faith, and the spirit of love. Group therapy is advanced as
           a means of dealing with unsocial tendencies, such as timidity,
           egocentricity, isolation, sense of inferiority, and aggres-
           siveness. Religious experiences can create healthy attitudes,
           like an appreciation of one's personal worth, a feeling of
           belonging to a fellowship, and a secure awareness that comes
           from living a disciplined life. The author holds that the
           healing results are acquired more readily in a group atmos-
           phere.

252.   Jones, Ernest. NIGHTMARES, WITCHES, AND DEVILS. New York: W.
           W. Norton, 1931. 374 pp.

           A collection of essays, originally published in German
           between 1909 and 1910. The author's main thesis is that an
           intensive study of nightmares and beliefs associated with them
           shows that religion is a valuable means of helping people
           cope with guilt and fear. In a chapter on witches, it is
           maintained that "the witch belief represents in the main an
           exteriorization of the repressed sexual conflict of women,
           especially those relating to the feminine counterpart of the
           infantile oedipus situation" (p. 190).

253.   Joyce, C. R. B., and R. M. C. Wellson. "The Objective
           Efficacy of Prayer: a Double-Bind Clinical Trial." JOURNAL
           OF CHRONIC DISEASES 18 (1965): 367-77.

           Reports on an attempt to assess the possible effect of
           intercessory prayer in an experiment conducted with patients
           selected from two outpatient clinics at a London hospital.
           Prayer groups that included subjects suffering from deterio-
           rating psychological diseases were formed. Medication was
           continued both in the experimental group and in the control
           group. The results were negative: prayer did not prove
           advantageous.

254.   Jung, Carl Gustav. "Psychotherapists and the Clergy."
           PASTORAL PSYCHOLOGY 7 (April 1963): 27-41. (Also in THE
           COLLECTED WORKS OF C. G. JUNG, item 78, vol. 11, pp. 327-
           54.)

           Criticizes Freudian and Adlerian theories for not giving
           much attention to the psychological need of giving meaning
           to life. The author states that in all his practice of over

35 years, the problem with his patients was, in the last analysis, that of finding a religious outlook on life. According to him, the decline of religious life has been accompanied by an increasing frequency of neurosis and hence one must take a patient's religious difficulties seriously. Because healing is a religious exercise, Jung sees a place for the clergy in the field of mental health.

255. Kahn, Marion. "Some Observations of the Role of Religion in Illness." SOCIAL WORK 3 (1958): 83-90.

Considers ways in which religious orientation has an impact on religion. Religious feelings are heightened during illness, and the sick person's beliefs may be a source of comfort or of anxiety, tension, and confusion. Religion can at times affect the adjustment to disability, recovery from illness, and attitudes toward death. The author stresses the need for the social worker to be aware of the impact of religion in illness and to work in conjunction with the clergyman.

256. Kanter, Arne. "Environmental Demands and Religious Needs." ACTA PSYCHIATRICA ET NEUROLOGICA 30 (1955): 709-20.

Discusses, in the context of two case histories, the importance of the environment for the religious beliefs and practices of the individual and the psychology and psychopathology of religion. It is the author's view that ecstasy and speaking in tongues are indications of a badly integrated personality. Many religious conflicts are due to the fact that people abandon the religion in which they were brought up and transfer their allegiance to a different religious tradition.

257. Kaufman, M. Ralph. "Religious Delusions in Schizophrenia." INTERNATIONAL JOURNAL OF PSYCHOANALYSIS 20 (1939): 363-76.

Discusses the process whereby delusions become religious beliefs in the context of several case studies of schizophrenic patients who belonged to different religious sects. Normal religion, which implies group adaptation, failed to provide satisfaction, and a more highly personal religion with delusional beliefs came into being. The religious beliefs of the patients are interpreted in Freudian terms.

258. Keene, James J. "Religious Behavior and Neuroticism, Spontaneity, and Worldmindedness." SOCIOMETRY 30 (1967): 137-57.

Points out that the disagreement about the effects of religion is based on several unresolved issues about the definition of religion, the sociological and psychological variables to which it is related, and the differences between religious groups. The study included Jews, Catholics, Protestants, Baha'is, and others and was limited to the investigation of several personality features, namely, the integration of

personality which was lacking in neurotic subjects, spontaneity, and worldmindedness--the last two being judged as conducive to psychological and social integration, respectively.
It was found that religious participation correlates with
adaptive behavior, but that an orthodox approach to religion
is linked with neuroticism.

259.   Kew, Clifton E. "Understanding Spiritual Healing." PASTORAL
        PSYCHOLOGY 12 (January 1962): 29-34.

        Maintains that the worship service helps the individual to
        attain self-identity, to feel accepted by the group, to have
        a feeling of belonging and togetherness, to arouse hope, and
        to provide some relief from suffering. Certain features of
        ritual, with the exception of "insight," are similar to group
        psychotherapy. The church service supplies the individual
        with a conceptual framework from which he/she can obtain a
        sense of direction.

260.   Kilpatrick, Milton E. "Mental Hygiene and Religion." MENTAL
        HYGIENE 24 (1940): 378-89.

        Broadly outlines the similarities and differences between
        the work of psychiatrists and of ministers of religion. The
        approach that the minister should take to develop mental
        hygiene in his parish is discussed. The underlying assumption
        is that religion contributes to psychological well-being.

261.   Knight, James A. A PSYCHIATRIST LOOKS AT RELIGION AND HEALTH.
        New York: Abingdon Press, 1964. 207 pp.

        Discusses, in the context of Jungian and Freudian theories,
        the relationship between religion and mental health and the
        use and misuse of religion by the emotionally disturbed. The
        positive, health-giving qualities of religion are numerous,
        but the neurotic and the psychotic can distort religious be-
        liefs. The author advocates cooperation between psychiatry
        and religion in the clinical situation.

262.   Krishnamurthy, N. "Social and Psychological Significance of
        Indian Rites and Ritual on the Indian Mind." TRANSACTIONS
        OF THE ALL-INDIA INSTITUTE OF MENTAL HEALTH 5 (1965): 86-93.

        Maintains that because rituals are ways of socialization
        and acculturation, they can be considered as techniques of
        creating satisfaction and confidence. They have, therefore,
        a positive and healthy effect on one's personality.

263.   Kysar, John E. "Mental Implications of Aggiornamento."
        JOURNAL OF RELIGION AND HEALTH 5 (1966): 35-42.

        Raises questions on the influence of Catholicism on person-
        ality, on the particular kind of conscience, superego, and
        ego ideal which the conservative leanings in the Church have
        tended to produce, and on the effects of the liberalizing
        movement since Vatican Council II. It is noted that exces-

sive severity of conscience, with consequent neurotic guilt feeling, self-depreciation and self-punishment, has often been the cause of mental illness. The changes which the Council set into motion may help Catholics toward better spiritual and mental health.

264. Lapsley, James N. "The Devotional Life and Mental Health." JOURNAL OF PASTORAL CARE 20 (1966): 136-48.

Assesses the probable effects of devotional reading (including THE IMITATION OF CHRIST by Thomas à Kempis, THE DARK NIGHT OF THE SOUL by St. John of the Cross, and CHRISTIAN DISCOURSES by Soren Kierkegaard) upon the mental health of their readers. These books are analyzed for the views they contain on: 1) attitudes towards self; 2) growth, development, and self-actualization; 3) self-integration; 4) autonomy; 5) perception of reality; and 6) mastery of one's environment. The author concludes that, on the whole, the readings may have a mixed effect on those who read them. If one takes into account the theme of suffering in these devotional classics, they can be easily seen as self-destructive. Spiritual books like those of Thomas à Kempis and St. John of the Cross are characterized by guilt, a low self-esteem, and a tendency to repression, and should be viewed as being primarily of historical interest.

265. Ligon, Ernest M. THE PSYCHOLOGY OF CHRISTIAN PERSONALITY. New York: Macmillan, 1961. x, 393 pp.

Considers the teaching of Jesus in the light of the psychology of personality. The basis for evaluating the Christian personality is to be found, according to the author, in the Sermon on the Mount, the teachings of which are examined from a psychological point of view and from the perspective of mental health. While admitting that not all religion is healthy, the author thinks that Christianity contributes to one's mental health by rooting out serious psychological problems, such as a sense of inferiority.

266. Linderthal, Jacob J., Jerome K. Meyers, Max P. Pepper, and Maxime S. Stern. "Mental Status of Religious Behavior." JOURNAL FOR THE SCIENTIFIC STUDY OF RELIGION 9 (1970): 143-49.

Reports on a two-year study of almost 100 individuals regarding their degree of pathology, their institutionalized religious participation, and their religious responses to life events. The researchers conclude that as the degree of illness increased: 1) the subjects' participation in organized religious activities decreased, 2) their church attendance was reduced in times of crisis, and 3) their prayer increased. Therefore, those who are mentally ill do not seem to make use of religious institutions to cope with reality nor do they turn to organized religion in times of crisis.

267.   Lowe, C. Marshall, and Roger O. Braaten. "Differences in
        Religious Attitudes and Mental Illness." JOURNAL FOR THE
        SCIENTIFIC STUDY OF RELIGION 5 (1966): 435-45.

        Points out that both Freudian theory and clinical evidence
        relates that heightened religious concern can lead to mental
        illness or disordered personality states. The author's goal
        was to measure religious attitudes of mentally ill people who
        needed hospitalization. Among his conclusions was the obser-
        vation that paranoid and schizoid subjects were no more
        religious than other mentally ill patients.

268.   MacKenzie, John G. NERVOUS DISORDERS AND RELIGION: A STUDY
        OF SOULS IN THE MAKING. London: Allen and Unwin, second
        edition, 1952. 183 pp.

        Deals with inner conflicts and guilt feelings which are part
        of human nature. Spiritual healing is accepted as a valid
        technique since prayer and faith have psychotherapeutic value
        and prevent the development of neurosis. Yet religion can
        also be the cause of psychological problems, especially when
        fear is stressed to such a degree that one's peace of mind is
        shaken. Similarly, those religious groups--such as Christian
        fundamentalists--which emphasize authority, often demand
        childish submission and compulsion, neglecting the human need
        for rationality and independence. Serious anxiety problems
        are the natural outcome. True commitment and faith, however,
        can bring an inner feeling of security which is essential
        for a healthy personality.

269.   Masserman, Jules H. "Faith and Delusion in Psychotherapy."
        AMERICAN JOURNAL OF PSYCHIATRY 110 (1953): 324-33.

        Proposes the view that three major religious beliefs,
        though ultimately delusional in character, are necessary to
        all human beings. These beliefs or delusions, namely, of
        invulnerability and immortality, of the omnipotent servant
        (or healer, or medicine man), and of mutual kindness between
        all people, are discussed. The question raised is whether
        "psychotherapy actually consists in the re-establishment of
        certain delusions necessary to all mankind" (p. 325).

270.   McConnell, Theodore A. "Confession in Cross-Disciplinary
        Perspective." JOURNAL OF RELIGION AND HEALTH 8 (1969):
        76-86.

        Explains the three dimensions of confession (religious,
        psychological, and legal) and argues that all must be taken
        into account for a more inclusive view. Confession is seen
        in the context of the healing process of therapy. It can be
        explained as a necessary attribute of one's personality, or
        as a dimension of pathology, or as a stage in the healing
        process of self-discovery and integration, the latter being
        the view espoused by the author.

271. Meadow, Arnold, and Harold J. Vetter. "Freudian Theory and
      the Judaic Value System," INTERNATIONAL JOURNAL OF SOCIAL
      PSYCHIATRY 5 (1959): 197-203.

      Analyzes the influence of Judaic cultural values on the
      Freudian theory of psychotherapy. Jewish attitudes towards
      worldliness and bodily pleasures, rationalism, Talmudic inter-
      pretation, methods of determining truth, and ideal family pat-
      terns are seen in the context of psychoanalytic theory. The
      author draws several parallels between psychoanalytic and
      Jewish thought and practice. The rabbi and the psychoanalyst
      are said to have the similar role of being arbiters in the
      problem of personal adjustment.

272. Medlicott, R. W. "St. Anthony Abbot and the Hazards of
      Asceticism: An Analysis of Artists' Representations of the
      Temptation." BRITISH JOURNAL OF MEDICAL PSYCHOLOGY 42
      (1969): 133-40.

      Examines the claims of asceticism in the context of St.
      Anthony's life as a hermit. Asceticism is viewed by the
      author not just as a form of discipline, but also as a deval-
      uation of material life. It favors regression in the service
      of the ego and plays a key role in creativity and mysticism.
      It is argued that asceticism has: 1) general religious, phil-
      osophical, and social hazards (like dualism, and the denial
      of the fullness of life and of social responsiblity); and 2)
      individual psychological dangers (like interference with ego
      functions, such as regression, defective reality-testing,
      ego-splitting, ego-disintegration, and distortion of drives,
      including masochism, activation of pregenital functioning,
      and recurrence of repressive and substitute gratifications).
      The way artists have handled the theme of asceticism is
      described in four historical stages starting from the thir-
      teenth to the first quarter of the twentieth century.

273. Meissner, W. W. "Notes on the Psychology of Faith." JOURNAL
      OF RELIGION AND HEALTH 8 (1969): 47-75.

      Discusses faith as a psychological process, as a return to
      basic needs and desires that characterize primitive human
      experiences. Although such a return is both regressive and
      recapitulative, it nevertheless leads to reorganization and
      revitalization. Deep faith is therefore ultimately conducive
      to a healthy personality.

274. Menninger, Karl A. MAN AGAINST HIMSELF. New York: Harcourt,
      Brace and Co., 1938. xii, 485 pp.

      Studies different kinds of human self-destructive tenden-
      cies, including asceticism and martyrdom. Various clinical
      studies in this area and the history of ascetics and martyrs
      are surveyed. The behavior of many of these religious men
      and women is, according to the author, self-defeating and
      self-destructive, whether the victim is revered as a saint,

admired for his or her heroism, or treated as a psychiatric
patient. Incidents from the lives of Christian saints are
quoted to show that their actions have the same components as
suicide attempts, that is, they are self-punitive, aggressive,
and erotic. Most people who indulge in ascetical practices
(such as fasting and celibacy) suffer from schizophrenia, the
classic syndrome of reality repudiation.

275. Meserve, Harry C. "Healthy and Unhealthy Religion." JOURNAL
     OF RELIGION AND HEALTH 4 (1965): 291-94.

     Explores the effects which a sound and healthy religion
     might have on a person. A healthy religion provides for the
     understanding of the world, gives meaning to life, brings
     unity in the world, and liberates rather than regresses the
     individual's sense of dignity and worth. Furthermore, healthy
     religion leads to that kind of security which puts an end to
     prejudice and which is prepared to receive, examine, and
     assimilate new truths. These qualities are universal and
     should be applicable to all religions.

276. Miller, Samuel H. "Religion: Healthy and Unhealthy." JOURNAL
     OF RELIGION AND HEALTH 4 (1965): 295-301.

     Maintains that a healthy religion provides for symbolic
     structures that give society its cohesiveness and the indi-
     vidual the support needed for the exercise of freedom. When
     religion leads to sectarianism and individualism, then it
     brings about mental illness in the individual and the deteri-
     oration of society. Faith can be misused and misinterpreted.
     In many sects, discipline can turn into masochism, anxiety
     can degenerate into scrupulosity, emphasis on orthodoxy can
     lead to sadism, and an atmosphere of suspicion easily creates
     heresy hunters. Healthy religion helps a person from succumb-
     ing to fear, anxiety, and hostility.

277. Mills, Robert. "The Synagogue as a Therapeutic Community."
     PASTORAL PSYCHOLOGY 23 (October 1972): 37-41.

     Proposes the view that the synagogue should be a counseling
     center that is concerned with human development and the
     healing of human ills. It can also provide answers to the
     current cry for relevance and for purposeful existence which
     all people crave.

278. Morgan, Norman C. "Religion in Psychotherapy." PASTORAL
     PSYCHOLOGY 8 (October 1957): 17-22.

     Believes that many people, without realizing it, go to
     psychiatrists for spiritual help and that successful therapy
     must take this factor into account. The author gives examples
     from his own practice of how to handle this problem. He out-
     lines some methods of interpreting various aspects of faith
     and religion to non-believing patients. Referral to clergymen
     is advised.

279.   Mowrer, O. H.   "Some Constructive Features of the Concept of
        Sin."   JOURNAL OF CONSELING PSYCHOLOGY 7 (1960): 185-88.

        Examines the rather negative reaction to the religious idea
        of sin among most psychiatrists who have been influenced by
        Freud. It is a common fallacy, according to the author, to
        hold that the idea and feeling of sin leads to neurosis or
        psychosis. He suggests that both religious and secular thera-
        peutic programs of the future will, like Alcoholics Anonymous,
        take guilt, confession, and expiation seriously.

280.   Murphy, Carol. RELIGION AND MENTAL ILLNESS. Wallingford,
        PA: Pendle Hill, 1955. 31 pp.

        Suggests several ways of looking at psychosis in an attempt
        to understand the mentally ill. The case of a paranoid indi-
        vidual is described and the author maintains that "vital
        religion" must somehow be able to assist the patient in his or
        her efforts for freedom from the many constrictions of mental
        illness.

281.   Musaph, Herman. "Religion and Mental Health Education."
        JOURNAL OF RELIGION AND HEALTH 8 (1969): 248-54.

        Discusses such questions as: 1) to what degree is a psychi-
        atrist competent to express an opinion on religion?, 2) to
        what extent can the psychiatrist assist the pastor in the
        latter's task?, and 3) how can religion make a contribution
        to mental health? It is held that religion offers a system
        of values and a path to happiness, thus contributing to one's
        psychological well-being. But it also fosters intolerance
        and belligerent attitudes, which lead to abnormality. The
        great demands which religion places on the individual can
        aggravate the sense of guilt, which could become pathological.

282.   Novey, Samuel. "Considerations on Religion in Relation to
        Psychoanalysis and Psychotherapy." JOURNAL OF NERVOUS AND
        MENTAL DISEASE 130 (1960): 315-21.

        Elaborates on the place of religious experiences in emo-
        tional disorders and in the state of emotional health.
        Paranoid religious delusions, as in the case of a person
        who assumes a prophetic and messianic role, can be either
        restitutive or destructive of one's psychological health.
        Infantile and regressive religious attitudes are often similar
        to demands of patients in therapy. Religion can, especially
        in time of turmoil, be a source of security and satisfaction,
        compensating for the lack of the required structured and
        stabilizing factors in one's life.

283.   Oates, Wayne E. WHEN RELIGION GETS SICK. Philadelphia:
        Westminster Press, 1970. 199 pp.

        Reviews those situations or conditions under which religion
        ceases to be a healthy factor in one's personality. Idolatry,

often manifested in bereavement, preoccupation with family
inheritance, and self-deification, disturbs one's mental
balance. Magic and superstitious rituals (like obsessive-
neurotic acts) are a sign of emotional instability and a
pathological distortion of healthy religious faith. The
pathology of religious leaders is also discussed.

284.   Oates, Wayne E. RELIGIOUS FACTORS IN MENTAL ILLNESS. New
        York: Association Press, 1957. 239 pp.

        Covers the problem of the relationship between religion
        and mental illness. Religion, it is claimed, can both hinder
        and help a mentally-ill person whose religion is often the
        projection of distorted family relations. The author draws
        several criteria for distinguishing between healthy and un-
        healthy religion. He stresses the need to know the psychic
        history of the individual before reaching any conclusions
        about the subject's religious ideas and their origin. When
        religious ideas are employed as concealment devices to justify
        the subject's participation in an unreal world, then one has a
        clear indication of mental illness. Among the signs of mental
        instability are complusive expressions of religious beliefs,
        the confusion between symbol and reality, and the literal and
        legalistic interpretation of symbols. Healthy religion binds
        people together. Religion can also be positively applied in
        therapy.

285.   Oates, Wayne E. "The Hindering and Helping Power of Reli-
        gion." PASTORAL PSYCHOLOGY 6 (May 1955): 43-49.

        Maintains that Freud's view that religion is a projection
        of the distortions of the parent-child relationship is true
        in folk religions, in the religions of authoritarianism, and
        in the religion of the mentally ill. But Freud's theory is
        not applicable to the Bible, more specifically to the teaching
        of Jesus. In this case religion leads to freedom and insight.
        The Christian concept of conscience, as distinct from Freud's
        "superego," is an essential part of religion that leads to
        maturity.

286.   Oates, Wayne E. "The Role of Religion in the Psychoses."
        JOURNAL OF PASTORAL CARE 3 (1949): 21-30.

        Maintains that religion can either facilitate mental health
        or else breed pathology. The author took part in a nine-week
        pastoral institute in a Kentucky State hospital. He found
        out that in several cases the psychotic condition was
        immediately preceded by a marked religious conflict over
        loyalty to a "Holy Roller" sect. This type of conflict arose
        as a spontaneous expression of the religious needs of those
        people who belong to socially, economically, and educationally
        marginal minorities. Further, there was a high incidence of
        religious ideas and experiences in the precipitation, func-
        tion, and causation of different types of psychoses. The
        role of the minister is discussed. The author thinks that

many counterfeit prophets often end up in mental hospitals after having spread their pathological ideas abroad.

287.   O'Doherty, E. F.   RELIGION AND PERSONALITY PROBLEMS.   New York: Alba House, 1964.   240 pp.

Dwells at length on the relationship between religion and mental health, which often seem to be in conflict.   Certain issues are explored: the spiritual formation of the adolescent, brainwashing, psychopathology and mystical phenomena, and the emotional development of ecclesiastical students. The author states that psychology and psychopathology have nothing positive to contribute to mysticism (inspired contemplation), which is brought about by God's grace and does not destroy but perfects and elevates a person's natural talents. Visions and revelations, which can be genuine revelatory events in one's religious life, are often nothing else by hysterical and hallucinatory phenomena.

288.   Ostow, Mortimer.   "Religion."   AMERICAN HANDBOOK OF PSYCHIATRY (item 3), vol. 2, pp. 1789-1801.

Discusses the relationship between religion and psychiatry and the use of religion and psychiatry by psychiatrists and clergymen, respectively.   The author exposes a number of areas of conflict and misunderstanding and the relationship between religion and human needs.   He alludes to ways in which clergy and psychiatrists can help each other.   He assumes throughout that religion can have therapeutic value.

289.   Ostow, Mortimer.   "The Nature of Religious Controls." AMERICAN PSYCHOLOGIST 13 (1958): 571-74.

Points out that religion influences human behavior by imitation, communication of affect, intervention in the pursuit of gratification, and obedience.   Further, religion uses controlled regression to facilitate the regulation of behavior.   Thus religious experience may bring relief from psychic distress by offering social sanctions.   The author seems to suggest that religious controls are healthy and that they could be made use of more wisely.

290.   Overstreet, Bonaro W.   "Guilt Feelings: Creative and Uncreative."   PASTORAL PSYCHOLOGY 6 (May 1955): 16-22.

Contrasts the religious point-of-view which holds that a sense of one's shortcomings is a spiritual necessity, with the common psychiatric position that one must get rid of one's guilt to be healthy.   A distinction is made between creative and uncreative guilt feelings and states.   Religion is concerned with the former and, therefore, affirms life and motivates people to do what is right.

291.   Page, F. Hilton.   "The Psychology of Religion After Fifty Years."   CANADIAN JOURNAL OF PSYCHOLOGY 5 (1951): 60-67.

Reflects on the general psychological attitude toward religion, which is summarized as one of disregard and neglect. "The unspoken implication is that adult religion is the same kind of thing as primitive, psychopathic, or adolescent religion irrationally and incongruously projected into later stage and development" (p. 64).

292.   Pattison, E. Mansell. "Social and Psychological Aspects of Religion and Psychotherapy." INSIGHT: QUARTERLY REVIEW OF RELIGION AND MENTAL HEALTH 5.2 (1966): 27-35.

A slightly different version of item 293.

293.   Pattison, E. Mansell. "Social and Psychological Aspects of Religion in Psychotherapy." JOURNAL OF NERVOUS AND MENTAL DISEASE 141 (1965): 586-97.

Examines the various definitions of the social role and task of psychotherapy as seen from both psychological and spiritual points-of-view. The psychological and religious goals involved in the process of psychotherapy are outlined. The author discusses the importance of the sociocultural context of psychotherapy and argues that certain forms of treatment might be enhanced by closer ties with religious therapy.

294.   Pattison, E. Mansell, editor. CLINICAL PSYCHIATRY AND RELIGION. Boston: Little, Brown and Co., 1968. xv, 327 pp.

Provides mental health professionals with information on religious issues that affect clinical practice. Two major areas are broadly covered: 1) what the clinician needs to know about religion to effectively evaluate and treat religious patients; and 2) how counseling professionals can collaborate with religious personnel to treat sick people. Of particular interest are studies on the mental health of those who (like cult members) are involved full-time in religious matters (see, for example, items 415 and 416). This volume contains useful, though dated, bibliographies.

Contains items 39, 169, 579.

295.   Persinger, John. "Religion and Mental Health—Compatible or Incompatible?" RELIGION IN THE FACE OF AMERICA. Edited by Jane C. Zahn. Berkeley: University Extension of the University of California, 1958, pp. 43-53.

Maintains that since religion is a philosophy and psychotherapy a method, the two cannot be compared. While many psychopathological religious practices have been recorded, it is argued that true religious experiences are still possible. The author points out that the city of Los Angeles, with its many religious sects and groups, has fewer sick people because religion provides a sense of identity and helps people cover up or ward-off mental illness.

296.   Petersen, Geoffrey. "Regression in Healing and Salvation."
       PASTORAL PSYCHOLOGY 19 (September 1968): 33-38.

       Points out that regression can be either an illness or a
       therapeutic means to better one's health. Some case histories
       from psychiatric literature are given to show this healing
       process. Regression, which could be a positive psychological
       process, is discussed with references to primitive societies
       and to Scripture. The words of Jesus about children and St.
       Paul's view of baptism are taken as examples of regressions,
       both of which have the power to lead to maturity of faith.

297.   Pfister, Oscar. CHRISTIANITY AND FEAR: A STUDY IN HISTORY
       AND IN THE PSYCHOLOGY AND HYGIENE OF RELIGION. Translated
       by W. H. Johnston. London: Allen and Unwin, 1948. 589 pp.

       After proposing a theory of fear as a problem in collective
       psychology, the author outlines both the solution and func-
       tion of fear in the history of the Judeo-Christian tradition.
       Chapters on this latter topic cover the Jewish religion, the
       teachings of Jesus and Paul, and the view of the main Chris-
       tian churches. The position held throughout is that Jesus
       laid out a plan for the best possible individual and social
       hygiene. Applying analytic theory, the author thinks that
       Jesus cures fear through love. Although there are clear
       elements of warning and fear in the sayings of Jesus, they
       are well-intentioned cautions designed to keep people on the
       right path. The churches may not have been very successful
       in maintaining this original balance.

298.   Powell, L. Mack. "Efforts by the Mentally Ill to Solve
       Problems through Religion." PASTORAL COUNSELOR 3 (1965):
       29-32.

       Grapples with the relationship between religion and mental
       health. Mentally-ill people often use religious ideas and
       practices to deal with their problems and to bolster their
       egos. Though religious behavior can often hinder restoration
       to health, the author maintains that these patients must
       first be met at their level before any progress can be made.
       Religion can then be used therapeutically as a curing aid.
       To what extent, if at all, religion can be said to be the
       original cause of their problems is not given much attention.

299.   Pruyser, Paul W. "Assessment of Patient's Religious Attitude
       in the Psychiatric Case Study." BULLETIN OF THE MENNINGER
       CLINIC 35 (1971): 272-91.

       Reacts to the common psychiatric approach that religious
       beliefs are irrelevant and argues that religion is a major
       coping device which can serve equilibrating, homeostatic,
       or defensive functions. Religion, therefore, can be central
       both in personality development as well as in helping an
       individual overcome psychological problems. The author cites
       the then-current religious revival in support of his theory.

300.   Rank, James G. "Religious Conservatism-Liberalism and Mental
        Health." PASTORAL PSYCHOLOGY 12 (March 1961): 34-40.

        Reports on a study of 8,000 male Protestant theological
        students which was conducted to determine the relationship
        between personality and conservative versus liberal theolog-
        ical attitudes and beliefs. Conservatism, as opposed to
        liberalism, was found to be linked with prejudice against
        outsiders, authoritarian aggression and submissiveness, iden-
        tification with power figures, and punitiveness. The charac-
        terization of conservatives as psychologically immature and
        liberals as mature was judged to be based on factual evidence.
        Authoritarianism in extreme religious conservative groups may
        be a sign of severe pathology. However, several psychopatho-
        logical syndromes, like hysteria, hypochondria, depression,
        persecution mania, and obsessive-compulsive behavior, had no
        significant relationship with either conservative or liberal
        religious ideologies. The author thinks that religious beliefs
        and attitudes can be more successfully correlated with one's
        early family environment.

301.   Reid, Fred W. "Resurrection and Mental Health." PASTORAL
        PSYCHOLOGY 19 (September 1968): 39-42.

        Argues that belief in the resurrection of Christ affects
        positively one's mental as well as spiritual health because
        of the hope that this doctrine brings.

302.   Reider, Norman. "The Demonology of Modern Psychiatry."
        AMERICAN JOURNAL OF PSYCHIATRY 111 (1955): 851-56.

        Maintains that magical gestures and words made up the core
        of primitive psychotherapy and that such practices persist
        in present-day treatment where white magic has been replaced
        by "scientific therapeusis," and black magic has evolved into
        controlled experimentation with "pathogens." The author
        insists that we manifest the relics of primitive magic when
        we project or personify our concepts as if they were substan-
        tial, material, or demonic spirits. Anxiety, hostility,
        ambivalence, and inhibition are often used in psychiatric
        practice like magical devices. It is held that those systems
        of psychotherapy, religious or otherwise, which stress faith
        in the healing system seem to rely more on magical techniques.

303.   Reik, T. "Final Phase of Belief Found in Religion and in
        Obsessional Neurosis." INTERNATIONAL JOURNAL OF PSYCHOANAL-
        YSIS 11 (1930): 278-91.

        Tries to show that the mental processes and mechanisms found
        in various rituals, such as the Jewish ceremony of extinguish-
        ing a light on Friday and fortune-telling in many societies,
        are the same as those producing the characteristic expression
        of obsessional neurosis. In typical Freudian fashion, the
        author tends to interpret religious expressions as forms of
        mental illness.

304.   Reik, T. "The Therapy of the Neurosis and Religion." INTER-
        NATIONAL JOURNAL OF PSYCHOANALYSIS 10 (1929): 292-302.

        Favors the Freudian position that culture is a repressive
        force and that religion is a collective, suppressive influence,
        primarily because it creates guilt feelings. The author
        refers to the ministers of thousands of cults who thrive on
        inculcating the fear of God in those who follow them. Reli-
        gious concepts must be studied to help people in therapy,
        because religion grasped the sense of guilt a long time ago.

305.   Rubins, Jack. "Religion, Mental Health, and the Psycho-
        analyst." AMERICAN JOURNAL OF PSYCHOANALYSIS 30 (1970):
        127-34.

        Observes that many changes and upheavals are taking place
        in religion with the result that the antagonism between reli-
        gion and science is decreasing and a new rapprochement is
        being forged between religion and the mental health profession.
        Religion is assuming a greater importance in therapy because
        it is one of the sociocultural factors which may influence
        (for better or for worse) the growth of one's personality.
        It is postulated that the emotional force of religion comes
        from its involvement in the neurotic process. Since religion
        can both resolve personal conflicts and create them, a neu-
        tral, scientific view is suggested as the best way to handle
        potential difficulties.

306.   Sadler, William S. "Religion as a Remedy for Personal and
        Social Maladjustments." RELIGION AND CONDUCT (item 204),
        pp. 164-77.

        States that all religions have therapeutic value in that
        they contribute to the relief of mental anguish and physical
        suffering. A patient who has a strong belief in God and in
        an afterlife is psychologically in a better position to come
        to grips with the problems of daily life. Religion provides
        an antidote to monotony. It stimulates one's speculative
        faculties, broadens one's horizons, and gives a universal
        outlook on life. Christianity is particularly therapeutic
        because it strikes at the root of most mental disorders by
        substituting faith for fear.

307.   Salzman, Leon. "Guilt, Responsibility, and the Unconscious."
        PASTORAL PSYCHOLOGY 15 (1964): 17-26.

        Discusses Freud's concept of the unconscious with its
        implications for religious behavior. The author thinks that
        the acts of mortification by many Christian saints are maso-
        chistic and, therefore, are indications of distorted reli-
        gion. People who think they are the "second Christ," and
        by implication those who claim prophetic insight or deliver
        revelatory messages, are judged to be psychopaths, suffering
        from paranoia. The meaning of guilt and responsibility in
        this context is discussed.

308.   Sanua, Victor D. "Religion, Mental Health, and Psychiatry: A
        Review of Empirical Studies." AMERICAN JOURNAL OF PSYCHI-
        ATRY 123 (1969): 1203-13.

        Argues that the contention that religion as an institution
        fosters well-being, creativity, honesty, and other desirable
        qualities is not supported by empirical data. There is no
        scientific evidence that religion is capable of serving mental
        health. Studies relating religiousness to 1) psychological
        adjustment, 2) social pathology and deviancy, 3) authoritar-
        ianism, 4) prejudice, and 5) social values are surveyed. The
        results are largely negative, particularly with regards to
        authoritarianism, which has often been singled out as a major
        characteristic of contemporary cults. A useful bibliography
        is appended.

309.   Schoben, Edward J. "Sin and Guilt in Psychotherapy: Some
        Research Implications." JOURNAL OF COUNSELING PSYCHOLOGY
        7 (1960): 197-201.

        Responds to Mowrer's (item 279) and Curran's (item 222)
        exchange on the psychotherapeutic value of the religious
        concepts of sin and guilt. He finds some common ground but
        urges further study. "Research on the nature of responsi-
        bility and its relation to mental health, and what has been
        called the redemptive sequence, may yield a new and signifi-
        cant dimension to psychological knowledge" (p. 220).

310.   Scott, Edward M. "'Will' and Religion as Useful Adjuncts in
        Psychotherapy." PSYCHOLOGICAL REPORTS 1 (1955): 379-81.

        Comments on the growing interest in free will and religion
        among psychologists. Two cases are presented to show that
        free will as well as religious beliefs and practices can be
        psychotherapeutically beneficial. The author thinks that
        the clients' need for religion should be respected no matter
        what the therapist's own personal position might be.

311.   Smith, M. Brewster. "'Mental Health' Reconsidered: A Special
        Case of the Problem of Values in Psychology." AMERICAN
        PSYCHOLOGIST 16 (1961): 299-306.

        Points out that it is now recognized in psychology that
        mental health is an evaluative term. The author holds that
        this intrusion of values in psychology is legitimate but
        argues that evaluating criteria for personality should not be
        linked with mental health. The cross-cultural implications
        when starting with a list of personality traits, which are
        taken as a gauge of mental health, are recognized. The author
        suggests that the concept of "mental health" should be used
        like a "rubric," a "label for the common concerns of various
        disciplines" (p. 304).

312.   Spilka, Bernard, and Paul H. Werme. "Religion and Mental
        Disorder: A Research Perspective." RESEARCH IN RELIGIOUS
        DEVELOPMENT. Edited by Merton P. Strommen. New York:
        Hawthorn, 1971, pp. 461-81.

Examines the relationship between religion and mental illness and explores, more specifically, the role of religion as
1) an outlet expressing or encouraging mental aberration; 2)
a suppressor of symptomatic behavior, serving as a socializing
agent; 3) a refuge from those stresses in life which can lead
to mental illness; and 4) a therapeutic or prophylactic for
handling stress and problems, for self-actualization, and
for the more effective use of one's capabilities. The many
positive functions which institutionalized religion performs
are emphasized.

313. Stark, Rodney. "Psychopathology and Religious Commitment."
      REVIEW OF RELIGIOUS RESEARCH 12 (1971): 165-76.

Examines and refutes the hypothesis that mental illness and
religious commitment are related. The author distinguishes
between conventional religious commitment and extremist or
pathological forms and argues that conclusions drawn from the
latter cannot be applied to the former. Reference is made to
the San Mateo County study on psychopathology and religious
experience, a study which concluded that the two are not
related. Authoritarianism is also not linked with the various
forms of conventional religious commitment. The conclusion is
that the mentally ill are less likely to be committed to a
conventional religion. The implications of this for the study
of new religious movements are not discussed.

314. Steere, David A. "Anton Boisen: Figure of the Future."
      JOURNAL OF RELIGION AND HEALTH 8 (1969): 359-74.

A good account of Boisen's contribution to the psychology
of religion and to the relationship between religious beliefs
and practices to mental illness. The author lists the traditional Christian doctrines and shows which ones, according
to Boisen, came to the fore in personal crises and which
could have beneficial and/or pathological effects.

315. Stevens, Samuel N. "Method of Applying Religion as a Thera-
      peutic Agent." RELIGION AND CONDUCT (item 204), pp. 177-84.

Points out that prayer and ritual can be employed as therapeutic agents, because they help the individual develop an
intellectual perspective about one's problems, and because,
in an atmosphere of relaxation, they counteract negative
emotional tensions. Religious emotion can be the basis of
an effective reintegration and reorganization of one's
emotional life.

316. Stevenson, Beaumont. "Confession and Psychotherapy."
      JOURNAL OF PASTORAL CARE 20 (1966): 10-15.

Maintains that, although auricular confession is a painful
experience, its results are generally beneficial. The
similarities and differences between confession and psychotherapy are outlined. Confession can deal with real guilt
which lies outside the scope of psychotherapy.

317.   Stevenson, Ian. "Assumptions of Religion and Psychiatry."
        PASTORAL PSYCHOLOGY 20 (June 1969): 41-50.

        Compares psychiatry to religion and argues that both aim
        at helping a person change oneself, the former by talking
        about one's problems with an expert, the latter by mystical
        techniques which are common in different religious traditions.
        Psychiatrists have criticized religion for providing an escape
        from reality and for leading the individual back to infantile
        experiences. Both views are rejected by the author who argues
        that regression is used regularly in psychotherapy and that
        religion provides a sense of unity, which brings with it a
        constructive attitude to life. Religious people, unlike
        psychoanalysts, believe that they can change themselves by
        consciously altering their own thoughts. The author thinks
        that the different assumptions made by psychiatry and religion
        should be seen as complementary rather than mutually exclusive.

318.   Stolz, Karl R. THE CHURCH AND PSYCHOTHERAPY. New York:
        Abingdon, 1943. 312 pp.

        Proposes the view that the Christian church has "an almost
        unlimited therapeutic value of which multitudes stand in
        need" (p. 11). The author, after outlining the healing minis-
        try of Jesus, shows how the church anticipated psychiatry by
        confession and forgiveness, preaching and education, prayer,
        assurance, and suggestion. "That the church does mediate
        grace which releases a disordered personality from over-
        compensation, social maladjustment, inward turmoil, and
        torturing impulsions cannot be contested" (p. 148). Fellow-
        ship in some sects is therapeutic, even though some of their
        practices, like glossolalia, may be an example of "weird
        psychic exhibition."

319.   Stolz, Karl R. THE PSYCHOLOGY OF PRAYER. New York: Abingdon,
        1923. 247 pp.

        Discusses the relationship between prayer and suggestion.
        The author's viewpoint is that "suggestion in prayer is a
        mental process which the religious impulse originates and
        uses as a means to an end" (p. 51). This topic is then
        discussed almost exclusively within the Christian context,
        though there are some references to other religions. The
        "Yoga cult" of India is said to be an extreme method of self-
        hypnosis.

320.   Szasz, Thomas S. "The Uses of Naming and the Origin of the
        Myth of Mental Illness." AMERICAN PSYCHOLOGIST 16 (1961):
        59-65.

        Aims at clarifying the concept of mental illness and to
        trace its hidden, historical antecedents and ethical implica-
        tions. It is explained how language in psychiatry can be
        promotive rather than, or in place of, informative. Calling
        a person psychologically ill, a "malingerer," a hysteric, or

mentally ill could be reflective of an ethical standard
rather than descriptive of the individual's actual condition.
The author illustrates his position with several examples
and concludes by stating that the expression "mentally ill"
has become a derogatory label connoting unpleasant and
socially deviant behavior.

321. Tageson, Carroll, F. "Psychological Problems in the Reli-
        gious." PSYCHOLOGICAL ASPECTS OF SPIRITUAL DEVELOPMENT.
        Edited by Michael J. O'Brien and Raymond J. Steimel.
        Washington, DC: Catholic University of America Press, 1965,
        pp. 106-25.

        Explores the roots of emotional disorders among members of
        religious orders. It is pointed out that the cause of these
        difficulties can be traced to their pre-religious days and
        that religious life itself could have intensified these early
        trends. Training methods used in spiritual formation may be
        partly responsible for accentuating psychotic and neurotic
        tendencies. Several symptoms of these disorders, like
        immature mysticism and intense, prolonged scruples, are
        listed. The implications for counseling are discussed.

322. Thomas, Jackson M. "Fragments of a Schizophrenic's 'Virgin
        Mary' Delusions." AMERICAN JOURNAL OF PSYCHIATRY 89 (1932):
        285-93.

        A typical Freudian analysis of the delusions of a schizo-
        phrenic who for six years proclaimed herself to be the Virgin
        Mary. The essay focuses on the specific content and formal
        presentation of the subject's pathological beliefs. Her
        experiences are related to those of primitive people. The
        identification with the Virgin Mary revealed unconscious
        desires and instinctive urges and helped her cope with them.

323. Tillich, Paul. "The Relation of Religion and Health."
        PASTORAL PSYCHOLOGY 5 (May 1954): 41-52.

        Distinguishes between religious, naturalistic, and magical
        healing and shows how all have been practiced from ancient
        times. The author tries to clarify the difference between
        religion and magic and stresses the need for developing
        criteria, especially because of spiritualistic movements and
        their claims of revelation. One could easily conclude that
        the latter are magical and not healthy forms of religion.

324. Trew, Albert. "The Religious Factors in Mental Illness."
        PASTORAL PSYCHOLOGY 22 (May 1977): 21-28.

        Maintains that some types of religion, like the fundamen-
        talist sects, which demand perfection, are legalistic,
        restrictive, and authoritarian, and tend to curtail natural
        inclinations by means of innumerable prohibitions, which are
        likely to produce feelings of guilt and to inhibit religious
        development in the individual. A religion which stresses and

builds self-respect, one's sense of dignity, and the meaning-
fulness of life contributes to mental health. Those religious experiences which free the individual from morbid guilt
feelings, create a sense of security and a feeling of belonging, and contribute to personal interaction are therapeutic.

325.   Van der Horst, L. "Mental Health and Religion." PASTORAL
       PSYCHOLOGY 6 (February 1955): 15-21.

       Discusses the question whether psychological treatment
       should also include the spiritual life and whether spiritual
       care embodies a therapeutic factor. It is stated that dreams
       are not always expressive of wishes, but may at times be the
       voice of conscience. Many psychic disorders, particularly
       anxiety, are attributed to the neglect of religious insights
       and values. Without religion and morality, mental health is
       bound to suffer.

326.   Vandervelt, James. "Religion and Mental Health." MENTAL
       HYGIENE 35 (1951): 177-89.

       Outlines the relationship between religion and mental
       health and strongly denies the Freudian position that
       dependency on God is a sign of immaturity. Religion, by
       helping a person accept the frustrations and sufferings of
       life, by supplying answers to ultimate questions, and by
       supporting morality, contributes to the psychological well-
       being of the individual.

327.   Vaughan, R. P. MENTAL ILLNESS AND RELIGIOUS LIFE. Milwaukee:
       Bruce Publishing Company, 1962. 198 pp.

       Deals with mental illness in monastic and religious insti-
       tutions and shows how it can undermine spiritual growth,
       interfere with personal relationships, and limit one's work.
       Topics such as scrupulosity and alcoholism are among those
       treated. The position adopted is that religious beliefs and
       practices do not cause mental illness, but once a person
       becomes ill, there can be serious religious repercussions.
       Thus, a religious person suffering from schizophrenia could
       have visions and other heavenly manifestations which are
       hallucinatory. Those who are mentally ill are encouraged to
       seek professional assistance. The relationship between
       spiritual guidance and psychotherapy is also considered.

328.   Von Domarus, Eilhard. "Religion." AMERICAN HANDBOOK OF
       PSYCHIATRY (item 3), vol. 2, pp. 1802-10.

       Points out some of the differences between Eastern and
       Western approaches to life and stresses that both acknowledge
       the same human problems. To solve these problems, the West
       has used the method of free association and scientific dream-
       interpretation, while East has preferred the mystical method
       of meditation. Hinduism, Buddhism, Confucianism, and Taoism
       are examined with regard to the role they might play in
       complementing modern scientific endeavors.

329.   Walters, Orville, S. "Religion and Psychotherapy." COMPAR-
        ATIVE PSYCHIATRY 5 (1964): 24-35.

        Evaluates James's varieties of religious psychopathology
        and Freud's analogy between obsessional neurosis and
        religious practices. Both authors are criticized for not
        developing criteria for distinguishing between normal and
        pathological religious experiences. Boisen's views that
        psychosis is a religious process and schizophrenia is a
        purposeful, problem-solving experience and that both could
        lead to either a healthy or sick individual are refuted. The
        author states that both neurosis and schizophrenia distort
        religious experience and that an acquaintance with normative
        religious experience is needed.

330.   Weatherhead, Leslie D. PSYCHOLOGY, RELIGION, AND HEALING.
        London: Hodder and Stoughton, 1951. 544 pp.

        Aims "to review every known method of healing through the
        mind and spirit, to assess the place of psychology and reli-
        gion in the field of non-physical healing, to pass a critical
        judgment on the methods used to attain health in this field,
        and to ascertain along which lines modern techniques might
        usefully proceed" (xv). The earliest methods of healing
        through religion (miracles) and through psychology (hypnotism
        and suggestion) are reviewed. Modern healing through reli-
        gion, like pilgrimages to Lourdes, Christian Science, and
        the Emmanuel Movement in Boston, as well as modern methods of
        psychological healing, like those of Freud, Jung, and Adler,
        are critically surveyed. The relationship between the two
        methods is discussed and it is concluded that both are neces-
        sary for the integration of human personality. Religious
        experience could, for example, help towards personal fulfill-
        ment, provided it does not become an escape from reality.

331.   Webb, Sam C. "An Exploratory Investigation of Some Needs Met
        Through Religious Behavior." JOURNAL FOR THE SCIENTIFIC
        STUDY OF RELIGION 5 (1965): 51-58.

        A study to determine the possibility of identifying the
        specific needs served by religion. The findings point to
        religion as a means of providing peace of mind. Since relief
        from tension and anxiety through worship, relaxation, etc.,
        is linked with religious thoughts and feelings, one could
        support the claim of the therapeutic effects of religion.

332.   Welford, A. T. "Is Religious Behavior Dependent Upon Affect
        or Frustration?" JOURNAL OF ABNORMAL AND SOCIAL PSYCHOLOGY
        42 (1947): 310-19.

        Discusses the psychological processes involved in the moti-
        vation and function of religion and outlines several problems
        which must be taken into consideration in any attempt to
        determine what causes religious behavior. The author's main

area of investigation are the individual and environmental
factors that accompany and seemingly produce religious activity, particularly prayer. His scope is to test Flower's
view (item 70) that religious behavior is based on a specific kind of response which relieves the affective tensions
resulting from frustration. Sixty-three subjects, all university and theological seminary male students, were tested.
It is concluded that prayer is not merely a response to
distressing forces in the environment and cannot be accounted
for adaquately by frustration or effect. Prayer is a means
of active adjustment to situations. It is not a mere escape,
but rather acts as a means through which the individual gets
help when needed.

333.   Wieman, Henry N. "How Religion Cures Human Ills." JOURNAL
       OF RELIGION 7 (1927): 263-76.

       Shows, with examples, how religion has helped human beings
       adjust rightly to new, difficult situations and thus became
       the source of the prevention or cure of many human problems,
       such as social wrongdoing, mental illness, and impoverished
       life. Religion supplies the believer with a strong purpose
       for improvement by offering salvation. It helps one cope
       with increased sensitivity through worship and gives one the
       patience to handle problems reflectively.

334.   Young, Richard K., and Albert L. Meiberg. SPIRITUAL THERAPY:
       HOW THE PHYSICIAN, PSYCHIATRIST, AND MINISTER COLLABORATE
       IN HEALING. New York: Harper and Brothers, 1960. 184 pp.

       Contains a chapter on spiritual therapy for the patient
       who suffers from anxiety and is likely to have a conversion
       experience. It is observed that an individual with conver-
       sion hysteria uses religion in an unhealthy way to control
       anxiety. Pastors should be aware that the anxiety-ridden and
       hysterial patient can easily become a victim of unscrupulous
       religious quacks.

                    C. GENERAL STUDIES ON CULTS AND SECTS

    The study of new religious movements and their leaders is not
new in psychology. The so-called "Great Awakenings" in the United
States provide ample material both in the variety of movements and
the types of religious leaders which emerged. It is not surprising
that the bulk of writings on cults deals with, or relies heavily
upon, data from faith-healing and evangelical groups, among which
Christian Science, New Thought, the Emmanuel Movement, and Father
Divine are frequently mentioned. Eastern religious movements, like
Theosophy and Yoga, also provide a plethora of material for discussing the question of religious orthodoxy by way of comparison and
the issue of the mental or psychological health of those who become
committed to a cult.

Besides the studies which are mainly descriptive, one comes across psychological literature which evaluates the new cults with regard to their negative or positive effects on those who join them. Although the word "cult," particularly in early literature, is frequently used in its original sense to mean "worship" or "approved ritual," it has a history of derogatory connotation.

From a negative viewpoint, new religious movements are said to bring out into the open primitive and uncontrolled mental, intellectual, and nervous human traits. It is sometimes contended that healing cults are but harmful fads, covering up a person's mental illness. Since they stress healing to an unrealistic degree, these cults can impede health and create anxiety and guilt in those individuals who uselessly await a cure. They cater to unstable people and do nothing to bring about a betterment in their condition. Revival meetings tend to attract extroverts and hysterics and are definitely linked with emotional disorders. Many fundamentalist Christian sects insist on some degree of social isolation, which could lead to mental illness and social maladjustment. The narrow-mindedness and intolerance which sects encourage are a sign of mental and psychological weakness. Cults, it is often admitted, come into being to solve personal and social problems and offer some hope in periods of cultural disintegration. However, they are generally a haven for the restless and discontented, and rather than alleviate problems, they often cause serious abnormalities. The main pathological aspects of these new groups are exposed in their hysterical behavior. Fanaticism, superstition, and sexual neuroses are some of the effects that cults have on people. Millennial movements suffer from a paranoid delusion syndrome. It has been asserted that those cults which promise physical, mental, or psychological improvement do not, in fact, use divine power to heal but rather have recourse to the power of suggestion and self-hypnosis. In the long run, they will be replaced by modern medicine and psycho-therapy.

This disparaging interpretation of new cults is reflected in the psychological evaluation of religious leaders. Biblical figures, religious founders, charismatic leaders, and the clergy have all been subjected to psychological scrutiny, and the results are at times devastating. The assertion that the great prophets in Biblical literature were neurotic and hysterical has been taken for granted in some quarters. Paranoid schizophrenia was the diagnosis made of some of them, while pathological thinking manifested in hallucinations and delusions was a main symptom they all shared. St. Paul's views on sex, as well as Saint Augustine's relationship with his mother, are subjected to the typical psychoanalytic interpretation that they are expressions of personal sexual problems.

Founders of religion or of religious sects have not escaped the denunciation by psychiatrists. Albert Schweitzer (item 444) strongly rebutted common psychiatric arguments which portrayed Christ as a deluded lunatic. Among the many evangelists and faith healers of the nineteenth and early twentieth centuries who were said to be psychologically sick, Mary Baker Eddy has probably received the harshest judgment. To many psychiatrists observing the religious scene, she seemed to typify the hysterical and neurotic woman who takes refuge in religion and uses it for her own paranoid ends.

The clergy are equally prone to similar psychological assessments. The well-known study by Dittes (item 370), for instance, concluded that 95 percent of them were mentally ill. They were found lacking especially in interpersonal relationships. Those who go into the religious ministry or who join religious orders are sometimes said to have serious problems before their commitment.

There is, however, another line of approach which contradicts this gloomy picture of religious sects or cults and intense religious involvement. Many writers have observed that faith-healing movements have positive effects especially on psychosomatic illnesses and could, therefore, be regarded as therapeutic. Joining one of these groups fulfills the need for emotional release, which is a kind of therapy. Some experiments (see, for example, items 388-90) lead one to conclude that healing by the laying on of hands, a common ritual among faith healers, is not just a symbolic practice but can have genuine curing effects which might be tested empirically. The experience of being saved, which is evoked in many evangelical revival tent-meetings, restores or strengthens one's self-esteem and one's ability to relate well to others. Cults might be transient but also contribute to a healthy religious development. The deprivation theory of cult formation, commonly held by scholars in different academic backgrounds, maintains that the cults fulfill many religious, economic, political, and social needs which have been neglected or ignored. They therefore play an important role in enabling people to adapt, mentally and psychologically, to harsh sociocultural environments.

In defense of the sanity of the prophets and founders of religious sects, Boisen's theory is adapted to explain their apparently erratic and unusual behavior. Thus, Biblical figures are admittedly maladjusted to their own culture, but they differ from the mentally ill in that they did not isolate themselves from society. Many religious leaders, like Fox and Bunyan, seem to have moved from some kind of mental disorder to personal integration. The ministers of these religious cults or groups are at times referred to as therapists. The Hasidic rabbi, the Yogi, the Christian Scientist practitioner, and the Zen master all perform the task of a trained counselor or therapist who helps individuals find meaning in life, grow in self-knowledge, and solve or come to terms with their psychological problems.

The acceptance in the West of Eastern ways of thought and action is not always viewed as a threat to religion and society or as a breakdown in an individual's mental and psychological well-being. Eastern spiritualities, which have genuine religious value, may also contain healing qualities. Some scholars claim that they contribute to the development of consciousness, which is an aid to therapy. It took quite a long time before Western scholars began to realize that there are systems of Eastern psychologies which deserve to be viewed as ways of understanding the human psyche and of curing its ills.

A good example of this more positive approach to Eastern culture and religion is seen in the evaluation of Yoga and Zen Buddhism. Several psychologists have expressed the view that these two Eastern

practices are not just strange religious activities, but also long
traditions of thought containing psychological insights which might
further the development of Western psychological theories. People
might be drawn to Eastern religious groups not because of unresolved
mental and psychological problems, but because of the simple fact
that these religions exhibit positive, attractive features which
seem lacking in their Western counterparts. Eastern religions and
psychologies leave the impression that they are more personalistic
and that they are, consequently, more conducive to an open awareness
and a less stressful life. They promise to help a person achieve
fulfillment and cope with alienation. Further, they emphasize a much
more cooperative relationship with the environment. This harmonious
interacting with nature produces peace of mind and alleviates many of
the conflicts which are inherent in a society that appears dominated
by impersonal technology.

This section will cover general works on new religious movements,
some background material necessary to understand their religious
context, and studies on different founders and leaders of religious
churches and groups in general.

335. Ali Beg, Moazziz. "The Theory of Personality in the Bhagavad
      Gita." PSYCHOLOGIA 15 (1970): 12-17.

      Presents a brief outline of the theory of personality found
      in this popular Hindu religious text and discusses its mean-
      ing from the point of view of transpersonal psychology. It
      is shown that the "Bhagavad Gita" bases its psychology on three
      states of existence, "tamas," "rajas," and "sattwas," which
      refer, respectively, to three orientations and main goals in
      life, namely, 1) sexual pleasure, 2) power and wealth, and
      3) spiritual development. The concept of adjustment is
      related to this theory and implies a threefold dynamic pro-
      cess: adjustment to self, to others, and to things and objects.
      The emphasis on transcendental values, ethical behavior, and
      spiritual states corresponds to focus on self-actualization
      and self-realization in transpersonal psychology.

336. Ali Beg, Moazziz. "A Note on the Concept of Self, and the
      Theory and Practice of Psychological Help in the Sufi
      Tradition." INTERPERSONAL DEVELOPMENT 1 (1970): 58-64.

      Discusses Sufi ideas regarding the nature of the self and
      of the inner resources which lead to happiness and serenity.
      The main goal of Sufism is to revitalize the individual and
      to develop a psychological immunity against afflictions (like
      envy, pride, deception, and anxiety) and thus open the way to
      self-fulfillment. Various states or conditions of the self in
      Sufi thought--the sick self, the impoverished self, and the
      abundant self--are described. Since the person needs help to
      attain self-fulfillment, the Sufi system contains a theory
      and a method of rendering psychological help, a system which
      the author briefly outlines.

337.   Anant, Santokh Singh. "The Guru as Psychotherapist." R. M.
        BUCKE MEMORIAL SOCIETY: NEWSLETTER-REVIEW 4 (1971): 43-48.

        Finds many similarities between the Sikh guru and the
        psychotherapist, both of whom are healers. The processes
        that are operative in the standard forms of psychotherapy,
        namely, the therapeutic relationship, expression of feel-
        ing, transference, and new behavior, are also present in
        the guru-disciple relationship. The emphasis on moral
        principles as requisites for mental health is common among
        gurus, religious leaders, and psychotherapists alike.

338.   Anderson, Felix A. "Psychopathological Glimpses at the
        Behavoir of Some Biblical Characters." PSYCHOANALYTIC
        REVIEW 14 (1927): 56-70.

        Selects Biblical figures (Jacob, David, and Paul) who lived
        in different historical periods and represent diverse person-
        ality types, and through their behavior deduces "echoes of
        the tumultuous strife, waged in the unconscious depth of the
        personality" (p. 57). Jacob's incestuous fixation resulted
        in the strong narcissistic tendencies that controlled his
        life. He was a typical neurotic under the control of primi-
        tive emotions. David, whose love-life makes him comparable
        to Don Juan, had a personality beset with neurosis and psycho-
        pathology. Finally, St. Paul is seen as a person who, in the
        midst of insoluble personal problems, takes shelter behind
        the assurance of an unusual hallucination on the road to
        Damascus. The author considers Paul to represent a fairly
        typical hysterical personality.

339.   Arlow, Jacob A. "The Consecration of the Prophet." PSYCHO-
        ANALYTIC QUARTERLY 20 (1951): 374-97.

        Sees a relationship between the personal struggle of the
        Old Testament prophets and their divine calling, which is
        explained as a solution to their problems and conflicts.
        When the prophet is consecrated, he is temporarily experi-
        encing a "schizophrenoid abandonment of reality." But then
        he re-establishes contact with reality by involving his
        fellow men and women in his delusions. His message is heard
        because it corresponds to emotions waiting to be stirred.
        The true prophet thus expresses emergent, but inarticulate,
        dreams and aspirations of his people.

340.   Aslam, Q. M. "Muhammad, a Psychological Study." CONFINIA
        PSYCHIATRICA 11 (1968): 225-35.

        Attempts to understand Muhammad both as a mystic and a
        prophet. Several Quranic references (like the splitting of
        the breast in Surah 94 and the night journeys in Surahs 17,
        53, etc.) are interpreted as mystical experiences. It is held
        that the prophet should not be understood (as psychologists
        are inclined to) by looking at his bizarre and paranormal
        religious behavior, but rather by his achievements and
        influence.

341. Atkins, Gaius G. MODERN RELIGIOUS CULTS AND MOVEMENTS. New
      York: AMS Press, 1971. 359 pp. A reprint of the 1923 edi-
      tion.

      Discusses mainly faith-healing cults, particularly New
      Thought, Christian Science, Theosophy, and spiritualism.
      While admitting that these groups, which depend on creating
      an atmosphere of mystery, perform a service to their members,
      the author thinks that psychotherapy will replace them. He
      further argues that the intimate association between religion
      and healing has not been beneficial either for religion or
      healing. All faith and mental healing can be ultimately ex-
      plained in terms of suggestion, and spiritualism can be
      readily understood with reference to the individual's person-
      ality traits.

342. Aumann, Jordan. "Sanctity and Neurosis." FAITH, REASON,
      AND MODERN PSYCHIATRY: SOURCES FOR A SYNTHESIS. Edited by
      Francis J. Braceland. New York: P. J. Kenedy and Sons,
      1955, pp. 267-94.

      Discusses whether many Christian saints, like St. Paul, St.
      Teresa of Avila, and St. Catherine of Siena, suffered from
      "mental derangement." A brief outline of the theology of
      Christian perfection is given. The author distinguishes
      between true and false mysticism and insists that not all
      saints and mystics are abnormal. Though pathological phenom-
      ena (like scrupulosity and hysteria) may be similar to the
      way in which a person responds to grace, the two are not
      to be identified. "The ordinary mystical phenomena are
      perfectly normal within the orbit of grace and the super-
      natural. In such cases the phenomena themselves are only
      materially pathological at best" (p. 287).

343. Bakan, David. "Some Thoughts on Reading Augustine's 'Con-
      fessions.'" JOURNAL FOR THE SCIENTIFIC STUDY OF RELIGION
      5 (1963): 149-52.

      Notes that Augustine's greatness, mystical leanings, and
      style of self-examination are not immune from psychoanalytic
      reflections. The way Augustine carried out a self-examination
      is compared to the psychoanalytic process. The author thinks
      that the oedipal elements in Augustine are patent and that they
      are carried over into the nature of his religious concerns.

344. Binder, Louis R. MODERN RELIGIOUS CULTS AND SOCIETY: A SOCIAL
      INTERPRETATION OF A MODERN RELIGIOUS PHENOMENON. Boston:
      Gorham Press, 1933. vii, 213 pp.

      Mainly a social study of various cults and sects, including
      Christian Science, the Shakers, Mormonism, the United School
      of Christianity, and Spiritualism. The ways these various
      groups try to adjust to society is discussed. One section
      is dedicated to the "pathological" aspects of many of these
      communities, such as refusal to accept medical treatment,

hysterical behavior seen in their many emotional outbursts
and superstitious beliefs and practices, religious fanaticism, religious excesses which aim at mystification, and
sexual neuroses. The cults are religious abnormalities; they
are unproductive and lead to social maladjustment and the
abandonment of social responsibilities. Those who join the
cults have a strange psychological makeup and their leaders
have disordered intellects and magnetic personalities.

345.   Bishop, George. FAITH HEALING: GOD OR FRAUD? Los Angeles:
        Sherbourne Press, 1967. 256 pp.

        Presents a somewhat unfavorable account of various religious
        healing movements, including the work of such evangelists as
        Kathryn Kuhlman and Oral Roberts. The former's religious
        meetings are more like stage shows catering to emotionally
        unstable people who are eager for public recognition. The
        latter's elaborate and dramatic presentations are compared to
        a circus show where reality is suspended for a brief period
        of time. Faith healers, according to the author, fulfill the
        needs for physical relief, spiritual salvation, and emotional
        release.

346.   Boggs, Wade H. FAITH HEALING AND THE CHRISTIAN CHURCH.
        Richmond, VA: John Knox Press, 1956. 216 pp.

        Discusses faith healing from a Christian point of view.
        The efficacy of faith healers and their power to perform
        miracles is evaluated in the light of Biblical teaching.
        Christian Science, the miracles at Lourdes, New Thought and
        Unity movements, Father Divine's church, and the work of
        evangelists like Oral Roberts and Aimee McPherson are
        all considered. The author seems inclined to concede that
        faith healing movements can have a positive effect on
        psychosomatic illnesses and that their results are similar
        to other therapeutic treatments.

347.   Boisen, Anton T. RELIGION IN CRISIS AND CUSTOM: A SOCIAL
        AND PSYCHOLOGICAL STUDY. New York: Harper, 1955. 271 pp.

        Deals mainly with crisis experiences which lead to the
        organization of the person and group and to the reconsider-
        ation of fundamental issues. The result may be a return to a
        rigid pattern of belief and/or practice or else to a creative
        change and to a new purpose in life. Studying crisis experi-
        ence is one way of understanding spiritual groups and move-
        ments which often serve to revitalize religious faith from
        routine adherence. A new process develops in which new reli-
        gious beliefs and practices emerge and then later become a
        matter of custom. Boisen sees this taking place particularly
        in the Christian Churches in America.

348.   Boisen, Anton T. "The Role of the Leader in Religious
        Movements." PASTORAL PSYCHOLOGY 6 (October 1955): 43-49.

A selection from one chapter in his RELIGION IN CRISIS AND CUSTOM. One particular leader, Joe Campbell, is chosen as an example. His life and activities are described and the conditions of the time are said to have been ripe for his type of ministry. Disagreeing with other scholars, the author holds that mystical experiences, such as those of Campbell, could be favorable to the creative process. The motive and character of the new leader should be the yardstick by which his message should be evaluated. Four types of mystical experiences are distinguished; those found in: 1) Buddhism; 2) in the devotees of the holiness movements; 3) in the Hebrew prophets; and 4) in those suffering from acute schizophrenia. The author seems to believe that the mystical experience of the Hebrew prophets was the only genuine one. In other instances, it is induced artificially, pursued for self-centered reasons, and unlikely to produce new insights.

349.   Boisen, Anton T. "The New Evangelism." CHICAGO THEOLOGICAL SEMINARY REGISTER 35 (March 1935): 9-12.

Deals with the inner conflict that is often present in those who join new evangelical movements. The main issue discussed is the acute emotional disturbance which psychiatrists and religious counselors encounter in those patients who participate in revival meetings. The author argues that outstanding religious men, like George Fox and John Bunyan, have passed through periods of mental disorder in the process of finding themselves.

350.   Bridges, Leonard Hal. AMERICAN MYSTICISM: FROM WILLIAM JAMES TO ZEN. New York: Harper and Row, 1970. xi, 208 pp.

Describes the mystical experiences of various people, like the Quaker Rufus Jones, Joshua Heschel, and Thomas Merton. The presence of Vedanta and Zen Buddhism, particularly the oriental form of mysticism they encourage, is also covered. It is stressed that twentieth-century American mystics "have understandably refused to regard mystical experiences as pathological, and on the contrary have argued that it can enhance mental health" (p. 7).

351.   Broome, Edwin C. "Ezechiel's Abnormal Personality." JOURNAL OF BIBLICAL LITERATURE 65 (1946): 277-92.

Maintains that in the Book of Ezekiel there is mounting evidence that the prophet exhibited behavioristic abnormalities consistent with paranoid schizophrenia. Periods of catatonia, narcissistic-masochistic conflicts, and delusions of grandeur are evidently manifested in Ezekiel's personality. This diagnosis, however, does not impair the truly religious significance of his role.

352.   Brown, Charles Reynolds. FAITH AND HEALTH. New York: Thomas Crowell, 1910. vi, 234 pp.

Evaluates some of the main arguments advanced in support of
faith healing. Christ's miraculous cures are discussed and
then modern faith healing claims are evaluated. The author
considers at length the pros and cons of Christian Science
and, while he concedes that it can cure some people who suffer
from psychosomatic diseases, he dismisses it as a "colossal
humbug" (p. 63) and as "a piece of cruel and wicked humbug"
(p. 85) which can seriously imperil the community's organic
and functional health. His view of the Emmanuel Movement is
somewhat more positive, for he thinks that its leaders have
used the healing power of suggestion effectively.

353.   Buckley, James M. FAITH HEALING, CHRISTIAN SCIENCE, AND
        KINDRED PHENOMENA. New York: The Century Co., 1906.
        308 pp.

Evaluates various occult phenomena like astrology, divination, visions, dreams, and witchcraft in the context of faith
healing practices. A brief account of the origin of Christian
Science and of its theory and practice is given. Examples of
successful Christian Science treatment are narrated. The
author appears to take for granted the effectiveness of faith
healing and mind cures.

354.   Cantril, Hadley. THE PSYCHOLOGY OF SOCIAL MOVEMENTS. New
        York: Wiley and Sons, 1941. xv, 274 pp.

Examines first the individual's mental context, the pursuit
of meaning and motivation in social life, and then describes
specific social and religious movements, like the lynch mob,
the Nazi Party, the Townsend Plan, and especially the Kingdom
of Father Divine (pp. 123-44). The author thinks that all
these groups serve the same psychological functions (see item
494).

355.   Casey, Robert P. "Transient Cults." PSYCHIATRY 4 (1941):
        525-34.

Describes some of the new sects which flourished in Paris
in the early part of the twentieth century. Two types are
distinguished: 1) those which, in the spirit of eclecticism
and gnosticism, are Christian in substance (e.g., Christian
Science, the Seventh-Day Adventists, and the Salvation Army);
and 2) those which are largely or wholly non-Christian (e.g.,
Mazdaznam and various semi-religious organizations). All
cults are said to be "the vehicles of deep-seated instinctive
desires" (p. 533) which are either repressed or controlled
before they reach consciousness. All these cults, the author
insists, are transient. They represent a continuous process
of flux and leave nothing behind. They do, however, make
some contribution to healthy religious development.

356.   Caycedo, Alfonso. INDIA OF YOGIS. Delhi, India: National
        Publishing House, 1966. iii, 253 pp.

Describes the visits the author made to various centers in
India where Yoga is prescribed as a way of therapy and as a
mode of psycho-physical training. The reader is first introduced to the phenomenon of Yoga. Then many ashrams, including
those of Sivananada, Radhaswami, and Aurobindo, are described.
The author deals with the application of Yoga in the field of
medicine. It is held that the attempt to bring about a synthesis between Yoga and medicine is a step in the right
direction. Yoga is shown to be a means to maintain health
and vitality. A final section is dedicated to Tibetan Yoga.
Yoga produces a state of consciousness which contributes to
both physical and psychological well-being.

357.   Chikes, Tibot. "Problems of Faith Healing." JOURNAL OF
        RELIGION AND HEALTH 4 (1965): 336-41.

Argues that the very term "faith healing" creates an unreal
dichotomy between medical and non-medical cures and that a
unified view of healing should be developed. The church is
warned against using gimmicks of healing as a means of pleas-
ing and attracting customers. Faith healing is unhealthy if
it is sensational, commercialized and overemotional.

358.   Christensen, Carl W. "The Mental Health of the Clergy."
        CLINICAL PSYCHIATRY AND RELIGION (item 294), pp. 191-200.

Examines the occurrence of mental disorder among clergymen
and finds that it is essentially the same as in the general
population. The predispositions, special stresses, and
characteristic problems of these religious specialists are
described. One of their major problems is their inability
to love and be loved, a condition which creates anxiety and
conflict. They seek in their religious vocation the uncondi-
tional love of infancy and, not being able to find it, become
depressed and hostile. Preoccupation with their own identity
and with sexuality can also be the cause of serious pathology.
Most ministers of religion with mental disorders use religious
beliefs to solve intra-psychic problems.

359.   Chung, Chang Y. "Differences of the Ego, As Demanded in
        Psychotherapy, in the East and West." PSYCHOLOGIA 12
        (1969): 55-58.

Starts from the generally agreed-upon assumption that
psychotherapy should make the patient mature, satisfied, and
independent. The author shows how Buddhist emancipation of
the soul is of greater value than Western psychoanalysis in
achieving these results in the patient. Both, however, are
necessary for the promotion and enlightenment of the ego.
Psychoanalysis is a good first step to the Buddhist approach
which overcomes both normal and abnormal anxiety.

360.   Clark, Elmer T. THE SMALL SECTS IN AMERICA. New York:
        Abingdon-Cokesbury, 1949. 266 pp.

An informative study of the "sectarian spirit" in America.
The author groups the large variety of sects into five major
types: 1) pessimistic or adventist; 2) perfectionist or sub-
jectivist; 3) charismatic or pentecostal; 4) communistic; and
5) legalistic. Among the common features of these sects are
puritan morality, conservatism, and bizarre ideas, beliefs, and
practices. Because the author sees the sects as "refuges of
the poor" and of the "emotionally starved" and as reflecting
the "craving for objectivity of many people," he seems to be
espousing a deprivation theory of sect or cult formation. To
what extent these needs are satisfied by sect membership is
left unanswered.

361.   Cohen, Norman. THE PURSUIT OF THE MILLENNIUM. London: Secker
        and Warburg, 1957. xvi, 476 pp.

        A historical study of Western millenarian movements in the
        Middle Ages. Various Christian sects and religious groups
        such as the Cathars, the Flagellants, and the Anabaptists as
        well as some popular messianic figures like John of Leyden
        are considered. The author detects paranoid patterns in the
        eschatologies of this historical period. Several features of
        the paranoid delusion syndrome, namely, the megalomanic view
        of considering oneself part of the elect, the attribution of
        demonic powers to the adversary, the tendency to assume a
        stance of moral and intellectual infallibility, and the ob-
        session with inerrable prophecies are present in most of
        these movements. Social conditions, according to the author,
        may produce emotional disturbances which find effective
        relief in a sudden, collective, and fanatical pursuit of the
        millennium.

362.   Cohen, Sheldon. "The Ontogenesis of Prophetic Behavior. A
        Study in Creative Conscious Formation." PSYCHOANALYSIS
        AND THE PSYCHOANALYTIC REVIEW 49 (1962): 100-22.

        An empirical and theoretical investigation of the thought
        processes related to prophetic behavior. The prophetic books
        of the Old Testament reveal several symptoms of psychopatho-
        logical thought-processes. Among these symptoms are listed
        strong personal anxiety and guilt, hallucinations, delusions,
        thinking in primitive modes, obsessive thinking, and a distort-
        ed sense of time and space. The author thinks that patholog-
        ical elements in prophetic thinking and behavior occur in
        the transition from a heteronomous to an autonomous creative
        conscience. During this phase a rebellion takes place and
        mental illness comes into being. In spite of this somewhat
        negative view of prophets, the author still thinks that they
        have a high degree of social and spiritual consciousness.

363.   Cotton, William R. "What Kind of People Does a Religious
        Cult Attract?" AMERICAN SOCIOLOGICAL REVIEW 22 (1957):
        561-66.

        Discusses what motivations would lead a person to join a
        new religious group in the context of an unspecified messianic
        cult which the author studied in Seattle, Washington, in 1952.

Seekers, as opposed to observers, tend to have strong religious interests that are not being satisfied by the churches of their upbringing. Hence they are more likely to accept the claims of a new leader. Cult joiners have qualities which can be easily identified. The author adopts a deprivation theory to explain why people join new movements.

364. Coyle, F. A., and Philip Erdberg. "A Liberalizing Approach to Maladaptive Fundamentalist Hyperreligiosity." PSYCHOTHERAPY: THEORY, RESEARCH, AND PRACTICE 6 (1969): 140-42.

Discusses the problems a psychotherapist encounters in dealing with Christian fundamentalist patients. While the authors maintain that the religious behavior is part of their clients' difficulties, causing seriously impaired functioning and inner conflict, they think that to attempt to change the patient's belief system is not a therapeutic approach. It is suggested that the therapist should make an effort to broaden and liberalize the patient's framework. The use of the Bible to counteract feelings of unworthiness, sinfulness, and guilt is advocated.

365. Cutten, George Barton. THREE THOUSAND YEARS OF MENTAL HEALING. New York: Charles Scribner's Sons, 1911. viii, 318 pp.

Discusses the power of the mind to cure, particularly in psychosomatic illness. The devout religious attitude makes a person more amenable to suggestion and promotes confidence in the sick person. Mental therapies are said to be of two kinds: those that deny the existence of matter and evil and heal by stressing the belief that disease cannot possibly be present; and those that, recognizing the existence of illness, heal by stressing faith in God, or in objects, or in the power of suggestion. Various types of healings in diverse cultures and the use of charms, amulets, relics, and shrines in the healing process are dealt with. The rise of mesmerism and the healing cults of the nineteenth and early twentieth centuries are among the major topics covered. Brief descriptions of such groups as Christian Science, the Christian Catholic Apostolic Church of Zion, and the Emmanuel Church are provided. The author's views on the founders of these groups is sometimes negative, as is the case with his opinion of Mary Baker Eddy as a hysterical and neurotic woman.

366. Davenport, F. M. PRIMITIVE TRAITS IN RELIGIOUS REVIVALS: A STUDY IN MENTAL AND SOCIAL EVOLUTION. New York: Negro University Press, 1968. First published in 1906. 323 pp.

Interprets religious revivals as a form of impulsive social action aided by the psychology of the crowd which, if left unrestrained, brings into the open primitive and uncontrolled mental and nervous traits. The following revivals are discussed: the American Indian Ghost Dance, the religion of the American Blacks, the Scottish-Irish revivals in Kentucky in

1800 and in Ulster in 1859, and the movements initiated by
Jonathan Edwards in New England, John Wesley in the United
Kingdom, and others. The author sees several similarities,
like speaking in tongues and conversion, between these groups
and other religious movements in different historical periods
and cultures. Tongue-speaking is interpreted as a loss of
rational self-control which can take place in primitive,
ignorant, and highly excitable individuals in the context of
an emotionally aroused crowd.

367.   Dean, Stanley. "The Ultraconscious Mind." BEHAVIORAL NEURO-
        PSYCHIATRY 2 (1970): 32-36.

        Makes a plea for the scientific recognition and investiga-
        tion of the ultraconscious mind which is a supra-rational,
        supra-sensory level of awareness known as mysticism, satori,
        nirvana, samadhi, unio mystica, and others. The author
        argues that in spite of the fact that many cults and reli-
        gious groups propound their own method of mysticism as the
        best, there is a common denominator underlying them all.
        Zen is used as an example of the state of ultraconsciousness,
        a tendency probably latent in all people. Eastern spiritual-
        ities have healing potential which might enrich Western
        psychotherapy.

368.   Dean, Stanley. "Is There an Ultraconscious Beyond the Con-
        scious?" CANADIAN PSYCHIATRIC ASSOCIATION JOURNAL 15
        (1970): 57-72.

        Discusses the supra-mental, supra-sensory level of awareness
        which is called by different names, like nirvana, satori, and
        Zen. The main features of Bucke's "cosmic consciousness"
        (kairos) are described. The author thinks that the develop-
        ment of this consciousness is probably open to all people.
        It can also be encouraged in the patient and used as an aid
        to psychotherapy.

369.   Dittes, James E. "Continuities Between the Life and Thought
        of Augustine." JOURNAL FOR THE SCIENTIFIC STUDY OF RELIGION
        5 (1965): 130-40.

        Attempts to understand why Augustine took particular stances
        on several issues, including the stress on God's sovereignty
        and human freedom. It is stated that there is both direct
        and indirect evidence of Augustine's ambivalent and oedipal
        relationship with his mother, which accounts for his hostility
        and fearful aloofness. Ways in which Augustine's career and
        behavior seem to have dealt with this conflict are explored.
        His conversion is said to make sense in the context of this
        conflict regarding his autonomy or independence.

370.   Dittes, James E. "Facts and Fantasy in (the Minister's) Men-
        tal Health." PASTORAL PSYCHOLOGY 19 (March 1959): 15-24.

        Raises the issue of the mental health of the clergy and
        outlines some methods of evaluating the psychological
        condition of ministers of religion. The author remarks

that, depending on one's definition of mental illness, one
could show that 95 percent of clergymen (or of lawyers, or
doctors) suffer from mental illness.

371.   Edsman, Carl-Martin. "A Swedish Female Folk Healer From
       the Beginning of the 18th Century." STUDIES IN SHAMANISM.
       Edited by Carl-Martin Edsman. Stockholm: Almquist and
       Wiksell, 1967, pp. 120-65.

Gives the historical background of Catherina Fagerberg, the
eighteenth-century folk healer whose behavior had striking
parallels to shamanism, and then describes the various supernatural interpretations of illness. Modern religious and
psychiatric explanations of possession are discussed. The
question of the mental health of people who have mystic or
ecstatic experiences is raised. The author is cautious and
does not seem to endorse any theory.

372.   Eickhoff, Andrew R. "A Psychoanalytic Study of St. Paul's
       Theology of Sex." PASTORAL PSYCHOLOGY 18 (April 1967):
       35-42.

Raises the issue of Paul's seemingly negative attitude
towards sex, an attitude which is endorsed by many fundamentalist Christians. The various misunderstandings of Paul's
theology of sex are enumerated. The author argues that today
it is clear that the male/female distinction and the values
implied are more cultural than natural, that our knowledge
of sex drives does not make woman a conscious tempter of men,
and that marriage is not an inferior state to celibacy.
Paul's own problem with sexuality is mentioned. The author
stops short of ascribing pathological illness to St. Paul,
but the reader is left with the impression that Paul's theology of sex wasn't quite healthy.

373.   Faris, E. "The Sect and the Sectarian." PUBLICATIONS OF THE
       AMERICAN SOCIOLOGICAL SOCIETY 22 (1927): 144-59.

Maintains that the sect is important in the study of social
psychology. Many kinds of people join sects during a period
of uncertainty and are then molded into the attitudes, life-
style, and world view of the particular group. Sects attract
people who want to be different. It is held that some characteristics of sect members, like social isolation, are to be
explained not in terms of mental illness, but rather of group
psychology.

374.   Farr, Clifford B., and Reuel L. Howe. "The Influence of
       Religious Ideas on the Etiology, Symptomatology, and Prog-
       nosis of the Psychoses." AMERICAN JOURNAL OF PSYCHIATRY
       91 (1932): 845-65.

Starts with the assumption that combined religious and
social isolation causes psychiatric stress and strain, as
has been clearly demonstrated among members of Pennsylvania

Dutch sects. This hypothesis is extended to include all types of religious problems observed in 500 hospital cases. Several case histories are given to illustrate the researchers' point of view.

375.   Fauset, Arthur H. BLACK GODS OF THE METROPOLIS: NEGRO RELI-
        GIOUS CULTS OF THE URBAN NORTH. New York: Octagon Books,
        1970. vii, 126 pp. First published in 1944.

Describes various black cults in the urban areas of the United States, in particular Mount Sinai Holy Church of America, United House of Prayer for All People (led by Bishop Grace), the Church of God (Black Jews), Moorish Science Temple of America, and Father Divine's movement, all of which were millennial. Cults attract people because of their desire to get close to supernatural power and to acquire new experiences and growth. They are successful because they offer relief from physical and mental illnesses and a haven to disillusioned churchgoers. These black cults make up for the economical, educational, and political needs of the black community.

376.   Feilding, Charles R. "Some Misunderstandings of Spiritual
        Healing." PASTORAL PSYCHOLOGY 15 (April 1964): 29-39.

Reflects somewhat negatively on the awakened interest in healing in the Christian churches. The author states that there is a clear distinction between pastoral and medical care and argues that the idea that there are spiritual methods of physical healing is "unhistorical and confusing." He berates the "silly claims, wild exaggerations, and false evidence" which are often adduced in support of spiritual healing of physical maladies. An interpretation of the New Testament passages on healing is provided. It is pointed out that the overemphasis on spiritual healing can lessen one's willingness to face the facts of life, impede the normal process of care and health, and create anxiety and guilt.

377.   Ferenczi, Sandor. "Spiritism." PSYCHOANALYTIC REVIEW 23
        (1936): 139-44.

Encourages the objective study of spiritism and does not dismiss it as fraud since it might lead to psychological knowledge of both our conscious and unconscious processes. Spiritist phenomena may be split into two kinds of mental functioning, one being a mirror of consciousness, the other an automatic and unconscious behavior which would explain some mediumistic actions.

378.   Festinger, Leon. A THEORY OF COGNITIVE DISSONANCE. Stanford,
        CA: Stanford University Press, 1957. xi, 291 pp.

Outlines the theory that the existence of dissonance, or inconsistency in one's cognitive elements, gives rise to pressures to reduce it and to avoid its increase by changing

one's behavior and knowledge and by minimizing one's exposure
to new information and new opinions. The implications of the
theory are carefully explored and relevant data brought forth
to support it. The author holds that his view is applicable
to different areas of human life, including new religious
movements. The Millerites of the nineteenth century are said
to be a good example of the theory. It is then shown how the
initial bewilderment at the failure of their major prophecy
led to an attempted rationale to change the date and an increase in proselytizing to reduce the dissonance.

379. Festinger, Leon, Henry W. Riechen, and Stanley Schachter.
      WHEN PROPHECY FAILS. Minneapolis: University of Minnesota
      Press, 1956. vii, 256 pp.

      Presents the theory that a person committed to a belief
      system will not only remain unshaken by evidence against his
      beliefs, but will emerge stronger in his or her faith with more
      fervor to convert others. The main part of the book focuses
      on showing why and how such a response to contradictory evi-
      dence comes about. The authors maintain that millenarian and
      messianic movements support their thesis and give one detailed
      example to illustrate their position. Their research centers
      around the prophecy of impending catastrophe foretold by a
      Mrs. Marian Keech, who claimed to have received messages from
      outer-space beings who had been visiting our planet in flying
      saucers. An account of the movement's ideology is given and
      the members are introduced with their personal history, their
      involvement in the cult, and their preparation for the coming
      flood. The group's reactions to the failure of the prophecy
      to come true are recorded at some length. The final dispersal
      of the members is accounted for by their ineffectiveness.

380. Fishbein, Morris. FADS AND QUACKERY IN HEALING. New York:
      Blue Ribbon Books, 1932. iv, 382 pp.

      Starts with the assumption that in times of crisis people
      abandon science and truth and resort to magic and prayer.
      Various medical beliefs and practices are considered and de-
      bunked. The gradual evolution of faith healing from the time
      of Paracelsus through the work of Mesmer and Mary Baker Eddy
      is traced. Even modern, scientific psychotherapy is not immune
      from faddism. A list of many of the extraordinary healing
      doctines and cures, including Divine and Spiritual Science,
      Christian Science, Pranayama, Zodiac Therapy, the Emmanuel
      Movement, and Theosophy, is provided. It is implied that all
      these fads can, in the long run, be harmful. Some people
      may, by getting involved in one of these movements, be using
      religious interest to cover up a mental illness.

381. Fodor, Nandor. "People Who Are Christ." PSYCHOANALYSIS AND
      THE PSYCHOANALYTIC REVIEW 45 (1958): 100-19.

      Describes the dreams of several patients who believed they
      were Jesus Christ, or the Messiah, or Judah, or the Devil.
      A thoroughly Freudian interpretation is given, with each

belief seen as revealing the same obsessive-compulsive or
psychotic picture. For instance, to the masochistic person,
the Christ fantasy is expressive of a victim of castration
complex. Identification with Christ seems to occur when the
boundary between reality and dreams is lost or obscured.

382.   Frank, Jerome D. PERSUASION AND HEALING: A COMPARATIVE STUDY
        OF PSYCHOTHERAPY. New York: Schocken Books, 1963. vi,
        282 pp.

        Discusses the many different types of psychotherapeutic
        treatments, including religious healing, which have been
        employed in different societies. Religion can have a great
        influence on health because it evokes hope. Practices of
        religious healing heighten one's self-worth and help the
        individual conceptualize, clarify, and reintegrate feelings
        and problems. Religious revival and thought reform are said
        to be ways of bringing about enduring modifications of the
        patient's worldview that will enable one to function more
        effectively. Thought reform and revivalism attempt to alter
        a person's attitude by recalling one's past history and
        arousing one's sense of guilt, leading to confession and
        atonement. Religious revivals, according to the author,
        attract extroverts, hysterical people, and those with undue
        fear of social disapproval.

383.   Gerlach, Luther P., and Virginia H. Hine. "Five Factors
        Crucial to the Growth of a Modern Religious Movement."
        JOURNAL FOR THE SCIENTIFIC STUDY OF RELIGION 7 (1968):
        23-40.

        Studies the recent resurgence of Pentecostal groups in the
        United States and questions the models of deprivation and
        disorganization that have been frequently applied to under-
        stand their revival. Admitting that these theories, including
        the one of psychological maladjustment, may be causal, the
        author prefers sociological explanations and suggests five
        set of factors "within the movement" for consideration:
        1) reticulate organization; 2) recruitment along pre-exist-
        ing lines of significant social relationships; 3) commitment
        act; 4) change-oriented and action-motivation ideology; and
        5) perception of real or imaginary opposition.

384.   Gewehr, Wesley M. THE GREAT AWAKENING IN VIRGINIA, 1740-1790.
        Durham, NC: Duke University Press, 1930. vii, 292 pp.

        Describes the American religious revival which, according
        to the author, produced many manifestations which were mis-
        taken for true religion. Chapters are dedicated to the
        Presbyterian, Baptist, and Methodist movements, respectively.
        The author argues that abnormal and irrational phenomena,
        which less-educated people are more likely to attribute to
        the power of God or of the devil, can be given a logical
        explanation by reference to "the operation of the laws of
        individual and social psychology" (p. 112). The powers of

suggestion and self-hypnosis frequently operate in revival
meetings which can, however, contribute to the betterment of
society and the individual.

385.   Glock, Charles Y. "The Role of Deprivation in the Origin
        and Evolution of Religious Groups." RELIGION AND SOCIAL
        CONFLICT. Edited by Robert Lee and Martin E. Marty. New
        York: Oxford University Press, 1964, pp. 24-36.

Proposes a general theory of deprivation to explain why
new religious movements come into being. Five types of
deprivation are distinguished: economic, social, organismic,
ethical, and psychic. Besides the situation of felt deprivation, the following conditions are needed for the rise of
new movements: 1) the deprivation must be shared; 2) no
alternative resolutions to the problem are perceived; and 3)
a leader must emerge. Both religious and social resolutions
to the above-mentioned deprivations are possible. "Religious movements emerge as sects when they are stimulated by
economic deprivation, as churches when the deprivation is
social, and as cults when it is psychic" (p. 33).

386.   Godin, André. "Belonging to a Church: What Does It Mean
        Psychologically." JOURNAL FOR THE SCIENTIFIC STUDY OF
        RELIGION 3 (1964): 204-15.

Attempts to delve into the psychological reasons why people
are not content with having a private belief system, but
value, or feel the need for, the support of a believing
community. Three particular circumstances are studied: 1)
the ambiguity of the signs of belonging; 2) the psychic over-
determination of motives; and 3) the attitude of belonging
and human ambivalence towards it. The author thinks that
such an approach could advance our understanding of the
psychology of commitment to a church. Given the common view
that belonging to a community of believers is one attractive
feature of modern cults, Godin indirectly suggests one area
of cultism which might be advantageously pursued.

387.   Goodman, H. "Value Judgments, Mental Health, and Psycho-
        therapy." AMERICAN JOURNAL OF PSYCHOTHERAPY 17 (1963):
        651-59.

Discusses some of the influences of value judgments on the
evaluation of mental health and illness, particularly in
psychotherapy. Adler's view that conformity to certain social
standards or values is an indication of mental health, is
contrasted with Freud's position that favors freedom of self-
expression and self-enhancement as the necessary means to
psychological well-being. The author advocates the position
that regards psychological autonomy, self-determination, and
personal responsibility as aspects of mental health. Though
the discussion does not include the question of cult involvement, it touches indirectly on the cults, which are often
accused of being psychologically deviant because they do not
conform to traditional patterns of behavior and because their
members lack autonomy.

388.   Grad, Bernard. "Healing By the Laying on of Hands: Review
        of Experiments and Implications." PASTORAL PSYCHOLOGY 21
        (September 1970): 19-26.

        Reports on experiments trying to assess whether mice and
        barley seedlings can be healed by the laying on of hands.
        The implication of the positive results are discussed with
        reference to people who claim that they can heal by laying
        their hands on sick people.

389.   Grad, Bernard. "Healing By the Laying on of Hands: A Review
        of Experiments." WAYS OF HEALTH (item 1326), pp. 267-88.

        Reviews the various experiments performed to test whether
        mice and plants can respond to the healing power of hands
        (item 390). The author discusses the part played by the
        placebo effect in the healing process. The implications of
        the practice of laying on of hands in psychotherapy are
        outlined.

390.   Grad, Bernard. "The 'Laying on of Hands': Implications for
        Psychotherapy, Gentling, and the Placebo Effect." JOURNAL
        OF THE AMERICAN SOCIETY FOR PSYCHICAL RESEARCH 61 (1967):
        286-305.

        Observes that healings by the laying on of hands and by
        other means were largely responsible for the success of many
        cults, and then proceeds to describe and to discuss the
        implications of a series of experiments on mice whose wounds
        were healed more quickly when a man with healing power laid
        his hands on them. The relationship between the phenomenon
        of laying on of hands, the placebo effect, and psychotherapy
        is drawn and several similarities between them are noted.
        Trust and faith in the healer or therapist, the unfavorable
        effects of the negative emotions of the therapist or physi-
        cian, and psychological factors like suggestion, are all
        operative in healings performed by the laying on of hands.

391.   Gross, Don H. THE CASE FOR SPIRITUAL HEALING. New York:
        Thomas Nelson and Sons, 1958. xiii, 263 pp.

        Argues, in the context of healing groups like the Emmanuel
        Movement and Christian Science, in favor of the healing
        ministries in the church. This volume reviews the various
        activities related to spiritual healing and sets them in a
        fuller theological background. Though the author clearly
        distinguishes between spiritual and psychological healing,
        he seems to assume that the former leads to the latter.

392.   Havens, Joseph. "Notes on Augustine's 'Confessions.'"
        JOURNAL FOR THE SCIENTIFIC STUDY OF RELIGION 5 (1965):
        141-43.

        Reflects on the conflict and decision of St. Augustine and
        explores the relationship between the psychological and theo-
        logical perspectives of his behavior. From a psychological

point of view Augustine's life is a paradigm of inner conflict and its resolution, while from a theological viewpoint it is an example of great apologetic and pastoral achievements. The author believes that these two perspectives cannot be reconciled.

393. Helming, O. C. "Modern Evangelism in the Light of Modern Psychiatry." BIBLICAL WORLD 36 (1910): 296-306.

Endeavors to present a psychological perspective of the factors and motives in religious appeals by evangelists. While not denying the value of Christian evangelism and the possibly good outcome of conversion, the author states that "the vice of revivalism is the straining for immediate effects, the misuse of the power of suggestibility, and the power to infatuate the crowd which yields to the will of the leader and is ostensibly converted without any moral change in itself" (pp. 299-300).

394. Heschel, A. J. THE PROPHETS. New York: Harper and Row, 1962. 518 pp.

Describes and analyzes the Biblical prophets' consciousness, that is, their awareness of their mission rather than of the content of their revelation or of their subjective personal experiences. The features which set the prophets apart are portrayed in general, and several of them, including Hosea, Isaiah, and Jeremiah, are chosen as examples. The psychopatho-logical symptoms which have so often been ascribed to them are refuted. The prophet, according to the author, is a person who is maladjusted to his society which he judges to be in a state of moral madness. His mind and behavior, like those of the psychotic, are out of tune with the rest of his con-temporaries. But unlike the mentally sick person, the prophet returns to reality and is able to apply his teachings to improve the society of his time.

395. Jacobs, Hans. WESTERN PSYCHOTHERAPY AND HINDU SADHANA: A CON-TRIBUTION TO COMPARATIVE STUDY IN PSYCHOLOGY AND METAPHYSICS. New York: International Universities Press, 1961. 231 pp.

Compares, discusses, and evaluates three approaches to psychology, namely Freudian, Jungian, and Hindu. The author contends that each one possesses merits and could, in certain therapeutic situations, become indispensable. The possible use of Yoga in the West is examined and several case examples given.

396. Johnson, Benton. "Do Holiness Sects Socialize in Dominant Values?" SOCIAL FORCES 39 (1961): 309-16.

Refutes the common deprivation theory which maintains that the function of holiness groups is to offer underprivileged groups an emotional and other-worldly escape from reality. Although holiness sects stress conversion, encourage members

to retreat from society, and endorse ascetical practices, it
is stated that their positive stress on self-application,
consistency, and achievement are in harmony with dominant
American values. Though the mental health of the members of
these religious groups is not discussed, the author sees
them as more conforming to culture than adopting unusual and
aberrant behavior.

397.   Johnson, Paul E. "Jesus as Psychologist." RELIGION AND HUMAN
       BEHAVIOR. Edited by Simon Doniger. New York: Association
       Press, 1954. Pp. 47-57.

       Maintains that one is justified in looking at Jesus as a
       psychologist because he worked with emotionally disturbed
       persons and found ways of relieving their needs. Jesus
       practiced his healing along the lines suggested by contem-
       porary psychotherapy. He diagnosed the human condition by
       insight and empathy (psychodiagnosis), understood that inner
       motives cause action, knew the fears and anxieties which
       cripple freedom, saw the anguish and frustration which can
       stifle growth (psychodynamics), and suggested remedies for
       healing inner conflicts and distresses (psychotherapy).

398.   Kamiat, Arnold H. "The Cosmic Phantasy." PSYCHOANALYTIC
       REVIEW 15 (1928): 210-19.

       Discusses the beliefs which are part of every creed, partic-
       ularly in fundamentalist groups and new religious movements,
       that the cosmos is a battleground between the forces of good
       and evil. The author maintains that such cosmic fantasies
       or hallucinations can be understood in terms of group psychol-
       ogy. They compensate for feelings of inadequacy by assuring
       believers that they are finally in possession of absolute
       values.

399.   Kelley, Mary William. "Depression in the Psychoses of Members
       of Religious Communities of Women." AMERICAN JOURNAL OF
       PSYCHIATRY 118 (1961): 423-25.

       Reflects on statistics which point to a significant increase
       in mental illness among religious sisters. The main problem
       seems to be a form of depressive psychosis which is symptom-
       atically common and which occurs at a higher rate than in other
       occupational or social classes. Cases of self-accusation,
       scrupulosity, sense of worthlessness and failure, and the
       desire to be destroyed, occurred frequently among these sub-
       jects. The author (herself a nun) points out that asceticism
       could lead to serious depression, that common religious life
       has within it a certain measure of insecurity, and that the
       demands associated with religious vows could instill a strong
       sense of guilt.

400.   Kelley, Mary William. "The Incidence of Hospitalized Mentally
       Ill Among Religious Sisters in the United States." AMERICAN
       JOURNAL OF PSYCHIATRY 115 (1958): 72-75.

Re-examines Moore's (items 422-23) hypothesis on the mental health of priests and religious and concludes that, while he may be right in his view that pre-psychotic personalities account for the mentally ill religious sisters, nevertheless the apparent increase in mental disorders among "active" religious women suggests that factors of life stress may be contributing more to their eventual breakdown than was previously thought. Religious life in a convent may bring about some of the psychiatric problems which sisters experience.

401.   Kelman, Harold. "Eastern Influences on Psychoanalytic Thinking." PSYCHOLOGIA 2 (1959): 71-78.

Outlines the contribution of Eastern thinking to psychoanalysis. The differences between Eastern and Western thought are discussed. The author looks favorably on Western interest in Eastern religions and philosophies—an interest manifested concretely in the presence of Zen in Western society.

402.   Kidorf, Irwin W. "The Shiva: A Form of Group Psychotherapy." JOURNAL OF RELIGION AND HEALTH 5 (1966): 43-46.

Explores the dynamics of a traditional Jewish rite, the Shiva. As in group psychotherapy, this ritual encourages a catharsis of feelings by the participants which brings about an amelioration of the surface-level aspects of the problem, provides a setting for psychodrama, and presents an opportunity for the projection of one's feelings on the group. In both situations, regression frequently occurs in the service of the ego.

403.   Klingerman, Charles. "A Psychoanalytic Study of the Confessions of St. Augustine." JOURNAL OF THE AMERICAN PSYCHOANALYTIC ASSOCIATION 5 (1957): 469-84.

Examines the major events in the life of Augustine, as narrated in his Confessions, and interprets them from a psychoanalytic point of view, stressing especially the ambivalent relationship between he and his mother, Monica. In his early childhood, Augustine was rather neurotic and his adolescence was marked by instinctual frustration, a vivid imagination, and a sensitive conscience, all of which were the cause of constant inner turmoil. The influence which Monica had on Augustine's adult life, especially on his conversion, is stressed and the oedipal element in their relationship noted. Augustine's conversion experience "was an identification with the mother and a passive feminine attitude to the father displaced by God" (p. 483).

404.   Knight, James A. "Calvinism and Psychoanalysis: A Comparative Study." PASTORAL PSYCHOLOGY 14 (December 1963): 10-17.

Considers the concepts, ideas, habits, and attitudes of Calvin and Freud, each with his respective "religion," and finds remarkable similarities. Both had ascetical practices,

were compulsive workers, were consumed by their interest in
religion, had similar concepts of God, man, and life, and
insisted on purity of doctrine. The question whether psychoanalysis is some kind of cult with Freud as its leader is
indirectly raised.

405.   Knight, Robert. P. "Why People Go to the Cultists." BULLETIN
         OF THE MENNINGER CLINIC 3 (1939): 137-47.

Written about a half-century ago, this essay captures the
mentality of many present-day psychiatrists when it states
that "the average physician looks with disdain on therapy as
practiced by cultists, brands it as unscientific, and cannot
understand how the cults can continue to thrive or how they
provide any real threat to organized scientific medicine"
(p. 139). Cults are judged to promote a childish, primitive,
and magical way of thinking to which the mentally ill are
easily attracted. The supercilious attitude of physicians,
which ignores the psychology of the person, is part of the
reason why people go to the cultists.

406.   Kobler, Frank J. "Screening Applicants for Religious Life."
         JOURNAL OF RELIGION AND HEALTH 3 (1964): 161-70.

Analyzes several studies on the incidence of schizophrenia
and obsessive-compulsive neurosis among members of Catholic
religious orders and congregations. The use of the MMPI is
discussed, especially regarding its usefulness in identifying the seriously disturbed individual who applies for entry
into religious life.

407.   Kretschmer, Wolfgang. "Meditative Techniques in Psycho-
         therapy." PSYCHOLOGIA 5 (1962): 76-83.

Describes various meditative techniques developed by German psychiatrists. Meditation helps the patient acquire an
expanded consciousness and an impersonal experience and knowledge. It also shortens treatment and eliminates transference.
In spite of the severe limitation caused the subjectivity of
both the patient and the therapist, meditation could become
one of the leading therapeutic methods.

408.   Lantis, Margaret. "The Symbol of a New Religion." PSYCHIATRY
         13 (1950): 101-13.

States that surveys show that the majority of people are
unsatisfied with institutional religion as it exists. The
strengths and weaknesses of Judeo-Christian symbols are
examined and found largely deficient since they do not conform to social reality and are thus unable to meet human
needs. The author's view is that there is a need for a "new
type of achieved, noncompetitive relationship" (p. 109)
expressed in a new symbol-system. The necessary conditions
for such a system to come into being, namely a leader who
dramatizes the symbols and who attracts disciples, are

described. Such a new religious symbolism would, in the author's view, be mentally healthy. Though written well before the rise of the new cults, this article indirectly throws some light on the causes and effects of new religious movements.

409. Liljencrants, Baron Johan. SPIRITISM AND RELIGION. New York: Devin-Adair Co., 1918. 205 pp.

Examines Spiritism (spiritualism) which originated as a religious movement in the West towards the middle of the nineteenth century, but which has existed for a long time in different parts of the world. The author covers: 1) the history of modern spiritualism, 2) the physical and psychic phenomena associated with it, and 3) genuine and spurious phenomena which occur during a session. The medium, who goes into a trance state, suffers a dissociation of personality and, during possession, is in a psychologically abnormal state.

410. Lorand, Sandor. "Psycho-analytic Therapy of Religious Devotees. (A Theoretical and Technical Contribution)." INTERNATIONAL JOURNAL OF PSYCHOANALYSIS 43 (1962): 50-56.

Studies religious devotees who developed neurotic difficulties and somatic illnesses from their childhood experiences and environment. The psychological features of these patients are outlined and it is stated that a long period of reconstruction is needed, since they react rather negatively to therapy. Several of the patients' problems, like hysterical symptoms and masochistic tendencies, are seen as originating in the oedipal relationship. Their neurosis is rooted in their identification with the mother. The patients' need to develop independence is underscored.

411. Lowe, Warner L. "Religious Beliefs and Religious Delusions: A Comparative Study of Religious Projection." AMERICAN JOURNAL OF PSYCHOTHERAPY 9 (1959): 54-61.

Analyzes the responses to a religious projection test administered to three groups, namely, Christian graduate students in psychology, students at a Bible college, and a group of hospitalized psychotic patients. Three major hypotheses were confirmed: 1) Bible students were more concerned with religious topics and more dogmatic than the psychology graduates; 2) these latter were less egocentric than the other two groups, that is, they were more objective, more relative in their views, and more flexible; and 3) the psychology students have a greater amount of personal conflict than the Bible students, who were more optimistic and self-confident and who enjoyed better family relationships.

412. Ludwig, Arnold M. "The Trance." COMPREHENSIVE PSYCHIATRY 8 (1967): 7-15.

Discusses the problems involved in defining "trance" and
points out that the major difficulty in describing its nature
is that most of its outward features are little more than
artifacts produced by hypnosis. The conditions necessary
for the emergence of trance are listed and the cultural and
historical influences are seen as important factors. Trance
phenomena are more widespread than is generally thought and
should be seen as normal rather than abnormal mental functioning. Some of the features of trance are discussed. In
conditions of trance, like Yoga, prayer, and meditation, the
individual's motivation is strengthened and one's energies
are concentrated on problem solving and creative activities.
Trance-like states appear to leave room for a greater social
cohesion.

413. Mathison, Richard P. FAITH, CULTS, AND SECTS IN AMERICA: FROM
      ATHEISM TO ZEN. New York: Bobbs-Merrill Co., 1960. 384 pp.

Gives a journalistic account of many cults including: 1)
established denominations, like Jehovah's Witnesses, Seventh-
Day Adventists, and Christian Scientists; 2) racial cults,
like Father Divine and Voodoo; 3) cults of sex and violence,
like the Satanic Mass and "Crowleyanity"; and 4) various fads
like flying saucers, Yoga, and Zen. Though largely descriptive in his presentation, the author does state that the cults
offer a haven for the restless and discontented. He does not
view them as healthy organizations. Cult leaders, he writes,
who are "opportunists, bunco artists, racketeers, confidence
men, and glib psychotics are also riding today's religious
ground swell, leaving chaos and tragedy in their wake" (p. 15).

414. Matthews, Ronald. ENGLISH MESSIAHS: STUDIES OF SIX ENGLISH
      RELIGIOUS PRETENDERS. London: Methuen, 1936. xvi, 230 pp.

A study of six English men and women who, claiming that
they were divine, attracted some followers, caused some contemporary stir, and advanced unorthodox religious beliefs.
The messiahs, some rather obscure, are identified as James
Nayler (1618-1660), Joanna Southcott (1750-1814), Richard
Brothers (1757-1824), John Nichols Tom (1799-1838), Henry
James Prince (1811-1899), and John Hugh Smyth-Pigott (1852-
1927). All these pretenders had abnormal personalities which
made them unfit to "cooperate harmoniously with society" (p.
201). While admitting that not all religious claims are
pathological or abnormal, the author insists that the above
mentioned "imposters" had succeeded "in escaping from their
difficulties of the real world into the gratification of a
delusive attitude to life" (p. 204). The path to normality
is disrupted by a process of psychic weaning too harsh or
abrupt for the child. The main results, namely paranoia,
dementia praecox (schizophrenia), hysteria, and melancholia,
are all found in the six self-styled messiahs. The author
thinks that only abnormal people were attracted to them.

415. McAllister, Robert J. "The Mental Health of Members of
      Religious Communities." CLINICAL PSYCHIATRY AND RELIGION
      (item 294), pp. 211-22.

      Comments on the common opinion that those who join a
      religious community are somewhat peculiar and eccentric, if
      not irrational. The relatively few studies on the subject
      are reviewed. The emotional stress in religious life and
      the problem of identity, together with the effect of family
      background and seminary training, are considered. The train-
      ing environment of religious candidates is one in which
      independent thought and behavior are stifled and close inter-
      personal relationships discouraged. Personality disorders,
      including paranoia and schizophrenia, account for nearly one
      half of the hospitalized clergy.

416. McAllister, Robert J., and Albert Vanderveldt. "Factors in
      Mental Illness Among Hospitalized Clergy." JOURNAL OF
      NERVOUS AND MENTAL DISEASE 132 (1961): 80-88.

      Reviews the somewhat scanty literature in the field and
      reports on a study of 100 Catholic priests who had been
      discharged from a psychiatric hospital after being treated
      for various problems, including anxiety, hallucinations,
      depression, and sexual deviations. Though it is admitted
      that "seminary training and the clerical life lend them-
      selves easily to a lack of duration and depth in inter-
      personal relationships" (p. 87), and can therefore be a
      source of psychopathology, most of the problems diagnosed
      indicate that the patterns of maladjustment had preceded
      the clerical state.

417. McComas, Henry C. THE PSYCHOLOGY OF RELIGIOUS SECTS: A
      COMPARISON OF TYPES. New York: Fleming Revell Co., 1912.
      235 pp.

      Points out that there are religious personality types which
      are based on certain fundamental differences in human nature
      and that, consequently, the diverse religious beliefs and
      practices found in Christian denominations have their basis
      in human dispositions and not in divine preferences. Three
      kinds of sects are distinguished: 1) the intellectual type,
      which stresses belief and doctrine and which is altruistic
      and aesthetic; 2) the emotional type, which values the experi-
      ence of the convert and tends to be suggestible; and 3) the
      action type, which aims at rousing the impulsive and instinc-
      tive response of the members. Various religious groups, like
      the Seventh-Day Adventists, the Baptists, the Christian Scien-
      tists, the Congregationalists, the Disciples of Christ, and
      the Latter-Day Saints (Mormons) are fitted into the author's
      threefold typology.

418. McComb, S. "Spiritual Healing in Europe." MENTAL HYGIENE
      12 (1928): 206-21.

Relates in conversational style the spiritual practices of
healing in Germany, France (Lourdes), and England. The cura-
tive methods employed, the psychic factors operative, and
the alleged successes are examined. The rise of interest in
spiritual healing is attributed mainly to Christian Science
and other New Thought Schools. Disclaiming the miraculous
element often brought forth to explain cures, the author
thinks that psychological healing is possible, but should be
practiced by those who are scientifically competent.

419.   McKenzie, J. G. PSYCHOLOGY, PSYCHOTHERAPY, AND EVANGELICAL-
        ISM. New York: Macmillan, 1940. xiii, 238 pp.

Examines evangelical experience and doctrine in the light
of psychology and psychotherapeutic principles. The evangelical experience and its emphasis on salvation is analyzed,
with special attention to conversion, guilt, sin, and forgiveness. Conversion differs, according to the author, from
psycho-neurosis because the former resolves conflict, while
the latter tries to escape from it.

420.   Metzner, Ralph. MAPS OF CONSCIOUSNESS. New York: Collier,
        1971. vii, 161 pp.

Discusses various techniques which can be used to free
human consciousness from its limitations of fixed mental,
emotional, perceptual, and behavioral patterns. The I Ching,
Tantra, Tarot, Alchemy, Astrology, and Actualism are among
the ways described and treated as methods of personal growth
and development. There seems to be an underlying assumption
that they are all psychologically beneficial to those who
apply them properly.

421.   Moody, Jesse. "The Psychological Difficulties of Mass Evange-
        listic Converts." PASTORAL PSYCHOLOGY 7 (December 1956):
        38-40.

Assesses the psychological problems of converts from a
questionnaire sent to several evangelists, including Billy
Graham. It is concluded that: 1) revivalists are becoming
more aware of the pathology of religious experience and the
need to do something about it; 2) they are not sure that the
one approach to evangelism is a cure-all for all converts;
and 3) they have not cooperated with health specialists.

422.   Moore, Thomas Vernier. "Insanity in Priests and Religious.
        Part II: The Detection of Psychotics Who Apply for Admis-
        sion to the Priesthood or Religious Community." ECCLESI-
        ASTICAL REVIEW 95 (1936): 601-13.

Continuing a previous study (item 423), the author gives
guidelines and comments on several areas which should be
carefully questioned when a person applies for the priesthood or for membership in a religious community. These areas
are: 1) family history; 2) personal history; 3) character;

and 4) emotional traits. While holding that people who
exhibit serious problems in the above areas should not be
turned down, he makes an exception for certain psychological
problems linked with adolescence. "From the candidate's point
of view, the religious life might be his hope for mental stability in the future. The relatively low incidence of mental
disorders in the religious life shows that there is no great
mental strain from the religious routine itself" (p. 603).

423.   Moore, Thomas Vernier. "Insanity in Priests and Religious.
        Part I: The Rate of Insanity in Priests and Religious."
        ECCLESIATICAL REVIEW 95 (1936): 485-98.

        Compares the rate of insanity of priests and religious
        with married and divorced people and finds that both priests
        and members (sisters and brothers) of religious orders
        suffered a much higher percentage of dementia praecox, manic
        depression, and paranoia. The strain of priestly or community
        life, according to the author, does not account for these high
        ratios and, hence, he has to conclude that those priests and
        members of religious orders who were mentally ill must have
        had a predisposition to the illness before their priestly or
        religious commitment.

424.   Murphy, Carol. "Spiritual Healing." JOURNAL OF PASTORAL
        CARE 17 (1963): 203-7.

        Expresses several reservations on spiritual healing and
        discusses faith healing in the context of Frankl's work. The
        link between spiritual and physical healing is discussed with
        special reference to Christian Science. It is concluded that:
        1) every illness has a spiritual significance and can influ-
        ence one's spiritual condition; 2) the quality of the patient-
        healer relationship is an important part of therapy; and 3)
        healing involves one's whole personality.

425.   Murphy, Gardner, and Lois B. Murphy, editors. ASIAN PSYCHOL-
        OGIES. New York: Basic Books, 1968. xv, 238 pp.

        A descriptive account of the psychologies of India, China,
        and Japan. The editors point out that these Asian systems
        are both mystical and practical, and that they start with the
        religious assumption that the goal of life is freedom from
        suffering and then propose religious and ethical practices
        which lead to freedom from delusions and self-imposed misery.
        This volume provides some philosophical and psychological
        background to many Eastern cults in the West.

426.   Nichol, John Thomas. PENTECOSTALISM. New York: Harper and
        Row, 1960. xvi, 264 pp.

        Surveys the rise and spread of the twentieth-century Pen-
        tecostal movement from its birthplace in the United States
        to its expansion in different parts of the world. Varieties
        of Pentecostalism (including the snake-handling groups) are

considered. The author attributes part of the initial
success of the movement to its ministry to the psychological
needs of people who found avenues for emotional release and
hopes for their future condition in Pentecostal piety.

427.   Northridge, William L.   RECENT PSYCHOLOGY AND EVANGELISTIC
        PREACHING. London: Epworth Press, 1924. 96 pp.

        Discusses various methods, namely conviction, confession,
        faith, and conversion, by which certain forms of religious
        experiences are brought about by evangelists. The author's
        view is that, in spite of the attempt by psychologists to
        reduce religious experience to a psychic process, psycholog-
        ical principles are not adequate to explain it. False
        evangelism, which uses the methods of suggestion and
        exhibitionism and produces results which can be brought
        about by hypnosis, can be wholly accounted for by psycho-
        logical laws. "True evangelism alters the foundation of
        individual character and men's conception of values" (p. 87).

428.   Oesterly, W. O. E., and Theodore H. Robinson. AN INTRODUCTION
        TO THE BOOKS OF THE OLD TESTAMENT. New York: Meridian
        Books, 1958. xvi, 454 pp.

        Introduces the various books of the Old Testament, out-
        lining their structure and content. Some attempts are made
        to interpret the prophets from a psychological point of view.
        Jeremiah is seen as a mournful pessimist, while Hosea is said
        to have suffered from an obsession with sex.

429.   Ornstein, Robert. E. THE PSYCHOLOGY OF CONSCIOUSNESS. New
        York: Viking Press, 1972. xii, 247 pp.

        Explores human consciousness using insights from both
        Western and Eastern traditions. The author examines "esoter-
        ic psychologies" in Buddhism, Yoga, and Sufism, all of which
        have stressed a personal, empirical approach, in contrast to
        the more objective and impersonal slant of Western psycholo-
        gies. Contemplation in Christianity, according to the author,
        performs the same function as Eastern techniques. Two forms
        of meditation exercises are considered: concentrative and
        "opening-up." The latter type causes a shift in the mode
        of consciousness, leading to increased self-knowledge and
        relaxation. The main psychological results could be a
        significant reduction in hypertension and stress.

430.   Pande, Shashi K. "The Mystique of 'Western' Psychotherapy:
        An Eastern Interpretation." JOURNAL OF NERVOUS AND MENTAL
        DISEASE 146 (1968): 425-32.

        Offers an interesting and insightful view of Western psycho-
        therapy as seen from the point of view of a psychiatrist from
        the East. The author considers psychotherapy as a decision-
        making process, as an integrating experience, as a critique

and overview of one's life-style, and as a redress from ego
alienation and isolation. Differences between the Eastern
and Western view of, for example, the concept of time and
the relationship between the ego and the environment, are
outlined. Though not written with the intention of explaining the current influx of Eastern views and practices in the
West, this essay may throw some light on why Eastern religions
may have some therapeutic effects.

431.   Penner, Wes. "Hippies' Attraction to Mysticism." ADOLESCENCE
        7 (1972): 199-210.

        Outlines several reasons why hippies are interested in
        occult matters, Eastern religions, and witchcraft. Hippies
        are dissatisfied with the greed and power of middle-class
        mentality and feel the need for cosmic consciousness. They
        are looking for increased awareness of self and environment,
        honesty and authenticity, and ways of expressing their emo-
        tions. These ideals have apparently been neglected in Western
        culture. Eastern religions and other movements may be helping
        them achieve personal fulfillment and cope with alienation.

432.   Perry, John Weir. "The Messianic Hero." JOURNAL OF ANA-
        LYTICAL PSYCHOLOGY 17 (1972): 184-98.

        Refers to the writer's discovery that in his schizophrenic
        patients there frequently appears a hero image that is regu-
        larly messianic, that is, intent on saving the world, changing
        society for the better, or reforming all nations. It is argued
        that this messianic figure, besides having a long and rich
        historical development spread over many cultures, has a valid
        function in the psychic process. Prophets and messiahs arise
        in times of sociocultural crises and lead to psychological
        reorientation and re-synthesis of new forms. The hero image
        embodies the psychological need to meet the pressing emotional
        issues of our times.

433.   Petersen, Severin. A CATALOG OF WAYS PEOPLE GROW. New York:
        Ballantine, 1971. xiii, 368 pp.

        Contains short descriptions of various methods which can be
        used for psychical and psychological growth and development.
        The list covers a variety of possibilities including several
        methods which are often connected with the cults. Astrology,
        ESP, Hasidism, different types of Yoga, meditation, Tran-
        scendental Meditation, contemplation, prayer, mysticism,
        shamanism, Synanon, and Zen all find a place in this encyclo-
        pedic collection, which, however, provides no help for the
        reader to evaluate their often conflicting methods. Since
        traditional psychotherapy and more recent forms of thera-
        peutic treatments, like family therapy and Gestalt, are also
        described, the assumption seems to be that all the methods
        mentioned in the catalog can be used therapeutically.

434.   Pruyser, Paul W. "Psychological Examination: Augustine."
        JOURNAL FOR THE SCIENTIFIC STUDY OF RELIGION 5 (1966):
        284-89.

Draws a psychological profile of Augustine by considering his perceptions, thought processes, thought content, language, behavior, emotions, relationships with others, and self-image. An aggressive, hypomanic, restless, and impulsive person who was too attached to his mother is the general picture which emerges from this account.

435.   Pruyser, Paul W. "Erikson's Young Man Luther: A New Chapter in the Psychology of Religion." JOURNAL FOR THE SCIENTIF- IC STUDY OF RELIGION 2 (1963): 238-42.

Compares Pfister's and Erikson's studies on Luther and holds that the latter's work is a major contribution to the psychology of religion. The author agrees with Erikson who, departing from such traditional themes as conversion and religious feeling, sees in Martin Luther a religious genius whose psychological makeup had both healthy and pathological aspects.

436.   Putney, Snell, and Russell Middleton. "Rebellion, Conformity, and Parental Religious Ideologies." SOCIOMETRY 24 (1961): 125-35.

Investigates the extent of rebellion from, and conformity to, parental religious beliefs among college students. A number of correlates, such as authoritarianism, status concern, and conservatism were utilized. Various influences on the students, together with the social and personality differences between those who rebel and those who conform, are explored. Study shows that deviation from parental belief systems has a history on college campuses. Since so many cult members are young college adults, this essay, written over 25 years ago, puts the cultic issue in a broader perspective.

437.   Rabinowitz, Seymour. "Developmental Problems in Catholic Seminarians." PSYCHIATRY 32 (1969): 107-17.

Discusses observations made in diagnostic, evaluative, and therapeutic work with 25 Catholic seminarians. The subjects were characterized as having poorly integrated into their lives the early psychosocial phases, and as having problems centering around trust, autonomy, initiative, and identity. Three types of psychopathology were noted: homosexuality, psychophysiological problems, and depression. Case studies of subjects show similarities in personality traits and family background. Some unique problems in the treatment of semi- narians are discussed.

438.   Rawcliffe, D. H. THE PSYCHOLOGY OF THE OCCULT. London: Derricke Ridgway, 1952. 551 pp.

Argues that the urge towards mysticism, the occult, and the supernatural is fundamental to human nature. The psycholog- ical factors which contribute to the creation and perpetua- tion of occult beliefs and practices are explored. Hypnotism, hallucination, crystal-gazing, automatic writing, mediumship,

mental healing, mystical experience and ecstasy, and Eastern
practices, such as Yoga, are among the many subjects considered. The author believes that mysticism frequently has a
hysterical or pathological origin and can be induced by drugs.
Some of the common symptoms of psychosis, like depersonalization, sense of union with the cosmos, and feelings of omnipotence, are evident in the mystical experience. St. Paul's
vision is quoted as an "excellent example of a hysterical
hallucination with a religious theme" (p. 241).

439.   Riley, I. Woodbridge. THE FOUNDER OF MORMONISM: A PSYCHO-
       LOGICAL STUDY OF JOSEPH SMITH. London: William Heinemann,
       1903. xix, 462 pp.

       Examines Smith's character and achievement from a psycho-
       logical point of view. His dreams are explained as illusions
       or hallucinations and his visions are said to furnish evidence
       of epilepsy which later developed into insanity. Smith suf-
       fered from serious emotional instability. The author reflects
       on the founder of Mormonism as: 1) a prophet, seer, and reve-
       lator; 2) an occultist; 3) an exorcist; and 4) a faith healer.
       It is concluded that Smith used the method of a trance-medium
       induced by auto-suggestion and that his claims to occult
       powers and to writing the BOOK OF MORMON reveal some conscious
       duplicity. Joseph Smith's ancestry is described as morbid,
       superstitious, and diseased, which explains his erratic and
       abnormal behavior.

440.   Rokeach, Milton. THE THREE CHRISTS OF YPSILANTI: A PSYCHO-
       LOGICAL STUDY. New York: Alfred Knopf, 1964. ix, 336 pp.

       Relates the author's counseling experience with three
       patients at Ypsilanti State Hospital in Michigan, each of whom
       claimed to be God or Christ. The author's main purpose was
       to explore the delusional beliefs and actions. The history
       of the patients and the way they related to one another when
       placed in the same room and confronted with each others'
       claims are recorded in some detail. All three patients are
       diagnosed as paranoid.

441.   Rose, Louis. FAITH HEALING. Harmondsworth, UK: Penguin
       Books, 1971. 194 pp.

       Investigates the claims of many Christian healers, includ-
       ing Mary Baker Eddy and two British healers, Christopher
       Woodward and Harry Edwards. The Christian orthodox view of
       such healings is outlined and some of the issues raised by
       these practices are discussed. The author's view is that
       there is no evidence that similar cures cannot be wrought
       by psychotherapy. The obvious conclusion that faith healing
       can have therapeutic effects is not brought up by the author.

442.   Schien, Stephen M. "The Ego in Need: the Mystic Way and
       the Consulting Room." INSIGHT: QUARTERLY REVIEW OF RELI-
       GION AND MENTAL HEALTH 5.1 (1966): 1-10.

Contrasts the psychiatrist's main concerns with those of
the mystic, the former concentrating on the concepts of the
unconscious, anxiety, transference, and intra-psychic conflict, the latter on the transformation of the individual,
the oneness with reality and communion with the infinite.
The former seeks explanation, the latter abandonment. Both,
however, want to go beyond the borders of consciousness.
Reasons for a rapprochement between psychiatry and mysticism
are explained and the distinction between mystics and schizophrenics is outlined. This study indirectly suggests that
those new movements which encourage mystical experience could,
in collaboration with the psychiatrist, promote mental health.

443.   Schneiderman, Leo. "Ramakrishna: Personality and Social
        Factors in the Growth of a Religious Movement." JOURNAL
        FOR THE SCIENTIFIC STUDY OF RELIGION 8 (1969): 160-71.

        Analyzes the nineteenth century Indian Ramakrishna mission
        as an example of a modern religious movement. The influence
        of Ramakrishna, the relationship with his followers, and the
        process whereby hero-worship was replaced by a service orien-
        tation are among the areas investigated. Ramaksrishna was
        the personification of a "god-intoxicated," prophetic leader
        who was permitted "to regress behaviorally while living an
        overpoweringly intense and dramatic fantasy life" (p. 63).

444.   Schweitzer, Albert. THE PSYCHIATRIC STUDY OF JESUS. Boston:
        Beacon Press, 1958. 79 pp. First published in 1948.

        Criticizes and refutes various studies (mostly in German)
        of Jesus which describe him as a pathological figure along
        with many other religious personalities. The author finds
        the material used to support this thesis unhistorical, taken
        out of context, and fabricated to conform with the diagnosis
        of psychological illness. The only facts about Jesus which
        could be discussed from a psychological point of view are his
        high opinion of himself and his ecstatic vision at his bap-
        tism, both of which, according to the author, fall outside
        the realm of mental illness.

445.   Slater, Eliot. "Neurosis and Religious Affiliation."
        JOURNAL OF MENTAL SCIENCE 93 (1947): 392-98.

        Makes a study of several thousand members of the military
        forces who were admitted to psychiatric wards. Jews and
        members of the Salvation Army were found to have a greater
        tendency to neurosis than Roman Catholics and Methodists who,
        in turn, were more neurotic than members of the Church of God.
        The higher incidence of mental disease among members of the
        Salvation Army is explained by the fact that they are, as a
        rule, recruited from the lower social classes.

446.   Spehn, Mel R. "The Small-Group Religions." PASTORAL PSYCHOL-
        OGY 23 (January 1972): 50-58.

        Compares the intensive group experience, for example, that
        at Esalen and Carl Rogers' Encounter Experience, with tradi-

tional religion. Several areas where both meet are mentioned:
the community, moral code, confession, penance, forgiveness,
the messiah, and the transcendent. The author seems to take
it for granted that these experiences are beneficial to the
individual, both from religious and humanistic points of view.

447.   Stanley, Gordon. "Personality and Attitude Characteristics
       of Fundamentalist Theological Students." AUSTRALIAN JOURNAL
       OF PSYCHOLOGY 15 (1963): 121-23.

       Administers several standard psychological tests to about
       350 theological students from eight different denominations.
       On the basis of their responses, the students were classified
       as fundamentalist and non-fundamentalist, the former being
       characterized by their belief in the literal truth of the
       Bible. Irrespective of their church membership, fundamental-
       ists registered a higher lie scale score and were more con-
       servative and dogmatic in their religious views. They are
       described as being close-minded.

448.   Stanley, Gordon. "Personality and Attitude Characteristics
       of Fundamentalist University Students." AUSTRALIAN JOURNAL
       OF PSYCHOLOGY 15 (1963): 199-200.

       Expands on a previous study (item 447) to include 72 uni-
       versity students of both sexes who are not studying for the
       ministry. Dogmaticism, authoritarianism, religious institu-
       tionalization, and conversion were positively related to
       fundamentalism but not to other personality traits (like
       extroversion, neuroticism, and mistrust). Brown's (item 352)
       general findings that fundamentalist beliefs are not asso-
       ciated with pathology are confirmed.

449.   Tart, Charles T., editor. ALTERED STATES OF CONSCIOUSNESS.
       New York: Doubleday, 2nd edition, 1969. ix, 589 pp.

       Covers various aspects of altered states of consciousness,
       through the use of psychedelic drugs, hypnosis, and meditation.

       Includes items 407, 504, 505, 564, 565.

450.   Taylor, W. S. "Science and Cult." PSYCHOLOGICAL REVIEW 37
       (1930): 166-68.

       Contrasts the intellectual attitudes of the scientist with
       those of the cult member. The former awaits proof, integrates
       acquired knowledge with allied scientists, accepts criticisms,
       and seeks facts. The latter accepts without any proof, rejects
       and resents any criticism of his or her views, is ignorant of,
       or disregards, other points of view, strives to vindicate one-
       self rather that to reach the truth, and appears to flourish
       on "inertia of thought." Cultishness leads to abnormality
       and requires psychotherapeutic treatment.

451.   Toch, Hans. THE SOCIAL PSYCHOLOGY OF SOCIAL MOVEMENTS. New
       York: Bobbs Merrill, 1965. xiv, 257 pp.

Examines the various social movements covering both secular
and religious groups in different cultural settings. Among
the many movements included are Alcoholics Anonymous, the
Black Muslims, Cargo cults, Father Divine's Church, Flying
Saucers Clubs, Jehovah's Witnesses, the Ras Tafari Brethren,
and millenarian and nativistic movements. In each case, three
general areas are explored: 1) the nature of the movement; 2)
the career of its members; and 3) the determinants and motives.
The view that social movements come into being as an attempt
to solve personal and social problems and are indirect agents
of change is endorsed.

452.   Van Dusen, W. "Wu Wei, No-Mind, and the Fertile Void in
        Psychotherapy." PSYCHOLOGIA 1 (1958): 293-96.

Maintains that at the heart of psychotherapeutic experience
lies "an awesome hole," which is only adequately described in
Oriental literature. Unlike the West, the East views this
void as fertile and is, therefore, not feared. Eastern
religions, instead of filling the void with many actions and
objects, as the West does, explore it, and thus lead the
individual to a therapeutic change.

453.   Waggett, J. MacPhail. MENTAL, DIVINE, AND FAITH HEALING:
        THEIR EXPLANATION AND PLACE. Boston: Gorham Press, 1919.
        259 pp.

Investigates the various healing practices based on faith.
Physical, psychological, and psycho-physical symptoms which
are the object of faith healing are described and their
treatment examined. The author thinks that the efficacy of
mental therapy when associated with organic disorders has
often been exaggerated. Three faith healing organizations
are considered, namely: Christian Science, New Thought, and
the Emmanuel Movement. Christian Science uses hypnosis to
bring about cures; New Thought stresses hygiene and the need
to develop a composed and tranquil mind; while the Emmanuel
movement places the efficacy of its healing on moral and
mental grounds.

454.   Wallis, Wilson D. MESSIAHS: THEIR ROLE IN CIVILIZATION.
        Washington, DC: American Council on Public Affairs, 1943.
        217 pp.

Gives an account of many messiahs that have appeared in
the course of human history. Early concepts of the messiah
and its supernatural, cultural, and political aspects are
dealt with. Messiahs in different religious traditions
and cultures, including Western civilization and primitive
societies, are described. Though this book is essentially
historical, it contains the germ of a psychological explanation since the author thinks that messianic movements come
into being in times of cultural disintegration and provide
hope to those struggling to survive.

455.   Watts, Alan W. PSYCHOTHERAPY, EAST AND WEST. New York:
        Ballantine Books, 1961. xiii, 220 pp.

Discusses the relationship between Western psychotherapy and Eastern practices like Yoga and Zen which, though not psychotherapies in the strict sense of the word, bear certain resemblances. Many psychoanalytic principles are challenged. The author urges that Eastern disciplines be linked with those forms of Western psychotherapy whose philosophy is social, interpersonal, and communicational, rather than with those which stress the unconscious and its archetypes. The link between psychotherapy and liberation and the different ways the latter is conceived in Eastern traditions are described.

456. Whiteman, Luther, and Samuel L. Lewis. GLORY ROADS: THE PSYCHOLOGICAL STATE OF CALIFORNIA. New York: Thomas Crowell, 1936. x, 267 pp.

Records some of the better known sociopolitical crusades of the depression years and the messiahs who led the movements or "cults." The Utopian Society of America, Dr. Townsend Crusade, Technocracy, and Dr. Sinclair and his EPIC are all considered. The authors adopt a socioeconomic deprivation theory to explain these new movements.

457. Wilson, William P. "Mental Health Benefits of Religious Salvation." DISEASES OF THE NERVOUS SYSTEM 33 (1972): 382-86.

Investigates, in the context of the emergence of religious movements in the late 1960s, the effects of the experience of salvation on individuals who had never been treated for psychiatric disorders. A lengthy questionnaire, which included items relating to the behavioral changes after salvation, was administered to 63 white Protestant subjects whose conversion experiences had occurred an average 11 years before they were interrogated. The collected data shows that salvation experiences produce positive results not only on the individual's affective state, but also on his or her relationship to others. The fruits of salvation described by James--freedom from worry, happiness, clear perception of truth, and a new perception of the world--are confirmed.

458. Woollcott, Philip. "Some Consideration of Creativity and Religious Experiences in St. Augustine of Hippo." JOURNAL FOR THE SCIENTIFIC STUDY OF RELIGION 5 (1966): 273-83.

Considers the "Confessions" of Augustine using insights from psychoanalysis. While admitting that Augustine was a creative genius who contributed many psychological insights, the author gives a typical Freudian interpretation of his mental development, conscience, and conversion. Augustine is depicted as having unresolved oedipal conflicts and an overbearing superego. His conversion is an example of a crisis leading to the regressive state of childlike proximity till he finally came to terms with his intrapsychic battles and experienced a new energy and a sense of liberation.

459. Woollcott, Philip. "Erikson's Luther: A Psychiatrist's View." JOURNAL FOR THE SCIENTIFIC STUDY OF RELIGION 2 (1963): 243-48.

Evaluates Erikson's view of Luther and criticizes it for
explaining areas of psychological interest, like the reform-
er's propensity for earthy, crude prose, and neglecting
important achievements, like Luther's excellent translation
of the Bible. While commending Erikson's study, the author
is disappointed with his tendency to leave out emotionally
significant experiences which contributed to Luther's strength
and to dwell instead on those aspects of his life which appear
pathological.

460.   Zygmunt, Joseph F. "Movement and Motives: Some Unresolved
        Issues in the Psychology of Social Movements." HUMAN
        RELATIONS 25 (1972): 449-67.

        Evaluates the motivational analysis which aims at identi-
        fying the psychological factors which attract and sustain
        membership in social movements, among which he includes
        millenarian groups. It is maintained that motivational
        analysis should not be limited to a study of the recruit-
        ment process, but must be grounded in an adequate theory of
        alienation, attraction, conversion, and membership management.

D.   STUDIES ON PARTICULAR CULTS AND SECTS

The study of particular religious sects or cults, which preceded
the current debate on cultism, covers a variety of movements from
the Christian revivals to Eastern and occult practices. The Holy
Rollers, Christian Science, the Church of Father Divine, the
Hutterites and Mennonites, and the Seventh-Day Adventists are among
the Christian groups explored. Buddhist and Japanese religions,
including various forms of meditation and Hindu practices, like
Yoga, start receiving some public attention in the 1960s.

The literature dealing with the effects of religion in general
and the studies on specific cults is divided about the psychological impact of religious beliefs and practices. One trend of
thought takes a definite stand against cultism. Revival meetings
are often frowned upon as expressions of hysteria and schizophrenia.
People who are attracted to them are under stress and maladjusted.
It is their pathology which makes them so responsive to such cultic
behavior. Their problems are often aggravated by the beliefs and
practices of the cult. Thus, the church founded by Father Divine has
bad effects on the social life of its members. Its members suffer
from benign psychosis. Because fear was a much stressed theme in
this group, those studying it concluded that becoming a member either
created psychological problems or else aggravated existing ones.
Glossolalia, common among many Christian sects, is an infantile
babble which, occurring in adults, is indicative of epilepsy, hysteria, or a state of personal disintegration.

Eastern religions are also at times looked upon suspiciously.
Buddhism openly denies the existence of reality and is, therefore,
conducive to pathology. The Buddhist monastic life aims at the

repression of all emotional life, which is unhealthy, while the quest for Nirvana is sadistic and narcissistic. Practices of meditation, Zen in particular, induce a state of trance, during which a person can readily succumb to a psychotic state. Zen is dangerous because it renders a sick person unresponsive to therapy.

Involvement in occult practices is also subjected to a negative psychological evaluation. Members of occult groups frequently suffer from schizophrenia and/or hysteria. Astrology is dangerous because it leads a person to give up one's responsibility and free will. It inculcates a blind determinism which causes fear and anxiety. Students of past European witchcraft practices see them not as an expression of genuine religious feelings, but rather as a manifest example of pathological behavior.

The literature covered in this chapter, however, is far from a general condemnation of sects and cults as signs or causes of pathology. On the contrary, the tendency to see positive results coming out of involvement in these religious movements is widespread. Those revival movements, which stress physical and psychological healing, often make a healthy contribution to those who become committed. The Emmanuel Movement, for example, healed psychosomatic problems; it could be regarded as a psychotherapy by suggestion and hypnosis. Many Pentecostal groups, even though they may be accused of fostering narrow-mindedness and regression, provide a context in which people can actually solve their problems. Conversion to the charismatic movement has produced impressive records of people who attribute to it their overcoming of alcoholism, or their rehabilitation from drug abuse, or the solution to their marital problems. Their tongue-speaking, far from being an expression of their pathological state, can be a source of strength and security which often brings about beneficial attitudinal and behavioral changes. It offers emotional release, lessens depression, and gives a sense of self-worth. The community life nurtured by many of the new movements, Christian or otherwise, is a source of emotional comfort, physical support, and mental balance. It further mitigates or resolves personality conflicts.

Eastern religious practices, particularly Zen meditation and Yoga, which became increasingly the subject of research from the late 1960s onwards, are considered to be forms of psychotherapy. Zen meditation is a means of acquiring a balanced and stable frame of mind. It fosters creativity and intuition and helps a person relate well to others. Yoga, a form of analytic therapy, is based on a well-developed Indian psychology that contains the principles for mental healing. The early studies of Transcendental Meditation concluded that its practice reduces stress and is conducive to a healthy personality. Eastern practices lessen the strains and worries brought about by modern technological society and help the individual come to grips with personality problems. They are attempts to probe the unconscious and should, therefore, be looked upon as comparable to modern psychiatric therapies developed in the West. They could, consequently, be profitably applied as alternatives or supplements to psychoanalysis.

Occult practices can also be evaluated in the same positive way. Astrology can promote different, and novel, interpersonal relationships. Involvement in the occult may be a way of coping with adversity. Even such obscure behavior as water-witching can reduce anxiety in situations where the control of the environment is not in human hands.

The deprivation theory is occasionally used to explain the rise and success of new movements. Many sociologists and social psychologists believe that the source of cultism is to be found in economic, social, educational, or religious dissatisfaction. Cults thrive on unfulfilled needs. They attract those people whose condition is unsatisfying and who are, consciously or not, ready for a change. Implicit in this theory is the view that the new movements offer some relief, even if the needs are not really met. The cults are, therefore, not seen as a problem, but rather as a temporary solution. Those who join these groups may have serious psychological problems which are not, however, caused by the cults, but rather by the cultural and/or religious situations experienced prior to their cultic involvement. This theory of deprivation is not universally accepted. It has been discussed at length in anthropological literature where it has been often adopted as a useful theory to account for the rise of various movements in non-literate societies. When analyzed in some depth it exhibits several weaknesses. Since there are many people who find the same needs satisfied in the religion of their upbringing, and many others who simply abandon all form of religious belief and practice, the theory leaves unanswered the question of why is it that a relative minority end-up joining a cult. It is, further, much too general to help us understand the presence of so many different religious innovations. Several generic human needs are lumped together and we are left in the dark as to what needs are satisfied by which cultic features. The theory, moreover, opts for a purely functional definition of religion which can be equally applied to other cultural elements, such as politics. Economic, political, educational, and social deprivations have, in fact, been proposed as explanations for the emergence of cults. The reason why the deprivation theory is popular among scholars is partly due to the fact that it is basically a utilitarian explanation. Its central thesis is that people in trouble find ways, consciously or not, to overcome crises and adapt to better and happier living conditions.

The literature on individual cults is far from huge. In-depth studies on one specific sect or denomination are relatively rare. The early debate on the cults or sects was conducted on a much lower key than the current exchanged among scholars. But the two polarized views, similar to those described in the Introduction, of what cults are and what effects they have on their members, are already evident.

461. Aikman, D. "The Holy Rollers." AMERICAN MERCURY 15 (1928): 180-91.

Provides a rather derisive description of the emotional meetings of the Holy Rollers and traces their roots to John

Wesley "who grandsired the modern cult" (p. 183). Disagreements within Methodism eventually led to the mitigation of its more extreme manifestations, like speaking in tongues and healing, causing the movement to split into many groups. The sects that expressed their beliefs in emotionally charged worship services became known as the Holy Rollers, some members of which need psychiatric treatment.

462.   Akishige, Yoshiharu. "A Historical Survey of the Psychological Studies of Zen." PSYCHOLOGICAL STUDIES ON ZEN (item 463), pp. 1-56.

Surveys studies on Zen in several areas: theoretical issues on the nature of Zen; the role of the Zen master; the practice of regulating one's body, breath, and mind; the process of Zen meditation and its effects; and Zen and psychotherapy. The author holds that Zen has the power of releasing the individual from many desires that torment him or her, with the result that freedom and enlightenment are reached. Zen contains the "principle of mental equilibrium" (p. 52). It leads to a balanced and stable mental state where suffering and anxiety are not felt. A lengthy bibliography of English articles published in Japanese journals is included.

463.   Akishige, Yoshiharu, editor. PSYCHOLOGICAL STUDIES ON ZEN. Fukuoka, Japan: The Faculty of Literature of Kyushu University, 1968. 280 pp.

Contains several physiological and psychological studies on Zen theory and practice.

Contains items 462, 540.

464.   Alexander, F. "Buddhist Training as an Artificial Catatonia." PSYCHOANALYTIC REVIEW 18 (1931): 129-45.

Views the ascetic training of Buddhist monks as an unhealthy suppression of all emotional life. The four steps to Nirvana, from the psychiatric point of view, are: 1) a sadistic, self-induced melancholy; 2) narcissism; 3) a diminution of the feeling of pleasure; and 4) a complete mental emptiness and uniformity. The Buddhist method is close to psychoanalysis in its striving to understand the unconscious. The main difference is that while Buddhism denies reality, psychoanalysis tries to adjust to it.

465.   Alland, Alexander. "'Possession' in a Revivalist Negro Church." JOURNAL FOR THE SCIENTIFIC STUDY OF RELIGION 1 (1962): 204-13.

A study of trance behavior in the United House for All People, a Black revivalist Christian Church founded by C. C. Sweet in the 1920s. The people's behavior during trance is described and the attempts of those "seeking" their first experience is outlined. The author rejects two common interpretations of trance which explain the phenomenon as a

hysterical or schizophrenic state. The theory that extreme
economic and psychological deprivation leads people to join
groups which stress trance experiences is also found wanting.
The author supports the view that trance is a form of hypnosis
which, in turn, is a form of regression in the service of the
ego.

466.   Alpert, Richard. "Baba Ram Das Lecture at the Menninger
        Foundation." JOURNAL OF TRANSPERSONAL PSYCHOLOGY 2.2
        (1970): 91-139.

        Transcribes a taped lecture of psychologist Alpert--turned
        Eastern guru. Various aspects of Buddhism, like the use of
        mantras, are discussed. Speaking from his experiences in the
        East, Alpert argues in favor of the psychotherapeutic use of
        Eastern religious practices.

467.   Ames, Van Meter. "William James and Zen." PSYCHOLOGIA 2
        (1955): 114-19.

        Shows how James's study on religion had much in common with
        Zen thought, especially with the stress on experience. The
        philosophy of James, like that of Zen, had a practical dimen-
        sion. The author seems to support the view that Zen could be
        used therapeutically.

468.   Anant, Santokh Singh. "Integrity Therapy and the Sikh Reli-
        gion." INSIGHT: QUARTERLY REVIEW OF RELIGION AND MENTAL
        HEALTH 5.1 (1966): 22-29.

        Describes the theory behind O. W. Mowrer's Integrity Therapy
        and its relation to basic morality, stressed particularly in
        the Sikh religion. The importance of adhering to moral and
        social values, the exercise of self-control, and the adoption
        of a simple life-style, all of which are exemplified in the
        Sikh community, are significant factors contributing to mental
        health since they not only cure mental illness, but also pre-
        vent it.

469.   Anderson, Robert D. "The History of Witchcraft: A Review with
        Some Psychiatric Comments." AMERICAN JOURNAL OF PSYCHIATRY
        126 (1970): 1727-35.

        Offers a psychological perspective of witchcraft and satan-
        ism as they developed in Western Europe until the witch
        trials of the seventeenth century. The author thinks that
        individual and group dynamics can explain the delusion of
        witchcraft. He maintains that the inclusion of perverse
        sexuality in the accusation against witches as well as the
        sadistic and aggressive reaction to them by the general
        public should also be taken into account. He also offers
        speculation on the illnesses (schizophrenia, hysteria, and
        delusional psychosis, in particular) which afflicted the
        accused witches (or satanists). To what degree his comments
        apply to the revival of satanism in the 1970s is a subject
        for debate.

470. Anonymous. "The Nervous Epidemic Connected With the Religious
      Revival in Ireland." AMERICAN JOURNAL OF INSANITY 16 (1986):
      356-58.

      Interprets the physical phenomena accompanying revivals as
      manifestations of catalepsy or epileptic seizures, which
      usually occur among people "of a low grade of intelligence."
      Among more intelligent people, revivals result in developed
      hallucinations, fanatical persuasions, and exotic beliefs,
      as is the case among the Millerites and spiritualists. Such
      physiological expressions are related to spiritual illumina-
      tion only incidentally. The author seems to assert that
      religious revivals are purely psychological phenomena.

471. Assagioli, Roberto. PSYCHOSYNTHESIS: A MANUAL OF PRINCIPLES
      AND TECHNIQUES. New York: Viking, 1965. xii, 323 pp.

      Propounds an existential method of psychotherapy which
      brings together various techniques, including meditation. The
      methods for personal, spiritual, and interpersonal psycho-
      therapy are described in detail.

472. Austin, Mary. ACUPUNCTURE THERAPY. New York: ASI Publishers,
      Inc., 1972. x, 290 pp.

      Presents a teaching guide for those studying the theory and
      practice of Chinese acupuncture. The book is divided into
      five parts, dealing respectively with: 1) organ meridians
      (i.e., peripheral energy paths) and the twelve pulses; 2) the
      five elements and acupuncture techniques; 3) organ meridians
      and factors of time; 4) the vessel meridians; and 5) acupunc-
      ture therapy. It is assumed throughout that physical, mental,
      and emotional disorders interact and that, therefore, acu-
      puncture is a system for treating both physical and psycholog-
      ical problems. The author maintains that though acupuncture
      is not to be taken as an alternative to psychoanalysis in all
      cases, its judicious use "can serve as an extremely useful
      technique for bringing about much more rapid results without
      torment and with great predictability" (p. 268). Anorexia,
      anxiety, depression, and general psychopathy are among the
      psychological disorders which can be successfully submitted
      to acupuncture treatment.

473. Bagchi, B. K. "Mental Hygiene and the Hindu Doctrine of
      Relaxation." MENTAL HYGIENE 20 (1936): 424-40.

      Admits that relaxation is a combined psychological and
      physiological process and that the Hindu view, while it has
      to be considered in relation to its geographical and cultural
      setting, contains some yogic techniques that are hygienically
      of value for all people. The practical stages are then dis-
      cussed: 1) the attitude of relaxation; 2) the relaxation of
      the mind; 3) relaxation through ideation; and 4) relaxation
      through uni-dimensional attention, which includes yogic breath-
      ing exercises. The author feels that the Western world can
      supplement its psychiatric, psychological, and medical methods
      by looking at some Indian theories and practices.

474.   Battle, Allen O. "Psychotherapy through Transcendence--Zen."
        INSIGHT: INTERDISCIPLINARY STUDIES OF MAN 6.3 (1968): 6-10.

        Explores Zen as a psychotherapy which aims not only to free
        patients from their problems but also to help them reach
        transcendence. Though insight cannot be given, one can pro-
        vide ways to it. It is necessary for a person to experience
        anxiety before he or she can acquire any of the higher states
        of awareness. Zen meditation assists an individual in deal-
        ing with one's own self and with the human condition.

475.   Becker, Ernest. "The Central Psychologic Role of Trace in
        'Zen Therapy.'" AMERICAN JOURNAL OF PSYCHOTHERAPY 15
        (1961): 645-51.

        Maintains that Zen brings about its psychotherapeutic
        change not by healing the individual, but by distorting his or
        her perspective through magical, self-hypnotic trance experi-
        ences. The partially negative psychoanalytic view of trance
        is presented and the place of trance in Zen practice, its use
        in Zen archery, and its place in conversion are all covered.
        Both forms of Zen, Soto and Rinzai, use various kinds of
        trance-inducing devices which can be traced to ancient
        psychologies of magical manipulation. Zen, in the author's
        opinion, places obstacles in the therapeutic situation and
        is fraught with dangers.

476.   Becker, Ernest. ZEN: A RATIONAL CRITIQUE. New York: Morton
        and Co., 1961. 192 pp.

        Examines the similarity between Zen practice and some
        important psychoanalytic techniques and crises, especially
        the frustration in the patient-therapist relationships, the
        resolution of ambivalence to authority figures, the careful
        weaning of patients from dependence on their respective
        analyst, and the final freedom of the patient from a con-
        stricting life-style. It is maintained that inducing trance
        is part of Zen training and is the basic psychological focus
        in the convert to Zen Buddhism. The trance state can provide
        an experience of reality distortion and a withdrawal from
        self, an experience which is parallel to the psychotic state.
        The ability to go into a trance also conveys a sense of power.
        The author discusses Zen and thought reform in the context
        of Chinese techniques and argues that oriental conversion
        therapies attain their maximum effectiveness by inducing the
        person to self-manipulation. Several reflections on the
        psychotherapeutic meeting of Eastern and Western traditions
        are offered.

477.   Becker, Ernest. "Psychotherapeutic Observations on the Zen
        Discipline: One Point of View." PSYCHOLOGIA 3 (1960):
        100-12.

        Criticizes the trend to equate Zen with psychoanalysis
        (particularly Stunkard's view, item 601). In Zen the close
        master-disciple relationship, the extreme authoritarian

poise of the master, and the apparently deep transference
that occurs create a dependency and an ambivalence which
therapy does not easily remove. Fromm is taken to task for
relying too much on the attraction of Zen values as ideal,
with little reflection on whether these values can be
achieved. An important difference between psychoanalysis
and Zen is that the former, unlike the latter, uses logic and
causal thinking throughout the process of therapy. Without
denying the possible healing potential of Zen, the author
states that "the two methods, Zen and psychoanalysis, cannot
possibly lead to the same end" (p. 110).

478. Ben-Avi, Aurum. "Zen Buddhism." AMERICAN HANDBOOK OF PSY-
      CHIATRY (item 3), vol. 2, pp. 1802-10.

      Deals with those central qualities of Zen which are related
      to the psychotherapeutic process. The following qualities of
      Zen are judged to be important: immediacy, concreteness,
      intensity, dedication, overwhelming tension, radicalism, and
      abruptness of experience, and the collaboration between the
      master and the disciple. A number of similarities between
      Zen and modern psychiatry are noted.

479. Bender, Lauretta, and M. A. Spaulding. "Behavior Problems in
      Children from the Homes of the Followers of Father Divine."
      JOURNAL OF NERVOUS AND MENTAL DISEASE 91 (1940): 460-472.

      Attempts to evaluate the effect of the teachings of Father
      Divine on the lives of the children of his followers. Eight
      case studies are recorded. The author thinks that Father
      Divine's teaching on family relationships led to the neglect
      of children by their parents with consequent physical and
      emotional deprivation. Because Father Divine's teachings
      attacked heterosexuality and family ties, children tended to
      experience difficulties, particularly with regard to their
      sexual identity. The net result is that many of them became
      asocial and needed institutionalized or supervised care.

480. Bender, Lauretta, and Zuleika Yarrell. "Psychosis Among
      Followers of Father Divine." JOURNAL OF NERVOUS AND MENTAL
      DISEASE 87 (1938): 419-49.

      Describes the condition of 18 devotees of Father Divine who
      were accepted in Bellevue Hospital, New York, for treatment
      while in a highly emotional or hysterical state. Most were
      diagnosed as suffering from psychosis which might have been
      precipitated or elicited by their involvement with the move-
      ment. Their search for a religious experience was an escape
      from unbearable problems. The authors judge the cases studied
      to be examples of "benign psychoses" (p. 446).

481. Benoit, Hubert. THE SUPREME DOCTRINE: PSYCHOLOGICAL STUDIES
      IN ZEN THOUGHT. New York: Pantheon, 1955. 248 pp.

      Starts by assuming that it is possible to improve our knowl-
      edge of what the human person is and then to radically alter

our natural state. The mechanism of anxiety, Zen unconscious-
ness, and metaphysical distress are dealt with. According to
the author, Zen throws light on these human problems and
provides means for coping with them effectively.

482.   Berger, Emmanuel. "Zen Buddhism, General Psychology, and
        Counseling Psychology." JOURNAL OF COUNSELING PSYCHOLOGY
        9 (1962): 122-27.

        After explaining how Zen aims at direct and intuitive
        experience by discouraging dualistic thought, subject-object
        relation, and attachment to form, the author states that Zen
        is psychologically relevant because it fosters creativity
        and intuition, both of which improve one's psychic skills.
        Moreover, Zen meditation can have an impact on counseling
        because it teaches one to look at the counselee as a person
        and to relate to him/her in a more profound way. Zen is thus
        useful both in the training of counselors and in the practice
        of therapy.

483.   Bergsma, Stuart. SPEAKING WITH TONGUES. Grand Rapids, MI:
        Baker Book House, 1965. 26 pp.

        Gives a brief introductory account of glossolalia in the
        New Testament and in the early church, considers the physio-
        logical elements relative to the phenomenon, and suggests
        that cybernetics can help us understand this. The various
        psychological factors involved are discussed and the motiva-
        tions which give rise to speaking in tongues are considered.
        The author maintains that glossolalia is "a pathological
        condition, a neurotic condition, in which anxieties are gone,
        the burdens and cares of this world banished" (p. 18).
        Modern glossolalia is not the same as the experience of speak-
        ing tongues in the early church and can be physiologically and
        psychologically explained.

484.   Bernard, Theos. HEAVEN LIES WITHIN US. New York: Scribner's
        Sons, 1939. xiv, 326 pp.

        Relates the author's initial interest in the practice of
        Yoga and his search in India leading to his final initiation.
        Relatively routine descriptions of the different stages of
        Yoga, the rules of those who seriously practice it, and the
        various postures and meditative techniques are provided.
        Yoga, it is argued, leads to bodily and mental health, and
        contributes to the growth in knowledge and the extension of
        life.

485.   Billings, R. A. "The Negro and His Church: A Psychogenetic
        Study." PSYCHOANALYTIC REVIEW 21 (1934): 425-41.

        Distinguishes American Black Christian churches according
        to three general types: those attended by lower-class, middle-
        class, and upper-class people, respectively. The church
        gatherings of lower-class Blacks are mechanisms of escape

and compensation for feelings of inadequacy, inferiority, and
deprivation, and provide various outlets for pent-up sexual
energies and expressions of sexual conflicts. Middle-class
churches provide a relief to their better educated and more
economically secure members who cannot attend ordinary amuse-
ment places. Church rituals repress the desire for prohibited
pleasures and act as an adequate substitution and rationalization. Finally, upper-class church members, who feel more
akin to the whites, are the most embittered and cynical of
all groups. Their church rituals ease their troubles and
offer an escape from the lower condition of their black
brethren. The religiosity of black people "has developed as
an adaptive reaction to definite environmental situations"
(p. 440).

486.   Blair, Margaret. "Meditation in the San Francisco Bay Area:
       An Introductory Survey." JOURNAL OF TRANSPERSONAL PSYCHOL-
       OGY 2.1 (1970): 61-70.

       Finds that both classic and new forms of meditation are
       flourishing in the Bay Area. Courses and classes are offered
       in many meditation centers. The conclusions reached are that
       meditation has taken a firm hold of this particular section
       of the country and that it may be used effectively in therapy.

487.   Boisen, Anton T. "Economic Distress and Religious Experi-
       ence: A Study of the Holy Rollers." PSYCHIATRY 2 (1939):
       185-94.

       Admits that there are some similarities between the beliefs
       and experiences of the Holy Rollers and mental patients, but
       affirms that there is a major difference in that the former,
       unlike the latter, are able to carry out their daily work
       without breaking down psychologically. The experiences of
       the majority of the Holy Rollers are constructive in that
       they help people reorganize their lives and face daily dif-
       ficulties more hopefully. This positive effect is ascribed
       to social influences which are absent in the environment of
       the mentally ill. It is, however, concluded that pentecostal-
       type churches, because of their eccentricity and repressive-
       ness, may cause serious psychological problems to their
       members.

488.   Boisen, Anton T. "Religion and Hard Times: A Study of the
       Holy Rollers." SOCIAL ACTION 5 (March 1939): 8-35.

       Reflects on the growth of the particular branch of Holiness
       Churches called the Holy Rollers because during their worship
       services their members exhibit such abnormal manifestations as
       dancing, jerking, falling on the floor, and going into trance
       states. The way these sects come into being, their source of
       membership, the content of their preaching, and the experiences
       they value are all accounted for. The author thinks that
       these sects are largely confined to the disinherited class
       and that they thrive in hard economic times, but that their

growth should not be related to mental disorder. Pentecostal
churches are eccentric and aggressive and their belief that
God is manifested in the unusual is, according to the author,
"highly dangerous" and found also among mentally ill people.
Some constructive elements are seen in these beliefs and
practices since the major focus is on healing those who are
spiritually sick.

489.   Boisen, Anton T. "The Holy Rollers Come to Town." CHICAGO
        THEOLOGICAL SEMINARY REGISTER 29 (January 1939): 5-8.

        Comments on the increase of enthusiasm among Pentecostal
        sects which have been successful among the socioeconomically
        depressed working class. Both cultural and religious factors
        are adduced to explain the rise of these sects. Pentecostal
        churches are, in the author's view, eccentric, fundamentalist,
        and regressive. Their belief that the divine is prompting
        their behavior is dangerous since it is found also among the
        mentally disturbed. They are criticized for their lack of
        social vision and for their inability to promise social
        salvation. Their narrow world view is bound to have a nega-
        tive influence on their children's development. They do
        have, however, some constructive features: the quest for a
        mystical experience, the expression of religious fervor, and
        the attempts at spiritual healing which bring hope, courage,
        and strength to many.

490.   Bourdreau, Leonce. "Transcendental Meditation and Yoga as
        Reciprocal Inhibitors." JOURNAL OF BEHAVIOR THERAPY AND
        EXPERIMENTAL PSYCHIATRY 3 (1972): 97-98.

        Shows briefly how two patients, one suffering from claus-
        trophobia, the other from profuse perspiration, responded to
        TM and Yoga when attempts at systematic desensitization had
        been only partially successful.

491.   Boyd, Thomas Parker. THE HOW AND WHY OF THE EMMANUEL MOVE-
        MENT: A HANDBOOK OF PSYCHO-THERAPEUTICS. San Francisco:
        The Whitaker and Ray Co., 1909. xvi, 143 pp.

        Gives an account of the healing techniques of the Emmanuel
        Movement with the aim of instructing people how they could
        use them alone or in cooperation with a physician or clergy-
        man. The author believes that the healings performed by
        Christ and the apostles justify the practices of this
        religious group. Several healing methods, like hypnotism,
        suggestion, and personal magnetism, are described. It is
        argued that the Emmanuel Movement offers a kind of psycho-
        therapy to be used mainly in psychosomatic illness.

492.   Brodie, Fawn M. NO MAN KNOWS MY HISTORY: THE LIFE OF JOSEPH
        SMITH, THE MORMON PROPHET. New York: Alfred Knopf, second
        edition, 1971. ix, 476 pp.

        Examines the contradictory documents relative to Smith's
        life in an attempt to draw a historical sketch of the founder

of Mormonism. Smith was both a religious and a political
leader. He was an ambitious and authoritarian dictator with
an army, a propaganda ministry, and a secret police. He is
depicted as a mythmaker and an impostor. The bibliography
contains his writings, the court records, various manuscripts,
and Mormon newspapers.

493. Bullock, F. W. B. EVANGELICAL CONVERSIONS IN GREAT BRITAIN,
      1696-1845. St. Leonards on Sea, Sussex, UK: Budd and
      Gillatt, 1959. xi, 287 pp.

      Presents a historical and psychological study of the con-
      version experiences of 30 converts in Great Britain, includ-
      ing John Wesley. Their pre-conversion backgrounds, their
      times of crises, and their post-conversion states are care-
      fully analyzed. Special conscious and unconscious features
      which characterized these conversions, like dreams, visions,
      and voices, are also considered. The value and validity of
      the experience of conversion are discussed in the light of
      the major psychological studies on religious experience (see,
      for example, items 118, 144, 180).

494. Cantril, Hadley, and Muzafa Sherif. "The Kingdom of Father
      Divine." JOURNAL OF ABNORMAL AND SOCIAL PSYCHOLOGY 33
      (1938): 147-67.

      Describes briefly the movement and points out the factors
      which created and maintained its world view. Father Divine's
      hypnotic power and the fear he instilled in his disciples
      acted as a powerful deterrent to defection. Three main
      reasons are brought forth to account for the early success
      of this cult: 1) it offered an escape from material hardships;
      2) it made life meaningful to its members; and 3) it raised
      the social status of its members. The cult was an escape
      mechanism for the weak, the powerless, and the ignorant.
      Because of the great fear instilled in its members, the cult
      was partly responsible for their psychological problems.

495. Carrigan, Robert L. "The Revival of Astrology. Its Impli-
      cations for Pastoral Care." PASTORAL PSYCHOLOGY 21 (Decem-
      ber 1970): 7-14.

      Considers the rise of interest in astrology as a new reli-
      gion and expresses surprise that in a scientific age people
      would dabble in magic. Possible reasons for this interest
      are examined. Several positive signs of astrology are out-
      lined: it helps people cope with adversities, fulfills the
      need to tune into a sense of the cosmos, presents a way of
      breaking out of one's social roles and games, develops novel
      ways of interpersonal relationships, and offers an alterna-
      tive to the ordered, predetermined, and logical system of
      Western thought and action. Three psychological dangers are
      mentioned: 1) the tendency to give up personal responsibility;
      2) the retreat from admitting failure in personal relation-
      ships; and 3) a fatalistic determinism which may encourage
      fear and anxiety. It is questioned whether astrology is an

expression of some unlimited fantasy about life and human
relationship and whether those seriously involved in
astrology are escaping from reality.

496.   Chaffee, Grace E. "The Isolated Religious Sect as an Object
        for Social Research." AMERICAN JOURNAL OF SOCIOLOGY 35
        (1930): 618-30.

        Examines the Amana Society, a communal group in Iowa. Its
        historical roots in German mysticism and pietism are traced.
        Though the author's main interest is the social aspects of
        the institution, he observes that the community is well-
        organized, and its members are calm and somewhat phlegmatic.
        The psychological effects of membership are beneficial since
        the "conflicts of personality which characterize American
        life even in conventional gestures are absent" (p. 629).

497.   Chuang, Yu-min. CHINESE ACUPUNCTURE. New York: Oriental
        Society, 1972. 283 pp.

        A manual of acupuncture, giving a short account of its
        origin and development and its theoretical basis, and de-
        scribing at length the points of treatment and the various
        diseases for which it can be applied. Though stressing the
        cure of physical illnesses, the author includes neurasthenia
        and hysteria as conditions for which acupuncture can be
        successfully used.

498.   Clark, Robert A. "Theosophical Occultism and Mental Hygiene."
        PSYCHIATRY 7 (1944); 237-43.

        Discusses occult groups like the Theosophical Society,
        Anthroposophy, Rosicrucianism, and the I Am Society, all of
        which fulfill many normal human needs, especially by supply-
        ing an opportunity for leadership to aggressive personalities.
        In general, occult groups propound irrational and unscien-
        tific doctrines and tend to foster the abnormal. They may
        precipitate such illnesses as schizophrenia and hysteria.
        Cults, however, should not be suppressed, but rather combated
        by education and possibly by legal action.

499.   Coster, Geraldine. YOGA AND WESTERN PSYCHOLOGY: A COMPARI-
        SON. London: Oxford University Press, 1934. 248 pp.

        Gives an account of analytical therapy and of the basic
        principles of Pantajali's Yoga. She finds a basis for com-
        parison in the yogist's state of confused perception and the
        mental and emotional condition of the analyst's subject. Yoga
        is a method of mind development which is quite as practical
        as analytical therapy. While the ideas of Yoga are univer-
        sally true for all people, Yoga techniques are not very
        suitable to Western life and temperament.

500.   Cunningham, Raymond J. "The Emmanuel Movement: A Variety of
        American Religious Experience." AMERICAN QUARTERLY 14
        (Spring 1962): 48-63.

Provides a short account of the rise of the Emmanuel Movement which was, according to the author, an attempt by some Episcopal clergymen and sympathetic physicians to stem the tide of healing cults like Christian Science. The Emmanuel Movement was a psychotherapeutic endeavor, bringing together several intellectual trends of the nineteenth century, including the new psychology. Its practitioners confined their treatment largely to functional disorders, though some tried to improve the mental and moral disposition of patients suffering from essentially organic ailments. The author's view seems to be that the church's practice of treating psychosomatic illnesses enjoyed a measure of success.

501. Cutten, George Barton. SPEAKING IN TONGUES: HISTORICALLY AND PSYCHOLOGICALLY CONSIDERED. New Haven: Yale University Press, 1927. xii, 193 pp.

Provides a historical overview of the phenomenon of speaking in tongues from the New Testament to the present. Its presence in various sects, like the Quakers, the Mormons, and the Irvingites, and several of its manifestations in the United States and elsewhere at the beginning of the twentieth century are described. Several cases are presented to show that non-religious types of glossolalia can also occur. From a psychological point of view, glossolalia is related to the experience of ecstasy which could be a form of catalepsy, hysteria, or hypnosis and is a state of personal disintegration. The author doesn't look favorably on glossolalia. "Those who speak with tongues are almost without exception devout, but ignorant and illiterate people" (p. 168).

502. Dai, Bingham. "Zen and Psychotherapy." RELIGIOUS SYSTEMS OF PSYCHOTHERAPY (item 1021), pp. 132-41.

Argues that Zen and psychotherapy have a common objective, namely, to enable individuals to enjoy the benefits of society and culture while living a full, creative, and spontaneous life, free from anxiety. Human nature, the genesis of human suffering, the methods used to alleviate pain, and the way that Zen and psychotherapy can learn from each other are considered. Both find narcissism to be the most important source of neurotic anxiety. Both claim that the capacity of altruistic love is the essential source of emotional health and strength. Zen's concept of selflessness, its style of meditation, and its stress on intuition are indispensable for therapy.

503. Danielou, Alain. YOGA: THE METHOD OF RE-INTEGRATION. New York: University Books, 1955. 164 pp.

Essentially a description of the different kinds of Yoga as ways of reintegration through strength (Hatha), through action (karma), through knowledge (jnana), through love (bhakti), and through the awakening of energy (kundalini). Though the relation of Yoga to psychological well-being is not brought up,

it is assumed throughout that Yoga leads to self-development
and self-realization, freeing those who practice it from both
physical and psychological illnesses. The yogi, the author
states, is like the psychiatrist who goes straight to the
root of the most powerful human instincts.

504. Deikman, Arthur J. "Implications of Experimentally Induced
     Contemplative Meditation." JOURNAL OF NERVOUS AND MENTAL
     DISEASE 142 (1966): 101-10.

     Tests the claims in both Eastern and Western mystical
     literature that contemplative meditation leads to the highest
     form of human experience. The author builds on his previous
     experiment (item 505) and discusses the perceptual phenomena
     of light, force, and motion of the meditator as he or she
     progresses from one meditation session to another. The var-
     ious internal stimuli, suggestion, projection, dreaming, and
     the hypnagogic state (i.e., a regression into autosyllabic
     thinking) are considered. The author thinks that the exper-
     imental data can be explained by postulating a process of
     "sensory translation" in which conflict repression, problem
     solving, and attention are seen through the sensation of
     light, color, and taste. The procedure of deautomatization,
     conceived as a liberating process, which takes place in medi-
     tation, and its implications are discussed. Perceptual ex-
     pansion is held to be one of the main beneficial results of
     the practice of meditation.

505. Deikman, Arthur J. "Experimental Meditation." JOURNAL OF
     NERVOUS AND MENTAL DISEASE 136 (1963): 329-43.

     Draws up and tests the following three hypotheses on medi-
     tation practice: 1) contemplative meditation is the main
     agent in producing mystical experience; 2) it leads to the
     creation of psychic barriers to distracting stimuli; and 3)
     the mystic experience is a partial deautomatization of the
     psychic structures that produce a different perception of
     stimuli. The experiments confirm the first and third hypoth-
     eses, while subjective reports support the second. Deauto-
     matization of one's perception and affective and cognitive
     controls is not a regression, but a change of pattern which
     permits a new and perhaps better experience and which may
     lead to a creative synthesis and to personal growth.

506. Devereux, George, editor. PSYCHOANALYSIS AND THE OCCULT.
     New York: International Universities Press, 1953. xv,
     432 pp.

     Contains 31 essays discussing various psychoanalytic inter-
     pretations of clinical data relating to occult phenomena
     including telepathy, premonition, extra sensory perception,
     and prophetic experiences. Six of Freud's relevant works on
     the subject and several studies by pioneers of psychoanalysis
     are included. While there seems to be no official psycho-
     analytic attitude to psi phenomena, this selection indicates
     a trend to interpret the occult in terms of transference and
     counter-transference.

507. DeVoto, Bernard. "The Centennial of Mormonism." AMERICAN
      MERCURY 19 (January 1930): 1-13.

      Attempts to explain why, out of so many new religious
      movements, Mormonism was the most successful. Its founder,
      Joseph Smith, is described as a despotic paranoid with the
      ability to command allegiance from his followers. He also
      experienced auditory hallucinations and had delusions of
      grandeur and persecution. Mormonism "originated among
      illiterate offscourings of the frontier; it has recruited
      always from the ignorant and bankrupt" (p. 12).

508. Dimond, Sydney G. THE PSYCHOLOGY OF THE METHODIST REVIVAL:
      AN EMPIRICAL AND DESCRIPTIVE STUDY. London: Oxford
      University Press, 1926. 296 pp.

      Sketches, mainly from memoirs and letters, the features of
      English society in Wesley's time and indicates those political
      and social events which influenced the rise of Methodism. The
      character and personality of John Wesley are depicted from the
      point of view of behaviorism and in relation to the psychology
      of sentiments. The revival is explained in terms of crowd
      psychology and of primary instincts. Several chapters are
      devoted to discussion of the psychological factors involved
      in conversion. The psychological features of Methodism are
      surveyed. It is maintained that "psychoanalysis contributes
      to the understanding of the pathological element in Wesley's
      conversion" (p. 95). Through his conversion, an experience
      of normal human nature, he overcame his conflicts and achieved
      mental harmony.

509. Eaton, Joseph W., and Robert J. Weil. CULTURE AND MENTAL
      DISORDER: A COMPARATIVE STUDY OF THE HUTTERITES AND OTHER
      POPULATIONS. Glencoe, IL: Free Press, 1955. 254 pp.

      Provides an in-depth study of whether cultural, social, and
      religious variables affect mental states. The Hutterites are
      chosen as a laboratory group because, while living in a modern
      technological society, they have kept themselves sufficiently
      apart from it to form an autonomous subculture. Incidences
      of psychosis, psychoneurosis, mental deficiency, epilepsy,
      and personality disorders are the main areas explored. The
      ways in which the Hutterites themselves identify, explain,
      and deal with members who have mental problems are described.
      Compared with modern psychiatric treatments, the Hutterite
      methods, seen in the context of their own faith, are judged
      to be effective and future-oriented, even though they stress
      repression. Hutterite psychiatry can be effective only for
      those who accept the whole value system. While the authors
      found many psychological stresses in the sect members, they
      also observed that these were ameliorated by the communal
      practices which encouraged those mentally disturbed people
      to get well and to function in a socially accepted manner.
      Religion gives the Hutterites a great sense of security,
      but also creates many feelings of guilt.

510. Eaton, Joseph W., and Robert J. Weil. "The Mental Health of
      the Hutterites." SCIENTIFIC AMERICAN 189.6 (December 1953):
      31-37.

      Reports on a three-year study of this isolated Anabaptist
      sect. Hutterite culture, the author found, does not provide
      immunity from mental disorders. Because of the greater need
      to live up to social expectations, the incidence of manic-
      depression was higher than that of schizophrenia. Antisocial
      and aggressive impulses are effectively repressed through
      adherence to social norms. The Hutterites do not represent
      a set of stereotyped personalities and the great majority of
      them have achieved a high level of psychological adjustment.
      Their culture has therapeutic effects only on those who con-
      form to its demands and limitations.

511. Eaton, Joseph W., Robert J. Weil, and Bert Kaplan. "The
      Hutterite Mental Health Study." MENNONITE QUARTERLY
      REVIEW 25 (1951): 47-59.

      Examines the U. S. Hutterites' reputation for good mental
      health and for considerable social cohesion and adjustment
      and finds that both are substantiated by research, though
      there are more exceptions than any superficial acquaintance
      with the sect would reveal. Several environmental factors,
      a number of cultural contradictions, and an unusually high
      degree of cooperation among the members of the community
      contribute to the Hutterite mental health.

512. England, R. W. "Some Aspects of Christian Science as
      Reflected in Letters of Testimony." AMERICAN JOURNAL OF
      SOCIOLOGY 59 (1954): 448-53.

      Attempts, by examining a sample of 100 letters of testimony
      published in the CHRISTIAN SCIENCE JOURNAL of the years 1929,
      1939, 1944, and 1946, to draw up the personality character-
      istics of those to whom Christian Science appeals, to deter-
      mine the basis of this appeal, and to explore the nature and
      dynamics of this sect. Several factors which motivate and
      sustain interest in the church and the mental attitudes of
      its members are outlined. Christian Science involves, accord-
      ing to the author, a transference and a hazy perception that
      illness can be of emotional origin. The role of the practi-
      tioner is not unlike that of the psychiatrist. The alleged
      effectiveness of the treatment is largely the result of the
      personal patient-client relationship established between the
      sick person and the practitioner.

513. Ericksen, Ephraim Edward. THE PSYCHOLOGICAL AND ETHICAL
      ASPECTS OF MORMON GROUP LIFE. Salt Lake City: University
      of Utah Press, 1975. xxii, 101 pp. First published in
      1922.

      Attempts to apply the principles of functional psychology
      to Mormon history that is conceived as a process of mental
      and social adaptation. Three areas are discussed: 1) the

psychological and social factors involved in the conflict
between the Mormons and the gentiles; 2) the problem of maladjustment between the Mormon people and nature in the desert
region of the Great Basin; and, finally, 3) the modern conflict between Mormon institutions and traditions and scientific innovation and democracy. The author tries to explain
Mormon community life "in terms of its whole life-process,
its conflicts, its struggles, its crises" (p. 9) which have
both created and maintained the basic Mormon sentiments.

514. Evans, W. N. "Notes on the Conversion of John Bunyan: A
      Study in English Puritanism." INTERNATIONAL JOURNAL OF
      PSYCHOANLYSIS 24 (1943): 176-85.

      Attempts to understand English Puritanism which, though
      being the "most repressive religious movement in history,"
      has played an important role in shaping British life and
      conduct. The religious experience of Bunyan is judged to be
      crucial for understanding the rise and spread of the puri-
      tanical movement. The four elements in Bunyan's conversion
      experience, namely, vision, conviction, absolution, and a
      sense of mission, are discussed. The author concludes that
      the typical Puritan is characterized by repression reinforced
      by discipline, jealousy, aggressive and ceaseless activity.

515. Feldman, A. Bronson. "Animal Magnetism and the Mother of
      Christian Science." PSYCHOANALYTIC REVIEW 50 (1963): 154-
      60.

      Discusses Mary Baker Eddy's fear of Malicious Animal
      Magnetism (MAM) in the context of her relationship with her
      mother. The author believes that Mrs. Eddy had definite
      trends to self-identification (that is, to see herself in
      another), which indicated serious phallic concerns. Many
      signs in her life show that she suffered from serious psycho-
      sexual problems, which are interpreted in typical Freudian
      terms.

516. Feuerstein, George, and Jeanine Miller. YOGA AND BEYOND:
      ESSAYS IN INDIAN PHILOSOPHY. New York: Schocken Books,
      1972. xiii, 176 pp.

      Offers a collection of essays by the two authors portraying
      the art and science of Yoga as the "living pulse" of Indian
      philosophy. Though the authors do not discuss the psychiatric
      implications of Yoga, they state at the very start that a
      study of Yoga could lead to remarkable discoveries in the
      field of psychology and psychoanalysis. The practice of Yoga
      will help toward a remodeling of human personality and could
      thus be therapeutic.

517. Fromm, Eric. "Psychoanalysis and Zen Buddhism." ZEN BUD-
      DHISM AND PSYCHOANALYSIS. Edited by D. T. Susuki, Eric
      Fromm, and Richard De Martino. New York: Harper Brothers,
      1960, pp. 77-141.

Presents, in some detail, those aspects of psychoanalysis
which are of immediate relevance in its relation to Zen
Buddhism. The major principles of both systems are compared.
In spite of the important differences in theory and method,
the author is impressed by their striking similarities. He
thinks that Zen can make a valuable contribution to our
understanding of the nature of insight. Zen "can have the
most fertile and clarifying influence on the theory and technique of psychoanalysis" (p. 140). Psychoanalysis, too, has
a role to play: it helps the Zen student avoid illusions.

518.   Fromm, Eric. "Psychoanalysis and Zen Buddhism." PSYCHOLOGIA
        2 (1959): 79-99.

Points out that while both psychoanalysis and Zen deal with
human nature and with a practice aimed at transforming it,
the differences seem to be much greater than their similarities. The author then outlines some of the minor and major
similarities and differences between the two systems. He
concludes that while the aim of both is the same, their
methods differ substantially. Zen, however, can have a
fertile and clarifying influence on both the theory and
technique of psychoanalysis.

519.   Garde, R. K. PRINCIPLES AND PRACTICE OF YOGA. Bombay, India:
        Taraporevala Sons, 1972. x, 131 pp.

Provides an outline of the physical and psychological benefits of Yoga practices, which can also be used as preventive
and rehabilitative measures. Psychological problems, like
hysteria, insomnia, and neurasthenia, can be successfully
subjected to Yoga therapy.

520.   Gelberman, Joseph H., and Dorothy Kobak. "Psychology and
        Modern Hasidism." JOURNAL OF PASTORAL CARE 17 (1963):
        27-30.

Considers the beliefs of Hasidism in three dimensions:
theological, psychological, and ethical. Similarities between modern psychiatric views and Hasidism are noted.
Both, for instance, attempt to free the individual from one's
imprisoned potential, both came into being as means of
counteracting human inhibitions, and both strive for wholeness. The Hasidic rabbi was, in the early days of the movement, an intuitive psychologist.

521.   Gerrard, Nathan L. "The Serpent-Handling Religion of West
        Virginia." TRANS-ACTION 5 (May 1968): 22-28.

Reports on a seven-year study of West Virginia serpent-
handling that aims at discovering the effect of this particular form of Christianity on the life of its adherents.
Some basic beliefs and the main ritual of this sect are
described. Important personality differences, especially
those relating to class structure, between serpent-handlers

and members of more conventional Christian churches are
discussed. Serpent-handlers are not pessimistic hypochon-
driacs. The author thinks that participation in their sect's
religious practices prevents them from becoming demoralized
or delinquent. Serpent-handlers tend to be more impulsive
and spontaneous, more hedonistic and exhibitionistic than
members of other churches. Religious snake-handling serves
as a "safety valve for many of the frustrations of life in
present-day Appalachia" (p. 28).

522.   Goodman, Felicitas D. "Glossolalia and Single-Limb Trance:
       Some Parallels." PSYCHOTHERAPY AND PSYCHOSOMATICS 19
       (1971): 92-103.

       Builds on a previous study (item 524) which showed that
       speaking in tongues was not a hypnotic, but rather a trance-
       produced, phenomenon. It is maintained that glossolalia is
       similar to those cases of trance of the arm alone, often
       reported in pre-literate societies and found in literate ones
       in those individuals who produced automatic or mediumistic
       writings. Two specific cases are discussed. Parallels be-
       tween glossolalia and single-limb trance are drawn up. Both,
       for instance, are characterized by "a switching off of a
       measure of cortical control" (p. 96). The major difference
       is that in glossolalia there is an overwhelming feeling of
       physical and emotional well-being which is not present in
       single-limb trance.

523.   Goodman, Felicitas D. "The Acquisition of Glossolalia Behav-
       ior." SEMIOTICA 3 (1971): 77-82.

       Maintains that glossolalia manifests three different lev-
       els or stages analogous to dreams: 1) kinetic preparation
       (including immobilization); 2) drowsiness (a new state of
       consciousness); and 3) deep sleep (which may include rapid
       eye movements). The glossolalic goes into the following
       comparable stages: 1) the configuration of the total body
       prior to speaking in tongues; 2) the entrance into a state of
       trance; and 3) the vocal utterances. Each stage is consid-
       ered in detail and it is shown how glossolalia is learned.
       The author's view that glossolalia is not a linguistic
       phenomenon but an artifact of the trance state is reasserted.

524.   Goodman, Felicitas D. "Glossolalia: Speaking in Tongues in
       Four Cultural Settings." CONFINIA PSYCHIATRICA 7 (1969):
       113-29.

       Insists that in the study of glossolalia, the totality of
       a given utterance and the cross-cultural and cross-linguistic
       dimensions should not be ignored. The author compares data
       from three English speaking groups: 1) a tent revivialist
       movement called the Stream of Power; 2) a mainline Pentecos-
       tal church; and 3) a Spanish group, the Mexican Pentecostal
       church. It is shown how several features of glossolalia,
       like the phonetic elements, its unproductivity, and its

uncommunicability, cut across cultural and linguistic
barriers. The author's view is that the person speaking in
tongues learns how to relinquish his or her control and to
reach a state of dissociation called trance. Glossolalia is
a direct artifact of this trance condition.

525.   Goyeche, John, T. Chihara, and H. Schimizu. "Two Concentra-
       tion Methods: A Preliminary Comparison." PSYCHOLOGIA 15
       (1972): 110-11.

       Compares Zen meditation with the ordinary state of concen-
       tration and finds the former easier to maintain and more
       productive of feelings of well-being.

526.   Greaves, George. "Meditation as an Adjunct to Psychotherapy."
       VOICES: THE ART AND SCIENCE OF PSYCHOTHERAPY 8 (Fall 1972):
       50-52.

       Describes the three kinds of "alone" assignments he gives
       his patients: 1) a form of Yoga meditation which consists of
       breathing exercises and repeating a mantra; 2) methods of
       emptying their thoughts and feelings as in Zazen; and 3)
       intensive introspection, flooding their consciousness with
       ideation. The author believes that these methods can be used
       without accepting the religious beliefs out of which they
       developed. He rejects the possibility that meditation might
       supplant psychotherapy, but strongly holds that it could be
       a very beneficial adjunct to help subjects with various
       psychological problems.

527.   Haglof, Anthony. "Psychology and the Pentecostal Experience."
       SPIRITUAL LIFE 17 (1971): 198-210.

       Cites psychological evidence in support of the view that
       religious conversion is a type of psychiatric healing. Some
       forms of behavior, like shrieking and convulsion, and a few
       less primitive manifestations, like ecstasy, tongue-speaking,
       visions, and hallucinations, are human reactions in the indi-
       vidual's progress towards perfection. "The total Pentecostal
       phenomenon can be seen objectively as a continuation of the
       basic method of psychotherapy, the aim of which is to enable
       a person to discern the direction in which his own psychic
       laws would lead him, and which he must take if he wishes to
       be free from the tensions which are to some extent inherent
       in human existence" (p. 207).

528.   Hardyck, Jane Allen, and Marcia Braden. "Prophecy Fails
       Again: A Report on a Failure to Replicate." JOURNAL OF
       ABNORMAL AND SOCIAL PSYCHOLOGY 65 (1962): 136-41.

       Discusses, in the context of Festinger's theory (item 379),
       the behavior of the Church of the True Word, an evangelical
       Pentecostal Christian sect whose prophetic leader had fore-
       told of an impending nuclear disaster. The conditions which
       Festinger lists to support the view that failure of pessimis-

tic predictions to materialize are likely to lead the members
to even greater fervor are tested and validated for this
group. However, contrary to expectation, their evangelistic
behavior did not increase. Two variables, namely, the degree
of social support available within the membership and the
amount of ridicule the group had to face, are suggested as
possible reasons for their unexpected behavior.

529.   Hart, Joseph. "The Zen of Hubert Benoit." JOURNAL OF TRANS-
        PERSONAL PSYCHOLOGY 2.2 (1970): 141-67.

        Draws upon the work of French psychoanalyst Benoit to
        reflect upon some of the psychological questions posed and
        answered by Zen. Satori, freedom, and illusion are among the
        topics brought up. Among the positive psychological effects
        of Zen is the modification of internal functioning leading
        to happiness.

530.   Hawley, Florence. "The Keresean Holy Rollers: An Adaptation
        to American Individualism." SOCIAL FORCES 26 (1948): 272-
        80.

        Describes the acceptance of an American Indian family by
        a black Holy Roller group in Albuquerque, New Mexico, the
        attempts of this family to proselytize the rest of the Pueblo
        Indians, and their subsequent banishment from their village.
        The author asks how this exotic cult, with its stress on
        individual experience, managed to gain a foothold among the
        community-oriented Pueblos. His conclusion is that personal
        stress and maladjustment led the original small group of
        Indians to ally themselves with the Holy Rollers.

531.   Hill, Wayne. "Some Aspects of Group Psychotherapy and Psycho-
        drama Used in a Modern Religious Cult." GROUP PSYCHOTHERAPY
        21 (1960): 214-18.

        Describes the now-defunct Process church with its initia-
        tion rites and group activities. Its members have developed
        methods for influencing behavior that have some similarities
        to psychotherapy. The magical atmosphere which pervades its
        meetings promotes regression and dependence and also hope for
        change. Resistance and individual initiative are reduced.
        Touching exercises, avoided by psychiatrists, are performed
        to lessen anxiety. The goal of the Process, unlike that of
        psychotherapy, is not to improve social relations and reality
        testing, but rather to bring about a new group identity.

532.   Hine, Virginia H. "Pentecostal Glossolalia: Toward a Func-
        tional Interpretation." JOURNAL FOR THE SCIENTIFIC STUDY
        OF RELIGION 8 (1969): 211-26.

        Reviews the literature on glossolalia, noting its predis-
        posing conditions and suggesting a functional interpretation
        of its role in spreading the Pentecostal movement. This
        essay covers both traditional Pentecostal sects and the more

recent Charismatic (neo-Pentecostal) renewal in communities
in the United States, Colombia, and Mexico. The various
psychological interpretations and testing methods are surveyed. The author favors a non-pathological explanation and
maintains that "Pentecostals as a group appear to be normally
adjusted and productive members of society" (p. 216). The
suspicion remains, however, that those who speak in tongues
are emotionally immature, overly anxious, and personally
inadequate. Suggestibility and hypnosis have also been advanced as non-pathological interpretations, while deprivation
and disorganization theories have been common among sociologists. The author discusses also the theory that glossolalia
is simply a form of behavior learned in a religious context.
Personal changes, as in conversion, fundamentalist ideology,
attitudes and behavior, and cognitive reorganization are
linked with the Pentecostal phenomenon of speaking in tongues.
The author interprets glossolalia as a form of non-pathological linguistic behavior, a component of the Pentecostal
movement facilitating its spread and providing motivation
for attitudinal and behavioral changes.

533.   Hinson, E. Glenn. "A Brief History of Glossolalia." GLOS-
        SOLALIA: TONGUE-SPEAKING IN BIBLICAL, HISTORICAL, AND
        PSYCHOLOGICAL PERSPECTIVE (item 597), pp. 45-75.

        Treats the history of speaking in tongues in Christianity
        in four historical sections, the last being from 1900 onwards.
        Several revival movements, the Cevenols (French Huguenots)
        of the seventeenth century, the Irvingites (English Presby-
        terians) of the early nineteenth century, the rise of the
        Methodist evangelical renewal both in England and in the
        United States, and the origin of Pentecostal churches in
        the twentieth century are described. Persecution, severe
        repression, and declining religious interest are the common
        conditions which lead to revival movements. Those who speak
        in tongues do not fit into a single personality stereotype.
        It is suggested that glossolalia supplies individuals with
        religious authority and assurance.

534.   Holmes, Stewart W. "Zen Buddhism and Transactional Psychol-
        ogy." ETC: A REVIEW OF GENERAL SEMANTICS 14 (1957): 243-
        49.

        Argues that there are three attitudes characteristic of Zen
        Buddhism which can be called transactional: 1) the attitude
        towards symbols, commonly found also in transactional psychol-
        ogy; 2) the Zen view toward the individual/environment com-
        plex where an empathetic relation with nature is fostered;
        and 3) the Zen tendency to stress intuitive experience. The
        author points out that between Zen and transactional psychol-
        ogy there are several similarities which are the bases of
        a meeting point between East and West.

535.   Holt, J. B. "Holiness Religion: Culture Shock and Social
        Organization." AMERICAN SOCIOLOGICAL REVIEW 5 (1940):
        740-77.

Proposes several theories to explain the factors in, and
the significance of, the growth of several sects known as the
Holy Rollers whose religious services are characterized by
highly emotional and physically energetic behavior. These
sects came into being in a time of change and conflict brought
about by swift migration to the cities. The culture shock
that resulted triggered a new religious revivalism which
led to reorganization and readjustment. The new religious
groups can therefore be called "healing" movements. The
reason why they occur outside mainstream religions is because
the established churches fail to provide for the needs of
those undergoing change and stress.

536.   Hora, Thomas. "Tao, Zen, and Existential Psychotherapy."
        PSYCHOLOGIA 2 (1955): 236-42.

Maintains that psychotherapy is a process of existential
encounter and that its goal is experiential and enlightening.
Cognition, consciousness, and authenticity of Being are the
major criteria of mental health. The philosophical bases
of both Tao and Zen contain such an existential psychology.

537.   Hostetler, John A., and Gertrude Enders Huntington. THE
        HUTTERITES OF NORTH AMERICA. New York: Holt, Rinehart and
        Winston, 1967. viii, 119 pp.

Gives an account of the world view and the life-style of
the Hutterites, stressing their technological, economic, and
family patterns. The authors attempt to understand the
behavior patterns of the Hutterite subculture from a personalistic point of view. They show how the Hutterite's well-
organized belief system protects members from the outside
world and offers them a solution to all their needs. The
Hutterites minimize aggression and dissent and are encouraged
to lose their identity to the culture of the group. No conclusion about their mental health is reached, but the reader
is left with the impression that Hutterite society is a closed
one, and that it has a tight socialization process which
maintains the status quo.

538.   Hughes, C. H. "Christopathy and Christian Science (so-
        called)." ALIENIST AND NEUROLOGIST 20 (1899): 611-28.

Comments on various religious delusions to which American
religion is making its contribution through such groups as
Christian Science. A clinical record of a morbid vision of
Christ, which a young female patient woman had, is described
and diagnosed as a form of hallucination. Christian Science
applies a kind of "buoyant" psychotherapy by providing psychic
support and exultation, even though it neglects proper hygiene
and ordinary medication. Christian Science is referred to as
an "insane sect" with a crazy creed.

539.   Hyman, Ray, and Elizabeth G. Cohen. "Water-Witching in the
        United States." AMERICAN SOCIOLOGICAL REVIEW 22 (1957):
        719-24.

Reports on a study which tried: 1) to estimate the number
of diviners in the United States; and 2) to ascertain the
conditions favorable to water-witching. The authors discovered that water-witching is usually practiced in those
rural areas where underground water is a problem, and they
concluded that water-witching is a ritual, the function of
which is, like that of magical rites in primitive societies,
to reduce anxiety.

540.   Ikegami, Ryutaro. "Psychological Study of Zen Posture."
        PSYCHOLOGICAL STUDY ON ZEN (item 463), pp. 105-133.

        Describes five experiments on Zen practice which: 1) com-
        pares the various sitting positions; 2) compares the sitting
        postures of the Zen priest and layperson; 3) draws up differ-
        ences which can be accounted for by age and experience;
        4) determines the effect of "mental set" on the different
        types of postures; and 5) assesses the effect of mental set
        on the maintenance of Zen practice. It is stressed that the
        regulation of the body is an integral part of Zen, leading
        to the state of mental concentration or "the release of
        personality."

541.   Jackson, John A. "Two Contemporary Cults." ADVANCEMENT OF
        OF SCIENCE, June 1966: 60-64.

        Outlines the belief systems of the Aetherius Society and
        Scientology. Like all cults, these two revolve around the
        major areas of cultural and social stress. They have devel-
        oped a comprehensive system of belief and practice which
        suggest that they are moving away from the more manipulative
        qualities of a cult. Their presence in a time of rapid
        social change may have considerable therapeutic effects.
        The author suggests that these movements might prevent
        psychological breakdowns by providing individuals with a
        theoretical framework for solving their problems.

542.   Jaiswal, Sita Ram. "The Psychology of the Bhagwad Gita."
        RESEARCH JOURNAL OF PHILOSOPHY AND THE SOCIAL SCIENCES
        1.2 (1964): 23-33.

        Gives a brief account of the psychological system found
        in the more popular Hindu texts. It is shown how the Gita
        explains the background of all the causes of human conflict,
        frustration, and pain. The belief in the immortality of the
        soul (central to the Gita) is beneficial to mental health
        since it removes fear, while the theories of rebirth and Karma
        lead to a peaceful life. The author maintains that the ideal
        personality, according to the Gita, does not merely possess
        emotional maturity and social adjustment, but also remains
        undisturbed in all situations of life. The Gita offers prac-
        tical guidance for facing the problems of life.

543.   Johansson, Rune E. THE PSYCHOLOGY OF NIRVANA: A COMPARISON
        BETWEEN THE NATURAL GOAL OF BUDDHISM AND THE AIMS OF MODERN
        WESTERN PSYCHOLOGY. New York: Doubleday, 1970. 141 pp.

Aims at understanding Nirvana by concentrating on one particular text, the Pali Nikayas, which is more psychologically
oriented than other ancient Buddhist literature. Though
Nirvana may not be ultimately a psychological concept, it may
have psychological aspects, conditions, or consequences. The
author's treatment covers, among other subjects, the cognitive
functions and the emotions in Nirvana, which is also examined
as a state of personality. The author compares the Western
concepts of mental health, which stress adaptation, adjustment, and integration, with Nirvana and finds a number of
similarities and differences. Happiness and satisfaction,
freedom from inner conflicts, adaptation to moral norms, an
emotionally stable life, and an integrated, harmonious personality are common goals in psychotherapy and in a person who
has reached Nirvana. The author thinks, however, that the
differences predominate, since the philosophies behind both
systems differ radically. Western psychology stresses more
the individual's success and adaptation to society, whereas
Buddhism is more concerned with internal freedom and the
detachment of the individual.

544.   Johnson, Paul E. "New Religions and Mental Health." JOURNAL
       OF RELIGION AND HEALTH 3 (1964): 327-34.

       Describes three new religions in Japan, namely, Tenrikyo
       (The Religion of Heavenly Wisdom), Konkokyo (The Religion of
       Golden Light), and Rissho Kosei Kai (Society of Laymen Who
       Seek Perfection of Character Through Religious Teaching).
       The rise of these new religions is seen in the context of
       personal and social stresses brought about by a rapidly
       changing world. The author reflects on these movements as
       means to mental health, which is defined as the fulfillment
       of the person through all of his or her relationships. The
       new Japanese religions are meeting vital human needs, offering
       hope for deliverance from all the ills of life, and promising
       fulfillment in a caring and healing environment.

545.   Jones, W. Lawson. "Some Psychological Conditions of the
       Development of Methodism to 1850." BRITISH JOURNAL OF
       MEDICAL PSYCHOLOGY 42 (1951): 345-54.

       Inquires into the psychological state linking Methodism in
       Great Britain with the social matrix in which it was born.
       The author examines in turn the development of church building
       in eight selected areas in England and Wales, the psychologi-
       cal influence of local leadership, the dynamics of the move-
       ment, leadership and fragmentation, and, finally, the family
       structure of Methodism. He believes that Methodism grew and
       prospered by its appeal to one of the deepest needs in human
       nature, namely, tenderness, which seems to be lacking in semi-
       industrialized and industrialized conditions of the time.

546.   Jung, Carl G. ON THE PSYCHOLOGY OF EASTERN MEDITATION.
       Translated by Carol Bauman. New York: The Analytical
       Psychology Club, 1949. 18 pp. Also in THE COLLECTED
       WORKS of C. G. Jung (item 78), vol. 11, pp. 558-75.

Presents the author's reflections on the psychical processes of Yoga, particularly as seen in a Mahayana Buddhist text,
the "Sutra of the Meditation on Amitays" (Amitaysu-Dhyana-
Sutra). Eastern and Western approaches in worship and meditation are contrasted. Yoga delves into the unconscious and
is therefore similar to Western psychoanalytic techniques.
Since the first step in psychological healing is the uncover-
ing of the unconscious level, Yoga can be therapeutic.

547. Kaplan, Bert, and Thomas F. A. Plaut. PERSONALITY IN A COM-
      MUNAL SOCIETY: AN ANALYSIS OF THE MENTAL HEALTH OF THE
      HUTTERITES. Lawrence: University of Kansas Press, 1956.
      xi, 116 pp.

      Studies the issue of the mental health of the Hutterites
      in the context of their subculture. After a description of
      the Hutterite culture and of the technique of personality
      study, the authors outline the personality of the Hutterites
      under three variables, that is, needs, stresses, and states.
      The Hutterite attitude to mental health is also outlined.
      Finally, a psychiatric evaluation of their mental health is
      made, particularly with regard to their guilt, fear and
      anxiety, love and sex, and deviance. It is concluded that
      while the Hutterites exhibit many signs of good health, they
      suffer from more pathological problems than the researchers
      expected to find. In general, however, the Hutterites leave
      a favorable impression when compared with other people.

548. Keene, James J. "Baha'i World Faith: Redefinition of Reli-
      gion." JOURNAL FOR THE SCIENTIFIC STUDY OF RELIGION 7
      (1967): 221-35.

      Finds that the members of the Baha'i faith are different
      from members of other religions in the structure of their
      religious behavior and in their personality makeup. The
      cognitive, experiential, self-defining, administrative, and
      meditative components of Baha'i life were found to contribute
      to a balanced religious activity, which was lacking in the
      adherents of other faiths. The strong involvement and commit-
      ment required by its members made participation in this move-
      ment both sociologically and psychologically beneficial.

549. Kido, Mantaro. "Origin of Japanese Psychology and Its Devel-
      opment." PSYCHOLOGIA 4 (1961): 1-10.

      Traces the history of Japanese psychology to Shintoism,
      Buddhism, and Confucianism. The views of some recent Japanese
      psychiatrists who have been influenced by Western theories is
      outlined. Points out that interest in the therapeutic value
      of Zen goes back to the 1920s.

550. Kiev, Ari, and John L. Francis. "Subud and Mental Illness.
      Psychiatric Illness in a Religious Sect." AMERICAN JOURNAL
      OF PSYCHOTHERAPY 18 (1968): 66-78.

Gives a brief description of the cosmology and philosophy
of this Indonesian sect which has a small following in the
Western world. The methods used bring about spiritual change
in those who join. Members often go through a "subud crisis,"
a state of anxiety and irritation with the slowness of their
progress, which may lead them to leave the group. Three case
studies are presented of patients whose participation in subud
lead to psychological problems. Subud seems to attract people
in distress and may fulfill some of the needs of dissatisfied
individuals. The practices of this sect may, however, enhance
anxiety, feelings of guilt, fear, and depression.

551. Kildahl, John P. THE PSYCHOLOGY OF SPEAKING IN TONGUES. New
York: Harper and Row, 1972. xiii, 110 pp.

Describes glossolalia both from the perspective of the outside observer and from the point of view of those who experience it. An overview of its history is given and several
of the major theses to explain it, like those of Cutten (item
501), Lapsley (items 558-59), and Oates (item 573) are
discussed. The author gives an account of his own research
and then concludes that tongue-speakers, when evaluated by a
broad criteria of emotional well-being, do not constitute
different personality types from those who do not speak in
tongues. There were differences, however, in a number of
personality variables such as dependency syndrome, speech
regression, and hypnotizability (the sine qua non of glossolalia). Among the characteristics of glossolalic group
behavior are divisiveness, projection of anger, histrionic
display, and preoccupation with their special endowment.
Glossolalia is, according to the author, a learned behavior.
Though the phenomenon does not theologically benefit wide
segments of the community, it has certain psychological
advantages, such as the lessening of depression and the feeling of worthlessness, and the increase of one's sense of
well-being.

552. Kirsh, James. "Affinities Between Zen and Analytical Psychology." PSYCHOLOGIA 3 (1960): 85-91.

Compares the practice of Zen to Western Jungian psychology
in the context of several dreams of his clients. The goal of
Zen, Satori, is identified with Jung's concept of the fulfillment of individuation. Though the Zen way to reach this goal
differs from psychotherapy, it achieves the same therapeutic
results.

553. Kondo, Akihisa. "Zen in Psychotherapy: The Virtue of Sitting." CHICAGO REVIEW 12.2 (1958): 57-64.

Encourages people who suffer from mental and psychological
ailments to sit in meditation because it helps them recover.
The author, himself a therapist and a practitioner of Zen,
holds that by sitting, people acquire the psychic energy to
work constructively on their problems. Zen is therapeuti-

cally valuable because it strengthens the individual and
gives stability, fullness, and harmony to one's personality.
It starts by freeing individuals to turn inward and to see
themselves as they really are--the first step one must take
in the healing process.

554.   Koya, Yoshiko, and Yoshiharu Akishige. "Psychological Study
        of Zen and Counseling." PSYCHOLOGICAL STUDIES ON ZEN (item
        463), pp. 57-76.

        Compares two Zen practices, zazen and mondo, from the view-
        point of the client-therapist relationship. The Zen view of
        human nature, as well as the life-style of a Zen monk, are
        described. The author maintains that "Sanshi-mompo" (hearing
        the teaching of the Zen master) should be considered counsel-
        ing in a broad sense. The Zen master is a trained therapist
        who helps his client-monk to realize his inmost nature. One
        can also examine the communal life of a Zen monastery from
        the perspective of group psychotherapy.

555.   Kumasaka, Y. "Soka Gakkai: Group Psychologic Study of a New
        Religio-Political Organization." AMERICAN JOURNAL OF
        PSYCHOTHERAPY 20 (1966): 462-70.

        Describes briefly the organizational structure, teachings,
        and the political, group, and individual activities of this
        Japanese Buddhist sect. The differences between Soka Gakkai
        (or Nichren Shoshu) in Japan and in the United States are
        listed. It is argued that their group meetings are a way of
        reducing anxiety. Members give one another emotional support
        and learn to relate constructively to one another.

556.   Kurokawa, Minako. "Psycho-social roles of Mennonite Children
        in a Changing Society." CANADIAN REVIEW OF SOCIOLOGY AND
        ANTHROPOLOGY 6 (1969): 15-35.

        Studies the way Mennonite children adjust to conflicting
        norms introduced from the outside and the roles they play in
        relation to their peers, teachers, and parents. It is con-
        cluded that among traditional Mennonites, where authority is
        stressed and children are expected to respond to their parents
        submissively, children are free from overt symptoms of mal-
        adjustment, but show covert signs. Children from transitional
        groups are more likely to express inconsistency in their
        values and to have a sense of inadequacy: their maladjustment
        is clear. The offspring of progressive Mennonites, though
        they exhibit overt symptoms of maladjustment, are still
        better adjusted than the other groups.

557.   La Barre, Weston. THEY SHALL TAKE UP SERPENTS: PSYCHOLOGY
        OF THE SOUTHERN SNAKE-HANDLING CULT. New York: Schocken
        Books, 1969. ix, 208 pp.

        Presents an ethnographic study and an account of the histor-
        ic spread of this cult, then explores its cultural prehistory
        in Africa and the Near East, and ends by making a clinical

study of the biography of a prominent snake-handling minister
to bring to the fore the psychological aspect of the cult
itself. The author gives the ritual of snake-handling a
Freudian interpretation, particularly in his analysis of the
cult leader's fear of his father. Snake-handling is a drama
which expresses repressed sexuality. It is a typical crisis
cult.

558.   Lapsley, James N., and John H. Simpson. "Speaking in Tongues:
       Infantile Babble or Song of the Self? Part II." PASTORAL
       PSYCHOLOGY 15 (September 1964): 16-24.

       Describes Pentecostals as uncommonly troubled people,
       exhibiting anxiety and instability, and tending to come from
       unusually disturbed home situations. They are likely to be
       problem-oriented and somewhat credulous. Further, they are
       more intellectual than older Pentecostals and they explain
       their experience in Jungian terms as "a song of the depth of
       the self, bursting the barrier of the unconscious" (p. 17).
       The intrapsychic function of tongue-speaking is outlined.
       The authors conclude that glossolalia is a regression of the
       ego for the sake of maintaining, and not disintegrating, the
       personality. It also has a self-aggrandizing, narcissistic
       component. While it reduces inner conflict and could lead to
       social interaction and individual productivity, it does not
       directly lead to personal integration. It can probably be
       best described as a "dissociate expression of truncated
       personality development."

559.   Lapsley, James N., and John H. Simpson. "Speaking in Tongues:
       Infantile Babble or Song of the Self? Part I." PASTORAL
       PSYCHOLOGY 15 (May 1964): 48-55.

       Aims at throwing some light on the nature and function of
       the neo-Pentecostal movement. Glossolalia is likened to
       trance states, somnambulism, mediumship, and automatic writ-
       ing. The authors compare speaking in tongues in the New
       Testament with similar phenomena today, give the historical
       background to the movement, and describe a modern Pentecostal
       group. Those who join such a group are fringe people who
       need personal security and emotional experience not found in
       the churches. Pentecostal leaders have a history of frus-
       trated vocational experience and lack self-fulfillment.

560.   Mackie, Alexander. THE GIFTS OF TONGUES: A STUDY OF THE
       PATHOLOGICAL ASPECTS OF CHRISTIANITY. New York: George H.
       Doran, 1921. xiv, 275 pp.

       Discusses glossolalia throughout the Western world, begin-
       ning with New Testament times and covering new religious
       movements in the Middle Ages, the Wesleyan revival, and
       spiritualism. Specific chapters are devoted to: 1) the
       Ursuline nuns and the Devils of Loudun; 2) the Camisards, or
       French prophets, of the seventeenth century; 3) the Shakers
       and the millennial church; 4) the Irvingites; and 5) the
       Mormons. Speaking in tongues is, according to the author,

always associated with pathological phenomena like atavistic
elements, perverse sexual tendencies, and egomania. The
author also considers the ethical aspects of glossolalia
which he links with the "criminaloid type."

561.   Malhotra, J. C. "Yoga and Psychiatry: A Review." JOURNAL OF
        NEUROPSYCHIATRY 4 (1963): 375-85.

        Discusses the neurophysiological, psychosomatic, social,
        religious, and therapeutic effects of Yoga. Five systems of
        Yoga are described and the aims of Yoga are outlined with
        particular reference to Pantajali's classical work. Those
        who practice Yoga are, in the author's opinion, mystics and
        should not be compared to schizophrenics, who have manifest
        asocial and antisocial symptoms definitely not found in
        mystics. Some of the benefits of Yoga, like the reduction
        of anxiety, are listed.

562.   Mann, Felix. ACUPUNCTURE: CURE OF MANY DISEASES. London:
        William Heinemann, 1971. vii, 121 pp.

        Outlines the theory and practice of acupuncture, pointing
        to the connection between psychological states and their
        physical sources. Depression is, for example, said to be a
        disease of the liver, while obsession is traced to the spleen.
        Many psychological problems, including nervousness, anxiety,
        phobias, neurasthenia, and stage fright are curable by acu-
        puncture treatment. Case histories are reported throughout
        the book.

563.   Maupin, Edward M. "Meditation." WAYS OF GROWTH: APPROACHES
        TO EXPANDING AWARENESS. Edited by H. A. Otto and J. Mann.
        New York: Gossman, 1968, pp. 200-10.

        Integrates some themes in the literature on meditation and
        presents several techniques of meditating. Several psycho-
        somatic benefits of its practice are mentioned: a greater
        ability to cope with stress situations; improved sleep; more
        and direct awareness. The existential element of meditation
        is emphasized. All methods seem to aim at establishing the
        same psychological state, namely, a relaxed awareness in
        which thought flow is reduced and detached observation main-
        tained.

564.   Maupin, Edward W. "On Meditation." ALTERED STATES OF CON-
        SCIOUSNESS (item 449), pp. 181-90.

        Discusses some of the criticism leveled at meditation,
        particularly its tendency to produce catatonic withdrawal.
        The author, however, thinks that the practice of meditation
        has the beneficial result of expanding one's awareness. It
        further produces calmness, a greater ability to cope with
        tense situations, and several psychophysiological benefits.
        The general principles regarding meditation are briefly
        sketched and several techniques are outlined for the reader
        to try.

565.   Maupin, Edward W. "Individual Difference in Response to Zen
       Meditation Exercise." JOURNAL OF CONSULTING PSYCHOLOGY 29
       (1965): 139-45.

       Outlines first some main features of Zen meditation which
       are similar to psychoanalytic procedures. The author then
       describes an experiment with 28 college student volunteers
       who were instructed in the practice of Zen meditation.
       Their attention, tolerance of unrealistic experience, and
       capacity for regression in the service of the ego were
       measured after two or three weeks of meditation and compared
       with results taken before the experiment. Both tolerance
       for unrealistic experience and capacity for regression
       registered a positive response to meditation. Satori, it is
       concluded, "seems to fit into the class of psychologically
       adaptive regressions described in psychoanalytic literature"
       (p. 144).

566.   Maupin, Edward W. "Zen Buddhism: A Psychological Review."
       JOURNAL OF CONSULTING PSYCHOLOGY 26 (1962): 362-78.

       Provides an overview of Satori and Zen training and surveys
       the psychological literature on these experiences and on their
       relevance to the concept of regression in the service of the
       ego. Realization therapy in Zen and Western psychotherapy is
       explored and the therapeutic application of Zen is examined.
       Zen is of interest to psychotherapy because the experience of
       Satori is described as living an increasingly satisfying and
       effective life. It is suggested that Zazen might be used to
       help subjects face and experience pre-oedipal levels of the
       unconscious that are less amenable to Western therapy.

567.   McDonnell, Kilian. CATHOLIC PENTECOSTALISM: PROBLEMS IN
       EVALUATION. Pecos, NM: Dove Publications, 1970. 58 pp.

       Essentially a theological evaluation of the Catholic
       charismatic renewal with a short outline of its history and
       its relation to traditional Pentecostalism. The author
       admits that certain outward expressions seen at charismatic
       meetings may be signs of emotional instability and hysteria.
       He argues, however, that charismatics are not psychologically
       deprived. They are, compared to non-charismatics, more gen-
       erous and outgoing in their personal relationships. Healing
       from alcoholism and drug addiction and the solution of mari-
       tal problems are some of the results of involvement in the
       charismatic movement.

568.   Mishra, Rammurti S. THE TEXTBOOK OF YOGA PSYCHOLOGY: A NEW
       TRANSLATION AND INTERPRETATION OF PANTAJALI'S YOGA SUTRAS
       FOR MEANINGFUL APPLICATION IN ALL MODERN PSYCHOLOGICAL
       DISCIPLINES. London: Lyrebird Press, 1972. 401 pp.

       Provides a thorough introduction to Yoga philosophy and
       practice and gives the text, with translation and commentary,
       of Pantajali's classic work on Yoga. The author maintains

that Yoga exercises lead to beneficial personality changes,
among which are included tranquility, peace of mind, and
self-control.

569. Naranjo, Claudio, and Robert E. Ornstein. ON THE PSYCHOLOGY
      OF MEDITATION. New York: Viking Press, 1971. 248 pp.

      Contains two lengthy essays: the first, written by Naranjo,
      describes the spirit and techniques of meditation, showing
      how some psychological processes, like "letting go," lie at
      its roots; the second, by Ornstein, aims at evaluating the
      implication of this practice for modern psychology. The
      essential similarities between esoteric and modern psychol-
      ogies of awareness are pointed out. The effects and after-
      effects of meditation, which is basically a self-regulatory
      technique, are also considered. Jewish and Christian prayer,
      Zen, Yoga, Tantra, and Sufi practices are among the many
      examples provided.

570. Nelson, Geoffrey K. "The Membership of a Cult: The Spiri-
      tualist National Union." REVIEW OF RELIGIOUS RESEARCH 13
      (1972): 170-77.

      Maintains in common with many sociologists that technology
      and certain related social changes not only destroy old
      systems, but also provide the basis for the development of new
      systems of belief. Cult members suffer from "psychic depri-
      vation," especially with regard to meaning and are concerned
      with the problem of understanding mystical experiences. Gen-
      eralizing from his study of the Spiritualist National Union in
      Great Britain, the author states that cults fulfill genuine
      needs and could thus be regarded as therapeutic.

571. Nibley, Hugh. NO, MA'AM, THAT'S NOT HISTORY: A BRIEF REVIEW
      OF MRS. BRODIE'S RELUCTANT VINDICATION OF A PROPHET SHE
      SEEKS TO EXPOSE. Salt Lake City, UT: Bookcraft, 1946.
      62 pp.

      Presents a short, apologetic rebuttal of Mrs. Brodie's life
      of Joseph Smith, the founder of Mormonism, whom she depicts
      not as totally depraved or insane, but rather as an inten-
      tional impostor. Brodie is criticized for her methodology
      and for her refusal to recognize the stability of Mormon
      teachings.

572. Noyes, Humphrey F. "Meditation: Doorway to Wholeness." MAIN
      CURRENTS IN MODERN THOUGHT 22.2 (1965): 35-40.

      Encourages the practice of meditation which not only brings
      deep relaxation and refreshment, but also leads to spontaneity
      and renewal. The existential despair of some people in our
      modern world can be counteracted by meditation, which gives
      wholeness of self and does away with the neurosis of ego-
      domination. Meditation is recommended as a useful technique
      in education because of its benefits.

573.   Oates, Wayne E. "A Social-psychological Study of Glossola-
          lia." GLOSSOLALIA: TONGUE SPEAKING IN BIBLICAL, HISTORICAL,
          AND PSYCHOLOGICAL PERSPECTIVE (item 597), pp. 76-99.

          Discusses the reasons for the revival of glossolalia, then
          compares speaking in tongues with the development of speech
          in children, and, finally, deals with the pastoral problems
          raised by its practice. The "turbulent upheavals and expres-
          sions of pent-up feelings, such as we find in speaking in
          tongues" (p. 83), are related to the sociocultural condition
          where the expression of religious feelings is suppressed.
          The author, relying on research in child psychology by several
          prominent scholars in the field (e.g., Piaget and Erikson),
          thinks that speaking in tongues is a regression to childhood,
          but it need not always be a sign of pathology. When people
          are speaking in tongues, a build-up of tension occurs, height-
          ened by the hypnotic impact of the group, and is then released
          in ecstatic behavior. Glossolalia can represent pathological
          symptoms of overdependence on alcohol and the absence of
          a clear-cut family structure. Church leaders are advised to
          be sympathetic listeners, to create openings of community
          and fellowship, and to provide means for the expression of
          creativity.

574.   Oates, Wayne E. "The Billy Graham Evangelistic Crusade: An
          Evaluation." PASTORAL PSYCHOLOGY 7 (December 1956): 17-26.

          Reports on a field-study and evaluates one of Graham's
          month-long crusades in Louisville, Kentucky. These meetings
          are seen in the context of religious revivals in general.
          From a psychological point of view, they give people hope
          and religious security. Billy Graham has not, however,
          developed a view of personality to go with the biblical idea
          of the wholeness of man. His message has, further, ignored
          any consideration of the pathological factors of religious
          experience. The rituals he constantly encourages--Bible
          reading, daily prayer, church attendance, and personal wit-
          nessing for Christ--can attract paranoid individuals. The
          author judges the counseling given during these crusades and
          the follow-up procedures to be unsatisfactory.

575.   O'Connell, Daniel C., and Ernest T. Bryant. "Some Psycho-
          logical Reflections on Glossolalia." REVIEW FOR RELIGIOUS
          31 (1972): 974-77.

          Discusses briefly some of the major psychological theories
          on glossolalia, with particular reference to Samarin's view
          (items 583-87). The author accepts Samarin's opinion that
          glossolalia is not pathological and states that the phenome-
          non itself is "just a pedestrian sort of vocalized nonsense"
          (p. 977).

576.   Oman, John B. "On 'Speaking in Tongues': A Psychological
          Analysis." PASTORAL PSYCHOLOGY 14 (December 1963): 48-51.

Comments on the glossolalia phenomenon that is appearing
in the mainline denominations. Speaking in tongues is a
disorder of association, a lack of integration which can
cause neurosis. It produces no original material and no
religious insights and is a person's return to infantile
megalomania where confidence is restored and the feeling of
guilt removed.

577.   Pálos, Stephen. THE CHINESE ART OF HEALING. New York:
        Herder and Herder, 1971. xv, 235 pp.

Outlines the general principles of Chinese medicine and
describes traditional methods of treatment, including
acupuncture, respiratory exercises, and remedial massage.
The author maintains that Chinese medicine was cognizant of
psychophysiological relationships and of psychosomatic illnesses. The book covers mainly physical diseases, but the
author points out that certain nervous exhaustion and depressive conditions associated with physical disorders can be
treated, but not cured, by respiration therapy.

578.   Parker, Robert Allerton. THE INCREDIBLE MESSIAH: THE DEIFI-
        CATION OF FATHER DIVINE. Boston: Little, Brown, and Co.,
        1937. xiii, 323 pp.

Attempts to present the "whole psychic field" of a messianic
cult, which is taken as representative of messianism throughout the ages. The success of Father Divine is attributed to
the troubled and chaotic Black community of Harlem, New York
City. The response to his mission is related to mental anxiety,
insecurity, social injustice, and racial prejudice. The movement is seen as a return to primitive consciousness or a mass
regression into the subconscious. The author insists that
one should not easily "dismiss Father Divine as a fantastic
anachronism, a psychological or biological 'sport,' an isolated aberration of social disorder" (p. 303). He should, on
the contrary, be judged in the context of other messianic
figures.

579.   Pattison, E. Mansell, and Robert L. Casey. "Glossolalia: A
        Contemporary Mystical Experience." CLINICAL PSYCHIATRY AND
        RELIGION (item 294), pp. 133-48.

Reviews briefly the phenomenon of glossolalia both in Western and non-Western societies and then reflects on its psycholinguistic and intrapsychic aspects, as well as its possible
links with psychopathology. Surveying some of the major
studies the authors conclude that "it would seem that
glossolalia can be produced experimentally, as a by-product
of psychotic disorganization, as a mechanism of expression
of neurotic conflict, or as a normal expectation and behavior
of a normal population" (p. 141). Glossolalia practice as
part of an expected ritual is not psychopathological. If,
however, it is not a cultural expectation, or if the group
is already part of a deviant culture, then the phenomenon of
glossolalia is pathological.

580. Philpott, Harry M. "Conversion Techniques Used by the Newer
      Sects in the South." RELIGIOUS EDUCATION 38 (1943): 174-79.

      Studies the psychological elements in the methods used to
      bring about a conversion experience in two Pentecostal Holi-
      ness Churches in South Carolina and Virginia. The preacher
      is said to arouse and manipulate the crowd by making people
      feel at home and experience a sense of belonging to a larger
      whole. All are urged to participate in singing hymns, giving
      testimonies, and in discussing family problems. Imitation,
      desire for conformity, suggestibility, and the emotions of
      fear and joy are all employed as social pressures. The
      function of these sects is seen, in part at least, as a way
      of compensating for the stress of life.

581. Robbins, Thomas. "Eastern Mysticism and the Resocialization
      of Drug Users: The Meyer Baba Cult." JOURNAL FOR THE
      SCIENTIFIC STUDY OF RELIGION 7 (1969): 308-17.

      Outlines briefly the history of the Meyer Baba cult and
      describes some of its main religious tenets. The followers
      of Baba, most of whom had been on psychedelic drugs, shift
      their emphasis from an inward, contemplative life-style to
      a more outward, social-service oriented one. The author's
      thesis is that Eastern mystical movements in the United
      States, including Meyer Baba, are "half-way houses" which
      rehabilitate many drug addicts into the mainstream of conven-
      tional society.

582. Sadler, A. W. "Glossolalia and Possession: An Appeal to the
      Episcopal Study Commission." JOURNAL FOR THE SCIENTIFIC
      STUDY OF RELIGION 4 (1964): 84-90.

      Comments on the Commission's study of the new cults and,
      while finding its Biblical and theological approach competent,
      faults it on psychological grounds and cultural meaning. The
      conclusion that glossolalia could also be a sign of mental
      illness or satanic possession is refuted. The author holds
      that the phenomenon in question could be a healthy outlet
      for some people as well as a sign of a creative personality.

583. Samarin, William J. "Sociolinguistics vs. Neurophysiological
      Explanations for Glossolalia: Comment of Goodman's Paper."
      JOURNAL FOR THE SCIENTIFIC STUDY OF RELIGION 11 (1972):
      293-96.

      Argues strongly that glossolalia is not to be understood
      in psychological terms of pathology but, rather, theologi-
      cally, as an expression of one's belief, and/or sociologically,
      as a sign of membership in the neo-Pentecostal movement. The
      author observes that the glossolalist always has the option
      to pray or praise God in the usual language or in tongues.
      The arguments of Goodman (see items 522-24), who maintains
      that glossolalia is a production of the dissociative state
      of trance, are refuted.

584.   Samarin, William J. "Variations and Variables in Religious
        Glossolalia." LANGUAGE IN SOCIETY 1 (1972): 121-30.

        Limits itself to contemporary Christian glossolalia which
        should not be identified with apparently similar phenomena
        elsewhere. The common psychological interpretation, taken
        for granted, that tongue-speaking is an artifact of the
        abnormal state of trance and is, therefore, an indication of
        pathology, is rebutted. It is argued that if one sees the
        phenomenon of glossolalia in its cultural context, then it
        becomes clear that the person who speaks in tongues cannot
        be judged to be pathological. By becoming a member of the
        Pentecostal subculture, the individual is led to tongue-
        speaking, that is, one learns how to talk religiously just
        as one learns the values and beliefs which go with one's
        commitment. Several factors that determine glossolalic
        utterances--for instance, the role of the speaker and the
        purpose and setting of the speech act--are discussed. It is
        the author's strong opinion that glossolalia is not a state
        of dissociation, but rather an expression of one's religious
        experience and that it can best be understood subjectively.

585.   Samarin, William J. TONGUES OF MEN AND ANGELS: THE RELIGIOUS
        LANGUAGE OF PENTECOSTALISM. New York: Macmillan, 1970. xv,
        277 pp.

        Studies glossolalia in general, describing it linguisti-
        cally, contrasting it with ordinary language, and comparing
        it with other forms of speech. An account is given of how
        glossolalia is acquired and used. One chapter is dedicated
        to reviewing the various psychical and psychological inter-
        pretations. The former tend to see speaking in tongues as a
        manifestation of altered states of consciousness or of trance
        experience, or of automatism. The latter prefer to explain
        the phenomenon as a form of repression, emotional release,
        or regression. While rejecting all these interpretations as
        unsatisfactory, the author thinks that glossolalia is not an
        indication of aberrant behavior or abnormality. Neither can
        it be linked with a specific personality type, though it is
        admitted that certain types may be attracted to those reli-
        gious groups or gatherings where speaking in tongues is
        practiced. Glossolalia is not a supernatural phenomena, but
        rather one of the many types of religious language. It is a
        linguistic symbol of the sacred and becomes a central part
        of a personal affective religion.

586.   Samarin, William J. "Glossolalia As Learned Behavior."
        CANADIAN JOURNAL OF THEOLOGY 15 (1969): 60-64.

        Refutes the view that glossolalia is a state of abnormality
        and that it is associated with trance. It is stressed that
        speaking in tongues is a form of pseudo-language and can be
        used in a normal state. The way glossolalia is acquired is
        discussed. The author argues that one "does not learn to
        talk in tongues" (p. 64), though one can be exposed to glos-

solalia and retain some information, like its intonational
patterns. Glossolalia is interpreted theologically: it is
a unique element within one's religious experience and is
linked with baptism, the charismatic rite of passage.

587.   Samarin, William J. "The Linguisticality of Glossolalia."
       HARTFORD QUARTERLY 8.4 (1968): 49-75.

       Discusses glossolalia from a linguistic point of view. The
       author distinguishes glossolalia from xenoglossia, the former
       consisting of meaningless utterances, the latter of foreign
       words unknown by the speaker. Different kinds of glossolalic
       speech utterances are compared with one another and with the
       speakers' native tongues. From a psychological point of view
       the author thinks that the study of glossolalia might shed
       some light on the use of language as "an expression of the
       ineffable." The theory that people who speak in tongues are
       psychologically abnormal is rejected.

588.   Sato, Koji. "Zen, Tendai Sen, and Naikan." PSYCHOLOGIA 13
       (1970): 2-4.

       Discusses various Japanese Buddhist techniques and proposes
       that they should be integrated with the training of psycholo-
       gists. The assumption is that these Japanese methods can be
       used as therapeutic aids in clinical situations.

589.   Sato, Koji. "Zen from a Personalistic Viewpoint." PSYCHO-
       LOGIA 11 (1968): 3-24.

       Reviews research on the history of Zen, the traditional
       structure of Zen training and its effects, and the general
       psychotherapeutic implications. Zen teaching is relevant
       for contemporary Western society because it can improve the
       educational system, help us adapt to the environment, and
       contribute to mental stability and proper personality
       functions.

590.   Sato, Koji. "Neurasthenia and Seiza of Dr. Sanzaburo Koba-
       yachi." PSYCHOLOGIA 9 (1966): 187-91.

       Describes the life and work of Kobayachi (1863-1926) who
       studied surgery in the United States and practiced medicine
       in Hawaii for fifteen years. On his return to Japan he cured
       his own "neurasthenia" by practicing "seiza," that is Zen
       sitting, and then used the method along with modern medicine
       to help his patients.

591.   Sato, Koji. "Psychoanalytic Implications of Zen." PSYCHO-
       LOGIA 1 (1958): 213-18.

       Presents Zen as an important psychotherapeutic technique
       which has much to teach Western psychotherapists. In Zen
       training, psychological health is restored by the adjustment
       of the posture, the breathing, and the mind. The effects of

these corrections bring about physical improvements, like the
increase of vitality and psychological amelioration, as a
change from a melancholic to a cheerful attitude. The main
differences between Zen and Western psychotherapy are briefly
outlined and some weaknesses of both systems are exposed.

592.   Scherzer, Carl J. "The Emmanuel Movement." PASTORAL PSYCHOL-
        OGY 2 (February 1951): 27-33.

        Describes the Boston-based healing movement of the second
        half of the nineteenth century. The author claims that its
        success, and that of other healing groups like Christian
        Science, was partly due to the fact that the churches had
        ignored healing. The Emmanuel Movement was a religiously and
        scientifically sound attempt to treat the whole person.

593.   Schwarz, Berthold E. "Ordeals by Serpents, Fire, and Strych-
        nine: A Study of Some Provocative Psychosomatic Phenomena."
        PSYCHIATRIC QUARTERLY 34 (1960): 405-29.

        Presents the author's field studies of the Free Pentecostal
        Holiness Churches in the southern parts of the United States.
        Psychiatric examination of some of these church members showed
        evidence of neurotic, psychotic, or other psychopathological
        disorders. Their meetings have a cathartic affect on the
        participants who act out their conflicts and the tragedies of
        life. The rituals of handling snakes, of putting one's hand
        over an open fire, and of drinking strychnine are described
        and discussed. The first is related to the dissociative
        state of trance of the snake-handlers and to the possible
        hypnotic effect on the snakes themselves. Various possible
        explanations for the fire ritual, like hypnotic anesthesia
        and the trance-effect of body cooling, are considered and
        rejected. The worshippers' gradual build-up of exultation
        prepares them to drink poison and to counteract its harmful
        effects.

594.   Seeman, William, Sanford Nidich, and Thomas Banta. "Influ-
        ence of Transcendental Meditation as a Measure of Self-
        Actualization." JOURNAL OF COUNSELING PSYCHOLOGY 19 (1972):
        184-87.

        Shows from a study of college undergraduates that TM influ-
        ences, in a positive direction, the criteria derived from
        Shostrom's Personal Orientation Inventory (POI), which centers
        on self-actualization. The conclusion one draws is that TM
        leads to a healthy personality.

595.   Sinha, Ajit Kumar. "Yoga and Western Psychology." RESEARCH
        JOURNAL OF PHILOSOPHY AND THE SOCIAL SCIENCES 1.2 (1964):
        80-92.

        Describes the Yoga system of Pantajali with its eightfold
        path. Yoga is said to inhibit behaviors which are harmful
        to human development, to help a person acquire a stable per-

sonality, and to release one's creative powers. Western
psychology and Yoga, which are both imperfect sciences, are
compared and contrasted and it is maintained that they may
profit from each other.

596.   Sleeper, David E. "Comments on Wardwell's 'Christian Science
        Healing.'" JOURNAL FOR THE SCIENTIFIC STUDY OF RELIGION 5
        (1966): 296-98.

        Criticizes Wardwell's evaluation (item 615) of Christian
        Science healing practices for ignoring the "personal meaning"
        in Christian Science therapy, which is so evident in its
        basic text, SCIENCE AND HEALTH, WITH A KEY TO THE SCRIPTURES,
        and in its Church Manual. The author contends that the
        experiences of Christian Scientists testify to the fact that
        their healing is not based on the denial of objective reality,
        but on a positive assertion of God's presence, power, and
        goodness.

597.   Stagg, Frank, E., Glenn Hinson, and Wayne E. Oates. GLOSSO-
        LALIA: TONGUE-SPEAKING IN BIBLICAL, HISTORICAL, AND PSYCHO-
        LOGICAL PERSPECTIVE. Nashville, TN: Abingdon, 1967. 110 pp.

        Considers the renaissance of Pentecostalism in Western
        society with special emphasis on glossolalia. The success
        of the movement is attributed to its achievements, namely,
        an improved morality, the cessation of alcoholism, the
        integration of disturbed personality, and the cure of both
        psychological and physical disorders.

        Contains items 533, 573.

598.   Stolee, H. J. PENTECOSTALISM: THE PROBLEM OF THE MODERN
        TONGUES MOVEMENT. Minneapolis: Augsburg, 1936. x, 142 pp.

        Discusses Pentecostalism as a religious movement and the
        place of tongue-speaking in scripture. Tongues movements
        like the Irvingites and the Holiness churches are described.
        The author states that the most serious delusion of those
        who speak in tongues is their tendency to subordinate the
        interpretation of scripture to mere intuition or subjective
        experience. The question is raised whether serious nervous
        disease makes an individual vulnerable to recruitment by
        Pentecostalist groups.

599.   Stone, Simon. "The Miller Delusion: A Comparative Study of
        Mass Psychology." AMERICAN JOURNAL OF PSYCHIATRY 91 (1934):
        593-623.

        Considers the religious millenarian revival which was
        started by William Miller in Vermont and which reached its
        peak in the United States in the middle of the nineteenth
        century. The author gives a short life history of Miller
        and detects a developing religious paranoia. A report on
        24 hospital cases of people who had joined the Millerites is

provided. The Miller delusion "represents a main reaction
to a certain stimulus when the time was ripe and the emotional
state of the public ready for its reception" (p. 622).

600.   Strunk, Orlo. "Motivational Factors and Psychotherapeutic
        Aspects of a Healing Cult." JOURNAL OF PASTORAL CARE 9
        (1955): 213-220.

        Examines over 500 samples of testimonies written by mem-
        bers of the Church of Christian Science and published in the
        CHRISTIAN SCIENCE JOURNAL. The psychotherapeutic implications
        are stressed. This cult can rightly boast of a number of
        healing accomplishments, particularly in overcoming addiction
        to alcohol, caffeine, and smoking and in coping with bereave-
        ment. England's conclusion (item 512) that Christian Science
        practitioners act as empathetic psychotherapists is corrobo-
        rated. The relationship between Christian Science practi-
        tioners and their clients is compared to that of psychiatrists
        and their patients. What attracts new adult members to this
        movement is mainly its stress on, and apparent success in,
        healing.

601.   Stunkard, Albert. "Some Interpersonal Aspects of an Oriental
        Religion." PSYCHIATRY 14 (1951): 419-31.

        Maintains that Zen encourages an interpersonal situation
        that is strikingly similar to transference manifestations
        in psychotherapy. In spite of its irrationality, Zen is
        a "meaningful operation" (p. 422), a method which involves
        a relationship and interaction between the Zen master and
        the meditator. The slappings and enigmatic questions (koans)
        are related to psychotherapeutic techniques for dealing with
        defenses against feeling. Some fundamental differences
        between Zen and psychotherapy are alluded to.

602.   Subbannacher, N. V. "The Problem of Consciousness: Modern
        Psychology and Sri Aurobindo." RESEARCH JOURNAL OF PHILOS-
        OPHY AND THE SOCIAL SCIENCES 1 (1964): 102-20.

        Criticizes the methods and goals of various Western psy-
        chologies for their materialistic and mechanistic bent which
        fails to deal with the dynamic orientation of human life.
        The Integral Yoga of Sri Aurobindo is proposed as an alter-
        native therapy which raises the level of human consciousness
        and prepares one for spiritual evolution. The meaning of
        consciousness in Aurobindo's thought is discussed in relation
        to modern psychology.

603.   Sullivan, Francis A. "The Pentecostal Movement." GREGORIANUM
        53 (1972): 237-65.

        Reflects on the Catholic Charismatic Renewal and discusses
        some of its theological and spiritual problems. The author
        rejects the view that Pentecostalism, with its glossolalia,
        is rooted in emotional disturbance and hence pathological.

604.   Swift, Edgar J. THE JUNGLE OF THE MIND. New York: Scribner,
        1931. ix, 340 pp.

        Discusses many occult phenomena, like astrology, spiritual
        mediumship, telepathy, and healing practices, all of which are
        said to be fads, cults, and credulities to which people have
        succumbed. Criticizing both behaviorists and psychoanalysts,
        the author insists that accurate reasoning is necessary to
        prevent us from falling victim to these unscientific beliefs.
        Since the occult is considered irrational, involvement in its
        practices could be pathological.

605.   Tart, Charles T. "A Psychologist's Experience With Transcen-
        dental Meditation." JOURNAL OF TRANSPERSONAL PSYCHOLOGY 2
        (1971): 135-40.

        Relates the author's initiation into TM and mentions some
        of the physical and psychological benefits of meditating.
        TM seems to enable the regular meditator "to work off a large
        accumulation of poorly processed experience" (p. 138). Some
        similarity with psychoanalytic technique is suggested.

606.   Tellegen, Auke, et al. "Personality Characteristics of
        Members of a Serpent-Handling Religious Cult." MMPI:
        RESEARCH DEVELOPMENTS AND CLINICAL APPLICATIONS. Edited
        by James N. Butcher. New York: McGraw-Hill, 1968, pp.
        221-42.

        Criticizes La Barre's theory (item 557) and conducts a
        survey of serpent-handlers using the MMPI, a test which has
        been found useful in assessing psychopathology. It is con-
        cluded that individual disposition may account in part for
        the fact that only certain members of a subculture become
        serpent-handlers. The authors maintain that non-conformity,
        excitablity, impulsivity, emotionality, and extraversion
        rather than neurotic conflicts and deviancy are character-
        istic of these cult members. They also found that older
        members of conventional church groups may have more depres-
        sive symptoms than their counterparts in snake-handling
        cults.

607.   Thiessen, Irmgard, Morgan W. Wright, and George Sisler. "A
        Comparison of Personality Characteristics of Mennonites
        with Non-Mennonites." CANADIAN PSYCHOLOGIST 10 (1969):
        129-37.

        The first of a series of studies of the relationship between
        the value system of the Mennonites in Manitoba, Canada, and
        the types of symptoms developed at the time of mental illness,
        the subsequent course of the illness, and the pattern of
        recovery. Samples of rural and urban Mennonites are compared
        with those of non-Mennonites, and all are given a battery of
        psychological tests. The researchers concluded that the
        Mennonites are generally more guilt-ridden (or morally-
        oriented), have a greater feeling of responsibility to the

group, and are more inflexible and rigid in their response
to authority figures and concepts. The authors are unsure
whether these features are a sign of mental health or illness.

608.   Thorne, F. C. "Zen Buddhism and Clinical Psychology."
        JOURNAL OF CLINICAL PSYCHOLOGY 16 (1960): 452-53.

        Comments, in an editorial, on the work of Harold Helman,
        who compared the mind structure of the West with that of the
        East. Thorne concludes that: 1) "Zen masters were, in effect,
        real psychologists dealing directly with the behaviors which
        are the subject matter of Western psychologists" (p. 453);
        2) direct first-hand experience with Zen should be pursued by
        Western psychologists; and 3) clinicians must direct them-
        selves to experience and be concerned with the behavior at
        issue.

609.   Tingling, David C. "Voodoo, Root Work, and Medicine."
        PSYCHOSOMATIC MEDICINE 29 (1967): 483-90.

        Deals with the Voodoo belief that illness and death may be
        brought about by hexes. The author is concerned about the
        treatment of migrant southern Blacks in industrialized
        northern cities where professional counselors do not under-
        stand the problem and are unable to help patients. Several
        case reports are present from a study conducted in Rochester,
        New York. It is suggested that, in appropriate cases, the
        issue of root work be raised, even though the patient may
        be reluctant to talk about it. Treatment, according to the
        author, includes listening to the patient's complaints,
        reciting incantations, using powders and liquids as counter-
        spells, and giving specific advice for future behavior.

610.   Vahia, N. S., S. L. Vinekar, and D. R. Doongaji. "Psycho-
        physiologic Therapy Based on the Concepts of Pantajali:
        A New Approach to the Treatment of Neurotic and Psycho-
        somatic Disorders." AMERICAN JOURNAL OF PSYCHOTHERAPY
        27 (1972): 557-65.

        Outlines briefly the theoretical and therapeutic concepts
        implicit in Pantajali's system of Yoga and presents the
        results of its application to 250 patients suffering from
        neurotic and psychosomatic disorders. In disagreement with
        general Western psychiatry, Pantajali held that the criterion
        of social adjustment is not a satisfactory yardstick of men-
        tal health and normality. On the contrary, any stress on
        social adaptation tends to increase anxiety and other psychi-
        atric problems. Instead, Pantajali's Yoga proposes that one
        should aim to make use of one's abilities in any given envi-
        ronment without preoccupation about reward or fear of punish-
        ment. The five main steps of Yoga which can be applied to
        achieve this end are described. The results confirm the
        value of Pantajali's Yoga for treating the above-mentioned
        disorders.

611.   Vahia, N. S., S. L. Vinekar, and D. R. Doongaji. "Some
       Ancient Indian Concepts in the Treatment of Psychiatric
       Disorders." BRITISH JOURNAL OF PSYCHIATRY 112 (1966):
       1089-96.

       Outlines the authors' endeavors to treat their psychiatric
       patients with Yoga techniques, based on Indian philosophical
       concepts of the nature of the human being and the basic prob-
       lems of life. The loss of peace of mind is singled out as
       the major cause of psychiatric problems and disorders. The
       treatment by Yoga is, according to these authors, not part
       of the Hindu religion and has, therefore, universal applica-
       bility. 30 case studies are schematically presented with a
       record of their symptoms, diagnoses, social incapacity,
       physical findings, and results.

612.   Valentine, Alonzo M. "Zen and the Psychology of Education."
       JOURNAL OF PSYCHOLOGY 79 (1971): 103-10.

       Maintains that with the infiltration of Zen wisdom in the
       West, another way of investigating the experience of the self
       is possible. Because Zen does not seek to construct a logical
       scheme that is supposed to define one's preconceived self-
       identity, it avoids the problem of this concept. Zen, there-
       fore, opens new educational possibilities which might have
       better psychological effects on people.

613.   Van Dusen, Wilson. "Zen and Western Psychotherapy." PSYCHO-
       LOGIA 1 (1958): 229-30.

       States that in spite of its suspicions of Zen, the West
       has shown an increasing interest in this Eastern meditative
       practice. The use of existential analysis in counseling and
       treatment was originally used by Zen, which insists that a
       person must center on the here and now. Zen as Buddhism and
       Zen as philosophy are less important, according to the author,
       than Zen as a therapeutic technique.

614.   Vithaldas, Yogi. THE YOGA SYSTEM OF HEALTH AND RELIEF FROM
       TENSION. New York: Bell Publishing Co., 1957. 125 pp.

       Views Yoga as an extended system of psychotherapy which
       should be adopted by the Western world. Besides physical
       disorders, Yoga can cure hysteria, depression, and other
       psychological illnesses. The various bodily postures,
       breathing exercises, and methods of concentration and medi-
       tation are described.

615.   Wardwell, Walter I. "Christian Science Healing." JOURNAL
       FOR THE SCIENTIFIC STUDY OF RELIGION 4 (1965): 175-81.

       Outlines the Christian Science method of healing and spec-
       ulates on the reason why the denial of reality is central
       in the system. It is pointed out that such denial occurs at
       different psychological levels. Christian Scientists seem to

be rejecting their own weaknesses and inadequacies as well
as their aggressive impulses; the latter are projected onto
other people who are perceived as dangerous. The belief in
Malicious Animal Magnetism (MAM) resembles delusions of
persecution inflicted by imaginary ememies. Because Christian Scientists repress or deny their fundamental human
drives and desires, they suffer from unconscious feelings of
depression and guilt that are only partly relieved by their
explanations.

616.   Whitehead, George. AN INQUIRY INTO SPIRITUALISM. London:
       John Bale, Sons, and Danielsson, 1934. vii, 466 pp.

       Surveys the various beliefs and practices connected with
       spiritualism, including mediumship, clairvoyance, and demonic
       possession. The author holds that spiritualism has its roots
       in savage and infantile psychology and is symptomatic of men-
       tal delusion. Belief in various spirits is explained with
       reference to the subconscious and mediumship is treated as an
       example of hypnotic suggestion. Fraud, hallucinations, and
       faulty memories are often sufficient to account for many of
       the phenomena which come under the topic of spiritualism.

617.   Wimberly, Howard. "The Knights of the Golden Lotus."
       ETHNOLOGY 11 (1972): 173-86.

       Examines a lay organization within the political branch
       of one of the new Japanese religions, namely, Seicho-no-ie
       ("House of Growth"), which has a few branches in the United
       States. The formation of the Knights is described, and it
       is shown how the group functions as an analogical extension
       of the family archetype. The ritual therapy of this new
       religious movement brings about a readjustment of domestic
       relationships and attitudes which clash with traditional
       values. The result is that conflict is often resolved and
       illness averted. The Knights are, through their political
       involvement, taking care of the psychological needs brought
       about by domestic problems.

618.   Winslow, David J. "Bishop E. E. Everett and Some Aspects of
       Occultism and Folk Religion in Negro Philadelphia." KEY-
       STONE FOLKLORE QUARTERLY 14 (1969); 59-90.

       Studies an occult bookstore in Philadelphia in the late
       1960s. The physical setting and the merchandise are care-
       fully described. The author concludes that Bishop Everett,
       the black minister who ran the store, brought hope, security,
       satisfaction, and happiness to those living in the ghetto by
       combining folk and official religious beliefs and practices.
       He succeeded in helping the blacks to a greater degree than
       all the poverty programs that were trying to solve the urban
       problems of the time.

619.   Wintrob, Ronald M. "Hexes, Roots, Snake Eyes? M.D. vs Occult."
       MEDICAL OPINION 1 (1972): 55-61.

Concerns the author's black patients in the Hartford, Connecticut, area who believed that certain misfortunes cannot be counteracted by scientific means, because they were caused by magical potions extracted from roots, and had to be treated by Voodoo priests or root doctors. The author argues that the persistence of such beliefs cannot be explained by the theory that their black adherents are poor or culturally deprived. He prefers the functional theory that explains root work as an expression of the suppressed rage and feelings of many Blacks, who are politically and economically powerless. Their inferior condition creates uncertainty and leads them to alternative belief systems. Root work is a kind of therapy and can coexist with modern treatments.

620. Wood, William W. CULTURE AND PERSONALITY ASPECTS OF THE PENTECOSTAL HOLINESS RELIGION. The Hague, Netherlands: Mouton, 1965. xi, 125 pp.

Attempts to show, by applying Rorschach tests, that those people who take part in highly emotional religions will have different personalities from members of more sedate, or mainline, religious organizations. The author describes briefly the religious patterns of Calvinism, Wesleyanism, and American Pentecostalism; analyzes a camp meeting; gives information on Pentecostal beliefs; examines feelings of social solidarity and subjective experience; and discusses two southern Pentecostal churches. Pentecostalism, he holds, is a form of enthusiastic religion which arises in situations of social and cultural disorganization. Those who join a Pentecostal church lack an adequate value-attitude system. They are, furthermore, uncertain and threatened individuals who are searching for satisfactory relationships and personal integrity. These needs are satisfied by involvement in Pentecostalism.

621. Worcester, Elwood, and Samuel McComb. THE CHRISTIAN RELIGION AS A HEALING POWER: A DEFENSE AND EXPOSITION OF THE EMMANUEL MOVEMENT. New York: Moffat, Yard and Co., 1909. 130 pp.

An insider's defense against the criticism leveled at the Emmanuel Movement. The psychological objection that religion has nothing to do with psychotherapy is first refuted. The relationship between the movement's theory and practice and the various psychologies is outlined. The authors state that the aim of this religious movement is to bring together the physician, the clergyman, and the social worker to help alleviate certain disorders of the nervous system, which may involve a defect of character and a more or less complete mental dissociation. The efforts of the Emmanuel Movement are directed towards functional disorders.

622. Worcester, Elwood, Samuel McComb, and Isador H. Coriat. RELIGION AND MEDICINE: THE SOCIAL CONTROL OF NERVOUS DISORDERS. New York: Moffat, Yard and Co., 1908. vii, 427 pp.

Embarks on a description of faith healing in Emmanuel
Church, Boston. It is argued that hysteria, alcoholism,
hypochondria, and other psychiatric conditions have a direct
impact on the personality and are traceable to moral causes.
Faith-healing movements are regarded as new religious movements which point to areas where Christianity has failed.
After examining the causes of nervousness and the nature and
therapeutic value of hypnotism, the authors discuss the therapeutic value of prayer and faith, which can have healing power
in certain circumstances. Healing cults, including Christian
Science, "dissipate various kinds of neuroses, afford moral
uplift to the depressed and create an atmosphere of faith,
hope and courage..." (p. 302). The authors think that such
things as automatic writing and crystal gazing are diseases
of the subconscious and that the ecstatic state of Hindu
mystics is achieved by autosuggestion and hypnosis.

623.   Yarnell, Helen. "An Example of the Psychopathology of Reli-
        gion: The Seventh-Day Adventist Denomination." JOURNAL OF
        NERVOUS AND MENTAL DISEASE 125 (1957): 202-12.

        Describes the historical background of the church and its
        main beliefs, giving special attention to two of the move-
        ment's leaders, William Miller and Ellen White. It is held
        that this sect does not have any psychopathologies that set
        it apart from the mainline Protestant denominations. Its
        preoccupation, however, with the second coming of Christ is
        indicative of neurosis. The church tends to attract those
        who have reached a hopeless despair and those persons who
        are probably immature, needing a more effective control over
        their lives.

624.   Yesudian, Selvarajan, and Elizabeth Haich. YOGA AND HEALTH.
        New York: Harper and Row, 1953. 190 pp.

        Maintains that the purpose of Yoga is to make human con-
        sciousness dependent on the will, to expand one's awareness,
        and to strengthen the nervous system. The practice of Yoga
        leads to both physical and mental health. The various yogic
        breathing exercises with their corresponding therapeutic
        effects are explained.

CHAPTER III

PSYCHIATRY AND THE CULTS IN CROSS-CULTURAL PERSPECTIVE

The rise of new religious movements in different societies around the world has been studied with vigor by anthropologists since the second half of the last century. These religious groups, frequently called nativistic or millenarian cults, or revitalization movements, have been very numerous, especially among non-literate societies. Many studies have been sociologically-oriented and have attempted to relate the new cults to sociocultural changes sparked by the contact between non-literate societies and one of the larger civilizations, particularly the industrialized Western world. Other studies have pursued a holistic approach which seeks to understand the relationship between individual cults and other aspects of culture, and the impact the new movements have on the society or community.

The functions of religion have played a key role in anthropological studies of religion. The most common psychological functions assigned to religion are emotional. Religion, by giving the person identity, security, and courage, succeeds in reducing, relieving, and allaying anxiety, fear, tension, and stress. The rise of new movements is amenable to similar interpretations. Because they arise in times of social and/or cultural changes, cults can be readily seen as a solution to both personal and social problems. More recently, anthropologists have stressed the adaptive functions of religious beliefs and rituals. Religion is a means by which human beings adjust to the environment and utilize it for their needs. New religious movements have also been explained as ways of adapting to a changing world. Since they help a person come to grips with new sociocultural conditions, cults could be psychologically beneficial, if not therapeutic.

In this chapter, we concentrate on those studies on non-Western societies which make direct or indirect reference to the psychological and/or psychiatric functions of these new groups, and to those which discuss native therapeutic techniques, several of which have found their way into the West either through immigrants or through propagation by new cults. Section One lists theoretical and general studies on transcultural psychiatry and on non-Western traditional and folk therapy. Specific works on indigenous psychiatric treatments are also included. Because many new religions in the West have adopted medical folk practices popular in other countries, evaluating these practices in their own cultural context might enhance understanding of their apparent success and popularity in the

185

West. Studies of specific non-Western therapies (like Morita and
Naikan) are also listed here. Section Two annotates studies of
individual movements, such as cargo cults, spiritism, curanderismo,
and glossolalia, which is usually referred to as a tongue-speaking
movement. Section Three contains material on, or relating to, the
phenomenon of shamanism, which has occupied a prominent place in
anthropological studies of religion. Because shamanism is often
linked with spirit possession or with procedures that bring about a
radical alteration of one's state of consciousness, it bears some
similarity to trance and possession states which have been recorded
in Western culture.

A. THEORETICAL STUDIES ON, AND SPECIFIC EXAMPLES OF, FOLK PSYCHIATRY

The student of new religious movements is struck by the similarity between some of their beliefs and healing practices and those
commonly referred to as folk medicine. Anthropology has contributed
many descriptive studies of indigenous beliefs and practices regarding illness and its cure. Psychological anthropology has explored
the native views about human nature and its operation. Cultural
psychiatry has recently studied the possible healing effects of folk
therapies and compared them with those attributed to Western psychiatric treatments. Many of the following studies challenge, directly
or indirectly, several of the assumptions which Western psychiatrists
frequently make. The first of these is to take for granted the universal applicability of Western psychological principles and psychotherapeutic treatments; the second, to assume that religious elements
should either be ignored in the curing process or, more negatively,
be considered a therapeutic hindrance.

In spite of the many problems which indigenous psychiatry has to
face, particularly in a changing world, the general consensus is
that it is a genuine healing technique. Folk therapy, like any
Western psychiatric treatment, may not always be successful. It
has, however, a healing potential based on similar principles which
operate in the West, namely faith, suggestion, group support, reliance on a therapist/client relationship, and catharsis. Although
there are many differences between folk therapy and Western treatment, many psychiatrists agree that 1) knowledge of the patient's
culture is necessary for successful therapy, 2) that the two systems
could occasionally be combined with better results, and 3) that
therapists from both traditions might collaborate in the healing
process.

625.   Ademuwagun, Z. A., John A. Agoade, Ire E. Harrison, and
          Dennis M. Warren, editors. THE AFRICAN THERAPEUTIC SYSTEMS.
          Waltham, MA: Brandeis University, 1979. 273 pp.

          Presents a collection of 40 essays and two reference ar-
          ticles on the interpretation of therapeutic systems in 14

African societies. The material is divided into three parts:
1) African treatments for physical and psychological disease;
2) African concepts of disease; and 3) the interaction between
African and Western medicine. The problems resulting from the
coexistence of both systems and the possibility of a fruitful
integration of them are discussed.

626. Aleksandrowicz, Malca. "The Art of a Native Therapist."
      BULLETIN OF THE MENNINGER CLINIC 36 (1972): 596-608.

Studies the case of a highly successful Jewish folk healer
in Israel whose treatments are confined mainly to cases of
neurosis and psychosomatic disorders. Her domineering
personality is characterized by both greed and the ability
to manipulate others. She also suffers from several pathological problems, including a deep-seated depression, a great
fear of death, poor reality testing, and fantasies of grandeur
and immortality. Her curing techniques are briefly described
and illustrated by several case studies. The author discusses
the needs for such folk therapists in Israel, their successes
where Western psychiatry has failed, and what the latter can
learn from folk healing techniques.

627. Algeria, Daniel, Ernesto Guerra, Cervando Martinez, and
      George C. Meyer. "El Hospital Invisible: A Study of
      'Curanderismo.'" ARCHIVES OF GENERAL PSYCHIATRY 34 (1977):
      1354-57.

Presents the conclusion drawn from interviews with 16
Mexican-American folk healers (curanderos and curanderas) in
San Antonio, Texas, where they are still called on to perform
healings, especially among older people. The process of
becoming a healer, the referral practices, the types of disorders treated, and the actual methods are described. The
authors doubt whether folk techniques can be incorporated
into Western medical practices and suggest that healers, who
perform valuable services to the people they treat, should be
informed of existing modern health care systems and instructed
about the symptoms of serious disease.

628. Araneta, Enrique. "'Scientific' Psychiatry and 'Community'
      Healers." TRADITIONAL HEALING (item 735), pp. 65-79.

Maintains that cultural psychology, which is also concerned
with relating the mentally ill to their cultural environment,
is not only scientific, but also the most effective and therapeutic approach. The objections to the collaboration between
Western psychiatrists and folk healers of minority groups in
the United States are discussed and refuted. The author
thinks that the arguments that 1) Western therapy is more
successful, and 2) the use of folk therapy fosters magical
thought, do not withstand critical examination.

629. Bergman, Robert L. "A School for Medicine Men." AMERICAN
      JOURNAL OF PSYCHIATRY 130 (1973): 663-66.

Provides a short account of how a Navajo Indian community
established its own medical school and how a non-Indian
psychiatrist participated in it. The background of Navajo
practitioners is given and the rituals, which the author
believes have healing powers, are described. The author cites
his work as a good example of cooperation between Western
psychiatrists and native therapists.

630.   Bilu, Y. "The Taming of the Deviants and Beyond: An Analysis
       of 'Dybbuk' Possession and Exorcism in Judaism." PSYCHO-
       ANALYTIC STUDY OF SOCIETY 11 (1985): 1-32.

       Attempts to clarify, in terms of its sociocultural compo-
       nents, the phenomenon of "Dybbuk" possession, cases of which
       have been documented in Jewish sources since the sixteenth
       century. Sixty-three cases of possession, which involved
       spirits of the dead as possessing agents, are analyzed. The
       author emphasizes the collective or control level, three
       elements of which are identified: 1) direct cultural molding
       of aberrant impulses; 2) rectification of deviance by exor-
       cism; and 3) the strengthening of the community through the
       actual possession. The author contends that "Dybbuk" posses-
       sion is a culture-specific syndrome in which "deviance is
       transferred into enhanced conformity." Cases of possession
       were prevalent in times of crises precipitated by rapid
       sociocultural changes.

631.   Bilu, Y. "General Characteristics of Referrals to Traditional
       Healers in Israel." ISRAELI ANNALS OF PSYCHIATRY AND
       RELATED DISCIPLINES 15 (1977): 245-52.

       Studies some elements of Jewish-Moroccan ethnopsychiatry.
       Observing that many people in Israel are still using these
       traditional resources of therapy, the author covers the range
       of problems treated. Romantic, marital, and sexual issues,
       interpersonal conflicts, and demon-caused diseases are more
       frequently the reasons why a person consults a local healer.
       The general characteristics of the patients--such as age, sex,
       family condition, and socioeconomic status--are presented.
       Some principles for choosing a healer are listed. It is held
       that the traditional system operates when modern medicine has
       no satisfactory answer.

632.   Bolman, W. M. "Cross-Cultural Psychotherapy." AMERICAN
       JOURNAL OF PSYCHIATRY 124 (1968): 1237-44.

       Discusses the need to adapt Western scientific approaches
       and mental health services in different culture areas. Since
       the availability of counselors who can be competent bridges
       between two cultures is rare, the author suggests that two
       professionals, one from each culture, be involved and that
       collaboration between Western psychiatrists and traditional
       healers be adopted as the norm.

633.   Boyer, L. Bryce. "Approaching Cross-Cultural Psychotherapy."
       JOURNAL OF PSYCHOANALYTIC ANTHROPOLOGY 6 (1983): 237-45.

Deals with the discrepancy between the patient's and therapist's goals, a discrepancy clearly seen especially in ethnic
minorities where shamanism, spiritism, and voodoo are practiced. Faith-healing and insight-oriented psychotherapy are
compared and contrasted. The former is said to rely on
supernatural powers and use exhortation and suggestion; the
latter stresses empirical evidence, urges the patient to
self-reflection, and interprets suggestion as a manifestation
of counter-transference problems. A number of problems which
psychiatrists encounter in the treatment of patients from
minority groups are discussed.

634.   Breckenridge, S. N., and M. A. C. Breckenridge. "Indigenous
        Healers of the Plantation of Sri Lanka." READINGS IN TRANS-
        CULTURAL PSYCHIATRY. Edited by A. Kiev and A. Venkoba.
        Madras, India: Macmillan, 1982, pp. 119-23.

Describes the native system of disease and the various types
of healers, astrologers, priests, and diviners, which may be
called to cure both physical and psychological illnesses. The
authors suggest that community health programs organized along
Western standards might benefit by the use of indigenous healers in a modified role.

635.   Bruhn, John G., and Raymond G. Fuentes. "Cultural Factors
        Affecting Utilization of Services by Mexican Americans."
        PSYCHIATRIC ANNALS 7.12 (1977): 20-29.

Discusses the health problems of Mexican-Americans and the
various cultural factors which must be taken into account in
order that medical and psychiatric care can be made available
to them and adapted to their needs. The cultural differences
between Mexicans and Americans, particularly the former's belief in supernaturally-caused illnesses, are described. The
philosophical basis of faith healing is explained and the role
of the curanderos in treating the patient is stressed. While
there are cultural barriers to the acceptance of modern, Western medicine, the authors believe that the two health care
systems can be used together for the benefit of the sick
individual.

636.   Buckley, Peter. "Altered States of Consciousness During Psy-
        chotherapy: A Historical and Cultural Perspective." INTER-
        NATIONAL JOURNAL OF SOCIAL PSYCHIATRY 25 (1975): 118-24.

Reviews some of the historical evidence which supports the
useful application of altered states of consciousness as a
form of therapeutic treatment in pre-modern psychiatry and in
non-Western cultures. The worship of Dionysius and the rites
performed in the temple of Asclepius are taken as an example
of healing in the context of drastic changes of consciousness.
The same link between altered states and religious rituals is
traced to the Middle Ages when, for example, many pilgrims
traveled to the shrine of St. Almedha in Wales and invoked a
trance-like state in order to be cured. Mesmerism marked a

dramatic shift from a religious to a scientific setting, but
the basic idea of placing healing in the context of a change
of awareness remained. Examples from North and South American
Indians and from Haitian Voodoo point to the same connection.
In psychoanalysis both the patient and the analyst should be
in "a state of free-floating awareness," implying a change of
consciousness. In contemporary times the therapeutic use of
altered states is common, Transcendental Meditation being an
excellent example. How central the altered state is to therapeutic efficacy remains an open question.

637.   Buhrmann, M. V., and J. Mqaba Gqomfa. "The Xhosa Healers of
        Southern Africa: A Family Therapy Session With a Dream as
        Central Content." JOURNAL OF ANALYTICAL PSYCHOLOGY 27
        (1982): 41-57.

        Reports and analyzes a healing ceremony in such a way that
        the reader can share the African experience. The ritual deals
        with tensions, anxieties, and concerns that are expressed in
        dreams. The author discusses the dream material and clearly
        depicts its main themes. The healer clarifies the obscure,
        makes the unconscious conscious, and brings order out of chaos
        and light out of darkness. By the end of the ritual, the par-
        ticipants are transformed into happy, joyous individuals. All
        of them had made their contribution to the healing experience.

638.   Carstairs, G. M. "Healing Ceremonies in Primitive Societies."
        LISTENER 72 (1964): 195-97.

        Examines many ritual healings in non-literate cultures and
        suggests that abreaction, which implies the free expression
        of unconscious painful feelings, is a central part of the
        cure. The participation of family and friends in primitive
        healing ceremonies is also psychologically beneficial. Prim-
        itive healing is likened to psychodrama, a form of highly
        emotional group therapy. Neurotic conflicts are sometimes
        resolved by granting the forbidden impulse an indirect expres-
        sion as socially approved behavior. Western psychology, the
        author maintains, has a lot to learn from primitive healing
        rituals.

639.   Chang, Suk C. "Morita Therapy." AMERICAN JOURNAL OF PSYCHO-
        THERAPY 28 (1974): 208-11.

        Discusses Japanese Morita therapy as a psychotherapeutic
        system. The four stages of treatment are described and a
        case study is presented. The author maintains that Morita
        therapy converges with the philosophy of Zen and has been
        found to be effective in curing many neurotic problems. It
        aims at a basic change in the patient's personality structure
        and not merely at the symptoms. In accordance with Zen prin-
        ciples, this therapy enables the subject to confront his own
        neurosis completely for a sustained period of time till the
        psychic conflict attains an "autonomous resolution" and thus
        allows him or her to gain a new perspective on life. The

applicability of Morita therapy to other cultures is discussed
and the author states that it is the metaphysical aspects of
Western culture and not the therapy's main elements that make
its use in the West rather difficult.

640.   Chang, Suk C. "The Cultural Context of Japanese Psychiatry
        and Psychotherapy." AMERICAN JOURNAL OF PSYCHOTHERAPY 19
        (1965): 593-600.

        Discusses the cultural and historical background of Japanese
        psychiatry and psychotherapeutic treatments, particularly
        Morita therapy, the goals and methods of which are described
        in the context of Zen Buddhism and its goal of Satori.

641.   Colson, Anthony C., and Karen E. Selby. "Medical Anthropol-
        ogy." ANNUAL REVIEW OF ANTHROPOLOGY. Edited by Bernard
        J. Siegel, Alan Beals, and Stephen A. Tyler. Palo Alto,
        CA: Annual Reviews, 1974, vol. 3, pp. 245-62.

        Surveys the literature in the rapidly growing field of medi-
        cal anthropology. Fours areas are covered: 1) ethnomedicine;
        2) medical ecology; 3) health research problems; and 4) health
        care delivery systems. The last section discusses the diffi-
        culties of using Western psychiatric approaches in a different
        cultural setting. There are 154 references.

642.   Corin, Ellen, and Giles Bibeau. "Psychiatric Perspectives in
        Africa. Part II: The Traditional Viewpoint." TRANSCULTURAL
        PSYCHIATRIC RESEARCH REVIEW 7 (1980): 205-33.

        Presents an overview of what is known about the ways tradi-
        tional African societies name, classify, explain, and treat
        mental disorders. African classification of disease and
        explanations of its origin are interpreted as operating on
        two distinct levels: 1) the natural or empirical, and 2) the
        interpretative or symbolic. These levels are also operative
        in the therapeutic system. Possession cults are seen as an
        integral part of the African medical system which provide
        treatment for patients as well as training for therapists.
        The African structure of beliefs and practices makes up a
        genuine and original psychiatric system, one which is under-
        going transformation during the current process of cultural
        change. A comprehensive bibliography (pp. 226-33) is
        included.

643.   Corin, Ellen, and H. B. M. Murphy. "Psychiatric Perspectives
        in Africa. Part I: The Western Viewpoint." TRANSCULTURAL
        PSYCHIATRIC RESEARCH REVIEW 16 (1979): 147-77.

        Examines the literature on African mental illness and its
        native treatment from a Western psychiatric point of view.
        Hospitalization data, classification of diseases and their
        incidences, distribution and control are outlined, and the
        etiological factors (pan-cultural and culture-linked) con-

sidered. Ethnopsychoanalysis has been employed as a special approach to understanding mental illness in Africa. A lengthy bibliography (pp. 169-78) is added.

644.   Crapanzano, V. THE HAMADSHA: A STUDY IN MOROCCAN ETHNO-
        PSYCHIATRY. Berkeley: University of California Press,
        1973. 258 pp.

Studies a Moroccan brotherhood which traces its origin to two Muslim saints of the late seventeenth century. Part One investigates the historical aspects of the brotherhood which, though linked with the Sufi tradition, employs the holiness of the saints as a power to heal and protect against the harmful effects of spirits. Part Two deals with the institutions and interrelationships of the brotherhood. Part Three is devoted to its therapeutic activities. The author relates the dynamics of the healing process to several factors, including the tension between the sexes in Moroccan society.

645.   Devereux, George. "Cultural Thought Models in Primitive and
        Modern Psychiatric Theories." PSYCHIATRY 21 (1958): 359-74.

Discusses the influence of non-scientific and culturally determined thought models upon psychiatric theories. Various cultural aspects of primitive and modern psychiatry are examined. The author thinks that a "reculturalization of psychoanalysis" is taking place and that psychoanalysis will cease to be an objective science.

646.   Doi, L. Takeo. "Morita Therapy and Psychoanalysis." PSYCHO-
        LOGIA 5 (1962): 117-23.

Attempts an exposition of the Japanese Morita therapy with its four stages leading to a cure and interprets it in psychoanalytic terms. The author argues that although there are definite links between Morita Therapy and Zen Buddhism, the two should not be identified or confused. Compared with this Eastern method, Western psychotherapy is found wanting because the latter encourages a spirit of authoritarianism and an attitude of dependency. Morita treatment, moreover, takes only a few months to complete, as compared to the much longer period needed in Western psychotherapeutic procedures.

647.   Douglas, Florence M. "Prescientific Psychiatry in the Urban
        Context." AMERICAN JOURNAL OF PSYCHIATRY 131 (1974): 279-
        82.

Studies the belief in ghosts and spirits in urban Los Angeles and examines the reliance on indigenous practitioners, who are believed to have some control over the supernatural. The therapeutic and antitherapeutic effects of beliefs in prescientific psychological concepts and practices are explored. Because healing is multi-dimensional, prescientific psychiatric treatment may have a measure of success because, among other reasons, many people find consolation in believing in

spiritual entities. Four case studies are presented. An
exchange of ideas between indigenous practitioners and psychiatrists and counselors is urged.

648. Easthope, Gard. "Marginal Healers." SICKNESS AND SECTARIAN-
ISM (item 1238), pp. 52-67.

Draws a picture of an ideal folk healer as a caring, sympathetic, disinterested, knowledgeable, and authoritative
individual. The author reviews the literature on the placebo
effect which, he claims, explains partially the success of
folk healers. Patients suffering from the uncertain outcome
of their problems are easily influenced by trustworthy and
authoritative healers. The author insists that placebo healing is real healing.

649. Edgerton, Robert B. "A Traditional African Psychiatrist."
SOUTHWESTERN JOURNAL OF ANTHROPOLOGY 27 (1971): 259-78.

Relates an account of a traditional psychiatrist in the
Hele tribe of Tanzania. His training and practice are briefly
outlined. Catharsis, group support, and suggestion are used
routinely as are numerous drugs and herbs. The author states
that even though the African psychiatrist operates with a
system of supernatural beliefs, there is evidence of
scientific use of medication.

650. Fabrega, Horacio. "Medical Anthropology." BIENNIAL REVIEW
OF ANTHROPOLOGY. Edited by Bernard J. Siegal. Stanford,
CA: Stanford University Press, 1972, pp. 167-229.

Presents an evaluative bibliographic survey of anthropological works on cross-cultural medicine. The material is
divided into three sections: 1) general works; 2) ethnomedical
studies, which include studies on the personality attributes
of shamans and other folk healers; and 3) medical ecology and
epidemiology. There are over 300 references.

651. Favazza, Armando R., and Mary Oman. "Anthropology and Psychi-
atry." COMPREHENSIVE TEXTBOOK OF PSYCHIATRY. Edited by
H. I. Kaplan, A. M. Freedman and B. J. Sadock. Baltimore:
Williams and Wilkins, 1980, vol. 1, pp. 485-504.

Provides an overview of studies which have been made to
integrate specific cultures with psychiatric theory and
practice. Various works in different areas are covered: 1)
culture, mental health, and psychoanalysis; 2) culture and
personality; and 3) cross-cultural research. Several studies
on the folk theory of mental illness, its diagnosis and treatment, and on the work of folk healers are also summarized. A
short description of Christian beliefs about mental illness
is given with reference to the current charismatic approach
to sickness and healing. The authors suggest that scientific psychiatry may be enhanced by the application of cross-
cultural insights. A lengthy bibliography is included.

652.   Foster, George M. "Disease Etiologies in non-Western Medical
        Systems." AMERICAN ANTHROPOLOGIST 78 (1976): 773-78.

        Draws up the similarities and differences between Western
        medical systems and those used in non-Western countries. The
        former stress the naturalistic view of illness and regard
        religion and magic as largely unrelated to illness, while the
        latter are personalistic and consider religion and magic as
        intimately linked with sickness. Curers in non-Western
        societies, like shamans and folk healers, have a therapeutic
        role to play in their respective communities.

653.   Foster, George M., and Barbara Gallatin Anderson. MEDICAL
        ANTHROPOLOGY. New York: Wiley and Sons, 1978. x, 354 pp.

        Provides a general overview of the relatively new field
        of medical anthropology, stressing the sociocultural dimen-
        sions which have been brought to the fore. Two basic
        assumptions seem to underlie the authors' treatment of the
        subject: 1) health-related behavior in both Western and Third
        World countries is adaptive, consciously or unconsciously
        promoting the survival and the increase of the population;
        2) a cross-cultural perspective provides the greatest insight
        into the dynamics of health behavior. Chapters on ethno-
        psychiatry and on shamans and other curers discuss, respec-
        tively, the problems of how traditional societies view and
        deal with mental illness, and of the roles of healers and
        patients. The positive and negative aspects of non-Western
        therapies are outlined with reference to the major anthropo-
        logical writings on the topic. The authors state that Western
        medicine, although not without flaws, is a more satisfactory
        way of meeting the needs of contemporary people.

654.   Foulks, Edward F., Ronald M. Wintrob, Joseph Westermeyer,
        and Armando R. Favazza, editors. CURRENT PERSPECTIVES IN
        CULTURAL PSYCHIATRY. New York: Spectrum Books, 1977.
        275 pp.

        Contains 18 essays dealing with: 1) anthropological theory
        in psychiatry; 2) current research in cultural psychiatry in
        the United States; 3) cross-cultural research by American
        psychiatrists; and 4) the future of cultural psychiatry.

        Contains items 775, 881.

655.   Green, Edward C. "Roles for Traditional African Healers in
        Mental Health Care." MEDICAL ANTHROPOLOGY 4 (1980): 489-
        522.

        Discusses the much-debated issue of whether native healers
        should have a part in modern health care. The strengths and
        weaknesses of African healers and the roles they play are
        examined. The main features of traditional healing practices
        are drawn up and the author analyzes the possible practical
        policies which may be implemented. Among his proposals to

the World Health Organization (WHO) Regional Commission for
Africa (1976), the author recommends: 1) registration of
native healers; 2) their legal recognition based on competency
tests; and 3) their possible integration in health teams.

656.   Hallowell, A. Irving. "Psychic Stress and Cultural Patterns."
       AMERICAN JOURNAL OF PSYCHIATRY 92 (1936): 1291-310.

       Examines the influence of cultural factors on the incidence,
       etiology, and symptomatology of certain mental disorders.
       Taking examples from the Salteaux, an American Indian tribe
       in Manitoba, Canada, the author shows how: 1) institution-
       alized confession is used as a means of relieving psychic
       stress; 2) an appeal to love magic may serve to lessen shame,
       embarrassment, and social ridicule; and 3) a theory of dream
       interpretation can play a role in the resolution of stressful
       situations. It is questioned whether "windigo" psychosis is
       a unitary type of mental disorder.

657.   Heelas, Paul, and Andrew Lock, editors. INDIGENOUS PSYCHOL-
       OGIES: THE ANTHROPOLOGY OF THE SELF. New York: Academic
       Press, 1981. xviii, 322 pp.

       Presents 16 essays discussing psychological theories of the
       human person in different cultures. The material is divided
       into three areas: 1) The Indigenous and the Universal; 2)
       Anthropological Perspectives; and 3) Psychological Perspec-
       tives.

       Contains item 1574.

658.   Hoch, Erna M. "Pir, Faqir, and Psychologist." HUMAN CONTEXT
       6 (1974): 668-77.

       Provides an account of two native healers in Kashmir: the
       "pir," or wise man, and the "faqir," or adept. The indigenous
       healer, unlike the Western psychiatrist, strives to achieve a
       cure in a single session, usually works in public, and often
       involves the family of the patient. Both native and modern
       procedures involve some form of transference which may take
       the form of psychodrama or traditional possession and exor-
       cism. The key difference between the types of therapy is the
       use of possession by the traditional healer. Many people in
       Kashmir have recourse to both healer and psychiatrist.

659.   Hoenig, J., and C. Wijesinghe. "Religious Beliefs and Psychi-
       atric Disorder in Sri Lanka." CONFINIA PSYCHIATRICA 22.1
       (1979): 19-33.

       Describes some popular beliefs about the causes of illness
       and the ceremonies held to cure them. Supernatural beliefs
       can influence various aspects of psychiatric disorder and
       practice. Mythology, for instance, can become the content
       of psychotic experiences and can also offer a therapeutic

approach to bring about a cure. Several cases are given and
the authors suggest, in each case, whether Western psychiatry
or native treatment would have been more successful.

660.   Holdstock, T. L. "Indigenous Healing in South Africa: A
        Neglected Potential." SOUTH AFRICAN JOURNAL OF PSYCHOLOGY
        9 (1979): 118-24.

        Outlines several reasons why psychologists should take
        serious note of indigenous healing in Africa. The African
        healer takes care of both the emotional needs and spiritual
        values of his clients. Western psychological approaches, it
        is argued, are inadequate when applied to other cultures.

661.   Holland, William R., and Roland G. Tharp. "Highland Maya
        Psychotherapy." AMERICAN ANTHROPOLOGIST 66 (1964): 41-52.

        Evaluates the psychotherapeutic aspects of a typical curing
        ritual for the "disease of the spirit" carried out by the
        Tzotzil Indians of Mexico. An account of the world view of
        these Indians is given and examples of the healing practices,
        which include emotional catharsis, confidence in the healer,
        and reassurance, are provided. The ceremonial phase is
        likened to group and family psychotherapy. Like modern
        psychotherapy, curing rituals are attempts to induce change
        in the emotional state, attitude, and social behavior of the
        persons undergoing treatment.

662.   Ishida, Rokuro. "Naikan-Analysis." PSYCHOLOGIA 12 (1969):
        81-92.

        Explains the original Naikan technique as systematized and
        developed by Ishiru Yoshimoto and the way he tried to improve
        it by combining it with hypnotherapy and autogenic training.
        Several cases are presented to show both the effectiveness
        and deficiences of the original and the new methods. The
        author holds that Naikan theory is in agreement with several
        Freudian principles, including free association. Parallels
        are drawn between Naikan therapy and hypnosis, both of which,
        for example, rely on the patient's emotions for effective
        treatment. The method of systematized Naikan analysis can be
        an effective and relatively short psychotherapy for neuroses,
        psychosomatic problems, and bad habits.

663.   Iwai, Hiroshi. "East and West." PSYCHOTHERAPY AND PSYCHO-
        SOMATICS 31 (1979): 357-60.

        Gives a brief history of psychotherapy in Japan and outlines
        the similarities and differences between Western and Eastern
        psychotherapies. The author suggests that certain features
        are mutually useful. It is pointed out that Naikan therapy
        is similar to psychotherapy in that both ask the patient to
        reflect on his or her life from early childhood, and that
        Morita therapy lies somewhere between Eastern and Western
        therapy and incorporates techniques similar to behaviorism
        and transactional analysis.

664.   Iwai, H., A. Homma, H. Amamoto, and M. Asakura. "Morita
       Psychotherapeutic Process." PSYCHOTHERAPY AND PSYCHOSO-
       MATICS 29 (1978): 330-32.

       Gives a short outline of Morita therapy and points out the
       way it differs from psychoanalysis. Morita therapy, unlike
       psychoanalysis, looks upon neurosis as part of human nature,
       makes no effort to analyze anxiety to find its cause, con-
       centrates on outward traits, and admits the weakness of human
       character and the ability to realize higher goals. Morita
       therapy aims to discover the solution to human ills through
       the integration and harmony between humankind and the environ-
       ment. Psychoanalysis is criticized for its rationalistic
       approach to human psychological problems.

665.   Iwai, Hiroshi, and David Reynolds. "Morita Therapy: The
       Views From the West." AMERICAN JOURNAL OF PSYCHIATRY 126
       (1970): 1031-36.

       Discusses the various interpretations of Morita therapy.
       Five topics, which usually appear in Western literature on the
       subject, are overviewed: 1) the relationship between Morita
       therapy and Zen Buddhism; 2) the concept of "arugamana," i.e.,
       the acceptance of phenomenal reality as it is; 3) absolute
       bed therapy as prescribed by Morita treatment; 4) work
       therapy; and 5) the effects of Morita therapy outside its
       Japanese cultural context. The authors observe that scholars
       from Western European countries have adopted a more favorable
       attitude to Morita's method than scholars elsewhere. They
       think that personal, social, and research backgrounds of
       Western researchers have influenced the various understandings
       of Morita therapy.

666.   Jacobson, Avrohm, and Albert N. Berenberg. "Japanese Psychi-
       atry and Psychotherapy." AMERICAN JOURNAL OF PSYCHIATRY
       109 (1952): 321-29.

       Deals with Dr. Morita's theories of mental illnesses and
       their cure. After describing the three types of psychologi-
       cal problems and the four stages of cure offered by this
       treatment, the essay dwells on how certain aspects of Japanese
       culture is reflected in the treatment, an example being the
       planned and rigid system used in Morita therapy. Several
       principles common to Morita therapy and Zen are drawn up:
       1) both aim at "a calm and well-integrated mind"; 2) both
       stress the need for performing one's duties and tasks with
       such absorption that one is hardly aware of one's self; and
       3) both rely on self-discipline.

667.   Jahoda, Gustav. "Traditional Healers and Other Institutions
       Concerned With Mental Illness in Ghana." INTERNATIONAL
       JOURNAL OF SOCIAL PSYCHIATRY 7 (1961): 245-68.

       Discusses the part played by traditional healers, a healing
       church, and one mental hospital in Ghana. A general overview
       of the work of these healers, their clients, and the physical

and mental ailments that are treated is presented. More
specifically, the spiritual and magical activities of a pas-
tor of an independent church, and his healing and counseling
methods in problems relating to love and marriage and in
anxiety before exams, are described. Case materials from the
government mental hospital are also recorded. The author
argues that traditional healers are still able to meet their
clients effectively. New institutions have sprung up to deal
with contemporary problems and traditional healers themselves
have adapted their techniques to deal with their new needs.

668.   Jilek, Wolfgang G. "Native Renaissance: The Survival and
       Revival of Indigenous Therapeutic Ceremonials Among North
       American Indians." TRANSCULTURAL PSYCHIATRIC RESEARCH
       REVIEW 15 (1978): 117-47.

       Reviews the literature on the therapeutic rituals of the
       Navajo, Iroquois, Dakota Sioux, and the contemporary Amer-
       indian Cult Movement (Gourd Dance, Sun Dance, and Winter
       Spirit Dance), and Peyotism. Evidence for the revival and
       revitalization of the ceremonials is presented and an attempt
       is made to determine the main therapeutic mechanisms operant
       in the various ritual procedures. Three theories which have
       been advanced to explain the survival of indigenous therapies
       and shamanism are briefly outlined: 1) their value as cultur-
       al symbols of native identity, superiority and resistance;
       2) the interest and support they receive from modern writers,
       especially social scientists, and from some of the clergy;
       and 3) the relative inadequacy of Western medicine and health
       care.

669.   Jilek, Wolfgang G. "Indian Healing Power: Indigenous Thera-
       peutic Practices in the Pacific Northwest." PSYCHIATRIC
       ANNALS 4.11 (1974): 13-21.

       Reports on his work with the Salish Indians and on how he
       found Western psychiatry insufficient to cure mentally ill
       people. A conjunction of native and Western therapeutic
       methods is found to be more effective. It is pointed out
       that the spirit dance, which takes place at initiation and
       which involves an ordeal that creates an altered state of
       consciousness, is a healing process based on the therapeutic
       symbol of death and rebirth. The ceremonies, according to
       the author, combat the state of anomie, provide group therapy,
       channel cathartic abreactions, and instill self-confidence in
       the dancers.

670.   Jilek, Wolfgang G., and Norman Todd. "Witchdoctors Succeed
       Where Doctors Fail: Psychotherapy Among the Coast Salish
       Indians." CANADIAN PSYCHIATRIC ASSOCIATION JOURNAL 19
       (1974): 351-56.

       Describes the healing practices of indigenous healers and
       therapists in this American Indian tribe and gives several
       case examples. Traditional healing seems to be restricted
       to the area of psychoreactive and psychophysiologic mecha-

nisms. The authors maintain that the therapeutic effectiveness of these witch doctors is comparable to the Western
treatment, as far as the Indians are concerned.

671.   Katz, Richard. "Towards a Paradigm of Healing: Data From the
       Hunting-Gathering !Kung." PERSONNEL AND GUIDANCE JOURNAL
       61 (1985): 494-97.

       Describes the healing practices of a nomadic tribe in
       Botswana, Namibia, and South Angola. An all-night dance, the
       center of their healing ritual, provides both psychological
       and sociological benefits to the individual and gives healers
       themselves opportunities for fulfillment and growth. The
       author characterizes their approach to healing as transfor-
       mational. He thinks that Western therapy can learn from this
       kind of healing, which is based on a broader view of reality
       "which would allow for transformation and for a source of
       healing beyond the person" (p. 497).

672.   Kawai, Hiroshi, and Koyoichi Kondo. "Discussion on Morita
       Therapy." PSYCHOLOGIA 3 (1960): 92-99.

       Summarizes the discussion on Morita therapy held in Japan
       in 1958. Criticism of Morita therapy by the psychoanalytic
       school, the main theory of hypochondria in Morita therapy,
       and the review of this Japanese technique from the standpoint
       of comparative psychiatry are covered. Morita Therapy is
       described as a reformation of a person's attitudes towards
       life leading to insight through personal experience. The
       author does not doubt the therapeutic qualities of this
       Japanese practice.

673.   Kennedy, John G. "Cultural Psychiatry." HANDBOOK OF SOCIAL
       AND CULTURAL ANTHROPOLOGY. Edited by J. Honigmann.
       Chicago: Rand McNally, 1973, pp. 1119-98.

       A comprehensive survey of anthropological literature on
       the relationships between sociocultural factors and emo-
       tional disorders, highlighting the main interests, and
       discussing the methodology and theoretical problems of the
       field. The areas covered are: 1) epidemiology; 2) cultural
       factors in mental illness, which presents the view from
       Western psychiatry; 3) cultural factors in mental disorders,
       which examines the question of culture-specific syndromes;
       4) non-Western psychiatric practices; and 5) additional topics
       in cultural psychiatry. Faith, suggestion, group support,
       and catharsis are the most common reasons advanced to
       account for the effectiveness of native cures. Regression
       and dissociation in the service of the ego have also been
       utilized to explain how altered states of consciousness dur-
       ing the healing process can ultimately lead to an improved
       condition. The anthropological debate on the psychological
       condition of the shaman is sketched (pp. 1145-52). Well over
       300 references (pp. 1185-98) present an excellent anthropo-
       logical bibliography up to 1972.

674.   Kiev, Ari. "Magic, Faith, and Healing in Modern Psychiatry."
       RELIGIOUS SYSTEMS OF PSYCHOTHERAPY (item 1021), pp. 225-35.

       Explains various primitive views of illness and healing
       and compares them to modern psychiatry, pointing out those
       features of healing practices which are universal. Taboo
       violation, witchcraft, spirit intrusion, and community re-
       sponsibility are among the topics covered. Attitudes during
       treatment, participation in the treatment of the subject's
       family, and the therapist's own influence are common factors
       which psychiatrists think contribute to the healing process.
       The psychiatrist, like the native healer, often acts as a
       mediator.

675.   Kiev, Ari. TRANSCULTURAL PSYCHIATRY. New York: Free Press,
       1972. xii, 223 pp.

       Attempts an introduction to the growing field of trans-
       cultural psychiatry, formulating its boundaries and assessing
       the current state of knowledge in the early seventies. Many
       issues relevant to contemporary cults, such as trance (unusual
       mental state), spirit possession (dissociation state), and
       Pentecostalism, are discussed. Cult groups, it is held, serve
       rehabilitation and prophylactic goals in many developing
       countries and contribute to group integration. The author
       discusses the issue of whether methods of religious conver-
       sion that promote intense religious experiences set into
       motion underlying pathological processes. Various culture-
       bound disorders, like bewitchment (an anxiety state),
       "Shinkeishitsu" (an obsessional neurosis treated by Morita
       therapy), and the evil eye (a phobic state) are considered.

676.   Kiev, Ari. "Prescientific Psychiatry." AMERICAN HANDBOOK OF
       PSYCHIATRY. Edited by Silvano Arieti. New York: Basic
       Books, 1966, vol. 3, pp. 166-79.

       Discusses the practice of (folk) psychiatry in non-Western
       societies. Four main areas are covered: 1) prescientific
       theories of mental illness; 2) prescientific treatment of
       the mentally ill; 3) contemporary practices of prescientific
       psychiatry, of which the West Indian Pentecostal church in
       London is given as an example; and 4) the therapeutic values
       of prescientific psychiatry. The author maintains that many
       of the non-scientific treatments found in healing cults are
       beneficial, though some adverse effects have occasionally
       been observed. Over 90 references are given.

677.   Kiev, Ari. "The Psychotherapeutic Aspects of Primitive
       Medicine." HUMAN ORGANIZATION 21 (1965): 25-29.

       Focuses on the role the witch doctor plays when treating
       patients in three types of societies, namely, food-gathering,
       fishing-hunting, and agricultural. The author observes that
       in the first two types of societies the conviction that the

healer has the power to cure is dominant, while in agricultural societies, cures seem to be attributed to the power
in the medicines themselves, rather than to the supernatural
qualities of the practitioner. It is concluded that: 1) not
all primitive societies have the same view of therapy; 2) the
nature of the medical role seems to be related to the nature
of the social organization; and 3) with increasing complexity
the medicine man shares the responsibility for treatment
success with his patients. In agricultural societies the
healer, like Western therapists, thinks that psychiatric illness is due primarily to the interpersonal and intrapsychic
conflicts of the patient. It is assumed throughout that
primitive medicine can be therapeutic.

678.   Kiev, Ari. "The Study of Folk Psychiatry." MAGIC, FAITH,
       AND HEALING (item 679), pp. 3-35.

       Stresses the impact of cultural factors on psychiatric
       theories and treatment showing how each society contributes
       to personality function and psychic conflict as well as to
       the development and management of mental illness. It is
       argued that, partly because of biological limits, there are
       some basic similarities in all psychotherapies. There is a
       short history of how Western psychiatrists have evaluated
       primitive psychologies and treatment of illness. Although
       primitive therapies are fundamentally magical, they may
       still contain some elements of rational treatment. The main
       topics dealt with are primitive medicine, cult, psychopa-
       thology, and primitive psychiatry.

679.   Kiev, Ari, editor. MAGIC, FAITH, AND HEALING: STUDIES IN
       PRIMITIVE PSYCHIATRY TODAY. New York: Free Press, 1964.
       xv, 475 pp.

       Presents a basic manual on the study of folk psychiatry in
       primitive and underdeveloped societies. Sixteen essays,
       describing and discussing healing systems in various cultures,
       are included.

       Contains items 678, 686, 709, 729, 802, 920, 942, 969.

680.   Kondo, Akihisa. "Morita Therapy: A Japanese Therapy for
       Neurosis." AMERICAN JOURNAL OF PSYCHOANALYSIS 13 (1953):
       31-37.

       Explains how Doctor Morita views the neurotic as a person
       who has made the tragic mistake of understanding egocentric
       development as the growth of the real self—a danger of which
       Buddhist philosophy constantly warns us. The therapy devel-
       oped by Morita is then described, stressing the need for the
       patients to engage in manual labor. The author sees a strong
       link between Zen and Morita, and speculates that a re-exami-
       nation of Zen Buddhism can help Morita therapy develop more
       effectively and profoundly.

681.   Kondo, Akihisa. "Morita Therapy: Its Sociocultural Context."
        NEW DIMENSIONS IN PSYCHIATRY: A WORLD VIEW. Edited by S.
        Arieti and G. Chrzanowski. New York: Wiley and Sons, 1975,
        pp. 236-60.

        Discusses Morita theory and treatment in its historical and
        cultural settings, particularly after the Meiji reformation
        in Japan in 1868. The author describes the type of Japanese
        neurosis, called "shinkeishitsu," which includes hypochondria,
        anxiety, and a number of compulsive and obsessive symptoms.
        It is pointed out that these neurotic problems developed when
        Japan established contact with Western culture with its great
        stress on individualism. Examples are given of people who
        had this type of neurosis, and the way they were treated by
        Morita therapy is outlined.

682.   Kondo, Kyoichi. "The Origin of Morita Therapy." CULTURE-
        BOUND SYNDROMES, ETHNOPSYCHIATRY, AND ALTERNATE THERAPIES
        (item, 690), pp. 250-58.

        Describes very briefly the forerunners of Morita therapy:
        rest therapy, occupational therapy, life-normalization
        method, and the technique of persuasion and hypnosis. Morita
        therapy itself is outlined with its goals to help the subject
        understand human nature, admit the psychic reality of human
        life, respect the value of constructive efforts, and improve
        and evaluate one's daily life. The author observes that,
        although Dr. Morita's method is based on Zen Buddhism, Morita
        himself denied such a link.

683.   Kora, Takehisa. "Morita Therapy." INTERNATIONAL JOURNAL OF
        PSYCHIATRY 1 (1965): 611-40.

        Attempts a comprehensive description of Morita therapy,
        covering the following main areas: 1) the symptoms leading
        to the use of Morita (i.e., a form of neurosis called
        "shinkeishitsu"); 2) the classification of the types of
        neuroses; 3) the mechanism of development and fixation of
        symptoms; 4) the salient points of the therapy; and 5) the
        individual symptoms and the treatments to counteract them.
        Excerpts from the diary of a patient who was cured are given.
        The positive results were confirmed by psychological tests.

684.   Kora, Takehisa, and Kenshiro Ohara. "Morita Therapy."
        PSYCHOLOGY TODAY 6 (March 1973): 63-68.

        Describes the Japanese Morita therapy and the three types
        of neuroses ("shinkeishitsu") it treats, namely, neurasthenia,
        anxiety neurosis, and obsessional fears. The characteristics
        of these illnesses are then outlined and the four periods of
        treatment sketched. The author admits that the basic author-
        itarianism, which is evident in the rigidly-structured treat-
        ment, has often be criticized.

685.   Kora, Takehisa, and Koji Sato. "Morita Therapy: A Psycho-
        therapy in the Way of Zen." PSYCHOLOGIA 1 (1958): 219-25.

Portrays the Zen type of psychotherapy developed by Shoma Morita (1874-1938) to treat obsessive and anxiety neuroses, conditions which he labeled "nervosity." Therapy consists of four stages of hospitalized treatment which stress self-acceptance and guide the patient to a normal life. Hints are given for those going through the treatment. Some psychoanalytic critique of Morita therapy is also provided.

686. La Barre, Weston. "Confession as Cathartic Therapy in American Indian Tribes." MAGIC, FAITH, AND HEALING (item 679), pp. 36-49.

Reflects on the ritual confession of sins among many American Indian tribes, a custom which apparently existed before the advent of Christianity. Examples from various tribes are provided. The author states that public confession was a "genuinely aboriginal therapeutic technique" (p. 45) leading to the removal of anxiety.

687. Lambo, T. A. "Psychotherapy in Africa." PSYCHOTHERAPY AND PSYCHOSOMATICS 24 (1974): 311-26.

Relates Western psychoanalytic theories to African cultures and argues that psychotherapy is built into African social and religious life. The methods employed in Africa vary from magico-religious rites to clearly formulated and defined procedures which include trance, hypnosis, suggestion, and the mystic invocation of spirits. All these techniques, according to the author, promote mental health.

688. Landy, David, editor. CULTURE, DISEASE, AND HEALING: STUDIES IN MEDICAL ANTHROPOLOGY. New York: Macmillan, 1977. xv, 559 pp.

Presents an edition of previously published essays dealing with physical medicine and psychological treatment in various cultures. Sections are included on emotional states and cultural constraints and on the status and roles of both patients and healers. A useful, lengthy bibliography (pp. 519-59) is added.

Contains items 649, 835, 947.

689. Lebra, Takie S. JAPANESE PATTERNS OF BEHAVIOR. Honolulu: University of Hawaii Press, 1976. xvii, 295 pp.

Studies Japanese behavior in the cultural context. Chapters on Naikan (pp. 201-14) and Morita (pp. 215-31) therapies are included.

Contains item 850.

690. Lebra, William P., editor. CULTURE-BOUND SYNDROMES, ETHNO-PSYCHIATRY, AND ALTERNATE THERAPIES. Vol. IV of MENTAL HEALTH RESEARCH IN ASIA AND THE PACIFIC. Honolulu: University of Hawaii Press, 1976. x, 302 pp.

Contains the majority of papers presented at the Fourth
Conference on Culture and Mental Health in Asia and the
Pacific held in March of 1972. Assuming a linkage between
culture and mental illness, the papers explore the effectiveness of folk therapies and the ways in which modern psychiatry
can cooperate with native healing techniques. Most of the
papers in this volume deal with 1) possession, 2) shamans
and other folk therapists, and 3) ethnopsychiatry and alternate
therapies.

Contains items 682, 698, 766, 850, 886, 952, 961.

691.   Lederer, Wolfgang. "Primitive Psychotherapy." PSYCHIATRY
       22 (1959): 255-65.

Considers unusual therapeutic methods and draws some conclusions regarding the fundamental elements which make them
effective. Several detailed examples, such as an exorcism
from sixteenth-century France, a treatment for witchcraft
by African medicine men, and the use of Zen in Japan, are
provided. All these methods are thought to bring about real
improvement in the emotionally disturbed subjects. The author
notes that all of them stress the relationship between therapist and patient. There is a common principle between Western
and primitive therapy: in both, the therapist can approach the
patient with a certain confidence and lack of anxiety.

692.   Leighton, Alexander H., and Dorothea C. Leighton. "Elements
       of Psychotherapy in Navaho Religion." PSYCHIATRY 4 (1941):
       515-23.

Observes that anthropology offers psychiatrists a wide
range of valuable data for comparison and for understanding
pathology in different cultures. Navajo religion is then
taken as an example to show how knowledge of indigenous
religious beliefs and practices has an impact on psychiatric
evaluation. Navajo rituals have a powerful appeal to the
emotions, give strong reassurance to the believers, and
supply them with both an occupation and a diversion. These
rituals are not important simply because of their symbolic
qualities, but also because they produce effects on the nervous system similar to "hydrotherapy." Navajo religion
builds up morale, provides a sense of security, and lessens
anxiety.

693.   Marsella, Anthony, Roland G. Tharp, and Thomas J. Ciborowski,
       editors. PERSPECTIVES ON CROSS-CULTURAL PSYCHOLOGY. New
       York: Academic Press, 1979. xv, 413 pp.

Contains papers presented at a conference on cross-cultural
psychology held at the University of Hawaii in 1978. The
material is organized under four headings: 1) foundations;
2) complex human behavior; 3) application; and 4) the future.
Although the issue of cults is not discussed, the essays present the necessary background for understanding non-Western

psychology, mental disorders across cultures, and psychotherapeutic treatments in different societies. Comprehensive
bibliographies are appended to most of the papers in this
volume.

Contains items 705, 745.

694.   Marsella, Anthony J., and Geoffrey M. White, editors. CUL-
       TURAL CONCEPTIONS OF MENTAL HEALTH AND THERAPY. Boston:
       Reidel Publishing Co., 1982. xii, 414 pp.

       A collection of 16 essays discussing cross-cultural issues
       in psychotherapy. The importance of sociocultural variables
       in determining mental health is portrayed through a comparison
       of a variety of conceptions of the person, of mental illness,
       and of what constitutes the right treatment in selected Asian
       and Pacific societies. The essays are divided into four main
       sections: 1) cultural conceptions of the person and health;
       2) cultural conceptions of mental disorder; 3) cultural con-
       ceptions of therapy; and 4) an overview of the issues and
       directions.

       Contains item 962.

695.   Messing, Simon D. "Traditional Healing and the Health Center
       in Ethiopia." TRADITIONAL HEALING (item 735), pp. 52-64.

       Discusses one example of collaboration between Western
       psychiatry and traditional healers in a Third World country.

696.   Meyer, George G. "The Professional in the Chicano Community."
       PSYCHIATRIC ANNALS 7.12 (1977): 9-19.

       Gives an account of some of the problems a psychiatrist has
       to face when dealing with people who have a different cultural
       background, particularly with Mexicans living in the United
       States. The author suggests the use of co-therapists,
       namely, the Mexican folk healers (curanderos) who have been
       effective in treating illnesses which are believed to be
       brought about by supernatural means, such as anxiety, fear,
       the evil eye, and bewitchment. Psychiatrists, it is argued,
       should have some knowledge of the curanderos and should refer
       patients to them if the circumstances warrant it.

697.   Miura, Monoshiga, and Shin-ichi Usa. "A Psychotherapy of
       Neurosis: Morita Therapy." PSYCHOLOGIA 15 (1970): 18-34.

       Gives an account of the origin and development of Morita
       therapy. The article explains the theory of "Nervosity"
       ("shinkeishitsu") and its classification into three types of
       diseases. The psychological basis of the therapy and its
       four-stage process is described. Some criticism of Morita
       is offered. A lengthy bibliography, including many works in
       Japanese, is appended.

698.   Murase, Takao. "Naikan Therapy." CULTURE-BOUND SYNDROMES,
        ETHNOPSYCHIATRY, AND ALTERNATE THERAPIES (item 690), pp.
        259-69.

        Attempts an outline of Naikan therapy, a form of guided
        introspection directed towards attitude and personality change,
        and based on a method derived from a Jodo Shin sect of Japa-
        nese Buddhism. Its method, process, and outcome are described
        and a couple of case studies are given. It is observed that
        this method has proven effective with many types of patients,
        including delinquents, criminals, and drug addicts, but not
        with psychotics. The author also discusses the therapeutic
        value of the acknowledgment of guilt, which is central to
        Naikan therapy.

699.   Murase, Takao, and Frank Johnson. "Naikan, Morita, and Wes-
        tern Psychotherapy." ARCHIVES OF GENERAL PSYCHIATRY 31
        (1974): 121-28.

        Describes two forms of Japanese therapeutic treatments and
        contrasts them with Western psychotherapy. In spite of the
        differences between the Japanese treatments, both, in contrast
        to Western therapy, hospitalize the patient voluntarily and
        for a relatively short period of time. They also establish a
        simpler and more goal-oriented psychotherapeutic relationship
        between subject and therapist, stress the need for achieving
        a positive and active adaptation to the world, and advise
        against seeking an intellectual understanding of one's prob-
        lems. Furthermore, they tend to keep transference issues
        simplified, and to handle resistance as a problem which arises
        during the treatment, rather than as an indication that the
        patient's past difficulties are resurfacing. These differ-
        ences are explained in terms of cultural values. It is argued
        that these Japanese therapies may be equally effective when
        applied outside their cultural context.

700.   Neki, J. S. "Sahaja: An Indian Ideal of Mental Health."
        PSYCHIATRY 38 (1975): 1-10.

        Examines the nature of "Sahaja" (innate nature), which is
        an Indian ideal of mental and spiritual health, especially
        stressed in Sikh scriptures. The author attempts to divest
        the concept from the esoteric, mystic connotations which
        Tantric cults have ascribed to it. Sahaja is described as
        a transcendental state, beyond the ordinary level of con-
        sciousness, beyond ordinary modes of living, and beyond the
        stage of duality. Sahaja stresses illumination, equipoise,
        spontaneity, freedom, and harmony. Criticizing Western
        psychotherapy, the author contends that the therapeutic
        relationship between therapists and their clients should be
        modeled on the relationship between guru and his chela
        (disciple).

701.   Ness, Robert C., and Ronald M. Wintrob. "Folk Healing: A
        Description and Synthesis." AMERICAN JOURNAL OF PSYCHIATRY
        138 (1981): 1477-81.

Reviews various systems of folk healing in different sub-
cultural groups in the United States--faith-healing by
Christian fundamentalists, root work in the southeastern part
of the country, curanderismo among Mexican-Americans, and
espiritismo among Puerto Ricans. Some generic therapeutic
aspects of these systems and their relevance to patient
management are discussed. Folk healers raise people's hope
and trust, which are essential for recovery. The suggestive
power of those healers who go into trance is also an important
factor in the cure. Further, the dissociative state, which
the client might enter, may enhance the therapeutic process,
often by cathartic release. The authors, aware that many
people go both to folk healers and to Western doctors and
psychiatrists, discuss ways of improving psychiatric treatment, which can be complemented by indigenous techniques.

702.   Odejide, A. O. "Traditional (Native) Psychiatric Practice:
        Its Role in Modern Psychiatry in a Developing Country."
        PSYCHIATRIC JOURNAL OF THE UNIVERSITY OF OTTAWA 4 (1979):
        297-301.

        Reviews the role of native healers in modern psychiatric
        practice among the Yoruba of Nigeria. The author finds some
        similarities between the native diagnosis and treatment of
        illness and modern medical practices. In spite of the short-
        comings of indigenous treatment, it is suggested that cooper-
        ation between folk healers in Nigeria and specialists in
        modern medicine will be beneficial to those who seek help.

703.   Ohara, Kenshiro, and David Reynolds. "Changing Methods in
        Morita Psychotherapy." INTERNATIONAL JOURNAL OF SOCIAL
        PSYCHIATRY 14 (1968): 304-10.

        Presents a brief outline of this Japanese therapy and its
        various implementations. The factors which have affected its
        application since its inception early in the twentieth century
        are examined. Morita scholars, under the influence of Western
        psychiatrists, are clarifying its theoretical foundations.
        Because Morita assumed that behavior change preceded symptom
        reduction, no systematic attempt was made to investigate the
        deep-rooted origin of neurosis, to analyze dream material, or
        to deal with repressed material. Over 70 percent of those
        who were treated registered some improvement, while over 60
        percent were cured. Morita therapists are interested in the
        possibility of applying the therapy in different cultural
        settings.

704.   Pattison, E. Mansell. "Exorcism and Psychotherapy: A Case of
        Collaboration." RELIGIOUS SYSTEMS OF PSYCHOTHERAPY (item
        1021), pp. 284-95.

        Describes how a psychotherapist collaborated with native
        healers of an American Indian tribe to heal a mentally ill,
        adolescent Indian girl. The therapist supported the common
        belief that the patient was suffering from spirit possession

and encouraged the family to hold an exorcism. The author
stresses the importance of the subject's belief system in
the healing process.

705.   Pedersen, Paul. "Non-Western Psychology: The Search for
        Alternatives." PERSPECTIVES ON CROSS-CULTURAL PSYCHOLOGY
        (item 693), pp. 77-98.

        Raises the timely question of the universality of Western
        psychology. A short history of how Western psychology has
        interpreted human behavior is given, with some focus on the
        meaning of Yoga. The critical issues, brought out by con-
        trasting Western and non-Western viewpoints, are discussed.
        Because some youths in the West have adopted elements of non-
        Western psychology, the author thinks that openness to healing
        alternatives is needed. A lengthy bibliography is included.

706.   Peters, Larry G., and Douglas Price-Williams. "A Phenomeno-
        logical Overview of Trance." TRANSCULTURAL PSYCHIATRIC
        RESEARCH REVIEW 20 (1983): 5-39.

        Reviews the literature on trance published mainly during
        the 1970s, and then attempts to identify some of the more
        prevalent contemporary theories and concepts. The authors
        classify the various ways in which trance conditions, or
        altered states of consciousness (ASC), have been explained
        in five different models: 1) discrete and continuous; 2)
        neurobiological; 3) synthesis; 4) psychodynamic and psycho-
        therapeutic; and 5) pathological. It is concluded that "most
        authors would agree that all ASC experiences may be creative,
        therapeutic, and involve regression and dissociation in the
        service of the self if utilized within cultural contexts"
        (p. 29). The author maintains that these states have the
        same tripartite structure as rites of passage.

707.   Prince, Raymond. "Variations in Psychotherapeutic Proce-
        dures." HANDBOOK OF CROSS-CULTURAL PSYCHOLOGY (item 744),
        vol. 6, pp. 291-349.

        Discusses the problem of cross-cultural psychotherapy and
        surveys the literature in the area. The author subscribes to
        the opinion that there are several commonly-shared features
        in all therapies: 1) the healer-patient relationship; 2) a
        shared world view between the two of them; 3) the labeling
        and attribution of the cause of illness; and 4) the important
        role of suggestion. In studying these exogenous elements,
        however, there has been a neglect of endogenous healing mech-
        anisms like sleep, rest, social isolation, trance, and altered
        states of consciousness--the latter including meditative,
        mystical, and dissociation states--and the shaman's ecstasy.
        The author shows, by reference to many cultures, how healers
        all over the world have learned to manipulate these mechanisms
        and to bring about the resolution of crises and the allevia-
        tion of suffering. Psychoanalysis is compared to other
        psychotherapeutic systems and, though judged to be a better

way of understanding psychopathology, is hampered by more
limitations with regard to its application than many other
forms of treatment.

708.   Prince, Raymond. "Psychotherapy as the Manipulation of Endog-
        enous Healing Mechanisms: A Transcultural Survey." TRANS-
        CULTURAL PSYCHIATRIC RESEARCH REVIEW 13 (1976): 115-33.

        Reviews the literature which concentrates on those elements
        or mechanisms of healing that are endogenous (i.e., which stem
        from inside the person), as opposed to exogenous ones (i.e.,
        those that arise from cultural and interpersonal factors out-
        side the individual). It is argued that all individuals under
        stress will resort to automatic self-healing techniques, the
        most important of which is an altered state of consciousness,
        such as dreams, dissociation states, religious experiences,
        and psychotic reactions. Many examples are provided: dream
        interpretation in the cult of Asclepius in ancient Greece and
        Rome and among the Iroquois Indians in the seventeenth century;
        mystical states and meditations in world religions; trance
        and dissociation states, as in the Zar Cult; and shamanism
        in primitive and other cultures. The author concludes by
        summarizing some of the ways in which endogenous mechanisms
        can be therapeutic by contrasting them to psychoanalysis. He
        believes that while psychoanalysis may be a superior form of
        therapy, its application, when compared to the above-mentioned
        methods, is rather limited. A lengthy bibliography is added.

709.   Prince, Raymond. "Indigenous Yoruba Psychiatry." MAGIC,
        FAITH, AND HEALING (item 679), pp. 84-120.

        Presents a study based on 46 practicing Yoruba healers in
        Nigeria. Besides a brief cultural background, the native
        psychiatric nomenclature and the various causes of particular
        illnesses are given. The two types of healing institutions,
        namely, the treatment center and the "Orissa" cult groups,
        together with the therapies they each use, are described.
        The following psychotherapeutic elements in folk healing are
        noted: suggestion, sacrifice, manipulation of the environ-
        ment, ego-strengthening elements, abreaction and group ther-
        apy, and personality growth factors. The author thinks that
        the therapy of Yoruba healers can be effective, even though
        there are some undesirable features, like the use of some
        herbs, in the treatment. He concludes by stating that
        "Western psychiatric techniques are not in my opinion demon-
        strably superior to many indigenous Yoruba practices" (p. 116).

710.   Prince, Raymond. "Delusions, Dogma, and Mental Health."
        R. M. BUCKE MEMORIAL SOCIETY: NEWSLETTER REVIEW 4 (Spring
        1971): 54-59.

        Explores the nature of group beliefs and shows how they
        differ from individual delusions. Many religious groups
        come into being to relieve tensions when there is conflict
        between cultures, especially in colonial times. Cargo cults

in the Pacific are taken as an example of the religion of
the oppressed. Their unrealistic beliefs are discussed and
it is argued that they come into being in situations of apathy
and despair when there is little or no realistic basis for
hope. The group beliefs of such cults have a healthy integrating function. The mental health of an individual when
he or she joins one of these cults is also explored.

711.   Rappaport, Herbert. "The Tenacity of Folk Psychotherapy: A
        Functional Interpretation." SOCIAL PSYCHIATRY 12 (1977):
        127-32.

        Attempts to identify those features of folk psychotherapy
        which persist in spite of the impact of Western medicine.
        The research was conducted among several tribal areas in
        Tanzania. The training, role, function, and practices of the
        medicine man, as well as the underlying conceptual framework
        to his work, are described. The folk system of psychotherapy
        is a dynamic and flourishing form of treatment. The author
        believes that the fundamental anxieties of the people can be
        better addressed within their traditional view of causation.
        The African therapist is in fact not a competitor of, but a
        collaborator with, the psychiatrist.

712.   Ratnavale, David N. "Psychiatry in Shanghai, China." AMER-
        ICAN JOURNAL OF PSYCHIATRY 130 (1973): 1082-87.

        Reports on the author's visit to China, describing the
        structure and organization of the Shanghai Psychiatric Insti-
        tute and the various treatments given patients. Acupuncture
        is widely used, with a measure of success, not only in anes-
        thesia, but also in cases of anxiety, apathy, catatonic stupor,
        and depression.

713.   Reynolds, David K. NAIKAN PSYCHOTHERAPY: MEDITATION FOR SELF-
        DEVELOPMENT. Chicago: University of Chicago Press, 1983.
        x, 170 pp.

        Describes the Japanese system of therapy known as Naikan,
        which means "inner observation." The author first provides
        an account of the practice of Naikan at the Nara Naikan Train-
        ing Center in the city of Korigama. Naikan techniques are
        listed and contrasted with the method of free association in
        psychoanalysis. The variations of this Japanese therapy (which
        include a Zen-oriented technique) are brought to the fore by
        a detailed examination of 11 Naikan facilities. The results
        of questionnaires given to both clients and therapists are
        summarized and the various criticisms leveled at Naikan ex-
        plored. A couple of chapters probe the theoretical aspects
        of the therapy. The author attempts to understand Naikan in
        the light of Japanese character, particularly its emotional
        side. Finally, the possible application of Naikan for West-
        erners is discussed. Naikan seems appropriate "for clients
        with difficulties in love relationships, histories of victim-
        ization with subsequent adoption of a generalized victim role,

parental and marital discord, some sorts of unemployment and job problems, and desires to deepen personal or spiritual growth" (p. 146).

714.   Reynolds, David K. "Naikan Psychotherapy." HANDBOOK OF INNOVATIVE PSYCHOTHERAPIES. Edited by Raymond J. Corsini. New York: Wiley and Sons, 1981, pp. 544-53.

Provides a general overview of this Buddhist-based psychotherapy with a sketch of its history, its theory and methodology, and its present state in Japan. Naikan has been applied to treat a variety of problems including neuroses, interpersonal difficulties, drug and alcohol addiction, and criminal behavior. It has also been employed with autogenic training, various other kinds of meditation, and Western psychotherapy. A case example is given to demonstrate how Naikan therapy works in a clinical context.

715.   Reynolds, David K. "Morita Psychotherapy." HANDBOOK OF INNOVATIVE PSYCHOTHERAPIES. Edited by Raymond J. Corsini. New York: Wiley and Sons, 1981, pp. 489-501.

Summarizes the history, current status, and theory of Morita therapy. The treatment of patients is described and its application to both Japanese and American patients is discussed. A lengthy case history illustrates how this Zen-oriented treatment functions in the clinical situation.

716.   Reynolds, D. K. THE QUIET THERAPIES. Honolulu: University Press of Hawaii, 1980. viii, 135 pp.

Describes five Japanese psychotherapies: Morita, Naikan, Seiza, Shadan, and Zen. The author maintains that these relatively new therapies may appear strange to Westerners. If one sees them, however, as the Japanese do, apart from their apparent mystical qualities, they represent practical advice and techniques for helping people deal with human problems. All these therapies have a history of clinical success in treating neurosis in Japan. The common themes which run through them all, namely, the regulation of the flow of consciousness as a major goal, the acceptance of inevitable reality, and resocialization, are discussed in a final chapter. Their usefulness to the West can only be discovered by testing them.

717.   Reynolds, David K. "Naikan Therapy--An Experiential View." INTERNATIONAL JOURNAL OF SOCIAL PSYCHIATRY 23 (1977) 252-63.

Provides a brief history and theoretical background to Naikan therapy--a form of Japanese meditation which has roots in the Jodo Shinshu sect of Buddhism. Many researchers have claimed that Naikan possesses therapeutic value, especially in treating various kinds of neuroses, psychosomatic disorders, and delinquency problems. The aim of Naikan therapy is to reconstruct the patient's view of one's past in order to re-

shape one's attitudes and behavior. It contains elements of
psychotherapy, religion, and public service. The author describes at some length his own experience with this Japanese
therapy.

718.   Reynolds, David K. MORITA THERAPY. Los Angeles: University
       of California Press, 1976. ix, 243 pp.

       Presents probably the best and most complete account of a
       Japanese method of treating neurosis, developed in the early
       twentieth century and still practiced successfully in Japan.
       The author adopts a form of presentation which stresses those
       aspects of Morita therapy that are readily understandable to
       a Western audience. The oriental, Zen-like qualities of this
       therapy are, therefore, downplayed. The book offers an over-
       view of the therapy and illustrates its method of operation
       by giving a detailed analysis of a Morita hospital. An
       attempt is made to understand Morita in its Japanese cultur-
       al context and to relate its development over its 50-year
       history to concomitant changes in Japanese society. Morita
       therapy is also compared to other Eastern treatments (like
       Zen and Naikan) and also to Western therapies (like psycho-
       analysis, behavior therapy, and logotherapy). To what extent
       Morita is applicable outside its cultural matrix was being
       tested when the book was published. A lengthy bibliography
       is appended.

719.   Reynolds, David K., and Christie W. Kiefer. "Cultural Adapt-
       ability as an Attribute of Therapies: The Case of Morita
       Therapy." CULTURE, MEDICINE, AND PSYCHIATRY 1 (1977):
       395-412.

       Comments on the growing interest in Morita Therapy and its
       application to patients in the United States. Some of its
       features, especially its philosophy and world view, are
       peculiar to its Japanese context, while others are flexible
       enough to be used in other cultural situations. Three types
       of variables are given for permitting Morita therapy to be
       applied cross-culturally: 1) structural factors (e.g., the
       looseness of the organization of therapists); 2) content
       factors (e.g., its stress on the need that patients should
       "live in reality," and the absence of spirit possession); and
       3) situational factors (e.g., the search for other forms of
       treatment in the West).

720.   Reynolds, David K., and Joe Yamamoto. "Morita Psychotherapy
       in Japan." CURRENT PSYCHIATRIC THERAPIES 13 (1973): 219-27.

       Describes briefly Morita therapy and presents it as an
       effective therapeutic system which provides the patient with
       several benefits: 1) a philosophy of life that fits one's
       cultural experience; 2) an experienced guide and model; 3)
       the use of culturally appropriate teaching tools; and 4) a
       treatment which can adapt to the individual patient and to
       the changing cultural environment. The authors believe that
       Morita therapy may someday have some influence in the West.

721. Reynolds, David K., and Joe Yamamoto. "East Meets West:
      Moritist and Freudian Psychotherapies." SCIENCE AND PSY-
      CHOANALYSIS. Edited by J. H. Masserman. New York: Grune
      and Stratton, 1972, vol. 21, pp. 187-85.

      Contrasts the two therapies in their respective cultures.
      It is shown how Freud's method fits in Western culture, which
      values rationality, individuality, and independence, while
      Morita's theory and method were conceived in a Zen Buddhist
      tradition which emphasizes the acceptance of phenomenological
      reality, controlled attention, intuitive knowledge, and famil-
      ial sharing. Both therapies are built on the theory that
      neurosis was caused by the misdirection of psychic interest,
      though Freud specified this as regression, while Morita saw
      it as obsession with self. In both cases the cure is to be
      achieved by releasing this misdirected interest. Morita
      therapy, unlike Freud's, discourages increased self-knowledge
      under some conditions. The cure, in Freud's view, consists
      in being freed from the symptoms, while in Morita's opinion,
      it is conceived of as becoming socially productive.

722. Romano, Octavio I. "Charismatic Medicine, Folk Healing, and
      Folk Sainthood." AMERICAN ANTHROPOLOGIST 67 (1965): 1151-
      73.

      Outlines the traditional, behavioral directives which govern
      the life of the South Texas Mexican-American community. The
      role and social position of the folk healer are defined. A
      special case of the rise of a folk healer from obscurity to
      sainthood is described. It is noted that folk healing and
      healer provide stability during periods of uncertainty brought
      about by illness.

723. Romanucci-Ross, Lola, Daniel E. Moerman, and Laurence R.
      Tancredi, editors. THE ANTHROPOLOGY OF MEDICINE: FROM
      CULTURE TO METHOD. New York: Praeger, 1983. xiii, 400 pp.

      Presents a collection of essays dealing with the problems
      of cross-cultural medicine and healing. Five major areas
      are covered: 1) the interaction of medical systems; 2) symbols
      and healing; 3) empirical analysis of non-Western practices
      and medical ecology; 4) psychiatry in modern medicine; and
      5) modern medicine: social structure and ritual in biomedicine.

      Contains items 797, 985.

724. Ruiz, Pedro. "Spiritism, Mental Health, and the Puerto
      Ricans: An Overview." TRANSCULTURAL PSYCHIATRIC RESEARCH
      REVIEW 16 (1979): 28-43.

      Reviews the literature on the practice of spiritism among
      the many Puerto Ricans who have migrated to the mainland of
      the United States. The major theoretical aspects of spirit-
      ism, particularly the various orders of spirits and the role
      of the medium, are outlined. The article stresses the impor-

tance of cultural factors in understanding the part played
by spiritism in the lives of the Puerto Ricans. Spiritism
may strengthen group cohesion, be an expression of emotional
illness, or serve as a means of counteracting anxiety. It
may also be therapeutic in some psychiatric conditions. The
new trend among psychiatrists is to utilize folk belief systems in the treatment of their patients, especially when
these beliefs contribute to their well-being. A case history
is provided to illustrate the implication of the practice of
spiritism on mental health services. A lengthy bibliography
is included.

725. Ruiz, Pedro. "Folk Healers as Associate Therapists." CURRENT
      PSYCHIATRIC THERAPIES 16 (1976): 269-75.

      Reports on the efforts of the staff of Lincoln Community
      Mental Health Center in the South Bronx, New York, to learn
      more about the belief system of their largely Puerto Rican
      clients. The author reports that a collaborative approach
      was worked out with the folk healers or spiritualists, an
      approach which aimed at benefiting the patients and to have
      both psychiatrist and folk healer accepted as professionals.
      In spite of the difference between the folk healers and
      psychiatrists and in their healing methods, their collabora-
      tion was an advantage to the community. Symptoms which would
      readily be recognized by psychiatrists as signs of mental
      illness were found to be a socially-accepted pattern of
      behavior.

726. Ruiz, Pedro, and John Langrod. "Psychiatrists and Spiritual
      Healers: Partners in Community Mental Health." ANTHROPOL-
      OGY AND MENTAL HEALTH. Edited by Joseph Westermeyer.
      The Hague: Mouton, 1976, pp. 77-82.

      Compares mental health services offered by spiritualist
      healers with those supplied by Western psychiatrists, and
      shows how the differences between the two can cause difficul-
      ties in the delivery of mental health care. It is maintained
      that the method of healing practiced by spiritualist healers
      offers a learning experience to Western psychological coun-
      selors and psychiatrists. A partnership between the two
      kinds of healers, initiated by the Lincoln Community Mental
      Health Center in New York in 1968, is described. Spiritu-
      alist healers see the patients' symptoms as an asset on which
      it is possible to build up an individual's ego-strength. They
      succeed in getting the extended family of their clients in-
      volved in the healing process. And their practices allow the
      expression of hostility and aggression. The authors believe
      that cooperation between both types of healers will benefit
      those who have certain kinds of psychological problems.

727. Ruiz, Pedro, and John Langrod. "The Ancient Art of Folk
      Healing: African Influence in a New York City Community
      Health Center." TRADITIONAL HEALING (item 735), pp. 80-95.

Discusses the encounter of modern psychiatry with the practice of "espiritismo," santeria, and brujeria among the Spanish-speaking population of the South Bronx, New York. These folk therapies are described and a detailed account of a séance which led to healing is presented. The authors favor the collaboration between psychiatrists and folk healers and argue that psychotherapy must take into consideration the cultural background of the patients for the success of the healing effort.

728. Salan, Rudy, and Thomas Maretzki. "Mental Health Services and Traditional Healing in Indonesia: Are the Roles Compatible?" CULTURE, MEDICINE, AND PSYCHIATRY 7 (1983): 377-412.

Summarizes the traditional and modern systems of medicine in Indonesia and attempts to integrate the different mental health services. Since most of the people still opt for the traditional healers, the authors think that research on the problems referred to such healers, client expectation, and methods and effectiveness of treatments, is necessary. The interaction between healer and client is an essential factor in the healing process. Traditional healers in Indonesia are not charlatans. They provide widely used and relatively successful treatments.

729. Schmidt, K. E. "Folk Psychiatry in Sarawak: A Tentative System of Psychiatry of the Iban." MAGIC, FAITH, AND HEALING (item 679), pp. 139-55.

Focuses on the group characteristics, the religion, and the psychiatric system of the Iban of Sarawak, a Malayan State in Borneo. The native system of classification of disease and of the causes of emotional disturbance is described in the context of their culture as a whole. There are healers who deal with mental illness, which they diagnose while in a trance. The author compares the Iban with the Western system and concludes that the psychiatric phenomena encountered in Iban society fits well within the referential framework of Western diagnostic categories. Some advantages of native healing, particularly the involvement of the family and neighbors of the sick person, are mentioned.

730. Scotch, Norman A. "Medical Anthropology." BIENNIAL REVIEW OF ANTHROPOLOGY. Edited by Bernard J. Siegel. Stanford, CA: Stanford University Press, 1963, pp. 30-68.

Surveys anthropological literature on the cultural dimensions of illness. The material is divided into four sections: 1) reviews, bibliographies, and collections of essays; 2) epidemiology; 3) ethnomedicine (under which folk therapies are included); and 4) modern public health programs in diverse cultural settings. There are 155 references.

731. Seguin, Carlos Alberto. "What Folklore Psychotherapy Can Teach Us." PSYCHOTHERAPY AND PSYCHOSOMATICS 24 (1974): 293-302.

Distinguishes folklore psychiatry, which is the study of
psychiatric conditions and their treatment maintained by
popular traditions in Western culture, from ethnopsychiatry
(or folk psychiatry) which is pre-scientific and common in
primitive societies where the shaman and medicine man play a
leading role in healing, and from charlatanism, where the
healer is a dishonest person whose main goal is profit.
Quoting several Peruvian studies, the author outlines some
of the factors which are instrumental in the success of the
folklore therapist. Aversion therapy and the use of several
psychological devices, such as psychodrama, healer-patient
relationship, and community psychotherapy, are commonly
employed. Knowledge from folklore therapists could be
incorporated into the training of psychotherapists.

732.   Seguin, Carlos Alberto. "Folklore Psychiatry." WORLD
        BIENNIAL OF PSYCHIATRY AND PSYCHOTHERAPY. Edited by S.
        Arieti. New York: Basic Books, 1971, vol. 1, pp. 165-77.

        Distinguishes between "folklore psychiatry" (the study of
        the ideas, beliefs, and practices concerning psychiatric con-
        ditions and their treatment and cure as they are maintained
        in each culture by popular tradition), and "ethnopsychiatry"
        (the study of mental illness as a function of the culture
        group to which the sick person belongs). A short history of
        folklore psychiatry is attempted, and an example of how it
        works in a small village in Northern Peru is given. The
        author thinks that native healers in this village could cure
        more than 30 percent of chronic alcoholics. He stresses
        the need to incorporate the study of folklore psychiatry in
        the training programs for psychiatrists and counselors.

733.   Shack, William A. "Hunger, Anxiety, and Ritual: Deprivation
        and Spirit Possession Among the Gurage of Ethiopia." MAN
        6 (1971): 30-43.

        Attempts to show that one form of anxiety aroused in the
        individuals of this tribe stems from institutionalized food
        deprivation, which finds its expression in experiences of
        spirit-possession. The author explains how the Gurage's
        cultural patterns of food production and consumption inten-
        sify their concern over food and increase their frustration.
        He also examines how their food habits affect their methods
        of feeding their infants. He claims there is a correlation
        between food distribution among children of opposite sexes
        and the sex pattern of spirit possession. The rise of exor-
        cism is both an expression and a resolution of a conflict
        built in the very structure of their values regarding food
        consumption.

734.   Shakman, Robert. "Indigenous Healing of Mental Illness in
        the Philippines." INTERNATIONAL JOURNAL OF SOCIAL PSYCHI-
        ATRY 15 (1969): 279-87.

        Investigates the types of mental illness which are appar-
        ently healed by native methods, the relation of successful

cures to the Filipino culture, and the role played by the healer. Several case histories are presented to illustrate the positive therapeutic effect of folk healers. The high degree of success folk therapists have in dealing with psychosomatic problems is best explained in the context of a culture which is characterized by expressions of volatile emotions, obstructions to the development of individual identity and responsibility, and frequent recourse to projection. In such situations, the most impressive supernatural rituals are the most effective ones.

735. Singer, Philip, editor. TRADITIONAL HEALING: NEW SCIENCE OR NEW COLONIALISM? New York: Conch Magazine Ltd., 1977. 260 pp.

Brings together theoretical and practical discussions on the problem and promise of the continuing use of medical and psychological folk healing and therapy in changing Third World countries. The editor raises the issue of whether the employment and promotion of traditional healers is "part of a continuing socioeconomic exploitation" by the West. He argues that traditional modes of therapy emphasize, as colonialism once did, the fact of dependency upon authority and do not favor collaboration.

Contains items 628, 695, 727, 909.

736. Singer, Philip, Enrique Arameta and Jamsie Naidoo. "Learning of Psychodynamics, History, and Diagnosis Management Therapy by a Kali Cult Indigenous Healer in Guiana." SPIRITS, SHAMANS, AND STARS (item 925), pp. 157-78.

Contrasts the Freudian interpretation of the goddess Kali with the native explanation and outlines the cooperation between Western psychiatrists and native healers in Guyana. The therapeutic value of the work of indigenous Kali healers is taken for granted.

737. Smith, Kendra, "Observations on Morita Therapy and Culture-Specific Interpretations." JOURNAL OF TRANSPERSONAL PSYCHOLOGY 13 (1981): 59-69.

Describes Morita therapy, stressing its Buddhist and Japanese aspects. It is suggested that a developmental and recapitulatory interpretation can make Morita therapy more understandable to Western psychiatrists.

738. Stewart, Horace. "A Pilot Study of the Afro-American Healers." PSYCHOENERGETIC SYSTEMS 1 (1976): 131-34.

Interviews several Afro-American healers and some of their clients in the State of Georgia with the aim of assessing the effectiveness of folk treatment. The training of healers (where present) in the procedure used in the healing process, the type of illness treated, and the fees charged are dealt with.

The clients are questioned about the problems which led them
to have recourse to folk healers and the way they went about
contacting a specific person. The author thinks that most
of the problems folk healers handle are psychosomatic ones,
which are sometimes difficult to heal with modern methods.
Personal involvement with the sick person and the special
status that the healer enjoys are important factors in the
cure. Some deceit, opportunism, and reliance on suggestion
were also observed.

739. Takeda, Ken. "Morita Therapy." JOURNAL OF RELIGION AND
      HEALTH 3 (1964): 335-44.

      Gives a short account of the psychotherapeutic method of
      the Japanese psychiatrist Morita. His concept of personality
      and the stages of actual treatment are described. Although
      patients who go through the treatment are not required to
      practice Zen meditation, it is considered important that
      psychotherapist themselves have a good understanding of Zen.
      The mentally sick person is thus helped indirectly through
      the influence of Zen on the therapist.

740. Takeuchi, Katashi. "On 'Naikan' Method." PSYCHOLOGIA 8
      (1965): 2-8.

      Describes the one-week process of Naikan therapy which
      transforms people and leads them to a better life. An out-
      line of the role of the teacher ("sensei") in guiding and
      relating to the patient is also given. Two basic principles
      of Naikan therapy are stressed, namely: 1) the fact that
      behavior towards others is the main factor in molding person-
      ality; and 2) the need for self-observation. Once the real
      self is awakened through Naikan therapy, then the subject
      begins to make progress smoothly. A short comparison between
      Naikan and psychoanalysis is attempted and some criticism of
      Naikan is mentioned and refuted.

741. Torrey, E. F. "What Western Psychotherapists Can Learn From
      Witchdoctors." AMERICAN JOURNAL OF ORTHOPSYCHIATRY 41
      (1972): 69-76.

      Criticizes Western psychotherapists for being ethnocentric
      and suggests that they can learn from their counterparts in
      other cultures. Basing his comments on his own observations
      of healers in Ethiopia, Sarawak, Bali, Hong Kong, and America,
      the author notes that native healers employ their personal
      qualities effectively, buttress their patients' expectations,
      and use specific techniques that are clearly understood by
      their subjects. Western psychiatrists should be less arrogant
      and more tolerant of other forms of treatment.

742. Torrey, E. F. THE MIND GAME: WITCHDOCTORS AND PSYCHIATRISTS.
      New York: Emerson Hall, 1972. xv, 236 pp.

      Attempts to draw up a framework for a general understanding
      of psychiatrists and their work. The focus is placed on the

healers whose therapeutic effectiveness comes from sharing a common world view with their patient. Part One outlines the four components of psychotherapy: 1) a shared world view between therapist and client; 2) the therapist's personal qualities; 3) the patient's expectations; and 4) the actual technique employed. Part Two examines the variety of therapists in the United States and in various other cultures. Part Three considers the future of psychotherapy. One of the main arguments is that the techniques used by witchdoctors and psychotherapists are basically the same.

743. Torrey, E. F. "Indigenous Psychotherapy: Theories and Techniques." CURRENT PSYCHIATRIC THERAPIES 10 (1970): 118-29.

Argues that both indigenous psychotherapy, including that of witchdoctors, shamans, and Mexican curanderos, and Western psychotherapy are based on the same theory and use similar techniques. Two theoretical aspects of psychotherapy, namely, the patient's expectations and the therapist's personal qualities, are discussed. Drugs, mild forms of shock treatment, confession, and suggestion are used in both primitive and Western therapies, though the last two mentioned are not stressed in modern psychiatric theory. Other methods, like dream interpretation, behavior techniques, and conditioning, are used by all. The study of the ways these treatments are applied would be mutually beneficial.

744. Triandis, H. C., et al. HANDBOOK OF CROSS-CULTURAL PSYCHOLOGY. Boston: Allyn and Bacon, 1980. 6 vols.

Provides a basic introductory and almost indispensable work for any counselor who is interested in the field of cross-cultural psychology and psychiatry. Six areas are covered: 1) general perspectives; 2) methodology; 3) basic psychological processes; 4) developmental psychology; 5) social psychology; and 6) psychopathology. One essay in particular (item 707) deals with psychotherapeutic processes in different cultures.

745. Tseng, Wen-Shing, and Jing Hsu. "Culture and Psychotherapy." PERSPECTIVES ON CROSS-CULTURAL PSYCHOLOGY (item 693), pp. 332-345.

Describes various psychotherapeutic practices, including trance-possession states, divination, Morita, Naikan, fortune-telling, and astrology, all of which are techniques related to their cultural setting. The author maintains that some elements are universal, like the inculcation of hope, the furthering of trust in the therapist, the involvement of the client's family in the treatment, and the presence of an authoritarian figure. To what degree, if at all, these non-Western therapies could be effective in the West is not discussed.

746.   Venkataramaiah, V., et al. "Possession Syndrome: An Epide-
        miological Study in West Karnataka." INDIAN JOURNAL OF
        PSYCHIATRY 23 (1981): 213-18.

        Surveys a local population in an Indian village to deter-
        mine the prevalence of possession syndromes and to study the
        people's attitude towards them. The common belief in the
        possibility of possession explains the rather high rate of
        occurrence of the phenomenon. The authors think that the
        "possession syndrome is a socioculturally induced phenomenon
        used by some to become healers and counselors, by some to
        take up a sick role and get healed" (p. 218). It can also,
        however, lead to harmful results.

747.   Wallace, Anthony F. C. "The Institutionalization of Cathar-
        tic and Social Control Strategies in Iroquois Religious
        Psychotherapy." CULTURE AND MENTAL HEALTH. Edited by
        Marvin K. Opler. New York: Macmillan, 1959, pp. 63-90.

        Reviews the procedures with which the Iroquois Indians of
        the seventeenth century treated mental illness when they were
        first contacted by white settlers and missionaries. The
        Indian methods relied on providing safe, ritual opportunities
        for the expression of wishes, especially those of passivity
        and dependence. These rituals, which included dream therapy,
        medicine societies, and death ceremonies, were a psychothera-
        peutic strategy for eliciting cathartic reactions. Under
        Western influence, the tribe moved from an organized to a
        disorganized sociocultural situation. New rituals--like con-
        fession and puritanical practices stressing self-control--
        arose to fulfill the same therapeutic ends.

748.   Ward, Colleen. "Thaipusan in Malaysia: A Psycho-Anthropolog-
        ical Analysis of Ritual Dance, Ceremonial Possession, and
        Self-Mortification Practices." ETHOS 12 (1984): 307-34.

        Studies a Hindu religious festival in Malaysia. The ritual,
        which includes a stereotyped trance, is analyzed in biologi-
        cal, psychological, and sociological terms, stressing the
        culture's beliefs, evaluation, and explanation of the phenom-
        enon. Trance and possession states are treated as altered
        states of consciousness and their features and methods of
        induction are described. The author outlines various psycho-
        physiological and psychosocial explanations of such trances.
        It is concluded that the ritual releases the individual's
        repressed emotions and fulfills the status needs of the Hindu
        community and Malaysian society as a whole.

749.   Wintrob, R. M. "The Influence of Others: Witchcraft and Root
        Work as Explanations of Behavior Disturbances." JOURNAL
        OF NERVOUS AND MENTAL DISEASE 156 (1973): 318-26.

        Considers the characteristics of supernatural beliefs about
        illness among two cultural groups, namely, Liberians and Black
        Americans. The range of behavior problems associated with

these beliefs is illustrated from case studies. Professionals could utilize a knowledge of supernatural systems to diagnose and treat their patients more effectively. Peaceful coexistence with folk therapists is advised.

750.   Wittkower, E. D., and Hsien Rim. "Transcultural Psychiatry." ARCHIVES OF GENERAL PSYCHIATRY 13 (1965): 387-94.

Surveys the field of transcultural psychiatry, pointing out the key concepts, the limits of the field of research, the methodological approaches, and the difficulties involved. Examples of psychological disorders in different countries are given. Culture-bound psychiatric disorders, like possession states in Voodoo ceremonies, are included.

751.   Worsley, Peter. "Non-Western Medical Systems." ANNUAL REVIEW OF ANTHROPOLOGY. Edited by Bernard J. Siegel, Alan R. Beals, and Stephen A. Tyler. Palo Alto, CA: Annual Reviews, Inc., 1982, vol. 2, pp. 315-48.

Considers the issues brought about by the contact between Western and non-Western medical systems. The author suggests that: 1) the growing mutual interchange between cultures in medical ideas and practices is a sign of an expanding medical pluralism; and 2) medical systems exist with a "meta-medical" framework of thought--implying that medical conceptions of illness and its cause are embedded within a wider sociological and ideological background which provides answers to "ultimate questions." The author believes that traditional medicine will, eventually, be incorporated into Western scientific medicine. The social role of the typical curer or therapist is among the topics dealt with. References to 82 books and essays are included.

752.   Yap, P. H. "The Possession Syndrome: A Comparison of Hong Kong and French Findings." JOURNAL OF MENTAL SCIENCE 106 (1960): 114-37.

Examines the possession syndrome, that is, the phenomena of spirit-communication in mediumistic trance, of spirit-possession, and of "demonpathy," in mental patients in Hong Kong and compares them with similar events among French Catholic patients. Literature, mainly in French, on the subject of possession and the major theories is reviewed. The possessed personality can be best understood in the light of the subject's own personality needs, life interaction, and cultural background. Possession is held to be both a hysterical illness and an imbalance of the personality.

753.   Yokoyama, Keigo. "Morita Therapy and Seiza." PSYCHOLOGIA 11 (1968): 179-84.

Points out that Morita therapy is similar to Zen, in spite of Dr. Morita's contention that he based his treatment on Western psychiatry. It is argued that the development of

Morita therapy should include the practice of Zazen (especially "Seiza," i.e, "quiet sitting"). The author concludes
from his own practice that Zen adds to Morita the power of
bodily and mental adjustment needed to improve hypersensi-
tivity.

754.   Young, Allan. "The Anthropology of Illness and Sickness."
        ANNUAL REVIEW OF ANTHROPOLOGY. Edited by Bernard J. Siegel,
        Alan R. Beals, and Stephen A. Tyler. Palo Alto, CA: Annual
        Reviews, Inc., 1982, vol. 2, pp. 257-83.

        Reflects on the advances in medical anthropology and out-
        lines the different methods anthropologists employ when
        writing about illness and sickness. The essay concentrates
        on the literature which relies on "an evolving conceptual
        system centered on the social and experiential particulari-
        ties of sickness and healing" (p. 261). The author contrasts
        the "anthropology of illness" which is concerned with indig-
        enous explanatory models of disease, with the "anthropology
        of sickness" which takes into account the social relations
        that produce the forms and distribution of sickness in a
        society. Although not directly related to new religious
        movements and their healing claims, this essay presents some
        of the theoretical background to understanding folk medicine.
        The author lists 189 references.

        B.   STUDIES ON SPECIFIC CULTS AND NEW MOVEMENTS

        The study of new religious movements or cults in non-Western
cultures provides a broader perspective for a better understanding
of the many cults which have been flourishing in the Western world.
The new cults may appear innovative to those who are not aware of
the religious ferment in different parts of the world. The fact of
the matter, however, is that what Western society has been experiencing since the late 1960s has its counterparts in different
historical eras and in diverse human cultures.

        Several elements in the anthropological study of new movements
might contribute both to the method and theory applied in the
investigation and interpretation of cults in the West. The non-
Western movements have been, by and large, researched by outsiders,
that is, by scholars whose cultural and religious traditions were
alien to the groups they were studying. Over the years, a methodology was developed to study these traditions, a methodology which,
although not without problems, incorporated a level of objectivity
and impartiality, which many of the studies of the new cults in the
West have certainly not enjoyed. Further, because anthropologists
were, as a rule, not emotionally involved in the religious turmoils
of the cultures under study, and because their personal loyalties
or commitments were not at stake, they were freer to explore the
ideology of the movements and more at liberty to speculate on their
possible causes and various levels of meaning. Unlike many contem-

porary Western psychiatrists who had already taken a personal, usually negative, stand on the issue of religion and mental health, anthropologists and cross-cultural psychologists and psychiatrists could, because of their methodological training to study other cultures impartially and non-judgmentally, approach their data with fewer preconceived ideas about its validity. People who joined one of the new cults in the West presented a challenge to the value systems and family traditions of the same Western psychiatrists and psychologists who were counseling parents of cult members and many ex-cult members who had left a cult, often under duress if not physical coercion.

There is, no doubt, debate in anthropological literature on the sociological and psychological functions that new movements in non-Western cultures might fulfill. Several authors, such as Burton-Bradley (see items 774-78) have favored the view that some cults are symptoms of pathology. By and large, however, the rise of the new movements in these societies has been seen as a relatively satisfying response to a variety of cultural and/or religious needs. Even hotly debated issues, like the psychological state of the shaman, have never been discussed on the same involved emotional level, which is so evident in some of the scholarly exchanges on contemporary cults in the West. It can certainly be shown that many psychiatric studies on new religious movements in the Western world sound more like diatribes or blanket denunciations than informed, academic statements. In such an atmosphere, the understanding of the cults is more likely to be obscured than enhanced. It must be stressed that understanding the cults must precede both the psychiatric evaluation of their ideologies and life-styles, and the counseling given to ex-cult and cult members and their families.

The following studies of individual cults in non-Western, mostly non-literate, societies contribute, in our opinion, to a more dispassionate approach to similar groups in the West and to a better understanding of the overall historical, cultural, and religious roles they have in a rapidly changing world.   Several studies of non-Western religious movements have direct relevance to the Western world. Studies of glossolalia in diverse cultures could certainly throw some light on this phenomenon, which has often been explained as a sign of infantile regression or pathological personality. Some of these cults, imported to the United States through the process of immigration, have now an established hold in our midst. Spiritism, Curanderismo, and Santeria are excellent examples of this cross-cultural fertilization. The practice of Voodoo has become more common especially in ethnic groups of African origins.

Anthropological literature is rich in ethnographic descriptions of new religious movements in non-Western cultures, a richness unmatched by comparable studies of the cults in the West. The reader versed in this anthropological material becomes aware both of the complexity of the problems and of the need to explore the cults in some depth before even attempting a psychiatric evaluation. The reader is further challenged to reconsider the Western concepts of deviancy and pathology and the way they have been applied to modern cultic movements.

755.   Abad, Vincent, Juan Ramos, and Elizabeth Boyce. "A Model
        for Delivery of Mental Health Services to Spanish Speaking
        Minorities". AMERICAN JOURNAL OF ORTHOPSYCHIATRY 44 (1944):
        584-95.

        Presents data from a Spanish clinic in a community mental
        health center where Puerto Ricans were treated with specially
        designed methods which took into consideration their cultural
        context. Common and cultic traits, as well as the subcultural
        differences between Puerto Ricans themselves, are described.
        The researchers think that awareness of the belief in Espiri-
        tismo is important to the clinician who attempts to deal with
        this group, since it frequently happens that a patient goes
        to the health clinic only after the folk healer has failed
        in his or her curing efforts. They recommend that close ties
        should be developed between the therapists and the Puerto
        Ricans and that ways of collaborating with indigenous folk
        healers should be explored.

756.   Aberle, David. "A Note on Relative Deprivation Theory as
        Applied to Millenarian and Other Cult Movements."
        MILLENNIAL DREAMS IN ACTION (item 899), pp. 209-14.

        Defines relative deprivation as "a negative discrepancy
        between legitimate expectation and actuality" (p. 209), and
        then discusses several types of deprivation. Millennial move-
        ments, like cults, are, according to the author, susceptible
        to analysis in terms of deprivation theory. Those people,
        who suffer from acute deprivation and cannot withdraw from
        the world, can only join sects of the elect, which compensate
        for the deprivation.

757.   Aberle, David F. "The Prophet Dance and Reactions to White
        Contact." SOUTHWESTERN JOURNAL OF ANTHROPOLOGY 15 (1959):
        74-83.

        Examines three forms of deprivation, that is, discrepancy
        between expectation and actuality, which might account for
        the rise of the Prophet dance among the Indians of the Ameri-
        can Northwest: 1) the general cultural decline of the tribe;
        2) its exposure to new desires which couldn't be satisfied;
        and 3) a differential shift in status among the members of
        the tribe. Another type of condition, namely, a general
        misunderstanding about the current state of affairs which
        have a pervading influence on culture, might also give rise
        to cult movements or make them acceptable to other tribes.
        The author appears to endorse cautiously the deprivation
        theory of cult origin. The implication is that the new move-
        ments satisfy the needs of the individual and of the group
        and could therefore be considered therapeutic.

758.   Allison, Stephen H., and H. Newton Malony. "Filipino Psychic
        Surgery: Myth, Magic, or Miracle." JOURNAL OF RELIGION AND
        HEALTH 20 (1981): 48-62.

Considers the Filipino folk healers who incorporate religious elements into their practice and who have organized
themselves into a religious group with many congregations.
Some of their beliefs and their healing methods such as
mystic, spiritual, and magnetic/psychic healings, are described. The medical questions raised by these practices
are discussed. Emotional disturbance and suggestibility
play an important role in all the alleged cures. The
emotional rapport between the healer and the patient is
probably the cause of all claims of emotional healing. The
authors speculate on the possibility of fraud and on the
cultural influences which guarantee success and acceptance.
The need for further research is underscored.

759.   Barber, Bernard. "Acculturation and Religious Experiences."
       AMERICAN SOCIOLOGICAL REVIEW 6 (1941): 663-69.

       Describes and analyzes the conditions under which the myths
       of a culture-hero among the North American Indians become the
       ideological basis for messianic movements, 20 of which have
       been recorded in the United States prior to 1890. These
       movements, which arose in periods of deprivation, serve to
       articulate the spiritual depression of the Indians and to
       stabilize society and culture. The author does not explore
       the correlation between the rise of the movements and the
       widespread deprivation. A bibliography of American Indian
       messianic movements is included.

760.   Barrett, H. G. INDIAN SHAKERS: A MESSIANIC CULT IN THE
       PACIFIC NORTHWEST. Carbondale: Southern Illinois Univer-
       sity Press, 1957. 278 pp.

       An anthropological study of an American Indian messianic
       cult in the nineteenth century with John Slocum (a member of
       the Squaxin tribe) as its prophetic leader. One section
       describes the cult's beginnings from Slocum's experience and
       its development into a full-blown movement. A detailed
       account of its doctrine, faith, and ceremonies is also pro-
       vided. The rise of the movement is related to the troubled
       times, caused particularly by the presence of white settlers.
       The author discusses briefly whether the tribe's leader
       suffered from some kind of nervous ailment, whether he was a
       victim of hysteria or epilepsy. The emotional experience of
       shaking is, in the author's view, a healing instrument.

761.   Barrett, Leonard E. THE RASTAFARIANS: SOUNDS OF CULTURAL
       DISSONANCE. Boston: Beacon Press, 1977. xviii, 257 pp.

       Studies a Jamaican messianic movement whose members are
       also found in the United States. The history of the cult,
       its cultural background, and its basic beliefs and practices
       are fully described. The author's view is that the cult is
       related to cultural deprivation and that its members are
       those who are denied the opportunity to perform the cultural
       roles that are normally expected of them. The implication
       is that the movement fulfills many social, political, and
       economic needs.

762.   Baugh, Timothy G. "Revitalization Movements Among the Kiowa
       and Kiowa-Apache." PAPERS IN ANTHROPOLOGY (University of
       Oklahoma) 2 (Spring 1970): 66-83.

       Applies Wallace's model of revitalization (item 903) to
       two Indian tribes in Southwest Oklahoma. Several religious
       revivals were attempted, all of which aimed at reducing the
       cultural stress inflicted on the Indians by the dominant
       white culture. Only the Peyote cult survived and still func-
       tions as a stress-reliever in a society in which the Indians
       play a secondary role.

763.   Berndt, R. M. "A Cargo Movement in the Eastern Central High-
       lands of New Guinea." OCEANIA 23 (1952-1953): 40-65, 137-
       58, 202-34.

       Studies a major Cargo cult in a non-literate society. The
       social, cultural, and historical backgrounds are given, and
       many ritual texts are included. The author accepts the com-
       mon anthropological theory that these cults not only express
       native dissatisfaction with existing conditions, but also
       attempt to reach a satisfactory adjustment. The cults can
       be said to be of some therapeutic value in the sense that they
       help individuals cope with existing socioeconomic problems.

764.   Binite, Ayo. "The Psychological Basis of Certain Culturally
       Held Beliefs." INTERNATIONAL JOURNAL OF SOCIAL PSYCHIATRY
       23 (1977): 204-8.

       Attempts to clarify the reasons why certain people are
       worried by the evil intention of spirits, witches, and other
       non-material beings, a situation common in Nigeria, particu-
       larly among semi-literate people. Several case studies are
       reported. The author seems to hold that these people are
       schizophrenics who are liable to suffer from various delu-
       sions, and that many of the so-called witches are actually
       insane.

765.   Bonilla, Edwardo S. "Spiritualism and Psychodrama." AMERI-
       CAN ANTHROPOLOGIST 71 (1969): 493-97.

       Observes that the four elements of psychodrama, namely,
       1) a protagonist (subject or patient), 2) the director (the
       chief therapist), 3) the auxiliary ego, and 4) the audience
       (or the group), are also found in a spiritualistic session
       which reenacts the intrapsychic conflict of the individual.
       An account of one particular spiritualist curing session in
       Puerto Rico is provided. There is, according to the author,
       a similarity between psychoanalysis and spiritualism in the
       conceptualization used to describe psychospiritual distur-
       bances. Spiritualist curing is effective, and its practice
       has possibly increased due to the breakdown of traditional
       patterns of social interaction with the consequent loss of
       security.

766. Bourguignon, Erika. "Possession and Trance in Cross-Cultural Studies of Mental Health." CULTURE-BOUND SYNDROMES, ETHNOPSYCHIATRY, AND ALTERNATE THERAPIES (item 690), pp. 47-55.

Presents some guidelines for distinguishing between possession and trance, which may be related to institutionalized forms of altered states of consciousness. These concepts are illustrated with data from the Pacific area. The difficult issue of whether possession and similar phenomena are psychopathological states is confronted, and it is maintained that their occurrence is not necessarily a sign of illness.

767. Bourguignon, Erika. "The Effectiveness of Religious Healing Movements: A Review of Recent Literature." TRANSCULTURAL PSYCHIATRY RESEARCH REVIEW 13 (1976): 5-21.

Reviews the literature, mostly of the 1960s and early 1970s, which deals with the effective results of religious healing activities in various parts of the world. The author discusses some terminological issues, as well as the meaning of effectiveness and healing in the context of religion. The area covered is mainly the therapeutic practices of shamans, diviners, and folk healers. It is stated that one can look at possession and faith-healing cults as largely "effective," if the alteration of life-style and self-image are judged to be desirable therapeutic goals. There is evidence that religious healing rites have resulted in the disappearance of symptoms. The author underscores the need for substantial field research to supply adequate medical and native diagnosis and other statistical information.

768. Bourguignon, Erika. POSSESSION. San Francisco: Chandler and Sharp, 1976. 71 pp.

Discusses the meaning of possession and illustrates its expression with reference to Haitian Voodoo. It is held that Voodoo has survived in a scientific age because it has an adaptive value for both the individual and for society. Those who participate in the rituals have a personality structure which leads to personal and social rewards. A short account of the beliefs about possession and of the trances, which include Pentecostal-type behavior like glossolalia, is given. Possession trance cults are, according to the author, signs of crises and expressions of human needs. They express anxiety, but offer no solution. Eastern mysticism in the West, with its trance behavior, is an indication that technology and rationalism have failed, thus leading people to retreat from accepting personal responsiblity and escaping into cult behavior.

769. Bourguignon, Erika. "Illness and Possession: Elements for a Comparative Study." R. M. BUCKE MEMORIAL SOCIETY: NEWSLETTER-REVIEW 7 (Spring 1974): 37-46.

Discusses dissociation states in the context of the author's own fieldwork in Haiti. The author makes an attempt to work out a typology of possession cults based on the indigenous explanations and treatments of illness. Two types of cults, West and East African, are proposed. The healing potential of these possession rituals seem to be taken for granted.

770.   Bourguignon, Erika. A CROSS-CULTURAL STUDY OF DISSOCIATIONAL STATES. Columbus: Ohio Research Foundation, Ohio State University, 1968. x, 303 pp.

Aims at surveying and developing a typology of dissociational states that are interpreted by the indigenous population as signs of spirit possession. The author, however, claims that this phenomenon is simply a type of trance or altered state of consciousness. She summarizes the results of four field studies in Micronesia, the United States, Brazil, and British West Indies. Her conclusion is that institutionalized dissociation states are a universal, psychobiological phenomenon, while belief in spirit possession is a less widespread cultural invention. No conclusion is made about the possible psychopathology of trance behavior. In some cases, however, possession may have been related to a positive reaction to stress.

771.   Bourguignon, Erika. "The Self, the Behavioral Environment, and the Theory of Spirit Possession." CONTEXT AND MEANING IN CULTURAL ANTHROPOLOGY. Edited by Melford Spiro. New York: Free Press, 1965, pp. 39-60.

Discusses the view that spirit possession is psychopathological in any society, with reference to a field study of Haitian peasants. It is held that ritualized possession or dissociation provides the self with an ultimate set of values in which unfulfilled desires can be achieved. "In a world of poverty, disease, and frustration, ritual possession, rather than destroying the integrity of the self, provides increased scope for fulfillment" (p. 57).

772.   Bourguignon, Erika, editor. RELIGION, ALTERED STATES OF CON-SCIOUSNESS, AND SOCIAL CHANGE. Columbus: Ohio State University Press, 1973. x, 389 pp.

Contains three cross-cultural studies on possession trance in Africa and four field studies of spirit mediums and religious change in various other cultures. Although most contributors stress the social correlates between spirit mediums and their culture, several psychological reflections are made on the healthy or unhealthy aspects of their trance states. The editor makes some observations on the implications of these studies and offers some reflections on religious innovation in contemporary America. She concludes that altered states of consciousness, which are a significant factor in contemporary religious movements in the West, can be important instruments of social change. She raises the question

of whether these trance experiences are but an escape from
history, and suggests that cult members are seeking a refuge
in the irrational.

Contains items 807, 820, 870.

773.   Bram, Joseph. "Spirits, Mediums, and Believers in Contempo-
       rary Puerto Rico." TRANSACTIONS OF THE NEW YORK ACADEMY
       OF SCIENCES 20 (1958): 340-47.

       Gives a many-sided picture of the spiritualist movement in
       Puerto Rico, showing the latitude and variety in levels of
       knowledge, ritual patterns, beliefs, and attitudes. The
       author maintains that the principal function of spiritualism
       is to reconcile human beings with the thought of death.

774.   Burton-Bradley, B. G. "Kung Fu for Cargo." JOURNAL OF NER-
       VOUS AND MENTAL DISEASE 166 (1978): 885-89.

       Reports on a patient, known as the Kung Fu man, from Port
       Moresby, Papua New Guinea. This person, after several mis-
       haps including head injuries and a kidnapping, developed the
       qualities of a Cargo cult leader. He was charismatic, very
       strong in his belief in his own power to deliver Cargo (i.e.,
       European goods), and able to attract a following. His psycho-
       pathology, a case of grandiose paranoia, was precipitated by
       head injuries. Many Cargo leaders suffer from serious mental
       disorders that are acknowledged by the natives themselves.

775.   Burton-Bradley, B. G. "Cannibalism for Cargo." JOURNAL OF
       NERVOUS AND MENTAL DISEASE 163 (1976): 428-31.

       Describes a unique case of cannibalism in the context of
       a Melanesian Cargo cult. This leader had an overt psychosis
       before, during, and after eating human flesh. The author
       states that this person had all the attributes of a Cargo
       cult leader. If he had been successful in attracting a
       large following and exerting his influence over a wide area,
       serious consequences, including social damage, would have
       followed.

776.   Burton-Bradley, B. G. "The Psychiatry of a Cargo Cult."
       MEDICAL JOURNAL OF AUSTRALIA 4 (1973): 388-92.

       Provides evidence for an expanded interpretation of Cargo
       cults, which takes into account the psychological disorders
       brought about by cultic activity and the mental problems of
       some of those who join them. A short survey is made of the
       literature, largely written by social or cultural anthropol-
       ogists. Various types of leaders are distinguished and
       it is held that many of them suffered from severe mental
       disorders, such as grandiose paranoia. Cargo anxiety is, in
       many instances, the emotional expresssion of pathology.

777.   Burton-Bradley, B. G. "Human Sacrifice for Cargo." MEDICAL
       JOURNAL OF AUSTRALIA 2 (1972): 668-70.

Discusses a case of a Cargo cult leader in the Solomon
Islands. The features of "Cargo cult thinking" are described.
An account is given of the leader who actually committed mur-
der that he tried to justify by referring to his prophetic
mission. The author insists that this person was mentally
ill, both from the point of view of his own cultural background and from Western psychiatric opinion. It is argued
that Cargo anxiety is prevalent in the area and is especially
an attribute of abnormal cult leaders who should be treated
as mentally ill patients.

778.   Burton-Bradley, B. G. "The Native Guinea Prophet: Is the
       Cultist Always Normal?" MEDICAL JOURNAL OF AUSTRALIA 1
       (1970): 124-29.

Refutes the view that psychotics are never leaders and
shows that, in Papua New Guinea, the leaders of Cargo cults
may suffer from serious psychiatric disorders. After a short
description of the general features of a Cargo cult and a
review of the pertinent literature, the author presents clinical material from several cases of leaders who were pathological. The problem of what constitutes mental illness in
the trans-cultural context is discussed.

779.   Calley, Malcolm J. C. GOD'S PEOPLE: WEST INDIAN PENTECOSTAL
       SECTS IN ENGLAND. London: Oxford University Press, 1965.
       xiv, 182 pp.

Studies of one group of Pentecostal sects which, according
to the author, has some social features of the early Christian
Church. The analysis focuses on the early stages of the movement when 1) organization is rather loose, 2) the charismatic
leader plays an important role, and 3) the boundaries of the
group are still vague. The doctrines, rituals, internal
organization, and relations with outsiders are discussed. The
presence of these sects in the West Indies is explained by
the theory of socioeconomic deprivation. Joining a cult provides not only a new set of values, but also an escape from
poverty, frustration, and personal inadequacy. The success of
the sects in England is attributed to the general difficulties
experienced by immigrants who moved from an agricultural to an
industrial way of life. The sects provide an opportunity for
participation in group life.

780.   Cannon, Walter B. "Voodoo Deaths." PSYCHOSOMATIC MEDICINE
       19 (1957): 182-90.

Gives several examples of Voodoo deaths from South America,
Africa, New Zealand, and Australia and examines the reliability of such reports. A number of explanations for Voodoo
deaths are recorded. The author thinks that a persistent
and profound emotional state may lead to a disastrous drop
in blood pressure, causing death. Voodoo death is possible
and may be accounted for by great emotional stress due to
manifest or repressed fear.

781. Christensen, Palle. THE MELANESIAN CARGO CULT: MILLENARIAN-
      ISM AS A FACTOR IN CULTURE CHANGE. Copenhagan, Denmark:
      Akademisk Forlag, 1969. 148 pp.

      Gives brief descriptions of three types of Cargo cults:
      1) a religious one; 2) a purely secular one; and 3) one which
      is partly religious and partly political. A structural and
      functional analysis is developed. The author examines var-
      ious deprivation, economic, and stress theories which have
      been advanced to explain them. Although nervous and hysteri-
      cal phenomena often accompany the activities of a Cargo cult,
      the author thinks that, nevertheless, their emotional and
      symbolic behaviors strengthen group solidarity, create a new
      group morale, and remove feelings of guilt. Many scholars
      agree that Cargo cults are links in the social and cultural
      processes of change.

782. Cosmas-Diaz, I. "Puerto-Rico Espiritismo and Psychotherapy."
      AMERICAN JOURNAL OF ORTHOPSYCHIATRY 51 (1981): 636-45.

      Discusses the use of native treatments of mental illness
      in Puerto Rico as an adaptive mechanism for coping with an
      alien environment and as a form of psychotherapy. Espiritismo
      has been employed 1) to help people in the midst of crises
      arising out of family problems, 2) to counteract the effects
      of hallucinations, and 3) to treat nervous and psychotic
      conditions. The theory and practice of this folk treatment
      are outlined and compared with modern psychotherapy. The
      author uses case studies to illustrate the role of the
      Western-trained therapist working with Puerto Ricans. The
      need to understand the cultural and religious background of
      the Puerto Ricans is emphasized. Belief in Espiritismo, the
      author states, "should not be viewed as primitive thinking,
      avoidance of responsibility, or a sign of pathology" (p. 644).

783. Counts, Dorothy E. "The Kaliai and the Story: Development
      and Frustration in New Britain." HUMAN ORGANIZATION 31
      (1972): 373-83.

      Studies Cargo cults among a New Guinea tribe and suggests
      that they are a cultural response to frustration. The author
      thinks that any attempts to suppress them are bound to fail,
      since they leave intact the indigenous belief system and the
      sources of discontent. She believes that a better approach
      would be to take positive steps to meet the pressing needs
      of these people, thus counteracting one of the conditions
      for the cults' origin and growth. Although basically a
      deprivation theory of new religious movements, this study
      intimates that there are beneficial social and psychological
      effects derived from Cargo cults. Concrete steps can be
      taken to address the underlying roots of the problem.

784. Crapanzano, Vincent, and Vivian Garrison. CASE STUDIES IN
      SPIRIT POSSESSION. New York: Wiley and Sons, 1977. xvi,
      457 pp.

Presents several studies of spirit possession in various
societies. The "most interesting aspect of this volume is
the light it sheds on the therapeutic value of the performances for individuals with frank psychiatric disorders"
(xiii). Ritual possession not only releases, by catharsis,
tensions caused by socially unacceptable behavior, but also
contains other therapeutic factors similar to those of modern
psychiatry. A lengthy introduction (pp. 1-40) by Crapanzano
provides an overview of the widespread nature of spirit
possession and of some of its many interpretations. The
bibliographies for the various essays furnish a comprehensive
guide to past and contemporary research on the subject.

Contains items 800, 887.

785.   Delgado, Melvin. "Puerto Rican Spiritualism and the Social
        Work Profession." SOCIAL CASEWORK 48 (1977): 451-58.

        Undertakes to examine "the psychotherapeutic merits of
        spiritualism in the Puerto Rican community, to compare the
        role of the medium with that of the social worker, and to
        make recommendations for the use of mediums and their methods
        as community resources" (p. 450). The hold of spiritualism
        over a large section of the population is functionally ex-
        plained as a means of coping with cultural and social changes.
        Mediums offer treatment for both physical and emotional ill-
        ness, thus stressing the unity of the person and avoiding the
        sharp distinction between body and psyche made in the West.
        Both mediums and social workers follow a task-oriented ther-
        apy, emphasize the role of the environment, and employ similar
        group and individual treatments. The mediums have the advan-
        tage of sharing a subculture with their clients. They are
        accepted as individuals possessing supernatural powers, which
        lends credence to their authority. They tend, however, to
        treat only the symptoms, while social workers strive to re-
        structure the personality of those who consult them. Several
        suggestions are made to increase the effectiveness of social
        workers.

786.   Dobkin, Marlene. "Fortune's Malice: Divination, Psychother-
        apy, and Folk Medicine in Peru." JOURNAL OF AMERICAN
        FOLKLORE 82 (1969): 132-41.

        Examines the psychotherapeutic techniques of divination by
        fortune-telling cards (called "naipes") used by folk healers
        in Peru. The article outlines the history and the structure
        of the procedure. The deck of cards is statistically "loaded
        not in the direction of good fortune but rather to highlight
        stress and conflict that may be present in the sociocultural
        milieu" (p. 138). The author suggests that the naipes may
        be an ethno-projective device comparable to free association,
        dream analysis, and projection tests.

787.   Dobkin de Rios, Marlene. "The Relation Between Witchcraft
        Beliefs and Psychosomatic Illness." ANTHROPOLOGY AND
        MENTAL HEALTH. Edited by Joseph Westermeyer. The Hague,
        Netherlands: Mouton, 1976, pp. 11-17.

Points out that witchcraft beliefs are a widespread index
of social and psychological strain, and that psychosomatic
illnesses are frequently viewed as infirmities of interpersonal relationships. Consequently, the correlation between
disease patterns and social stress inherent in witchcraft
should be carefully examined. Witchcraft beliefs in primitive societies reflect certain institutionalized patterns of
tension and anxiety, both of which in turn lead to psychosomatic disorders. The author thinks that these beliefs can be
adaptive because they contribute to the dispersal of popula-
tions when the resources of the environment are at the point
of being exhausted. Whether this theory can be modified to
explain witchcraft beliefs and practices in Western culture
is not discussed.

788.   Dumont, Jean-Paul. "Not in Ourselves, But in Our Stars."
        SPIRITS, SHAMANS, AND STARS (item 925), pp. 241-54.

        Attempts a structural analysis of astrological concepts
        among the Panare Indians of Venezuelan Guyana. The author
        elaborates on the social implication of astrological sexual-
        ity, namely, that all sexual departures from the cultural
        norm are believed to lead to death. He suggests that astrol-
        ogy reenforces social norms which receive justification not
        only from some force within us, but also from a power beyond
        us. To what extent this can be said to have a therapeutic
        value is not discussed.

789.   Egeland, Janice, and Abram M. Hostetter. "Affective Disorder
        Among the Amish, 1976-1980." AMERICAN JOURNAL OF PSYCHIA-
        TRY 140 (1983): 56-61.

        Contains the first of a series of essays (cf. item 823)
        reporting the results of a six-year study of the Amish who,
        because they form a culturally and genetic homogenous popu-
        lation and because they are not hampered by drug abuse and
        alcoholism, offer an excellent research setting. The authors
        describe the socioreligious background of the group and out-
        line their research methods and results. Among their con-
        clusions is the confirmation of the absence of alcoholism,
        hysteria, and sociopathy. A high percentage of manic-depres-
        sive patients, comparable to that found among the Hutterites
        (cf. item 509), was detected. Minor depression, chronic
        hypomanic disorder, and schizo-affective disorders were
        recorded.

790.   Egerton, Robert B., Marvin Karno, and Irma Fernandez.
        "Curanderismo in the Metropolis: The Diminished Role of
        Folk Psychiatry Among Los Angeles Mexican-Americans."
        AMERICAN JOURNAL OF PSYCHOTHERAPY 24 (1970): 124-34.

        Comments on several reports that curanderismo, a healing
        ritual performed by a specialist by virtue of a "gift from
        God" revealed in dreams, and often involving contact with a
        spirit, has been occasionally successful in healing and pre-

venting illness when psychiatric treatment failed. The
reseachers report that, while curanderismo still persists in
the East Los Angeles community studied, its importance has
diminished greatly.

791.   el Islam, M. F. "The Psychotherapeutic Basis of Some Arab
        Rituals." INTERNATIONAL JOURNAL OF SOCIAL PSYCHIATRY 13
        (1967): 265-68.

        Concentrates on the interpretation of two rituals, the
        visit to the tombs of dead sheikhs and the Zar ceremonies.
        In both cases, the clients express submission to the master.
        The author thinks that this is indicative of the need to
        submit to a parent figure which is, in these cases, trans-
        ferred to an imaginary superhuman entity. These rituals,
        though superstitious, are therapeutic.

792.   el Sendiony, M. F. "The Problem of Cultural Specificity of
        Mental Illness: The Egyptian Mental Disease and the Zar
        Ceremony." AUSTRALIAN AND NEW ZEALAND JOURNAL OF PSYCHI-
        ATRY 8.2 (1974): 103-7.

        Questions whether there are, in Egypt, mental illnesses
        which result specifically from the culture. The literature
        is reviewed and supplemented by the author's anthropological
        observations and Egyptian psychiatric reports. It is con-
        cluded that the pathological manifestations expressed in
        the Rabt and Zar cult phenomena are simply local varieties
        of a common disease process to which all people are
        vulnerable.

793.   Ewing, Katherine. "The Messengers of the 1890 Ghost Dance."
        PSYCHODYNAMIC PERSPECTIVES ON RELIGION, SECT, AND CULT
        (item 1226), pp. 73-92.

        Traces the origin and development of a North American In-
        dian movement that was based on the teachings of the prophet
        Wovoka, a member of the North Paiute tribe of Western Nevada
        and which spread to other Indian tribes. The author's view
        is that the crucial issue is not economic or political depri-
        vation, but "whether cultural patterns are available for
        securing cultural and individual self-esteem in such a situ-
        ation of deprivation and/or domination" (p. 74).

794.   Fakhouri, Hani. "The Zar Cult in an Egyptian Village."
        ANTHROPOLOGICAL QUARTERLY 41 (1968): 49-56.

        Provides a short description of a Zar possession ceremony
        and illustrates the symptomatology and treatment of two
        patients. Since most of the latter's problems are psycholog-
        ical in origin, the Zar rituals provide temporary relief.
        The core of the treatment consists of changing the patient's
        point of view or attitude. In serious cases, however, the
        Zar rituals, which induce hysterical behavior in the subject,
        are only a relatively ineffective handling of the problem.

795. Figge, Horst H. "Spirit Possession and Healing Cult Among
      the Brazilian Umbanda." PSYCHOTHERAPY AND PSYCHOSOMATICS
      25 (1975): 246-56.

      Describes the belief system and ritual practices of this
      South American cult. Four kinds of treatments are listed:
      counter magic, fluid manipulation, offerings, and mediumship.
      The ability of a person to fall into a trance is explained
      by the "internalization of the releaser."

796. Finkler, Kaja. SPIRITUALIST HEALERS IN MEXICO: SUCCESS AND
      FAILURE OF ALTERNATIVE THERAPEUTICS. New York: Bergin and
      Garvey, 1985. xii, 256 pp.

      Presents an anthropological study of Mexican spiritualism
      focused on two temples in the southern region of Hidalgo
      State. The world view of spiritualism as a religion, with
      its theory of the origin of illness and the ways to treat it,
      is described. The author demonstrates the patient's view-
      point of the effectiveness of spiritual healing. One must
      understand the historical, social, and economic factors which
      interact with the therapeutic system. The strength of spiri-
      tual healers lies in their providing symbolic treatments which
      modern Western medicine and therapy are unable to offer in an
      alien setting. Because illness must be treated and cured,
      not just by medicine, but by culturally significant symbols,
      patients turn to folk healers, especially when Western treat-
      ment fails. Spiritualist healing is seen as a complement to,
      rather than as a competitor of, modern medicine and therapy.

797. Finkler, Kaja. "Studying Outcomes of Mexican Spiritualist
      Therapy." THE ANTHROPOLOGY OF MEDICINE (item 723), pp.
      81-102.

      Investigates treatment outcomes in two spiritualist temples
      in rural Mexico. The cultural setting of Mexican spiritual-
      ism and the role played by the healers and their healing
      techniques are described. Various case studies are also dis-
      cussed. The author stresses the need for empirical studies
      which would throw light on the requirements for recovery and
      health care. Further cooperation between Western medicine
      and alternate healing systems of the spiritualist kind is
      anticipated.

798. Finkler, Kaja. "Non-Medical Treatments and their Outcomes.
      Part II. Focus on Adherents of Spiritualism." CULTURE,
      MEDICINE, AND PSYCHIATRY 5 (1982): 65-103.

      Continues the discussion of spiritual healing in a Mexican
      village, and concentrates on those patients who identify them-
      selves as spiritualists and who share the spiritist temple
      ideology and participate in temple life. The treatment in-
      cludes several therapeutic modalities, like patient-healer
      interaction, the healing trance, and the process of becoming
      a healer. The author presents a sample of 31 regular patients

with their symptoms, diagnoses, treatments, and results.
These patients have, as a rule, already consulted a Western
therapist and suffer from serious disorders. The spiritualist treatment reduces the subject's feeling of being sick by
a combination of sociological, psychological, and cultural
factors. Although the effect of spiritist healing of psychotic disorders is not evident, it is clear that the treatment eliminates the sick role and restores some of the
individual's pre-sickness behavior qualities. It could,
therefore, be counted as successful therapy.

799.   Finkler, Kaja. "Non-Medical Treatments and Their Outcomes."
        CULTURE, MEDICINE, AND PSYCHIATRY 4 (1980): 217-310.

        Examines the results of spiritual healing methods adminis-
        tered in a rural region of Mexico. The socioeconomic setting
        and the healing techniques are briefly sketched. The kind of
        ailments which lead both a first-time and a habitual patient
        to go to a traditional healer are recorded. The results show
        that spiritualist healers are not very successful in curing
        their patients, though there are some benefits accrued by
        those who suffer from minor physical problems or from minor
        psychiatric complaints. When success occurs, it is usually
        attributable to both the manipulation of psychological symp-
        toms and symbolic representations. In Mexico, the stress
        on cleanliness and purification that relate to healing is a
        factor which contributes to the therapy.

800.   Garrison, Vivian. "The 'Puerto Rican Syndrome' in Psychiatry
        and Espiritismo." CASE STUDIES IN SPIRIT POSSESSION (item
        784), pp. 383-449.

        Explores the biological, cultural, and psychological aspects
        of a nervous attack of a Puerto Rican woman, which was inter-
        preted as possession by three misguided spirits sent against
        her by the work of witchcraft. The background of the sub-
        ject, her episodes of spirit possession, the initial medical
        assessment, and the later psychiatric consultation are de-
        scribed at length. Six reunions or meetings in a spiritist
        center in the Bronx, New York, are outlined. The author
        maintains that there are several significant similarities and
        differences between the ways spiritists and psychodynamically
        oriented psychotherapists conceptualize, diagnose, and treat
        "spiritual" or "mental" states. Both tend to use sociodrama,
        family therapy, and an interactional theory of personality
        rather than a psychoanalytic approach.

801.   Gaviria, Moises, and Ronald Winthrob. "Spiritist or Psychi-
        atrist: Treatment of Mental Illness among Puerto Ricans in
        Two Connecticut Towns." JOURNAL OF OPERATIONAL PSYCHIATRY
        10 (1979): 40-46.

        Discusses the ways Puerto Ricans living in the United States
        react to mental illness. Those who conceive of their illness
        as being the result of natural causes consult a psychiatrist,

while those who attribute it to supernatural influence have
recourse to a folk healer (a curandero) who has been successful in his practice. The author thinks that the outcome of
therapy might depend more on the special skills and personal
qualities of the therapist than by the particular treatment
prescribed.

802.   Gelfand, Michael. "Psychiatric Disorders as Recognized By
       the Shona." MAGIC, FAITH, AND HEALING (item 679), pp.
       156-73.

       Gives an account of the system of mental health among the
       Shona of Southern Rhodesia (now Zimbabwe). While these
       Africans recognize certain psychological illnesses common
       also to Western psychiatry, they fail to distinguish between
       neurotic and psychotic disorders. Shona treatment is based
       entirely on suggestion, which is an important feature of every
       technique they use.

803.   Gilestra, Doris M. "Santeria and Psychotherapy." COMPREHEN-
       SIVE PSYCHOTHERAPY 3 (1981): 69-80.

       Presents Santeria, the theory and practice of Voodoo in
       Cuba, as a psychotherapy by comparing the diagnosis, treat-
       ment, and psychodynamic aspects of its healing methods to
       modern psychotherapy. The article sketches the historical
       background of Santeria's origins among the Yoruba tribe of
       Nigeria, and describes the way its treatment handles hysteria,
       phobias, antisocial behavior, obsessive-compulsive disorders,
       schizophrenic symptoms, and character disorders. Two specific
       ritual ways by which Santeria treats hysteria and compulsive
       stealing are compared to modern psychotherapy. The author
       thinks that Santeria is a form of psychotherapy which has
       unharnessed potential.

804.   Golden, Kenneth M. "Voodoo in Africa and the United States."
       AMERICAN JOURNAL OF PSYCHIATRY 134 (1977): 1425-27.

       Describes the psychological mechanisms of Voodoo as prac-
       ticed in Africa in order to understand similar customs in the
       United States. The reasons why Voodoo hexes are apparently
       successful are briefly outlined. The importance of the com-
       munal nature of the belief system, which brings overdepen-
       dency and a feeling of powerlessness, is stressed. The author
       thinks there is a need to develop effective treatments to deal
       with the psychological resistances of patients who believe
       they have been cursed.

805.   Goodman, Felicitas D. "Triggering of Altered States of Con-
       sciousness as Group Event: A New Case from Yucatán."
       CONFINIA PSYCHIATRICA 23 (1980): 26-34.

       Gives an example of a crisis cult which did not arise, as
       so many others do, in the context of severe social unrest.
       The group studied is a Mexican fundamentalist Christian Pen-

tecostal Church, where speaking in tongues is practiced. The author reports, through an informant, on an evening service during which several people experienced an altered state of consciousness. Since there was no evidence of a crisis or problem which might have been the cause of such an outburst, the author suggests that in this case the "trance" experience might have been set off by population pressure. She thinks that human beings, having a genetically-based propensity for assuming altered states of consciousness, might occasionally do so in a group atmosphere.

806.   Goodman, Felicitas D. "Disturbances in the Apostolic Church: A Trance Based Upheaval in Yucatán." TRANCE, HEALING, AND HALLUCINATION (item 812), pp. 277-364.

Presents a field study of a Mexican millenarian movement which lasted about two years and in which members went into uncontrolled trance behavior. The social and cultural backgrounds are described and a short history of the Pentecostal movement and its position in the society at large is given. Glossolalia, with its anxiety-reducing capabilities, is discussed. While agreeing with La Barre (item 31) that such movements can be labeled crisis cults, the author disagrees with the implication that they are necessarily pathological. She rather maintains that these cults include adaptive mechanisms, namely, altered states of consciousness, which are strategies of the organism to resolve stress. The author's findings contradict Wallace's emphasis (item 903) on two psychological processes, namely, mazeway synthesis and hysterical conversion as paths to culture change.

807.   Goodman, Felicitas D. "Apostolics of Yucatán: A Case Study of a Religious Movement." RELIGION, ALTERED STATES OF CONSCIOUSNESS, AND SOCIAL CHANGE (item 772), pp. 178-217.

Describes a tongue-speaking Pentecostal movement in Mexico. Glossolalia is said to be a hyperarousal, dissociative state in which the person loses some "cortical control" of his or her behavior. The author discusses the rise and fall of the movement in the context of social turmoil of the time. There is some suggestion that, in the author's view, glossolalia, prophesying, and extensive recourse to diabolical possession are aberrant reactions to change.

808.   Goodman, Felicitas D. "Glossolalia and Hallucinations in Pentecostal Congregations." PSYCHIATRIA CLINICA 6 (1973): 97-103.

Makes a diachronic study of glossolalic utterances in Apostolic congregations in Mexico City and in Yucatán. Two case studies of people who had hallucinatory visions are presented. These visions which, unlike speaking in tongues, are not ritualized, occur regularly in clinically healthy subjects and not in those under the influence of drugs or who suffer from hysterical psychosis. The author concludes

that "the regular evolution of certain hallucinatory experiences may provide a diagnostic tool for distinguishing
pathological or drug-induced behavior from pseudo-perception
of clinically healthy subjects, thus freeing certain religious
experiences from the odium inherent in the pathological model"
(pp. 102-3).

809.   Goodman, Felicitas D. SPEAKING IN TONGUES: A CROSS-CULTURAL
        STUDY OF GLOSSOLALIA. Chicago: University of Chicago Press,
        1972. xxii, 175 pp.

        Presents a comprehensive study of glossolalia which brings
        together several of the author's previously published articles.
        The data is collected from four main groups: 1) Streams of
        Power (St. Vincent in the Caribbean); 2) a Midwestern Tent
        Revival (Columbus, Ohio); 3) a mainline Protestant church
        (in Texas); and 4) Umbanda (São Paulo, Brazil). Many conver-
        sion stories of those who speak in tongues are narrated and
        analyzed. The author concludes that altered states of con-
        sciousness were the focus of the experience, with glossolalia
        playing a secondary role. She maintains that glossolalia is
        not just an utterance by a person in a state of dissociation,
        but rather "an artifact of the mental state, or rather of
        its neurophysiological processes" (p. 124).

810.   Goodman, Felicitas D. "Altered Mental State vs 'Style of
        Discourse': Reply to Samarin." JOURNAL FOR THE SCIENTIFIC
        STUDY OF RELIGION 11 (1972): 297-99.

        Replies to Samarin's critique of her views (item 583) and
        points out that in religious environments the speakers are
        often in a state of trance. Cross-cultural studies on
        glossolalia reveal distinct, common features which cannot be
        explained by Samarin's theory that charismatics simply learn
        to speak in tongues as they learn to speak their native
        tongue. Glossolalia is not just a style of religious dis-
        course but requires a psychological and neurological
        explanation.

811.   Goodman, Felicitas D. "Phonetic Analysis of Glossolalia in
        Four Cultural Settings." JOURNAL FOR THE SCIENTIFIC STUDY
        OF RELIGION 8 (1969): 227-39.

        Analyzes the phonology, accent pattern, and intonation of
        tongue-speaking in four English- and Spanish-speaking groups,
        and finds that, in spite of the diversity in culture and
        language, there are some significant similarities. It is
        postulated that this similarity exists because glossolalia
        is an artifact of the dissociative state of trance or altered
        state of consciousness. The author compares this glossolalic
        trance to breathing rhythms in Pentecostal groups, to mass
        trancing, as among the Shakers, and to curative dances of
        native societies. It seems to be assumed that participants
        gain some benefits from their trance activity.

812.   Goodman, Felicitas D., Jeannette H. Henney, and Esther
        Pressel. TRANCE, HEALING, AND HALLUCINATION: THREE FIELD
        STUDIES OF RELIGIOUS EXPERIENCE. New York: Wiley and Sons,
        1974. xxiii, 388 pp.

        Brings together three major studies (items 806, 821, 871)
        on spirit possession and glossolalia.

813.   Griffen, William B. "A North American Nativistic Movement,
        1684." ETHNOHISTORY 17 (1970): 95-116.

        Describes an Indian movement in Mexico during the Spanish
        Colonial period. The historical background as well as some
        of the movement's main features are presented. Wallace's
        theoretical scheme (item 903), which understands the rise
        of new religiopolitical groups as channels for the release
        of tension, is adopted.

814.   Griffith, Ezra E. "The Impact of Sociocultural Factors on
        a Church-Based Healing Model." AMERICAN JOURNAL OF ORTHO-
        PSYCHIATRY 53 (1983): 291-302.

        Examines health care systems that offer a combined Western-
        ized medicopsychological approach and Christian healing.
        The research presented in this paper centers on the impact
        that sociocultural factors have on a Baptist healing clinic
        in Jamaica. The structure of this clinic, in which a client
        could be referred to a physician, a psychological counselor,
        or a prayer partner, is described. Religious principles
        seemed to dominate the healing activity of the church, even
        though the use of traditional native healers was excluded.
        The author concludes that this holistic model was quite
        successful and thinks that the procedure is a step in the
        right direction.

815.   Griffith, Ezra E., and George E. Mahy. "Psychological Bene-
        fits of Spiritualist Baptist 'Mourning.'" AMERICAN JOURNAL
        OF PSYCHIATRY 141 (1984): 769-73.

        Studies the Black Spiritualist Church in Barbados, a church
        which has flourished in the Caribbean since the late nine-
        teenth century. The author concentrates on the practice of
        "mourning" which, based on a text from the Book of Daniel
        (chapter 10), consists of a ceremonial washing and anointing
        after which the mourners are isolated in a small chamber at
        the back of the church. While thus secluded, the fervent
        participants pray and fast. During this period, dream and
        vision experiences are usually reported. Several therapeutic
        effects of the whole experience are claimed by the 23 people
        involved in the study. Among the benefits listed are a relief
        effect on one's mood, the ability to foresee and avoid certain
        situations, an improvement in one's decision-making ability,
        a heightened facility to communicate with God and to meditate,
        and a clear appreciation of one's racial origins. These re-
        sults are compared to those observed by Frank (item 382).

816. Hallaji, Ja'Far. "Hypnotherapeutic Techniques in a Central
      Asian Community." INTERNATIONAL JOURNAL OF CLINICAL AND
      EXPERIMENTAL HYPNOSIS 10 (1962): 271-74.

      Describes the curing methods of a semi-monastic Sufi com-
      munity in Afghanistan. Uninfluenced by Western psychiatry
      and trained in secret, the Sufi mystics treat physical and
      psychosomatic disorders by a method similar to mesmerism.
      The author observed a healing service which included chant-
      ing, the dimming of lights, hand passes, and eye fixation.
      Patients appeared to enter into a hypnotic state in a matter
      of minutes and the majority claimed an instant cure. No
      evaluation is provided.

817. Harwood, Alan. "Puerto Rican Spiritualism: Parts I and II."
      CULTURE, MEDICINE, AND PSYCHIATRY 1 (1977): 69-95, 135-53.

      Offers some reflections on two trends in contemporary Amer-
      ican medicine, namely, an increased interest in healers from
      other cultural traditions and a shift to the healing process
      itself. Spiritism in Puerto Rico and its implications are
      then discussed. Its cosmology and social aspects as well as
      the practical diagnosis and treatment of illness are recorded.
      The therapeutic goals of spiritism and of mainstream Western
      psychiatry are compared, and it is theorized that what the
      former achieves symbolically by removal in space, the latter
      cures through removal in time. Some practical applications,
      like the role of the spiritist psychotherapist in community
      health, are drawn up. Areas for further study, which include
      the effectiveness of spiritist and Western therapies on Puerto
      Rican clients, are suggested.

818. Harwood, Alan. RX: SPIRITUALISM AS NEEDED: A STUDY OF PUERTO
      RICAN COMMUNITY MENTAL HEALTH RESOURCE. New York: Wiley
      and Sons, 1977. xvii, 251 pp.

      Focuses on the medical system underlying spiritualist ther-
      apy in Puerto Rico, the kind of problems which lead people
      to have recourse to indigenous healers, and the treatments
      applied. The author views spiritualism not just as a form
      of psychotherapy, but also as a cultural institution con-
      tributing to the social and psychological well-being of the
      people by serving as a voluntary organization which orders
      social relationships and gives individuals an identity. The
      nature of spiritualist psychotherapy is summarized and com-
      pared to mainstream psychotherapies. The role of spiritualist
      therapy in community health is finally discussed.

819. Henderson, Cynthia. "Self, Spirit Possession, and Worldview."
      INTERNATIONAL JOURNAL OF SOCIAL PSYCHIATRY 17 (1971): 194-
      209.

      Describes and analyzes the world view of a group of Egyptian
      women who belong to the spirit-possession Zar cult. It is
      pointed out that this cult expresses basic concepts of the

self and the world, including male/female relationships. The
Zar ceremony is sketched with special attention to the reasons
given by the participants for performing the ritual and to the
kind of people for whom it is held. Although this paper is
not concerned directly with the therapeutic function of Zar,
it offers some valuable insights into the relationship of Zar
to other aspects of culture, specifically the separation of
sexes, the low female status, the marriage ceremony, marital
instability, and the manipulation of authority.

820.   Henney, Jeannette H. "The Shakers of St. Vincent: A Stable
        Religion." RELIGION, ALTERED STATES OF CONSCIOUSNESS AND
        SOCIAL CHANGE (item 772), pp. 219-62.

        Describes the belief system and the rituals of a fundamen-
        talist Protestant church. The author asserts that Shakerism
        offers the lower-class people a meaningful, soothing ritual
        which bolsters their injured identity image. Possession
        trance is a reassuring experience in time of innovation.
        Shakerism drains away their frustrations in the release of
        dissociation and religious activities.

821.   Henney, Jeannette H. "Spirit-Possession Belief and Trance
        Behavior in Two Fundamentalist Groups in St. Vincent."
        TRANCE, HEALING, AND HALLUCINATIONS (item 812), pp. 1-111.

        Concentrates on two religious groups, the Shakers and the
        Streams of Power, a Dutch healing group, both of which have
        spread in the West Indies, and compares them with similar
        sects in the Caribbean. Although worshippers of both groups
        experience dissociative states called trance, they differ in
        several important aspects. Several functions of Shakerism
        are noted: it gives its worshippers some leisure time, affords
        them an outlet for aesthetic yearnings, provides opportunity
        for the achievement of prestige, and enhances the lower-class
        individual's self-image. Although unable to confirm specific
        therapeutic values in the dissociative state achieved by the
        Shakers, the author maintains that Shakerism serves a positive
        purpose for releasing tension and reducing anxiety.

822.   Hogg, Donald. THE CONVINCE CULT IN JAMAICA. New Haven, CT:
        Yale University Publications in Anthropology, No. 58, 1960.
        32 pp.

        Examines an indigenous cult and attempts to explain the
        historical and functional significance of its Jamaican con-
        text. Besides the historical and cultural backgrounds, the
        author provides a description of the cult's ritual practices.
        It is maintained that its presence had a functional utility.
        Its main themes can be interpreted as wish-fulfillments of op-
        pressed and dissatisfied people, or as symbolic expressions of
        their repressed desires. The decline of the cult is explained
        by the fact that the cultural conditions in Jamaica have
        changed.

823.   Hostetter, Abram, Janice E. Egeland, and Jean Endicott.
       "Amish Study II: Consensus Diagnosis and Reliability Re-
       sults." AMERICAN JOURNAL OF PSYCHIATRY 140 (1983): 62-66.

       Describes the methods used in their study of the Amish (cf.
       item 789) to control and eliminate bias in the ascertainment
       of psychiatric diagnosis and to specify the various types of
       diagnostic reliability studies that can be performed.

824.   Inglis, Judy. "Interpretation of Cargo Cults--Comments."
       OCEANIA 30 (1959): 155-58.

       Replies to Stanner's criticism (item 897) and restates her
       argument (item 825) that a strict explanation of Cargo cults
       is not possible because of the diversity of the people and
       conditions involved.

825.   Inglis, Judy. "Cargo Cults: The Problem of Interpretation."
       OCEANIA 27 (1957): 249-63.

       Examines various interpretations of different Cargo cults
       and discusses the difficulties in finding a general explana-
       tory theory. Cargo cults have been seen as new religious or
       political movements, as responses to charismatic leadership,
       as reactions or rebellions to economic dissatisfaction, as
       moral protests, or as expressions of a particular state of
       mind. The author maintains that it is not possible to for-
       mulate a general theory covering all Cargo cults and that
       functional explanations are not fully satisfactory. Cults,
       she argues, can also be seen as a quest for a richer life.
       Though she does not discuss explicitly the therapeutic value
       of cult involvement, it is clear that she does not consider
       them as manifestations of individual or social pathology.
       Her opinion of cult leaders, however, is less positive since
       she thinks they are unusual people who are more ambitious
       and more intelligent that the average, but also mentally
       unbalanced.

826.   Jarvie, I. C. "Theories of Cargo Cults: A Critical Analysis."
       OCEANIA 34 (1963): 1-32, 108-36.

       Examines various theories of Cargo cults, apocalyptic mil-
       lenarian movements primarily in Melanesia. The author finds
       that the causes of the cults cannot be considered apart from
       their pre-conditions and that the view that socioeconomic
       unrest is the main cause of cultism cannot be dealt with apart
       from millenarianism. While not providing any new theory of
       cultism, the author leans towards a sociological explanation.

827.   Jilek, Wolfgang G. "A Quest for Identity: Therapeutic Aspects
       of the Salish Indian Guardian Spirit Ceremonial." JOURNAL
       OF OPERATIONAL PSYCHIATRY 8.2 (1977): 46-51.

       Discusses spirit illness among these Indians as a form of
       "anomic depression," an affective syndrome which develops in
       reaction to the alienation from traditional culture under the

impact of Westernization. This sickness is also characterized by relative deprivation and cultural identity confusion.
Spirit dance initiation performed by contemporary American
Indians is seen as a curing process based on the therapeutic
myth of death and rebirth. Other psychological principles,
like group therapy and cathartic abreaction, operate to
help the Salish overcome, and resist falling into, anomic
depression.

828.   Jilek, Wolfgang G. "'Brainwashing' as Therapeutic Technique
        in Contemporary Canadian Spirit Dancing: A Case of Theory-
        Building." ANTHROPOLOGY AND MENTAL HEALTH. Edited by
        Joseph Westermeyer. The Hague: Mouton, 1976, pp. 201-13.

        Examines the rituals performed by the Salish Indians of
        the Pacific Coast of North America over native persons whose
        depression, anxiety, and somatic complaints do not respond to
        Western treatment, and who suffer from behavioral, alcoholic,
        and drug-related problems. The literature on the biology and
        psychology of altered states of consciousness is briefly sur-
        veyed and the therapeutic process of the ceremony described.
        Three major therapeutic processes are discerned: 1) depattern-
        ing through shock treatment; 2) physical training; and 3)
        indoctrination. It is concluded that the therapeutic effec-
        tiveness of indigenous treatments compares favorably with
        current Western therapies.

*   Johnson, Paul E. "New Religions and Mental Health." JOURNAL
        OF RELIGION AND HEALTH 3 (1964): 327-34. Cited above as
        item 544.

829.   Kahana, Yaal. "The Zar Spirits: A Category of Magic in the
        System of Mental Health Care in Ethiopia." INTERNATIONAL
        JOURNAL OF SOCIAL PSYCHIATRY 31 (1985): 125-43.

        Studies the beliefs about Zar spirits commonly found among
        the Christian Amhara and Jewish Falasha societies. The author
        distinguishes between magical and religious institutions, and
        shows how the Zar ritual is essentially magical because it
        attempts to manipulate the supernatural. The mental illnesses
        healed in the Zar cult are forms of hysteria and catatonic
        states mainly among women, and self-violent and epileptic
        states mostly among men. Various kinds of healers and their
        functions are described. The beneficial results of Zar heal-
        ing include relief from anxiety and stress.

830.   Katz, Richard. BOILING ENERGY: COMMUNITY HEALING AMONG THE
        KALAHARI !KUNG. Cambridge, MA: Harvard University Press,
        1982. xiv, 329 pp.

        Gives a vivid phenomenological account of ritual trances
        and healing in an African tribe. The author concentrates on
        exploring how "kia," an intense emotional state of conscious-
        ness and necessary condition for healing, and "num," the
        healing energy linked with this state, are used in the service
        of curing various kinds of ailments.

831.   Katz, Richard. "Accepting 'Boiling Energy': The Experience
        of !Kia Healing Among the !Kung." ETHOS 10 (1982): 344-68.

        Focuses on the experience of healing among this hunting-
        gathering people who live in parts of Botswana, Namibia, and
        Southern Angola. At the core of this experience is a trans-
        formation of consciousness which the healer undergoes, and
        which can be viewed as one possible paradigm for psychologi-
        cal and community development. The ethnographic background
        of the tribe is provided and both the training of a healer
        and the healing dance itself are described. The author holds
        that the individual and the community benefit from the ritual.

832.   Kearney, Michael. "Spiritualist Healing in Mexico." CULTURE
        AND CURING. Edited by Peter Morley and Roy Wallis. London:
        Peter Owen, 1978, pp. 19-59.

        Investigates the phenomenon of "espiritismo" in Mexico,
        and attempts to give a general outline of the relationship
        between folk medical concepts, symptoms, and therapeutic
        responses. The most common psychiatric symptoms--bodily
        complaints, paranoia, anxiety, and depression--are described
        and their treatment by folk healers is contrasted with that
        of Western psychiatrists. Successful folk treatment is due
        to several factors, among which are the friendly, warm support
        that paranoid people get from participation in spiritualism
        and the ability of this native treatment to deal with emo-
        tional problems by legitimizing outward expressions of
        catharsis. The mediums themselves profit not only socially
        and financially but also psychologically by acting out their
        repressed desires and impulses.

833.   Kehoe, Alice B., and Dody H. Giletti. "Women's Preponderance
        in Possession Cults: The Calcium-Deficiency Hypothesis Ex-
        tended." AMERICAN ANTHROPOLOGIST 83 (1981): 549-61.

        Argues that spirit possession is not evidence of psycholog-
        ical disturbance, nor is it a kind of political role used by
        powerless, low-status people to relieve frustration. Rather,
        the majority of women in spirit possession cults can be ex-
        plained by a direct relationship between diet and behavior.
        Several examples, particularly the Zar cult, are given to
        support this hypothesis as the best empirical explanation.
        The authors question Lewis's view (item 964) that possession
        cults are organized factions in class conflicts.

834.   Kennedy, John G. "Psychosocial Dynamics of Witchcraft Sys-
        tems." INTERNATIONAL JOURNAL OF SOCIAL PSYCHIATRY 15
        (1969): 165-78.

        Outlines the current theory of witchcraft and then explores
        its irrationality and dysfunction. The author maintains that
        ideas and practices related to witchcraft are largely the
        products of institutionalized individual psychopathology. He
        argues strongly against those anthropologists who hold that

witchcraft systems function positively to provide an intellectual framework for social and individual behavior and a
culturally-approved way of handling psychological problems.
He also objects to the neo-Freudian view that all groups find
a healthy, balanced level of functioning and that there are
no neurotic cultures. Witchcraft, the author insists, produces fear and stress rather than satisfaction, and must be
viewed as pathogenic.

835.   Kennedy, John G. "Nubian Zar Ceremonies as Psychotherapy."
       HUMAN ORGANIZATION 26 (1967): 185-94.

       Examines the form and content of the Zar ceremony in order
       to account for its therapeutic effectiveness in the allevia-
       tion of hysteria, anxiety, depression, and psychosis. The
       indigenous reason for performance of the ceremony, namely,
       to deal with demons that are believed to be the cause of
       certain psychological illnesses, is analyzed. The various
       forms of the ritual itself are described. It is maintained
       that the rite has both sociological and psychological func-
       tions. The Zar provides an ideal situation for the relief
       of persistent and regular anxieties and tensions arising from
       Nubian life conditions. The ritual provides intellectual and
       emotional support, gives people the opportunity for express-
       ing their emotions, and intensifies faith through group par-
       ticipation. The core members of the cult are, however,
       unstable and prone to emotional outbursts and hysterical fits.

836.   Kiev, Ari. CURANDERISMO: MEXICAN-AMERICAN FOLK PSYCHIATRY.
       New York: Free Press, 1968. xii, 207 pp.

       Studies and evaluates the psychological theories and treat-
       ment used in the Mexican-American subculture in the South-
       western part of the United States. Besides giving a general
       view of illness and death and of the diagnosis and treatment
       of disease, the author accounts for the role of the curandero
       in this subculture. The psychological conflicts of Mexican-
       Americans are also described. Curanderismo has therapeutic
       value in that: 1) it includes techniques designed to allay
       anxiety and fear; 2) it generates group experience which aims
       at reintegrating the patient into society; and 3) it provides
       a meaningful system to explain the causes of illness and to
       treat many diseases. Curanderismo differs from dynamic
       psychotherapy because it relies on traditional absolutes,
       faith, and obedience, while psychotherapy strives for objec-
       tivity, impartiality, and scientific evidence. The author
       states, however, that "there is no evidence that dynamic
       psychotherapy is of more value than such forms of treatment
       as curanderismo" (p. 183). While the curandero is less
       equipped than the psychiatrist to handle more serious psychot-
       ic and neurotic disorders (like obsession and schizophrenia),
       he is just as competent, if not more so, to treat the less
       severe forms of psychoses (like paranoid reactions and inter-
       personal and social stress).

837. Kiev, Ari. "Psychotherapy in Haitian Voodoo." AMERICAN
JOURNAL OF PSYCHIATRY 26 (1962): 469-76.

Outlines some of the features of Voodoo belief and practice
related to psychiatric illness. Voodoo priests recognize
psychiatric illness and offer both individual and group
therapy. It is concluded that the successful treatment by
the Voodoo priests warrants further investigation.

838. Kiev, Ari. "Brief Note: Primitive Holistic Medicine." INTER-
NATIONAL JOURNAL OF SOCIAL PSYCHIATRY 8 (1961-62): 58-61.

Addresses the nature of the setting in which traditional
healing practices in Haiti occur with the aim of investigat-
ing the holistic orientation of the native healers. Besides
the use of drugs and herbs, Voodoo priests employ psychotherapeutic elements, such as the belief that priests and
priestesses have the power to cure, to lessen an individual's
anxiety. These elements are, in fact, more effective than
the physical remedies prescribed. The relationship between
the healer and the patient is in itself therapeutic.

839. Kiev, Ari. "Folk Psychiatry in Haiti." JOURNAL OF NERVOUS
AND MENTAL DISEASE 132 (1961): 260-65.

Examines Voodoo religion and attempts to determine if the
Voodoo priest meets the criteria of modern psychotherapy.
The native views of personality, of psychiatric illness and
its treatment are described. It is argued that if psychiatry
means a system of treatment of disorders based on a theoretical model of normal human behavior, then Voodoo can be
considered a psychiatric technique. Voodoo acknowledges
various psychopathological problems, like acute schizophrenia,
hysteria, and paranoia, all of which are part and parcel of
Western psychiatric vocabulary. While Voodoo differs in
content and conception from Western psychotherapy, it has
similarities in therapeutic structures and identification
of syndromes. It has also developed a relationship between
the priest and the client which characterizes the psychotherapeutic relationship.

840. Kiev, Ari. "Spirit Possession in Haiti." AMERICAN JOURNAL
OF PSYCHIATRY 118 (1961): 133-38.

Discusses spirit possession in the context of Voodoo.
Three different patterns of behavior are sketched, namely,
the possessions of a priest, an adept, and a non-adept. The
native theory of insanity explains Voodoo as spirit possession. The author thinks that there are some personality
traits that predispose an individual to become possessed by
a spirit. The question as to whether possession is a form
of psychiatric disorder, or merely a culturally acceptable
patterned role-playing, is raised. It is argued that the
latter seems to be the more likely explanation. Possession
offers a cultural outlet for expressing "various ego dystonic

impulses and thoughts" (p. 137). It fulfills various public
and private needs of different people. The similarity between
possession phenomena and psychiatric illness is brought forth
as an argument in favor of the view that ritual possession in
Voodoo presents an acceptable form of "going crazy."

841.   Kitzenger, Sheila. "Protest and Mysticism: The Rastafari Cult
        of Jamaica." JOURNAL FOR THE SCIENTIFIC STUDY OF RELIGION
        8 (1969): 240-62.

        Presents an anthropological study of a predominantly male-
        oriented protest cult which centers around the messianic
        worship of the former Emperor Haile Selassie of Ethiopia and
        which anticipates a return to Africa. The Rastafari faith is
        seen as dysfunctional in the sense that it seeks the ultimate
        destruction of the existing social system. It is maintained
        that repressed psychological drives provide a basis for the
        cult's existence and success. A psychoanalytic explanation
        is offered, which sees in it a process of mother-rejection
        and father-identification, coupled with a canalization of
        hostility. The cult does not help the members adjust to
        their condition, though it does soften the disenchantment of
        the hopelessness of their cause.

842.   Koss, Joan D. "Social Process, Healing and Self-Defeat Among
        Puerto Rican Spiritists." AMERICAN ETHNOLOGIST 4 (1977):
        453-69.

        Discusses some of the processes that underlie the treatment
        of emotionally sick subjects by spiritists and shows how a
        spiritist cult can effect behavioral changes by relieving
        anxieties and frustrations. It is maintained that cures,
        psychological resyntheses through conversion, and identity
        changes are often achieved, but they are not sustained for
        a long period of time. A description of the belief and
        ritual systems of these Puerto Rican cults and an outline
        of their structure and organization are provided.

843.   Koss, Joan D. "Therapeutic Aspects of Puerto Rican Cult
        Practices." PSYCHIATRY 38 (1975): 160-70.

        Explains the phenomenon of possession trance as an active
        component in the development of significant personal relation-
        ships central to the organization and goal of some religious
        cults. It provides background data and information on re-
        cruitment to mediumship, role of cult leader, and methods of
        trance induction. It is argued that the cult practice of
        possession-trance "serves as a therapeutic tool in the cult-
        leader-adherent relationships" (p. 161). The cult leader
        assumes control of the client through the trance and then
        instigates changes in his or her life, often solving personal
        problems.

844.   Kriesman, Jerold J. "The Curandero's Apprentice: A Thera-
        peutic Integration of Folk and Medical Healing." AMERICAN
        JOURNAL OF PSYCHIATRY 132 (1975): 81-83.

Relates two case-reports which describe psychotic Mexican-Americans in Denver, Colorado, who were successfully treated with a technique uniting "curanderismo" (folk healing) and modern therapy, which by itself had proved ineffective. The author discusses the nature of folk illness, the need to recognize the problem, and the various possible approaches to treatment. The psychological advantages of using folk healing methods are mentioned.

*   La Barre, Weston. "Materials for a History of Studies of Crisis Cults: A Bibliographic Essay." Cited above as item 31.

845. La Barre, Weston. THE PEYOTE CULT. New York: Schocken Books, enlarged edition, 1969. xvii, 260 pp.

Presents the first detailed ethnographic monograph written on the American Indian Peyote religion. The botanical and physiological aspects of Peyote, its ethnology, and relation to other customs of using drugs in a religious context (as in the Native American Church) are described. The following psychological aspects of Peyotism are discussed: 1) its alleged powers to remove anxiety; 2) its apparent ability to act as an antidote to witchcraft; and 3) its role in personal adjustment. A survey of Peyote studies (pp. 193-213) is included.

846. La Barre, Weston. "Transference Cures in Religious Cults and Social Groups." JOURNAL OF PSYCHOANALYSIS IN GROUPS 1 (1962): 66-75.

Discusses some theoretical issues in group psychotherapy and explores several religious rituals, such as confession of sin in Voodoo, the Peyote cult among the American Indians, the shamanistic rituals of the Tungus of North-Central Siberia, and the snake-handling cults in the United States. While in all these rites there is an acting out of individual problems, there may also be some measure of group therapy. The Peyote rite and the shaman's ritual are judged to be therapeutic because they relieve or remove the individual's anxiety, while Voodooism promotes health because it relieves neurotic wishes. The snake-handling ritual of the Christian fundamentalists is said to be pathological and without therapeutic value.

847. La Barre, Weston. "Primitive Psychotherapy in Native American Culture: Peyotism and Confession." JOURNAL OF ABNORMAL AND SOCIAL PSYCHOLOGY 42 (1947): 294-309.

Describes the ritual of the Peyote cult among the American Indians of the Plains and the Great Basin. The author thinks that Peyotism functions like a living religion, offering consolation for troubles, advising people in their behavior, and reinforcing many traditional values. The practice of public confession tends to remove individual anxieties and is a "genuinely aboriginal psychotherapeutic technique" (p. 307).

848.   Lanternari, Vittorio. THE RELIGION OF THE OPPRESSED: A STUDY
       OF MODERN MESSIANIC CULTS. Translated from the Italian by
       Lisa Sergio. New York: Knopf, 1963. xx, 343 pp.

       Approaches new religious movements from a historical point
       of view in order to explain their nature, function, genesis,
       and dynamics. The cults dealt with are those which came into
       being in preliterate societies as a reaction to colonial rule.
       A large geographic area is covered, including Africa, Central
       and South America, Melanesia and Polynesia, and sections of
       North America and Asia. The rituals common to most of these
       movements are usually centered around experiences of posses-
       sion, trance, and visions, and are "a means of evasion in an
       atmosphere of exaltation and collective mystical up-lift"
       (p. 315). Though the author calls these rites a form of
       "collective psychosis," he maintains that they make a posi-
       tive contribution to the regeneration of society as a whole
       and to the individual. The Peyote cult, with its alleged
       therapeutic qualities is treated separately (pp. 63-113). A
       select bibliography arranged by country is appended.

849.   Leacock, Seth, and Ruth Leacock. SPIRITS OF THE DEEP: A
       STUDY OF AN AFRO-BRAZILIAN CULT. New York: Doubleday, 1972.
       x, 404 pp.

       A comprehensive description of the Batuque, a contemporary
       non-Christian religious sect in Belém, Brazil. The authors
       outline its belief system, organization, and rituals. The role
       and behavior of the trance medium are explained in the context
       of the cult's central beliefs. The authors state that from
       their day-to-day observations and interactions they reached
       the conclusion that Batuque mediums are, as a rule, normal,
       well-adjusted individuals.

850.   Lebra, Takie S. "Taking the Role of the Supernatural 'Other':
       Spirit Possession in a Japanese Healing Cult." JAPANESE
       PATTERNS OF BEHAVIOR (item 689), pp. 232-47. (Also in-
       cluded in CULTURE-BOUND SYNDROMES, ETHNOPSYCHIATRY, AND
       ALTERNATE THERAPIES, item 690, pp. 88-100.)

       Studies a Japanese salvation cult established in 1929. A
       short description is provided of the cult with its principal
       behavioral patterns of possession. The participants are
       said to take up one of the following roles: supernatural,
       suppliant, disciplinary, retaliatory, status-demonstrative,
       and informant. The aim of the study is to find out whether
       spirit possession, be it a pathological phenomenon or a
       therapeutic technique, gives any clues to Japanese cultural
       values. The author states that many members of this cult
       were deprived of the social roles available to them in Japan,
       and that the possession ritual afforded them the opportunity
       to overcome their deprivation, even if only for a relatively
       short period of time. The psychological effects of cult
       membership appear to have been beneficial.

851.   Lebra, Takie S. "The Interactional Perspective of Suffering
        and Curing in a Japanese Cult." INTERNATIONAL JOURNAL OF
        SOCIAL PSYCHIATRY 20 (1974): 281-86.

        Studies an unnamed, healing-oriented Japanese cult which
        was founded in 1925. Out of the 22 reported cases of heal-
        ing experienced within one year, 16 were judged to involve
        a physical or mental disorder or disability. Therapy in
        healing cults implies "compulsive sensitization of the suf-
        fering ego to mutual dependency and mutual interference
        between ego and alter(s) rather than just providing a passive
        role to be taken by the ego" (p. 280). The healing is dis-
        cussed from two points of view: 1) as a form of repercussion
        (in which the ego is seen as the cause of suffering); and
        2) as a form of dependency (where the alter-ego acquires a
        vicarious role). The interaction between patient and folk
        healer is placed in the context of Japanese culture. The
        cult mobilizes and intensifies underlying cultural values for
        therapeutic purposes.

852.   Lebra, Takie S. "Religious Conversion and Elimination of
        the Sick Role: A Japanese Sect in Hawaii." TRANSCULTURAL
        RESEARCH IN MENTAL HEALTH. Volume Two of MENTAL HEALTH
        RESEARCH IN ASIA AND THE PACIFIC. Edited by William Lebra.
        Honolulu: University of Hawaii Press, 1972, pp. 282-92.

        Provides a study of Tensho, a Japanese sect in which heal-
        ing is a major religious practice. The author focuses on an
        analysis and change of the sick role. Tensho views illness
        as a supernatural punishment for religiously or socially
        prohibited behavior. Its converts experience a deep sense of
        guilt. Joining the sect has several economic, interactional,
        affectional, and tactile rewards. The needs of the converts
        are met by the Tensho system of beliefs and practices.

853.   Lebra, Takie S. "Logic of Salvation: The Case of a Japanese
        Sect in Hawaii." INTERNATIONAL JOURNAL OF SOCIAL PSYCHI-
        ATRY 16 (1970): 45-53.

        Attempts to identify the specific set of mechanisms which
        are needed to maintain faith in salvation in the context of
        the Dancing Religion, a post-war Japanese sect. The author
        finds that the reasons brought forth to reinforce one's faith
        tended to be emotionally reassuring, but logically contradic-
        tory. He holds that conversion to this religion suddenly
        frees the neophyte from guilt and shame.

854.   Lidz, R. W., T. Lidz, and B. G. Burton-Bradley. "Cargo-
        Cultism: A Psychosocial Study of Melanesian Millenarianism."
        JOURNAL OF NERVOUS AND MENTAL DISEASE 157 (1973): 370-88.

        Denounces New Guinea Cargo cultism as a form of delusional
        thinking which takes the form of paranoid schizophrenia.
        Cargo cults are actually based on a childlike belief in the
        magical power of European goods and are a surviving form of

"preoperational thinking." Christian missionaries, who themselves opened the door for delusional ideas about Christian
teaching, and the ethnocentrism of traditional Papuan cultures are said to be responsible for the propagation of these
cults. The authors draw parallels between members of the
Cargo cults and the Jesus freaks who, finding no guidance in
the tenets of modern scientific society, seek to become
children of Jesus.

855.   Linton, Ralph. "Nativistic Movements." AMERICAN ANTHROPOL-
        OGIST 45 (1943): 230-40.

        Attempts to define and classify the types of nativistic
        movements that have occurred in culture-contact situations
        and to identify the various conditions under which they come
        into being. A fourfold typology of these movements is devel-
        oped: 1) revivalistic-magical; 2) revivalistic-rational;
        3) perpetuative-magical; and 4) perpetuative-rational. Most
        of the troubles which precede the appearance of new movements
        stem from exploitation and frustration. The second and fourth
        types of movements are the best mechanisms for dealing with
        feelings of inferiority, which members of these movements so
        often have.

856.   Lubchansky, Isaac, Gladys Egri, and Janet Stokes. "Puerto
        Rican Spiritualists View Mental Illness: The Faith Healer
        as Paraprofessional." AMERICAN JOURNAL OF PSYCHIATRY 127
        (1970): 88-97.

        Examines the beliefs about, and attitudes towards, mental
        illness among Puerto Rican faith healers in New York City,
        and compares them with those of leaders and household heads of
        the same community. The main method of faith healers, namely,
        the séance, is described. While stressing the difference
        in belief between the psychotherapist and the healer, the
        authors claim that, in practice, they both use similar treat-
        ments. Paraprofessionals, like faith healers, can contribute
        to mental health.

857.   Machovec, Frank J. "The Cult of Asklipios." AMERICAN JOURNAL
        OF CLINICAL HYPNOSIS 22 (1979): 85-90.

        Describes a cult which flourished in Greece some 25 centuries
        ago. The most common form of treatment to those suffering from
        various ailments was "temple sleep" or "dream healing," which
        was a form of hypnosis induced at the ritual. Seven distinct
        phases were part of the healing process: change of environment,
        cleansing of the body, sacrifice, repetition (chanting), trust
        in the method itself, focused attention, and emotional impact.
        The author asserts that "from the standpoint of contemporary
        psychotherapy, the Asklipians combined cognitive, affective,
        behavioral, social, physical, and spiritual treatment factors,
        a very powerful holistic combination" (p. 89). The study of
        this cult might lead to a better clinical use of altered
        states of consciousness to relieve suffering more effectively.

858. Martinez, Cervando. "Curanderos: Clinical Aspects." JOURNAL
      OF OPERATIONAL PSYCHIATRY 8.2 (1977): 35-38.

      Shows how curanderos (Mexican-American folk healers) fit
      into the mental health system of the Southwest, where they
      are consulted for, among other things, fear of evil and hexes,
      the former denoting a state of anxiety, the latter a psycho-
      logical condition bordering on catatonia. The author argues,
      contrary to Kiev (item 836), that the curanderos are not folk
      healers. They do not devote most of their efforts to dealing
      with psychiatric disorders, nor do they see themselves as
      psychiatrists, and much less do their clients perceive them
      as such. Curanderos can interact with the Western-oriented
      mental health system in a number of ways: they can be corrob-
      orators of mental illness, auxiliary therapists, or an
      initial treatment resource.

859. Martinez, Rafael, and Charles V. Wetli. "Santeria: A Magico-
      Religious System of Afro-Cuban Origin." AMERICAN JOURNAL
      OF PSYCHIATRY 2.3 (1982): 32-38.

      Presents an overview of Santeria beliefs and practices as
      experienced by the Cuban-American population in the Miami,
      Florida, area. The historical background and the basic syn-
      cretistic structure of the religion are briefly outlined.
      Various ritual treatments for all types of illnesses are
      described. Spirit possession, a common ecstatic experience,
      has a therapeutic value, in that it allows for the discharge
      of hostility into a supernatural realm. Black magic is
      understood as a cultural way of expressing interpersonal
      conflict and intrapsychic aggression. It not only contrib-
      utes to social stability but also supplies socially-accepted
      ways of performing otherwise disallowed activities. Santeria
      is generally seen as a supportive system that plays a role in
      the healing process of the individual.

860. May, L. Carlyle. "A Survey of Glossolalia and Related Phenom-
      ena in Non-Christian Religions." AMERICAN ANTHROPOLOGIST
      85 (1956): 75-96.

      Shows that glossolalia occurs in various forms in shaman-
      istic rites both in the New and the Old Worlds. The Christian
      tradition of glossolalia is traced to its biblical and extra-
      biblical sources, and its reappearance in the history of
      Christianity is briefly referred to. Several psychological
      studies of Christian glossolalia conducted in the first quar-
      ter of the twentieth century are examined and compared to
      cross-cultural research on the subject. The shamanistic
      phenomenon of glossolalia is described. The author also
      examines phenomena which have close similarities to tongue-
      speaking, such as the so-called "phonations clusters," which
      include sacerdotal language, animal cries, ventriloquism,
      xenoglossia, and the interpretation of sounds. "Glossolalia
      in one form or other is found in religions that are tolerant
      of highly emotional, individualistic behavior on the part of
      medicine men and their assistants" (p. 91).

861.   May, L. Carlyle. "The Dancing Religion: A Japanese Messianic
       Cult." SOUTHWESTERN JOURNAL OF ANTHROPOLOGY 10 (1954): 119-
       37.

       Describes a Japanese sect known as Tensho Kotai Jingukyo
       (The Religion of the Absolute Almighty God), which was founded
       by Mrs. Sayo Kitamura in 1945. Her background, the religion's
       main beliefs and rituals, and its educational, hierarchical,
       and economic status are described. The author thinks that
       the Dancing Religion is a revivalist sect which arose during
       the crisis of World War II. Mrs. Kitamura exhibited shaman-
       istic traits in her early religious period. The foundation
       of her sect gave her more self-confidence and helped her
       overcome her previous anxiety.

862.   McAll, R. K. "Demonosis or the Possession Syndrome." INTER-
       NATIONAL JOURNAL OF SOCIAL PSYCHIATRY 17 (1971): 150-58.

       Reviews some of the psychiatric theories and classifica-
       tions of possession states, particularly those relating to
       the Yap Islanders of Micronesia. It is maintained, with
       other psychiatrists, that the possession syndrome may be
       linked to psychosis or neurosis with concomitant abnormal
       sensations, weakness, anxiety, and depression. Many pos-
       sessed persons are atypical schizophrenics. The author
       advises people not to get involved with witchcraft and black
       magic, both of which might lead to possession syndromes.

863.   Messing, Simon D. "Group Therapy and Social Status in the
       Zar Cult of Ethiopia." AMERICAN ANTHROPOLOGIST 60 (1958):
       1120-26.

       Describes this healing cult which requires the active co-
       operation of the patient. The following cultic elements are
       described: Zar cosmology; individual vulnerability; the
       qualities of the practitioner; and his diagnosis and treat-
       ment. The author concludes that the Zar cult, which is not
       a deviant one, deals with many psychological disturbances
       ranging from frustrated, social ambition to acute mental ill-
       ness, and that it functions as a form of group therapy.

864.   Mischel, Walter, and Frances Mischel. "Psychological Aspects
       of Spirit Possession." AMERICAN ANTHROPOLOGIST 60 (1958):
       249-60.

       Offers a detailed description of spirit possession behavior,
       particularly among the Shango worshippers of Trinidad, and
       then attempts a psychological analysis using the learning
       theory. It is assumed that spirit possession takes place if
       it is somehow reinforced or rewarded by those who exhibit it.
       Spirit possession permits expression of sanctioned behavior
       or otherwise forbidden acts, supplies a socially approved
       framework for interpreting certain psychological and/or
       physical phenomena, and refers all serious problems to the
       "powers" for solution, thus giving the individual freedom

from responsibility for controlling and directing his or her
life. It also reenforces the conflict between the natives
and the Europeans.

865.   Modarressi, Taghi. "The Zar Cult in South Iran." TRANCE AND
        POSSESSION STATES (item 876), pp. 149-55.

Discusses the Persian origin of the name "Zar," and describes its peculiar features observed by the author in South
Iran, especially in the town of Bandar Abbas. Zar is seen
as a complex "disease-entity" which manifests psychogenic
disorders, but which is at the same time a healing process.
"Zar seems to be a safe means of expressing inner feelings
without shame or guilt" (p. 155). It is a way for attaining
social identity leading to security. The ambivalent attitude
to Zar, which is both desired and feared, is noted.

866.   Murphy, H. B. M. "Depression, Witchcraft Beliefs, and Super-
        Ego Development in Pre-literate Societies." CANADIAN
        JOURNAL OF PSYCHIATRY 24 (1979): 437-49.

Explores the possibility that the upsurge of witchcraft
beliefs can help us understand the relationship between group
ego and individual ego pathologies. The psychodynamics of
these beliefs are discussed and those features which distinguish them from all other types of supernatural knowledge are
outlined. The main issue is whether witchcraft represents a
psychological regression. The author's view is that heightened witchcraft beliefs and practices are a defense against
an individualizing change which has led to aggression and
reproach.

867.   O'Connell, M. C. "Spirit Possession and Role Stress Among
        the Xesibe of Eastern Transkei." ETHNOLOGY 21 (1982): 21-
        37.

Gives a brief account of the history of spirit possession
in this South African tribe, and then discusses the typical
male and female roles of Xesibe society. The author demonstrates that one does not have to explain spirit possession
in this culture by postulating an "innate female hysteria,"
or some other kind of female trauma. An explanation is
explored in terms of conflict between an individual's performance and the culturally prescribed role.

868.   Perez y Mena, Andres I. "Spiritualism as an Adaptive Mecha-
        nism Among Puerto Ricans in the United States." CORNELL
        JOURNAL OF SOCIAL STUDIES 12 (1977): 125-36.

Discusses the problems that Puerto Ricans immigrants to the
United States face and how a combination of spiritualism and
Santeria is being used to alleviate the stress. The psychological difficulties which people come across in their efforts
to adapt to a new culture can only be solved if their need
for a sense of relatedness and consolation are taken into

consideration. These can be dealt with more effectively by
spiritualism than by confinement in a modern psychiatric ward.
The way a spiritualist center operates is described. The
author sees spiritualism as a from of group therapy.

869.   Perinbanayagam, R. S. "Self, Other, and Astrology: Esoteric
       Therapy in Sri Lanka." PSYCHIATRY 44 (1981): 69-79.

       Describes the work of Hindu astrologers in Sri Lanka and
       reports on several people who consulted them. The author
       points out that there is a culture of astrological cure in
       which the client/shaman (or astrologer) relationship is sus-
       tained. It is concluded that astrology, coupled with the
       doctrine of Karma, establishes the cause of misfortune out-
       side the self and thus relieves the person from responsi-
       bility. The practice of consulting astrologers can conse-
       quently have a therapeutic effect.

870.   Pressel, Esther. "Umbanda in São Paulo: Religious Innovation
       in a Developing Society." RELIGION, ALTERED STATES OF CON-
       SCIOUSNESS, AND SOCIAL CHANGE (item 772), pp. 264-318.

       Describes a spiritualist religion in Brazil, a religion
       which emerged in the 1920s and which stresses consultation
       with spirits who possess mediums. This new religion is
       discussed in the context of Brazilian society, its class
       structure, economy, wealth, and distribution of power and
       prestige. Umbanda is a way of helping people solve their
       personal difficulties in a situation of sociopsychological
       stress. The author dwells at some length on the spirit
       medium's personality. Possession, a dissociative state, is
       usually due to some inability of the personality to function
       adequately in its sociocultural environment. To what extent
       this is a serious pathological factor is not made very clear.

871.   Pressel, Esther. "Umbanda Trance and Possession in São Paulo,
       Brazil." TRANCE, HEALING, AND HALLUCINATION (item 812),
       pp. 113-225.

       Describes and analyzes trance and possession in a rapidly
       expanding Brazilian religion called Umbanda and concentrates
       especially on the behavior of spirit mediums. The author
       observes that stress can precipitate trance and possession
       states and that, through becoming a medium, a person could
       be relieved of personal fault and possibly also of guilt. It
       is noted that the person learns how to behave when possessed
       by a spirit, and that certain pre- and post-trance actions
       are part of the pattern. Mediums are relaxed after the
       trance and any personal problems they might have had before
       are no longer present.

872.   Preston, Robert J., and Carl A. Hammerschlag. "The Native
       American Church." PSYCHODYNAMIC PERSPECTIVES OF RELIGION,
       SECT, AND CULT (item 1226), pp. 93-104.

Presents an account of the Native American Church which
incorporates Peyote in its main ritual. The authors point
out that many features of modern psychotherapy are present
in such healing rituals. Both psychotherapists and healers
mobilize guilt, heighten self-esteem, review the patient's
life, and reenforce values and behavior. The Native American
Church has been successful in dealing with alcoholism. Its
rituals expand one's awareness, which yields positive results.

873.   Prince, Raymond R. "The Problem of Spirit Possession as a
        Treatment for Psychiatric Disorder." ETHOS 2 (1974):
        315-33.

Studies the role of various types of "possession and mas-
querade" cults in the treatment of subjects of Yoruba healers
in Nigeria. The therapeutic potential of the initiation
procedure into, and of membership in, one of these possession
cults is examined in the light of psychoanalytic theory. The
Yoruba religious system in general and one cult in particular
(namely, the Sopono cult) are described, and the symbolism
and psychological process associated with these cults in
Nigeria and other countries are considered. The marked
alteration of consciousness generated by the ritual, and the
childlike learning process during these states are common
features of all possession cults studied. The author rejects
the view that initiation represents a temporary regression
and that it works on sensory deprivation, leading to "brainwashing" or forceful indoctrination. The most satisfactory
interpretation, according to the author, is the neurological
hypothesis that some persons have split brains with two
independent streams of conscious awareness.

874.   Prince, Raymond R. "Possession Cults and Social Cybernetics."
        TRANCE AND POSSESSION STATES (item 876), pp. 157-65.

Attempts to show that besides the individual cathartic and
release effects of possession states, there are wider therapeutic results which fall under social psychiatry and cybernetics. Several case studies from the author's field work
among the Yoruba of Nigeria are given, and it is argued that
these cases can be better explained by relating psychiatric
disorders to the social structure. One of the functions of
possession cults is to provide a "tightening of the social
structure" (p. 161). Further, the efforts of those involved
in the Yoruba ritual function as " a kind of homeostatic
mechanism to maintain the organization and coherence of the
community at an optimum level" (p. 163). Possession cults
come into being whenever there is an increase in social
pathology, and their performance helps people return to their
normal social conditions.

875.   Prince, Raymond R. "The Ras-Tafari of Jamaica: A Case Study
        of Group Beliefs and Social Stress." R. M. BUCKE MEMORIAL
        SOCIETY: NEWSLETTER-REVIEW 4 (Spring 1971): 48-54.

Offers a short description of this back-to-Africa movement
which originated in Jamaica in the early twentieth century.
The movement exemplified the similarities and differences
between the individual delusions of the psychotic and the
delusions shared by the group. The beliefs also serve as a
protection against an overwhelming fear of nothingness and
provide some measure of self-esteem and meaning in a life of
degradation.

876.   Prince. Raymond R., editor. TRANCE AND POSSESSION STATES:
        PROCEEDINGS OF THE SECOND ANNUAL CONFERENCE OF THE R. M.
        BUCKE MEMORIAL SOCIETY. Montreal: R. M. Bucke Memorial
        Society, 1966. xii, 200 pp.

        Consists of 14 papers which cover three major areas: 1) the
        distribution and patterns of trance and possession states;
        2) the nature and method of studying such states; and 3) their
        meaning and purpose. Several essays discuss possession states
        as forms of psychotherapy.

        Contains items 865, 874.

877.   Pugh, Judy F. "Astrological Counseling in India." CULTURE,
        MEDICINE, AND PSYCHIATRY 7 (1983): 279-99.

        Provides an evaluation of the theory that divination is a
        form of therapy while astrology provides a kind of situation-
        centered counseling. The discussion is conducted in the con-
        text of an advisory session between an Indian astrologer and
        his client. The concepts of dialogue, prediction, and remedy
        are used to throw light on the structure of divination inquiry
        and on the nature of its effectiveness in counseling. The
        idea of "therapeutic space" is used to include both the scene
        of an actual advising session and the client's daily life.
        The author sees Indian astrology as a vital system of counsel-
        ing and as a form of multi-faceted therapy.

878.   Ravenscroft, Kent. "Voodoo Possession: A Natural Experiment
        in Hypnosis." INTERNATIONAL JOURNAL OF CLINICAL AND
        EXPERIMENTAL HYPNOSIS 13 (1965): 157-82.

        Compares Haitian Voodoo possession to clinical and experi-
        mental hypnotic phenomena. The article sketches the Voodoo
        belief system and the way an individual is socialized into it.
        The state of possession, that is classified as ceremonial or
        non-ceremonial, with its various stages, is described. The
        alteration of one's identity and amnesia are both found in
        possession and hypnosis. The author thinks that the Voodoo
        priest plays a role similar, in some respects, to that of
        the hypnotist.

879.   Renshaw, Parke. "A New Religion for Brazilians." PRACTICAL
        ANTHROPOLOGY 13 (1966): 126-38.

        Gives an account of how a syncretism of Christianity and
        tribal religion has occurred in Brazil. Spiritism plays an

important role in the religious life and experience of many
people. This new religion is said to promote individual
fulfillment "in the harassed, inflation-pinched, unjust world
of the worker" (p. 130).

880. Rogler, Lloyd H., and August B. Hollingshead. "The Puerto
     Rican Spiritualist as Psychiatrist." AMERICAN JOURNAL OF
     SOCIOLOGY 67 (1961): 17-21.

     Focuses on the therapeutic role of a quasi-professional
     group, the spiritualists. It is proposed that people in the
     lower social classes rely upon spiritualist beliefs and prac-
     tices as therapeutic outlets for mental illness. Spiritualism
     is a form of folk psychotherapy which takes the stigma away
     from the afflicted participant. The persistent hallucinations
     of those who adhere to spiritualistic beliefs are not symp-
     toms of mental illness, but rather demonstrations of psychic
     faculties that might put the subject in contact with the
     invisible world. "Participation in a spiritualist group
     serves to structure, define, and render behavior institu-
     tionally meaningful that is otherwise perceived as aberrant"
     (p. 21).

881. Ruiz, Pedro, and Ezra H. Griffith. "Hex and Possession: Two
     Problematic Areas in the Psychiatrist's Approach to Reli-
     gion." CURRENT PERSPECTIVES IN CULTURAL PSYCHIATRY (item
     654), pp. 93-102.

     Discusses several problematic areas which hinder American
     psychiatrists in understanding spiritualism. The authors
     discuss a number of cases of hex and possession among Puerto
     Rican immigrants. They point out that in clear cases where
     a client believed he or she had been hexed, they found it
     advantageous to use a "dehexing" process besides using drugs
     to treat the schizophrenic symptoms. They also draw up some
     of the features of possession and observe that it is still
     unclear as to what are the criteria for assessing abnormal
     states of possession.

882. Sanada, Takaaki, and Edward Norbeck. "Prophecy Continues to
     Fail: A Japanese Sect." JOURNAL OF CROSS-CULTURAL PSYCHOL-
     OGY 6 (1975): 331-45.

     Studies a Japanese sect, Ichigen-no-Miya, whose leader made
     an unfulfilled prophecy that an earthquake would occur on June
     18, 1974. A short history of the sect and a brief description
     of its main religious beliefs and practices are given. The
     prophet's attempt to commit suicide when the disaster failed
     to materialize was later interpreted by his followers either
     as a sacrificial act which actually prevented the earthquake
     from taking place, or as an expression of gratitude to the
     gods for holding the disaster back, or as a suicide act by
     the prophet who had misunderstood the revelatory message.
     Although the leader dissolved the sect, many of his followers
     remained loyal. The theory of cognitive dissonance is used
     to explain their behavior.

883.   Sandoval, Mercedes C. "Santeria as a Mental Health Care
        System: An Historical Perspective." SOCIAL SCIENCE AND
        MEDICINE 13B (1979): 137-51.

        Explains why Santeria, an Afro-Cuban cult which has taken
        root in several urban areas in the United States, constitutes
        a vital and dynamic mental health care system. The main
        features of cult belief and practice are described and the
        cultural and historical conditions which have led to the
        cult's success both in Cuba and the United States are out-
        lined. The author sees Santeria as a psychotherapeutic sys-
        tem which handles matters relating to the soul and which can
        exist in collaboration with modern medical and psychiatric
        treatments.

884.   Sandova, Mercedes C. "Santeria: Afro-Cuban Concepts of
        Disease and Its Treatment in Miami." JOURNAL OF OPERA-
        TIONAL PSYCHIATRY 8.3 (1977): 52-63.

        Describes the Santeria belief system common among Cuban
        immigrants in the United States. Various supernatural causes
        of disease, like imitative or contagious magic, loss of
        soul, spirit intrusion, and anger of the gods, are briefly
        portrayed. Santeria has been successful in helping its
        adherents adjust to a new environment by offering a guilt-
        releasing set of beliefs. It has been used, with positive
        results, to deal with psychosomatic disorders. Although the
        beliefs and practices of Santeria are not often conducive to
        the growth of the subjects' inner strength, many times its
        priests are able to channel personality growth and develop-
        ment into constructive channels. Understanding Santeria
        and cooperating with its priests are recommended for improv-
        ing health care services among Cuban Americans.

885.   Sargant, William. "Witch Doctoring, Zar, and Voodoo: Their
        Relations to Modern Psychiatric Treatments." PROCEEDINGS
        OF THE ROYAL SOCIETY OF MEDICINE 60 (1967): 1055-60.

        Discusses traditional healing in Africa and the Zar cult
        in Ethiopia and holds that these techniques resemble the
        experimental findings of Pavlov. Witch doctors rely on the
        patients' suggestibility that is enhanced by abreactive
        simulation (that is, by the weakening or elimination of
        anxiety by reliving the original tension-evoking experience).
        Primitive healing relies on the acting out of one's emotions,
        angers, and fears, which occurs in a typical Voodoo séance.
        The training of the healer and the type of patients cured
        are accounted for. Chronic anxiety states, depression, and
        schizophrenia are among the psychological disorders treated
        with success. The author contends that there exists a common
        mechanism of healing which links primitive with modern
        psychiatry.

886.   Sasaki, Yuji. "Non-Medical Healing in Contemporary Japan:
        A Psychiatric Study." CULTURE-BOUND SYNDROMES, ETHNO-
        PSYCHIATRY, AND ALTERNATE THERAPIES (item 690), pp. 241-49.

Reports on an psychiatric field survey on Hachija Island, Japan, which the author takes as representative of contemporary Japan as a whole. Two unspecified religious sects employ popular non-medical healing therapies. It is claimed that the reason why people, in spite of modern medical resources, still flock to magicoreligious healing practices is that these bring about favorable changes among neurotics. "Religious conversion apparently produces a beneficial change for neurotics by facilitating greater insight, social awareness, and moral responsibility" (p. 249).

887. Saunders, Lucie Wood. "Variants of Zar Experience in an Egyptian Village." CASE STUDIES IN SPIRIT POSSESSION (item 784), pp. 177-91.

Gives a description of the Zar possession ceremonies and several examples of women who became possessed. The author concludes that "the multiple functions of the Zar permit women to react to it as a therapy, religious experience, or party, while using it for different ends in specific relationships" (p. 190).

888. Schwartz, Theodore. "Cult and Context: The Paranoid Ethos in Melanesia." ETHOS 1 (1973): 153-75.

Explains Cargo cults as a mode of psychocultural adjustment brought into being by the interaction of Melanesian and Western cultures. It is argued that Cargo cults are precipitated in the context of a paranoid ethos that is prevalent in the areas and to which religion has contributed. The individual lives in a society where institutionalized paranoia is the norm. The cult-oriented Melanesians are dominated by fantasies and inflated goals which are magical in nature. Cultism remains pathological because the goals are unrealistic and unrealizable.

889. Schwartz, Theodore. "The Noise: Cargo Cult Frenzy in the South Seas." PSYCHOLOGY TODAY 4 (March 1971): 51-54, 102-3.

Describes the rise of a prophetic movement on Admiralty Island in New Guinea and propounds the view (see item 888) that Cargo cults are, in part "a manifestation of a paranoid ethos under conditions of cultural contact and value dissonance" (p. 102). The author thinks that a similar period of intense cultural disruption is occurring in the United States and points to recent fads, like astrology, to illustrate his point. Various anthropological theories of Cargo cults are discussed.

890. Sharon, Douglas. "A Peruvian Curandero's Séance: Power and Balance." SPIRITS, SHAMANS, AND STARS (item 925), pp. 223-38.

Concentrates on the dynamics of the night séance of a curandero (folk healer) in Northern Peru. It is held that the central goal of the séance is the balance of power, which is

expressed in the symbolism of the ritual. The author lists
and briefly explains the many phases of the séance. The
power generated by the ritual is used to solve the patient's
problems.

891. Silverman, Philip. "Local Elites and the Nzila Ceremony
      Among the Lozi of Zambia." ETHOS 5 (1977): 379-87.

      Describes the practices of this African healing cult, which
      has some similarity to separatist religious sects, at a time
      when its popularity was on the rise. Nzila, which refers to
      both a disease and a congregation, afflicts a person when a
      spirit enters his or her body and causes discomfort, involv-
      ing some mental disorder such as speaking in tongues, and an
      inability to eat or sleep. A complex ritual performed by
      the Nzila doctor includes the use of roots and herbs, but not
      dancing, costumes, or ecstatic behavior. The cult, which
      attracts educated, marginal Zambians, is interpreted as a
      subtle mechanism to facilitate modernization and to provide
      effective vehicles for adjusting their belief and behavior
      patterns.

892. Simpson, George E. "The Ras Tafari Movement in Jamaica:
         Its Millennial Aspect." MILLENNIAL DREAMS IN ACTION (item
         899), pp. 160-65.

      Describes briefly the features of this movement which
      centers around the position of Haile Salassie, the former
      Emperor of Ethiopia. The author explains this religious cult
      as an "escapist-adjustive type of activity." The Ras Tafari
      is best seen as a deprivation movement arising out of pro-
      longed frustration.

893. Simpson, George E. RELIGIOUS SECTS OF THE CARIBBEAN: TRI-
         NIDAD, JAMAICA, AND HAITI. Rio Piedras: Institute of
         Caribbean Studies, University of Puerto Rico, 1970.
         308 pp.

      Studies three cults :1) the Shango cult of Nigeria and
      Trinidad; 2) the Ras Tafari movement in Jamaica; and 3) the
      Voodoo cult in Haiti. The author's approach is largely
      ethnographic with some sociological interpretation. There
      are, however, psychiatric reflections on each of the three
      cults. The possession which takes place in the Shango cult
      provides a release of aggressive impulses towards self and
      others. Participation in the Ras Tafari movement is an
      "escapist-aggressive" type of activity. And Voodoo gives
      its adherents a meaningful world view and guidance in their
      daily life.

894. Simpson, George E. "Religious Changes in Southwestern
         Nigeria." ANTHROPOLOGICAL QUARTERLY 43 (1970): 79-92.

      Offers a study of religious movements in Nigeria, pointing
      out that many of the sociological and psychological needs
      once met among the Yoruba through traditional forms of wor-

ship or cults are now being satisfied by several functional
alternatives, including Islam, Christianity, tribal and labor
unions, and political parties. Since, however, anxieties do
not decrease rapidly in a changing cultural situation, the
presence of cults is bound to persist.

895.   Solomon, Ted J. "The Response of Three Japanese Religions to
        the Crisis in the Japanese Value System." JOURNAL FOR THE
        SCIENTIFIC STUDY OF RELIGION 16 (1977): 1-14.

        Examines three new Japanese religions, Soka Gakkai, Rissho
        Kosei-Kai, and PL (Perfect Liberty) Kyodan, and explains them
        as a reaffirmation of the traditional values of loyalty and
        aestheticism. All three religions attempt to come to terms
        with modernity by reformulating the traditional system with
        respect to aesthetics, group work, political action, or
        nationalism. They all exemplify a response to the crisis in
        values engendered by the social and cultural changes of the
        twentieth century. They, therefore, alleviate anomie as they
        search for imaginative ways to encounter the sacred through
        the technological medium.

896.   Spier, Leslie, Wayne Sutters, and Melville J. Herskovits.
        "Comment on Aberle's Theory of Deprivation." SOUTHWESTERN
        JOURNAL OF ANTHROPOLOGY 15 (1955): 84-88.

        Examines Aberle's thesis (item 756) that cults arise in
        periods of deprivation and rejects it on the grounds that
        it is unsupported by facts.

897.   Stanner, W. E. H. "On the Interpretation of Cargo Cults."
        OCEANIA 29 (1958): 1-25.

        Discusses the problem of interpreting Cargo cults that
        are based on an inordinate valuation of alien wealth. These
        cults are crisis cults and, though the real crisis is secular,
        a religious dimension is imposed on them. To what degree the
        crisis is resolved and to what extent participation in the
        rituals help people to cope with the problem are left
        unanswered.

898.   Tambiah, S. J. "The Cosmological and Performative Signifi-
        cance of a Thai Cult of Healing." CULTURE, MEDICINE, AND
        PSYCHIATRY 1 (1977): 97-132.

        Analyzes the actual performance of a healing ritual and
        the shared meaning that the Buddhist participants bring to,
        and derive from, it. Although the patient's life history and
        symptoms are not dealt with in any depth, it is shown how the
        ritual encourages the sick person to transcend ill health by
        aspiring to a more enduring reality. The author holds that
        the treatment addresses the latent aspects of the patient's
        emotional life.

891.   Thrupp, Silvia L., editor. MILLENNIAL DREAMS IN ACTION:
        STUDIES IN REVOLUTIONARY RELIGIOUS MOVEMENTS. New York:
        Schocken Books, 1970. 229 pp.

Contains the papers presented at a conference held at the
University of Chicago in April, 1960. A historical and comparative essay as well as several studies of millennial movements
in different cultures are included. Although largely historically and sociologically oriented, these essays are typical of
the work done in the field of new religious movements, both in
primitive and Western societies. They provide the necessary
background for psychological interpretation.

Contains items 756, 892.

900.   Torrey, E. Fuller. "The Zar Cult in Ethiopia." INTERNA-
        TIONAL JOURNAL OF SOCIAL PSYCHIATRY 13 (1967): 216-23.

Surveys the most widely known possession cult, which
originated in Ethiopia and has spread to several Middle
Eastern countries. Three varieties of this cult are distinguished: 1) conversion Zar (a hysterical reaction which
occurs nearly always in women); 2) "seer" Zar (a less common,
fortune-telling ritual practiced mainly by men); and 3) group
therapy Zar (a somewhat rare ritual in which a healer directs
a group of people who are afflicted with Zar). The author
speculates that Zar doctors could become analogous to mental
health aides in Western clinics.

901.   Trotter, Robert T., and Juan Antonio Chavira. "Curanderismo:
        An Emic Theoretical Perspective of Mexican-American Folk
        Medicine." MEDICAL ANTHROPOLOGY 4 (1980)): 423-87.

Presents a study of curanderismo using the healers themselves as the main informants. The authors give an insider's
theoretical perspective of the healing system that is divided
into several levels, and show that some elements of the "myth"
commonly found in Western literature about it are not accurate.
Curanderismo is still a vital force, even though changes in
both theory and practice are taking place. It also appears
to be gaining in respectability and its therapeutic value is
taken for granted.

902.   Walker, Sheila S. CEREMONIAL SPIRIT POSSESSION IN AFRICA AND
        AFRO-AMERICA. Leiden, Netherlands: E. J. Brill, 1972. xii,
        179 pp.

Considers "the various elements involved in possession, such
as neurophysiology, hypnosis, socialization, and cultural
determinism, to see how each functions and what its role is
alone and in relation to the others" (p. 1). Among the topics
dealt with are : 1) possession and the individual; 2) possession, mental illness, and therapy; and 3) the normality and
abnormality of possession. The author holds that possession
not only allows the individual to express himself or herself,
but also presents the occasion for demonstrating the validity
of the belief system behind possession. Examples from Voodoo,
the Zar cult, and the Peyote ritual are given.

903.   Wallace, Anthony F. C. "Revitalization Movements." AMERICAN
        ANTHROPOLOGIST 58 (1956): 264-81.

Presents one of the seminal anthropological papers outlin-
ing a comprehensive theory of revitalization movements which
include Cargo cults, messianic and prophetic uprisings,
charismatic groups, and new sects. The concepts, assumptions,
and initial findings of these movements are described. Two
conditions for the birth of such movements are explored:
1) the high stress of the individual members of a society,
and 2) the disillusionment with a distorted cultural world
view. A series of functional stages through which the movements progress is delineated. The followers, it is stated,
achieve satisfaction of their dependency needs in charismatic
fellowship.

904.   Ward, Colleen. "Spirit Possession and Neuroticism in a West
        Indian Pentecostal Community." BRITISH JOURNAL OF CLINICAL
        PSYCHOLOGY 20 (1981): 295-96.

Studies a West Indian Pentecostal church, focusing on the
relationship between the belief in spirit possession and
neuroticism. The author concludes that spirit possession in
this community is a culture-bound neurotic disorder. She
cautions, however, that one cannot hold that "possession per
se is pathological" (p. 296).

905.   Ward, Colleen. "Therapeutic Aspects of Ritual Trance: The
        Shango Cult in Trinidad." JOURNAL OF ALTERED STATES OF
        CONSCIOUSNESS 5 (1979-80): 19-28.

Investigates the psychological aspects of a West Indian
syncretistic religion, which includes a ritual trance similar
to ceremonial possessions in other religious groups. The
main features of the rite and the way the trance is induced
are described. It is argued that this cult should not be
linked with psychosis or neurosis, taken as an indication of
hysteria or schizophrenia, or be related to susceptibility,
maladjustment, and anxiety. On the contrary, the author
contends that its main ritual operates as a kind of psychiatric abreaction and brings into being new emotional reactions
which lead the individual to a new level of autonomic balance.

906.   Ward, Colleen., and Michael Beaubrun. "Psychodynamics of
        Demon Possession." JOURNAL FOR THE SCIENTIFIC STUDY OF
        RELIGION 19 (1980): 201-7.

Examines cases of demon-possession in the Pentecostalism
of Trinidad, which is similar to the charismatic movement in
the United States. The authors conclude that, while local
folklore and belief are prerequisites for the possession
complex, the reaction is triggered by unusual stress or
emotional conflict. Four case studies are presented. It is
pointed out that, though the possessed individuals manifested
hysterical features, it was not possible to arrive at a single
psychiatric diagnosis. The possession had the following
advantages: 1) it allowed the possessed person to escape from
unpleasant situations; 2) it diminished one's responsibility
and guilt; and 3) it elicited group support.

907.   Ward, Colleen, and Michael Beaubrun. "Trance Induction and
        Hallucination in Spiritualist Baptist Mourning." JOURNAL
        OF PSYCHOLOGICAL ANTHROPOLOGY 2 (19790: 479-88.

        Unites anthropological and psychological perspectives to
        study mourning rites of Spiritualist Baptists in Trinidad.
        In these rituals the worshippers experience several altered
        states of consciousness including trance, hallucinations,
        and visions. The article explores the psychological features
        of altered states of consciousness and the sociological and
        psychological factors of trance and hallucinations. Although
        mourning can be a dangerous experience leading to serious
        psychological problems, it may also bring about psychological
        benefits, such as the release of tension, the reduction of
        anxiety, and social prestige. Since the subjective reports
        of the mourning experiences stress emotional satisfaction,
        it can be said that participation in the ritual could be
        therapeutic.

908.   Warner, Richard. "Witchcraft and Soul Loss: Implications
        for Community Problems." HOSPITAL AND COMMUNITY PSYCHIATRY
        28 (1977): 686-90.

        Utilizes a case study of a Chicano patient who believes in
        witchcraft and soul loss to show the significance of under-
        standing alternate theories of disease causation. The need
        to interpret the subjects' behavior in the context of their
        culture is underscored. The treatment of the curanderos has
        certain advantages in that the patient's confidence in the
        folk healer's power has considerable therapeutic effect. The
        author feels, however, that the active integration of folk
        healers in mental health programs is a difficult and unpro-
        ductive task.

909.   Williams, Charles Harrison. "Utilization of Persisting Cul-
        tural Values of Mexican-Americans by Western Practitioners."
        TRADITIONAL HEALING (item 735), pp. 108-22.

        Discusses the cultural framework of the Mexican-American
        concept of disease and the reason why curanderos persist in
        a modern American setting. The ethical and therapeutic prob-
        lems of incorporating folk therapy into modern psychotherapy
        are considered. The problems brought about by uniting native
        and Western beliefs are made apparent by alluding to several
        practical cases. Western therapists may have to consult
        traditional healers in order to understand the nature of the
        illnesses of their Mexican-American clients and to be able
        to apply an adequate treatment.

910.   Wilson, Michele. "Voodoo Believers: Some Sociological
        Insights." JOURNAL OF SOCIOLOGY AND SOCIAL WELFARE 9
        (1982): 375-83.

        Offers a study of Voodoo, concentrating on an unnamed city
        in the Deep South of the United States. The various possible
        interpretations of Voodoo, as an alternative medical system,

a religion, and a subculture are discussed. The author endorses the view that Voodoo is therapeutic and argues that
the tendency to consider believers as insincere, foolish, or
mentally ill is a shere expression of ethnocentrism.

911.   Wittkower, E. D. "Trance and Possession States." INTER-
        NATIONAL JOURNAL OF SOCIAL PSYCHIATRY 16 (1970): 153-60.

Recounts native cult rituals in Haiti, Liberia, and Brazil
to show the behavior patterns during trance and possession
states. Similarites between these and epileptic, hysteric,
and hypnotic conditions are noted, the latter being the most
conspicuous. Cult rituals have functionally adaptive value
both for the culture in which they appear and flourish and
also for the individual worshippers. These rituals may, at
times, relieve feelings of impotence and dependability produced by discrimination, oppression, and the rapid cultural
change brought about by Western influence.

912.   Yassa, Ramzy. "A Psychiatric Study of an Egyptian Phenome-
        non." AMERICAN JOURNAL OF PSYCHOTHERAPY 34 (1980): 246-51.

Describes various apparitions of, and miracles attributed
to, the Virgin Mary, all of which took place in Egypt after
the 1967 Israeli-Egyptian war. The author discusses some
interpretations of the events and concludes that they are
related to the massive loss of self-esteen the Egyptians
suffered as a result of their defeat.

913.   Young, Alan. "Why Amhara Get 'Kureyna': Sickness and
        Possession in an Ethipian 'Zar' Cult." AMERICAN ETHNOLO-
        GIST 2 (1975): 567-84.

Points out that many accounts assume that cults play a
homeostatic role. They are often interpreted as ways to
inhibit or safely redirect pathological behavior endemic to
the society in which they are found. A further assumption,
challenged here, is that the study of ritual possession or
trance is the best way to understand the adaptive features
of the cults. The author argues that certain social and
psychic advantages of belonging to a Zar cult explain, in
part, why people choose to participate.

        C. STUDIES ON SHAMANISM AND RELATED PHENOMENA

    The study of shamanism provides valuable insights on the cultic
phenomenon. The majority of studies on shamanism have been written
by anthropologists who are responsible for ethnographic monographs
of many shamanistic beliefs and practices, particularly in non-
literate and tribal societies. Anthropological studies have discussed at length both the social and religious roles shamans play
in their respective cultures. They have also debated the psychological state of shamans, whose trance behavior is comparable to
that of mediums in Western culture.

A central and universal feature of the behavior of shamans is their ability to go into a trance-like state and behave as if a spirit or spiritual power has taken control, thus giving them the unique ability to diagnose an illness and cure it, and to offer divinely-inspired advice. Many folk healers and medicine men and women in different cultural settings have exhibited shamanistic qualities (see, for example, item 371). Several modern leaders of religious movements are also highly acclaimed mediums by their followers, and could easily be classified as shamans (cf. item 979).

Shamanism has a long history of controversy. Although anthropologists have reached some agreement on the important role that shamans play in their respective societies, there is still plenty of debate about their psychological state. Three major trends in interpretation are clearly discernible. The first, often adopted by psychiatrists, is that shamans have serious personality problems and their trance behavior is a sign of dissociation. According to this view, shamans suffer from serious neurotic or psychotic problems, and frequently exhibit qualities similar to those of psychopaths in Western societies. Shamans have, therefore, been at times analyzed in terms of Freudian psychology.

A second opinion looks on shamans as individuals who had been originally psychologically disturbed, but who eventually overcame their conflicts. Their vocation as shamans was the means through which they surmounted their troubles and came to terms with reality. Because of their ability to go into trance and to act as mediums, they are an asset to other members of their society. Their past experiences of mental and/or psychological illness enables them to counsel and help many people in their daily troubles. This view is similar to the theory which explains religious experience as a regression in the service of the ego.

A third viewpoint considers shamans as psychologically normal but highly gifted individuals who play the role of healers and therapists in their communities. Their qualities, though eccentric and out-of-the-ordinary, are not a sign of pathology, but rather an indication of their profession; their behavior marks them as exceptional people who perform much-needed social and psychological functions. Their aberrant behavior is seen, not in terms of individual psychology, but in terms of cultural norms which an aspirant to the shamanic state has to adopt. Many writers, who accept this point of view, stress the religious and/or social position of shamans and the many services that they make available to their communities.

The debate as to whether one should adopt a sociological or psychological interpretation of religion is very evident in the studies on shamanism. No matter what stand one takes on the psychopathology or normality of these religious leaders or on their social status and role, studies on shamanism are important because they direct our attention to several considerations necessary for evaluating new religious leaders, prophets, and mediums. The universality of the shaman-type of religious person raises the issue of whether a psychiatric analysis is sufficient for understanding such a figure. The position commonly held by cultural and social anthropologists, that

the shaman's personality must be understood in the context of a particular culture, and that his or her social role should be the determining factor in any evaluation, has much to recommend it. Further,
because shamans experience an altered state of consciousness, the
issue may also revolve around a religious ideology which values and
seeks peak or transcendent experiences. Many of the new religious
movements explicitly promote such types of experience by the use of
meditation, Yoga, and other disciplines. In spite of the voluminous
studies on meditation, which show how much it allays anxiety and
relieves tension, its promoters have something else in mind. Meditation, as well as certain life-styles and other practices, is
recommended because it changes a person's perception of reality,
provides a different and allegedly more profound and satisfying
self-awareness, and develops new modes of relating to others. The
shaman is a person who is recognized as having achieved this new
mode of being, and who can go beyond the realm of this world into
that of the spirits.

Altered states of consciousness could, like intense religious
experiences, be a sign of mental or psychological illness. Not all
shamans or mediums are healthy individuals. Cross-cultural psychiatrists have the task of drawing up the criteria for distinguishing
between healthy and unhealthy forms of trance-like experiences. The
debate on the personality of the shaman has not solved the major
issues at stake. It has, however, provided new insights and warned
us of the pitfalls into which some psychiatric studies of contemporary cult leaders have so easily succumbed.

914.   Bahr, Donald M., Juan Gregorio, David I. Lopez, and Albert
        Alvarez. PIMAN SHAMANISM AND STAYING SICKNESS. Tucson:
        University of Arizona Press, 1974. xi, 332 pp.

        Presents a study of Papago Indian shamanism, which combines
        the research of an anthropologist and a linguist, as well as
        the assistance of a local shaman and a native interpreter.
        The main goals of the writers are to provide an introduction
        to the Piman theory of sickness and to contribute toward a
        comparative study of theories of illness. The nature of
        human sickness and its classifications, as conceived in Piman
        culture, are outlined. The diagnostic and ritualistic pro-
        cedures used by the shamans are described and various formulae
        pronounced during the healing process are recorded. Although
        the authors do not discuss explicitly the mental state of the
        shamans, their assumption throughout is that they are native
        healers working with a tenable theory of disease.

915.   Bartolomé, Miguel Alberto. "Shamanism Among the Avá-Chiripá."
        SPIRITS, SHAMANS, AND STARS (item 925), pp. 95-148.

        Offers a lengthy account of the institution of shamanism
        in Eastern Paraguay. The shaman's role as healer is high-
        lighted. It is stated that his or her functions contribute

to group solidarity and cohesion and provide consistent
reassurance regarding the people's relationships with their
environment. The considerable increase in the number of
yearly shamanistic rituals point to the growing internal tension that the rituals themselves tend to decrease.

916.   Beattie, John, and John Middleton, editors. SPIRIT MEDIUM-
        SHIP AND SOCIETY IN AFRICA. New York: Africana Publishing
        Corporation, 1969. xxx, 310 pp.

        Brings together selected essays on possession and mediumship
        in different parts of Africa. The main area of concern is
        the institution centering on spirit mediums. The main areas
        investigated are: 1) the ideological aspects of mediumship
        cults, especially their beliefs and values; 2) the behavior
        of those who get involved in them, particularly the mediums
        themselves and their rituals; and 3) the social and cultural
        contexts in which the cults flourish. Though the focus of
        this volume is not on the psychiatric interpretation of cultic
        behavior, it provides a broader context in which shamanism,
        glossolalia, possession, and mediumship can be considered.
        The issue of the mental illness of the medium is briefly con-
        sidered in several essays and there is disagreement about the
        matter.

917.   Belo, Jane. TRANCE IN BALI. New York: Columbia University
        Press, 1960. xiii, 284 pp.

        Gives a detailed account of the different kinds of ritual
        trances in Bali. The author describes various individual
        trances, the structure of the villages where they occur, and
        the situations in which they occurred. In her introduction,
        she presents these psychological interpretations of trance
        as cases of schizophrenia or hysteria. Her opinion is that
        trance is an essential part of Balinese social organization,
        making change possible. Consequently, trance should not be
        identified with pathology. Though trance seizures offer
        an outlet for the expression of neurotic tendencies, many
        Balinese trance subjects, outside their trance behavior,
        seemed indistinguishable psychologically from those who never
        experienced the state of trance.

918.   Blacker, Carmen. THE CATALPA BOW: A STUDY OF SHAMANISTIC
        PRACTICES IN JAPAN. London: Allen and Unwin, 1982. 376 pp.

        Describes Japanese shamanistic rituals and behavior which,
        the author thinks, are gradually fading out under the influ-
        ence of contemporary cultural pressures. This study includes
        many of the newer Japanese religious cults and sects, such as
        Tendai Buddhism, Tenrikyo, the Dancing Religion, World Messi-
        anity, and Nichren Shoshu, some of which have branches in the
        United States. The author does not refer to any psychiatric
        issues which involvement in these groups might give rise to.
        She tends to view shamanic practices as a kind of archaic
        mysticism.

919. Boyer, L. Bryce. "Further Remarks Concerning Shamans and
      Shamanism." ISRAELI ANNALS OF PSYCHIATRY AND RELATED
      DISCIPLINES 2 (1964): 235-57.

      Presents data of fieldwork done among the Apaches of the
      Mescalero Indian Reservation. An overview is provided of the
      literature describing the psychological state of the shaman
      and Apache socialization and personality development. Several
      cases of people who had been accorded the status of shaman are
      recorded. These shamans were not considered psychological
      deviants in their society. The author compares the results
      of her studies with the personality organization of Balinese
      and Chuckchee shamans. In Balinese culture, shamans are
      treated for some psychological illness before their initia-
      tion into their new religious role, while in Chuckchee
      society, shamans do not suffer from any acknowledged psycho-
      logical problem before they are accepted. All members of
      these three societies were suggestible and prone to halluci-
      natory experiences and trance-like states. They all lie in
      the range of the hysterical personality disorder, with the
      Balinese tending to schizophrenia more than the other two
      groups. Some shamans could in fact be less afflicted psycho-
      pathologically than the average members of their society.

920. Boyer, L. Bryce. "Folk Psychiatry of the Apaches of the
      Mescalero Indian Reservation." MAGIC, FAITH, AND HEALING
      (item 679), pp. 384-419.

      Describes briefly the social structure and socialization
      processes of the Apache who live in a New Mexico reservation,
      and the main features of their religion, medical practices,
      and shamanism. The treatment of psychogenic illnesses is
      said to be the forte of the shaman. Some points of compari-
      son are drawn up between Apache shamanism and Western psychi-
      atry. It is concluded that Apache shamanism is a form of
      faith healing.

921. Boyer, L. Bryce. "Remarks on the Personality of Shamans:
      With Special Reference to the Apache of the Mescalero
      Indian Reservation." PSYCHOANALYTIC STUDY OF SOCIETY 2
      (1962): 233-54.

      Attempts a systematic study of the psychology of the shaman.
      The pertinent anthropological literature is surveyed, and the
      author concludes that he finds no evidence of an anal fixation
      in shamans. Because shamans believe that they possess magical
      powers, they have the attributes of the oral phase. Shamans
      are in a state of psychological regression and exhibit both
      neurotic and psychotic symptoms. Hysterical tendencies and
      deceptive inclinations appear to be common among shamans who
      have problems with sexual identification, which shows that
      they may have become fixated in the phallic state. Judged
      from outside their culture, shamans seem psychologically
      deviant.

922.   Boyer, L. Bryce. "Notes on the Personality Structure of a
        North American Indian Shaman." JOURNAL OF THE HILLSIDE
        HOSPITAL 10 (1961): 14-33.

        Presents a case study from the Eastern Apache Indians to
        illustrate the hypothesis that the typical shaman has the
        traits of a hysterical personality and of an impostor, and
        that he/she is fixated in the oral and phallic phases. The
        particular shaman studied also lacked clear masculine iden-
        tity and suffered from latent homosexuality.

923.   Boyer, L. Bryce, George A. De Vos, and Ruth M. Boyer.
        "Crisis and Continuity in the Personality Structure of an
        Apache Shaman." PSYCHOANALYTIC STUDY OF SOCIETY 11 (1985):
        64-113.

        Summarizes relevant information concerning Apache religio-
        medical philosophy and practices, and re-examines some of the
        issues regarding the psychological state of the shamans in
        this society. A detailed comparison between the result of
        Rorschach tests administered two years apart is given. Sever-
        al psychoanalytic interpretations are offered. The authors
        conclude that "Rorschach protocols reveal that shamans who
        show psychotic propensities are in the distinct minority"
        (p. 108).

924.   Boyer, L. Bryce, Bruno Klopper, Florence Brawer, and Hayao
        Kawai. "Comparison of the Shamans and Pseudoshamans of the
        Apaches of the Mescalero Indian Reservation: A Rorschach
        Study." JOURNAL OF PROJECTIVE TECHNIQUES 28 (1984): 173-80.

        Tests and compares the personality structures of shamans
        and pseudoshamans, the former being those whose claim to the
        status of medicine men with supernatural power was recognized
        by the community at large. The results show that shamans
        possessed more hysterical features, were keener in observing
        peculiarities, were more interested in theoretical matters,
        and tended to regress in the service of the ego. Compared to
        the shamans, pseudoshamans were impoverished personalities.
        Rorschach tests indicated that the shamans were psychologi-
        cally better off than the normal group, while the pseudo-
        shamans were worse off. The findings appear to contradict
        Devereux's theory (item 935) that the shaman is a severely
        neurotic or psychotic person.

925.   Browman, D. L., and R. Schwarz, editors. SPIRITS, SHAMANS,
        AND STARS: PERSPECTIVES FROM SOUTH AMERICA. The Hague:
        Mouton, 1979. xiii, 276 pp.

        Offers a collection of papers presented at the Ninth Inter-
        national Congress of Anthropological and Ethnological Sciences
        held in 1973. The material is divided into three sections:
        1) perspectives on psychotropic drugs; 2) medical anthropol-
        ogy; and 3) spirits, structures, and stars.

        Contains items 736, 788, 890, 915.

926. Centlivres, Micheline, Pierre Centlivres, and Mark Slobin.
      "A Muslim Shaman of Afghan Turkestan." ETHNOLOGY 10 (1971):
      160-73.

      Deals primarily with the performance, role, and status of
      the shaman. The author reports on his attendance at a thera-
      peutic séance performed by one of the shamans in this society.

927. Chandrashekar, C. R. "A Victim of an Epidemic of Possession
      Syndrome." INDIAN JOURNAL OF PSYCHIATRY 23 (1981): 370-72.

      Examines the case of a young man who was one of four victims
      of an epidemic of possession by two spirits. The author con-
      cludes that such a possession need not always be interpreted
      as a sign of illness or pathology. Culture can lead a person
      to exhibit this phenomenon as an expected form of behavior
      in certain situations.

928. Chang, Suk C., and Kwang-iel Kim. "Psychiatry in South
      Korea." AMERICAN JOURNAL OF PSYCHIATRY 130 (1973): 667-69.

      Refers to four native traditions, namely Shamanism, Bud-
      dhism, Confucianism, and folk medicine, as "built-in socio-
      cultural mechanisms that had a preventive or even curative
      effect on man's psychological distress" (p. 667). The intro-
      duction and state of Western psychiatry in Korea are briefly
      described. Shin-Byong, a state of possession which often
      leads a person to become a shaman, is a culture-bound
      depersonalization syndrome, a psychosomatic illness which
      cures the person as he or she is transformed into a shaman.
      The author observes that the incidence of this disease is
      now decreasing, possibly as the result of the introduction
      of Western psychiatry.

929. Corin, Ellen. "A Possession Psychotherapy in an Urban Set-
      ting in Kinshasa." SOCIAL SCIENCE AND MEDICINE 13 B (1979):
      327-38.

      Describes a Mongo possession ritual (called Zebola) in
      Northwest Zaire and underlines the structure which makes it
      an effective psychotherapeutic tool. The indigenous inter-
      pretation of illness, the diagnostic process, and the trans-
      formation of the symptoms are portrayed. The therapy is built
      around three bipolar dichotomies: 1) the individual versus
      the group; 2) the traditional versus the modern; and 3) the
      sacred versus the profane. Zebola fulfills the important
      psychological function of establishing links between tradi-
      tion and modernity.

930. Covell, Alan Carter. ECSTASY: SHAMANISM IN KOREA. Eliza-
      beth, NJ: Hollym International Corporation, 1983. 107 pp.

      Gives an account of shamanism in Korea, illustrating it by
      many photographs and diagrams. The traditional symbols of
      shamans and their present-day rituals are among the main

areas covered. The shaman's role as a healer in modern Korea is briefly discussed. The author sees sexual overtones in Korean shamanism. Women, who make up 90 percent of the shamans, were so suppressed socially that in their rituals they "were acting out some of their repressed sexual feelings, striving for temporary escape from the official religion which put them in a subordinate position within society" (p. 97).

931.   Cramer, Marc. "Psychopathology and Shamanism in Rural Mexico: A Case Study of Spirit Possession." BRITISH JOURNAL OF MEDICAL PSYCHOLOGY 53 (1980): 67-73.

Presents a detailed examination of two occasions when a Chinese-American male was allegedly possessed by four entities, namely, three Catholic saints and the spirit of a medical doctor. The author, in an attempt to show the psychological and sociological processes involved, states that possession by benevolent spirits is a socially-accepted expression of psychological conflicts. This kind of possession functions as an agent of abreaction, communication, and status and helps the individual resolve cognitive and emotional stress.

*   Crapanzano, Vincent, and Vivian Garrison. CASE STUDIES IN SPIRIT POSSESSION. Cited above as item 784.

932.   Day, Richard, and Ronald H. Davidson. "Magic and Healing: An Ethnopsychoanalytic Examination." PSYCHOANALYTIC STUDY OF SOCIETY 7 (1976): 231-91.

Studies medicine men, sorcerers, and shamans who seek, through the alleviation of group anxiety, their own sense of identity and security. A conceptual overview is provided, using Devereux's idea of the "integrative capacity of the healer." The healer is able to stabilize his or her regressive tendencies and capacity for sublimation. A case example is given of a Filipino woman whose conflicts and crises led to a radical transformation of identity. Her life history and healing practices are described and the healer/patient relationship analyzed. The healer, after a period of personal regression, is able to remain integrated in society because the conflicts are located in his or her ethnic background. Through creative symbolic contact with others, healers achieve a sense of integration and belonging to society.

933.   Dean, Stanley R., and Denny Thong. "Transcultural Aspects of Metapsychiatry: Focus on Shamanism in Bali." PSYCHIATRY AND MYSTICISM (item 1024), pp. 271-82.

Studies psychogenic culture-bound reactive syndromes and their treatment by indigenous healers. These conditions, which share a common belief in spirit possession, sorcery, voodoo, trance states, and exorcism, resemble acute schizophrenic episodes. They are also alike in their outward

symptoms, which include transient attacks of depersonalization, dissociation, depression and autonism in the context
of paranoia, and projective and massive regressions. The
Bali syndrome, which has its replica in other cultures, is
described. The authors state that no specific type of psychotherapy has been devised for mental illness, that in all
healing practices the therapeutic personality of the healer
and the faith of the patient are the central features, and
that empathetic communication between healer and patient is
a necessary quality for the restoration of health. They
further maintain that indigenous healers should be treated
as psychiatrists and that future psychiatrists should be
evaluated for their therapeutic personality. The authors
list some of the shortcomings of shamanism and point out
that several lessons can be learned from it.

934.   Dean, Stanley R., and Denny Thong. "Shamanism Versus Psychi-
        atry in Bali, 'Isle of the Gods': Some Modern Implications."
        AMERICAN JOURNAL OF PSYCHIATRY 129 (1972): 59-62.

        Maintains that the wide spectrum of psychotherapy, from
        the practices of the witch doctor to those of modern Western
        psychiatry, is based on two common constants, the charisma
        of the therapist and the faith of the sick person. It is
        insisted that, in their professional training, modern psychi-
        atrists should be introduced to the work of native therapists
        and be tested for their therapeutic personality. The Balinese
        views on mental illness and their cures are described. Patho-
        logical syndromes can occur within the context of shamanism.
        One lesson from Balinese shamanism is that the stigma of
        some mental illnesses is removed and certain extraordinary
        experiences are accepted as part of the community's life.
        The shaman is a participant in the healing process and not
        just an observer or an objective doctor prescribing a parti-
        cular treatment.

935.   Devereux, George. "Shamans and Neurotics." AMERICAN ANTHRO-
        POLOGIST 63 (1961): 1088-90.

        States briefly the author's view that shamans are basically
        neurotic people who use socially-sanctioned defenses to ex-
        press their feelings. In spite of their psychiatric condi-
        tion, shamans can perform culturally valid social functions.

936.   Ducey, Charles. "The Life History and Creative Psychopathol-
        ogy of the Shaman: Ethnopsychoanalytic Perspectives."
        PSYCHOANALYTIC STUDY OF SOCIETY 7 (1976): 173-230.

        Discusses the theoretical problem of the shaman's psycho-
        pathology and proposes a general theory to explain shamanism.
        The shaman's initiation rites, hallucinations, fantasies,
        illusions, and curing techniques are assessed. Shamanistic
        behavior in general is judged to be childish and adolescent.
        "Shamanism is an attempted cure of a pre-existing mental dis-
        order, a defensive activity pitted against the reemergence

of potentially debilitating affects that continue to operate
behind the scenes" (p. 177). Shamans have healing capacities
in their sensitivity to psychological problems.

*   Edsman, Carl-Martin. "A Swedish Female Folk Healer From the
        Beginning of the 18th Century." Cited above as item 371.

937.   Eliade, Mircea. SHAMANISM: ARCHAIC TECHNIQUES OF ECSTASY.
        Translated from the French by Willard R. Task. New York:
        Pantheon House, Bollingen Series LXXVI, 1964. xiii, 610
        pp. First published in 1951.

        Presents an impressive book which has become the classic
        study of shamanism in the field of the history of religions.
        The author surveys the entire phenomenon in its universal
        manifestations. The shamans' vocation and initial sickness,
        the way they obtain their superhuman powers, their initiation,
        and the symbolism of their clothing and drums are described
        at some length. Various chapters deal with shamanism in
        different parts of the world. The theory that shamanism can
        be explained as a form of mental illness is rejected. The
        author treats shamans as religious persons and specialists.

938.   Fabrega, Horacio, and Daniel Silver. ILLNESS AND SHAMANISTIC
        CURING IN ZINACANTAN: AN ETHNOMEDICAL ANALYSIS. Stanford:
        Stanford University Press, 1973. xii, 285 pp.

        Explores and analyzes the ways by which the Maya Indians
        of Zinacantan, Mexico, orient themselves toward medical prob-
        lems and seek relief from illnesses. The main features of
        of the culture that bear on medical matters are reviewed. The
        shamans were tested on the Holtzman Inkblot Technique and
        showed no evidence of "pathological thinking."

939.   Fabrega, Horacio, and Daniel Silver. "Some Social and Psy-
        chological Properties of Zinacantaco Shamans." BEHAVIORAL
        SCIENCE 15 (1970): 471-86.

        Describes some of the features of shamans in the state of
        Chiapas, Mexico, and reports on the results of projective
        tests given to a group of shamans and non-shamans. The
        former tended to receive lower scores, reflecting participa-
        tion in ladino culture, and higher scores on several psycho-
        logical aspects, including anxiety, anger, and pathological
        thinking. Shamans are respected more for their social role
        than for their personality attributes.

940.   Felton, R. A. "The Healing Ritual." INTERNATIONAL JOURNAL
        OF SOCIAL PSYCHIATRY 21 (1975): 176-78.

        Portrays the rituals of the shaman healers in southern
        Chile and compares their procedures with modern therapeutic
        practices. Rituals, it is argued, are not just means of
        producing a placebo effect in psychosomatic disorders. They
        are also able to bring about dramatic changes in a person's

consciousness and could be employed as an effective aid to
psychotherapy. The obvious implication is that the Chilean
shamans are to be considered as respectable therapists.

941.   Freed, Stanley A., and Ruth S. Freed. "Spirit Possession as
       Illness in a North Indian Village." ETHNOLOGY 3 (1964):
       152-71.

       Discusses spirit possession as illness in Shanti Nagar, a
       North Indian village near Delhi, and compares it with similar
       phenomena in other parts of India. The possession of the
       sick person and the shaman's attempted cure are described.
       Spirit possession is related to difficulties and tensions
       with close relatives and often affects those whose expecta-
       tions of aid and support are low. While the person usually
       recovers, his or her condition can become a permanent psycho-
       logical affliction. The author discusses the common theory
       that spirit possession is a form of hysteria and thinks that,
       in certain cases, it may be better understood as a means of
       controlling one's relatives in a stressful situation. The
       possession by spirits, which occurs in uniform patterns in
       North India, has the effect of relieving tension and attract-
       ing sympathy and attention. It may, however, develop into
       schizophrenia.

942.   Fuchs, Stephen. "Magic Healing Techniques Among the Balahis
       in Central India." MAGIC, FAITH, AND HEALING (item 679),
       pp. 121-38.

       Describes the work of indigenous shamans ("Barwas") in cur-
       ing certain diseases that are believed to be of supernatural
       origin, and in freeing individuals from evil spirits. The
       shamans go into a self-induced trance which may be a form of
       autohypnosis. The author states that the shamans in this
       untouchable caste are often "men and women of hysterical
       disposition and psychic aptitude for hypnotizing themselves
       easily into a state of trance" (p. 130). He disagrees with
       the diagnostic opinion that a shaman is a typical example of
       a dissociated personality because the psychic state is always
       deliberately brought on. The author thinks that the psychi-
       atric problems brought about by industrialization cannot be
       adequately treated by shamans.

943.   Grim, John A. THE SHAMAN: PATTERNS OF SIBERIAN AND OJIBWA
       HEALING. Norman: University of Oklahoma Press, 1983. xiv,
       255 pp.

       Provides an ethnographic account of shamanism in two soci-
       eties and identifies four patterns in the shaman's experience,
       namely, cosmology, tribal sanction, ritual re-enactment, and
       trance. Although the personality of the shaman is not dis-
       cussed, the author maintains that "a therapeutic field is
       conveyed to the patient by means of the trance experience"
       (p. 138).

944.   Grim, John. REFLECTIONS ON SHAMANISM: THE TRIBAL LEADER AND
       THE TECHNOLOGICAL TRANCE. Chambersburg, PA: Anima Books,
       Teilhard Studies, No. 6, Fall 1981. 16 pp.

       Examines the religious dynamics of shamanism and describes
       four cross-cultural patterns, namely, cosmology, ritual re-
       enactment, trance experience, and tribal sanction, to inter-
       pret the many functions of the shaman. In the native American
       Indian tradition, the sense of power is expressed in the
       personality of the shaman, while in modern Western culture,
       the same sense is located in the technological and scientific
       processes. In both cases power can be used for personal
       aggrandizement.

945.   Halifax, Joan. SHAMAN: THE WOUNDED HEALER. New York: Cross-
       road, 1982. 96 pp.

       Contributes a short essay on shamanism, with many photo-
       graphic illustrations of shamanistic behavior throughout the
       world. The author offers a summary of the various forms of
       shamanism and a generalized model based on the psychosymbolic
       structures of many shamanic cultures. The focus of her
       observations lies on the inner journey that shamans make
       during a life crisis, and on the ways in which they bring
       order out of chaos and confusion. The psychiatric evaluation
       of the shaman as a pathological personality is rejected. The
       shaman is depicted as an individual who has passed through
       a serious personal crisis and is now in a position to help
       others.

946.   Halverson, John. "Dynamics of Exorcism: The Sinhalese Sanni-
       yakuma." JOURNAL OF RELIGION 10 (1971): 345-59.

       Describes a popular dramatic exorcism ritual in Sri Lanka.
       The rite centers around a psychologically disturbed person,
       whose symptoms may reach catatonic withdrawal, and aims to
       heal him and restore him to normalcy. The author argues that
       the ritual is comparable to psychoanalysis and that it some-
       times works. Therapeutic work with the patient involves the
       building up of confidence in the exorcist and his method and
       the allaying of fear. It is observed that there has been a
       decline of this ritual and a rising interest in Western
       psychotherapy.

947.   Hamer, John, and Irene Hamer. "Spirit Possession and Its
       Socio-Psychological Implications Among the Sidamo of
       Southwest Ethiopia." ETHNOLOGY 5 (1966): 392-408.

       Contends that spirit possession among these people provides
       a psychocultural outlet for the sense of failure in the
       struggle for power and prestige. The authors give an account
       of the native belief system and of the possession states that
       are associated with illness. People who are believed to be
       possessed show an unusual amount of dependency. Although
       possession is interpreted as a psychological state of disso-
       ciation, it is still, for many people, an adaptive technique
       which functions therapeutically.

948. Harner, Michael. THE WAY OF THE SHAMAN: A GUIDE TO POWER AND
      HEALING. San Francisco: Harper and Row, 1980. xviii, 167
      pp.

      Introduces the reader to shamanistic methods of health and
      healing. Shamanism is described as 1) a strategy for personal
      learning and acting upon the new knowledge, and 2) a system
      for mind-body healing. The author maintains that anyone can
      move from the ordinary to the shamanistic state of conscious-
      ness and become an effective healer.

949. Harner, Michael J., editor. HALLUCINOGENS AND SHAMANISM.
      New York: Oxford University Press, 1973. xv, 200 pp.

      Collects several essays on the use of hallucinogenic drugs
      during shamanistic ceremonies in different parts of the world.
      The editor contends that "long-standing controversies over the
      personality and psychopathology of shamans will undoubtedly
      benefit from a serious consideration of the potentiality of
      native psychedelics to temporarily transport almost any indi-
      vidual to another state of consciousness" (xiv). Most of the
      papers deal with shamanism in South America, particularly
      the Amazon region, with one essay, respectively, on American
      Indian and Mexican shamanism. One paper examines the role of
      hallucinogenic plants in European witchcraft.

950. Harris, Grace. "Possession 'Hysteria' in a Kenya Tribe."
      AMERICAN ANTHROPOLOGIST 59 (1957): 1046-66.

      Considers the case of spirit possession ("saka") among
      women in the Wataita people, a Bantu-speaking tribe in Kenya.
      The psychological interpretation that the possession makes
      up for the unfulfilled needs of those individuals who become
      possessed is rejected. The author prefers a ritual theory
      which looks on possession as symbolizing socially approved
      relationships between individuals and groups.

951. Hes, Josef Ph. "Shamanism and Psychotherapy." PSYCHOTHERAPY
      AND PSYCHOSOMATICS 25 (1975): 251-53.

      Raises the issue of the relationship between shamanism and
      modern therapy. The following pertinent questions are dis-
      cussed: Should one fight shamanism as an unmedical and un-
      scientific practice? Or should one find a compromise between
      the shaman and the Western therapist? Or should one simply
      accept the shaman as a healer and neglect many patients whose
      diseases are not recognized, much less treated, by the shaman?
      Noting that it is not easy to eradicate shamanistic practices,
      the author suggests that a patient, after seeking medical
      assistance, should go to a shaman, who may be better equipped
      to help the individual get rid of tensions and overcome feel-
      ings of guilt and inferiority. Psychotherapists should learn
      as much as they can from native healers in order to understand
      the needs of their patients.

952.   Hippler, Arthur E. "Shamans, Curers, and Personality: Sug-
        gestions Toward a Theoretical Model." CULTURE-BOUND
        SYNDROMES, ETHNOPSYCHIATRY, AND ALTERNATE THERAPIES (item
        690), pp. 103-14.

        Reviews the conflicting explanations of shamanistic behav-
        ior and concludes that shamanism is a method of working out
        individual psychological problems, a role which permits the
        deviant some degree of comfort, a folk healing method which
        permits personal integration, and a mature, creative and
        integrative life-style. While the shaman can definitely be
        an unconscious faker, he is also shrewd, competent, conserva-
        tive, adaptable, and highly organized. The author proposes
        several hypotheses to explain shamanistic behavior. He finds
        the phenomenon of shamanism rather ambivalent. Shamanism
        could be a refuge for the seriously disturbed person or a
        role for the more mature, "normal" person.

953.   Jilek, Wolfgang, and Louis Jilek-Aall. "The Psychiatrist
        and His Shaman Colleague: Cross-Cultural Collaboration
        With Traditional Amerindian Therapists." JOURNAL OF
        OPERATIONAL PSYCHIATRY 9.2 (1978): 32-39.

        Points out that the difference between modern Western and
        traditional therapists cannot be reduced to one between
        scientific and non-scientific methods of healing. Cultural
        premises lie at the root of the difference: Western society
        sees disease as a natural phenomenon without any moral impli-
        cation, while traditional societies tend to ascribe disease
        to supernatural causes and link it with moral behavior. Both
        kinds of healing have a common function or purpose, namely,
        the relief of distress, the alleviation of anxiety, and the
        development of feelings of well-being and security. The
        authors examine and refute the hypothesis that shamanistic
        behavior is pathological. They found that contemporary
        shamanistic healing among the American Indian Salish tribe
        of the West Coast is effective, especially in some cases of
        depression.

954.   Johnson, Colleen Leahy. "Psychoanalysis, Shamanism and
        Cultural Phenomena." JOURNAL OF THE AMERICAN ACADEMY OF
        PSYCHOANALYSIS 9 (1981): 311-18.

        Comments on the widespread, if not universal, presence of
        shamanism and its curing methods and searches for similari-
        ties between primitive and modern forms of healing. Two
        anthropological approaches to shamanism, one that stresses
        its universal aspect, the other its cultural relativity, are
        explained. The characteristics of the shaman and the various
        functions he or she performs are identified. It is concluded
        that the shaman is an individual, marginal to society, who
        undergoes an altered state of consciousness to achieve the
        required status and to perform curing rituals. The role of
        shamans parallels that of the psychoanalyst in the West, in
        that the success they achieve depends on their thorough knowl-

edge of their respective cultures. Shamanism addresses the psychological issues directly and permits psychotic episodes to be treated without removing the individual from his or her social milieu. In some cases, it also molds mental disorders into socially accepted syndromes. The author sees a number of similarities between shamanism and large-scale social movements like evangelical religious sects and messianic and reform movements.

955. Kabar, Sudhir. SHAMANS, MYSTICS, AND DOCTORS: A PSYCHOLOGI-
CAL INQUIRY INTO INDIA AND ITS HEALING TRADITIONS. Boston:
Beacon Press, 1982. x, 306 pp.

Explores those traditions in India that aim at restoring what is broadly called "mental health" in the West. The material covered is divided into three traditions, the folk, the mystical, and the medical. Under folk traditions are included the rituals of shamans in village and tribal India. The path of the saints, Tantric healing, and the cult of Mataji (in Delhi) are dealt with as mystical traditions. The final section explores Indian medicine and psychiatry based on the Ayurveda. Contrasts between Indian and Western views are drawn up and the nature of psychotherapy itself is discussed. One of the major distinguishing features of the Indian tradition is the reliance on the supportive-suggestive character of the therapy employed.

956. Kim, Wosnik. "A Further Study of Korean Shamanism and Hypnosis." AMERICAN JOURNAL OF CLINICAL HYPNOSIS 11 (1969):
183-90.

Reviews aspects of shamanism, the major religion of Korea. The shaman uses forms of auto- and hetero-hypnosis during which the spirits are believed to communicate knowledge and advice. Case studies are presented to illustrate the central role shamanism plays in people's lives. It is theorized that the subconscious mind may be actively involved in the manifestations of the shaman.

957. Kim, Wosnik. "Korean Shamanism and Hypnosis." AMERICAN
JOURNAL OF CLINICAL HYPNOSIS 9 (1967): 191-97.

Maintains that shamans uses hypnosis to treat their patients. The shaman is said to be a nervous, high-strung, and very suggestible individual who suffers from a special mental disorder (shaman disease), and who is often an epileptic. This disease has certain features: loss of appetite, nervousness, mental instability, and avoidance of contact with others. Conversations with spirits, presumably hallucinatory, sometimes take place. The author describes two initiation ceremonies and gives a case history of a female shaman. A comparison is made between the shaman's and the hypnotist's methods.

958. Kleinman, Arthur. "Why Do Indigenous Practitioners Successfully Heal?" SOCIAL SCIENCE AND MEDICINE 13 B (1979): 7-26.

Relates follow-up studies of patients treated by a shaman
in Taiwan to earlier findings from a larger study of Chinese
folk medicine and therapy. Most of the subjects suffered
from chronic, non-life threatening, psychological disorders.
The author admits that some indigenous therapy may have
beneficial results.

959.   Klopper, Bruno, and L. Bryce Boyer. "Notes on the Personal-
        ity of a North American Indian Shaman: Rorschach Inter-
        pretation." JOURNAL OF PROJECTIVE TECHNIQUES 25 (1961):
        170-78.

Records the results of Rorschach tests administered to one
of the shamans of the Apache tribe of the Mescalero Indian
Reservation. After carefully analyzing the shaman's responses, the conclusion reached previously by one of the
authors (cf. items 919-22) is questioned. It is doubtful
whether the shaman "had strong oral and phallic fixations
and suffered from a hysterical personality disorder, with
attributes of an imposter" (p. 170). This subject was definitely not a schizophrenic and his responses are indicative of
cultural influences rather than personality disorders.

960.   Kraus, Robert F. "A Psychoanalytic Interpretation of Shaman-
        ism." PSYCHOANALYTIC REVIEW 59 (1972): 19-32.

Develops two themes: 1) a model of shamanistic behavior as
reflecting aspects of great individual psychological significance and cultural importance; and 2) a view of shamans as
having personality traits which make them fit their social
role. The psychology of the shaman is reviewed and the author
points out that the emphasis has shifted from a preoccupation
with the normality or insanity of the shaman to a search for
his or her personality characteristics. The shaman has been
found to differ little from non-shamans. He or she is sensitive to environmental clues and capable of regression to
primary modes of thinking or perceiving. This regression is
not pathological, but occurs rather in the service of the
ego. It is suggested that the shamanistic séance is a social
institution which expresses symbolically the anxieties and
strivings of a society.

961.   Langness, Lewis. "Hysterical Psychoses and Possessions."
        CULTURAL-BOUND SYNDROMES, ETHNOPSYCHIATRY AND ALTERNATE
        THERAPIES (item 690), pp. 56-67.

Compares and contrasts hysterical psychoses and possessions and points out that the latter, unlike the former, are
actively sought after by the taking of drugs, fasting, ritual
drumming, and other means. The author holds that hysterical
psychoses are abnormal in a society, even if they are culturally learned and transmitted. Possession and psychoses
are both episodes of brief duration, predictable in form,
and learned. They occur in a limited segment of the population and stem from conflicts in the ethnic unconscious. Both
experiences exploit and canalize existing neurotic leanings,
thus relieving mental stress.

962.   Lebra, William T. "Shaman-Client Interchange in Okinawa:
        Performative Stages in Shamanic Therapy." CULTURAL CON-
        CEPTS OF MENTAL HEALTH AND THERAPY (item 694), pp. 303-15.

        Describes the main features of Okinawan shamanism and the
        process of shamanistic diagnosis and cure in three distinct
        stages: 1) negotiating shamanic reality; 2) determining
        spiritual causes; and 3) prescribing remedial action. The
        author labels Okinawan therapy "putative psychotherapy,"
        because there is no hard scientific evidence that it is
        effective. It does, however, have some validity for those
        Japanese patients who believe in it. The social-physical
        setting for the client is generally congenial and cathartic
        and thus might be somewhat therapeutic.

963.   Lévi-Strauss, Claude. STRUCTURALISM. New York: Basic Books,
        1963. xvi, 410 pp.

        Contains two essays, "The Sorcerer and His Magic" (pp. 167-
        85), and "The Effectiveness of Symbols" (pp. 185-205), both
        of which discuss the shamans' relationship to psychoanalysis.
        The author approaches the phenomenon of shamanism from a uni-
        versalist position and claims that its study can point to
        universal structures of the human psyche. Shamans and sor-
        cerers are the precursors of psychoanalysts. The study of
        shamanism can elucidate some of the more obscure points of
        Freudian theory regarding myth and the unconscious.

964.   Lewis, I. M. ECSTATIC RELIGION: AN ANTHROPOLOGICAL STUDY OF
        SPIRIT POSSESSION AND SHAMANISM. Harmondsworth, UK: Pen-
        guin, 1971. 221 pp.

        Discusses spiritual experiences and ecstatic behavior in
        different religions, particularly the religions of primitive
        or non-literate societies. The author points out that the
        states of altered consciousness and dissociation, however
        bizarre and eccentric they might seem, are culturally norma-
        tive experiences. Various cults of possession are analyzed.
        Finally, the author discusses and rejects the common psychi-
        atric view that the spirit-possessed shaman is "a conflict-
        torn personality who should be classified either as seriously
        neurotic or even psychotic" (p. 179). Equally refuted is the
        view that shamans are self-healed neurotics or psychotics.
        The author insists that the shamans are symbols of indepen-
        dence and hope to their community to which they minister by
        therapeutic rituals. There is a good introductory bibliog-
        raphy of anthropological works on shamanism.

965.   Lewis, I. M. "Spirit Possession and Deprivation Cults." MAN
        1 (1966): 307-29.

        Surveys studies of spirit possession which have stressed
        the psychological aspects of the trance states and the pos-
        sible therapeutic value of shamanistic healing. The author

prefers a sociologically-oriented theory that looks at spirit
possession as a behavior "by means of which women and other
depressed categories exert mystical pressures upon their
superiors in circumstances of deprivation and frustration
when few other sanctions are available to them" (p. 318).

966.   Maduro, Renaldo J. "Hoodoo Possession in San Francisco:
        Notes on Therapeutic Aspects of Regression." ETHOS 3
        (1975): 425-47.

        Presents the important ethnographic aspects of "Hoodoo,"
        (the rough equivalent of Voodoo in San Francisco), and
        describes a case of a possessed woman, stressing the notion
        of cultural relativity in clinical diagnosis and treatment,
        and showing that black Voodoo possession states are not
        necessarily pathological. Possession trance is a culturally
        constituted healing situation in which therapeutic aspects
        of regression are enhanced. Personal and social integration
        are often the end result.

967.   McNiff, Shaun. "From Shamanism to Art Therapy." ART PSYCHO-
        THERAPY 6(1979): 155-61.

        Compares the therapeutic treatment of the shaman with art
        therapy. The enactment of the psychological conflict by the
        shaman is paralleled with psychodrama where problematic
        situations are dramatized. Similarly, the shaman's struggle
        to find meaning and order can be related to the artistic
        process. Both the shaman and the artist go to the heart of
        one's inner problem and lead the person not only to emotional
        catharsis, but also to a deepened insight into the nature of
        human emotions. Moreover, the personality and training of
        both the shaman and the artist directly affect the healing
        process. The implications of shamanistic rituals for art
        psychotherapy are discussed.

968.   Miller, Casper J. FAITH-HEALERS IN THE HIMALAYAS: AN INVES-
        TIGATION OF TRADITIONAL HEALERS AND THEIR FESTIVALS IN THE
        DOLAKHA DISTRICT OF NEPAL. Kathmandu: Center for Nepal and
        Asian Studies, Tribhuvan University, n.d. xv, 201 pp.

        Investigates the main functions of traditional healers
        (shamans), their organization, and the way ordinary people
        view them. The different roles of the healer, priest, and
        doctor are discussed. The healer's state during the ritual
        is not one of cataleptic trance or epilepsy. He has the
        important function of serving the sick by relieving them of
        tensions and curing many of their psychosomatic illnesses.
        Although the author discusses the possibility of training the
        local shamans in modern methods of diagnosis and treatment,
        he also maintains that the traditional methods of curing,
        which are functionally successful, should not be uprooted.

969.   Murphy, Jane M. "Psychotherapeutic Aspects of Shamanism on
        St. Lawrence Island, Alaska." MAGIC, FAITH, AND HEALING
        (item 679), pp. 53-83.

Reports on research on Eskimo Shamanism conducted by two
anthropologists and two psychiatrists. This study describes
and analyzes information about shamanistic practices in order
to assess their therapeutic value. The indigenous etiologies
of various diseases and the treatments given are presented.
Though psychiatric disorder was not a requirement for a person to become a shaman, a variety of psychiatric symptoms
did at times heighten an individual's exceptionality and lead
him or her to assume the role of shaman. The following are
among the many psychotherapeutic techniques used in shamanism:
diagnosis, group participation, possession, and the involvement of the patient.

970.   Naka, Koichi, Seijun Tocuhci, et al. "Yuta (Shaman) and Com-
        munity Mental Health in Okinawa." INTERNATIONAL JOURNAL
        OF SOCIAL PSYCHIATRY 31 (1985): 266-73.

Reports on the relationship between the indigenous healer
and the community's mental health activities. The Yuta
position as a healer or folk therapist is described and
his contributions to decreasing stress and curing mentally
ill people are attested to. The need to combine folk treatment with modern psychiatric methods is underscored.

971.   Noll, Richard. "Shamanism and Schizophrenia: A State Spe-
        cific Approach to the 'Schizophrenic Metaphor.'" AMERICAN
        ETHNOLOGIST 10 (1983): 443-59.

Maintains that the shamanic state of consciousness is a
type of altered state of consciousness and should not be
compared to schizophrenia. The shaman, unlike the schizoid,
enters voluntarily into the experience. He does not suffer
from delusions and he is inclined to have hallucinatory
visions, rather than auditions. The psychological state of
the shaman during trance does have a permanent affect on his
or her normal functioning.

972.   Nordland, Odd. "Shamanism and the 'Unreal.'" STUDIES IN
        SHAMANISM. Edited by Carl-Martin Edsman. Stockholm:
        Almquist and Wiksell, 1967, pp. 166-85.

Discusses shamanism from various psychological points of
view. It is stated that monotony, destruction of personal
identity, and isolation are among the basic features of
shamanism. The personality of the shaman, as it appears
upon the administration of the Rorschach test, is outlined.
The author compares the shaman to an artist who has hysterical traits. While in a trance, the shaman goes into a
regression which is, however, in the service of the ego.
The shaman is endowed with an intuitive creativity which can
solve problems.

973.   Ohnuki-Tierney, Emiko. "Shaman and Imu: Among Two Groups.
        Towards a Cross-Cultural Model of Interpretation." ETHOS
        8 (1980): 204-28.

Suggests possible ways of understanding the interrelationships between shamans and culture-bound syndromes and their
sociocultural correlates in the context of two Japanese
groups. A brief description is given of the two societies
and a presentation is made of the major features of shamanism
and "imu," the state of trance or spirit possession into
which a shaman often goes. The author sees possession as a
culturally sanctioned mechanism with a definite therapeutic
function--to resolve some psychological difficulties through
the experience. Shamanism is a complex phenomenon and the
shaman may play several roles, that of a healer, religious
specialist, covert politician, or even theatrical performer.
It is, thus, not surprising that the interpretation of the
shaman's behavior has varied widely, from that of a psychotic
to that of a perfectly normal human being.

974.   Opler. M. E.   "Some Points of Comparison Between the Treat-
       ment of Functional Disorders by Apache Indians and Modern
       Psychiatric Practice." AMERICAN JOURNAL OF PSYCHIATRY 92
       (1936): 1371-87.

       Attempts to see the Apache shaman from a native point of
       view in order to determine the possible therapeutic functions
       of their treatments. It is maintained that the shaman's
       treatment of chronic pathology is worthless, but has some
       measure of success in cases of functional and mental problems.
       A description of the shamanistic ceremony is given. It is
       pointed out that while absolute confidence in the shaman is
       necessary, some confidence in the Western psychiatrist is
       needed to help the healing process. And that while both the
       shaman and the Western psychiatrist may make use of sugges-
       tion in therapy, the former treats only the symptoms. Those
       patients who go to the shaman run the risk of developing too
       great a dependence on him or her.

975.   Parin, Paul, and Goldy Parin-Matthey. "The Prophet and the
       Psychiatrist." JOURNAL OF PSYCHOLOGICAL ANTHROPOLOGY 3
       (1980): 87-117.

       Describes an interview with a messianic healer, Edjro Josué,
       of the Ivory Coast Republic, and examines the dynamic forces
       he projected and the effects he had on those he healed or
       converted. A short history of messianic movements in the
       Ivory Coast is given and some biographical data on Josué is
       provided. Two psychiatric interviews with this prophet are
       outlined and evaluated. Although his character tends to be
       phallic-narcissistic in structure, his ego functions well and
       there are no schizophrenic, hysterical, or other pathological
       traits. Prophethood is a type of conflict-resolution, a con-
       version which restores the person's health and peace of mind.
       The results of the prophet's healing activities were found to
       be mixed. Some clients were led to a healthier life, some to
       tragic outcomes.

976.   Peters, Larry G. ECSTASY AND HEALING IN NEPAL: AN ETHNO-
       PSYCHIATRIC STUDY OF TAMANG SHAMANISM. Malibu, CA: Undena
       Publications, 1981. ix, 179 pp.

Interprets the role of the shaman in this Nepalese tribe as analogous to the psychotherapist's role in the contemporary Western world. The author shows how the shamans relieve the mental tensions of their clients and restore equilibrium in disturbed interpersonal relationships. The training of shamans and psychotherapists is compared, and didactic and practical similarities are noted. This volume covers several topics, including cultural background, religious specialists, indigenous medical treatments, and the shaman's trance. In a chapter of "Psychotherapy in Tamang Society" (pp. 115-42), the author examines the cultural context of various physical symptoms, spirit possession, and soul loss, and outlines the ritual performances and techniques used by the shaman. It is maintained that suggestion, faith, catharsis, and group support are sufficient for mastery over most types of psychoneuroses.

977.   Peters, Larry G. "An Experiential Study of Nepalese Shamanism." JOURNAL OF TRANSPERSONAL PSYCHOLOGY 13 (1981): 1-26.

Describes the author's attempt to understand shamanism by adopting a participatory role which included taking a guru and being led to a shamanistic experience. A short description is given of Tamang shamanism in its sociocultural context and the initiation steps and the relationship with one's guru are described in some detail. Complete initiation includes mastery of altered states of consciousness, which the Tamang call spirit possession and soul journey. The common interpretation that these are pathological conditions is rejected. The author thinks that initiation into Tamang shamanism is a therapeutic system and that the altered states of consciousness are used in ritual context in the service of the community.

978.   Peters, Larry G. "Psychotherapy in Tamang Shamanism." ETHOS 6 (1978): 63-91.

Investigates the cultural context of the healing rituals among the Tamang people of Nepal and examines the techniques used by the shaman, comparing them with Western psychotherapeutic methods. Tamang healing provides a common vocabulary by which to name illnesses, a catharsis for the sick, and a well-defined set of rules and procedures. The psychotherapeutic effectiveness of symbolic communication is highlighted by the author. The healing ritual transforms the patient's symptoms and behavior into socially useful channels and reorganizes the emotions released by the traumatic experience. Shamanism is a mechanism for dealing with conflict and stress but, unlike Western psychotherapy, does not go to the root of the problem and cannot cure the patient permanently.

979.   Porterfield, Amanda. "Native American Shamanism and the American Mind-Cure Movement: A Comparative Study of Religious Healing." HORIZONS 11 (1984): 276-89.

Outlines the basic patterns of American Indian Shamanism
and compares them to the healing activities of mind-cure
movements in the second half of the nineteenth century, with
special attention given to the work of Phineas Quimby and
the activities of Mary Baker Eddy, who founded Christian
Science. Although there are philosophical and practical
differences between the two movements, both are seen as
"responses to perceived mysteries enveloping human life."
Shamans and mind-cure practitioners are able to bring about
recovery of the patient by invoking symbols of well-being.

980.   Posinsky, S. H. "Yoruk Shamanism." PSYCHIATRIC QUARTERLY
        39 (1965): 227-43.

Provides an ethnographic account of the training and practice of shamans, usually women, in this North American Indian
tribe. The author thinks that the shaman shows acute psychological and sociological insight in her treatment of various
forms of psychoses, neuroses, and psychosomatic ailments, and
in her decisions to limit child therapy to behavioral disorders. Shamanistic ritual is used to exorcise guilt and to
remove the sick person's ambivalence.

981.   Prince, Raymond, editor. "Shamans and Endorphins." ETHOS
        10 (1982): 299-423.

Contains papers presented at a conference held in Montreal
in October, 1981. The possibility was discussed that, since
shamanistic healing produced analgesia, euphoria, altered
states of consciousness, amnesia, and reduced anxiety, it
might have the therapeutic power to trigger or enhance the
mobilization of morphine- and valium-like substances in the
brain. The biological aspects of shamanic trances "are
intended to supplement rather than replace other highly
significant psychological and sociological dimensions" of
shamanism (pp. 419-20). This volume is indicative of one
trend in psychiatry, to explain human behavior as a product
of chemical reactions.

982.   Rappaport, Herbert. "The Tenacity of Folk Psychotherapy: A
        Functional Interpretation." SOCIAL PSYCHIATRY 12 (1977):
        127-32.

Examines over 30 Tanzanian shamans in order to find out
why their services are still requested. The differences
between the training of folk and Western therapists, and
between their techniques and underlying conceptual schemes,
are briefly outlined. The folk system of psychotherapy is
seen as a dynamic and flourishing form of treating psychosomatic disorders in East Africa, where the personalized style
of the shaman is preferred to the rather detached Western
approach. The author favors the integration of both
approaches.

983.   Rappaport, Herbert, and Preston L. Dent. "An Analysis of
        Contemporary East African Folk Psychotherapy." BRITISH
        JOURNAL OF MEDICAL PSYCHOLOGY 52 (1979): 49-54.

Studies 31 Tanzanian shamans with the goal of identifying
the characteristics of folk psychotherapy which could account
for its tenacity. Western and African therapies are compared
and contrasted. The former lays more stress on the technique
itself, while the latter relies largely on the charisma and
mysticism of the therapist and regards the search for meaning
to be central to the curing process. The authors consider
Western faith healers, who practice within diverse ethnic
and religious groups, as the counterpart of the medicine men.
They favor the cooperation between Western folk healers and
psychiatrists.

984. Rogers, Spencer L. THE SHAMAN'S HEALING WAY. Ramona, CA:
     Acoma Books, 1976. 40 pp.

Provides an account of primitive theories of disease and
of shamanism as a profession. The techniques used by the
shaman--like instructing his or her patients, eliciting their
confession, easing their fears, and arousing their emotions
to relieve states of depression--are successful psychotherapeutic treatments.

985. Rogers, Spencer L., and Lorraine Evernham. "Shamanistic
     Healing Among the Diegueno Indians of Southern California."
     THE ANTHROPOLOGY OF MEDICINE (item 723), pp. 103-18.

Gives an overview of shamanism in Diegueno cosmology, and
of the native theory of illness. The training of the shaman
and his healing techniques, like dream interpretation, are
described. Traditional beliefs and practices are compared
with more recent innovations. The work of the shaman in
treating both physical and mental illness and his role as
both religious and medical resource person have both waned
with the presence of doctors and therapists trained in Western techniques. These latter specialists, however, have not
been able to assist in establishing harmony within the Indian
community. The authors thinks that some traditional healing
practices could be incorporated in the modern mental health
programs.

986. Róheim, Géza. "Hungarian Shamanism." PSYCHOANALYSIS AND THE
     SOCIAL SCIENCES. Edited by Géza Róheim. New York: Inter-
     national Universities Press, 1951. Vol. 3, pp. 131-70.

Offers an explanation of the Hungarian male sorcerer and
healer with regard to both his ethnic origin and his latent
psychological makeup. Many of the features of the Hungarian
folk healer are representative of Siberian shamanism. The
author interprets the data from a psychoanalytic point of
view and tends to see in the behavior of the Hungarian shaman
a regression from the genital to the oral level.

987. Rosen, David M. "The Pursuit of One's Own Healing." AMERI-
     CAN JOURNAL OF PSYCHOANALYSIS 37 (1977): 37-41.

Believes that the West has much to learn from studying the
historical roots of psychiatry and observing parallels between

shamanism and modern psychiatry. Shamans differ from medicine
men in that they can heal themselves and are also able to cure
psychological disorders. Like psychiatrists, shamans have to
confront their own personal conflicts. The author thinks
that, while only the shaman undergoes a symbolic death and
rebirth ritual, both psychiatrist and shaman undergo a change
of role during their training. Like the shaman, the psychiatrist must allow the negative part of his or her ego to die
and to be reborn spiritually.

988.   Seltzer, Allan. "Psychodynamics of Spirit Possession Among
       the Inuit." CANADIAN JOURNAL OF PSYCHIATRY 28 (1983):
       52-56.

       Presents three cases to illustrate the psychodynamics of
       spirit possession or intrusion among an Eskimo tribe. The
       author explains the phenomenon of spirit possession with
       reference to the cultural change from a traditional society,
       where group ego was dominant, to modern society, which lays
       great stress on the individual ego and superego. In this
       transition stage, the Eskimos are exposed to the stress of
       social fragmentation and, consequently, to a regressive
       belief that supernatural forces can ward off the anxiety
       which comes with anomic individualism. There are hints that
       the belief that ancestral spirits are those who actually
       possess the individual has some erotic implications.

989.   Silverman, Julian. "Shamans and Acute Schizophrenia."
       AMERICAN ANTHROPOLOGIST 69 (1967): 21-31.

       Presents an analysis of the behavior of the shaman in
       primitive cultures and of certain schizophrenics in Western
       society. The theory is advanced that pathological and sha-
       manistic types of behavior and cognition are the result of a
       specific ordering of psychological events, and the essential
       difference between the two types is the degree of cultural
       acceptance and emotional support of the individual's resolu-
       tion of a life crisis. Five stages leading to a psychotic
       and shamanistic resolution are explained. It is pointed out
       that in Western culture there are no referential guides for
       understanding the experience, and thus the schizoid, unlike
       the shaman, undergoes an intensification of suffering.

990.   Spencer, Dorothy M. "The Recruitment of Shamans Among the
       Mundas." HISTORY OF RELIGIONS 10 (1970): 1-31.

       Gives a somewhat detailed account of the special features
       of shamanism among the Mundas, a tribal people in Bihar,
       India. The steps leading to the initiation are described
       and the conscious and unconscious factors which lead a
       person to choose to become a shaman are considered. The
       author thinks that emotional disorders are prevalent among
       those young boys who become pupils of established shamans,
       but that most shamans do not have a history of severe emo-

tional disorder. Shamanism can lead a person to rebuild and maintain self-esteem, which is deemed necessary to achieve one's goals in life.

991.   Torrey, E. Fuller. "Spiritualists and Shamans as Psycho-
        therapists: An Account of Original Anthropological Sin."
        RELIGIOUS MOVEMENTS IN CONTEMPORARY AMERICA (item 1360),
        pp. 330-37.

        Stresses the assumption that psychiatrists have a lot to
        learn from spiritualists and shamans who have been wrongfully
        categorized as mentally ill. The origin of this mistake is
        traced to the colonial attitudes of the eighteenth and nine-
        teenth centuries, attitudes which were often strengthened by
        anthropological literature. More recent anthropological
        studies tend to show that shamans and spiritualists are, as
        a rule, psychologically healthy persons and that most folk
        therapists in other cultures are unusually talented people
        who are emotionally stable and mature. The following common
        factors between Western therapists and shamans are noted:
        the importance of the personal qualities of the therapist;
        the various elements used to influence the patient's expecta-
        tions; and the employment of the same spectrum of healing
        techniques.

992.   Tseng, Wen-Shing. "Psychiatric Study of Shamanism in Taiwan."
        ARCHIVES OF GENERAL PSYCHIATRY 26 (1972): 561-65.

        Describes the general picture of shamanism in Taiwan and
        analyzes two cases, discussing shamanism both from psycho-
        logical and sociocultural points of view. Shamanism is
        similar to the state of hysterical dissociation because they
        both include a personality change, both have a tendency to
        claim amnesia, and both exhibit a premorbid personality which
        is theatrical, suggestive, immature, and suspicious. They
        differ in that the shamans, unlike hysterical patients, can
        control their trance conditions and, therefore, cannot be
        considered psychotic patients when in the state of possession.
        Shamans also satisfy their patients' need for explanations of
        life's misfortunes and for advice in coping with disaster.

993.   Warner, Richard. "Deception in Shamanism and Psychiatry."
        TRANSNATIONAL MENTAL HEALTH RESEARCH NEWSLETTER 18.3 (1976):
        2-12.

        Relates the author's treatment by a Huichol Indian medicine
        man of West-Central Mexico and discusses the use of deception
        and self-deception by primitive healers and psychiatrists.
        Tricks used at a healing ceremony are meant to impress people
        with the shaman's power. They have the value of reinforcing
        the patient's and community's belief and of contributing to
        the force of suggestion and the patient's expectation. Such
        tricks are compared to the use of placebos in the history of
        medicine. Shamans are sincere practitioners in spite of
        their intentional deception of their patients.

994.   Weakland, John H. "Shamans, Schizophrenia, and Scientific
        Unity." AMERICAN ANTHROPOLOGIST 70 (1968): 356.

        Briefly criticizes Silverman's essay (item 989) for not
        relating shamanism and schizophrenia properly, especially
        for not noting the fact that, while shamanism fits into its
        cultural context, the latter does not. It is argued that
        there are many studies which see the shaman as an essential
        part of his culture.

995.   Wijesinghe, C. P., S. A. W. Dissanayake, and N. Mendis.
        "Shamans, Schizophrenia, and Scientific Unity." AMERICAN
        ANTHROPOLOGIST 79 (1968): 356.

        Refutes Silverman's comparison between shamans and schizo-
        phrenics (see item 989). It is argued that while shamans
        are well-adapted to their social context, schizophrenics are
        not. Anthropological studies have consistently shown that
        shamans fit into their respective cultures and cannot, there-
        fore, be judged to be social and/or psychological deviants.

996.   Winiarz, W., and J. Wielawski. "Imu: A Psychoneurosis
        Occurring Among the Ainu." PSYCHOANALYTIC REVIEW 23 (1936):
        181-86.

        Discusses a (shamanic) possession state among this aborig-
        inal Japanese tribe, and concludes that it is a psychopatho-
        logical state which manifests itself in sporadic, trance-like
        attacks. Although the Ainu regard the "imu" condition as a
        special state of mystical and religious significance, the
        author insists that it "is a primitive form of reaction to
        fear, manifested by impulsive actions, by aggressiveness, by
        flight, or by other forms approaching to the cataleptic
        condition" (p. 186).

CHAPTER IV

CURRENT PSYCHOLOGICAL AND PSYCHIATRIC STUDIES ON THE NEW CULTS

The Jonestown suicide tragedy in 1978 is the major event in the history of contemporary cult experience which sealed the negative attitude towards involvement in cultism both in the public view and in some professional quarters. But the People's Temple case did not cast doubt solely on the nature and activity of "extremist" cults. It also created apprehension about many small traditional Christian churches and, further, raised once again the whole issue of the relationship between some form of religious beliefs and practices and mental health. The People's Temple had its legitimate beginning in a well-established Christian denomination. And although one can maintain that it is an exceptional instance of a religious group which degenerated into a closed society ruled by a tyrant, the question still remains whether other new religious groups run the risk of following the same path to destruction.

A. GENERAL STUDIES ON THE PSYCHOLOGY OF RELIGION AND ON RELIGION
AND MENTAL HEALTH

The issue of religion and mental health can be examined from two different aspects. The first is the general question of whether religion contributes to a person's mental and/or psychological well-being or whether it is an obstacle to intellectual and psychological growth. The second deals more specifically with the thorny issue of religious experience, and the mental health of those who claim to have had such an experience. It is important to note in this context that the emphasis on religious experience is not a unique cultic feature. It is found also in the mainline Christian churches and in the major religious traditions of the world.

Some observers (e.g., Pattison, item 1100) have observed that the relationship between religion and psychiatry has improved greatly since the early 1960s, and that cooperation between the two is being sought by both sides. This opinion, however, may be a somewhat optimistic overstatement. The tendency to look at religion as a obstacle to human psychological growth, and at deep religious experi-ence and commitment as an expression of mental and psychological illness, is still rampant in the counseling disciplines. One can distinguish three major trends in the relationship between religion and psychiatry.

The first is a continuation of the Freudian position which links
religion with mental illness. In this view, religiosity is judged
to be an index of emotional immaturity and psychological imbalance.
The less religious a person is, the healthier one is bound to be.
Several features of unhealthy religion are the topic of research
and discussion. Authoritarianism, ethnocentrism, dogmaticism, weak
ego-strength, and irrationality are often judged to be necessary
ingredients of any religion. Since all these traits tend to weaken
human beings both intellectually and emotionally, religion must be
regarded as a hindrance to mental health. Religion is, therefore,
a cause of illness; it creates serious problems and obstacles in an
individual's effort to adapt to changing cultural and environmental
situations. Studies of religious founders, Old Testament figures,
and religious leaders are adduced to show how religion fosters abnormal behavior. Messianic figures have frequently been considered
to be excellent examples of psychotic behavior. And those people
who so readily commit themselves to the teachings and life-styles
of these self-proclaimed saviors are said to suffer from hysterical
and inadequate personalities.

A second view of the relationship between religion and mental
health is defended by many psychologists and counselors, who are
themselves committed to a religious tradition. Religion and faith,
rather than being a cause of mental illness, have therapeutic value.
Deep commitment to a belief system cures emotional stress and illness, relieves guilt feelings, gives people a sense of worth, and
helps them cope with fears and anxieties. Religion offers emotional
support and is instrumental in altering maladaptive behavior. Religious rituals are therapeutic and can be compared to psychotherapy.
Prayer is not a flight from reality, but, on the contrary, a positive
way of handling and reducing some fundamental human anxieties.

A third position is endorsed mainly by humanitarian and transpersonal psychologists. While not explicitly religious in its
orientation, this view admits that religion caters to higher,
characteristically human aspirations and noble values, which can
lead to self-fulfillment and contribute to human welfare. There
are both healthy and unhealthy forms of religious belief and practice. A religion is healthy if it is comprehensive, open-ended,
and tolerant of ambiguity. Extreme forms of dogmatism, unyielding
authoritarianism, and intolerance are considered to be unhealthy
expressions of religion. Religion can, therefore, have a normal
integrative function in an individual's life, but it can also be a
neurotic defense mechanism.

The evaluation of religious and mystical experience, which has
been the hallmark of new religious movements, parallels the triple
division described above. The Freudian legacy leaves no doubt about
the illusory character of this claimed experience of the holy. The
qualities ascribed to it--loss of self, hallucination, psychotic
experience of time, and sense of unreality--are definite indices
of mental illness. Mysticism is often antirational and the mystic's
withdrawal from the world is a sign of pathology. The mystical experience is still compared to that of psychotics and/or neurotics.
Its expressive forms, like glossolalia, are signs of conflict or

mental disturbance. It is related to aggression, that is, it can
be explained as a reaction to one's own inner violence. Some psychiatrists have argued that mystical or religious experience is a
chemical or electrical imbalance in the brain that, like epilepsy,
can be controlled by medication.

The opposite view would insist on the beneficial results of religious and mystical experiences. The functional view that they are
therapeutic, creating calmness and relief from fear and anxiety, is
commonly held among religious psychologists. Some more cautious
scholars observe that, even though mysticism may not always be a
sign of a healthy life-style, it can still serve as a useful tool
to prevent suicide. Whether it is authentic or not and whether it
represents a flight from reality or an encounter with the holy, it
has potentially adaptive qualities.

Another area of investigation has arisen in connection with religious and mystical experience, namely, the study of altered states
of consciousness. Though the current psychiatric view is that a
person who cultivates, or goes spontaneously into, such states is
probably mentally ill, many psychologists are reassessing the evidence. A common view seems to be emerging that the experience of
such unusual human states of awareness can have either beneficial
or harmful results. Their healing potential has been stressed
particularly by Deikman (item 1024).

The different views described above are important because they
affect the therapeutic treatment in psychiatric situations. Thus,
while psychoanalysis and other forms of traditional therapy disregard the religious dimension and might indirectly lead the patients
to grow out of their religious involvement, religious and more human-
istically-inclined therapists tend to use the patient's religion as
part of the treatment. The need to respect and take into account
the subject's beliefs and values is given priority, no matter what
the therapist's own stand might be.

There are a number of issues which the discussions on religion
and mental health have not solved. The first deals with the criteria for judging whether a religion is healthy or not. There seems
to be some agreement that not all religious beliefs and actions
lead to a psychologically balanced life, and that some individuals
have expressed their religious commitment in a highly neurotic and/or
psychotic manner. The boundaries between religious pathology and
sanity are, however, far from clear. It is rather difficult, for
example, to decide when dogmaticism and ethnocentricity are pathological. For all religions advance their views as being true and
reject opposing opinions as mistaken or heretical. It is precisely
on this certainty of truth that the religious appeal, in part at
least, relies. How does one judge when a religious dogma has reached
a state of pathology? If creating a community with a distinct mission is essential to religious life, then some degree of ethnocentrism is likely to be present. How and where one draws the line
that separates an ethnocentrism which is a normal feature of group
identity, and an ethnocentrism which is characterized by pathological exclusivism, remains debatable.

The second problem revolves around the troublesome question of the nature of religious and mystical experience. It is admitted by all that such experience may be illusory. It is, however, not easy to draw up universally-accepted criteria to evaluate its genuineness. It is doubtful whether such a task belongs to the psychologist or psychiatrist. Even though some specific differences between the behavior of the mystic and that of the psychotic or neurotic are obvious, one still has to contend with the similarities between the two. Mystics, like psychotic patients, tend to withdraw from social life. But there are different kinds and levels of withdrawal and not all need be judged psychotic. The monk, who physically lives apart from the mainstream of social life and who abstains from becoming involved in social and political activism, may still be a rationally and emotionally healthy person.

These questions concerning religious experience and mental health can be discussed in the context of cultism. The claim to a unique and transforming religious experience, as well as the apparent attractiveness of a shared ideology and community life, are major features of the new religious movements. The general literature annotated in this section is judged to be important because it provides the background to the debate on the cults, and because it demonstrates that some major psychological issues are relevant to both traditional churches and new religious groups. It is not surprising to discover that some of the attacks against the cults are equally an attack against religion, or to find that, on some issues at least, several of the major religious organizations have sided with the cults.

997.   Aldworth, Thomas. SHAPING A HEALTHY PERSONALITY ESPECIALLY
        IF YOU ARE A CATHOLIC. Chicago: Thomas More Society,
        1985. 132 pp.

        Attempts to outline the features of a healthy religion.
        Writing from a Catholic perspective, the author states that
        Catholicism can help a person develop one's humanity, but it
        can also retard such development. Many themes are explored,
        including images of God, sin, the afterlife, and prayer. A
        healthy religion sets a person free, possesses a sense of
        humor, leads a person to involvement in the needs of others,
        helps the individual person develop a sense of responsibility,
        increases one's self-esteem, and has good intellectual roots.

998.   Bache, Christopher M. "A Reappraisal of Teresa of Avila's
        Supposed Hysteria." JOURNAL OF RELIGION AND HEALTH 24
        (1985): 300-15.

        Discusses Teresa of Avila's severe seizures which seem so
        characteristic of her mystical experiences that she has been
        called the "patron saint of hysterics." The author first
        gives a critical review of those theories which identify her
        experiences with hysteria. He then describes her physical
        and psychological symptoms. Next, he turns to an account of

perinatal symptomatology in LSD therapy. Finally, he compares Teresa's experiences with those produced by LSD subjects under medical control. He concludes that her experiences were not hysterical, emotional outbursts, but rather perinatal symptoms, that is, emotional and physical expressions of experiences of birth, physical pain, disease, aging, dying, and death. Perinatal symptoms are quite natural and occur in subjects who are heading toward a transcendental state of consciousness. They are progressive, rather than regressive. They reflect no pathology, but rather indicate the passage to a much deeper spiritual awareness.

999.   Batson, C. Daniel, and W. Larry Ventis. THE RELIGIOUS EXPERI-
       ENCE: A SOCIAL-PSYCHOLOGICAL PERSPECTIVE. New York: Oxford
       University Press, 1982. vii, 356 pp.

       Discusses the nature and consequences of religious experi-
       ence. Two chapters in particular are relevant to the study
       of the cults, one dealing with the issue of whether religion
       is freeing or enslaving, the other on the relationship be-
       tween religion and mental health. The authors think that
       conversion to the new movements involves nothing more than a
       powerful use of social influence. Adherence to cultic belief
       and practice is explained not by a pathological model, but by
       two rather normal human needs: 1) to make sense of one's life,
       and 2) to maintain an organized system of beliefs and values.
       These can, however, lead to an escalating involvement which
       produced the disaster at the People's Temple in Guyana.

1000. Beit-Hallahmi, Benjamin. "Religious Ideas and Psychiatric
       Disorders." INTERNATIONAL JOURNAL OF SOCIAL PSYCHIATRY 23
       (1977): 26-30.

       Discusses two major issues, namely, whether religious ideas
       occur in mental patients and whether intense religious
       experiences lead to mental disorder. The author holds that
       religious ideas are more likely to be connected with cases
       of affective disorders and of paranoid schizophrenia. Reli-
       gious experience, conversion, and glossolalia are linked with
       mental disorders. The need to take into account sociocultural
       factors is emphasized.

1001. Beit-Hallahmi, Benjamin. "Encountering Orthodox Religion in
       Psychotherapy." PSYCHOTHERAPY: THEORY, RESEARCH, AND PRAC-
       TICE 12 (1975): 357-59.

       Discusses the difficulties in counseling religious patients
       and provides case examples to illustrate ways of handling
       religious beliefs and practices in clinical contexts. The
       need to consider the clients' religiosity in both their
       religious and personal milieus is stressed. The author main-
       tains that those psychiatrists who respect their clients'
       belief systems will be more effective in the treatment
       prescribed.

1002.   Beit-Hallahmi, Benjamin, editor. RESEARCH IN RELIGIOUS BEHAV-
        IOR: SELECTED READINGS. Monterey, CA: Brooks/Cole, 1973.
        x, 414 pp.

        Contains selected essays on religious socialization, reli-
        gious beliefs, values and attitudes, religious belief and
        personal adjustment, intense religious experience, and reli-
        gious and political behavior. These articles were written
        long before the current debate on cultism became a debated
        issue in psychiatry.

        Contains items 101, 266, 465, 532.

1003.   Bergin, Allen E. "Religiosity and Mental Health: A Critical
        Reevaluation and Meta-Analysis." PROFESSIONAL PSYCHOLOGY:
        RESEARCH AND PRACTICE 14 (1983): 170-84.

        Rebuts the common psychological view that religiosity is
        antithetical to emotional health and rationality (See items
        1031, 1145). The values and ideological principles of pro-
        fessional psychology often exclude spiritual phenomena, with
        the result that the significance of religion in people's
        lives is either underestimated or else conceived of as a
        negative force. Many of the devices used to measure authori-
        tarianism, ethnocentrism, dogmatism, ego strength, and
        irrationality reflect this bias. The author overviews the
        ambiguities in field studies and elaborates on the difficulty
        in dividing religiosity into healthy and unhealthy types. He
        recommends consideration of the client's religious feeling,
        collaboration with religious leaders, and a broadening of
        horizons to include the spiritual perspective in clinical
        practice.

1004.   Bergin, Allen E. "Psychotherapy and Religious Values."
        JOURNAL OF CONSULTING AND CLINICAL PSYCHOLOGY 48 (1980):
        95-105.

        Reflects on the alienation of therapeutic psychology from
        religious values and proposes various ways in which religion
        could be included more systematically in psychological theory,
        research, and counseling. Theistic and clinical humanistic
        values are compared and contrasted, and the author thinks
        that there is no reason why religious values cannot be incor-
        porated into clinical practice. The author presents a number
        of hypotheses on the positive impact of religious beliefs
        and practices on psychological well-being.

1005.   Bergin, Allen E. "Religious and Humanistic Values: A Reply
        to Ellis and Walls." JOURNAL OF CONSULTING AND CLINICAL
        PSYCHOLOGY 48 (1980): 642-45.

        Responds to the critical review (items 1031, 1145) of his
        original article (item 1004), which stressed the need to take
        religious beliefs seriously in constructing theories of per-
        sonality and in treating patients. The issues involved in

distinguishing between benevolent and detrimental religious
aspects are discussed. The author maintains that religious
belief should not be construed as a sign of emotional disturbance and that religious values are not less rational than
other kinds of values.

1006. Bishop, John G. "Psychological Insights in St. Paul's Mysticism." THEOLOGY 78 (1975): 318-24.

Shows how Paul's mysticism differs widely from that found
in the main religious traditions since he does not seek, by
ascetical practices, any specific transcendental experiences,
and he remains essentially a man of action. Some psychological aspects in Paul's mysticism are compared to Jung's use
of reconciling symbols. Non-Christians are bound to interpret
Paul's experiences as obsessive and delusory. But given their
monotheistic and Christocentric contexts, the author argues,
they could be therapeutic.

1007. Blackburn, Lawrence H. "Spiritual Healing." JOURNAL OF
RELIGION AND HEALTH 15 (1976): 34-37.

Argues that spiritual healing, which can be defined as
"God's loving action in all and every part of our nature,"
is important to doctors because it cures emotional stress and
illness.

1008. Bonhoffer, Thomas. "Christianity and Fear Revisited." JOUR-
NAL OF RELIGION AND HEALTH 13 (1974): 239-50

A somewhat critical review of Pfister's book (item 297),
which discusses the place of fear in the Christian faith.
The author, however, seems to agree with Pfister's analysis
of anxiety as "a crack within the narcissistic fundamental
texture of our soul" (p. 250).

1009. Booth, Howard J. "Pioneering Literature in the Psychology
of Religion: A Reminder." JOURNAL OF PSYCHOLOGY AND THEOL-
OGY 6 (1978): 46-53.

Examines some of the major examples of psychological
studies on religion made in the first two decades of the
twentieth century. Included in this survey are the works
of G. Stanley Hall, Edwin Starbach, George Coe, William
James, James Pratt, Edward Ames, and James Leuba.

1010. Buckley, Peter. "Mystical Experience and Schizophrenia."
SCHIZOPHRENIA BULLETIN 7 (1981): 516-21.

Compares autobiographical accounts of mystical experience
and schizophrenia. The following similarities are observed:
a sense of noesis, a heightening of perception, feelings of
communion with the divine, exultation, loss of self-object
boundaries, and distortion of time. Disruption of thought is

not found in mystical experience which, unlike schizophrenia,
is self-limited and brief. Examples are given from Christian
mystics, members of cults, and Alcoholics Anonymous.

1011. Bulka, Reuven P., editor. MYSTICS AND MEDICS: A COMPARISON
       OF MYSTICAL AND PSYCHOTHERAPEUTIC ENCOUNTERS. New York:
       Human Sciences Press, 1979. 120 pp.

       Concerns itself with the mystical tradition and some of its
       similarities to modern clinical encounters. The essays, which
       had been published in an issue of the JOURNAL OF PSYCHOLOGY
       AND JUDAISM, deal with the Jewish tradition, particularly
       with Hasidism. In a concluding article, the editor compares
       Hasidism with psychology and maintains that Frankl's logo-
       therapy and Hasidic teachings have much in common. Both
       have similar ideas about free will, and the nature of love
       and human striving; both acknowledge the need for value
       orientation and meaning; and both share similar attitudes
       towards despair, suffering, death, work, and material gain.
       They both aim at reforming distorted thinking.

       Contains items 1796, 1809.

1012. Byrnes, Joseph F. THE PSYCHOLOGY OF RELIGION. New York:
       Free Press, 1984. xi, 308 pp.

       Summarizes the main writings in the psychology of religion
       in four major areas: 1) the psychology of religious experi-
       ence, including conversion; 2) religion within the context
       of personality; 3) religious development through social
       interaction; and 4) religion in psychological research and
       theory. Several studies on the new religious movements are
       included. A number of clinical approaches (conflict, ful-
       fillment, conditioning, and group therapy) for patients with
       religious problems are outlined with examples, and a brief
       evaluation of their usefulness is given.

1013. Carbine, Michael F. "Religion, Psychology, and Mental Health:
       The Problems of Partnership." JOURNAL OF RELIGION AND
       HEALTH 19 (1980): 40-47.

       Considers religion and psychology as therapeutic systems
       in that they both offer values, guidelines, alleviating
       devices, and normative explanations for the unknown factors
       of everyday life. The rise of "pop psychology" with its
       frequent "religious therapeutic matrix" is discussed, to-
       gether with its assumptions and goals. Religion, the author
       maintains, plays an important role in psychological well-
       being. It can bring about a renewed sense of community and
       family and a reevaluation of such psychodynamic categories as
       sin, guilt, anxiety, and conflict.

1014. Carroll, Michael P. "Visions of the Virgin Mary: The Ef-
       fect of Family Structures on Marian Apparitions." JOURNAL
       FOR THE SCIENTIFIC STUDY OF RELIGION 22 (1983): 205-21.

Studies well-documented Marian apparitions which occurred
between 1100-1896. The author states that these apparitions
are as likely to occur to males as to females, that those who
have them are usually adult individuals who have no sexual
partners, and that Italy has a disproportionate percentage of
seers. A Freudian interpretation is given. Marian apparitions are produced by the intensification of certain aspects
of the oedipal process. Males and females find in these
visions an ideal way of sublimating their sexual desires for
their mothers and fathers, respectively.

1015. Charry, Dana. "The High Priest, the Day of Atonement, and the
      Preparation for Psychotherapy." JOURNAL OF PASTORAL CARE
      36 (1982): 87-93.

      Examines four aspects of the Jewish High priest's prepara-
      tion for the Day of Atonement, namely, separation, humility,
      awesome expectation, and self-examination. The author thinks
      that the psychotherapist goes through a similar preparation
      for his therapy sessions. Psychotherapy and the Day of
      Atonement share similar aims of purification from sin and
      restoration of harmony with God.

1016. Clark, John H. A MAP OF MENTAL STATES. London: Routledge
      and Kegan Paul, 1983. xxiii, 242 pp.

      Describes the whole range of mental states, including mys-
      ticism. Mystical literature is examined and various mystical
      experiences are analyzed. Different methods of reaching the
      mystical state, such as meditation, are presented and the
      Yoga system of Pantajali is outlined. Various theories of
      mysticism are discussed. The author views mystics as "an
      informal and determined group of applied psychologists"
      (p. 3).

1017. Clark, Robert A. "Religious Delusions Among the Jews."
      AMERICAN JOURNAL OF PSYCHOTHERAPY 34 (1980): 62-71.

      Points out that religious delusions are common among the
      Jews and sets out to discover the typical forms these delu-
      sions take. Five case studies are presented. The messianic
      idea, shared by Jews and Christians, is discussed in the
      context of Sabbatai Sevi. Modern Jews, the author thinks,
      are ripe for messianic fantasies. The ferment in our age
      can lead to religious delusions among the unstable and the
      schizoid.

1018. Clark, Walter Houston, H. Newton Malony, et al. RELIGIOUS
      EXPERIENCE: ITS NATURE AND FUNCTION IN THE HUMAN PSYCHE.
      Springfield, IL: Charles C. Thomas, 1973. xi, 151 pp.

      Contains the proceedings of the First John G. Finch Sympo-
      sium on Psychology and Religion held at Fuller Theological
      Seminary in 1971. Several papers by Clark are included as
      well as responses to them by a theologian, a psychologist,

and an anthropologist. Clark's theory that a person has an
inner capacity for religious experience and that it could be
induced by drugs is among the issues debated.

1019.   Cohen, Eric J. "Holiness and Health: An Examination of the
        Relationship Between Christian Holiness and Mental Health."
        JOURNAL OF PSYCHOLOGY AND THEOLOGY 5 (1977): 285-91.

        Explores the issue whether holiness and mental health go
        together or whether they are opposed to one another. The
        meaning of holiness is explained and some integration of
        health and holiness is espoused. It is stressed that holi-
        ness should be given priority and that the promotion of
        health is no substitute for holiness.

1020.   Committee on Psychiatry and Religion. MYSTICISM: SPIRITUAL
        QUEST OR PSYCHIC DISORDER. New York: Group for the Advance-
        ment of Psychiatry 11, Publication No. 97, (1976): 713-822.

        Examines the mystic's experience and life-style to deter-
        mine its normal and/or pathologic psychic organization and
        function. The following topics are discussed: the nature of
        mysticism and the current mystical scene: Jewish, Christian,
        and Hindu mysticism; Jacob Frank and the Frankists; a Polish
        Jewish movement of the eighteenth century; and Ignatius Loyola
        and the Society of Jesus. Mystical phenomena are of interest
        to the psychiatrist because they exhibit both normal and psy-
        chotic forms of behavior and because they are a form of ego
        regression in the service of self-defense. From a psycho-
        logical point of view, the mystic is a person who finds living
        in society stressful and who seeks relief by retreating from
        reality and regressing to an infantile state. This retreat
        is strengthened by his joining an elite group of mystically-
        minded persons and by adhering to a supernatural, revelatory,
        or experiential authority. There are both significant simi-
        larities and differences between mystics and schizophrenics.
        The mystic's retreat from reality is--unlike the schizo-
        phrenic's,--partial, voluntary, and communal. Mysticism is
        also related to creativity.

1021.   Cox, Richard H., editor. RELIGIOUS SYSTEMS OF PSYCHOTHERAPY.
        Springfield, IL: Charles C. Thomas, 1973. xxiv, 519 pp.

        Presents a collection of 37 essays, some previously pub-
        lished, discussing the relationship between psychiatry and
        diverse religious systems. The material is divided into
        three parts: 1) major religious systems; 2) indigenous and
        emergent religious systems; and 3) pluralism (multiple sys-
        tems). Besides essays on Christianity, Protestantism,
        Orthodox Christianity, Islam, and Buddhism, several studies
        on traditional sects, like Seventh-Day Adventism, Christian
        Science, and Mormonism, are included.

        Contains items 502, 674, 691, 704, 1106, 1257, 1753, 1815.

1022. Dean, Stanley R. "Metapsychiatry: The Confluence of Psychi-
       atry and Mysticism." PSYCHIATRY AND MYSTICISM (item 1024),
       pp. 3-17.

       Discusses metapsychiatry, a term coined by the author to
       include parapsychology and all other supernatural manifesta-
       tions of human consciousness. Supra-consciousness, which
       refers to a supersensory level of mental awareness, is de-
       scribed with its distinct characteristics. Several questions
       about the nature of consciousness are raised. It is admitted
       that the search for a higher state of consciousness is not an
       unmixed blessing, because such a state-of-being can have a
       healing quality, but can also lead to pathology. The cultist,
       the dilettante, and the charlatan cannot contribute to the
       development of this "cosmic consciousness."

1023. Dean, Stanley R. "Metapsychiatry: The Interface Between
       Psychiatry and Mysticism." AMERICAN JOURNAL OF PSYCHIATRY
       130 (1973): 1036-38.

       Maintains that psychic research should focus on the state
       of mysticism (or cosmic consciousness, or ultra-conscious-
       ness), under which is included Nirvana, Satori, Samadhi,
       kairos, and "unio mystica." The author points out that the
       visions and other supernatural experiences of Zen monks,
       sages, and prophets need not be equated, as is frequently
       done, with schizophrenia or other forms of psychoses. The
       psychiatrist should be interested in the healing potential
       of the ultra-conscious state, ten distinguishing features of
       which are listed.

1024. Dean, Stanley R., editor. PSYCHIATRY AND MYSTICISM. Chicago:
       Nelson-Hall, 1975. xxii, 424 pp.

       Brings together 26 essays as part of "a major multi-disci-
       plinary project aimed at bridging the gap and establishing
       rapport between medical science and psychic research" (xix).
       Four general areas are covered: 1) metapsychiatry, the branch
       of psychiatry which deals with psychic phenomena; 2) the
       current state of psychic research; 3) psychic phenomena and
       healing; and 4) altered states of consciousness.

       Contains items 933, 1022.

1025. Deikman, Arthur J. THE OBSERVING SELF: MYSTICISM AND PSYCHO-
       THERAPY. Boston: Beacon Press, 1981. xiii, 194 pp.

       Regards mysticism as a type of science which can increase
       the effectiveness of psychotherapy and deepen our understand-
       ing of human life. The book focuses on providing a bridge
       between mysticism and psychotherapy, both of which are said
       to contribute to a person's increase in knowledge. Mysticism
       supplies human life with a meaning and purpose, thus combating
       boredom, despair, and depression. The author thinks that
       mysticism doesn't have to be expressed in religious or esote-

ric language and that many virtues encouraged in its practice,
like renunciation and selflessness, have a functional value in
human life. Meditation, the best known technique of mystical
experience, can be used as an adjunct in psychotherapy, though
one should be aware of some of its adverse effects, like withdrawal as a defense against intimacy and, in those who meditate too much, psychotic decompensation.

1026. Deikman, Arthur J. "Bimodal Consciousness and the Mystic Ex-
      perience." UNDERSTANDING MYSTICISM (item 1154), pp. 261-69.

      Maintains that a human being has components of two modes
      of organization and consciousness: an "action mode" and a
      "receptive mode." The former manipulates the environment,
      the latter receives it. Renunciation and monastic training
      are intended to make the receptive mode the dominant orien-
      tation in the individual's life. Life in a Zen monastery of
      the Soto sect is taken as an example of this training. In
      everyday life the receptive mode is used to solve problems
      by creative intuition, which is a quality claimed by mystics.
      It is argued that the two modes are complementary.

1027. Edkins, William. "Psychoanalysis and Religious Experience."
      JOURNAL OF PSYCHOLOGY AND CHRISTIANITY 4.2 (1985): 86-90.

      Discusses a way of understanding religious language and
      experience in the context of a specific male patient who was
      struggling with personal and family problems. The treatment
      suggested was to help him relate well to others without
      "splitting defensively into an omnipotent, wrathful God who
      must do away with his weak and needy self by hating and
      attacking it" (p. 90).

1028. Egan, Harvey D. "Christian Mysticism and Psychedelic Drug
      Experience." STUDIES IN FORMATIVE SPIRITUALITY 5 (1984):
      33-41.

      Contends that the claims made for the mystical effects of
      psychedelic drugs are false ones. These drugs tend to alter
      consciousness and to diminish personal integrity and are to
      be viewed as leading to pernicious and pseudo-mystical
      experiences. Nevertheless, they often leave their users
      with a sense of transcendence that may be a catalyst for Zen
      enlightenment or Christian conversion. It is suggested that
      an unrestricted love affair between God and the mystic con-
      stitutes Christian mysticism.

1029. Egan, Harvey D. WHAT ARE THEY SAYING ABOUT MYSTICISM. New
      York: Paulist Press, 1982. 134 pp.

      Surveys theologically-oriented literature on mysticism.
      Two chapters are dedicated to psychological studies, which
      are divided into two major trends. One revolves around the
      research of James, Bucke, and Stacey; the other around that
      of Prince, Savage, and Maven. The former scholars distinguish

mysticism from insanity and the occult, and maintain that
mysticism has some positive features; the latter reduce mystical experience to biologism or infantile regression.

1030. Ellens, J. Harold. "Anxiety and the Rise of Religious Experience." JOURNAL OF PSYCHOLOGY AND THEOLOGY 3 (1975): 11-18.

Theorizes that religious experience arises from the native
and universal human experience of anxiety. Four strategies
are used to cope with this experience: 1) rationalization of
anxiety; 2) its denial; 3) its narcotization; and 4) the
avoidance of thoughts and feelings which might cause anxiety.
Religion is the process of reducing this anxiety about the
brutal facts of life and of presenting a way to salvation.
This anxiety could reach pathological proportions because
"much of what goes for Judaic and Christian religion is
psychological distortion or full-blown pathology" (p. 17).
When evaluating religious experience, it is necessary to distinguish between what is authentic spirituality and what is
psychic pathology.

1031. Ellis, Albert. "Psychotherapy and Atheistic Values: A
Response to A. E. Bergin's 'Psychotherapy and Religious
Values.'" JOURNAL OF CONSULTING AND CLINICAL PSYCHOLOGY
48 (1980): 635-39.

Responds to Bergin's view (item 1004) that psychotherapists
should take the religious beliefs of their clients seriously.
It is argued that most psychological problems stem from religious dogmatism, inflexibility, and absolutism, and that
extreme religiosity is essentially an emotional disturbance.
The less religious one is, the more emotionally healthy one
tends to become. The clinical, humanistic, and atheistic
values are schematically drawn up. Several theses illustrate
the main points in the probabilistic atheistic position on
psychotherapy and religion.

1032. Falk, Avner. "The Messiah and the Qelippoth: On the Mental
Illness of Sabbatai Sevi." JOURNAL OF PSYCHOLOGY AND
JUDAISM 7 (1982): 5-29.

Surveys the psychoanalytic theories of manic-depressive
illness and endeavors to find out whether they are applicable to facts of the life of Sabbatai Sevi, the seventeenth
century Jewish mystic. The author presents evidence to show
that Sevi suffered from an acute mental disease, more specifically a manic-depressive (affective) psychosis, rather than
paranoia or homosexuality. Moreover, his illness was emotional and psychological, and not physical or constitutional.
Sevi's life is understood as a product of unsolved unconscious
conflicts of his soul. His personal psychopathology is manifested in his mystical experiences and occult practices of
the Kabbalah, both of which are replete with sexual and famil-
ial symbolism.

1033. Field, William E., and Sandra Wilkerson. "Religiosity as a
       Psychiatric Symptom." PERSPECTIVES IN PSYCHIATRIC CARE 11
       (1973): 99-105.

       Defines religiosity as "a morbid concern with religion, a
       concern which, upon investigation, reveals a basic disturbance
       in personality" (p. 99). An overview of how religious beliefs
       and practices are acquired through acculturation is presented.
       Using Allport's distinction between mature and immature reli-
       gion, the author points out that some adults never grow out
       of their immature religious beliefs of childhood. Both social
       and personal crises can generate religious symptomatology.
       Fundamentalism and authoritarianism are at the root of reli-
       gious preoccupations, which can be traced to early emotional
       insecurity and lead to neurosis.

1034. Finney, John R., and H. Newton Malony. "Empirical Studies of
       Christian Prayer: A Review of the Literature." JOURNAL OF
       PSYCHOLOGY AND THEOLOGY 13 (1985): 104-15.

       Reviews empirical works on verbal and contemplative Chris-
       tian prayer under four categories: 1) developmental studies
       on prayer; 2) research on motivation for prayer; 3) studies
       on the effects of prayer; and 4) studies on the effects of
       contemplative prayer. The literature supports the views that
       A) prayer is not a neurotic flight from anxiety, B) verbal
       prayer is generally ineffective in reducing anxiety, and
       C) contemplative prayer can be effective as a therapeutic
       intervention.

1035. Floyd, William A. "Another Psychotherapist Looks at Religion:
       A Reply to Albert Ellis." PSYCHOLOGY: A JOURNAL OF HUMAN
       BEHAVIOR 18 (Spring 1981): 26-29.

       Reacts to Ellis's negative evaluation of the use of religion
       in therapy (see item 1031), and discusses the essential traits
       of religion and their relation to human freedom. He insists
       that religion is not a commitment to dogma, but a system of
       symbols and rituals. Certain belief systems, commonly taught
       by many evangelical and mainline churches, are antithetical
       to the goals of the mental health movement. It is admitted
       that many fundamentalist churches curb human thinking and
       restrict freedom. Theistic beliefs, according to the author,
       could, but need not, enhance a person's neurotic behavior.

1036. Francis, Leslie, Paul R. Pearson, Marian Carter, and William
       K. Kay. "The Relationship Between Neuroticism and Religi-
       osity Among English 15- and 16-Year Olds." JOURNAL OF
       SOCIAL PSYCHOLOGY 114 (1981): 99-102.

       Tests over 1000 English students in 25 state schools, and
       concludes that religiosity is not related to instability of
       character. Religion does not foster emotional instability,
       nor does it attract people who are emotionally sick.

*   Franck, Loren, et al. SEVEN YEARS OF RELIGIOUS CONVERSION:
      A SELECTED BIBLIOGRAPHY, 1975-1981. Cited above as item 20.

1037.   Frank, Jerome D. "Nature and Function of Belief Systems:
       Humanism and Transcendental Religion." AMERICAN PSYCHOLO-
       GIST 32 (1977): 555-59.

       Shows how belief systems seem to differ much less in their
       ethical content than in their metaphysical beliefs. All be-
       lief systems have similar functions: 1) to enable the believer
       to control events; 2) to bind people to each other; and 3) to
       help them counteract "ontological anxiety," that is, the fear
       of losing their identity with death. The shortcomings of the
       scientific-humanistic belief system and of transcendental
       religions are enumerated. The latter can give their adherents
       hope, security, and peace, but they can also instill fear and
       guilt. Although the scientific and mystical realities cannot
       be reconciled, they may overlap in several areas, especially in
       that of subatomic physics. Science and mysticism can enrich
       each other.

1038.   Gass, Charlton S. "Orthodox Christian Values Related to
       Psychotherapy and Mental Health." JOURNAL OF PSYCHOLOGY
       AND THEOLOGY 12 (1984): 230-37.

       Tests the hypothesis that orthodox religious values, reli-
       gious faith, prayer, meditation, and biblical teaching are
       positively related to mental health. The need for the thera-
       pist to be sensitive to these values is underscored. It is
       argued that Christian values can be used in therapy to foster
       emotional support and to change maladaptive behavior.

1039.   Geels, Anton. "Mystical Experience and the Emergence of
       Creativity." RELIGIOUS ECSTASY (item 1057), pp. 27-62.

       Discusses whether mysticism and creativity have a common
       theoretical base, and whether there is a common model for
       understanding religious and profane creativity. Some major
       works on schizophrenia and creativity and Deikman's study
       on meditation (item 1434) are outlined. The author holds
       that modern research on the psychology of creativity can be
       used to provide a partially new method for research on
       mysticism.

1040.   Gilberg, Arnold L. "Asceticism and the Analysis of a Nun."
       JOURNAL OF THE AMERICAN PSYCHOANALYTIC ASSOCIATION 22
       (1974): 381-93.

       Outlines the various psychological and psychoanalytic views
       of ascetical behavior, and then presents the case of a Catho-
       lic nun to show the hazards of asceticism both to society and
       the individual. Asceticism can lead to a dualistic view of
       the universe. It tends to deny the fullness of life and stifle
       heterosexual maturity; the result is a distortion of ego func-
       tioning. The ascetic is seen as a person who passes through

the oedipal stage without being able to synthesize it. Asceticism does, however, have its benefits in its desire for
psychic equilibrium. The nun's entry into the convent is
given a psychoanalytic interpretation in terms of the oedipus
complex. Commenting on the new religious movements, the
author states that some of them, such as the Self-Realization
Fellowship and the Hare Krishna movement, demonstrate an adaptation to asceticism, which is not a defense against sexuality
but "a desperate attempt to avoid loneliness and abandonment
and, in fantasy, to recapture it through the church or religious life-style" (p. 392).

1041. Godin, André. THE PSYCHOLOGICAL DYNAMICS OF RELIGIOUS EXPERI-
        ENCE. Birmingham, AL: Religious Education Press, 1985.
        279 pp.

        Presents an introductory study of Christian religious experi-
        ence. The first part is dedicated to the place religion and
        religious experience have in the believer's life, and to their
        psychological functions of calming fears, gratifying wishes,
        reinforcing beliefs, and tightening group membership. The
        second part examines several types of religious experiences,
        including sudden, intense conversions. Finally, the issue
        of whether religion deals with realities or wishful fantasies
        is examined in Freudian terms.

1042. Goldman, Norman Saul. "The Placebo and the Therapeutic Uses
        of Faith." JOURNAL OF RELIGION AND HEALTH 24 (1985): 103-
        16.

        Discusses the relationship between religion and medicine,
        a relationship which has been brought to the fore by the
        holistic movement. The author believes that a theological
        analysis of the placebo effect may throw light on the impact
        that religious faith has on a person's health. He suggests
        that the placebo works like faith-healing and/or suggestion.

1043. Goleman, Daniel, and Richard J. Davison. CONSCIOUSNESS: THE
        BRAIN, STATES OF AWARENESS, AND ALTERNATE REALITIES. New
        York: Irvington Publishers, 1979. xvii, 220 pp.

        Offers a collection of previously published essays and
        selections from various books divided into four sections: 1)
        the brain and consciousness; 2) the ordinary states of con-
        sciousness; 3) altered states of consciousness; and 4) the
        politics of consciousness.

        Contains item 989 and selections from items 1283, 1387, 1475.

1044. Golner, Joseph H. "The Sabbath and Mental Health Intervention:
        Some Parallels." JOURNAL OF RELIGION AND HEALTH 21 (1982):
        132-44.

        Compares the celebration of the Jewish Sabbath with some
        mental health interventions, particularly those proposed by
        the Family Centered Education, an approach initiated by the

author himself. Five interventions are examined, namely:
1) simulation; 2) emphasis on the here and now; 3) private
reflection; 4) stress on process; and 5) positive feedback.
The author concludes that the celebration of the Sabbath is
therapeutic.

1045. Gottesfeld, Mary, L. "Mystical Aspects of Psychotherapeutic
      Efficacy." PSYCHOANALYTIC REVIEW 72 (1985): 589-97.

Describes the mystic as a person who undergoes a profound
change, "not through the head (knowledge), but through the
heart (experience)" (p. 592). Ecstatic or trance-like states
are found both in mysticism and in psychosis. Mystics, unlike psychotics, are not attached to, or fixated on, such a
state. The author sees an affinity between the mystical
journey and the psychotherapeutic experience. Both use paradox
and metaphor, and both alter the subject's view of reality.

1046. Gowan, John Curtis. "Altered States of Consciousness: A
      Taxonomy." JOURNAL OF ALTERED STATES OF CONSCIOUSNESS 4
      (1978-79): 141-56.

Presents the view that altered states of consciousness occur
when the right hemisphere in the brain is active and produces
exterior hallucinations or interior imagery. During these
states, the left hemisphere is in abeyance. A taxonomy of the
various states of consciousness expresses the relationship
between the conscious ego and the collective unconscious.
The individual's level of developmental maturity determines
whether the experience is dreadful, as in schizophrenia and
possession trance, or benign, as in samadhi or mysticism.
Three modes of experiences are distinguished (cf. item 1047).
The properties of the various trance states--schizophrenia,
possession, mediumship, hypnotism, shamanism, glossolalia,
and mystical experience--are then compared. As shown in the
author's chart, schizophrenia and mysticism are at opposite
ends of the spectrum, the latter lacking most of the elements
contained in the former. Possession and mediumship are closer
to schizophrenia, while shamanism and glossolalia are allied
with mysticism.

1047. Gowan, John Curtis. TRANCE, ART, AND CREATIVITY. Buffalo,
      NY: Creative Education Foundation, 1975. xxvi, 448 pp.

Addresses itself to the question of how a person gets
in touch with the "ground of being" without losing self-
consciousness. The various methods of enlightenment are
divided into three modes: 1) "prototaxic" modes, that is,
states of complete cognitive chaos (e.g., schizophrenia)
and other types of dissociation and trance; 2) "parataxic"
modes, which provide a middle ground involving "successive
totemization of the numinous element by the conscious ego";
and 3) the "syntaxic" mode, where there is some cognitive
control, as in biofeedback and meditation. This book is
wide in scope, covering various forms of meditation, new

religions, and human growth movements, and discussing several
issues involving their therapeutic value and morality. Many
theories are surveyed. Transcendental Meditation is given a
favorable review. The author's introductory statement that
"this is a demanding book which should be read only by serious
adults in good health" (vii) should be taken seriously.

1048. Graves, Carl C. "Counterpoint: Religion--Cause or Cure?"
      PERSPECTIVES IN PSYCHIATRIC CARE 21.1 (1983): 27, 36-38.

      Reflects on the problem of defining religion and of assign-
      ing it a function in the healing process. The author makes
      a distinction between religion and religionism, the latter
      being characterized by its dogmatic stance. Religionism
      brings several dangers into psychiatric treatment: 1) it is
      linked to a morbid preoccupation with religious problems; 2)
      it is indicative of thought disorder; and 3) it subtly forces
      dogma on the patient. Religionism creates "a short-term pal-
      liative effect which evaporates under hyperstress" (p. 37).

1049. Hanson, David J. AUTHORITARIANISM, DOGMATICISM, AND RELIGION:
      A REVIEW. Washington, DC: American Psychological Associa-
      tion, 1977. Psychological Documents, MS 1528. 11 pp.

      Reviews studies on the relationship between authoritarianism
      and religion. Conflicting findings suggest that the research
      done so far has neglected two major points: 1) there are many
      factors which influence denominational affiliation, which may
      not be related to religious belief and orientation; and 2)
      there is an important distinction between the content of
      beliefs and the manner in which they are held. More research
      is encouraged.

1050. Hartocollis, Peter. "Aggression and Mysticism." CONTEMPO-
      RARY PSYCHOANALYSIS 12 (1976): 214-26.

      Relates mystical movements to aggressive tendencies in the
      sense that the search for the mystical is evidence of a
      potential for violence. An overview of psychological and
      psychoanalytic views of mysticism is given. Several case
      examples of patients are presented to show how the quest for
      mystical experiences stems from an intolerance of one's own
      inner violence, directed particularly against the hated
      oedipal father. What distinguishes the introvertive from
      the extrovertive kind of mysticism is the degree of aggres-
      siveness. Modern mystical movements are characterized by
      their anti-war sentiments and quietistic attitudes that
      the author interprets as a protest against the inward and
      outward violence that surrounds them.

1051. Hay, David. EXPLORING INNER SPACE: SCIENTISTS AND RELIGIOUS
      EXPERIENCE. Hammondsworth, UK: Penguin, 1982. 256 pp.

      Examines religious experience from a scientific point of
      view. The author first outlines the pervasiveness of re-

ligion in space and time, and discusses the theories that
explain away religious experience. Secondly, he answers the
question of whether personal religious experience still exists.
The early works of William James and Stanley Hall are judged
to be "abortive" and the theories that explain religious experience as an outlet for mental aberration, a suppressor of
discontent, or a haven for the inadequate, are all rejected
as insufficient to account for the data gathered by modern
research. The author proposes the theory that religious experience is something biologically natural to the individual.

1052. Hay, David. "Religious Experience and Its Induction."
      ADVANCES IN THE PSYCHOLOGY OF RELIGION. Edited by L. B.
      Brown. New York: Pergamon Press, 1985, pp. 130-50.

      Surveys some of the recent research on religious experience
      conducted in the United States and in the United Kingdom.
      Several explanations of how religious experience is brought
      about or facilitated are discussed: pharmacology (the use of
      psychedelic drugs like LSD, and endogenous substances like
      endorphins), epilepsy, physical shamanistic techniques (which
      include hyperventilation and sleep deprivation), meditation,
      and prayer. Researchers who study religious experience as a
      mechanically induced state, without reference to its religious
      and cultural setting, are criticized.

1053. Hay, David, and Ann Morisy. "Reports of Ecstatic, Paranormal,
      or Religious Experiences in Great Britain and the United
      States--A Comparison of Trends." JOURNAL FOR THE SCIENTIFIC
      STUDY OF RELIGION 17 (1978): 255-68.

      Examines the widespread occurrences of religious experiences
      in Western Society, and compares the research conducted on the
      subject in Great Britain and the United States. The unanimous
      conclusion is that there is a definite relationship between
      religious experience and psychological well-being.

1054. Haynal, André, Miklos Molnar, and Gérard de Puymège. FANAT-
      ICISM: A HISTORICAL AND PSYCHOANALYTIC STUDY. Translated
      by Linda Butler Korseogler. New York: Schocken Books,
      1983. 282 pp.

      Discusses the origin of fanaticism, which is linked with
      excessive religious enthusiasm. Fanatic people are those
      who, mistakenly, think that they have discovered the absolute
      truth which makes them omniscient, omnipotent, and invulner-
      able. Fanaticism is a form of infantile regression which is
      accompanied by narcissism. The fanatic suffers from paranoia
      and megalomania, and indulges in psychopathological behavior.
      The Crusades, the Inquisition, sectarianism, and witch hunts
      are cited as historical examples of fanaticism. Charles
      Manson's family, Jim Jones's People's Temple, and Reverend
      Moon's Unification Church are given as examples of contempo-
      rary fanatical behavior.

1055. Herrenkohl, Ellen C. "Parallels in the Process of Achieving
       Personal Growth By Abusing Parents Through Participation
       in Group Therapy Programs or in Religious Groups." FAMILY
       COORDINATOR 27 (1978): 279-82.

       Reports on research carried out in Eastern Pennsylvania
       which concluded that abusive parents can alter their behavior
       towards their children either by group therapy or by a reli-
       gious conversion, which leads them to full participation in a
       religious group. Both group therapy and church affiliation
       provide a source of surrogate parental love and acceptance,
       which can be considered therapeutic.

1056. Hohn, Nils G. "Ecstasy Research in the Twentieth Century:
       An Introduction." RELIGIOUS ECSTASY (item 1057), pp. 7-26.

       Gives a brief survey of the various definitions of ecstasy,
       which has been linked with trance, mysticism, possession,
       altered states of consciousness, and hypnosis. The literature
       reviewed is divided into two sections: 1) early twentieth-
       century research; and 2) more recent anthropological, socio-
       logical, and psychological studies. Glossolalia in the
       Pentecostal movement is given as an example to show how the
       focus of research on ecstasy has shifted from the field of
       abnormal psychology to that of group dynamics. Modern studies
       have attempted to understand ecstatic experiences from the
       perspective of normal psychology.

1057. Hohn, Nils G., editor. RELIGIOUS ECSTASY. Stockholm: Alm-
       quist and Wiskell, 1982. 306 pp.

       Presents a collection of papers read at the Symposium on
       Religious Ecstasy held in Finland in August, 1981. The
       phenomenon of mystical experience is dealt with from psycho-
       logical, social, and religious perspectives.

       Contains items 1039, 1056, 1706.

1058. Hood, Ralph W. "Conceptual Reconstruction of Regressive
       Explanations of Mysticism." REVIEW OF RELIGIOUS RESEARCH
       17 (1976): 179-88.

       Defines mysticism as an experience of the loss of self in
       a state of ultimate union. Regressive explanations of mysti-
       cism, which owe their origin to Freud, have been common in
       psychology. The author rejects the view which evaluates
       mystics as unhealthy personalities, and argues that mystical
       experiences may be a sign of psychological well-being.

1059. Hood, Ralph W. "Psychological Strength and the Report of
       Intense Religious Experience." JOURNAL FOR THE SCIENTIFIC
       STUDY OF RELIGION 13 (1974): 65-71.

       Comments on the theoretical debate between Freud and the
       humanistic psychologists, like Maslow, on the pathological
       meaning of religious experience, and presents studies which

aim at determining the relationship between religious experience and pathology. Hood's Religious Experience Episodes
Measure (REEM), the Minnesota Multiphasic Personality Inventory
(MMPI), and Starks's Index of Psychic Inadequacy (IPI) were
used in this study. It was found that the relationship between ego strength and reported religious experience is low
when the former is measured independently of religious commitment. On the other hand, those who scored high on Starks's
IPI were more likely to report an intense religious experience. The findings, according to the author, are not
conclusive, but rather indicative of the need for further
research. He argues that much of the similarity between
mystical states and the infantile ego is unfounded, and that
mystical states cannot be said to be regressive.

1060. Hood, Ralph W. "Forms of Religious Commitment and Intense
       Religious Experience." REVIEW OF RELIGIOUS RESEARCH 15
       (1973): 29-36.

       Pursues the author's interest in measuring religious commit-
       ment by relating it to intense religious experiences. Two
       areas of study are explored: 1) the classification of reli-
       giously committed persons into two groups, dependent on
       whether their commitment was personal or institutional; and
       2) an exploration of the nature of the intense religious
       experience for each type of commitment. The hypothesis that
       institutionalized religious commitment would be accompanied
       by a less intense personal religious commitment is confirmed.
       Because mysticism seems to occur outside institutionalized
       contexts, research into reasons why people defect from the
       religion of their upbringing is encouraged.

1061. Horne, James R. BEYOND MYSTICISM. Waterloo, Ontario: Cana-
       dian Corporation for Studies in Religion, SR Supplements 6,
       1978. Vol. V, 156 pp.

       Attempts to answer six major questions on mysticism:
       1) can mysticism be defined?; 2) are there different types
       of mystical experiences?; 3) can the mystical experience
       itself be described?; 4) is mysticism rational?; 5) are some
       mystics more reliable than others?; and 6) what does the
       mystical experience mean? It is maintained that the defini-
       tion of mysticism as a psychological phenomenon, in which a
       person undergoes a saving transformation--with emotional,
       intellectual, and frequently visionary elements, at a crucial
       point in one's life--is not a sufficient explanation. The
       author thinks that mysticism is an experience of selfhood and
       of a refined self-awareness.

1062. Horton, Paul C. "The Mystical Experience: Substance of an
       Illusion." JOURNAL OF THE AMERICAN PSYCHOANALYTIC ASSOCIA-
       TION 22 (1974): 364-80.

       Presents a case history as the basis of a discussion of
       mystical experience. The author's view is that this experi-

ence, which is often transitory, is an upsurge of residual
primary narcissism, which can serve as a defense against
overwhelming loneliness. Thus, while the experience itself
may be illusory, it is a potentially adaptive ego mechanism.

1063. Horton, Paul C. "The Mystical Experience as a Suicide Pre-
       ventive." AMERICAN JOURNAL OF PSYCHIATRY 130 (1973):
       294-96.

       Gives an account of three schizophrenic subjects whose
       mystical experiences seemed to lessen, if not abolish, the
       inclination to suicide, a state of mind equivalent to primi-
       tive narcissism. The author regards the mystical experience
       not as a delusional mental state which has to be untangled,
       but rather as a potential transitional phenomenon which can
       soothe individuals and lead them to maturity. The mystical
       experience itself is not part of a healthy religious life-
       style, but a useful tool in preventing people from committing
       suicide.

1064. Hufford, David. "Christian Religious Healing." JOURNAL OF
       OPERATIONAL PSYCHIATRY 8 (1977): 22-27.

       Investigates the interaction between religious beliefs and
       modern Western surgical and psychiatric medicine. Religious
       and medical world views are both seen as valid cultural systems.
       Within the unorthodox health systems are included the activi-
       ties of Christian Science, of fundamentalist preachers like
       Oral Roberts, and the practice of the anointing of the sick
       in the Catholic Church. Two sets of questions, seen within
       the context of the respective world views, are posed: 1) how
       complex and integrated is this religious healing system?, and
       2) is it likely to have negative health implications? The
       author thinks that Christian healing has the potential for
       both adaptive and maladaptive consequences.

1065. Hunt, Harry T. "A Cognitive Psychology of Mystical and
       Altered Experience." PERCEPTUAL AND MOTOR SKILLS 58 (1984):
       467-513.

       Attempts to reconcile two opposing views of religious
       mysticism and altered states of consciousness, namely, the
       Freudian which associates them with schizophrenia, regression,
       and primitivity, and the Jungian which interprets them more
       positively as higher paths of self-development and self-
       actualization. The author analyzes the potentially cognitive
       attributes of the sense of the numinous and related phenomena,
       and develops a holistic-cognitive approach towards understand-
       ing the nature of religious experience and ecstatic trance.
       Religious experience is seen as a full exteriorization and
       completion of "human cross-modal synaesthetic capacity."

1066. Hyder, O. Quentin. "On the Mental Health of Jesus Christ."
       JOURNAL OF PSYCHOLOGY AND THEOLOGY 5 (1977): 3-12.

Refutes the view that Jesus Christ was a deluded madman in his claim that he was the Son of God. The author first outlines the psychiatric view of what a lunatic is, showing how such a person thinks, speaks, behaves, and relates to others. Then he discusses whether Jesus fits into the picture. Finally, on a more positive note, the psychological makeup of Jesus is compared to the features of mental health. It is concluded that Jesus did not suffer from paranoia or delusion, but that he rather exemplified the psychiatric image of good mental health by his balanced sense of self-esteem, his unequivocal concern for the sufferings and needs of others, his responsible fulfillment of the demands of living, and his teachings--especially those contained in the Sermon on the Mount.

1067. Jones, Fowler C., Glen O. Gabbard, and Stuart W. Twemlow. "Psychological and Demographic Characteristics of Persons Reporting Out-of-Body Experiences." HILLSIDE JOURNAL OF CLINICAL PSYCHIATRY 6 (1984): 105-15.

Attempts to answer several questions about people who report out-of-body experiences (OBEs), which are connected with religious and mystical ones: 1) are OBEs more prone to imagery and fantasy?; 2) do they lead to lower anxiety about death?; 3) are they indicative of hysteria or psychosis?; and 4) do people who report them show greater psychological adjustment? The researchers conclude that out-of-body experiences are not delusional, hallucinatory, or drug-induced. People who have such experiences do not have a distinct psychological profile, and are, on the contrary, better adjusted psychologically.

1068. Kallstad, Thorvald. "Ignatius Loyola and the Spiritual Exercises: A Psychological Study." PSYCHOLOGICAL STUDIES ON RELIGIOUS MAN (item 1070), pp. 13-45.

Explores the events and experiences in the life of St. Ignatius that influenced the development of his personality and the formation of the spiritual exercises. During his illness, Ignatius was "in a cognitive process that had characteristics of dissonance" (p. 16). Both his physical and psychological weaknesses probably intensified his crisis. The author shows how the practices outlined in the exercises, namely, examination of conscience, meditation, contemplation, and prayer, were aimed at leading the individual to religious experience and behavior.

1069. Kallstad, Thorvald. JOHN WESLEY AND THE BIBLE: A PSYCHOLOGICAL STUDY. Stockholm: Nya Bokforlags, 1974. 356 pp.

Argues that the few psychological studies on John Wesley have stressed the psychoanalytical viewpoint and neglected Wesley's own religious development. The author aims to explore "the importance of the Biblical tradition and religious system on the development of his personality" (p. 27). Wesley's family background and religious influences are investigated. Major events in his life, like the opposition

to Oxford Methodism, his voyage to America, his reactions to
stress situations, and his attraction to some forms of mysticism, are studied in the framework of the ongoing religious
development of his personality.

1070. Kallstad, Thorvald, editor. PSYCHOLOGICAL STUDIES ON RELI-
        GIOUS MAN. Stockholm: Almquist and Wiksell, 1978.
        252 pp.

        Contains the results of a seminar on the psychology of re-
        ligion, held at the Faculty of Theology at Uppsala University.
        The areas covered are religious personalities, religious atti-
        tudes, religion and group process, and religion and health.

        Includes items 1068, 1141, 1150, 1663, 1670.

1071. Kiely, William F. "Critique of Mystical States: A Reply."
        JOURNAL OF NERVOUS AND MENTAL DISEASE 159 (1974): 196-97.

        Responds to the critique of Mills and Campbell (item 1089)
        by insisting on the tentative and limited scope of the
        investigation on the neurophysiological and clinical aspects
        of mysticism which he had conducted with Ernst Gelhorn (see
        item 134).

1072. Knapp, Bettina L. "The Golem and Ecstatic Mysticism."
        JOURNAL OF ALTERED STATES OF CONSCIOUSNESS 3 (1977-78):
        355-69.

        Examines the Golem legend which was created by the Jewish
        mystic, Rabbi Judah Loew, in sixteenth-century Prague. This
        story, it is maintained, answered specific needs of the Jews
        living in the ghetto, particularly the need for survival.
        The Golem-making ritual is analyzed in Jungian terms and de-
        scribed in six steps. The Golem, a being without a soul, was
        a psychological projection which acted as a catalyst, a force
        which helped the Jewish community overcome persecution.

1073. Lange, Mark K. "Prayer and Psychotherapy: Beliefs and Prac-
        tice." JOURNAL OF PSYCHOLOGY AND CHRISTIANITY 2 (1983):
        36-49.

        Reports on a survey conducted on the members of the Chris-
        tian Association for Psychological Studies to assess their
        belief in prayer and their use of it in therapeutic settings.
        It is concluded that while these Christian psychologists
        believed both in the efficacy of prayer and its potential
        healing qualities, they never used it as a replacement for
        therapy.

1074. Lea, Gary. "Religion, Mental Health, and Clinical Issues."
        JOURNAL OF RELIGION AND HEALTH 21 (1982): 336-51.

        Points out that the response to the mass suicide at Jim
        Jones's People's Temple has raised the question whether reli-

gious beliefs and practices in cults, sects, and mainline
denominations alike have a negative impact on the mental
health and behavior of believers. Social scientific literature on the relation between religion, mental health, and
social behavior are surveyed. Several standard works on
religious pathology and neurotic conversion are evaluated.
A good, lengthy bibliography is included.

1075. Lenz, Hermann. "Belief and Delusion: Their Common Origin
       But Different Course of Development." ZYGON: A JOURNAL
       OF RELIGION AND SCIENCE 18 (1983): 117-37.

       Describes the mystic experience from abstracts from the
       biographies of Teresa of Avila and Ignatius of Loyola, state-
       ments by Zen Buddhist monks, and reports by artists and finds
       that their conditions were similar to that of 25 mentally-ill
       persons. The sense of mission, suspension of time, halluci-
       nations, and extremes of mood were among the common elements
       observed. Many differences, however, appeared as the experi-
       ences developed. In the mystic, hope and doubt leave room
       for growth, while among the mentally ill, paralyzed belief
       persisted. The mystic's faith, unlike that of the patients
       examined, led to freedom and to interaction between other
       people and with society at large.

1076. Lukoff, David. "The Diagnosis of Mystical Experience With
       Psychotic Features." JOURNAL OF TRANSPERSONAL PSYCHOLOGY
       17 (1985): 255-81.

       Presents a model delineating the overlap between mystical
       experience and psychotic states, and suggests guidelines for
       making diagnostic and treatment decisions. Several themes
       are identified as occurring commonly in mystical experiences
       with psychotic elements: rebirth (new identity), journey
       (sense of mission), magical powers (telepathy), new society
       (new age), and divine union. It is held that when these
       mythic themes are projected onto outward reality, they
       meet the psychiatric criteria for delusions.

1077. MacDonald, Coval B., and Jeffrey B. Luckett. "Religious
       Affiliation and Psychiatric Diagnosis." JOURNAL FOR THE
       SCIENTIFIC STUDY OF RELIGION 22 (1983): 15-37.

       Examines the relation between religious affiliation and
       emotional disorders. Over 7000 subjects from 23 different
       religious groups were included in this study. The results
       show that drug and alcohol use and paranoid schizophrenia
       were not linked with any religious preference. Non-mainline
       Protestant church members registered high on anxiety, explo-
       sive personality, and depression. These same problems were
       observed also among mainline Protestants, who suffered from
       personality disorders, and among Catholics, who showed a
       tendency to hysterical personality. Members of sects like
       Christian Science, Jehovah's Witnesses, Mormons, and Seventh-
       Day Adventists registered a higher frequency of hysterical
       neurosis and inadequate personality.

1078. Margolis, Robert D., and Kirk W. Elifson. "Validation of a
       Typology of Religious Experience and Its Relationship to
       the Psychotic Experience." JOURNAL OF PSYCHOLOGY AND
       THEOLOGY 11 (1983): 135-41.

       Attempts to draw up criteria for distinguishing genuine
       religious experiences from other human experiences. Subjects
       included members of traditional denominations and of Eastern
       religious sects. Three types of experiences are distinguished,
       namely, 1) genuine religious, 2) fabricated religious, and
       3) psychotic. The author concludes that the genuine reli-
       gious experience is not to be identified with the psychotic
       one.

1079. Margolis, Robert D., and Kirk W. Elifson. "A Typology of
       Religious Experience: Construction, Validation, and Rela-
       tionship to the Psychotic Experience." JOURNAL FOR THE
       SCIENTIFIC STUDY OF RELIGION 18 (1978): 61-67.

       Discusses various typologies of religious experience and
       suggests a new one based on interviews with 45 people who
       claimed to have had such experiences. Four basic types are
       distinguished: 1) transcendental experience, which is the
       same as in classical mysticism and which brings with it peace,
       ecstasy, and security; 2) vertigo experience, which is brought
       about by drugs and music, and which causes a temporary dis-
       orientation of the subject; 3) life-change experience, leading
       to a change in the individual's feelings and cognition; and
       4) visionary experience, which includes visual and/or auditory
       sensations. A sense of unity, ineffability, noetic quality,
       and time/space distortion are the major common features of
       all religious experiences.

1080. Matheson, George. "Hypnotic Aspect of Religious Experience."
       JOURNAL OF PSYCHOLOGY AND THEOLOGY 7 (1979): 13-21.

       Presents the hypothesis that hypnosis is a good perspective
       from which to analyze some religious events. A history of
       hypnosis and its use in medical and psychological disorders
       is drawn up. It is argued that religious experiences, espe-
       cially the salvation experience in evangelical crusades and
       non-medical healings, reveals processes and phenomena similar
       to the hypnotic state. Prayer and the healing of memories
       are methods of inducing hypnosis. The author thinks that
       hypnosis, if it can be dissociated from evil and the occult,
       may be a useful means for understanding religious experiences.

1081. McNamara, William. "Psychology and the Christian Mystic
       Tradition." TRANSPERSONAL PSYCHOLOGIES (item 1338), pp.
       391-430.

       Discusses the place of psychology in Christian mysticism.
       Four areas are covered: 1) an overall description of the
       mystical experience; 2) the philosophical basis of the Chris-

tian mystical tradition; 3) its origin and history; and 4)
the path to mystical experience (with 12 features of the
mystic way, seven techniques and experiential exercises, and
ten dangers). Psychopathology is said to be one of the main
dangers. Like most people, mystics are normal, in the sense
that they conduct their lives without grotesque or bizarre
behavior, and abnormal, in the sense that their vitality,
sensitivity, and powers of knowing and loving are richer and
deeper.

1082. Meadow, Mary Jo, and Richard D. Kahoe. PSYCHOLOGY AND RELI-
       GION: RELIGION IN INDIVIDUAL LIVES. New York: Harper and
       Row, 1984. xxiv, 488 pp.

       Gives a general introduction to the psychology of religion
       covering: 1) the origin and function of religiousness; 2)
       religious experiences, including conversion, trance, faith-
       healing, and mysticism; 3) psychological variables in reli-
       gious perspective; 4) characteristics and measurement of
       religiousness; and 5) critical evaluation of religion, in
       which is included a discussion of religion and psychopathol-
       ogy. The author observes that most cases of religious con-
       version among psychotherapy patients are examples either of
       regressive pathology or of integrative maturity. These
       conversions could, therefore, be a step in religious develop-
       ment. Similarly, religion can directly precipitate serious
       disturbances, but can also contribute to one's well-being and
       to the solution of one's personal problems. The author favors
       a partnership between religion and psychotherapy.

1083. Meadow, Mary Jo, et al. SYMPOSIUM: THE SPIRITUAL AND/VERSUS
       THE TRANSPERSONAL. Washington, DC: American Psychological
       Association, 1979. Psychological Documents MS 1960.
       24 pp.

       Contains the papers presented at a symposium held at the
       1978 annual meeting of the American Psychological Association
       in Toronto. The main discussion topic was the relationship
       between religious or spiritual experiences and other altered
       states of consciousness. Psychedelic drugs, meditation, con-
       version, psi-phenomena, and out-of-body experiences are among
       the topics covered. In the discussions held among the parti-
       cipants, a hierarchy of altered states is offered and the
       proposal to conduct research with the purpose of refuting
       arguments for a "physicalistic-monistic view of consciousness"
       is considered.

1084. Medlicott, R. W. "The Case of Joseph: The Strengths and
       Hazards of Narcissistic Omnipotence." BRITISH JOURNAL OF
       MEDICAL PSYCHOLOGY 53 (1980): 187-90.

       Examines this biblical figure in the context of the psycho-
       analytic framework of personality development, stressing its
       narcissistic elements. Joseph is seen as an illustration of

"the narcissistic omnipotence of the 'special' child who
avoids resolution of the oedipal conflict by identifying with
the powerful father" (p. 190).

1085.   Menz, Robert L.   "The Denial of Death and the Out-Of-The-
        Body Experience."   JOURNAL OF RELIGION AND HEALTH 23
        (1984): 317-29.

        Explores the possible relation between the denial of death
        and the out-of-the-body experiences. The questions about
        who denies death and how, why, when, and where such denials
        occur are discussed. The pharmacological, physiological,
        neurological, spiritual, and psychological interpretations of
        out-of-the-body experiences are briefly outlined. The author
        opts for a psychological explanation, which sees these experi-
        ences as defense mechanisms that are employed as attempts
        to deny the occurrence of death. Such experiences are hallu-
        cinations caused by traumatic events, rather than genuine
        previews of the afterlife.

1086.   Mester, Roberto, and Hillel Klein.   "The Young Jewish Reviv-
        alist: A Therapist's Dilemma."   BRITISH JOURNAL OF MEDICAL
        PSYCHOLOGY 54 (1981): 299-306.

        Discusses the cases of young Jews who became so devoted
        to their religion that they ceased to perform the tasks and
        duties which their social environment required of them, and
        who exhibited symptoms of mental disease and severe social
        maladjustment. The patients' main characteristics, the hos-
        pital staff's initial reaction, and the possible meaning of
        the patients' behavior are discussed. Their new religious
        behavior could be interpreted as a cluster of neurotic,
        obsessive-compulsive symptoms, or as the first stage of a
        psychotic breakdown. Methods of handling these patients are
        given. The need to take their religion into consideration
        is stressed.

1087.   Mikulas, William L.   "Buddhism and Behavior Modification."
        PSYCHOLOGICAL RECORD 31 (1981): 331-42.

        Traces briefly the nature and history of Buddhism. The
        author holds that meditation can be profitably used in cer-
        tain behavior modification practices. Both Buddhism and
        behavior modification are ahistorical, stressing the present
        condition of the individual. Both aim at objectivity by
        attempting to perceive reality as it is, with a minimum of
        distortion and interpretation and with little theoretical
        and metaphysical constructs. Both question the concept of
        an individualized self or separate entity. The cultivation
        of empathy in Buddhism is likened to the behavior modification
        practice of distinguishing between the behavior of the person,
        and the person performing the actions. The stress on the
        changing nature of reality and behavior, and on the need to
        develop unattachment, or to accept what one cannot change,
        is central to both systems. The interrelationship of Buddhism

and behavior modification has repercussions on behavioral,
personal, and transpersonal levels, and leads to the development of psychological principles and therapeutic practices.

1088. Mikulas, William L. "Four Noble Truths of Buddhism Related
       to Behavior Therapy." PSYCHOLOGICAL RECORD 28 (1978):
       59-67.

Considers the bases of Buddhism philosophy and action as
they are related to clinical practice in general and behavior
therapy in particular. It is suggested that both Buddhism
and behavior modification can be combined to facilitate self-
integration. Meditation, the basic method of Buddhism, is a
potentially important tool in the hands of the behavior therapists. The author believes, however, that the reliance on
meditation as the major technique to overcome attachments is
a weakness in the Buddhist approach, a weakness which can be
remedied by the use of behavior therapy methods.

1089. Mills, Gary K., and Ken Campbell. "A Critique of Gellhorn
       and Kielly's Mystical State of Consciousness: Neuro-
       physiological and Clinical Aspects." JOURNAL OF NERVOUS
       AND MENTAL DISEASE 159 (1974): 191-95.

Criticizes Gellhorn and Kielly's view (item 134) for several
reasons, including their failure to take into consideration
the differences between the various meditation techniques,
and to consider important published evidence on Yoga. It is
argued that Zen and Yoga differ philosophically, psychologically and physiologically, and hence one cannot easily allude
to their common therapeutic value.

1090. Morris, Ronald J., and Ralph W. Hood. "Religious and Unity
       Criteria of Baptists and Nomes in Reports of Mystical
       Experience." PSYCHOLOGICAL REPORTS 46 (1980): 728-30.

Examines the relationship between reports of religious
experience and church membership. Forty Baptists and 40
persons with no religious affiliation (Nomes) were tested.
The results show that both groups had gone through several
religious experiences. The authors think that the experience of unity may be a major feature of mysticism in both
groups.

1091. Narrone, Bruce. "Guilt: Its Universal Hidden Presence."
       JOURNAL OF PSYCHOLOGY AND THEOLOGY 2 (1974): 104-15.

Maintains that the emotion of guilt is to some degree involved in the etiology of all psychological maladjustments.
Also discussed are the origin of sin in the book of Genesis,
and the major defensive processes used to negate or distort
the subjective experience of guilt. The author outlines the
psychological and theological implications of the failure to
recognize the part played by guilt in pathology. Indirectly,

the question is raised as to whether fundamentalist Christian
sects and cults, where guilt is frequently stressed, are a
source of psychological harm to members.

1092.   Nelson, Scott H., and E. Fuller Torrey. "The Religious
         Functions of Psychiatry." AMERICAN JOURNAL OF PSYCHIATRY
         43 (1973): 362-67.

         Shows how many of the functions of religion, particularly
         the explanation of the unknown, the definition of values, and
         the provision of social centers, have now been transferred to
         psychiatry. The implications of such a shift, especially
         for the relationship between the clergyman and the psychia-
         trist, are discussed. The therapeutic value of religious
         and faith healing is taken for granted.

1093.   Nicholi, Armand N. "A New Dimension of the Youth Culture."
         AMERICAN JOURNAL OF PSYCHIATRY 131 (1974): 396-400.

         Focuses on 17 college students who claimed to have had a
         religious experience. The author explains how this phenomenon
         comes about, points out the social and psychological factors
         that trigger it, and traces its relationship to the modern
         drug culture. The changes in life-style and attitudes after
         conversion are described under the following topics: drugs,
         self-image, relationships, parents, sexuality, and affect.
         The discussion then shifts to whether the experience promotes
         adaptation or tends to be destructive. The author thinks
         that, through the experience, the controlling functions of
         the ego which foster adaptation are strengthened.

1094.   Nilsen, E. Anker. RELIGION AND PERSONALITY INTEGRATION.
         Stockholm: Almquist and Wiksell, 1980. 173 pp.

         Raises the issue of whether religion promotes or impedes
         the integration and development of one's personality. A
         theory of personality is constructed, and the value system
         in psychotherapy and in actual life situations are discussed.
         Religion can be unhealthy, when the crisis in one's religious
         life becomes permanent. Some kinds of religious beliefs may
         encourage neurosis and psychosis, and the conversion experi-
         ence, which occurs at a time of crisis, may be neurotic. A
         comparison is made between psychiatry, psychotherapy, and
         pastoral counseling. Healthy religion, which is based on the
         theological interpretation of the New Testament, promotes
         personality growth and integration. Various ways in which
         religion and psychotherapy can cooperate are proposed.

1095.   Nusbaum, Kurt. "Abnormal and Mental Phenomena in the Proph-
         ets." JOURNAL OF RELIGION AND HEALTH 13 (1974): 194-200.

         Concedes that abnormal mental phenomena of varying emo-
         tional depth are found frequently in the earlier Old Testa-
         ment prophets. Three levels of these phenomena are described:
         1) inspiration, a state of excitement with well-preserved

reality controls; 2) ecstasy, a state in which reality control
has been temporarily lost; and 3) eidetic imagery, which is
characterized by dreams and visions. The prophets may have
been psychotics, mystics, poets, or people endowed with great
psychic gifts, but their apparent abnormal behavior is not
subject to easy interpretation. The author thinks that it
rather the people whom these prophets addressed who suffered
from psychological disorders.

1096.   Oakland, James A. "Self-Actualization and Sanctification."
        JOURNAL OF PSYCHOLOGY AND THEOLOGY 2 (1974): 202-9.

        Argues that the Wesleyan view of sanctification corresponds
        to the psychological perspective of self-actualization.
        Christ is presented as the outstanding example of a self-
        actualized person.

1097.   Oates, Wayne E. THE PSYCHOLOGY OF RELIGION. Waco, TX: Word
        Books, 1973. 291 pp.

        Presents a very comprehensive introduction to the psychology
        of religion, including coverage of such topics as conversion,
        ecstatic experiences, mysticism, and the relation between re-
        ligion and mental illness. Much of the material is discussed
        within the context of the counterculture of the late 1960s,
        though no explicit reference is made to cults, except a few
        minor ones in connection with the Jesus Movement. There are
        brief comments on Hinduism and Buddhism. A chapter on the
        expansion of consciousness deals with the use of psychedelic
        drugs and with the human potential movement. Commitment,
        seen as a learned response, is discussed, together with the
        sense of alienation and the counterculture. The author holds
        that it is not easy to draw the line between creative reli-
        gious experience and mental illness, and maintains that the
        latter should be related, in some instances at least, to
        demonic possession.

1098.   Ostow, Mortimer. "Religion and Psychiatry." COMPREHENSIVE
        TEXTBOOK OF PSYCHIATRY (item 29), vol. III, pp. 3197-208.

        Discusses the psychodynamics of religious practice from a
        Freudian perspective and explores some mental mechanisms that
        appear in both religious practice and mental illness. The
        part played by religion in obsessive-compulsive disorders,
        phobias, hysteria, depression, schizophrenia, and paranoia
        is considered. The rise of new religious cults is also ex-
        amined, and the clinical syndrome of those who join them is
        explained in pathological terms. Cult members are seen as
        masochistic, inadequate, and depressive persons whose feel-
        ings of helplessness and incompetency lead them to resort
        to three major primitive mechanisms, namely, those of self-
        effacement, self-degradation, and self-sacrifice. The
        problem of counseling parents of cult members is taken into
        account. The author doesn't favor deprogramming because,
        among other reasons, cult members are usually neither minors,
        nor are they clinically psychotic.

1099. Paloutzian, Raymond F. INVITATION TO THE PSYCHOLOGY OF
       RELIGION. Glenview, IL: Scott, Foresman, and Co., 1983.
       213 pp.

       Gives a standard introduction to the psychology of religion,
       covering the history of the subject, the psychology of reli-
       gious development, conversion, moral attitudes, and religious
       personality. Various types of conversions—sudden, gradual,
       and unconscious—are distinguished. The Lofland/Stark model
       of cult conversion (item 1870) is explained and a list of
       cultic features, based largely on Conway and Siegelman's ana-
       lysis (item 1188), is presented. Among the psychological
       issues discussed are religion as a psychopathological crutch,
       the conversion/brainwashing debate, and the deprogramming of
       cult members. The author states that a "clear resolution of
       the issues has yet to be done" (pp. 106-7).

1100. Pattison, E. Mansell. "Psychiatry and Religion Circa 1978:
       Analysis of a Decade. Parts I and II." PASTORAL PSYCHOLOGY
       27 (1978): 8-25, 119-41.

       Surveys the history and recent development of the relation-
       ship between religion and psychiatry. In Part One, the common
       origin of religious practitioners and psychiatrists is traced
       to shamanism. The stages of the relationship between the two
       disciplines from 1900-65 is sketched. Part Two deals with
       the years 1966-77, during which period the alliance between
       psychiatry and religion is attributed to organizational devel-
       opment, the religious orientation of some mental health pro-
       fessionals, and the concern about mental health among the
       clergy. Some current trends in the following areas are out-
       lined: studies of the clergy; community and church; conceptual
       studies on psychiatry and religion; psychopathology and reli-
       gion; religion and medicine; and indigenous healers. An
       extensive bibliography, containing 230 items, is included.

1101. Perez, Leon. "The Messianic Psychotic Patient." ISRAELI
       ANNALS OF PSYCHIATRY AND RELATED DISCIPLINES 15 (1977):
       364-74.

       Examines over seventy cases of Jewish and Arab clients
       who believed that they had been chosen by God to perform some
       special task, and that to this end they had been given super-
       natural powers. The majority of them are diagnosed as para-
       noid schizophrenics. Several differences between the Jewish
       and Christian conception of messianism are drawn up, and the
       author observes that some of his patients crossed this
       cultural boundary.

1102. Persinger, M. A. "People Who Report Religious Experiences
       May Also Display Enhanced Temporal-Lobe Signs." PERCEPTUAL
       AND MOTOR SKILLS 58 (1984): 963-75.

       Tests the hypothesis that religious experiences are caused
       by transient electrical stimulations in the temporal lobe.

According to this view, temporal lobe epilepsy and psychosis could be linked with proneness to exotic philosophy and mystical ideas. Various psychological tests, such as the Personal Philosophy Inventory (PPI), were administered to several subjects to find out whether the above effects of temporal lobe signs could be discerned by a self-evaluation method. The results are said to support the thesis that religious experiences are normal consequences of temporal lobe function.

1103. Persinger, M. A. "Religious and Mystical Experiences as Artifacts of Temporal Lobe Function: A General Hypothesis." PERCEPTUAL AND MOTOR SKILLS 57 (1983): 1255-62.

Examines the neurophysiological basis of religious and mystical experiences and suggests that they are "normal" consequences of "spontaneous biogenic stimulation of temporal lobe structures." These transient electrical impulses are also responsible for psychic experiences. Their frequency, duration, and intensity determine the extent of pathology present in the subject. Life-crises, exotic yogic postures, the repetition of mantras, and drastic diet changes could trigger the mechanism and create a "religious" experience, which the author labels a temporal lobe transient (TLT). The implications of the possible use of these experiences as potent modifiers of human behavior are considered.

1104. Peteet, John R. "Issues in the Treatment of Religious Patients." AMERICAN JOURNAL OF PSYCHOTHERAPY 35 (1981): 559-64.

Explains how religious patients are often difficult to treat, not only when it comes to ethical issues, but also in such areas as resistance to treatment, therapeutic issues, and countertransference. Some religious groups spurn psychiatry on principle. Religious patients are usually troubled with guilt feelings and the depression which accompanies them. They may also be hampered by their inability to think independently because of their membership in an authoritarian church. Therapy may undermine their religious faith. The ethical issues involved in treating these clients are discussed.

1105. Prince, Raymond. "Religious Experience and Psychosis." JOURNAL OF ALTERED STATES OF CONSCIOUSNESS 5 (1979-80): 167-81.

Presents the view that religious experience and psychosis are on a continuum. The frequency, distribution, and varieties of religious experiences are described with a number of case examples. The author's view is that psychosis and religious experience represent, more or less, unsuccessful or successful adaptation attempts on the part of people experiencing life-stress. While not identified with psychological disease as such, religious experience appears to be capable of creating or aggravating personal problems.

1106. Prince, Raymond. "Mystical Experience and the Certainty of
       Belonging: An Alternative to Insight and Suggestion in
       Psychotherapy." RELIGIOUS SYSTEMS OF PSYCHOTHERAPY (item
       1021), pp. 307-18.

       Explores the alleged psychotherapeutic effects of mystical
       states and the theories that have been proposed to explain
       them. The good effects of mystical experiences cannot be
       attributed to insight in the psychoanalytical sense, nor
       simply to the power of suggestion. The author believes that
       one can better understand them within the framework of more
       primitive modes of therapy, namely, "the integration of the
       individual into a supportive religiosocial network with peri-
       odically reinforced convictions and significant sacrifices,
       balanced by significant benefits" (p. 314).

1107. Pritchard, Warren. "Mysticism and Psychotherapy." JOURNAL
       OF CONTEMPORARY PSYCHOTHERAPY 6 (1974): 141-45.

       Proposes that mysticism is a necessary element in successful
       psychotherapy which, in part, replaces religion and shamanism.
       Several views, including those of Freud and Jung, are surveyed.
       It is noted that primitive tribes and great civilizations have
       rituals to help people prepare for death and other difficult
       thresholds of transformation. In modern Western culture,
       psychotherapy fills this role. LSD therapy in terminal ill-
       ness is cited as an example of the mystical element in psycho-
       therapy.

1108. Pruyser, Paul W. "The Seamy Side of Current Religious Be-
       liefs." BULLETIN OF THE MENNINGER CLINIC 41 (1977): 329-48.

       Discusses the psychological weaknesses of religion, partic-
       ularly the sacrifice of the intellect, wishful compromises,
       and authoritarianism. The resurgence of folk religion is
       viewed as a regressive trend. Several forms of religious
       pathology, including magic, ritual, and symbolism, are ex-
       plained. Among the criteria of neurotic religion, the follow-
       ing are listed: ill-adaptive, growth-stunting, regressive,
       shrinking of personal freedom, curbing of human potentialities.

1109. Reyniere, James H. "Behavior Therapy and Job's Recovery."
       JOURNAL OF PSYCHOLOGY AND THEOLOGY 3 (1975): 187-94.

       Continues the argument of his earlier essay (item 1110)
       and examines the role of behavior therapy techniques and the
       recovery of Job. Behavior therapy in the laboratory is out-
       lined and it is shown how the same method was also used in
       Job's case. The initial therapeutic process, which began with
       the appearance of Job's friends, is equated with systematic
       desensitization. Elihu (Job chs. 32-37) distracts Job from
       his own affliction and leads him to see God's greatness. The
       voice from the whirlwind (Job 38:1-21) culminates the thera-
       peutic process and is similar to the behavior technique of
       flooding. Job is cured of his helpless state of depression.

1110.   Reyniere, James H. "A Behavioristic Analysis of the Book of
        Job." JOURNAL OF PSYCHOLOGY AND THEOLOGY 3 (1975): 75-81.

        Attempts to apply some learning principles of behavioral
        psychology, rather than traditional psychoanalysis, to inter-
        pret Job's behavior and conversion. Job's situation is seen
        as one of physical and psychological helplessness, a condition
        commonly observed in institutionalized psychotics and labor-
        atory animals. Job's condition was "learned helplessness"
        with its concomitant maladaptive pattern of behavior (depres-
        sion). The article draws heavily on the Book of Job for
        documenting this interpretation.

1111.   Reynolds, Mildred M. "Religious Institutions and the Preven-
        tion of Mental Illness." JOURNAL OF RELIGION AND HEALTH 21
        (1982): 245-53.

        Recognizes the positive role of religious institutions in
        preventing mental illness by providing support in a community.
        Various types of programs found supportive by the President's
        Commission on Mental Health (1978) are referred to, and the
        support system of one particular church, Cedar Lane Unitarian
        Church in Bethesda, Maryland, is outlined.

1112.   Ricardo, Martin. MYSTICAL CONSCIOUSNESS: EXPLORING AN EXTRA-
        ORDINARY STATE OF AWARENESS. Burbank, CA: MVR Books, 1977.
        144 pp.

        Provides an overview of mysticism, giving some of its dis-
        tinguishing marks, its various types, and the methods used
        to attain it (particularly meditation). The claims that
        meditation has beneficial results, physical and mental, on
        those who practice are examined. The benefits of meditation
        are discussed in the context of Transcendental Meditation
        where the placebo effect, the receptivity of the person, and
        other psychological factors account for the good results.
        The most significant change reported after mystical enlight-
        enment is the elimination of the fear of death.

1113.   Rosen, Irving B. "Some Contributions of Religion to Mental
        Health." JOURNAL OF RELIGION AND HEALTH 3 (1974): 289-94.

        Argues against those psychologists who hold that religion
        does not contribute to mental health. The author holds that
        in the Bible and other religious literature, one comes across
        many insights which are of value to medicine and psychotherapy.
        The minister of religion often acts as a helpful listener to
        one's troubles. Religious beliefs and practices, like medi-
        tation, meet needs that are dealt with in modern psychotherapy
        by relieving people of their guilt feelings and by helping
        them cope with their anxieties, insecurities, and fears. The
        possible health-related functions of clergymen are outlined.

1114.   Rossi, Albert, editor. SPIRITUAL PRACTICE AND PSYCHOTHERAPY:
        A SYMPOSIUM. Washington, DC: American Psychological Associ-
        ation, 1981. Psychological Documents, MS 2449. 22 pp.

Contains the papers presented at the American Psychological
Association convention in Montreal, September 1980. These
short essays, which draw upon both Western and Eastern religious traditions, address the variables included in spiritual
practice as experienced by clients in psychotherapy. It is
stressed by several of the authors that the common belief in
a spiritual, transcendent reality cannot be ignored in psychotherapeutic practice.

Contains item 1334.

1115. Rottschafer, Ronald H. "The Passive Christian: Personality
       Disorder or Role Play." JOURNAL OF PSYCHOLOGY AND CHRIS-
       TIANITY 3 (1984): 42-51.

       Discusses whether Christianity, which appears to encourage
       passivity, attracts people with weak personalities, or whether
       those who become committed Christians develop psychological
       problems. Passivity becomes pathological when it ceases to
       be a well-chosen quietness, a careful withdrawal to gather
       strength, and becomes an expression of anxiety and fear. Four
       possible disorders linked with passivity--asocial actions,
       submissiveness, narcissism, and obsessive compulsion--and
       examples of Christians who fit into them, are outlined.
       Biblical teaching, prayer life, and church structure are
       three areas of Christianity which suggest a definite leaning
       towards passivity. Arguments are offered to show that Chris-
       tianity is ideally against all pathological forms of passivity.
       In a passing reference to the new cults, the author thinks
       that they are an example of the weak gravitating towards a
       somewhat satisfying system.

1116. Rowan, John. "The Real Self and Mystical Experience."
       JOURNAL OF HUMANISTIC PSYCHOLOGY 23.2 (1983): 9-27.

       Outlines seven separate and distinct mystical experiences
       which can be achieved through meditation. The author holds
       that, through therapy, "we learn how to open up to our inner
       process," while, through mysticism, "we learn how to carry
       on with that same process" (p. 25).

1117. Rumbaut, Ruben D. "Saints and Psychiatry." JOURNAL OF RELI-
       GION AND HEALTH 15 (1976): 54-61.

       Argues, in a somewhat apologetic tone, that Christian
       Scientists have made important contributions to health. Three
       Christian saints, St. Dympna, St. Vincent de Paul, and St.
       John of God, are said to have had an indisputable role in the
       advancement of psychiatry.

1118. Runions, J. Ernest. "The Mystic Experience: A Psychiatric
       Reflection." CANADIAN JOURNAL OF PSYCHIATRY 24 (1979):
       147-51.

       Observes that the psychiatrist is interested in the mystical
       experience and in cosmic consciousness, because they are

similar to the experiences of psychotics and neurotics, and
because they have played a role in the history of Western
medicine. The essential features of mysticism, namely, in-
evitability, noesis, transiency, passivity, and unio mystica,
are described, and the setting in which the experience occurs
is explored. The author warns against two possible fallacies:
1) the tendency to reductionism, that is, to explain mystical
experience solely in terms of pathology; and 2) the inclination to speculate on the psychological function of mysticism
without the adequate philosophical and theological tools.

1119. Runions, J. Ernest. "Religion and Psychiatric Practice."
       CANADIAN PSYCHIATRIC ASSOCIATION JOURNAL 19 (1974): 79-85.

       Reviews a series of 70 patients who were referred to him
       because of his known religious commitment. It is suggested
       that religion plays a normal integrative function in human
       life, but that it can also be used as a neurotic-defense
       mechanism, or as an aggressive tool to meet dependency needs.
       In certain situations, religion can protect one from anxiety
       arising out of inner conflicts and guard against awareness
       of the impact of one's actions upon others. The following
       features of manic religiosity are listed: "its intensity, its
       mystical quality without obvious integrating benefits, its
       volubility, its ecstasy, its superficiality" (p. 84).

1120. Sacerdote, Paul. "Application of Hypnotically Elicited
       Mystical States to the Treatment of Physical and Emotional
       Pain." INTERNATIONAL JOURNAL OF CLINICAL AND EXPERIMENTAL
       HYPNOSIS 25 (1977): 309-22.

       Studies those mystical experiences, or states of ecstasy,
       rapture, and trance, which occur spontaneously during hypnosis
       and transcendental meditation, the latter being viewed as a
       variety of the former. A distinction is made between intro-
       verted experiences of nothingness and extroverted mystical
       states. The former may lead to sensory and emotional isola-
       tion, which can in turn facilitate dissociation from the
       problems leading to calm and serenity. The latter, which are
       experiences of universal awareness, could lead the patient to
       deal in an entirely new way with problems of guilt and punish-
       ment, and of life and death. The author illustrates the above
       by presenting four subjects in whom he induced the mystical
       experience.

1121. Sacks, Howard L. "The Effect of Spiritual Exercises on the
       Integration of Self-Esteem." JOURNAL FOR THE SCIENTIFIC
       STUDY OF RELIGION 18 (1979): 46-50.

       Investigates the effects of the 30-day spiritual exercises
       of St. Ignatius of Loyola on 46 Jesuit novices to test the
       hypothesis that these meditative exercises, which are similar
       to religious experiences, result in "increased cognitive
       integration for the individual" (p. 47). The results confirm

the hypothesis, but leave unanswered the question as to which aspects of the exercises are primarily responsible for the positive change in the self-esteem of the participants.

1122.   Saffady, William. "New Developments in the Psychoanalytical Study of Religion: A Bibliographic Review of Literature since 1960." PSYCHOANALYTIC REVIEW 63 (1976): 291-99.

Points to various signs of renewed vitality in the psychoanalytic study of religion since the early 1960s, namely, the stress on the importance of the pre-oedipal period and ego-psychology, the combination of psychoanalytically-oriented historians and anthropologists, and the attempts to integrate psychoanalysis and religious thought. Several major criticisms of the psychoanalytic study of religion are outlined. Current literature favors the view that, in religion manifestations, psychoanalysts do not encounter a mystery beyond human comprehension and that "religion must now demonstrate that it can be healthy" (p. 297).

1123.   Scharfstein, Ben-Ami. MYSTICAL EXPERIENCE. Baltimore: Penguin, 1974. 195 pp.

Reviews different types, techniques, defenses, and claims of mysticism as practiced in both Eastern and Western cultures. The Yoga of Pantajali is discussed in relation to Freud's psychoanalytic theories. Both Yoga and psychoanalysis deal with common human problems, instincts, and regression, even though their aims are opposite. The author judges the goals and achievements of Yoga to be selfish and fanciful. He also describes certain qualities of the mystical experience, such as the loss of self or identity and fusion with others, hallucinations, psychotic experiences of time, certainty and bliss, and a sense of unreality.

1124.   Scholem, Gershom. SABBATAI SEVI: THE MYSTICAL MESSIAH. Princeton, NJ: Princeton University Press, 1973. xxvii, 1000 pp.

Presents a lengthy and detailed historical study of the life of a Jewish messiah in the seventeenth century, and the rise and growth of his movement in Palestine and its spread all over the Middle East and Europe. The author discusses (pp. 125 ff.) the mental health of Sevi, and concludes that there is hardly any doubt that he suffered from a manic-depressive psychosis coupled with paranoia. This diagnosis, however, does not say anything about the value of his thoughts and actions.

1125.   Scobie, Geoffrey E. W. PSYCHOLOGY OF RELIGION. New York: Wiley and Sons, 1975. 189 pp.

Provides a general introduction to the psychological study of religion, reviewing the various theories and research methods in the field. Religion is classified under three

headings, namely, world religions, denominations, and conversions. The latter can be of three types: 1) unconscious
conversion, a product of socialization; 2) gradual conversion
brought about by various conflicts and frustrations; and
3) sudden conversion, which occurs among those who are more
suggestible or subjected to physiological persuasion. Many
religious beliefs and practices linked with conversion, such
as glossolalia and mysticism, are dealt with. Because these
phenomena are also found in non-Christian and pseudo-religious
groups, the author thinks that they can be explained by psychological mechanisms. Several factors, like suggestibility,
prejudice, authoritarianism, and neuroticism, which have often
been connected with religion, are discussed.

1126. Sevensky, Robert L. "Religion, Psychology, and Mental Health."
AMERICAN JOURNAL OF PSYCHOTHERAPY 38 (1984): 73-86.

Attempts to further the dialogue between religion and
psychology by considering: 1) the prevalence of religious
involvement in mental care; 2) the effect of religion on our
view of human nature; 3) the way in which religion may manifest itself in mental illness; and 4) the question whether
religion can foster mental healthy or not. The author thinks
that religion should not be taken as evidence of psychopathology. Because religion is part of psychic life, it can easily
be distorted, and thus negatively affect one's mental health.
Among the unhealthy religious signs are listed demonic possession, inability to feel forgiven, feeling of abandonment
by God, glossolalia, and sudden religious conversion. A
healthy religion is comprehensive, open and seeking, tolerant
of ambiguity, and flexible. Therapists should not overlook
the resources available to understand religious beliefs and
practices. They should also not neglect the religious concerns of their patients.

1127. Snow, Loudell F. "Sorcerers, Saints, and Charlatans: Black
Folk Healers in Urban America." CULTURE, MEDICINE, AND
PSYCHIATRY 2 (1976): 69-106.

Reviews the literature on case histories of Black Americans
who, believing that illnesses may be caused by sorcery, have
consulted folk healers who often advertise in large city newspapers. The belief system about the origin, diagnosis, and
cure of disease is sketched. The author thinks that some
healers provide a useful service to their clients, but others
do nothing but extract money from the poor and gullible. In
either case, the root of the problems brought to the folk
healers lies in unemployment, poverty, and negative self-image
and cannot, therefore, be cured by magical means.

1128. Solignac, Pierre. THE CHRISTIAN NEUROSIS. Translated from
the French by John Bowden. New York: Crossroads, 1982.
168 pp.

Argues that traditional Christian education encourages
neurotic troubles with the consequent psychosomatic ailments.

Clinical examples of a priest, a physics teacher, a nun, a married priest, and a Catholic medical doctor are given to show that religious education was based on anxiety and fear, lack of confidence in human nature, and scorn for the body and sexuality. The church herself, according to the author, suffers from institutional neurosis, which can be seen in her inability to communicate with herself and with the world at large. Several suggestions are offered for a new education and a new church.

1129. Spero, Moshe H. "Religious Patients in Psychotherapy: Comments on Mester and Klein (1981)'s 'The Young Jewish Revivalist.'" BRITISH JOURNAL OF MEDICAL PSYCHOLOGY 56 (1983): 287-91.

Criticizes the views of Mester and Klein (item 1086) and illustrates the danger of misidentifying and generalizing on pathological aspects of the peculiarities of religiously-oriented patients. Their diagnostic process and, consequently, their conclusions, are questioned.

1130. Spero, Moshe H. "Counter Transference in Religious Therapists and Religious Patients." AMERICAN JOURNAL OF PSYCHOTHERAPY 35 (1981): 365-75.

Discusses the unique relationship between psychotherapists and their patients who share similar religious beliefs. Various distinctive counter-transference reactions may arise in the counseling context. These reactions stem mainly from a neurotic need for religious belief. Several guidelines for the therapist are listed, including the advice that the therapist "must be able to tolerate the patient's normal need for an area of emotional, and not necessarily rational, commitment and belief" (p. 573).

1131. Spilka, Bernard, Ralph W. Hood, and Richard L. Gorusch. THE PSYCHOLOGY OF RELIGION: AN EMPIRICAL APPROACH. Englewood Cliffs, NJ: Prentice-Hall, 1985. lx, 388 pp.

Introduces the reader to the psychology of religion. The main topics explored are: 1) the nature of religion; 2) religious development and change; 3) religious organization; 4) religious experience (including mysticism and conversion); and 5) religious belief and behavior (including mental disorder). Mystical experience, speaking in tongues, and sudden conversion could be manifestations of personal conflicts, psychological problems, or mental disturbances, but they could also have therapeutic effects. Cults are dealt with in several chapters, and three models of cult formation, namely pathological, entrepreneurial, and vertical are discussed. The authors maintain that brainwashing cannot account for conversions to the new religious movements.

1132. Staal, Frits. EXPLORING MYSTICISM: A METHODOLOGICAL ESSAY. Berkeley, CA: University of California Press, 1975. xix, 230 pp.

Reviews the methods by which mysticism is usually studied. New and more fruitful ways of analyzing the mystical experience are explored. In discussing the irrationality of mysticism, particularly in relation to Christ and Buddha, the author contends that these two religious founders exhibited a rational structure comparable to those found in modern scientists. Mysticism and rationality are thus compatible. Psychological approaches to mysticism are criticized as mostly impressionistic and should be largely avoided. The future of the psychology of mysticism looks promising, especially if one looks at the pioneering work of Deikman (items 504-5) on the psychology of meditation.

1133. Stettner, John W. "What to Do With Visions." JOURNAL OF RELIGION AND HEALTH 13 (1974): 229-38.

Sees a relationship between some of the extraordinary events related in the Bible, such as the visions of the prophets, the transfiguration of Jesus, his walking on the water, and Paul's experience on the road to Damascus, and contemporary claims of visions, psychic phenomena, and UFO sightings. Eschewing the common psychological interpretation which considers the above phenomena as indicative of pathology, the author points out how Anton Boisen and Carl Jung had to face similar experiences and integrate them in their lives. The author seems to assume throughout that these phenomena are not as abnormal as they appear, and that they may have a healthy effect on the individual.

1134. Stillwell, William. "The Process of Mysticism." JOURNAL OF HUMANISTIC PSYCHOLOGY 19.4 (1979): 7-29.

Proposes the view, based on Carlos Castaneda's studies, that mysticism is the initiate's process of being trapped in a series of paradoxical situations, and subsequent release. Similarities between mysticism and other intense experiences, like psychotherapeutic cures, creativity, and scientific discovery, are explored. The main features of mystical learning, common in many religious traditions, are outlined, and several paradoxical situations examined. Intrapersonal alienation, a form of neurosis, is present in all paradoxical situations and can, therefore be also found in mysticism. The mystic differs from the psychotic in that the latter is forced to withdraw from everyday life and only partially returns to it, while the former goes back to a full social life after a period of withdrawal.

1135. Switzer, David K. "Considerations of the Religious Dimensions of Emotional Disorder." PASTORAL PSYCHOLOGY 24 (1976): 317-28.

Investigates some of the different forms of relationships between religion and emotional disorder in the context of the author's counseling experience in a private psychiatric hospital. Three possible roles which religion might play in a person's emotional life are discussed: religion as a cause of one's problems; faith as an organization center in one's life; and religion as providing material for delusions and hallucinations. The following therapeutic suggestions are made: 1) consultation with peers; 2) short-term educational and interactional groups which focus on religious belief systems; and 3) opportunity for worship designed for patients.

1136. Szasz, Thomas. "The Myth of Psychotherapy." PSYCHOTHERAPY
        AND PSYCHOSOMATICS 24 (1974): 212-21.

        Proposes the view that there is no mental illness. While human misery, conflict, and prohibited social behavior definitely exist, they are not signs of human weakness, and cannot be listed as types of mental disorders. Psychotherapeutic interventions are metaphorical in character. The author states that "Psychotherapy is secular ethics; that is to say, it is the religion of the formally irreligious--with its language, which is not Latin, but mental jargon; with its theology, which is not Christianity, but positivism; and with its ultimate source of meaning and value, which is not God, but science" (p. 220). Although obviously a minority view in psychotherapy, this position raises some serious questions both on the nature of mental illness and of the dominant view of religion in the psychological sciences.

1137. Tart, Charles T. "Transpersonal Experience: Realities or
        Neurophysiological Illness?" JOURNAL OF INDIAN PSYCHOLOGY
        2 (1979): 93-113.

        Explains how the current scientific position, by equating consciousness with brain functioning, reduces the contents of transpersonal and religious experiences to chemical changes in the brain. The author argues that experiments refute this extreme view, and proposes a theory of "emergent interactionism" to account for human consciousness. Transpersonal experiences are interpreted not as illusions, but as valid and important insights into the nature of human consciousness.

1138. Tart, Charles T. "Some Assumptions of Orthodox, Western
        Psychology." TRANSPERSONAL PSYCHOLOGIES (item 1338), pp.
        61-111.

        Draws up in detail the underlying assumptions which Western psychology makes about the nature of the universe. The psychological view about the place of human beings in the universe, the nature of human consciousness, and life after death, are contrasted with the tenets of spiritual psychology. The current psychological view is that a person who spontaneously goes into, or cultivates, altered states of consciousness is probably mentally ill. Detachment from worldly things, which is invariably stressed by mystics, is a sign of pathology.

1139. Thomas, L. Eugene, and Pamela E. Cooper. "Incidence and
        Psychological Correlates of Intense Spiritual Experiences."
        JOURNAL OF TRANSPERSONAL PSYCHOLOGY 12 (1980): 75-85.

Explores the domain of peak or intense spiritual phenomena
in order to determine what exactly people experience, and
whether certain personality traits are linked with the experience. The results point to only one measurable personality
trait, namely, the intolerance of ambiguity, which actually
distinguished those who had the experience from those who had
not. The authors think that the influence of these religious
or spiritual experiences on personality growth and development
is significant.

1140. Tisdale, John R. "Mystical Experience: Normal and Normative."
       RELIGION IN LIFE 44 (1975): 370-74.

       Stresses the fact that mystical experiences are common in
       all religions and could be produced by drugs. The author
       relies on the works of Ornstein (item 569), Maslow (item 158),
       and Hood (items 1058-60) to support his insistence that non-
       rational mystical experience is universal to the human
       species, has clear psychological roots, and is necessary for
       a person's fullest development.

1141. Unger, Johan. "Is Religion a System of Adaptation?" PSYCHO-
       LOGICAL STUDIES ON RELIGIOUS MAN (item 1070), pp. 117-37.

       Discusses the psychological meaning of religion in the
       context of the theories of Allport, Jung, Freud, and others.
       The relationship between the image of God and one's personal-
       ity and self-concept is elaborated upon. The author draws
       the conclusion that "religion can contribute to give the
       individual meaning in what happens and thereby facilitates
       the individual's adaptation to his existence. However, reli-
       gion cannot give meaning to the different problem situations
       that the individual meets; it also creates problem situations"
       (pp. 135-6). Religion can thus be both a help and hindrance.

1142. Vanderpool, Harold Y. "Religion and Medicine: A Theoretical
       Overview." JOURNAL OF RELIGION AND HEALTH 19 (1980): 7-17.

       Maintains that recent scholarship calls for a reassessment
       of the nature of the relationship between medicine and reli-
       gion because, among other things, the results of "certain
       empirical studies in psychosomatic medicine and biofeedback
       are beginning to indicate the great degree to which human
       health and physiology are influenced by mental states, includ-
       ing those formed or informed by religion" (p. 9). Major areas
       of interaction are identified and outlined: the influence of
       religion on mental and emotional states; medical and religious
       explanations of disease; the therapy employed by both; and
       health behavior that is a direct consequence of religious
       beliefs.

1143. Vassallo, Janice N. "Psychological Perspectives of Buddhism:
       Implications for Counseling." COUNSELING AND VALUES 28
       (1984): 179-91.

Attempts to clarify the Buddhist perspective of the universal human problem of ignorance and craving for existence, and
suggests that wisdom and compassion--the Buddhist solution--
be used in therapy. The method of reaching enlightenment,
namely meditation, is then outlined. The counseling process
would involve the investigation of the individual's assumptions and belief system. The subject's energy and attention
should then be directed through specific meditation techniques
for the purpose of recognizing the incorrect view of reality
and its manifestations. The counseling relationship in which
both the counseling and the client are on the path that leads
to transpersonal actualization is stressed. Meditation should
be integrated into regular counseling procedures.

1144. Wainwright, William J. MYSTICISM: A STUDY OF ITS NATURE,
      COGNITIVE VALUE, AND MORAL IMPLICATIONS. Madison: Univer-
      sity of Wisconsin Press, 1981. xv, 244 pp.

      Discusses various theories on the nature of the mystical
      experience, especially the scientific explanations which have
      been put forward to account for it. The similarities and
      differences between mystical and psychotic experiences are
      registered. The author asserts that the fact that psychotic
      patients have mystical experiences leading to paranoia, does
      not cast doubt on the cognitive validity of the mystical
      experience. Cosmic consciousness cannot be dismissed as a
      sheer delusion which occurs in mentally ill people.

1145. Walls, Gary B. "Values and Psychotherapy: A Comment on
      'Psychotherapy and Religious Values.'" JOURNAL OF CONSULT-
      ING AND CLINICAL PSYCHOLOGY 48 (1980): 640-41.

      Criticizes Bergins's (item 1004) characterization of human-
      istic values for giving a false and degrading picture of what
      humanism really is, and offers an alternative expression of
      the values central in a humanistic world view. Bergin's sug-
      gestion that theism should be included in theories of psychol-
      ogy and psychotherapy is rejected on the grounds that it
      leads to an abdication of human responsibility to justify and
      critically assess human values.

1146. Ware, Kallistos T. "The Mystical Tradition of the Christian
      East: Cultural Varieties of Mysticism." R. M. BUCKE MEMO-
      RIAL SOCIETY: NEWSLETTER-REVIEW 7 (1974): 3-26.

      Considers three themes common to Eastern mystical tradition:
      1) the negative or "apophatic" approach to God; 2) the
      practice of the Jesus prayer; and 3) the experience of light.
      Similarities and differences between the Jesus prayer and
      Buddhist and Islamic forms of prayer are noted. The author
      also discusses the relationship between mysticism and society,
      particularly the mystic tendency to withdraw from the world,
      a tendency which is interpreted by psychologists as a sign
      of pathology. Quoting various Eastern Christian writers, the
      author insists that mysticism and social involvement are not
      necessarily incompatible.

1147. Welwood, John, editor. THE MEETING OF THE WAYS: EXPLORATIONS
       IN EAST/WEST PSYCHOLOGY. New York: Schocken Books, 1979.
       xvi, 240 pp.

       Presents a collection of previously published essays which
       were designed to offer new perspectives on the nature of human
       consciousness, personal identity, sanity, and psychotherapy.
       The editor's view is that Eastern psychology complements West-
       ern psychology, because the former is primarily rooted in
       direct experience, always sees human beings holistically, and
       is mainly concerned with understanding human experience,
       especially from the viewpoint of an enlightened state of mind.

       Contains items 613, 1416, 1432, and excerpts from item 569.

1148. Whiteman, J. H. M. "An Introduction to the Mystical Model
       for Psychotherapy." JOURNAL OF ALTERED STATES OF CONSCIOUS-
       NESS 5 (1979-80): 31-52.

       Argues against the medical model of psychopathology which
       lists distinct mental illnesses, and favors a mystical model
       which contains images of both behavior disorders and healthy
       features. This second model is traced back to the Buddha,
       Plato, the New Testament, and Swedenborg, and is in conformity
       with modern physics as well as Freudian theory. Behavior
       disorders are "escapes" provided when the development of
       higher integrative or mystical powers is in question.

1149. Whitlock, F. A., and J. V. Hymes. "Religious Stigmatization:
       An Historical and Psychophysiological Inquiry." PSYCHOLOG-
       ICAL MEDICINE 8 (1978): 185-202.

       Surveys the history of the stigmata phenomenon in Chris-
       tianity, and points out that those who suffered from it often
       underwent a long period of physical and psychological ill
       health. Though some of those who claimed to have received
       the stigmata are frauds, there are genuine cases which call
       for an explanation. Several theories, including the one which
       traces the cause of stigmata to hysteria, are discussed. The
       authors favor a neurological or physiological explanation. A
       lengthy bibliography is provided.

1150. Wikström, Owe. "Religion in Psychiatric Press 1972-76.
       A Literature Survey." PSYCHOLOGICAL STUDIES ON RELIGIOUS
       MAN (item 1070), pp. 195-218.

       Surveys the psychiatric literature listed in the inter-
       national data bank, Medline. Several areas are explored: the
       relationship between psychiatry and religion; possession,
       witchcraft, and exorcism; faith healing and stigmata; and
       transcultural psychiatry. The author concludes that the psy-
       chology of religion has not influenced psychiatry, and that
       Freud's psychoanalytic theory is still dominant. Because
       this survey uses a narrow, dynamic theory of religion, "the

therapeutic potential of a theory of religion as a goal-
directed, mature, ego-strengthening experience" is automat-
ically excluded.

1151. Wilbur, Ken. "Of Shadows and Symbols: Physics and Mysticism."
       REVISION: A JOURNAL OF CONSCIOUSNESS AND CHANGE 7.1 (1984):
       3-11.

       Discusses the relationship between modern physics and mys-
       ticism, and the attempts which have been made to stress their
       similar world views. The founders of modern physics are
       virtually in agreement in their view that developments in
       physics support the existence of mystical and transcendental
       levels of human life. Religion and science deal with differ-
       ent dimensions of reality and cannot be in conflict or in
       agreement.

1152. Wilson, William P. "Utilization of Christian Belief in Psy-
       chotherapy." JOURNAL OF PSYCHOLOGY AND THEOLOGY 2 (1974):
       125-31.

       Comments that past evidence has pointed to the therapeutic
       effects of strong religious faith on individuals suffering
       from a variety of psychological problems. The author thinks
       that Christian beliefs should be used in therapy rather than
       ignored or attacked. Symptomatic relief was obtained in 16
       out of 18 of the author's patients, when the Christian view of
       commitment, and Christian teaching on confession, forgiveness,
       and fellowship were used in conjunction with conventional
       psychotherapy.

1153. Wood, Barry G. "The Religion of Psychoanalysis." AMERICAN
       JOURNAL OF PSYCHOANALYSIS 40 (1980): 13-22.

       Discusses the healthy and neurotic aspects of religion in
       the context of Karen Horney's NEUROSIS AND HUMAN GROWTH and
       Charles Glock's five dimensions of religion. Both psycho-
       therapy and religion use rituals which can have either con-
       structive or damaging effects on the individual. Rituals that
       provide a constant context to explore the inconstant aspects
       of life, like the liturgical reading of scripture, are healthy.
       But any absolutized ritual is neurotic. The author attempts
       to lay down principles to distinguish healthy from neurotic
       elements in religious experiences.

1154. Woods, Richard, editor. UNDERSTANDING MYSTICISM. New York:
       Doubleday, 1980. xi, 586 pp.

       Offers a collection of essays and selections from books, all
       of which have been published over a period of almost three
       quarters of a century (1912-78). The material is divided
       into five parts dealing respectively with: 1) descriptions,
       analyses, and methodological concerns; 2) mysticism in world
       religions; 3) scientific (including psychological) investiga-

tions; 4) philosophical and aesthetic evaluations; and
5) theological appraisals.

Contains items 124, 143, 145, 186, 1026.

1155. Wootton, Raymond J., and David F. Allen. "Dramatic Religious
       Conversion and Schizophrenic Decompensation." JOURNAL OF
       RELIGION AND HEALTH 22 (1985): 212-20.

       Discusses the relationship, if any, between religious experi-
       ence and schizophrenic psychosis, and the possible ways of
       distinguishing between the two. Both phenomena are said to:
       1) begin in a series of characteristically identifiable stages;
       2) have similar or identical conditions; and 3) contain cor-
       responding stages in the processes of religious conversion
       and schizophrenic decompensation. In the former, however,
       the process ends up in a rapid and complete reintegration of
       the ego; in the latter, in the failure of one's defensive
       mechanism leading to the worsening of one's condition.

1156. Worthen, Valerie. "Psychotherapy and Catholic Confession."
       JOURNAL OF RELIGION AND HEALTH 13 (1974): 275-84.

       Summarizes the position of Jung on the values of both
       psychotherapy and Catholic confession. The author discusses
       the meaning of psychotherapy and confession, the possibility
       of comparing the former with the latter, the similarities and
       differences between them, and the possibilities of uniting
       them in one efficient method. It is concluded that while
       psychotherapy and confession are based on different and irrec-
       oncilable views on the nature of sin, both deal with similar
       human problems, namely, guilt, anger, hostility, jealousy,
       and loneliness. They could thus meet on common ground and
       contribute to psychological healing. Although the author does
       not discuss the cults, her observations are applicable to many
       of those sectarian religious groups which employ some form of
       confession in their rituals.

1157. Zales, Michael R. "Mysticism: Psychodynamics and Relationship
       to Psychopathology." EXPANDING DIMENSIONS OF CONSCIOUSNESS.
       Edited by A. Arthur Sugarman and Ralph E. Tarter. New York:
       Springer Publishing Co., 1978, pp. 253-72.

       Maintains that since mysticism is a universal phenomenon, it
       possibly serves certain psychic needs, or else solves common
       human problems. The mystical union, the mystic way, and the
       trance state (the latter being a less common form of mysticism)
       are described in the terminology of the mystics themselves.
       Three major differences between mystics and schizophrenics
       are noted: 1) the mystic's retreat from reality is not oblig-
       atory; 2) this retreat in the mystic is partial, rather than
       complete; 3) mystics maintain affective ties with other
       mystics. Though many mystics exhibit pathological symptoms
       and mental disturbances, others are very creative and
       adaptive.

1158. Ziff, Joel D. "Shabbat as Therapy: Psychosynthesis and
          Shabbat Ritual." JOURNAL OF PSYCHOLOGY AND JUDAISM 7
          (1983): 118-34.

          Attempts to understand the therapeutic effects of the
          Shabbat ritual practice through an analysis taken from the
          framework of psychosynthesis, which is briefly described.
          The Jewish day of rest is seen as a therapy system in four
          stages, namely, preparation, cessation of productive labor,
          the Meshamah Yetuyran (the extra or enlarged soul one receives
          on the Shabbat), and integration. The observance of this holy
          day provides an opportunity to withdraw, relax, and examine
          one's self--activities which lead to the satisfaction of
          one's true needs and the development of new insights. Shabbat
          and psychosynthesis might enhance one another in healing and
          in preventing illness.

1159. Zucker, Arnold H. "Conflict, Crisis, and Resolution in the
          Life of Maimonides." JOURNAL OF THE AMERICAN ACADEMY OF
          PSYCHOANALYSIS 2 (1974): 369-80.

          Gives an overview of the life of Moses Maimonides and con-
          siders his growth and maturation through crisis and resolution
          in the context of Freud's theory of the oedipus complex. The
          experience of Maimonides is relevant to those who are in crisis
          today, a crisis brought about by materialism, aggressive com-
          petition, and the craving for self-aggrandizement.

                     B.   GENERAL WORKS ON CULTS AND SECTS

     A commonly shared opinion exists that not all the new religious
movements or cults necessarily offer a viable alternative to traditional religions. The aggressive evangelical behavior of some of
them can be, at best, a nuisance. Many cults seem to promote extreme
forms of behavior, such as personal hardships or restrictive life-
styles, which might cause physical and psychological problems to
their adherents. Scholars, however, disagree strongly on the relation between cults and the traditional churches or synagogues, on
the status of Eastern religions in the West, and especially on the
definition of an "extremist" cult. Obviously not all cults are the
same. Attempts have been made to establish criteria to distinguish
between those cults which are genuine religious expressions and those
which are not (cf. Deikman, item 1192, and Welwood, item 1354). But
such endeavors have not resulted in a universally-accepted method of
evaluating fringe religious groups.

     Debate also flourishes on the significance of the new cults. Some
scholars and other observers of the cultic scene regard them as fads,
most of which will pass away, leaving a negligible impact on society
or religion. Others think that the cults, even those which will not
survive, indicate future religious trends and have already left their
mark on our culture and religion. Still others think that the cults
are a serious threat to Western civilization and should, therefore,
be suppressed.

In psychological literature, a distinction is sometimes made between pro-cult and anti-cult scholars. The result is that scientific scholarship concerning the new movements is split into two sharply divided camps. The anti-cult scholars recognize the danger of the cults and support their control or eradication by legal means, if necessary. Scant distinction is made between one cult and another. Since cult members are believed to have been tricked into joining, and the freedom of members to leave the cult is thought to be severely restricted, efforts to remove members by force have been frequently employed or encouraged. Pro-cult scholars are seen as defenders of the cults. They hold that there are some similarities between cults and traditional religious groups. They object to lumping all of the new religious movements together as extremist or destructive cults. They further insist that individual freedom has to be respected and that anti-cult legislation may have a negative impact on all religions. Pro-cult scholars are interpreted as being sympathizers of the cults with leanings towards their theological or philosophical principles.

It must be admitted that a few so-called pro-cult scholars have become personally involved in some of the new religious movements. But there is no evidence that the majority of these scholars agree with cultic ideology or approve of cultic practices. The anti-/pro-cult dichotomy is unrealistic. It is a rather unprofessional way of expressing differences of opinion and engaging in academic debate. It hinders understanding of the presence of the new movements and of their impact on culture and on individuals. Moreover, it is not therapeutically helpful. The controversy increases the anxiety of parents of cult members. It alienates cultists who need help from the traditional mental health services. There is apparent agreement, however, that membership in a cult is not a simple matter of religious conversion. The sociopolitical stress resulting from World War II and the strain which the rapidly changing cultural situation has created are considered to be the immediate causes of cult formation. Further, there is some indication that both the family situation as well as the individual's psychological makeup have a bearing on why a person decides to join a religious movement.

The issue arises whether traditional therapies can cope with the new problem or be adapted to treat the psychological difficulties of young adults in the second half of the twentieth century. Many relatively new therapies (like Gestalt and Transactional Analysis), though still on the fringe of traditional psychotherapy, have gained some popularity and respect within the psychological disciplines. The question is whether traditional psychotherapy can solve or relieve all psychological problems, including those of young adults who become cult members. A search for alternative therapies in an age of cultural change is expected. To what extent the new cults can succeed as alternative or complementary treatments to psychotherapy is debatable. The new religious movements, particularly those stemming from the East, have introduced to the Western world novel philosophical and psychological systems, new views of human nature and personality, and different religious answers to the meaning and goal of life. The new religions offer novel ideas about the main problems of life and their cure. Different life-styles, religious ideologies,

and spiritual practices have emerged. Numerous psychologists have
undertaken the study of the new psychology, be it Hindu or Buddhist.
Although Eastern psychologies appear inextricably linked with religious beliefs and practices, some scholars insist that they contain
a psychology which is distinct and separate from religion. Applied
Yoga psychology allegedly promotes human growth and self-development,
and Buddhism has been compared to behavior modification and Gestalt
therapy.

Several difficulties remain for the proponents of Eastern psychologies. Granted that Eastern religions comprise a well-developed
psychological system, it is difficult, however, to extricate this
system from its religious or spiritual matrix. Eastern religions
and several branches thereof have come to the West primarily as
spiritual systems offering salvation, and only secondarily as psychologies. Scholars who have investigated Eastern psychologies are
of the opinion that Western culture could derive new insights about
the human psyche by consideration of both the theory and practical
application of Eastern psychological systems. In the West, it has
often been assumed that traditional psychotherapy has cross-cultural
validity and that few insights, if any, can be acquired from non-
Western cultures. Theoretical studies of Eastern psychologies and
their incorporation into clinical practice have challenged this
ethnocentric viewpoint.

Another issue is the applicability and adaptability of Eastern
religions and psychologies to the West. Put in simpler terms: are
the Eastern psychologies so culture-bound that they are not cross-
culturally transportable? The only way to answer this question is
to check the empirical data over a relatively long period of time.

Accompanying the rise of interest in the religious psychology of
the East is the development of Christian psychology. The latter is
especially evident in Christian fundamentalist sects who look for
answers to all human psychological ills in the Bible. The proper
ways to raise children, to solve marital conflict, and to relate to
other people, are drawn from Christian principles and not from the
fundamental assumptions about human nature and psyche implicit in
current psychotherapy.

Because the new religious movements are promulgating new psychological and psychotherapeutic systems, the study of these systems
is a prerequisite for understanding their attractiveness and success.
Understanding these systems is required in counseling ex-cult members
who may have already adopted some of the psychological principles of
Eastern religious groups. The so-called "re-entry" problems experienced by those who have, willingly or forcibly, left the cults,
stem, in part at least, from the psychological change of returning
to a Western life-style and philosophical orientation. One example
will suffice to demonstrate the delicate task of the counselor or
therapist. In Western culture, independence and self-development
are stressed from childhood. In fact, one way of assessing an
individual's psychological health is to check his or her "field
independence" and "ego-strength." In many Eastern cultures, on the
contrary, belonging to an extended family group has priority. One
simply does not act on one's own initiative irrespective of what

family members think. Counselors of foreign students in the West
are well-acquainted with the difference. What are taken to be signs
of pathology in Western students may be indications of a balanced
and healthy mind in students who were brought up in an Eastern
country. Understanding Eastern psychology may also prove to be useful in the counseling of cult members and their parents. One major
problem which parents have to face is the lack of conceptual tools
to evaluate how their offspring changed both before joining a cult
and after they had become cult members. Some psychological changes
are the direct result of an acceptance of a different life-style and
value system, which teaches quite a different view of human nature
and provides a different answer to life's ultimate questions. The
clash between opposing values is what the counselor has to face in
many cult-related cases.

1160. Addis, Marsha, Judith Schulman-Miller, and Meyer Lightman.
        "The Cultic Clinic Helps Families in Crises." SOCIAL CASE-
        WORK 65 (1984): 515-22.

        Addresses the counseling and educational needs of troubled
        families of cult members and describes efforts of the Los
        Angeles Jewish Family Services to meet them. Accepting the
        theory that cult membership is dangerous, the authors show
        how the parents and siblings react to the loss of a family
        member, and how the cults themselves threaten family struc-
        ture. The clinic helps families by teaching them about mind
        control and cult recruitment methods, by developing communi-
        cation techniques to assist them in relating to their child-
        ren's involvement in cults, and by pointing out strategies
        that can be used to urge cult members to reevaluate their
        new commitment.

1161. Adler, Nathan. "Ritual, Release, and Orientation: Maintenance
        of Self in the Antinomian Personality." RELIGIOUS MOVEMENTS
        IN CONTEMPORARY AMERICA (item 1360), pp. 283-97.

        Supports the view that there is a relationship between new
        movements and their stressful, changing social environments.
        Calling these religious groups "antinomian," because of their
        "characteristic opposition to established values," the author
        argues that they act as a psychological mechanism, helping the
        individual adapt to current crises, which have brought into
        being problems of self-identification and personal orientation.
        The basic function of new religious movements is to resanctify
        experience. A common feature of modern movements is their
        repudiation of rational knowledge in favor of an intuitive,
        visionary gnosis which astrology, among others, so clearly
        demonstrates. The charismatic leader's social role is
        stressed. The author states that "in time of crisis and
        change the pathologic may find a social platform and a pub-
        lic which validates its nay-saying. In new roles, deviants
        thus achieve prominence and are confirmed in modes of be-
        havior that otherwise might be stigmatized as as sickness"
        (p. 297).

344

1162. Allen, Mark. CHRYSALIS: A JOURNEY INTO THE NEW SPIRITUAL
       AMERICA. Berkeley, CA: PAN Publishing, 1978. 179 pp.

       Reports the author's own personal encounter with many new
       religious movements, including Zen, Tibetan Buddhism, and
       Silva Mind Control, all of which are interpreted positively
       as ways to expand human consciousness. In a section on the
       study of psychology, the author stresses that the West has
       much to learn from Eastern psychology.

1163. American Family Foundation. CULTISM: A CONFERENCE FOR
       SCHOLARS AND POLICY MAKERS. Weston, MA: American Family
       Foundation, 1985. 16 pp.

       Outlines the topics discussed at the "Wingspread Conference
       on Cultism" in Racine, Wisconsin. The problems of cultism,
       and research and educational recommendations are the two major
       items covered. A negative definition of extremist cults,
       which are detrimental to the individuals who join them, their
       families, and the community, is adopted. Cult-related con-
       cerns are said to overflow into government, business, and
       education. The resolution adopted by the European Parliament
       on May 22, 1984, is included.

1164. American Family Foundation. YOUNG PEOPLE AND CULTS: A PRE-
       VENTIVE APPROACH. RESOURCE HANDBOOK. Weston, MA: American
       Family Foundation, 1983. 59 pp.

       A workbook on cultism, listing some major resources and
       reproducing selected readings. A destructive cult is defined
       as one which utilizes extreme and unethical manipulation,
       frequently causing psychological and physical harm to indi-
       viduals. Among the psychologically negative effects of cult
       membership are distancing oneself from or rejecting one's
       family, diminished independent critical thinking, and a slow-
       down of personality development. The theory of brainwashing
       seems to dominate the material selected in this collection.

1165. Appel, Willa. CULTS IN AMERICA: PROGRAMMED FOR PARADISE.
       New York: Rinehart and Winston, 1983. 204 pp.

       Discusses contemporary cults, which are seen as provoking
       controversy because they are counter-culture, undemocratic,
       and anti-social groups. The messianic visions which they
       offer are compared to fairy tales. Most cult members are
       said to be ordinary people who face the problems created by
       insecurities of life and who are then warped by the indoc-
       trination techniques, such as meditation, used to control them.
       The author has no doubt that cults are psychologically harm-
       ful to their members, and that ex-members are left emotionally
       sick, requiring special therapy and rehabilitation. Several
       ways of counseling ex-cult members are proposed.

1166. Applebaum, Stephen A. "Challenges to Traditional Psycho-
       therapies from the 'New Therapies.'" AMERICAN PSYCHOLOGIST
       37 (1982): 1002-8.

Responds to the criticism leveled at traditional psychotherapies by the human potential movement, which encompasses
Gestalt, psychosynthesis, Rolfing, bioenergetics, Est, Silva
Mind Control, meditation, biofeedback, and other psychological
techniques for self-development. While the author thinks
that psychoanalysis needs improvement and refinement, he does
not see the new therapies as an effective substitute. At
best, "the new therapies can be viewed as an informal, inex-
pensive laboratory for testing new ideas and practices, for
stimulating discourse, for forcing conventional therapies
either to adopt and espouse new ideas or to refine their own"
(p. 1008).

1167. Applebaum, Stephen A. OUT IN INNER SPACE: A PSYCHOLOGIST
ELPLORES THE NEW THERAPIES. Garden City, NY: Anchor Press/
Doubleday, 1979. xxii, 529 pp.

Examines several of the new therapies, including Est, Silva
Mind Control, Yoga, and Transcendental Meditation, and considers several influences, like the placebo effect, suggestion,
and the relationship between the patient and the therapist,
which are operative in some of them. In general, the author
finds these new techniques beneficial. Est, for example,
encourages an attitude of detachment, interrupts any morbid
self-preoccupation, limits unpleasant feelings, and controls
the individual's tendency to take everything too seriously.
He is inclined to see the new therapies as complementary to
traditional psychotherapy, though he has some minor reservations, expressed by the label "Fast Food Chains," which he
applies to them.

1168. Ash, Stephen. "Cult-Induced Psychopathology, Part I: Clinical
Picture." CULTIC STUDIES JOURNAL 2 (1985): 31-90.

Synthesizes the available literature on the psychopathological results of cult membership into a theoretical overview.
In extremist cults there is a direct link between the cult
conversion process and its resulting pathological impairment.
Several factors which render people vulnerable to cults are
outlined: cultural disillusionment, moderately dysfunctional
family systems, lack of intrinsic religious belief systems,
and dependent personality tendencies. It is argued that, in
extremist cults, conversion, isolation, induction of a dissociative state (through physical debilitation and lack of
sleep), and indoctrination into cultic views and life-style
are the major operative elements in the recruitment and maintenance of devotees. The stages of a person's dissociation
from a cult are discussed, and the model adopted by the
American Family Foundation (see item 1164) is evaluated.
An overview of the clinical picture, which includes the ego
functions, the physical appearance, the affect, and the problems of cult members, is given, using the DSM-III as a
reference guide. A lengthy bibliography is appended.

1169. Ash, Stephen. "Avoiding the Extremes in Defining Extremist
Cults." CULTIC STUDIES JOURNAL 1 (1984): 37-63.

Examines the two major interpretations of cults, namely,
one which considers them as other religious groups (the
"pro-cult" position), and the other which sees them as quite
different organizations, creating special problems for the
individuals who join them and for society as a whole (the
"anti-cult" position). Criteria for distinguishing extremist
cults are proposed. It is the author's view that such cults
are psychologically harmful to their members.

1170. Ashby, Robert H. "The Guru Syndrome." THE SATAN TRAP (item
        1201), pp. 34-52.

        Comments on the tendency of those people who uncritically
        accept as facts what is but honest opinion, who develop un-
        bridled admiration for anyone with apparent credentials for
        psychic abilities, and who misplace their faith on people
        who claim they are illuminated. Such attraction towards
        gurus is labeled "the Guru Syndrome," which is an exagger-
        ated enthusiasm liable to create psychological problems.
        Several examples of this syndrome are provided. One can
        avoid falling into this trap by using one's critical acumen
        and by maintaining a balanced view on psychic issues.

1171. Atwood, George E. "On the Origins and Dynamics of Messianic
        Salvation Fantasies." INTERNATIONAL REVIEW OF PSYCHO-
        ANALYSIS 5 (1978): 85-96.

        Presents a brief description of three hospitalized patients
        whose lives were dominated by messianic themes and salvation
        imagery, and then offers a psychoanalytic interpretation of
        their condition. Several features of the "salvation fantasy"
        are listed: 1) the experience of sympathetic identification
        with the suffering of all people; 2) the feeling of an obli-
        gation to relieve others from pain, even if one's own happi-
        ness is sacrificed; and 3) the belief that the mission is part
        of one's higher calling. The author explains the salvation
        fantasy as "the product of a series of psychological adapta-
        tions to certain traumatic experiences which begin during the
        early phases of childhood" (p. 89). These experiences include
        disappointments or losses in relationships with early love
        objects, and a great desire to recover the previously peace-
        ful situation, a desire which is incompatible with one's
        hostile and vindictive feelings. This dilemma is solved by
        a retreat into a world of fantasy in which negative feelings
        are suppressed and positive images idealized. The patient
        finally personalizes and identifies himself or herself with
        the positive image. The shadowy side of salvation fantasies
        and their defensive functions are described. The author
        distinguishes three variants of salvation fantasy, namely,
        depressive, paranoid, and moral.

1172. Avens, Robert. "Silencing the Question of God: The Ways
        of Jung and Suzuki." JOURNAL OF RELIGION AND HEALTH 15
        (1976): 115-35.

Aims at understanding the religious aspect of Jung's thought
through the Satori of Zen Buddhism, and throwing light on the
latter by using Jung's concept of individuation. The author
considers the collective unconscious and the archetypes, and
describes the unconscious and the experience of Satori as
expounded by Suzuki. Satori is said to be an experience of
reality. Zen and Jungian psychology are conceived as psychological processes, which "endeavor to silence the question
of God by reorienting our attention to the inward man" (pp.
131-32).

1173. Bailey, Larry W. "Focus of Fulfillment." JOURNAL OF PSYCHOL-
      OGY AND THEOLOGY 3 (1975): 294-97.

Comments on the popular quest for fulfillment and self-
actualization, which has been central in several new religious
movements and in the work of humanistic psychologists. The
author tries to reconcile the teachings of Jesus on self-
denial and the findings of Maslow on self-development. It
is maintained that, in both cases, the locus of fulfillment
and of a healthy personality is to be found not in the self,
but rather outside the self.

1174. Barkun, Michael. DISASTER AND THE MILLENNIUM. New Haven, CT:
      Yale University Press, 1974. x, 246 pp.

Examines the relation between two dissimilar concepts: a
disaster, which suggests death and desolation, and the
millennium, which points to salvation and fulfillment. The
nature and scope of millenarian movements, their origin in
disasterous events and conditions, and the relation between
conversion and catastrophe are among the topics dealt with.
One chapter discusses whether these movements are instances
of rational behavior or cases of mass psychopathology. The
three most frequently used perspectives to explain cults,
namely, epidemic hysteria, paranoia, and the religious ecstacy,
are surveyed. The author prefers the last-mentioned theory.
He sees these groups not as evidence of mental instability,
but as an energizing device which resocializes the individual,
and as a contrived means for recapturing the "disaster utopia."
Millenarianism in the modern world and the changing pattern
of disasters are finally considered.

1175. Beckford, James. "The World Images of New Religions and
      Healing Movements." SICKNESS AND SECTARIANISM (item 1238),
      pp. 72-93.

Gives a rapid and sketchy review of social scientific
literature on new religious movements which, in the author's
view, has minimized the importance of healing within these
groups. Historical studies have been more aware of the
connection between religion and healing. The discussion of
healing in the new movements has been concerned with three
major areas: 1) the mental health of participants; 2) the
applicability of the mental health model to the new religions;

and 3) the attitudes towards psychotherapy among members of
the new cults. The author suggests that the current debate
would be more profitably centered on the assumptions, themes,
and images underlying the healing practices of the new movements.

1176.   Bender, Hans. "Psychosis in the Séance Room." THE SATAN
        TRAP (item 1201), pp. 231-8.

        Maintains that pathological conditions are present in those
        who participate in, or lead, a mediumistic sitting. Several
        examples are given to show that spiritualistic practices are
        emotionally charged situations which may be psychologically
        dangerous.

1177.   Benor, Daniel J. "Psychic Healing." ALTERNATIVE MEDICINES
        (item 1309), pp. 165-302.

        Surveys the popular field of psychic healing. The main
        principles in such healing, and the way they differ from
        modern conventional medicine are outlined. The psychic
        healer, the author suggests, might be a psychotherapist, and
        his successes may be explained by psychosomatic mechanisms.
        Just by listening to the client's problem, the healer may be
        instrumental in reducing anxiety and tension. The author
        concludes that the potential benefits inherent in psychic
        healing are bound to have an impact on medicine, psychology,
        and theology.

1178.   Bloomgarden, Andrea, and Michael D. Langone. "Preventive Edu-
        cation on Cultism for High-School Students: A Comparison of
        Different Programs' Effects on Potential Vulnerability to
        Cults." CULTIC STUDIES JOURNAL 1 (1984): 167-77.

        Points out that the cult crisis has suggested four ways of
        reacting to their influence: deprogramming, legislative pro-
        posals, voluntary counseling, and preventive education, the
        last mentioned being theoretically the most attractive sugges-
        tion. The authors compare the effects on 190 students of
        four types of preventive programs: 1) presentation by an ex-
        cult member; 2) a video of that presentation; 3) a film on
        the cults; and 4) a number of filmstrips. Educators are
        encouraged to avoid scare programs. Various limitations of
        this study are listed: the sample was not representative;
        there was lack of psychometric testing on the questions
        asked; and the research question itself is slanted towards
        a definite (and negative) view of cult education theory.

1179.   Boorstein, Sylvia. "Notes on Right Speech as a Psychothera-
        peutic Technique." JOURNAL OF TRANSPERSONAL PSYCHOLOGY
        17 (1985): 47-56.

        Suggests that the use of Right Speech can be used outside
        its context of the Buddhist Eightfold Path to treat patients
        with difficulties related to their style of speaking. The

writer explains how this is done in clinical situations, and
presents three case studies to illustrate the technique.
Right Speech can be used effectively to bring about personal
changes, especially when there is no underlying psychopathology. It should be used as an adjunct to, rather than a
substitute for, traditional psychotherapy.

1180. Bromberg, Walter. FROM SHAMAN TO PSYCHOTHERAPIST: A HISTORY
OF THE TREATMENT OF MENTAL ILLNESS. Chicago: Henry Regnery,
1975. vii, 360 pp.

Gives a historical overview of the healing of mental illness. All forms of healing procedures, from magical rites to
modern psychotherapy, are covered. Shamanism and faith healing in different ancient and modern societies are described.
Nineteenth-century healing practices, like mesmerism and
Christian Science, and twentieth-century procedures, like
witchcraft, Zen, and Yoga, are among the methods considered.
"The present scene in this country represents virtually a
recapitulation of the entire history of the art and science
of mental healing" (p. 347). The author's view is that the
skill and deceit of the curer or psychotherapist, together
with magical thinking and omnipotence fantasies, are at the
root of the specific healing systems, including psychotherapy,
hypnosis, behavior modification, and faith healing.

1181. Camic, Charles. "Charisma: Its Varieties, Pre-conditions,
and Consequences." SOCIOLOGICAL INQUIRY 50 (1980): 5-23.

Maintains that progress in the sociological study of
charisma has been limited, and suggests that Freud's work
could throw light on the matter. Since the conditions for
the rise of charisma are extraordinary psychological needs,
the author thinks that charisma should be differentiated into
four phenomena: omnipresence, excellence, sacredness, and the
uncanny. Charisma is defined as the formation of immediate
relationship with need-gratifying figures, characterized by
awe, devotion, and obedience.

1182. Chaudhuri, Haridas. "Yoga Psychology." TRANSPERSONAL PSY-
CHOLOGIES (item 1338), pp. 233-80.

Gives the history, philosophical basis, and personality
theory of Yoga. Yoga psychology encompasses all kinds of
human experience, including the mystical. The various disciplines of Yoga are intended for the attainment of personal
self-realization. It is assumed that Yoga, in spite of some
dangers, leads to a healthy personality.

1183. Clark, John G. "Cults." JOURNAL OF THE AMERICAN MEDICAL
ASSOCIATION 242 (July 1979): 279-81.

Gives a general description of cult members, and attempts
to explain their susceptibility to conversion to those groups
whose goals are expansion by recruitment and the amassing of

money. The negative effects of conversion, and the rejection
of modern medicine which often follows it, are briefly dealt
with. Many of the cults, according to the author, are
intolerant of others and destructive.

1184. Clark, John G. "Problems in Referral of Cult Members."
        NATIONAL ASSOCIATION OF PRIVATE PSYCHIATRIC HOSPITALS
        JOURNAL 9.4 (1978): 27-29.

        Outlines what is expected from hospitals when a cult or ex-
        cult member is enrolled for treatment, namely: professional
        consultation; special and unique diagnostic and treatment
        services; and protection of patient and community. Several
        case examples are given to illustrate the problems in deal-
        ing with cult members. Because some cults are dangerous and
        have a corrupting influence on young adults, their members
        might require special treatment.

1185. Clark, John G., and Michael D. Langone. "The Treatment of
        Cult Victims." HANDBOOK OF PSYCHIATRIC CONSULTATION WITH
        CHILDREN AND YOUTH. Edited by Norman R. Bernstein and
        James Sussex. New York: SP Medical and Scientific Books,
        1984, pp. 373-86.

        Makes several counseling suggestions for treating members
        of destructive cults. An assessment of cultists should be
        the first step. Their mental status, family relations, his-
        tory, nature of their involvement, and various psychological
        traits should be examined. Former cult members suffer from
        "an impaired capacity to exhibit an adaptive autonomy in their
        daily functioning" (p. 376). The counselor should help them
        cope with their daily tasks, make a connection with their
        pre-cult experiences, and confront the cult experience itself.
        Theological debates should be avoided. In the treatment of
        parents of cult members, the counselor should create an
        atmosphere of safety, examine and verify their feelings and
        beliefs, deal with the caretaker urge they feel toward their
        offspring, and help them promote their offsprings' post-cult
        psychological development. Clinicians are advised to be care-
        ful before recommending, or participating in, any type of
        deprogramming.

1186. Clifford, Terry. TIBETAN BUDDHIST MEDICINE AND PSYCHIATRY:
        THE DIAMOND HEALING. York Beach, ME: Samuel Weiser, 1984.
        xx, 268 pp.

        Introduces the reader to Tibetan Buddhist medicine and
        psychiatry as seen in their religious, cultural, and his-
        torical contexts. Several areas are covered: 1) medical
        psychiatry; 2) demons (invisible energies and forces) in
        medical psychiatry; 3) three chapters from the Four Tantras
        (Gyu-Zhi); and 4) the pharmacology of Tibetan Buddhist medi-
        cal psychiatry. Parallels between specific types of psycho-
        pathology in Tibetan and Western traditions are noted. The
        Tibetan approach to healing is holistic, combining mental,

spiritual, and mystical techniques with the regular practice
of medicine, and can be applied in the treatment of serious
mental disorders. Tibetan healing also requires a high degree
of morality and kindness on the part of the healer. Buddhist
therapy is not psychoanalysis, but rather a transformation
of self through the development of morality, meditation, and
wisdom. Charts of substances used in Tibetan psychiatric
remedies are provided.

1187. Collins, Gary R. "Popular Christian Psychologies: Some
Reflections." JOURNAL OF PSYCHOLOGY AND THEOLOGY 3 (1975):
127-32.

Discusses the rise of popular Christian counselors, whose
advice as to how to rear children, have a better marriage,
and settle quarrels is followed uncritically by many people.
The main features of these popularizers are listed: relevance;
simplicity; practicality; avoidance of academic matters;
communication skills; personal appeal; biblical orientation;
reactionary nature; and uniqueness. The appeal of these
Christian psychologists is discussed. The author thinks that
the enthusiastic disciples of various Christian counselors
"create a cult-like atmosphere around a somewhat reluctant
guru" (p. 130). Guidelines for evaluating these popular
Christian psychologists are given.

1188. Conway, Flo, and Jim Siegelman. SNAPPING: AMERICA'S EPIDEMIC
OF SUDDEN PERSONALITY CHANGE. New York: J. B. Lippincott,
1978. 254 pp.

Outlines the popular view that converts to the new religious
and evangelical movements experience a sudden personality
change called "snapping." According to the authors, such a
conversion may lead to an "information disease," characterized by impaired awareness, irrationality, disorientation,
and delusion, and sometimes violent, destructive acts. What
happens to members of the new cults is not simply hypnosis
or brainwashing. The fundamental working of their minds is
drastically altered. Examples from many of the new cults,
such as the Children of God, Scientology, the Unification
Church, Yoga groups, the International Society of Krishna
Consciousness, and Transcendental Meditation, are given to
expound in detail the information disease theory.

1189. Coukoulis, Peter. GURU, PSYCHOTHERAPIST, AND SELF: A COM-
PARATIVE STUDY OF THE GURU-DISCIPLE RELATIONSHIP AND THE
JUNGIAN ANALYTIC PROCESS. Marina del Rey, CA: DeVorss and
Co., 1976. 120 pp.

Pursues three main goals: 1) the investigation of the
psychological aspects of the guru-disciple relationship as
found in Eastern traditions; 2) the comparison of this relationship with the Jungian analyst and his patient; and
3) the delineation of those features in the guru-disciple
relationship which throws light on its Jungian counterpart.

Eastern and Jungian concepts of the self and of the personal
goal of realization are presented and compared. Three Eastern
gurus, Milarepa, Sri Ramakrishna, and Sri Aurobindo, are examined from the standpoint of analytical psychology. In both
relationships, the essential goal is to eliminate the rule
of the ego. Just as the guru is only a means to the divine,
so the Jungian analyst is just a means through which his subject establishes a connection with the collective unconscious.
The end result is that disciples and patients will no longer
need their gurus and analysts respectively.

1190. Cushman, Philip. "The Politics of Vulnerability: Youth
       in Religious Cults." PSYCHOHISTORY REVIEW 12 (1984): 5-17.

       Argues that the new cults make a premeditated attack on the
       "self" of potential recruits, thus precipitating a narcissis-
       tic crisis, which makes the individual more willing to make
       a commitment. Most young people are especially vulnerable
       because of sociopolitical stresses since World War II. Cults
       offer young people the fantasies of instant friendship, free-
       dom from anxiety, reliable authority, and spiritual meaning.
       Deprogramming is defined as non-forceful exit-counseling,
       which is needed by the great majority of those who leave the
       cults. The major symptoms of cult life are enumerated:
       1) dissociation, depersonalization, and retardation of adult-
       hood (or regression); 2) fragmentation and dissociation of
       self; and 3) a narcissistic symbiosis with the cult leader.
       The process of becoming a cult member is outlined in several
       stages.

1191. Dean, Roger A. "Youth: Moonies' Target Population."
       ADOLESCENCE 17 (1982): 567-74.

       Looks at some of the psychological, social, and emotional
       experiences of youth in order to understand why they are
       vulnerable to the cults. The stages of normative develop-
       ment, namely, identity struggle, idealism, intellectual
       curiosity, and disillusionment, are examined. The author,
       using members of the Unification Church as examples, believes
       that these stages are the necessary preambles to cult involve-
       ment. A traumatic experience may also increase a person's
       susceptibility to recruitment tactics. Some groups, like
       the Unification Church, offer discontented people a new and
       concrete option for the reconstruction of their lives.

1192. Deikman, Arthur J. "The Evaluation of Spiritual and Utopian
       Groups." JOURNAL OF HUMANISTIC PSYCHOLOGY 23.3 (1983):
       8-18.

       Argues that one can discriminate between genuine and spu-
       rious religious groups by examining how a group's activities
       are suited to their stated claims. Selfless orientation is
       a major feature of true spirituality. Those movements which
       use fear to discourage members from defecting, condemn all
       ex-members, manipulate guilt, and indoctrinate their members

into a rigid system of belief and practice cannot promote
spiritual development. Genuine leaders, religious or otherwise, do not use their followers for personal gain. Similar
functional criteria should be employed to evaluate those
groups which claim that they provide therapeutic benefits for
their members. The group can be judged to be healthy if it
helps people to work and to love, and if it encourages them
to be autonomous.

1193. Denning, Melita, and Osborne Philips. THE MAGICAL PHILOSOPHY.
BOOK 1: ROBE AND RING. St. Paul, MN: Llewellyn Publications,
1974. 192 pp.

Attempts a historical overview of Western spiritual ideals
and their developments in religion, philosophy, and magic.
The part played by alchemy in human development and transformation into an integrated personality is presented. Also
outlined is the merger of magical principles in modern psychology, and the relevance of the latter to modern "magick."
Several exercises or techniques (such as physical postures,
breathing methods, and meditation) for awakening one's higher
faculties are described.

1194. De Silva, Padmal. "Buddhism and Behavior Modification."
BEHAVIOR RESEARCH AND THERAPY 22 (1984): 661-78.

Examines the early Buddhist literature to determine how
Buddhist techniques compare to those used in behavior modification. The author thinks that the Buddhist approach is
very close to methods of behavior modification since Buddhism
adopts an experimental and empiricist standpoint, endorses a
relation between ethics and doctrine, and stresses action.
The following behavior change methods in early Buddhism are
described: setting an example; fear reduction by reciprocal
inhibition; stimulus control; mastery of intrusive thoughts;
thought-control through mindfulness; meditation as a therapeutic method; and cognitive therapy. The implications for
modern behavior modification are discussed. Buddhist techniques are wide-ranging, and can be combined with current
behavior therapy methods for a better system of behavior
change, which can be applied cross-culturally. Buddhist
concepts and practices can also be valuable in the prevention
of some common psychological disorders.

1195. De Silva, Padmasiri. AN INTRODUCTION TO BUDDHIST PSYCHOLOGY.
New York: Macmillan, 1979. xii, 134 pp.

Describes the basic features of Buddhist philosophy and the
part cognition, motivation, and emotion play in the system.
The relationship between Buddhism and Western psychologies and
their similarities in the therapeutic situation are discussed.
Buddhism offers important points of convergence with psychoanalysis, humanistic psychology, and existential therapy.
The author detects a gap between Buddhism and behavior
therapy, since the former prefers insight and self-under-

standing to counter-conditioning and desensitization. It
is demonstrated how Buddhism can be applied to contemporary
Western social pathology, specifically to the West's
depersonalization tendencies, identity crisis, narcissism,
loneliness, sexuality, boredom, and encounter with emptiness.

1196. Deutsch, Alexander, and Michael J. Miller. "Conflict, Char-
       acter, and Conversion: Study of a 'New Religion' Member."
       ADOLESCENT PSYCHIATRY 7 (1979): 257-68.

       Presents a case of a young Catholic woman who joined a new
       religious movement, and focuses especially on certain psychic
       conflicts and character trends that attracted her to the group
       and its teachings, particularly those regarding sexuality and
       universal messianism. The subject's childhood guilt and inhi-
       bition in relation to sex were central to her inner struggle.
       Because of the lack of external support and guidance, her
       sense of confusion, isolation, and helplessness increased.
       Her conversion is interpreted as a partial abandonment of a
       punitive parental authority, and its replacement with a new
       one which provided strong external support for superego con-
       tent. The new teachings about sex fitted the subject's needs.
       She was "employing multiple hysterical and obsessional defenses
       to avert sexual and aggressive impulses" (p. 266).

1197. Dillbeck, Michael C. "Testing the Vedic Psychology of the
       Bhagavad-Gita." PSYCHOLOGIA 26 (1983): 62-72.

       Outlines the psychological theory contained in this popular
       Hindu text, and explores its themes of suffering, transcen-
       dence, and enlightenment. The state of freedom from suffering,
       which can only be achieved through non-attachment to outer
       sources of joy, requires the development of a transcendental
       state of consciousness (enlightenment). Inner fulfillment is
       the final result. The psychology of the Gita is beneficial
       for self-development and personal growth.

1198. Dole, Arthur A., and Steve K. Dubrow Eichel. "Some New Reli-
       gions are Dangerous." CULTIC STUDIES JOURNAL 2 (1985): 17-
       30.

       Challenges Kilbourne and Richardson's position (item 1245)
       on the therapeutic function of cults, and charges them with
       neglecting evidence of drug smuggling, manufacture of weapons,
       mass suicides in Jonestown, and child abuse. It is maintained
       that the dangerous and destructive nature of cults has been
       amply demonstrated by cult critics, and is central to any
       serious discussion of the effects these new movements have on
       those who join them. An exhaustive list of these experts'
       ratings of destructive cult practices is supplied. Many new
       cults manipulate, abuse, coerce, threaten, enslave, and
       neglect their members and, unlike traditional psychothera-
       peutic practices, have no accountability to the public and
       little concern for ethical issues.

1199. Dowling, Joseph A. "Millenarianism and Psychology." JOURNAL
       OF PSYCHOHISTORY 5 (1977): 121-30.

       Reviews several issues which millenarian beliefs and
       practices raise. Two basic questions are addressed. To the
       first question, why should millennial movements occur, the
       author suggests the Freudian answer that our constant conflict
       with a repressive civilization is the cause. However, though
       these movements exhibit regression, they need not be patho-
       logical, but could help the healthy interests of the ego. To
       the second question, why do these movements erupt in certain
       times and places, the author points out that socioeconomic
       theories of culture-conflict and deprivation have been domi-
       nant. His own position is that only a psychoanalytic theory
       can ultimately account for the rise of new movements.

1200. Ebon, Martin, editor. THE WORLD'S WEIRDEST CULTS. New York:
       New American Library, 1979. 177 pp.

       Describes several of the "strangest" cults, including the
       Rastafarians, Jim Jones's People's Temple, snake-handling in
       Tennessee, UFO groups, the Aetherius Society, Satanism, the
       Hell Fire Club, and the Hitler cult. "Cults," the author
       states, "tend to have a touch of madness" (p. 1). Since the
       cults are a distortion of true religion, they can be called
       the religion of the sick soul. Cults are signs of emotional
       illness, demanding complete surrender and fostering intolerance.

       Contains item 1718.

1201. Ebon, Martin, editor. THE SATAN TRAP: DANGERS OF THE OCCULT.
       Garden City, NY: Doubleday, 1976. xii, 276 pp.

       Presents a collection of 25 articles, several of which had
       been previously published, discussing occult topics. The
       material is divided into four parts: 1) prophets, false and
       real (including psychic phenomena); 2) the mind in danger
       (covering also witchcraft); 3) possession and exorcism; and
       4) the Scientific Diagnosis (with essays on ESP and telepathy).
       An essay by the editor describes the Edgar Cayce cult. The
       editor thinks that occult powers open people to influences
       that are unknown and, at times, uncontrollable. The occult,
       he thinks, appeals to those who are emotionally unstable.

       Contains items 1170, 1176.

1202. Eichel, Steve K. Dubrow, Linda Dubrow Eichel, and Robert
       Cobrin Eisenberg. "Mental Health Interventions in Cult-
       Related Cases: A Preliminary Investigation of Outcomes."
       CULTIC STUDIES JOURNAL 1 (1984): 156-66.

       Records data from 19 cult-related mental health consulta-
       tions carried out at the Re-Entry Therapy Information and
       Referral Network (RETIRN), and tries to describe the kind of
       interventions made and to suggest ways of evaluating their
       success. The authors provide some interesting data, and

conclude that in 60 percent of the determining cases the
counseling procedure was successful. They also admit that
their research had several limitations, namely: 1) there was
no sampling strategy, or comparisons, or multiple treatments;
2) the mind-control paradigm was used throughout the procedures; and; 3) there was a selection bias in their data. The
researchers seem unaware that these significant limitations
seriously challenge, if not invalidate, their results.

1203. Fauteux, Kevin. "Good/Bad Splitting in Religious Experience."
       AMERICAN JOURNAL OF PSYCHOANALYSIS 41 (1981): 261-67.

       Observes that in cult disciples, who appear to be function-
       ing normally, and in schizophrenics one can observe the same
       "raptured eyes, frozen smiles, dull affect, repressed aggres-
       sion." It is argued that the negative and positive images
       of the mother present in early infancy reemerge in adult re-
       ligious experiences, which dichotomize between the omniscent
       guru and the saved disciples on the one hand, and the lost
       non-believers on the other. Some cultists continue to seek
       an illusory world of total goodness and a state of continuous
       euphoria, where all anxieties are wiped out and the miraculous
       is an everyday occurrence. These people will cling to their
       guru just as the life-long neurotic clings tenaciously to
       the security of the idealized mother.

1204. Feinstein, Sherman C. "The Cult Phenomenon: Transition, Re-
       pression, and Regression." ADOLESCENT PSYCHIATRY 8 (1980):
       113-22.

       Attempts to understand the reasons why young people join
       new religious movements. People who are attracted to cults
       show no evidence of previous pathological conditions, but
       are characterized by a dissatisfaction with their status quo
       and by a slow resolution of their identity crisis. Conversion
       did produce considerable and sustained relief from neurotic
       distress, but this may actually be a "pathological resolution
       of the existential anxiety with which these people are strug-
       gling prior to conversion" (p. 118). Deprogrammed ex-cult
       members exhibit a post-psychotic state, which points to the
       need for counseling or therapy.

1205. Fenwick, Peter, Stephen Galliano, et al. "'Psychic Sensi-
       tivity,' Mystical Experience, Head Injury and Brain Patho-
       logy." BRITISH JOURNAL OF MEDICAL PSYCHOLOGY 58 (1985):
       35-44.

       Compares, by using various standard psychological tests,
       the psychic experiences, such as telepathy, clairvoyance,
       mediumship, preconception, and mystical states, of 17 stu-
       dents from the College of Psychic Studies with those of 17
       church-going subjects. The so-called "sensitives" (those
       manifesting psychic gifts) were more likely than the control
       subjects to be single or divorced who had consulted a psychi-
       atrist, or to have suffered head-injuries or other serious
       illness. The hypothesis that the experiencing of psychic

gifts can be directly related in time to the occurrence of
brain trauma is supported, to some degree, by the authors'
findings. It is also possible to interpret the data as
pointing to a relationship between the claim of psychic
abilities and psychiatric illness.

1206.   Flammonde, Paris. THE MYSTIC HEALERS. New York: Stein and
        Day, 1974. 252 pp.

Discusses the issue of non-scientific healing with reference to many healers in the West like Franz Mesmer, Mary
Eddy Baker, Edgar Cayce, Oral Roberts, Rex Humbard, Kathryn
Kuhlman, and L. Ron Hubbard. The success of some of these
healers is acknowledged and explained through hypnotic power,
reversal of a hysterical condition, or spontaneous remission.
These healers, it is implied, use crowd psychology to influence and, in some cases, to manipulate people.

1207.   Friedman, Maurice. "Aiming at the Self: A Paradox of the
        Encounter and Human Potential Movements." JOURNAL OF
        HUMANISTIC PSYCHOLOGY 16.2 (1976): 5-34.

Discusses some of the problems in encounter movements which
openly stress the pursuit of self-development. The author
doubts whether we can define ourselves or our potentialities
apart from what we become in relation to others. Too much
concern with methods for achieving self-development leads to
such artificial situations as "planned spontaneity." "Cults,"
he insists, "give their members the fake security that they
are in the know and that everyone else is really outside.
Cults destroy the person by destroying his or her responsibility before the other who does not fit the model of the
group. They also destroy the reality of the group because
people do not meet each other in the freedom of fellowship"
(pp. 23-24).

1208.   Gabbard, Glen O., and Stuart W. Twemlow. WITH THE EYES OF
        THE MIND: AN EMPIRICAL STUDY OF OUT-OF-BODY STATES. New
        York: Praeger, 1984. xii, 272 pp.

Approaches the study of out-of-body experiences (OBEs) with
a more open mind and without dismissing them as delusions or
fakery. The material is divided into four sections: 1) definition and description of an OBE experience, and a report on
a questionnaire survey; 2) differentiation of OBEs from both
pathological and normal states; 3) the near-death experience;
and 4) an integrated view from various disciplines. Several
psychological theories (pp. 188-90) are briefly reviewed and
judged to be inadequate to provide a model for understanding
the singular, idiosyncratic nature of a given individual's
experience. The authors think that altered states of consciousness are a necessary context for OBEs to occur. They
claim that, during an OBE, an uncoupling of the bodily ego
and the mental ego takes place. There is no mention of cults,
but OBEs are linked with Transcendental and other forms of
meditation.

1209. Galanter, Marc.   "Charismatic Religious Sects and Psychiatry:
       An Overview."   AMERICAN JOURNAL OF PSYCHIATRY 139 (1982):
       1539-48.

       Studies the nature of membership in new religious movements
       or cults in order to assess their psychiatric impact on those
       who join. The factors that lead to membership and the psychi-
       atric issues related to joining are considered. It is found
       that psychological distress and some major pathology are fre-
       quent antecedents among joiners. The issue of sudden religious
       conversion, as a pseudo-solution to extreme personal conflict,
       is discussed. The author thinks that mystical experience has
       a role in the resolution of major psychopathology, including
       tendencies to suicide, schizophrenia, and affective psychosis.
       Similarities between the cults and other groups, such as
       Alcoholics Anonymous and Recovery Inc., are noted. Cognitive
       dissonance and attribution theory, rather than brainwashing,
       are proposed as ways of understanding belief systems and con-
       sensual validation. The use of systems theory for assessing
       the relationship between group influence in these sects,
       current conceptions of individual pathology, and normal adap-
       tation is proposed.

1210. Galanter, Marc.   "The 'Relief Effect': A Sociobiological Model
       for Neurotic Distress and Large-Group Therapy."   AMERICAN
       JOURNAL OF PSYCHIATRY 135 (1976): 588-91.

       Examines the adaptive value of neurotic distress symptoms,
       such as anxiety and depression, which are alleviated when
       people join a closely-knit group. A highly cohesive sect or
       association can lead to the decline of attempted suicides,
       anomie, and behavioral and emotional problems. The author
       finds both anthropological and ethological support from his
       theory, thereby establishing a direct relationship between
       attitudes reflecting group unity and the degree of symptom
       relief. Zealous movements having messianic goals often
       function as homogeneous groups, supplying group therapy to
       their members.

1211. Gallegos, Eligio Stephen.   "Animal Imagery, the Chakra System,
       and Psychotherapy."   JOURNAL OF TRANSPERSONAL PSYCHOLOGY 15
       (1983): 125-36.

       Contrasts Western with Eastern views of human nature, and
       suggests that Western visualization-therapy techniques can be
       combined with certain aspects of the "chakra" system in thera-
       peutic sessions. The introductory visualization procedure
       is outlined, and ways for contacting personal characteristics
       through animal imagery are proposed. A case study is presented
       to illustrate the method.

1212. Galper, Marvin F.   "The Cult Phenomenon: Behavioral Science
       Perspective Applied to Therapy."   CULTS AND THE FAMILY
       (item 1242), pp. 141-49.

       Maintains that the new cults are a challenge to the estab-
       lished religions and to the biological family, and that they

should be studied as totalistic organizations which debase
humanistic values and lead to a regressive form of adaptation.
Ways of treating cult-related problems are suggested. For
those suffering from severe pathology, involvement in a cult
appears to bring about some kind of adjustment.

1213. Gay, Volney Y. "Individual Needs and Charismatic Figures."
      JOURNAL OF RELIGION AND HEALTH 19 (1980): 24-39.

      Describes why and how a young female client had become a
      devotee of a charismatic person, whose small group believed
      itself to be the beginning of God's kingdom on earth. The
      life history of both the leader and this particular follower
      is described. The profile of the leader and his devotee are
      compared and it is explained how the former corresponded to
      the latter's infantile ideal of adult functioning, which her
      father never fulfilled. This devotee was a psychologically
      sick woman who had a masochistic relationship with an
      extremely narcissistic man. The patient eventually replaced
      the cult leader and his book with Jesus Christ and the Bible.
      The author hesitates to explore further since psychoanalysis
      has ceased analyzing the personality of Jesus since Schweitzer
      (item 444) criticized the psychoanalytic theories of Jesus.

1214. Geis, Larry, and Alta Picchi Kelly, editors. THE NEW HEALERS:
      HEALING THE WHOLE PERSON. Berkeley, CA: And/Or Press, Inc.,
      1980. viii, 147 pp.

      Contains articles on: 1) the basis of holistic health; 2)
      physical awareness and healing; 3) mental awareness and heal-
      ing; 4) the life cycle; and 5) spiritual awareness and healing.

      Contains item 1332.

1215. Gibbard, Graham S., and John J. Hartman. "The Significance
      of Utopian Fantasies in Small Groups." INTERNATIONAL JOUR-
      NAL OF GROUP PSYCHOTHERAPY 23 (1973): 125-47.

      Attempts to demonstrate that the belief that one's community
      is a utopia reflects the emergence of oedipal and pre-oedipal
      themes. The author first presents a case study of two self-
      analytic classroom groups, and underlines the parallels be-
      tween them and sensitivity training groups. Secondly, he
      speculates on the theoretical implications of the utopian fan-
      tasy. Finally, he considers the practical application of
      these theories in a clinical setting. It is concluded that
      such groups could be an institutionalized defense against
      anxiety and depression. They may be offering pseudo-solutions
      to several psychological problems.

1216. Gilbert, Albin R. "Toward a Scientific Technique of Mind
      Expansion in the Future of Mankind." PSYCHOLOGIA 21 (1978):
      124-27.

      Holds that mind expansion, or "enlightenment," is part and
      parcel of human nature and is based on: 1) a reduction of

motivational over-determination to unidirectional determination; and 2) "purgation," that is, simple, frugal living, as
proposed by the Buddhist Middle Path, which is opposed to
over-indulgence in sexual pleasures. Among the effects of
mind expansion are the state of relaxation, improved capacity
to solve problems, and better self-control. It is pointed out
that the path to enlightenment is hard and arduous, and that
enlightened persons who occupy important positions in society
will become "healers of social fragmentation."

1217. Goldberg, Carl. "Courage and Fanaticism: The Charismatic
        Leader and Modern Religious Cults." PSYCHODYNAMIC PER-
        PPECTIVES OF RELIGION, SECT, AND CULT (item 1226), pp.
        163-85.

        Describes cults as pseudo-religious organizations which
        manipulate the vulnerability of young people. The cults
        foster emotional dependency on cultic authority, which hin-
        ders the natural maturation into adulthood. Their rituals
        and other practices are physically and psychologically harm-
        ful. Further, the experience they provide is the last defense
        before psychological breakdown or suicide. The cult leader is
        usually a paranoid personality. Jim Jones and his People's
        Temple are taken as typical examples of leaders and their
        cultic organizations.

1218. Goleman, Daniel. "Buddhist and Western Psychology: Some
        Commonalities and Differences." JOURNAL OF TRANSPERSONAL
        PSYCHOLOGY 13 (1981): 125-36.

        Briefly sketches the principles of Buddhist psychology as
        presented in the "Adhidhamma" and compares them to Western
        psychological theory. In spite of some similarities, there
        are several major differences in the goals and methods used
        to achieve self-actualization and mental health. Buddhist
        psychology aims at a deep transformation of consciousness,
        which is not even envisaged by its Western counterparts.

1219. Goleman, Daniel. "Mental Health in Classical Buddhist Psychol-
        ogy." JOURNAL OF TRANSPERSONAL PSYCHOLOGY 9 (1975): 176-81.

        Outlines the primary mental factors in classical Buddhist
        psychology as found in the "Adhidhamma," distinguishing be-
        tween cognitive and affective reality and diverse unhealthy
        elements. The goal of Buddhist psychology, with the "arhat,"
        or saint, as a prototype model of sanity, is briefly pre-
        sented. Buddhism supplies meditators with a checklist of
        healthy qualities they should be striving for.

1220. Gordon, James S. "The Cult Phenomenon and the Psychothera-
        peutic Response." JOURNAL OF THE AMERICAN ACADEMY OF
        PSYCHOANALYSIS 11 (1983): 603-15.

        Points out that therapists should be aware that people
        entering cults do not show signs of pathology greater than
        the average population. The common psychological bias on

religious matters hinders our understanding of the spiritual
quest of those seeking membership in one of the new cults.
Some of the therapeutic issues that arise in the treatment
of those who have left new religious movements are discussed.
The fully-committed member who leaves always suffers a deep
disorientation and a disturbing experience. The author rejects
the theory of forceful conversion to cults, but admits that
deception in recruitment, pressure to conform, abdication of
personal responsiblity, and poor treatment of women exist
in some of the new religious groups. The therapist is seen
as "a bridge to the rest of the world" and "an aid to understanding and dealing with it" (p. 614).

1221. Grossinger, Richard. FROM STONE AGE SHAMANISM TO POST-INDUS-
      TRIAL HEALING. Boulder, CO: Shambala Publications, revised
      edition, 1982. 436 pp.

      Discusses the art of healing from ancient times to modern
      traditional medicine to the current movement of holistic heal-
      ing. The work of the shaman as spiritual ethnomedicine as
      well as the contributions of Freud and Reich are covered.
      In the epilogue, the author surveys the present state of
      holistic health and makes suggestions as to how to choose
      a healer. Meditation and prayer are among the many forms of
      healing listed.

1222. Hall, Arthur L., and Peter G. Bourne. "Indigenous Therapists
      in a Southern Black Urban Community." ARCHIVES OF GENERAL
      PSYCHIATRY 28 (1973): 137-41.

      Concludes from a study of a black ghetto in South Atlanta,
      Georgia, that in spite of modern medical health programs,
      root doctors, faith healers, magic vendors, and neighborhood
      prophets still provide an important health care resource in
      many communities, especially among older people. The attempts
      made to incorporate the work of these local, untrained thera-
      pists into the practice of the health center have been almost
      universally unsuccessful.

1223. Hall, Manley P. BUDDHISM AND PSYCHOTHERAPY. Los Angeles:
      Philosophical Research Society, second revised edition,
      1979. 330 pp.

      Describes the author's visits to Japanese Buddhist temples
      which, he claims, have the therapeutic value of bestowing
      calmness on visitors. Religion is seen as a defense against
      the disintegration of culture and the disorientation of the
      mind and heart. Moreover, it removes uncertainties. The
      essentials of Buddhist psychotherapy are not the same as
      those in Western scientific treatments. The former consist
      mainly of providing a universal purpose to life and a hope
      in the afterlife, both of which lead to psychological health.
      The author describes his book as a pilgrimage in search of
      realities bringing peace to the spirit.

1224. Halperin, David A. "Training Issues for Cult Treatment
       Programs." CULTIC STUDIES JOURNAL 1 (1984): 136-42.

       Discusses the need to train health-care specialists to deal
       with cult problems. Two areas are covered: 1) the cultists'
       angry family members, who come for advice and immediate
       action; and 2) ex-cult members, who need help to integrate
       the cult experience in their lives. Therapists are advised
       not to over-identify themselves with ex-cult members, nor to
       minimize the problems that parents face. Deprogramming is
       not a panacea, and not all cult members need psychoanalysis.
       Intense religious experience should not be readily dismissed
       as pathological. The author thinks that one must distinguish
       between "the authoritative mainstream religious leader and
       the totalitarian cult leader" (p. 141).

1225. Halperin, David A. "Group Processes in Cult Affiliation and
       Recruitment." GROUP 6.2 (1982): 13-24.

       Discusses cult recruitment procedures with reference to
       the Unification Church, whose methods are seen as ways of
       manipulating potential recruits who are not aware of the
       goals of the recruiters. A therapeutic group must be distin-
       guished from a recruiting group. In the former, all members
       are treated equally; they are encouraged to share their ex-
       periences in an atmosphere which permits them to question
       the leader's (i.e., therapist's) authority. The author thinks
       that a person's affiliation with a cult may be the expression
       of individual pathology and vulnerability or evidence of
       familial dysfunction. It could also be a reflection of
       destructive group processes.

1226. Halperin, David A., editor. PSYCHODYNAMIC PERSPECTIVES ON
       RELIGION, SECT, AND CULT. Boston: John Wright, 1983.
       xxii, 384 pp.

       Contains 25 essays, some previously published, on various
       psychological dimensions of the cultic phenomenon. The pa-
       pers are grouped under three headings: 1) historical sketches,
       which include studies on the Albigenses, the Mormons, the
       American Indian Ghost Dance, and Father Feeney's movement;
       2) cult affiliation and religious identification; and 3)
       therapeutic approaches and issues.

       Contains items 793, 1217, 1321, 1352, 1748.

1227. Hand, Wayland D. AMERICAN FOLK MEDICINE: A SYMPOSIUM. Berke-
       ley: University of California Press, 1976. viii, 347 pp.

       Offers a collection of 25 papers presented at the UCLA
       Conference of American Folk Medicine, held in December, 1973.
       The traditions and practices of several American Indian
       tribes, and of the Spanish- and French-American populations
       are described and discussed. A number of essays on shamanism
       are included. Both physical and psychotherapeutic treatments
       are covered.

1228. Hargrove, Barbara. "Mental Health and the New Religions."
       ILIFF REVIEW 40.2 (Spring 1983): 25-36.

       Examines mental health from the viewpoint of the sociology
       of knowledge. It is contended that at least some of the new
       movements represent a search for an alternative world view,
       and, as such, are attractive not to people on the fringe of
       society but to those who occupy central positions in it.
       The author examines Clark's (see items 1183-85) anti-cult
       position that cult members are mentally ill, and the rebuttal
       of Robbins and Anthony (see especially item 1890). She favors
       a balanced view and stresses the need to distinguish between
       the various cults. "Often our labelling of 'cults' as cre-
       ators of mental illness is a defense against treating seriously
       the critique they raise against current social definitions of
       normality" (p. 35).

1229. Henderson, C. William. AWAKENING: WAYS TO PSYCHOSPIRITUAL
       GROWTH. Englewood Cliffs, NJ: Prentice-Hall, 1975. xi,
       244 pp.

       Gives an account of the many new religious and spiritual
       movements, which the author presents as organizations offer-
       ing methods of psychological and spiritual development. Among
       the many institutions mentioned are Silva Mind Control, Est,
       the Church of Scientology, the Jesus Movement, Transcendental
       Meditation, Ananda Marga, Zen Centers, Integral Yoga Institute,
       and ISKCON. It is argued that, since some of these methods
       may fit a person's needs and character, "the real problem is
       to find the best ones specifically suited for you" (p. 204).
       A now dated partial list of "psycho-spiritual schools" is
       appended.

1230. Hidas, Andrew M. "Psychotherapy and Surrender: A Spiritual
       Perspective." JOURNAL OF TRANSPERSONAL PSYCHOLOGY 13 (1981):
       27-32.

       Defines surrender as a psychological experience which,
       though initially negative, brings the individual in contact
       with unitive forces and, hence, to positive personality
       changes. Surrender, unlike conversion, is marked by a sense
       of "emptiness," a concept found in both Christian and Buddhist
       spiritualities. The author holds that the act of surrender,
       in spite of its vulnerability and risk, can have broad impli-
       cations for the psychotherapeutic process. It is not clear
       whether personal integration is an effect of self-surrender,
       or whether a healthy personality is a pre-requirement.

1231. Hopkins, Robert P. "The Hospital Viewpoint: Mental Illness
       or Social Maladjustment." NATIONAL ASSOCIATION OF PRIVATE
       PSYCHIATRIC HOSPITALS JOURNAL 9.4 (1978): 19-26.

       Outlines some of the problems of treating mental illness
       resulting from cult membership, especially in groups like the
       Unification Church, ISKCON, the Divine Light Mission, and the

Children of God. Several reasons why people join cults and
some case histories are presented. Though not all subjects
examined showed signs of psychotic illness, there was always
a slight deterioration in their social and intellectual functioning after joining the group. Whether cult members are
mentally ill, whether they should be committed to psychiatric institutions, and whether hospitals should get involved,
are some of the questions raised.

1232. Hulke, Malcolm, editor. THE ENCYCLOPEDIA OF ALTERNATIVE
        MEDICINE AND SELF-HELP. New York: Shocken Books, 1979.
        243 pp.

        Lists and describes different, unorthodox healing techniques
        without recommending or criticizing any of them. Acupuncture,
        which can be employed to heal anxiety and depression, and
        Yoga, which is an effective treatment for hypertension, are
        among the subjects included. A directory of associations,
        products, training and treatment centers, health spas and
        resorts, health magazines, and a short bibliography are added.

1233. Irwin, H. J. FLIGHT OF MIND: A PSYCHOLOGICAL STUDY OF THE
        OUT-OF-BODY EXPERIENCE. Metuchen, NJ: Scarecrow Press,
        1985. viii, 374 pp.

        Provides a comprehensive survey of the empirical literature
        on out-of-body experiences (OBEs), and examines the directions
        in which a scientific appreciation of them might be usefully
        pursued. The phenomenology of the experience, the circum-
        stances of its occurrence, the character of the experiment,
        the methods of OBEs research, and the principle theories
        brought forth to explain the phenomenon are systematically
        reviewed. Theories of OBEs are categorized into two major
        groups: 1) ecsomatic theories, which take a literal inter-
        pretation of the experience; and 2) imaginal theories, which
        assume that there are physiological and/or psychological
        explanations, and which classify OBEs as an hallucinatory
        phenomenon bordering on the psychotic or schizophrenic. The
        author proposes an imaginal theory, which does not discount
        the ecsomatic approach, and hypothesizes that the origins of
        OBEs "lie in a confluence of absorption factors" (p. 307),
        which might be heightened by meditation. There are no refer-
        ences to any specific cults. This study may be useful in
        studying those new religious groups, like Eckankar, which
        stress astral projection and OBEs. A lenghty bibliography
        (pp. 325-54) is added.

1234. Isser, Natalie. "The Linneweil Affair: A Study of Adoles-
        cent Vulnerability." ADOLESCENCE 19 (1984): 629-42.

        Maintains that many young people who are unhappy, lonely,
        alienated, or disoriented are vulnerable to cults. A his-
        torical example, the Linneweil Affair in nineteenth-century
        France--which is the case of a Jewish girl who, brought up
        away from her Jewish parents, eventually became a Catholic--

is described in detail. Although not exhibiting any clear
signs of psychopathology or maladaptability, the subject was
an insecure individual caught up in a moment of decision and
filled with fear of the unknown. In the parents' attempts
to reclaim her, her social bonds to her foster parents and
surroundings were a source of conflict. The author sees
parallels in today's cults in that people are drawn to cultic
beliefs because of their social association with cult members.

1235. Jacobs, Janet. "The Economy of Love in Religious Commitment:
        The Deconversion of Women from Nontraditional Religious
        Movements." JOURNAL FOR THE SCIENTIFIC STUDY OF RELIGION
        23 (1984): 155-71.

        Studies the process of deconversion of 17 women from var-
        ious new religious groups, ranging from charismatic Chris-
        tianity to Eastern mysticism. The author found that, in all
        these cults, the work of women was delineated by their sex
        roles and was characterized by domestic obligations, fund-
        raising and recruitment, sexual relations with the guru, and
        abusive and degrading expressions of commitment. A sense of
        violation leads women to abandon the groups they joined so
        eagerly. The author's findings support the view that for
        many women involvement in a cult is often psychologically and
        physically harmful.

1236. Jarvis, William J. "Food Faddism, Cultism, and Quackery."
        ANNUAL REVIEW OF NUTRITION 3 (1983): 35-52.

        Describes the current food faddism, which exaggerates the
        effects of nutrition upon health and disease prevention, and
        which becomes cultic when a religious component is part of
        it. Magical thinking about food, the reason why food faddism
        persists, and the harm it can cause are discussed. Current
        practices on health food, including the publication of books,
        magazines, and "pseudoscientific journals" are criticized.
        The author believes that the devotees of food faddism behave
        delusionally and accept uncritically the unscientific teach-
        ings of charismatic authority figures. Ways of coping with
        the problem are suggested. A useful, lengthy bibliography is
        added.

1237. Johnson, Ann Braden. "A Temple of Last Resorts: Youth and
        Shared Narcissism." THE NARCISSISTIC CONDITION. Edited
        by Marie Coleman Nelson. New York: Human Sciences Press,
        1977, pp. 27-65.

        Discusses the psychological condition of troubled, unhappy
        people who join exclusive cults that reject the larger
        culture. Such groups are characterized by a rejection or
        avoidance of the adult world through a regressive, narcis-
        sistic retreat from reality. Zen Buddhism, ISKCON, the Divine
        Light Mission, and the Meyer Baba movement are the main groups
        described. Their members are said to be trapped in an extended
        adolescence. Those people who join these cults are so over-

whelmed and frightened by the modern world that they prefer
to "wrap themselves in the security blanket of compulsive
chanting to the 'illusion' that is their lives" (p. 65).

1238. Jones, Kenneth J., editor. SICKNESS AND SECTARIANISM: EXPLOR-
        ATORY STUDIES IN MEDICAL AND RELIGIOUS SECTARIANISM.
        Aldershot, UK: Gower, 1985. ix, 158 pp.

        Contains essays on various aspects of medical and psycho-
        therapeutic practices among both traditional sects and new
        cults.

        Contains items 648, 1175.

1239. Kara, Ashok. "The Guru and the Therapist: Goals and Tech-
        niques in Regard to the Chela and the Patient." PSYCHO-
        THERAPY: THEORY, RESEARCH, AND PRACTICE 16 (1979): 61-71.

        Argues that the Eastern guru and Western therapist differ
        in their assumptions about human life, and function quite
        differently in their relation to the "chela" (or devotee) and
        client, respectively. Enlightenment is diametrically opposed
        to the self-acutalization sought in therapy. The author com-
        pares the theoretical assumptions and techniques of the guru
        and the psychotherapist, and concludes that both can teach
        each other some important lessons. The author has some reser-
        vations regarding the guru's professional work, since some
        of the questions dealt with by the guru are rejected as delu-
        sional by the therapist.

1240. Kaslof, Leslie J., compiler and editor. WHOLISTIC DIMENSIONS
        ON HEALING: A RESOURCE GUIDE. New York: Dolphin Books, 1978.
        295 pp.

        Contains one chapter on psychic and spiritual healing and
        includes a section on "the potential use of therapeutic touch
        in healing."

1241. Kaslow, Florence, and Lita L. Schwartz. "Vulnerability and
        Invulnerability to the Cults: An Assessment of Family
        Dynamics, Functioning, and Values." MARITAL AND FAMILY
        THERAPY: NEW PERSPECTIVES IN THEORY, RESEARCH, AND PRAC-
        TICE. Edited by Dennis A. Bagarossi, Anthony P. Jurich,
        and Robert W. Jackson. New York: Human Sciences Press,
        1983, pp. 165-90.

        Presents several variables according to which all families
        can be evaluated: systems orientation; boundaries; context;
        power; autonomy and initiative; affect; conflict negotiation
        and task performance; and transcendental values. An over-
        view, based on Conway and Siegelman's theory of the contem-
        porary cult phenomenon (item 1188), is given. The authors
        make a comparative study of ex-cult, non-cult members, and
        their families in the light of the above-mentioned variables.
        A tentative profile of cult members and their families is

depicted. "Those who are vulnerable to cults appear to come
from midrange and dysfunctional families" (p. 182). Treatment approaches and applications are discussed.

1242. Kaslow, Florence, and Marvin B. Sussman, editors. CULTS AND
THE FAMILY. New York: Hayworth Press, 1982. 192 pp.

Presents a collection of papers originally published in THE
MARRIAGE AND FAMILY REVIEW (vol. 4, 1981). The family issues
brought about by the new cults are discussed from psychological, psychiatric, and social perspectives.

Contains items 1212, 1289.

1243. Katz, Nathan, editor. BUDDHIST AND WESTERN PSYCHOLOGY.
Boulder, CO: Prajna Press, 1983. xi, 271 pp.

Discusses the psychological implication of four varieties
of Buddhism, that is, Pali, Sanskrit, Tibetan, and Japanese.
Comparisons between Buddhist psychology and Western psychoanalysis are made. It is assumed and stated throughout most
of the contributions to this volume that not only has Buddhism
developed a psychology on a par with its Western counterpart,
but that it also has a therapeutic system which can contribute
to the refinement of Western treatments.

1244. Kelsey, Morton T. HEALING AND CHRISTIANITY IN ANCIENT
THOUGHT AND MODERN TIMES. New York: Harper and Row, 1973.
xi, 398 pp.

Provides a comprehensive history of healing in the Christian
church from Biblical times to the present. After discussing
the case against Christian healing, the author shows how healing was practiced and justified in the early church and how
it eventually ceased to be central in the Church's ministry.
The revival of healing in modern times, particularly with the
rise of Christian sects, is outlined. The relationship between the body, the emotions, and healing is considered, and
the possibility that religious experience and faith may be
significant factors in the health of the human psyche by
releasing positive emotions and counteracting negative ones,
is fully discussed. The collaboration of physicians, psychotherapists, and religious ministers in the healing of the
whole person is advocated.

1245. Kilbourne, Brock, and James T. Richardson. "Psychotherapy
and New Religions in a Pluralistic Society." AMERICAN
PSYCHOLOGIST 39 (1984): 237-51.

Views the new religious groups and traditional psychotherapy
as competitors in the marketplace, and attempts to critically
examine the nature and origin of this competition and conflict.
Some common features shared by the new religions and psychotherapy are identified: sociohistorical context, type of
members, underlying deep structures, common functions, and

similar cognitive and interactive styles. New religions may
be offering some badly needed alternatives in contemporary
society.

1246. Krieger, Dolores. THERAPEUTIC TOUCH: HOW TO USE YOUR HANDS
TO HELP AND TO HEAL. Englewood Cliffs, NJ: Prentice-Hall,
1979. xiii, 168 pp.

Develops the method of therapeutic touch, which is derived
from the laying on of hands. The author, a nurse who explored
the healing possibilities of Eastern medical treatments including Yoga, maintains that healing is a natural potential
that can be actualized under the appropriate conditions. The
basis of the therapeutic touch "lies in the intelligent direction of significant life energies from the person playing the
role of healer to the healee" (p. 23). Several phases of the
therapeutic touch are described. Its effects include a profound relaxation response, the alleviation of pain, especially
that linked with the nervous system, and the cure of stress-
related illnesses. Reports from a personal journal, which
recorded the experiences of people exercising the therapeutic
touch, are provided.

1247. Krieger, Dolores. "Therapeutic Touch: The Imprimatur of
Nursing." AMERICAN JOURNAL OF NURSING 75 (1975): 7840-47.

Reviews early studies on the potential healing qualities of
touch (or of the laying on of hands) and reports on experiments which showed that this practice raised hemoglobin levels
of sick people. The possibility of nurses using such healing
powers is explored. Tests on nurses, who were taught the
method of therapeutic touch, registered good scores on inner
directedness, independence, self-support, expression of feelings, sense of worth, self-acceptance, and capacity for
intimate contact. The improvement of patients was significant
after they experienced the healing touch of their nurses.

1248. Kriegman, Daniel, and Leonard Solomon. "Psychotherapy and
the 'New Religions': Are They the Same?" CULTIC STUDIES
JOURNAL 2 (1985): 2-16.

Examines Kilbourne and Richardson's view (item 1245) that
cults may be an alternate form of therapy in the light of the
authors' own studies on the devotees of the Divine Light
Mission. It is argued, among other things, that even if the
cults relieved anxiety, it doesn't follow that they can be
placed on the same level as psychotherapy. The differences
between cults, which are dogmatic and authoritarian institutions energetically involved in gaining new converts, and
psychotherapy, which is an ethically and scientifically-minded
profession, are too substantial even to warrant a comparison.

1249. Krippner, Stanley. "'Psychic Healing' and Psychotherapy."
JOURNAL OF INDIAN PSYCHOLOGY 2.1 (1979): 35-44.

Gives a brief history of psychic healers who are divided
into four categories: shamans, spiritists, esoterics, and
intuitives. Their procedures are said to contain the four
basic components of psychotherapy, which are: 1) identification of illness; 2) qualities of the therapist; 3) patient
expectation; and 4) psychotherapeutic methods, such as drugs,
shock treatment, and group therapy. The paranormal concepts
and techniques of these psychic healers include discarnate
entities, divine intervention, life after death, out-of-body
experiences, laying on of hands, and magical remedies and
rites. The success of these healers has been widespread,
especially where Western methods are not available. The
author refers to the endeavors of some Western psychotherapists to work with native healers and to incorporate some
of their methods.

1250. LaDage, Alta J. OCCULT PSYCHOLOGY: A COMPARISON BETWEEN
       JUNGIAN PSYCHOLOGY AND THE MODERN QABALAH. St. Paul, MN:
       Llewellyn Publications, 1978. x, 193 pp.

Introduces the reader 1) to the Jewish Qabalah, tracing its
roots and presenting its teachings, and 2) to the basis of
Jungian psychology with its collective unconscious, archetypes, and the four human functions of thinking, feeling,
sensation, and intuition. Various correlations between
Jungian psychology and occult theory and practice are drawn.
The author thinks that Jung's views fit surprisingly well
within the framework of the Qabalah. Individuation and spiritual growth are seen as the goals of occult psychology which,
unlike psychoanalysis, not only raises the psyche's uncon-
sciousness contents to awareness, but also helps one deal with
them effectively.

1251. Langone, Michael D. "Cult Involvement: Suggestions for Con-
       cerned Parents and Professional." CULTIC STUDIES JOURNAL
       2 (1985): 148-68.

Offers suggestions to parents to help their children freely
reevaluate their cult involvement. The ethical issue of the
parents' interference with their offspring's new life-style
is discussed, and parents are advised to avoid using manipulative techniques of influence merely to fulfill their goals
or needs. Ways of promoting reevaluation, like collecting
information, communication, modeling, education, and strategy,
are outlined.

1252. Langone, Michael D. FAMILY CULT QUESTIONNAIRE: GUIDELINES
       FOR PROFESSIONALS. Weston, MA: American Family Foundation,
       1983. 21 pp.

Outlines the way counselors should proceed when they are
approached with cult-related problems. The questionnaire is
designed to collect general information, family and religious
backgrounds, family's experiences with the cult, the developmental and psychological history of the cult member, and the

convert's response to the cult. A three-page bibliography, mainly of materials describing the negative features of cultism, is included.

1253. Langone, Michael D. DESTRUCTIVE CULTISM: QUESTIONS AND ANSWERS. Weston, MA: American Family Foundation, 1982. 22 pp.

A pamphlet, set in a question/answer format, which deals with some of the major issues of cultism. The author draws a distinction between a cult and a destructive cult. The former refers to a group gathered around a specific deity or person, which has significantly different beliefs and practices from the major world religions and the minor sects, while the latter is a highly manipulative group that exploits and sometimes harms its members. Destructive cults practice mind control, deprive those who join them of their respective autonomy, and interfere with their psychological development. Why and how people become cult members, what can parents do when their daughter or son joins a cult, and how they can help their offspring reevaluate their commitment are some of the questions dealt with.

1254. Langone, Michael D. COUNSELING INDIVIDUALS AND FAMILIES TROUBLED BY CULT INVOLVEMENT. Weston, MA: American Family Foundation, n.d. 17 pp.

Offers general guidelines for counseling families whose offspring are cult or ex-cult members. The author holds that the advice given parents should be consistent with "a person-situation view of cult conversion," a position which takes into consideration both the conversion and the brainwashing models of cult involvement. The situational and personal variables are described. Among the former are listed manipulation and exploitive preoccupation, which include trance inducement, control of information, and physical debilitation; among the latter one finds anxiety, unassertiveness, gullibility, dependency, low tolerance of ambiguity, alienation, and naive idealism. Treatment is suggested under three headings: reevaluation counseling, reentry counseling, and family counseling.

1255. Larsen, John A. "Dysfunction in the Evangelical Family: Treatment Considerations." FAMILY COORDINATOR 27 (1978): 261-67.

Discusses psychological problems in religious families, who are a unique challenge to many non-religious therapists. The evangelical family, in which the parents and their adolescent children are in conflict, is the focus of the author's study. Two copying mechanisms used by these familes, namely, authoritarianism and spiritualizing, are examined and several treatment considerations are made. The author believes that therapists who work with evangelical families should be sensitive to their religious feelings, and thus be able to tap powerful religious resources to assist them in their therapeutic work.

1256. Lauer, Roger. "A Medium for Mental Health." RELIGIOUS MOVE-
       MENTS IN CONTEMPORARY AMERICA (item 1360), pp. 338-54.

       Describes the counseling and therapeutic activities of a
       psychic in a large city in the Pacific Northwest United
       States. The background of the psychic, the six psycho-
       therapists who enlisted as his students, and the counseling
       setting are given. The teachings, sermon outlines, and the
       content and method of the psychic's performance are also de-
       scribed. Psychic therapy utilizes many commonly accepted
       clinical principles and appears to be effective, not only
       on the basis of client satisfaction, but also from the point
       of view of psychiatric theory. It is concluded that other
       types of mediumistic counseling can successfully be used to
       treat emotionally disturbed people. Collaboration between
       psychics and psychiatrists is endorsed, in spite of the
       obstacles that will certainly be encountered.

1257. Lauer, Roger. "Master of Metaphysics." RELIGIOUS SYSTEMS
       OF PSYCHOTHERAPY (item 1021), pp. 254-67.

       Examines psychic counseling on the Pacific Coast and in a
       mid-Atlantic metropolitan area and presents examples of such
       well-known counselors as Eva Jansen, Mrs. Donner, Ludmilla
       Kosa, and Dave Johnson. It is noted that these practitio-
       ners, who prefer such titles as spiritual readers, spiritual
       advisors, and psychic mediums, have certain acknowledged
       similarities with mental health professionals. The author
       thinks that psychotherapists and folk healers should collabo-
       rate, because both provide useful and effective service to
       clients who are psychologically disturbed.

1258. Leahey, Thomas Hardy, and Grace Evans Leahey. PSYCHOLOGY'S
       OCCULT DOUBLES. Chicago: Nelson Hall, 1983. xii, 277 pp.

       Studies, from a psychological perspective, occult phenomena,
       including such topics as phrenology, mesmerism, spiritualism,
       psychical research, and contemporary therapeutic cults. The
       authors outline the origins of these various forms of pseudo-
       science. While trance mediums could be good therapists, in
       that they sometimes console the bereaved person who asks for
       help, they more often prey on the distressed person's fears
       and worries and use their clients' dependence to make a
       living. Scientology and the Process are presented as two
       groups which started as therapies and developed into cults,
       while Transcendental Meditation and the Divine Light Mission
       are examples of groups which tried to adapt Eastern ideas to
       Western scientific language. All these groups came into being
       to serve people's needs for meaning and order. Their thera-
       peutic value is superficial, at best.

1259. Levine, Edward M. "Religious Cults: Implications for Society
       and the Democratic Process." POLITICAL PSYCHOLOGY 3.3-4
       (1981-82): 34-49.

Maintains that several of the new cults, such as the Unification Church, the Divine Light Mission, the Children of God,
ISKCON, the Way International, and the Alamo Foundation are
significantly different from those of preceding generations
and cultures. The new cults do not offer genuine, thought-
ful, and meaningful religious alternatives to young adults
with dependency problems. They manipulate and exploit those
who turn to them to meet certain pressing needs. Almost all
of them use some form of mind control. Worst of all, they
are eroding the morals and values that are basic to any
democratic institution.

1260. Levine, Edward M. "Rural Communes and Religious Cults: Ref-
      uges for Middle-Class Youth." ADOLESCENT PSYCHIATRY 8
      (1980): 138-53.

      Argues that, in spite of the differences in life-styles,
      members of communes and cults share certain personality
      characteristics. When young adults join a cult, they are
      escaping from freedom. Though the conversion experience may
      relieve many of them of emotional stress, there is reason to
      believe that this relief is temporary. Their dependency
      needs, which are assuaged by a change of personal identity
      and by a life of abnegation in a closed cultic environment,
      might reappear later in life, especially if they leave the
      cult.

1261. Levine, Saul V. RADICAL DEPARTURES: DESPERATE DETOURS TO
      GROWING UP. San Diego: Harcourt Brace Jovanovich, 1984.
      xvi, 196 pp.

      Reflects on the several years of counseling members of
      religious cults, political fringe groups, and therapeutic
      communities. The author tries to answer the most-often-asked
      questions about cults: why do people join them, and does their
      involvement bring about serious psychological harm. He con-
      cludes that participating in cultic life does not cause harm,
      and that cult members use their experience "in the service of
      growing up." Cult joiners are rebellious youths seeking,
      without success, to gain independence from their parents.
      They usually have low self-esteem and are not yet committed
      to any value system. They can be described as perfectionists
      in search of radical and more satisfying answers in a communal
      life-style. Parents are advised to supply acceptable forms
      of commitment and community, which their children are desper-
      ately looking for.

1262. Levine, Saul V. "Radical Departures." PSYCHOLOGY TODAY 18
      (August 1984): 20-24.

      Provides a brief presentation of the author's published
      work, RADICAL DEPARTURES (item 1261).

1263. Levine, Saul V. "Cults and Mental Health: Clinical Considera-
      tions." CANADIAN JOURNAL OF PSYCHIATRY 26 (1981): 534-39.

Comments on the current debate on the mental health of
cultists and ex-cultists, and argues that there is more
rhetoric than fact to the many allegations brought into the
picture. On the basis of several studies, the author draws
ten conclusions on the relationship between the cults and
mental health. His view is that cults do not attract more
clinically disturbed persons, nor do they adversely affect
their members more than any other demanding organization.
Cults rather tend to reduce stress, fulfill crucial psychological needs, and create a therapeutic milieu for members
with serious problems. On the other hand, they also bring
into being some emotional problems and lead to cognitive and
behavior patterns that are harmful to their members. While
cults can wield great power over their committed members by
creating ethnocentric communities, what ultimately makes a
person accept the group's ideology is not brainwashing, but
the individual's own susceptibility and "autohypnosis."

1264. Levine, Saul V. "Adolescents: Believing and Belonging."
       ANNALS OF THE AMERICAN SOCIETY OF ADOLESCENT PSYCHIATRY
       7 (1979): 41-53.

       Develops the thesis that adolescents have two basic psycho-
       social needs, namely, for a belief system and a sense of
       belonging, which enable them to cope better with those criti-
       cal years and with life in general. The author thinks that
       these needs can be used in rehabilitative, correctional, and
       therapeutic work with many adolescents.

1265. Levine, Saul V. "Role of Psychiatry in the Phenomenon of
       Cults." CANADIAN JOURNAL OF PSYCHIATRY 24 (1979): 593-603.

       Deals with a variety of theoretical and practical issues
       which have received prominence, especially after the tragic
       events at Jonestown. Basing his reflections on clinical work
       with over two hundred cult members and many of their parents,
       the author discusses the meaning of a cult and the background
       of those who become members. The role of the psychiatrist,
       who should not assume a blanket condemnation or approval, is
       considered. Four stages of cult involvement are outlined:
       1) prior to conversion; 2) commitment; 3) doubt; and 4) post-
       cult condition. The issue of deprogramming, which the author
       doesn't support, is also debated.

1266. Levine, Saul V. "Youth and Religious Cults: A Societal and
       Clinical Dilemma." ADOLESCENT PSYCHIATRY 6 (1978): 75-89.

       Endeavors to clarify some of the fundamental issues which
       the presence of the new religious movements have brought to
       the fore. Five major questions are asked: 1) are cult members
       a particularly vulnerable or pathological group of people?;
       2) what makes the new movements attractive?; 3) are the
       experiences of cult members positive or meaningful, or are
       they deleterious and destructive?; 4) what is the experience
       of their families?; and 5) will fringe religions eventually

become part of the mainstream or are they just fads? The
author thinks that many cult members had borderline personality disorders, such as neurotic anxiety and depression,
before they joined a cult. Membership in a cult, he maintains, is largely beneficial, at least for a short period of
time.

1267. Levine, Saul V. "The Mythology of Contemporary Youth."
        CANADIAN MEDICAL ASSOCIATION JOURNAL 113 (1975): 501-4.

        Discusses, in the context of the emergence of new religions,
        the myths about contemporary youth, which adults create to
        handle young people's quest for a millennium and for answers
        to their existential questions. The following myths are de-
        scribed: those of youth's adulators, youth's detractors, and
        adulthood. The author states that many people who found no
        answers in psychotherapy achieved a sense of self, a feeling
        of self-esteem and self-realization, and a reduction of
        pathlogical symptoms by exploring a new belief system and way
        of life.

1268. Levine, Saul V., and Nancy E. Slater. "Youth and Contempo-
        rary Religious Movements: Psychosocial Findings." CANADIAN
        PSYCHIATRIC ASSOCIATION JOURNAL 21 (1976): 411-20.

        Attempts to answer four fundamental questions about new
        religious movements: 1) Are those who are attracted to them a
        particularly vulnerable group of people? 2) What makes them
        appealing to young adults? 3) Are the experiences of those
        who join meaningful and positive or harmful? 4) Will the
        fringe religions become mainstream or will they fade away?
        The authors, basing their conclusions on interviews with many
        cult members, state that demoralized, unhappy, and alienated,
        though definitely not sick, young adults are attracted to the
        new movements. Both their vulnerability and the movements'
        ability to fulfill their needs are the cause of the latter's
        success. Some benefits are accrued from conversion, but the
        negative result of close-mindedness is common. In some cases
        severe emotional problems were evident prior to cultic in-
        volvement. Most of the new cults, according to the authors,
        will eventually fizzle out.

1269. Levinson, Peritz. "Religious Delusions in Counter-Culture
        Patients." AMERICAN JOURNAL OF PSYCHIATRY 130 (1973):
        1265-69.

        Summarizes the research made on eight hospitalized patients
        who claimed messianic or prophetic calling, and whose behavior
        had appropriate practices linked with the counterculture prac-
        tices, such as meditation, vegetarianism, and the occult.
        These delusionary forms of behavior are identified as belief
        in one's omnipotence, avoidance of affect-laden experiences,
        asceticism, and the tendency to form symbiotic relationships.
        The author supplies clinical examples to demonstrate the de-
        fence mechanisms of religious delusions, the influence of the

counterculture, and the part played by meditation. Special
treatment which can be given to these subjects is considered.
Schizophrenia, narcissistic personality, and emotionally-empty
relationships are the major issues the clinician has to deal
with.

1270. Lieberman, M. A., and J. R. Gardner. "Institutional Alterna-
       tive to Psychotherapy: A Study of Growth Center Users."
       ARCHIVES OF GENERAL PSYCHIATRY 33 (1976): 157-62.

       Studies encounter groups (including those which make use
       of meditation, sensory awareness, and transcendental experi-
       ences) which stress health, normality, and the development
       of sensitivity. The aim of the study was to determine the
       societal function of the centers. "Were these centers
       alternatives to psychotherapy or were they specialized edu-
       cational activities that facilitated a person's individual
       development?" (p. 157). The subjects were measured for the
       degree of life-stress, numerous psychiatric symptoms, and
       acknowledged help-seeking goals. It is concluded that most
       users of growth centers are experiencing stress and join the
       group for psychotherapeutic reasons. These centers, however,
       cannot be an alternative to traditional psychotherapy, but
       could be a useful addition to it.

1271. Lockwood, George. "Rational-Emotive Therapy and Extremist
       Religious Cults." JOURNAL OF RATIONAL-EMOTIVE THERAPY
       16 (1981): 13-17.

       Adopts the view that conversion to a cult is coercive, and
       that involement in it is pathological. A case example, the
       author's own sister, is provided to illustrate the potential
       of rational-emotive principles in dealing with cult conversion.
       By undertaking a direct, logical refutation of her beliefs,
       the author was able to trigger her independent and critical
       thought until she was led to reexamine her newly-acquired
       belief system.

1272. MacHovec, Frank J. "Current Therapies and the Ancient East."
       AMERICAN JOURNAL OF PSYCHOTHERAPY 38 (1984): 87-96.

       Explains several root ideas from Taoist, Confucian, and
       Buddhist Zen sources which relate to contemporary psychother-
       apy. Concepts from Gestalt, psychoanalysis, Transactional
       Analysis, and existential, cognitive, and family therapies
       are traced to these ancient Eastern forerunners. The authors
       maintain that Yoga is a "sequential experiential therapy
       system," and that the Four Noble Truths and the Eightfold
       Path of Buddhism are relevant to our contemporary problems of
       life adjustment and are a useful guide to counseling and
       therapy.

1273. Maleson, Franklin G. "Dilemmas in the Evaluation and Manage-
       ment of Religious Cultists." AMERICAN JOURNAL OF PSYCHIATRY
       138 (1981): 925-29.

Highlights some of the difficulties in dealing with patients
who are or have been members of religious cults. Notwith-
standing the debate on the matter, the author insists that
cult members are neither psychotics nor mentally ill persons
in the legal sense. On the contrary, they are generally
happier in the group than they were outside it. Two contrast-
ing case histories are presented. The psychiatrist should not
readily accept the brainwashing hypothesis, but should seek
an explanation in other areas, such as the adolescent search
for identity and meaning, faith healing, dissociation and
altered states of consciousness, and predisposing psychopathology. The life-style in a cult may have been a satisfying
solution to the joiner's needs. Some guidelines for advising
parents of cult members are proposed.

1274. Markowitz, Arnold, and David Halperin. "Cults and Children:
      The Abuse of the Young." CULTIC STUDIES JOURNAL 1 (1984):
      143-55.

      Focuses on the potential and factual abuse, neglect, and
      mistreatment of children in the cults. Jonestown is taken as
      an example of what some cults might be doing to young children.
      The authors identify the psychological factors which lead
      parents to narcissistic and often sadistic behavior towards
      their offspring. The cult environment, dictated and con-
      trolled by the guru, easily fosters child abuse and neglect.
      Examples of this are the downplaying of the need for medical
      care, the use of strange diets, the sexist education prac-
      tices, and the belittlement of the role of the biological
      parents.

1275. Marks, David, and Richard Kamman. THE PSYCHOLOGY OF THE
      PSYCHIC. Buffalo, NY: Promotheus Books, 1980. 232 pp.

      Offers an exposition of all psychic phenomena as fraudulent
      and deceptive. The psychic claims of two of the most well-
      known psychics, Kreskin and Uri Geller, are challenged. The
      author thinks that belief in paranormal, extrasensory percep-
      tion, and psychic abilities borders on the pathological. In
      the light of many psychic claims by leaders of religious cults,
      this book offers some stimulating discussion. One appendix in
      this book (pp. 223-26) gives a set of rules for evaluating the
      evidence for psychic phenomena (including testimonials). The
      authors believe that the evidence brought forth to sustain
      the claims of psychic happenings is rather poor and could
      easily be dismissed.

1276. Masserman, Jules H. "Threescore and Thirteen Tangential
      Therapies--A Review and Integration." CURRENT PSYCHI-
      ATRIC THERAPIES 18 (1978): 3-37.

      Lists and briefly describes over seventy non-traditional
      therapies including Esalen, Est, faith healing, Silva Mind
      Control, Morita Therapy, Synanon, Transcendental Meditation,
      Yoga, and Zen. Several experiential analogies between them
      are cited, and an analysis of their common dynamics is pro-
      posed. A comprehensive bibliography is included.

1277. McGuire, Meredith B. "Words of Power: Personal Empowerment and Healing." CULTURE, MEDICINE, AND PSYCHIATRY 7 (1983): 221-40.

Studies the ritual use of words in modern alternative healing groups, Christian groups (like Pentecostal and fundamental churches and healing cults), Meditation and Human Potential groups (Zen, various forms of Buddhist, and Eastern meditation), metaphysical groups (Christian Science, I Am Movement, and Theosophy) and occult and eclectic groups (like witchcraft). The beliefs about language used in these movements and the centrality of ritual language in the healing process are discussed. The author thinks that ritual language has healing power because it mobilizes the individual's resources. She maintains that, in the groups she studied, quackery and refusal of medical treatment is not a major problem. Alternative healing methods are not incompatible with orthodox medicine.

1278. Meissner, W. W. "The Cult Phenomenon: Psychoanalytic Perspective." PSYCHOANALYTIC STUDY OF SOCIETY 10 (1984): 91-111.

Discusses the sociological analysis of church, sect, and cult, and sees the latter as a deviant religious group which tends "to become a repository for psychopathology" (p. 93). The following elements of mental illness are examined: 1) sacrifice of the intellect, leading to the surrender of freedom; 2) a subtle form of thought control, which underlies authoritarianism; 3) the consequent regressive surrender of ego controls and responsibility; and 4) the development of paranoia. Pathological narcissism often becomes an operative factor in a cult. Because paranoid mechanisms project undesirable and feared qualities onto the outside group, participation in a cult may lead to some relief of inner feelings of inadequacy, powerlessness, and meaninglessness. One central feature of cultism, namely, the attraction and attachment to a leader, has libidinal and hysterical components and is basically a form of narcissism which can be easily exploited. Converts to cults suffer from a higher neurotic distress and have a greater incidence of psychotic problems, but are inclined to find greater emotional relief and stability in the cult itself. The emergence of Cargo cults in Melanesia and the snake-handling sects in the United States are taken as examples of the pathology of cults. While stressing the pathological elements of cults, which may be found in varying degrees in all forms of religious organizations, the author states that the process and mechanism of cult formation may lead to human growth and strength as well as to constructive adaptation.

1279. Melton, J. Gordon, and Robert L. Moore. THE CULT EXPERIENCE: RESPONDING TO THE NEW RELIGIOUS PLURALISM. New York: Pilgrim Press, 1982. x, 180 pp.

Provides a general overview of the cult phenomenon and the problems it has created in many segments of society. The

meaning of the word "cult" is discussed, and the origin and
appeal of the new movements briefly sketched. The authors
raise the issue of whether cult members have been brainwashed
or converted, and propose the view that cults are rites of
passage into adulthood. The question of deprogramming and
the reaction of anti-cult movements are also given some attention. The authors give specific guidelines (pp. 112-23) for
helping families of cult members cope with their children's
involvement in cults.

1280. Miller, Claude E. "Human Potential Movements." AMERICAN
        JOURNAL OF PSYCHOANALYSIS 37 (1977): 99-109.

Remarks on the conflict between the human potential movement and psychotherapy, and the uneasy truce which has marked
the relationship between psychotherapists and the leaders of
the Human Potential Movement, including Michael Murphy, the
founder of Esalen, and Robert Assagioli who developed psychosynthesis (cf. item 471). The author proposes that in psychic
life, there are two phases, the diastolic or filling state,
and the systolic or contracting state. Human potential modes,
such as meditation and biofeedback, are related to the diastolic phase, while classical psychotherapy is linked with
the systolic phase. These two phases are complementary and
must be integrated. Human potential movements, which include
TM, Est, and other forms of meditation, are fulfilling a need
of experiencing oneself in a diastolic phase, a need which our
culture tends to ignore.

1281. Mosatche, Harriet S. SEARCHING: PRACTICES AND BELIEFS OF
        THE RELIGIOUS CULTS AND HUMAN POTENTIAL GROUPS. New York:
        Stravon Education Press, 1983. 437 pp.

Purports to be a social-psychological analysis of nine
organizations and their members, namely, Est, the Unification
Church, Scientology, the Association for Research and Enlightenment, the Himalayan International Institute, the Institute
for Psycho-Integrity, the Divine Light Mission, Wainright
House, and the Hare Kirshna movement. An evaluation of each
group is provided. The brainwashing/conversion controversy
is considered, and it is concluded that manipulation, deceptive practices and pressures, and indoctrination in the cults
are probably the same as those found in some other respectable
organizations.

1282. Needleman, Jacob, and Denise Lewis, editors. ON THE WAY TO
        SELF-KNOWLEDGE. New York: Alfred Knopf, 1976. xii, 241 pp.

Presents a collection of essays discussing the relationship
between sacred tradition and psychotherapy in the context of
the rise of the new religious movements in the West. Because
Western psychiatrists are now using ideas and methods from the
ancient spiritual traditions of Asia and spiritual leaders
are employing the language of modern psychology, the editors
think that a synthesis between psychiatry and religion is

being gradually forged. The various essays discuss the principles, aims, and practices of both psychiatry and religion and the benefits and dangers when they are combined. The question is raised as to whether modern men and women, faced with cultural and religious changes, need spiritual or psychological help, or both.

1283. Neki, J. S. "Reappraisal of the Guru-Chela Relationship as a Therapeutic Paradigm." INTERNATIONAL MENTAL HEALTH RESEARCH NEWSLETTER 16.1 (1974): 2, 17.

Compares and contrasts the attitude towards the dependency relationship between patient and therapist in Western culture and the approach to the dependency between guru and disciple in Indian society. Western psychiatrists make all efforts to avoid the relationship, while Indian psychiatrists exploit it. The Western model need not, according to the author, be universally imposed.

1284. Neki, J. S. "Guru-Chela Relationship: The Possibility of a Therapeutic Paradigm." AMERICAN JOURNAL OF ORTHOPSYCHIATRY 43 (1973): 755-66.

Contrasts the psychotherapeutic strategies of Eastern and Western cultures and suggests that, for Indian patients, the relationship between therapist and subject might be better patterned after the guru-chela (master/disciple) relationship in Eastern cultures. The role and function of the guru (spiritual director, or cult leader), and the steps in the relationship with his or her disciples, are described. The goals therapy--relief of symptoms, self-realization, and adjustment--could also be fulfilled, if psychotherapy takes place within the context of a guru-chela relationship. The author seems to suggest that this relationship is not suitable to Western culture.

1285. Nelson, Geoffrey K. "Cults and the New Religions: Towards a Sociology of Religious Creativity." SOCIOLOGY AND SOCIAL RESEARCH 68 (1984): 301-325.

Reviews the literature on cults and maintains that the new religious movements are indicative of creative efforts to satisfy spiritual needs, and that their rise is to be related to the process of secularization, to the movement toward an ideational society, and to greater contact with Eastern cultures. The author seems to imply that the new religious movements provide some benefits to their followers.

1286. Newman, Ruth G. "Thoughts on Superstars of Charism: Pipers in our Midst." AMERICAN JOURNAL OF ORTHOPSYCHIATRY 53 (1983): 201-8.

Draws an analogy between charismatic cult leaders, such as Father Divine, Jim Jones, and the Reverend Moon, and the Pied Piper of Hamelin, stressing their attractive power which

can be used for both good and evil. These leaders prey on
human dependency needs and work among the isolated, lonely,
oppressed, and depressed people, offering them a purpose and
meaning in life and an answer to all their problems. Such
needs, though natural, leave one vulnerable to narcissistic
leaders and to psychotic charismatics, who can turn their
followers back to an infantile stage.

1287. Olsson, Peter A. "Adolescent Involvement With the Super-
        natural and Cults: Some Psychoanalytic Considerations."
        ANNALS OF PSYCHOANALYSIS 8 (1980): 171-96.

        Presents three clinical cases of female adolescents whose
        psychopathology was linked with their supernatural beliefs
        and preoccupations. Freud's views on the supernatual and
        the uncanny are then briefly described. The cases examined
        typified the predominant "pre-oedipal" borderline state and
        high narcissistic trends of the patients. The author holds
        that adolescent preoccupation with the cults and the super-
        natural is reflective of psycho-dynamic, psycho-economic,
        and psycho-genetic issues and does not necessarily affect
        their intrapsychic structure and functioning.

1288. Ott, Herbert A., and James W. Knight, editors. DIMENSIONS IN
        WHOLISTIC HEALING: NEW FRONTIERS IN THE TREATMENT OF THE
        WHOLE PERSON. Chicago: Nelson-Hall, 1979. xx, 543 pp.

        Deals with the current interest in wholistic health. The
        basis of wholistic healing and Western and non-Western
        approaches to healing are among the broad areas covered.

        Contains items 1486, 1544, 1766.

1289. Ottenberg, Donald J. "Therapeutic Community and the Danger
        of the Cult Phenomenon." CULTS AND THE FAMILY (item 1242),
        pp. 151-173.

        Points out that the cult is an alternative form of therapy,
        although radically different from the established religions,
        which are also therapeutic communities. Using Synanon as an
        example, the author shows how a therapeutic community can
        degenerate into a cult, points to some safeguards for prevent-
        ing such corruption, and examines cult-like aspects of thera-
        peutic communities. Cults differ from these in the location
        of power (the guru), area of interest (the millennium or
        apocalypse), goals (strengthening of the cult itself), right
        to challenge (obedience and false compliance), accountability
        (protected by religious exemption), openness to the outside
        world (severely limited in cults), pre-entry information
        (minimal), aftercare (nonexistent), and change of personality
        (induced pathology). Several lessons from the therapeutic
        community are drawn.

1290. Owens, Claire Myers. "Zen Buddhism." TRANSPERSONAL PSYCHOL-
        OGIES (item 1338) Edited by Charles T. Tart. pp. 155-202.

Includes, besides some basic history and philosophy of
Buddhism, a comparison and contrast between the spiritual
psychology of Zen and the various psychologies of the West.
In Zen, Jungian psychology, and the psychologies of Houston
and Masters, the goals of self-realization, the psychological
process, and the transformation of one's personality are
similar. Because Zen meditation leads to one's true self
and to a personality that is loving, strong, creative, and
able to solve daily problems, the obvious conclusion is drawn
that Zen is an effective treatment for human problems.

1291. Pattison, E. Mansell. "Religious Youth Cults: Alternative
      Healing Social Networks." JOURNAL OF RELIGION AND HEALTH
      19 (1980): 275-86.

      Compares traditional psychotherapy with modern cults, which
      are seen as "alternative healing systems" that share many
      of their goals, but differ in method, content, and context.
      Religious cults are an indication that a shift in Western
      cosmologies and family structure is under way. Of three
      types of social networks--normal, neurotic, and psychotic--
      the normal one is said to reduce stress and anxiety. Those
      young adults who join cults exhibit existential stress and
      cultural maladaptation problems, which some cults deal with.

1292. Pattison, E. Mansell. "Psychosocial Interpretations of
      Exorcism." JOURNAL OF OPERATIONAL PSYCHIATRY 3.2 (1977):
      5-21.

      Concerns itself with the widespread interest in the super-
      natural, the mystical, and the magical in contemporary Western
      society, particularly as seen in the rise of folk healers.
      Naturalistic versus supernaturalistic systems of health and
      illness are contrasted, and beliefs in demon possession and
      exorcism are placed within the context of supernaturalism.
      Western society is said to be ripe for the reemergence of
      these beliefs, which can be interpreted as part of the social
      repudiation of scientific determinism. Three areas distin-
      guishing exorcism from psychoanalysis are challenged: 1) the
      supernatural description of the possession state is less
      accurate than the natural one; 2) folk healing tends to be
      less thorough in dealing with possession than psychoanalysis;
      3) and the rite of exorcism is less effective than psycho-
      therapy in dealing with subjects who manifest signs of
      possession. The author's view is that exorcism is an example
      of the powerful use of symbolic transformations in healing
      rituals, and that psychoanalysis itself is a form of exorcism.

1293. Paul, Robert A. "A Mantra and Its Meaning." PSYCHOANALYTIC
      STUDY OF SOCIETY 9 (1981): 85-91.

      Gives a psychoanalytic interpretation of the Tibetan mantra
      "Ome Mani Padme Hum," the references to the mystical union of
      male and female principles, and the metaphoric references to
      sexual union. The recitation of the mantra leads to an experi-

ence of blissful contentment (child nursing), followed by
deprivation and desire, with a final return to the object of
desire. The mantra "provides a culturally valued symbol, the
utilization of which enables either a wish to regress or
regression itself to be accomplished" (p. 90). The repetition
of the mantra infuses the attitude of submission with powerful
sexual cathexis.

1294. Pavlos, Andrew J. THE CULT EXPERIENCE. Westport, CT: Green-
wood Press, 1982. xii, 209 pp.

Presents a general survey overview of the new religious
movements, accounting for their origin and growth in Western
society. The steps leading to conversion into, and identity
with, a cult are traced. The roots of the cult belief system
and the charismatic qualities of cult leaders are also considered. Although the author thinks that extreme forms of
behavior are clear in many cults, and that many people who
join become psychologically disabled, he nevertheless holds
that some deprogramming methods are questionable. The success
of the cults is related to the continuing youthful search for
a positive self-image and identity and a new spiritual sensi-
bility. Synanon, the Unification Church, Scientology, Jim
Jones's People's Temple, the Children of God, the Divine Light
Mission, and the Hare Krishna are among those cults cited
throughout the book.

1295. Pruyser, Paul W. "Narcissism in Contemporary Religion."
JOURNAL OF PASTORAL CARE 32 (1978): 219-31.

Examines, from a Freudian perspective, 1) narcissistic motives, like salvation, providence, and election, in the
Judeo-Christian tradition, 2) narcissistic trends in modern
society, where the cult of self-centeredness is prominent,
and 3) narcissistic features in current religious beliefs and
practices. The quest for instant mysticism, which the author
identifies as a contemporary trend, is interpreted as a
regressive step. Narcissism is evident in the charismatic
movement and in those groups with strong leadership, which
demand total subjugation.

1296. Reiser, Morton F. "Psychosomatic Medicine: A Meeting Ground
for Oriental and Occidental Medical Therapy and Practice."
PSYCHOTHERAPY AND PSYCHOSOMATICS 31 (1979): 315-22.

Argues that the field of psychosomatic medicine is a meeting ground for East and West. The difference between the
treatment of psychological disorders in Eastern and Western
cultures has been that the former prefers the use of religious
theories and practices, like Yoga and Zen, while the latter
takes a much more mechanical approach. The author believes
that, because of theoretical and practical reasons, the gap
has become narrower since the early 1960s.

1297. Richardson, Herbert, editor. NEW RELIGIONS AND MENTAL HEALTH:
UNDERSTANDING THE ISSUES. New York: Edwin Mellen Press,
1980. lv, 177 pp.

Contains 16 essays on the psychiatric and legal issues
which the new religious movements have raised. The articles
are grouped in four parts: 1) definition of the problem;
2) special interest groups; 3) judicial decisions and govern-
mental studies; and 4)conversion, a theological view. Included is the "Conclusion of the Study on Mind Development Groups,
Sects, and Cults in Ontario" by Paul G. Hill. The editor, in
a lengthy introduction, reviews the entire material, and compares the anti-cult ferment with anti-Catholicism and anti-
Semitism. He concludes that parents and psychiatrists have
overreacted to the presence of the cults, that there is no
need for legislation to control or limit their activities,
and that part of the reason why there is so much antagonism
against the cults is that they are viable competitors to
traditional psychiatry.

1298. Richardson, James T. "Psychological and Psychiatric Studies
        on New Religions." ADVANCES IN THE PSYCHOLOGY OF RELIGION.
        Edited by L. B. Brown. New York: Pergamon Press, 1985, pp.
        209-23.

        Reviews psychological and psychiatric literature on the new
        movements. The major personality assessment findings of
        researchers, who used standardized instruments to evaluate
        cult members, are outlined. Included are works on: the Jesus
        Movement which, in spite of some deviance, led to healing,
        rehabilitation, and reintegration of members into society;
        Ananda Marga Yoga Society, membership in which did not sug-
        gest personality disorders or major psychopathology; and the
        Unification Church and the Divine Light Mission, both of
        which can be interpreted as alternate therapies. Some nega-
        tive views on the new movements are discussed. The author
        concludes by stating that "there is little data to support
        the almost completely negative picture painted by a few
        psychiatrists who have been involved in the controversy over
        the new religions" (p. 223).

1299. Robbins, Thomas. "A Comment on Ash's Conception of Extrem-
        ist Cults: With a Postscript on Models of Thought Reform."
        CULTIC STUDIES JOURNAL 1 (1984): 120-26.

        Questions the conclusions of Ash regarding extremist cults,
        especially the connection which he makes between cult member-
        ship and psychological harm. The author points out that
        different individuals may react differently to the same social
        conditions, and may get involved in a cult on quite different
        levels. It is argued that sectarian zealotry is not psycho-
        pathology. The need to clarify such concepts as brainwashing
        and deception, and not to apply them in their extreme form to
        all cults, is underscored.

1300. Rome, Howard P. "Limits of the Human Mind." PSYCHIATRIC
        ANNALS 7 (November 1977): 11-31.

        Discusses, among other things, Latter-Day Millenarianism,
        which is "a coping reaction" in times of domestic or spiritual

trouble. The Unification Church, Transcendental Meditation, and Est are taken as examples of contemporary millenarian or messianic movements. Joining one of these groups brings several rewards to the individual: religious salvation, political power and prestige, and the psychosocial benefits of an enhanced sense of personal security and control.

1301. Rosen, R. D. PSYCHOBABBLE: FAST TALK AND QUICK CURE IN THE ERA OF FEELING. New York: Avon Books, 1975. 250 pp.

Depicts and interprets several therapeutic trends of the 1970s, with chapters on Est and Scientology. It is contended that psychotherapeutic and spiritual objectives have been blurred and merged, mainly because of the influx of Eastern mysticism. The new therapies are seen as using meaningless jargon. While their clients may reap some therapeutic benefits, they run the risk of losing their ability to develop more independent judgments about themselves. Some of the new therapies (like Transactional Analysis) have converted psychoanalytic principles into more expedient therapies with a new terminology.

1302. Rosenthal, Raymond F., and James S. Gordon. NEW DIRECTIONS IN MEDICINE: A DIRECTORY OF LEARNING OPPORTUNITIES. Washington, DC: Aurora Associates, 1984. xix, 215 pp.

Contains over 150 entries of health professionals who offer their expertise as resource persons or teachers to medical students, interns, and residents. The directory is written "to supplement and encourage biomedical training to be a window on new and undiscovered concepts and practice in preventive medicine and health care, and to promote students with educational opportunities to mentors who might not otherwise be available to them" (xi). The glossary includes brief descriptions of many alternative healing practices, including acupuncture, (Hatha) Yoga, Mantra, meditation, psychic healing, shaman, and Zen.

1303. Rosten, Leo, editor. RELIGIONS OF AMERICA: FERMENT AND FAITH IN AN AGE OF CRISIS. New York: Simon and Schuster, 1975. 672 pp.

Deals mainly with traditional churches. In a short section on the Pentecostal and charismatic movements of the 1970s, some groups are judged to be theologically aberrant. People in these groups achieve hallucinations and visions by their loud and noisy behavior. People who are emotionally starved and disturbed (like those who join the Hare Krishna movement) seem to be suffering from serious psychological problems bordering on pathology.

1304. Rubins, Jack L. "The Personality Cult in Psychoanalysis." AMERICAN JOURNAL OF PSYCHOANALYSIS 34 (1974): 129-33.

Discusses the irrational attachment of a number of people to an idealized leader whose followers accept his/her ideals

as the final truth. This cult of personality is "peculiarly
notable in psychoanalysis" (p. 129). The condition for the
rise of this type of leader and the motives of those who
accept his/her views are described. The author holds that
personality cultism is not always necessarily bad or obstruc-
tive to progress.

1305. Rudin, James, and Marcia Rudin. PRISON OR PARADISE: THE NEW
       RELIGIOUS CULTS. Philadelphia: Fortress Press, 1980.
       164 pp.

       Discusses the main religious cults, among which are listed
       the Unification Church, ISKCON, the Way International, the
       Alamo Foundation, the Children of God, and Scientology. The
       cults are attacked for using deceptive means to recruit fol-
       lowers, for discouraging rational thought, for manipulating
       guilt, for isolating members from the outside world, and for
       instigating violence. They are psychologically dangerous,
       liable to cause serious mental breakdowns. The authors
       speculate on their attractive features, and propose ways of
       counteracting them. Ex-cult members are often in need of
       counseling and rehabilitation.

1306. Rudin, Marcia. "Women, Elderly, and Children in Religious
       Cults." CULTIC STUDIES JOURNAL 1 (1984): 8-26.

       Relying almost exclusively on newspaper reports and con-
       versations with ex-cult members, concludes that there is a
       negative impact of cults on women, children, and the elderly.
       Women, besides being generally poorly treated and abused, are
       not allowed to make their own decisions regarding marriage,
       sex, and childbearing. The elderly frequently suffer from
       financial exploitation, and children, particularly in funda-
       mentalist churches, are in many cases separated from their
       parents, denied proper diet and medical care, and meted out
       harsh physical punishments. Cultic life-style does not bene-
       fit the physical and psychological well-being of women,
       children, and the elderly. Legal means are recommended to
       remedy the problem.

1307. Saliba, John A. "Psychiatry and the New Cults, Part I: The
       New Cults: Dangerous Institutions Causing Mental Illness."
       ACADEMIC PSYCHOLOGY BULLETIN 7 (1985): 39-55.

       Attempts an objective and impartial examination of current
       psychiatric views on the effect of cult membership. The
       first part examines the theory that the new cults are danger-
       ous organizations which have added a new dimension to mental
       health problems. The cultic features and effects as typified
       by the analysis of Margaret Singer and her colleagues are out-
       lined and evaluated. Her views are found wanting, both in
       theory and method. It is concluded that her completely nega-
       tive picture of the cult phenomenon is unrealistic and betrays
       a psychoanalytical bias against religion.

1308. Saliba, John A. "Psychiatry and the New Cults, Part II: The
       New Cults: Helpful Organizations Providing Alternative
       Therapy." ACADEMIC PSYCHOLOGY BULLETIN 7 (1985): 361-75.

       Examines the view that the cults have a beneficial thera-
       peutic effect on those who join them. The position of Marc
       Galanter, which typifies that of several psychiatrists, is
       outlined and evaluated. It is concluded that, though found
       wanting in several respects, his view is theoretically and
       methodologically superior to Margaret Singer's analysis of the
       cults. The attitude towards religion of many psychologists
       and psychiatrists is criticized, and several suggestions are
       made as to how an improved method and a more positive theory
       can help toward a better understanding of the cult phenomenon.

1309. Salmon, Warren J., editor. ALTERNATIVE MEDICINES: POPULAR
       AND POLICY PERSPECTIVES. New York: Tavistock Publications,
       1984. x, 302 pp.

       Brings together a series of papers discussing the rise and
       spread of non-Western ways of healing, which are often viewed
       as competing with traditional scientific medicine. Chinese
       medicine, indigenous systems of healing, and psychic healing
       are among the areas covered. Two survey articles analyze
       the encounter between alternative and traditional medicine
       in the United Kingdom and in the United States, and holistic
       health centers in the latter country. Several of the authors
       reflect on the practical policies and clinical implications
       of the new therapies.

       Includes item 1177.

1310. Sargant, William. THE MIND POSSESSED: A PHYSIOLOGY OF POS-
       SESSION, MYSTICISM, AND FAITH HEALING. Philadelphia: J. B.
       Lippincott Company, 1974. xii, 212 pp.

       Raises the question whether mysticism, faith healing, and
       similar phenomena are mechanistic tools created by human
       beings rather than spiritual phenomena. Various rituals of
       possession and exorcism in different countries--the Zar rit-
       ual in Ethiopia, Voodoo in Haiti, and religious revivals in
       the United States--are among the many areas covered. The same
       physiological processes that underlie possession, trance, and
       tongue-speaking are found in the behavior of those undergoing
       hypnosis, taking certain drugs, or experiencing sexual excite-
       ment. A person's vulnerability to fall into one of these
       states depends on his/her inherited neurological system.
       While admitting that some healing methods are effective, the
       author leaves the reader with the impression that all these
       practices dealing with possession and exorcism are somewhat
       dangerous and more likely, in the long run, to be harmful than
       beneficial.

1311. Schecter, R. E., editor. COUNSELING CULTISTS AND THEIR
       FAMILIES. Weston, MA: American Family Foundation, 1985.
       51 pp.

A collection of essays, previously published in THE ADVISOR, and written by people who have been involved in counseling ex-cult members and their families. Several of the authors are themselves former members of a cult. Topics, such as "non-coercive exit counseling" and undoing the effects of mind control, are discussed. The programs used by two centers, namely, "Unbound: Iowa Rehabilitation Center," and the "Norfolk Enrichment Center," are described.

1312. Schoen, Stephen. "Gestalt Therapy and the Teachings of Bud-dhism." GESTALT JOURNAL 1 (1978): 103-15.

Observes that there are two major parallels between Gestalt therapy and Buddhist teachings, namely, that both have faith in the human capacity for rehabilitation, and both stress the awareness of, and response to, the present situation as a reaction to something new. While both agree that egotism is the source of all the symptoms of neurosis, such as anxiety, depression, and obsessional thought, they differ radically as to the meaning and extent of egotism. Buddhism stresses a fundamentally changing theory of personality, while Gestalt therapy emphasizes the integrity of, and responsibility to, a personal identity or subject. The Buddhist view of mental health is judged to be better, since it realizes that the ego, and not just egotism, is the root of the problem. Buddhist teaching can make a profound contribution to psychotherapy.

1313. Schultz, James. "Stages on the Spiritual Path: A Buddhist Perspective." JOURNAL OF TRANSPERSONAL PSYCHOLOGY 7 (1975): 14-28.

Expounds the Buddhist spiritual path in five stages, namely: 1) childhood precursors as the foundation of worldly knowl-edge; 2) peak experiences and aspiration for enlightenment; 3) community, compassion, and strength; 4) deep psychological experiences and spirituality such as "tantra"; and 5) fulfill-ment, enlightenment, and union with the lineage of original teachers. These stages are related to psychological processes as developed in Western psychology. It is held that the Bud-dhist approach is both theoretically and practically useful.

1314. Schuster, Richard. "Towards a Synthesis of Eastern Psychol-ogy and Western Psychotherapy." PSYCHOLOGY: A JOURNAL OF HUMAN BEHAVIOR 14.1 (1977): 3-13.

Argues that a synthesis of Western and Eastern psychologies takes place in the attitude and understanding of the psycho-therapist with no great change in setting or techniques. The orientation of Eastern and Western cultures towards human suffering are contrasted, the former aiming at producing a transcendent or mystical experience, the latter at solving personal problems in one's life. The West prefers a negative path, removing those aspects of personality which thwart ego-development, while the East opts for a positive approach, one

which develops equanimity, compassion, and ego-transcendence.
The author demonstrates, by presenting a case study, how both
ways can be combined in a psychotherapeutic setting.

1315. Schwartz, Lita Linzer. "Family Therapists and Families of
       Cult Members." INTERNATIONAL JOURNAL OF FAMILY THERAPY 5
       (1983): 168-78.

       Presents information on cults in general, cult members, and
       families of cult members in order to help psychologists and
       therapists who encounter cult-related problems in their clin-
       ical practice. Cults, according to the author, govern the
       minds of their members by indoctrination techniques. Many cult
       members have had a history of psychological problems involv-
       ing a search for a meaningful purpose to life and a coherent
       value system. Once they leave the cult, more often than not
       through some kind of pressure, they suffer from additional
       problems, particularly "floating," the tendency of the ex-cult
       member to drift back into the cultic state of mind, or altered
       state of consciousness, from which he/she had been rescued.
       The ex-cult patient is not a typical clinical case. Parents
       who seek advice after one of their children has joined or
       left a cult pose different therapeutic challenges, and the
       author suggests ways of dealing with them.

1316. Schwartz, Lita Linzer. "Cults and Family Therapists." INTER-
       ACTION 2 (1979): 145-54.

       Describes those features of cults which distinguish them
       from religious sects, the characteristics of people who are
       vulnerable to the appeal of cultic groups, and the techniques
       used by the cults. Cults differ from sects (like the Mormons,
       the Quakers, the Amish, and the Hasidic Jews) in that the
       former, unlike the latter, have an absolute leader to whom
       everybody in the group is subservient, practice physiological
       deprivation (like vegetarianism), and demand that the total
       earnings of the cult members be given over to the institution.
       Appropriate and inappropriate intervention strategies are
       discussed. The author thinks that the medical model is not
       appropriate, and that the treatment of family members should
       not be modeled after death therapy. The family can, in a
       non-judgmental way, explore its feelings and thoughts about
       why one of its members joined a cult, and thus be relieved of
       some of its guilt feelings. A support network is encouraged.
       Some methods used for dealing with the family members of drug
       abusers might be profitably applied to the families of those
       people who join cults.

1317. Shapiro, Eli. "Destructive Cultism." FAMILY PHYSICIAN 15.2
       (1977): 80-83.

       Views the cults as harmful organizations, both to the
       physical and emotional health of their members. "Destructive
       cultism" is a distinct syndrome with several unique features,
       including the demand for complete obedience, separation from

society, and brainwashing maintained through destructive behavior modification techniques. Suggestions for helping ex-
cult members are proposed.

1318. Shapiro, S. A. "A Classification Scheme for Out-of-Body Phe-
        nomena." JOURNAL OF ALTERED STATES OF CONSCIOUSNESS 2
        (1975-76): 259-65.

Presents guidelines and criteria for identifying and distinguishing the various (physical) out-of-body experiences
(OBEs). Besides the commonly-accepted three distinct states
of consciousness, namely, waking, sleeping, and dreaming,
the author suggests a fourth, which lies somewhere between
the waking and the dreaming states. In this new state, the
physical body is asleep, but the level of awareness is close
to being fully awake. Although the psychological condition
of those having OBEs is not discussed, the assumption is that
these experiences are not a sign of pathology.

1319. Shealy, C. Norman, with Arthur S. Freese. OCCULT MEDICINE
        CAN SAVE YOUR LIFE: A DOCTOR LOOKS AT UNCONVENTIONAL MEDI-
        CINE. New York: Dial Press, 1975. 214 pp.

Describes the author's explorations of occult practices as
they relate to the healing of physical, psychological, and
psychosomatic disorders. A short history of occult medicine
is provided and numerous topics, such as astrology, palm-
istry, and faith-healing, are dealt with. Faith healing and
shamanism are seen as psychotherapeutic methods. Guidelines
as to how to choose a real psychic and avoid quacks are given.

1320. Sherwood, Keith. THE ART OF SPIRITUAL HEALING: A PRACTICAL
        GUIDE TO HEALING POWER. St. Paul, MN: Llewellyn Publica-
        tions, 1985. 209 pp.

Argues that everybody has the potential of healing oneself,
and of becoming a channel for healing others. Ways of diag-
nosing human illnesses by examining the aura are described.
Mental healing, chakra healing, and the laying on of hands
are among the methods which can improve one's physical and
psychological health.

1321. Shneidman, J. Leo, and Conalee Levine Shneidman. "The
        Albigensian Cathari." PSYCHODYNAMIC PERSPECTIVES ON RELI-
        GION, SECT, AND CULT (item 1226), pp. 45-58.

Gives a brief account of this early medieval Christian sect
which flourished in southern France and other parts of Europe.
A brief overview of the political and theological developments
leading to the rise of this movement is provided. The author
adopts the view that Catharism was a pessimistic rejection
and denial of the world at the time, and that it functioned
as a defense against the anxieties of changing sociocultural
conditions.

1322. Shupe, Anson D. SIX PERSPECTIVES ON NEW RELIGIONS: A CASE
       STUDY APPROACH. New York: Edwin Mellen Press, 1981. x,
       235 pp.

       Discusses different interpretations of "fringe religions,"
       and examines them from six different perspectives, namely:
       criminological, philosophical, anthropological, social psycho-
       logical, social structural, and historical. In the social
       psychological perspective (pp. 113-53), four models of cult
       formation are discussed: deprivation, interactionist, role
       theory, and brainwashing. The last mentioned model is,
       according to the author, "obviously the most badly reduction-
       ist, for it does not even accord many fringe groups legitimacy
       as religion" (p. 135). Festinger theory of prophecy (item
       379), and Lofland and Stark's view of religious conversion
       (item 1870), are presented as case studies.

1323. Singer, Margaret Thaler. "In Search of Self: The Cult Cul-
       ture." ISRAELI HORIZONS 27.6 (1979): 19-21.

       Lists eight negative characteristics of cults, and shows
       how lonely and depressed people are attracted to them. Var-
       ious problems, which cult members experience when they leave
       the group, particularly that of re-entering society, are
       discussed.

1324. Singer, Margaret Thaler. "Coming Out of the Cults." PSYCHOL-
       OGY TODAY 12 (January 1979): 72-83.

       Discusses several problems which ex-cult members have to
       face: depression, indecisiveness, blurring of mental activity,
       passivity, fear of the cult, and the "fishbowl effect." The
       author seems to hold that many of these problems are actually
       caused by the cultic life-style. One of the main difficulties
       that ex-cult members have is to explain why they were unable
       to walk away from the cult. According to the author, the
       social and psychological coercion and indoctrination practices
       employed in many cults explain why people find it so hard to
       leave.

1325. Singer, Margaret Thaler. "Therapy with Ex-Cult Members."
       NATIONAL ASSOCIATION OF PRIVATE PSYCHIATRIC HOSPITALS JOUR-
       NAL 9.4 (1978): 15-19.

       Comments on the need for counselors to learn more about
       the cults if they are to assist ex-cult members effectively.
       Several negative cultic characteristics, such as the simplis-
       tic answers they provide and the pressure they put on members
       to solicit funds, are discussed. Ex-cult members suffer from
       "thought and conversational inefficiencies," tend to go into
       an altered state of consciousness (floating), and have to deal
       with the "fishbowl effect" (the awareness that they are being
       watched lest they return to the cult). Group therapy is
       recommended.

1326. Sobel, David S., editor. WAYS OF HEALTH: HOLISTIC APPROACHES
       TO ANCIENT AND CONTEMPORARY MEDICINE. New York: Harcourt
       Brace Jovanovich, 1979. xiii, 497 pp.

       Presents a collection of 20 essays, some previously pub-
       lished, advocating a holistic approach to mental and physical
       healing. The volume is divided into five main sections:
       1) holistic approaches to health; 2) ancient systems of medi-
       cine; 3) unorthodox medicines; 4) techniques of self-regulation;
       and 5) an ecological view of health. A lengthy supplementary
       bibliography (pp. 479-92) is added.

       Contains item 389 and selections from item 382.

1327. Spanos, Nichols P. "Witchcraft in Histories of Psychiatry:
       A Critical Analysis and an Alternative Conceptualization."
       PSYCHOLOGICAL BULLETIN 85 (1978): 417-39.

       Examines the common psychiatric view that those accused of
       witchcraft from the late medieval to early modern times were
       mentally disturbed. The arguments brought forth in support
       of this view are found wanting because of the unreliability
       of the psychiatric diagnosis and the failure to consider
       situational influences on human behavior. The accusations
       of witchcraft and the confessions of the witches themselves
       are discussed. It is concluded that the belief that a person
       was a witch was not the outcome of irrational thinking, and
       that the persecutions of witches in Western Europe from the
       fifteenth through the seventeenth centuries "cannot be
       adequately explained in terms of psychiatric disorders" (p.
       434). The author proposes that witchcraft should be under-
       stood with reference to 1) the importance of sociopolitical
       factors in the evolution and maintenance of witch beliefs
       and persecutions, and 2) certain situational elements, such
       as torture, intervillage conflict, and local superstitions.
       A good bibliography, comprising over 150 references mainly in
       English, is appended.

1328. Spanos, Nichols P., and Jack Gottlieb. "Demonic Possession,
       Mesmerism, and Hysteria: A Social Psychological Perspective
       on their Historical Interrelations." JOURNAL OF ABNORMAL
       PSYCHOLOGY 88 (1979): 527-44.

       Deals with the historical relationship between demonic
       possession, mesmerism, and hysteria, three phenomena which
       have helped to shape modern conceptions of mental illness and
       its treatment. The following areas are covered: 1) mesmerism,
       with the roles of the mesmerized subject and the mesmerist,
       and the transcendental phenomena commonly attributed to the
       former; 2) demonic possession, with the roles of the demoniac
       and the exorcist, and the paranormal acts of the former. The
       current psychiatric view that manifestations of both mesmerism
       and demonic possessions are symptoms of hysteria is discussed.
       While agreeing that there are several behavioral similarities
       among these three phenomena, the authors maintain that they

cannot be explained by one simple theory of mental illness.
Instead, they suggest the adoption of a social role theory,
which sees the manifestations of the demonic role as a cul-
turally-consistent explanation for various physical disorders
and other inexplicable occurrences. A large selection of over
180 titles in English and French is added.

1329. Spero, Moshe H.   "Some Pre- and Post-treatment Characteris-
      tics of Cult Devotees." PERCEPTUAL AND MOTOR SKILLS 58
      (1984): 749-50.

      Maintains that initial interest in the type of community
      offered by cults is relative to the field independence, and to
      the overall ego quality of the psychological differentiation
      of the individual. Membership in a cult could also influence
      the same psychological features.

1330. Spero, Moshe H.   "The Stimulus Value of Religion to Cultic
      Personality Types." JOURNAL OF PSYCHOLOGY AND JUDAISM 4
      (1980): 161-70.

      Points out that religion can have therapeutic effects on
      disturbed individuals, and that pseudo-religious cults can
      occasionally have similar results on some of their members.
      What the author calls a penitent personality is potentially
      disposed to religious or cultic affiliation, which may offer
      merely temporary symptomatic relief. Religions and cults are
      attractive because they present alternative solutions to the
      critical conflicts of adolescence. The author believes that
      cultic indoctrination is especially dangerous, because it
      contributes to the process of depersonalization. Cultic
      involvement, which is a kind of superficial religious commit-
      ment, is a magical, infantile escape from the paradoxes, fears,
      and crises of growing up. Cults disguise problems rather than
      solve them.

1331. Spero, Moshe H.   "Cults: Some Theoretical and Practical Per-
      spectives." JOURNAL OF JEWISH COMMUNAL SERVICE 53 (1977):
      330-39.

      Argues strongly in favor of the view that cultic belief
      and religiosity are pathological, since they represent commit-
      ment to regressive doctrines, stunt or retard the individual's
      growth, and lead the cult member to break contact with friends
      and family. Two basic cult profiles are described: 1) signi-
      ficant constriction in cognitive processes; and 2) manic
      denial of depressive trends. Both are weak in critical
      judgment and reason, have clear narcissistic trends, and
      are strongly pre-oedipal in their personality stage.

1332. Stapleton, Ruth Carter. "Spiritual Healing." THE NEW
      HEALERS (item 1214), pp. 139-44.

      Contains an autobiographical account of the author's view
      of spiritual healing, which she calls "inner healing," and
      which she understands as being "psychological."

1333. Steiner, Lee R. PSYCHIC SELF-HEALING FOR PSYCHOLOGICAL PROB-
       LEMS. Englewood Cliffs, NJ: Prentice-Hall, 1977. 167 pp.

       Discusses the method of psychological diagnosis through the
       human aura, using Kirlian photography. It is argued that
       these photos are more valid, graphic, accurate, and easier to
       interpret than the current psychological tests and therapies
       for measuring the extent of emotional distress, and the extent
       of success which modern treatment can provide. Kirlian pho-
       tography shows that psychic energy clearly denotes emotional
       stability. How psychic healing teaches a person to utilize
       his or her own intellectual and emotional powers is discussed.

1334. Stern, E. Mark. "Psychotherapy for the Guru." SPIRITUAL
       PRACTICE AND PSYCHOTHERAPY: A SYMPOSIUM (item 1114), pp. 1-5.

       Gives an account of a client who went to the author for
       psychotherapy after a period of leadership in a special
       branch of one of the new cults. The author believes that
       "guruism" is a "diabolical process," and that his patient, a
       law student, encountered his own diabolism during the period
       spent in the cult. Manic behavior, linked with obsession and
       paranoid fears, was one of the symptoms which had to be
       dealt with in therapy.

1335. Streiker, Lowell D. "Freedom Counseling Center: An Innova-
       tive Approach." UPDATE: A QUARTERLY JOURNAL ON THE NEW
       RELIGIOUS MOVEMENTS 6.2 (1982): 50-61.

       Describes the author's own initiative in starting "Amer-
       ica's only professional counseling agency in the mental
       health field wholly dedicated to assisting individuals and
       families whose lives have been disturbed by cults, sects,
       communes, mass therapies (for example, Est, Lifespring), and
       other authoritarian groups" (p. 52). The center's goal is
       not to use coercive persuasion or deprogramming to deconvert
       people, but rather to support their return to autonomy and
       adulthood. A "mediated dialog to challenge the subject's
       assumptions about his conversion" (p. 59) is the major tech-
       nique employed. A case example is presented to illustrate
       this method. Although the author admits the possibility of
       conversion, his assumptions and counseling procedures seem to
       indicate that he thinks that cults, sects, and many other
       small religious groups are psychologically harmful to their
       members.

1336. Sullivan, Lawrence Bennett. "Counseling and Involvements in
       New Religious Groups." CULTIC STUDIES JOURNAL 1 (1984):
       178-95.

       Analyzes the results of a survey of cult counseling agencies,
       and the background and training of those who run them. The
       questionnaire focused on 17 persons throughout the United
       States who specialize in cult counseling. Most of the general
       counseling institutions and agencies report very few cases of

cult and ex-cult members who were referred to them for therapy.
The extent of the counseling experience and the training and
personal characteristics of the counselors are submitted.
Practically all counselors and therapists agree with family
members that coercive and deceptive recruitment and conversion practices explain why people join cults and, at times,
remain members.

1337. Sullivan, Lawrence Bennett. "Family Perspectives on Involve-
       ments in New Religious Movements." CULTIC STUDIES JOURNAL
       1 (1984): 79-102.

       Describes and discusses a report of 105 family members of
       persons involved in cults. A questionnaire was set up to get
       the parents' view of the characteristics of cult-members,
       the way they were recruited, the need for services, and the
       legal/moral ramifications. It is admitted that the respon-
       dents may have been predisposed to be critical of their kin's
       involvement. The author questions the limits of religious
       freedom and the protection which cults, as religious groups,
       enjoy under the law. It is recommended that safeguards are
       necessary to prevent and correct abuses.

1338. Tart, Charles T., editor. TRANSPERSONAL PSYCHOLOGIES. New
       York: Harper and Row, 1975. 502 pp.

       Points out that transpersonal psychologies, unlike tradi-
       tional Western psychology, have become integral parts of
       various spiritual disciplines. The essays in this volume
       generally react against Western psychology, which has tended
       either to ignore the spiritual dimension of human life or to
       intrepret it as a pathological condition. The editor favors
       attempts to bridge the gap between traditional Western
       psychology and transpersonal psychologies.

       Contains items 1081, 1138, 1182, 1290, 1473, 1771, 1789.

1339. Temerlin, Maurice K., and Kane W. Temerlin. "Psychotherapy
       Cults: An Iatrogenic Perversion." PSYCHOTHERAPY: THEORY,
       RESEARCH, AND PRACTICE 19 (1982): 131-41.

       Shows how psychotherapy itself can be misused to produce
       cults. A comparison is made between psychotherapy and reli-
       gious cults based on West and Singer's (item 1355) analysis
       of the negative cult features. Both types of cults suffer
       from paranoia, which is a determined function of four vari-
       ables, namely, misuse of sex, fusion and identification with
       the leader, lack of experiential boundaries, and displacement
       of hostility. The author fears that the cult mentality within
       psychotherapy may be widespread, and could be just as detri-
       mental to one's psychological health as membership in a
       religious cult.

1340. Tendzin, Osel. "The Wheel of Life." NAROPA INSTITUTE JOURNAL
       OF PSYCHOLOGY 1.1 (1980): 145-57.

Starts with the view that the Buddhist Wheel of Life is a
practical guide to liberation or enlightenment. The Buddhist
perception of suffering and its origin is explained. Meditation is the discipline that leads to the cessation of suffering, leading to health and to the overcoming of neurotic
problems.

1341. Trungpa, Chogyam. "Becoming a Full Human Being." NAROPA
       INSTITUTE JOURNAL OF PSYCHOLOGY 1.1 (1980): 4-20.

       Discusses, in question-and-answer form, Buddhist and Western
       approaches to psychotherapy, past and present orientation in
       therapy, and the importance of the environmental and social
       contexts. Buddhist sitting meditation is said to be "central
       to our journey toward becoming more sane."

1342. Tseng, W. S., and J. F. McDermott. "Psychotherapy: Historical
       Roots, Universal Elements, and Cultural Visions." AMERICAN
       JOURNAL OF PSYCHIATRY 132 (1975): 378-84.

       Traces the history of therapeutic treatment from its earli-
       est and still-practiced forms, like shamanism, divination,
       fortune-telling, and astrology. It is argued that all psycho-
       therapies share some characteristics, in particular the stress
       on the relationship between the healer and his or her client,
       and the cognitive, emotional, and behavioral influence which
       the former has on the latter. Examples from various cultures,
       such as Morita and Naikan therapies, are provided. It is con-
       cluded that modern psychotherapists should be aware of these
       universal elements and cultural variety, so as to broaden
       their horizon and to improve their treatment.

1343. Ungerleider, T. Thomas. THE NEW RELIGIONS: INSIGHTS INTO THE
       CULT PHENOMENON. An interview with J. Thomas Ungerleider.
       New York: Merck, Sharp, and Dohme, n.d. 20 pp.

       Presents, in question-and-answer format, the views of Dr.
       Ungerleider, a psychiatrist at the UCLA Medical Center. The
       meaning of the word "cult," the attractive power and success
       of cults, and the individual's freedom in deciding to join a
       cult are among the topics dealt with. The author maintains
       that cult members are not seriously impaired from a psycho-
       logical point of view. Many, however, were disturbed before
       joining, and their membership prolonged their stage of depen-
       dency. Deprogramming, the author claims, resembles coercive
       persuasion more than the indoctrination techniques of the
       cults. Suggestions for helping the families of cult members
       are given.

1344. Vanderpool, Harold Y. "Miracle and Faith Healing: Conceptual
       and Historical Perspectives." ENCYCLOPEDIA OF BIOETHICS.
       Edited by Warren T. Reich. New York: Free Press, 1978,
       vol. 3, pp. 1120-24.

       Presents major categories and assumptions about the nature
       of illness and the ways it is treated by miracles and faith-

healing. A brief history of Christian healing, including the
practices of Christian Science, is given. The contemporary
relevance of religious healing traditions is assessed. The
author thinks that these traditions offer intensive interpersonal rewards, bestow a great sense of certainty in the
face of anxiety and depersonalizing influences of the modern
age, and provide an affirmation of human life. The positive
implications for health care are acknowledged.

1345. Vaughan, Francis. "A Question of Balance: Health and Pathology in the New Religious Movements." JOURNAL OF HUMANISTIC
PSYCHOLOGY 23.3 (1980): 20-41.

Examines the health of the new religious movements from the
perspective of transpersonal psychology. The various motives
for joining a new religion are explored. The author distinguishes between those groups that encourage dependency and
regression, and those which support transcendence of the ego
and contribute to authentic personal development. She makes
a clear differentiation between ego-mastery and spiritual
mastery, and delineates the features of the latter. Moreover,
she suggests a balanced use of intuition and reason to draw
up criteria for discriminating between healthy and unhealthy
religious groups. Those which manipulate fear and guilt for
social control and that appeal to their members' greed are
pathogenic. Those which develop acceptance, love, and forgiveness, facilitate self-transcendence, and appreciate both
unity and diversity, create a healthy environment for self-
development.

1346. Von Franz, Marie-Louise. ALCHEMY: AN INTRODUCTION TO THE
SYMBOLISM AND THE PSYCHOLOGY. Toronto: Inner City Books,
1980. 280 pp.

Transcribes a series of lectures on old Greek, Arabic, and
European alchemy, seen from the standpoint of Jungian psychology. The symbolisms and archetypes are explored, and several
psychiatric-like incidents are interpreted as an eruption of
an unconscious archetypal image.

1347. Wallis, Roy. SALVATION AND PROTEST: STUDIES OF SOCIAL AND
RELIGIOUS MOVEMENTS. New York: St. Martin's Press, 1979.
231 pp.

Addresses the issues of why people join together to form
religious and/or social movements, what conditions favor the
emergence of such movements, and why they often founder.
Three main areas are discussed: 1) sociological aspects of
new movements; 2) the sociology of moral crusades; and
3) problems of theory and method. Among the cults and sects
studied are the Children of God, Christian Science, Dianetics,
Spiritualism, the Aetherius Society, and the Nationwide Fes-
tival of Light (a British moral crusade). The author criticizes the deprivation theory of cult formation (pp. 3-6).
He states that the theory of Festinger, et al., (item 379)
supports his findings on the character and dynamics of new
movements.

1348. Walsh, Roger, and Dean H. Shapiro, editors. BEYOND HEALTH AND
       NORMALITY: EXPLORATIONS OF EXCEPTIONAL PSYCHOLOGICAL WELL-
       BEING. New York: Van Nostrand Reinhold Co., 1983. xii,
       516 pp.

       Offers a collection of essays describing Eastern and Western
       psychological approaches to human growth and development and
       the possibility of an integrated psychology of health combin-
       ing both traditions. Articles on meditation, Zen, and Sufism,
       and their respective contributions to mental health are
       included.

1349. Wardwell, Walter I. "Limited and Marginal Practitioners."
       HANDBOOK OF MEDICAL PSYCHOLOGY. Edited by Howard E. Free-
       man, Sol Levine, and Leo G. Reeder. Englewood Cliffs, NJ:
       Prentice-Hall, third edition, 1979, pp. 230-50.

       Discusses medical practitioners who either 1) limit their
       treatments to certain parts of the human body (like dentists,
       podiatrists, etc.), or 2) use unorthodox therapies for heal-
       in purposes (like osteopaths, who were originally considered
       cultists, and chiropractors). A short section on quasi-
       practitioners considers quacks and magical and faith healers.
       The author thinks that medical personnel can cooperate with
       folk healers, when the patient can benefit from it.

1350. Washington, Joseph R. BLACK SECTS AND CULTS. Garden City,
       NY: Doubleday, 1973. xii, 176 pp.

       Examines the many black religious movements in the United
       States and outlines their African roots. Black sects and
       cults are grouped into two major divisions: 1) Methodists and
       Baptists: the Established Sectarians; and 2) Holiness and
       Pentecostal Blacks: the Permanent Sects. The common sociolog-
       ical view that black cults come into being because of psycho-
       logical instability caused by social disorder, is refuted.
       "What the black cults prove is that at bottom black people
       are a moral people seeking community" (p. 138). The cults
       express the legitimate search for social and community
       identity. The movement of Father Divine, the Black Muslims,
       the Shrine of the Black Madonna, Voodoo, and spiritualist
       cults are among the groups mentioned.

1351. Watts, Alan. "Psychotherapy and Eastern Religion: Metaphys-
       ical Bases of Psychiatry." JOURNAL OF TRANSPERSONAL
       PSYCHOLOGY 1 (1974): 18-31.

       Presents a lecture explaining why the treatment of psychi-
       atric patients must be based on some metaphysical view of
       life. Some trends in modern Western culture, like the stress
       on technology, are criticized for not being realistic, because
       they do not take into account the processes of life. Eastern
       philosophical approaches, which stress naturalness and the
       quiet acceptance of death, should be adopted and applied to
       the way patients are treated.

1352. Weber, Vanessa. "Modern Cults and Gnosticism: Some Observa-
       tions on Religious and Totalitarian Movements." PSYCHO-
       DYNAMIC PERSPECTIVES ON RELIGION, SECT, AND CULT (item
       1226), pp. 31-42.

       Compares Gnostic theology with that of modern cults to
       determine the cognitive content and the psychology of cult
       affiliation. By means of a brief historical survey of Gnos-
       ticism and a description of its main features, the author
       aims to show how modern cults can be interpreted as a new
       Gnostic rising. Lifton's model of brainwashing (see item
       1865) is applied to both classic Gnosticism and to the new
       cults.

1353. Weil, Andrew. HEALTH AND HEALING: UNDERSTANDING CONVENTIONAL
       AND ALTERNATIVE MEDICINE. Boston: Houghton Mifflin, 1983.
       296 pp.

       Discusses the nature and meaning of health, and lists
       several principles which underlie our concepts of health and
       illness. A number of therapeutic choices are described:
       allopathic medicine, chiropractic medicine, Chinese medicine,
       shamanism, mind cure and faith-healing, psychic healing,
       holistic medicine, and quackery. All the above treatments
       share some characteristics and rely on the belief in the
       treatment itself. Many of the cures of faith healers are
       restricted to psychosomatic illnesses. Some speculations
       about the future of health and healing are made.

1354. Welwood, John. "On Spiritual Authority: Genuine and Counter-
       feit." JOURNAL OF HUMANISTIC PSYCHOLOGY 23 (1983): 42-60.

       Explores ways of discerning between false prophets and gen-
       uine spiritual masters, between misguided cults and wholesome
       spiritual communities. Several features of "spiritual pathol-
       ogy" are enumerated: 1) total power of leaders to judge
       their devotees; 2) allegiance to a cause which keeps the group
       together; 3) manipulation of emotions by leader to keep
       followers in line; 4) the stress on the group's exclusivity;
       and 5) the self-styled nature of the prophethood adopted by
       cult leaders. Other criteria are required to distinguish
       genuine from false authority, the former being marked by sur-
       render, the latter by submission. Respect for human dignity,
       allowance of tolerance and paradox, and appeal to the natural
       intelligence of the devotees are some of the positive signs
       of genuine authority.

1355. West, Louis J., and Margaret Thaler Singer. "Cults, Quacks,
       and Non-professional Psychotherapies." COMPREHENSIVE TEXT-
       BOOK OF PSYCHIATRY. Cited above as item 29. Vol. III, pp.
       3245-58.

       Discusses the issues raised by the new religious movements,
       which are considered to be psychologically damaging to their
       adherents. Various features of the cultic phenomenon are

outlined, and the recruitment and indoctrination methods are
described. It is contended that there is a "cult indoctrination syndrome," making new cult members victims of a traumatic
neurosis. The difficulties which ex-cult members face and
the legal ramifications brought about by cultic behavior are
overviewed. Transcendental Meditation, psychic healers,
Scientology, and occult practices are among the areas covered.
The authors feel that these cults and non-professional forms
of treatment may have some beneficial results, but they can
also create serious hazards.

1356. Westley, Francis R. "Merger and Separation: Autistic Symbolism in New Religious Movements." JOURNAL OF PSYCHOANALYT-
IC ANTHROPOLOGY 5 (1982): 137-54.

Argues that the symbolism of psychologically disturbed,
autistic children exhibits similarities to the behavior of
cult members. Several interpretations of infant autism are
described, and the symbolism of joining (merger) and isolating
(separation) is seen as central. The same symbolism can be
observed in several groups, such as Est, Arica, Silva Mind
Control, and Scientology, whose training includes highly
ritualistic exercises of self-examination and self-stimulation.
Several examples are given to illustrate the author's main
thesis. The author states, however, that one should not
conclude that the adherents of cults are psychotic autistics.
What he, rather, wants to show is that the study of ritual in
the new cults can help us understand how they came into being.

1357. Wilbur, Ken. NO BOUNDARY: EASTERN AND WESTERN APPROACHES TO
PERSONAL GROWTH. Los Angeles: Center Publications, 1980.
160 pp.

Explores the human quest for personal growth. Several
chapters are dedicated to the quest for "unity consciousness."
The growth of the individual on different levels, that is,
the total organism, the ego, and the persona, are explained.
Various Eastern and Western therapies are used to enable a
person to come in contact with these levels. Some Eastern
practices, like Yoga, are seen as alternate therapies.

1358. Wright, Fred, and Phyllis Wright. "The Charismatic Leader
and the Violent Surrogate Family." ANNALS OF THE NEW YORK
ACADEMY OF SCIENCES 347 (1980): 266-76.

Discusses several family-type cults (such as the People's
Temple, Charles Manson's group, and the Church of the Lamb of
God), where coercion and violence seem to be common features.
The authors reject the views that cult members experience
some relief from emotional distress and that their membership
satisfies their need for an ideology, and accept instead the
Freudian position that conversion to a cult represents a
search for a father figure. Dependency on a cult leader
creates some security, reduces ambiguity, and achieves clari-
fication of goals, but brings with it weakness and bondage.

The leaders help their followers control their hostility
towards their families, and at the same time express it.
Several explanations of irrational group behavior, applicable
to the cult and to its leader, are examined.

1359. Zaretsky, Irving I. "Youth and Religious Movements."
       ADOLESCENT PSYCHIATRY 8 (1980): 281-87.

       Summarizes the current religious revival and its periodic
       appearance since the middle of the nineteenth century. From
       an anthropological point of view the distinctive religiosity
       of the new movements is not pathological. The author points
       out that our knowledge of the long-term effects of partici-
       pation in these groups is minimal, and that until we acquire
       such information our evaluation of, and response to, them are
       premature.

1360. Zaretsky, Irving I., and Mark P. Leone, editors. RELIGIOUS
       MOVEMENTS IN CONTEMPORARY AMERICA. Princeton: Princeton
       University Press, 1974. xxxvi, 837 pp.

       Represents one of the first large volumes discussing the
       new religions from different perspectives: theological, legal,
       linguistic, philosophical, religious, symbolical, and socio-
       logical. One section (pp. 255-455) contains several essays
       on the psychological dimensions of the new religious groups.

       Contains items 991, 1161, 1256, 1659, 1682, 1775, 1781.

                      C. STUDIES ON INDIVIDUAL CULTS AND SECTS

1. Meditation and Yoga

    The study of Eastern meditation has received great attention from
psychologists and psychiatrists over the last 20 years. Since so
many of the new religious movements advance their own meditation
techniques, psychiatric evaluation of these methods can help determine the influence of a cult on its members.

    The practice of meditation has been given, by and large, a posi-
tive assessment. It has been recommended as a form of relaxation
which reduces stress and leads to mental catharsis. The result is
psychological growth and development. Several experiments have
demonstrated that those who dedicate some time every day to meditation register an intensification of performance and endurance in
their tasks. The following are said to be the main benefits of
pursuing a meditation program: reduced anxiety; heightened awareness; increased self-knowledge, self-control, and self-acceptance;
reduction in the level of hostility and aggression; and cure of drug
addiction. Some have been so encouraged by the results of experiments that they have compared meditation to a benign form of self-

hypnosis, or to altered states of consciousness. Its clinical use has been proposed as an alternative, or complement to, traditional therapy.

Not all reports on meditation have, however, been unqualified endorsements. Several disturbing side effects have been recorded. Insularity, self-centeredness, and acquisitiveness are frequently the outcome of meditative practices. More serious psychological problems have also been observed. Depersonalization seems to be a possible consequence. Suppressed conflicts are, at times, brought to the surface. Intense meditation may also be the direct cause of psychotic behavior. Further, in some cases, meditation tends to increase, rather than diminish, a person's anxiety and tension. There is, therefore, some doubt as to whether meditation can be proposed as a universally applicable solution or help in a clinical setting. Its practice may be more suitable for those who already enjoy a normal level of psychological health. The view that meditation is not a form of therapy, but rather a soteriology, has much to recommend it. There is also some doubt as to whether meditation, even if it is beneficial, has anything more to offer than other well-established techniques for relaxation and rest.

Three forms of meditation in particular, namely, Transcendental Meditation, Yoga, and Buddhist Meditation, have been subjected to numerous experiments. The research into the psychological effects of TM has been voluminous. Many of those who joined the TM movement in the late 1960s and early 1970s embarked on a mission to show how its practice is a simple, safe method to tackle most human problems. TM is said to reduce individual and social stress, to eliminate neurotic traits, and to lessen or eradicate dependency on alcohol and drugs. It has been propounded as an effective cure for depressed people contemplating suicide and for those struggling with academic deficiency, sexual problems, and marital conflicts. It has been advanced as a novel approach to the rehabilitation of prison inmates. TM furthers the individual's self-development, fulfillment, and actualization, and should be a part of any system of education. It augments one's creative faculties, improves work achievement, and develops field independence. Because it cultivates empathy, TM should be incorporated in the training of counselors. In glowing terms, supporters of the TM program insist that its practice leads to pure awareness, and this, they claim, is the solution to all human problems, be they individual or social.

Research on the effects of TM has been hampered by both theoretical and methodological problems. Much of the early experimentation was conducted by enthusiastic supporters. This led to questions about the objectivity of the tests, which seemed to corroborate the positive assumptions about its potential therapeutic benefits. Expectancy, suggestibility, and the placebo effect can account for many, if not all, of the claimed psychological improvements. TM may, after all, have nothing new to offer, since its results can be duplicated by other methods, such as Benson's relaxation response, biofeedback, hypnosis, and psychoanalysis. One wonders whether a regular, short period of relaxation, without the mystical aura of Maharishi Mahesh Yogi, could produce precisely the same results.

Not all researchers have unequivocally endorsed TM. It is now recognized by many scholars that TM is certainly not a cure to all human problems, as has been so often advertised. It could create, rather than solve, difficulties. People with emotional troubles may get worse by meditating. Since TM is a method of stilling the mind, it may bring compelling, and possibly harmful, fantasies to one's consciousness and arouse primitive distressing thoughts. The outcome could be psychopathological regression. Long practice of TM could cause serious problems: anxiety, confusion, depression, frustration, neurotic dependency, and psychotic behavior. TM could be hazardous to one's health. The fact that a large number of meditators have given up its practice might lend support to the view that those who enthusiastically took up the program discovered that it had few long-term benefits and possibly some undesirable effects. Certain claims that TM improves a person's psychic ability, including the ability to levitate, have not only exposed meditation to ridicule, but also raised questions about the sanity of those who seriously take up the practice.

Studies on Yoga and Buddhist meditation do not compare to those on TM in their intensity or claims. Yoga therapy, which includes both physical and mental exercises, has been related to progressive relaxation, Gestalt therapy, behavior therapy, and psychoanalysis. Some of the purported results of TM have also been ascribed to Yoga, the practice of which decreases stress, helps drug addicts overcome their problem, and increases one's motivation. Yoga, it is argued, is based on a well-developed psychological system, which goes to the roots of one's emotional and intellectual problems and is, therefore, better than Western therapy. It has also been recognized that the practice of Yoga could be harmful in some neuroses.

Buddhist meditation, particularly Zen, has also been studied for its possible therapeutic qualities. Zen develops the qualities of selflessness, non-attachment, and self-examination. It is a method for self-actualization and for developing empathy. The Zen meditator allegedly becomes less aggressive, less manipulative, less ambitious, less independent, and less concerned with planning for the future. Whether all these qualities are a clear sign of psychological health is debatable. One form of Buddhist Meditation (Vissipana, or Insight Meditation) removes, according to some, unwholesome features of one's personality; it could also, however, attract those whose view of self is pathological.

The evaluations of meditation, when it is practiced within its religious and philosophical traditions, are, therefore, mixed. Many clinicians, however, maintain that one can detach meditation from its religious matrix and mystical connotations and use it simply as a method of treating some common psychological problems. What Patricia Carrington (see items 1407-1413) and other psychiatrists are advocating is a non-cultic and non-religious form of meditation which can be standardized and used clinically, preferably in conjunction with any other well-established form of therapy. Benson's relaxation response (item 1387) is basically an adaptation of Transcendental Meditation without the mystique of its initiation rite, the magical qualities of its mantra, and the presence of a charismatic guru. Meditation could be seen as a mechanical way of bringing about neurophysiological changes in the brain.

The problem, however, is whether meditation, extracted from its religious matrix, actually becomes something else, a new Westernized technique, with only the trappings of an Eastern name.   Several psychotherapists seem to be ignoring the essential fact that Eastern meditation, no matter what its physical expressions (e.g., breathing, sitting in Yoga posture, and reciting a mantra) and its neurophysiological components might be, is inseparably linked with a religious philosophy about the nature of human personality and the ultimate goal of life.   Non-religious meditation as proposed by many psychiatrists fails to answer the ultimate questions which those who join cults or who embark on a religiously-oriented meditation program are seeking.

It is not surprising that the research results on meditation are contradictory and confusing. It is conceivable that what produces the reported beneficial results, say, of TM, is not the rather easy exercise of sitting down and repeating, in robot-like fashion, one's assigned mantra for two short 20-minute sessions a day, but the fact that one does so in the context of belonging to a world-wide organization, which provides the meditator with a cross-cultural ideology and with noble aspirations for the betterment of the human condition. From a religio-philosophical point of view, "non-cultic meditation," as it has been called, appears to be a trivialization of traditional Eastern meditation methods, which cannot be separated from the soteriology that lies at their very heart. Benson himself (item 1386) has pointed out that faith certainly makes an important contribution to the therapeutic benefits. Those who have joined a new religious movement, which encourages a specific form of meditation, end up by making a faith commitment which may be more therapeutic than the meditation exercise itself.

1361.   Abrams, Allan I., and Larry M. Siegel. "The Transcendental Meditation Program and Rehabilitation at Folsom State Prison: A Cross-Validation Study." CRIMINAL JUSTICE AND BEHAVIOR 5 (1978): 3-20.

Investigates the possible use of TM as an alternative (or additional) treatment in a maximum-security federal prison located in California. The aim of the study was to test whether TM could prepare the inmates to reenter society. Previous findings had concluded that TM reduces anxiety and hostility, improves physiological ability, sleep patterns and behavior, and reduces cigarette smoking. The subjects participating in the experiment, the procedure used, and the psychological tests administered are recorded. The results confirm the previous findings that "the TM program is a scientific method of personal development applicable to rehabilitation" (p. 15). The authors think that this program is the most self-efficient and potent rehabilitation treatment for prisoners available.

1362. Abrams, Allan I., and Larry M. Siegel. "Transcendental Medi-
      tation and Rehabilitation at Folsom Prison: Response to a
      Critique." CRIMINAL JUSTICE AND BEHAVIOR 6 (1979): 13-22.

      Replies to Allen's critique (item 1370) of their experiment
      with the TM program on prison inmates. The previous results
      are reasserted, because they are backed by the enthusiastic
      acceptance of the inmates and by other positive results
      obtained by other researchers.

1363. Aiken, Robert. "Zen Practice and Psychotherapy." JOURNAL
      OF TRANSPERSONAL PSYCHOLOGY 14 (1982): 161-70.

      Argues that Zen is not therapy, because it does not make
      the individual better and because it usually differs from
      the therapeutic approach. The use of Zen for mental health
      and the various Zen techniques which differ from other East-
      ern methods, like Yoga, are discussed. Zen guides people
      "from self-concern to the strength to forget the self and
      personify the ideal of coping creatively with the environment"
      (p. 169).

1364. Ajaya, Swami. PSYCHOTHERAPY, EAST AND WEST: A UNIFYING PARA-
      DIGM. Homesdale, PA: Himalayan International Institute of
      Yoga Science and Philosophy, 1983. xiv, 345 pp.

      Describes the world views and methods of Yogic sages, and
      compares them with those of Western psychotherapists. The
      author holds that the Yoga system is an ancient, comprehen-
      sive, and tested strategy, while the Western system is modern,
      experimental, and still evolving. Part I contrasts the two
      therapies with their different ideas on projection, trans-
      ference, and diverse treatments. Part II deals with the
      application of Yoga therapy and contains chapters on body
      and behavioral techniques, the relationship between therapist
      and client, the collective unconscious from the Yogic per-
      spective, and the spiritual aspects of psychotherapy.

1365. Ajaya, Swami. YOGA PSYCHOLOGY: A PRACTICAL GUIDE TO MEDITA-
      TION. Glenview, IL: Himalayan International Institute of
      Yoga Science and Philosophy, 2nd revised edition, 1976.
      115 pp.

      Acknowledges that meditation is an important need in human
      life. The practice of meditation helps put order into the
      mind and improves proficiency and creativity. Methods of
      practicing Yoga and ways of using a mantra are described.

1366. Ajaya, Swami, editor. MEDITATIONAL THERAPY. Glenview, IL:
      Himalayan International Institute for Yoga Science and Phi-
      losophy, 1977. vii, 92 pp.

      Presents the third in a series of books comparing Yoga to
      modern psychology. The articles show how Yoga can be used

with modern methods to treat stress-related dysfunctions in
society. Several essays deal with the relation between Yoga,
meditation, and biofeedback.

Contains items 1599, 1607.

1367. Ajaya, Swami, editor. PSYCHOLOGY: EAST AND WEST. Glenview,
       IL: The Himalayan Institute, 1976. xi, 103 pp.

       Illustrates the current trend to integrate Eastern and
       Western psychological insights.

       Contains items 1382, 1489, 1550, 1616.

1368. Akers, Thomas K., Don M. Tucker, Randy S. Roth, and John S.
       Kidloff. "Personality Correlates of EEG Change During
       Meditation." PSYCHOLOGICAL REPORTS 40 (1977): 439-44.

       Administers the MMPI test to 15 seminary students who regu-
       larly practiced some form of meditation, and records the EEG
       signals. The research concludes that further study is needed
       to find out if there are personality variables which might
       predict response to meditation. Only then can one consider
       the possibility of adopting a selective use of meditation as
       a therapeutic procedure.

1369. Akishige, Yoshiharu. "The Principles of Psychology of Zen."
       MEDITATION: CLASSICAL AND CONTEMPORARY APPROACHES (item 45),
       pp. 686-89.

       Describes some of the common features of Zen Buddhism, and
       maintains that Zen practices and states contribute to the
       cultivation and development of a new field of psychology.
       Zen teaches selflessness and non-attachment and fosters
       world peace.

1370. Allen, Don. "TM at Folsom Prison: A Critique of Abrams and
       Siegel." CRIMINAL JUSTICE AND BEHAVIOR 6 (1979): 9-12.

       Criticizes the procedures used and data obtained by Abrams
       and Siegel (item 1361), and suggests that their evaluation of
       the potential of TM is overstated. Particularly deficient is
       their failure to use any form of placebo control. The relia-
       ability of prison inmates who were encouraged to have high
       expectations in the effects of the program is questioned.

1371. American Psychiatric Association. "Position Statement on
       Meditation." AMERICAN JOURNAL OF PSYCHIATRY 134 (1977):
       720.

       Recommends that research be undertaken to assess the pos-
       sible therapeutic value of meditation and to assess its
       dangers. Meditation may facilitate the therapeutic process,
       even though the evidence that it can be a substitute for

psychiatric treatment is not forthcoming. Relatively new
religious groups, like the Self-Realization Fellowship, Zen
Buddhist centers, Sufi circles, and Transcendental Meditation,
are specified as contemporary organizations teaching some form
of meditation.

1372. Amodeo, John. "Focusing Applied to a Case of Disorientation
      In Meditation." JOURNAL OF TRANSPERSONAL PSYCHOLOGY (1981):
      149-54.

      Reports on a subject who during meditation developed a
      strong tendency to dissociate from her current experience
      with the result of intense fear. This might have happened
      both because of some inherent dangers in the concentrative
      type of meditation, and because of mistakes which the medi-
      tator might have made. The subject's fear and dissociation
      were favorably affected by the use of "focusing," where "a
      trained guide asks questions to lead the client systematically
      to an awareness of the felt-body sense which, if successful,
      results in a felt-shift in the client's perception of his
      and her more pressing problem, conflict, or life concern"
      (pp. 153-54). Focusing could be of help to those who experi-
      ence a diffusion or floating during meditation.

1373. Aron, Elaine N., and Arthur Aron. "The Patterns of Drug and
      Alcohol Use Among Transcendental Meditation Participants."
      BULLETIN OF THE SOCIETY OF PSYCHOLOGISTS IN ADDICTIVE
      BEHAVIOR 2 (1983): 28-33.

      Reports on a study of 60 TM participants who had stopped
      using alcohol, tobacco, and marijuana. While only two had
      given up their addiction immediately following their initia-
      tion, the rest registered a gradual decline in their habit
      over a period of two years or more. The authors explore the
      various reasons (experiential, improved functioning, changed
      attitudes, and social influence) the subjects gave to explain
      their withdrawal.

1374. Aron, Elaine N., and Arthur Aron. "Transcendental Meditation
      Program and Marital Adjustment." PSYCHOLOGICAL REPORTS 51
      (1982): 887-90.

      Administers Locke's Marital Adjustment Inventory to 17
      married women who had received instruction on TM and to an
      equal number of control subjects. The former exhibited a
      significantly higher degree of marital satisfaction. Their
      interpersonal relationships were less fraught with problems.
      It is concluded that the TM program "seems a promising support
      in marital adjustment."

1375. Aron, Elaine N., and Arthur Aron. "An Introduction to
      Maharishi's Theory of Creativity: Its Empirical Basis and
      Description of the Creative Process." JOURNAL OF CREATIVE
      BEHAVIOR 16 (1982): 29-49.

Discusses the deepest phase of the practice of TM, namely, the experience of pure awareness, and the strong association this has with performance on the Torrance Test of Creative Thinking. The Maharishi's model of the ideal creative process is outlined, and it is stated that its essential ingredient is a coherent nervous system. Conscious awareness and control of the creative process, envisaged in the TM program, are of vital importance in any psychological theory of human behavior. Although its application to the psychotherapeutic process is not immediately evident, the TM theory of creativity opens up possibilities for self-development and for overcoming one's psychological weaknesses.

1376.   Aron, Elaine N., and Arthur Aron.   "The Transcendental Meditation Program for the Reduction of Stress-Related Conditions." JOURNAL OF CHRONIC DISEASES AND THERAPEUTIC RESEARCH 3.9 (1979): 11-21.

Examines some of the research data relevant to the view that TM reduces stress, and also has a major positive influence on the health of the individual and on the social environment. Two areas are covered: 1) the TM program as a stress immunizer, with consequent psychological and social improvements; and 2) the use of TM as a treatment for mental illness, substance abuse, and the rehabilitation of prisoners. The authors are optimistic about the therapeutic benefits of TM.

1377.   Avila, Donald, and Renaye Nummela. "Transcendental Meditation: A Psychological Interpretation." JOURNAL OF CLINICAL PSYCHOLOGY 33 (1977): 842-44.

Argues that meditation should become one of the basic tools for the helping professions, and that TM is the most suitable form of meditation, since it is simple and easily applicable to most people and since its value has been proven by many empirical tests. The subject, while meditating, enters a fourth state of consciousness, in which reconditioning takes place more effectively than in desensitization. Several of the standard psychological benefits of TM are enumerated.

1378.   Bache, Christopher M. "On the Emergence of Perinatal Symptoms in Buddhist Meditation." JOURNAL FOR THE SCIENTIFIC STUDY OF RELIGION 20 (1980): 339-50.

Examines the experience of traumatic physical seizures and strong disruptive emotions, that advanced Zen meditators often experience. Finding no explanation in the Buddhist tradition, the author proposes a solution by bringing together material from LSD research, object-relations theory, and transpersonal psychology. The seizures are interpreted as "birth-trauma memories." Just as the fetus is subjected to "radical-impingement," resulting in fear, so the meditator goes through an ego-death, reliving his or her primordial experience. During meditation "the past is resolving itself, allowing the meditator to live more fully in the present" (p. 349).

1379. Badaracco, Marie R. "Psychoanalysis as Altering States of
       Consciousness." JOURNAL OF THE AMERICAN ACADEMY OF PSYCHO-
       ANALYSIS 3 (1975): 205-10.

       Compares the process of psychoanalysis with meditation, and
       concludes that both tap one's needs and capacities for effort
       and relaxation. Psychoanalysis develops these by altering
       one's state of consciousness. A clinical example is present-
       ed, showing how a patient moved to a greater self-awareness
       and became able to control himself and to experience rest.

1380. Bahrke, Michael S. "Exercise, Meditation, and Anxiety Reduc-
       tion: A Review." AMERICAN CORRECTIVE THERAPY JOURNAL 33.2
       (March/April 1979): 41-44.

       Reviews the literature which deals with the ability of both
       acute physical exercise and meditation-relaxation techniques
       to reduce tension and improve psychological states. Although
       exercise and meditation are opposed to one another, both seem
       to be equally effective in reducing anxiety.

1381. Bahrke, Michael S., and William P. Morgan. "Anxiety Reduction
       Following Exercise and Meditation." COGNITIVE THERAPY AND
       RESEARCH 2 (1978): 323-33.

       Compares the influence which acute physical activity and
       "non-cultic" meditation have on anxiety. Seventy-five male
       volunteers were divided into three groups, two of which were
       randomly assigned a period for exercise or meditation, with
       the third serving as a control group. The conclusion reached
       was that vigorous physical activity, non-cultic meditation,
       and quiet rest periods are equally effective in reducing both
       low and high levels of anxiety. Whether cultic meditation
       produces different results is not considered.

1382. Ballantine, Rudolph M. "Yoga and Psychoanalysis." PSYCHOL-
       OGY: EAST AND WEST (item 1367), pp. 1-21.

       Uses the eight steps of Raja Yoga as a framework for com-
       paring Yoga with the techniques of psychoanalysis and later
       methods developed by Wilhelm Reich and Alexander Lowen. Both
       psychoanalysis and Yoga deal with body posture, sensory with-
       drawal, regulation of one's life, and the observation of one's
       mental processes. The relationship between the therapist and
       the patient is compared to that between the guru and his or
       her devotee. Although the methods of Yoga and psychoanalysis
       differ, their goals are in many respects shared. The latter,
       however, in the author's view, falls short of Yogic training.

1383. Balodhi, J. P., and H. Mishra. "Pantajali Yoga and Behavior
       Therapy." BEHAVIOR THERAPIST 6 (1983): 196-97.

       Maintains that Pantajali established a system of Yoga which
       stresses behavior therapy and cognitive control, and which is
       based on the psychophysiological processes that lie at the root

of psychosomatic health or illness. The nine pathological
stages of mind and the eight stages to control and modify
them are enumerated. The authors draw similarities between
progressive relaxation, autogenic training, and reciprocal
inhibition, and the Yoga corpse posture (shavasana), deep-
breathing (pranayama) and meditation (samayama), respectively.
Research efforts which used Yoga in clinical tests to relieve
anxiety states, psychosomatic problems, and psychoneuroses
are briefly alluded to.

1384. Balogh, Penelope. "Gestalt Awareness: A Way of Being as a
        Yoga for the West." INTERNATIONAL JOURNAL OF SOCIAL
        PSYCHIATRY 22 (1976): 64-66.

        Points out some of the similarities between Gestalt Therapy
        and Yoga, both of which are based on Eastern philosophical
        tradition, which stress a sense of unity of the universe,
        and which tend to be monistic rather than dualistic. Though
        the techniques they use differ, both have the same goal.

1385. Barmark, Susanne, and Samuel C. B. Gaunitz. "Transcendental
        Meditation and Heterohypnosis as Altered States of Con-
        sciousness." INTERNATIONAL JOURNAL OF CLINICAL AND EXPER-
        IMENTAL HYPNOSIS 27 (1979): 227-39.

        Discusses whether the state of consciousness achieved by
        TM techniques differs from normal and hypnotic states. Forty-
        two subjects, including 19 persons who were susceptible to
        hypnosis, took part in the experiment. Subjective reports
        about attentional processes, body image, and experience of
        time were recorded, and three physiological variables--heart
        rate, respiration rate, and finger skin-temperature--were
        registered. The researchers conclude that TM is "a phenome-
        nologically altered state of consciousness which resembles
        the hypnotically altered state" (p. 237).

1386. Benson, Herbert. "Looking Beyond the Relaxation Response: An
        Interview with Herbert Benson." REVISION: A JOURNAL OF
        CONSCIOUSNESS AND CHANGE 7.1 (Spring 1984): 50-55.

        Discusses the author's own research (item 1387) on the
        relaxation response. His view that religious faith adds to
        the therapeutic benefit is explained.

1387. Benson, Herbert. THE RELAXATION RESPONSE. New York: Avon
        Books, 1976. 221 pp.

        Proposes the use of controlled meditation, which can be
        easily learned as a therapeutic technique to relax and to
        overcome psychological tension and stress. The relaxation
        response is the normal bodily mechanism's reply to overstress
        and brings about physical changes that decrease the heart
        rate, lower the metabolism, and slow down breathing--all of
        which contribute to physical health and, consequently, to

one's psychological well-being. Benson's method is similar
to Transcendental Meditation, especially in its use of a
mantra. It is, however, completely devoid of religious and
philosophical trappings.

1388. Benson, Herbert, John F. Beary, and Michael P. Carol. "The
       Relaxation Response." PSYCHIATRY 37 (1974): 37-46.

Outlines the authors' thesis that progressive relaxation,
hypnosis, Yoga, Zen, and Transcendental Meditation elicit
what they call the "relaxation response," which contributes
to the physical and psychological well-being of the individual. Various techniques of relaxation are listed, and the
literature in support of it is mentioned. Some negative side
effects of the relaxation response, ranging from insomnia to
psychotic manifestations and hallucinatory behavior, are
possible. Belief in the technique may be an important factor
in the relaxation process.

1389. Berwick, P., and C. J. Oziel. "The Use of Meditation as a
       Behavior Technique." BEHAVIOR THERAPY 4 (1973): 743-45.

Reports on the success the authors had with altering the
behavior patterns of one patient by reducing her anxiety
through regular meditation. It is argued that by diminish-
ing anxiety, meditation allows the individual to learn new
adaptive relaxation responses.

1390. Block, Bruce. "Transcendental Meditation as a Required Inhib-
       itor in Psychotherapy." JOURNAL OF CONTEMPORARY PSYCHOLOGY
       9 (1977): 78-82.

Argues that TM, used as a relaxation method, has particular
advantages not shared with other techniques, such as hypnosis,
progressive relaxation, and biofeedback. TM achieves results
faster, easier, and with less equipment and can be used long
after therapy sessions have come to an end. It further helps
the patient cope with his or her environment, develops therapeutic insight, and enables people to cease indulging in
childish, immature feelings.

1391. Bloomfield, Harold H., and Robert B. Kory. HAPPINESS: THE
       TM PROGRAM, PSYCHIATRY, AND ENLIGHTENMENT. New York: Simon
       and Schuster, 1976. xxxii, 312 pp.

Explains how the TM program can contribute to the development of an enduring happiness, free from all anxieties. TM
is compared to such other therapeutic methods as hypnosis,
Benson's relaxation technique (item 1387), and biofeedback.
The authors contend that TM is effective in treating psychosomatic disorders and in preventing many of them. It also
promotes emotional well-being. Psychiatrists are encouraged
to practice TM and to use it as a therapeutic method for
helping their patients.

1392. Bloomfield, Harold H., Michael P. Cain, and Dennis T. Jaffe.
      TM: DISCOVERING INNER ENERGY AND OVERCOMING STRESS. New
      York: Delacorte Press, 1975. xxvii, 290 pp.

      Presents a study of TM as a system of contacting pure aware-
      ness, leading to the solution of many problems caused by the
      crises of modern life. One chapter (Ch. 5, pp. 91-114) out-
      lines the beneficial psychological benefits of TM practice
      from personal accounts of those who claim to have been trans-
      formed by it. Improved performance in practically all aspects
      of life, and the cure of such maladaptive behavior as drug
      abuse, are among its major effects. The authors propose TM
      as a system of psychotherapy, comparable to psychoanalysis
      and other Western treatments, and as a technique for expanding
      a person's creative intelligence and bringing about fulfill-
      ment and self-actualization.

1393. Boals, Gordon F. "Toward a Cognitive Reconceptualization of
      Meditation." JOURNAL OF TRANSPERSONAL PSYCHOLOGY 10 (1978):
      143-82.

      Presents the theory that meditation, practiced as a form
      of relaxation, has outlived its usefulness, and that a cogni-
      tive perspective should be adopted. The research on medita-
      tion is reviewed and criticized, particularly because it does
      not explain the negative consequences which sometimes follow
      extensive meditation, nor account for the different effects
      of similar relaxation techniques, such as Yoga, Zen, autogenic
      training, hypnosis, and biofeedback. The central problem
      facing any attempt to explain meditation, from a cognitive
      perspective, is to show how the shifts in attention produce
      relaxation and other psychological benefits to the meditator.
      The implications for research and psychotherapy of considering
      meditation as "a process involving complex patterns of deploy-
      ing attention" (p. 168) are discussed.

1394. Bono, Joseph. "Psychological Assessment of Transcendental
      Meditation." MEDITATION: CLASSICAL AND CONTEMPORARY
      APPROACHES (item 45), pp. 209-17.

      Clarifies what TM is and what it does by referring to
      the psychological assessment of individuals who practice it.
      Personality traits, perception, learning ability, and several
      psychological factors were explored in prospective TM subjects
      and regular meditators. These latter showed a significant
      shift toward field independence and a rise in their self-
      esteem after six months of meditating. While the practice
      of TM leads to improved physiological homeostasis, this effect
      is not necessarily a unique function of TM.

1395. Boorstein, Seymour. "The Use of Bibliotherapy and Mindful-
      ness Meditation in a Psychiatric Setting." JOURNAL OF
      TRANSPERSONAL PSYCHOLOGY 15 (1973): 173-79.

      Reports on a patient who suffered from paranoia and depres-
      sion, and whose problems and test patterns indicated that

standard psychotherapy was not likely to be effective. He
was treated instead with bibliotherapy, a kind of interaction
which employs both reading and discussion, and then, as a
second step, some rudimentary forms of Buddhist meditation.
The progress of the subject is mapped out, and his sustained
improvement is confirmed by independent evaluation and by
follow-up reviews. Increased self-esteem and psychological
growth were among the results noted.

1396. Boswell, Philip C., and Edward J. Murray. "Effects of Medi-
        tation on Psychological and Physiological Measures of
        Anxiety." JOURNAL OF CONSULTING AND CLINICAL PSYCHOLOGY 47
        (1979): 606-7.

        Discovers, in a test conducted on mantra meditators and
        non-meditators, that the former showed no evidence that their
        meditation practice reduced their anxiety more than that of
        the control group.

1397. Brooks, James S., and Thomas Scarano. "Transcendental
        Meditation in the Treatment of Post-Vietnam Adjustment."
        JOURNAL OF COUNSELING AND DEVELOPMENT 64 (1985): 212-15.

        Compares Transcendental Meditation with psychotherapy in
        the treatment of Vietnam veterans, who are having serious
        problems in readjusting to civilian life. A number of vari-
        ables, including anxiety, emotional and family problems,
        depression, and alcohol addiction, are examined. The authors
        discovered that meditation practice, used alone or in con-
        junction with regular therapy, did prove beneficial, even
        though they are somewhat cautious about the general applica-
        bility of the program.

1398. Brown, Daniel P., and Jack Engler. "An Outcome Study of
        Intensive Mindfulness Meditation." PSYCHOANALYTIC STUDY
        OF SOCIETY 10 (1984): 163-225.

        Examines at length the two commonly used models for defin-
        ing meditation, namely, stress reduction and psychotherapy,
        and suggests a "stage model," which emerged out of a three-
        month study of indigenous Buddhist meditation practitioners
        and an examination of the textbook tradition. The researchers
        conclude that "the prospect of quick advance along the path
        of meditation is not realistic" (p. 220), and that meditation
        "is not a form of therapy but a soteriology, i.e., a means
        of liberation" (p. 221).

1399. Brown, Daniel P., and Jack Engler. "The Stages of Mindfulness
        Meditation: A Validation Study." JOURNAL OF TRANSPERSONAL
        PSYCHOLOGY 12 (1980): 143-189.

        Presents a preliminary report of a study of Buddhist medi-
        tation practitioners and the various traditional texts on
        which meditation is based. The study restricts itself to the
        Buddhist Vissipana tradition, which divides the entire system

of meditation into three stages, namely, preliminary training (moral stage), concentration training, and insight training, the first of which is recommended for beginners. Three independent projects are included in this report: a three-month study of intensive-meditation students; data collected from advanced Western students at the Insight Meditation Center in Barre, Massachusetts; and a study of South Asian enlightened Masters. The Rorschach test was used on all subjects, and it was concluded that "the prospect of quick advancement along the path of meditation is not realistic" (p. 188). Meditation, in the authors' view, is not a form of therapy, but a means of liberation.

1400. Brown, Daniel P., Michael Forte, and Michael Dysart. Differences in Visual Sensitivity Among Mindfulness Meditators and Non-Meditators." PERCEPTUAL AND MOTOR SKILLS 58 (1984): 727-33.

Describes briefly mindfulness meditation as taught by the major Burmese schools of Buddhism, and tries to determine, by experiments with light flashes on various groups of subjects, whether this form of meditation affected their visual sensitivity. The staff and retreatants of the Insight Meditation Society in Barre, Massachusetts, and Western and Eastern meditation teachers were the main participants in the experiment. The results indicate that meditators do perform better than non-meditators in detecting light flashes, but not in discriminating between successive light flashes. Few differences were recorded between the different groups of meditators.

1401. Brown, Daniel P., Michael Forte, and Michael Dysart. "Visual Sensitivity and Mindfulness Meditation." PERCEPTUAL AND MOTOR SKILLS 58 (1984): 775-84.

Tests practitioners of Buddhist mindfulness meditation before and immediately after a three-month retreat, and tries to determine what changes, if any, occurred in their visual sensitivity. After the retreat, meditators were found able to detect shorter light flashes, and to differentiate correctly successive flashes in a shorter period of time. The researchers state that meditators could become conscious of the pre-attentive process. Mindfulness meditation could consequently make them gain insight into, and voluntary control over, perceptual biases, which could affect their psychological well-being.

1402. Burns, Douglas, and Ron Jonah Ohayv. "Psychological Changes in Meditating Western Monks in Thailand." JOURNAL OF TRANS-PERSONAL PSYCHOLOGY 12 (1980): 11-24.

Gives an edited transcription between Ron Ohayv and Dr. Burns, an American psychiatrist who studied meditation as a form of psychological self-therapy. Burns' research shows that meditators registered an increase in self-confidence and a drop in defensiveness. On the negative side, he concludes that some meditators have become extremely insular in their views.

1403.   Busby, Keith, and Joseph De Konick. "Short-Term Effects of
        Strategies for Self-Regulation on Personality Dimensions
        and Dream Content." PERCEPTUAL AND MOTOR SKILLS 50 (1980):
        751-65.

        Tests the hypothesis that self-regulation strategies, par-
        ticularly Transcendental Meditation, induce psychological
        changes, which would be clearly reflected in dream content.
        The authors speculate that the subjects' dreams would, after
        meditation, express less anxious, aggressive, and negative
        themes, and dwell more on positive motifs, such as friendli-
        ness, success, and fortune. It was found, however, that
        meditation, while it did induce significant positive psycho-
        logical changes, was not more effective than simple relaxation.
        Some changes in dream content, e.g., an increase in fantasy
        and good fortune themes, were recorded, but it is not clear
        whether the changes had any lasting value. A lengthy bibli-
        ography is appended.

1404.   Campbell, Anthony. SEVEN STATES OF CONSCIOUSNESS: A VISION
        OF POSSIBILITIES SUGGESTED BY THE TEACHING OF MAHARISHI
        MAHESH YOGI. London: Gollancz, 1973. 175 pp.

        Gives an account of the author's own involvement in Tran-
        scendental Meditation and of the philosophical theory behind
        it. The emphasis throughout the book is that the practice
        of this form of meditation leads to self-development, self-
        actualization, and greater creativity. The view that all
        mystical experience is pathological is rejected.

1405.   Candelent, Thomas, and Gillian Candelent. "Teaching Tran-
        scendental Meditation in a Psychiatric Setting."   HOSPITAL
        AND COMMUNITY PSYCHIATRY 26 (1975): 156-59.

        Describes the TM instruction given to patients at the
        Institute of Living in Hartford, Connecticut, and lists some
        of the benefits of its regular practice. TM was used as an
        adjunct to regular therapy, because of its ability to bring
        about relaxation and to reduce anxiety. The role of the staff
        in administering the program and the relationship between
        nurses and TM instructors are outlined. The authors consider
        TM to be an effective therapeutic process.

1406.   Carpenter, J. Tyler. "Meditation, Esoteric Traditions: Con-
        tributions to Psychotherapy." AMERICAN JOURNAL OF PSYCHO-
        THERAPY 3 (1977): 394-404.

        Reflects on the contemporary increase in clinical papers
        on the effects of Eastern meditation and points out that the
        difference between Eastern traditions of liberation and West-
        ern systems of psychotherapy is one of focus rather than of
        kind. The Japanese Morita and Naikan therapies, as well as
        the Maitri Space (Tantric) therapy of the Tibetan Master
        Chogyam Trungpa Rimpoche, are described. The current appli-
        cations of these techniques are discussed. The author
        maintains that Eastern meditation traditions can enrich the

practice of psychotherapy and can be psychotherapeutically effective methods in changing self-defeating patterns of behavior, desensitizing painful thoughts, and training the central nervous system.

1407. Carrington, Patricia. "Modern Forms of Meditation." PRINCIPLES AND PRACTICE OF STRESS-MANAGEMENT. Edited by Robert L. Woolfolk and Paul M. Lehrer. New York: The Guilford Press, 1984, pp. 108-41.

Presents her view that meditation techniques, divested of their religious trappings, are therapeutic and have the same impact as biofeedback and relaxation methods. She maintains that TM has not been used more frequently in therapy because it has clear religious overtones. She also discusses various theories which explain why non-cultic meditation is effective. The common effects of meditation are listed. Guidelines are given to assess the suitability of meditation to a particular patient. The limitations of the method and the cautions one should take are discussed. Finally, the clinically standardized meditation practice is described.

1408. Carrington, Patricia. "Meditation Techniques in Clinical Practice." THE NEW THERAPIES: A SOURCEBOOK. Edited by Lawrence E. Apt and Irving R. Stewart. New York: Van Nostrand, 1984, pp. 60-78.

Points out that meditation is not a strange or unfamiliar state of consciousness, and then explores the question of how it can interact with psychotherapy. The ways in which meditation might affect personality are explored: reduction of tension, increase of productivity, lowering of anxiety, mood elevation, lessening of self-blame, and increase of sense of identity. Several reasons, such as the effects of rhythm (mantra), global desensitization (behavior therapy), and shift in hemispheric dominance to the right (linked with holistic, intuitive, and wordless thinking), are outlined. The author thinks that there are two main problems in the use of meditation: 1) the possible negative tension-release side effects, and 2) the rapid behavioral change which might threaten a patient's pathological life-style. Carrington's position is that meditation can be used clinically, as an adjunct to traditional psychotherapy, without dependence on a religious organization.

1409. Carrington, Patricia. "The Uses of Meditation in Psychotherapy." EXPANDING DIMENSIONS OF CONSCIOUSNESS. Edited by A. Arthur Sugarman and Ralph E. Tarter. New York: Springer Publishing Co., 1978, pp. 81-98.

Proposes the view that uniting meditation techniques with psychotherapeutic approaches promises to be one of the most exciting and potentially fruitful applications of meditation to modern life. The author limits herself to secular meditation, implying that meditation methods can be employed to achieve not only spiritual goals, but also material benefits.

Benson's relaxation response, TM, and clinically standardized
meditation are cited as examples, though the author has some
reservations about TM. The following effects of meditation
are listed: decrease in the level of tension and dependency
on drugs; increase in energy level, self-esteem, and sense
of identity; mood elevation; expression of previously
suppressed feelings; and stress release. Several reasons
why meditation works are given. The author thinks that
meditation is different from, but complementary to, conventional psychotherapy and, in spite of its limits and dangers,
can be applied therapeutically. Psychologists can also reap
personal benefits by pursuing a meditation program.

1410. Carrington, Patricia. FREEDOM IN MEDITATION. Garden City,
       NY: Anchor Press/Doubleday, 1977. xxii, 384 pp.

       Divides the treatment of meditation into four basic areas:
       1) the scientific exploration of meditation, where its phys-
       ical and psychological effects have become a subject of
       research and debate; 2) the way one uses meditation, including
       the TM mantra, particularly under stress; 3) meditation and
       personal growth, with a section on the therapist's point of
       view; and 4) explanation of why meditation works as a mode
       of sensory deprivation, a shift in cognition, or a method of
       desensitization. The author states that the basic findings
       that meditation relaxes people, reduces stress, and brings
       about several side effects have not been reversed, but thinks
       that the therapeutic benefits of meditation are incomplete,
       and that it should not be used by itself to treat psychiatric
       disorders. In conclusion, she discusses the problem of the
       use of meditation in medicine, psychiatry, education, busi-
       ness, and industry. It is her belief that meditation could
       change ways of viewing human destiny and our role in the
       cosmos.

1411. Carrington, Patricia, Gilbert H. Collins, et al. "The Use
       of Meditation-Relaxation Techniques for the Management of
       Stress in a Working Population." JOURNAL OF OCCUPATIONAL
       MEDICINE 22 (1980): 221-31.

       Compares relaxation and control conditions as part of a
       program for stress-reduction in industry. The study was
       carried out among New York telephone employees with the aim
       of discovering whether meditation-relaxation methods can re-
       duce stress among workers, whether some techniques are better
       suited than others for this purpose, and whether all employees
       can benefit from these methods. The method of research is
       described and plenty of statistical data is supplied. The
       authors conclude that meditation-relaxation techniques can
       effectively reduce stress, and that meditation can become a
       permanent coping strategy which can be applied when needed.

1412. Carrington, Patricia, and Harmon Ephron. "Meditation as an
       Adjunct to Psychotherapy." NEW DIMENSIONS ON PSYCHIATRY:
       A WORLD VIEW. Edited by S. Arieti and G. Chrzanowski.
       New York: Wiley and Sons, 1975, pp. 261-91.

Describes the meditation process and its relation to free association. The following effects of meditation are then discussed: reduction of tension, increased productivity, lessening of anxiety, modification of the superego, and overcoming of drug addictions. Although meditation is not a panacea, the authors think that it is a "facilitator of the psychotherapeutic process." It can be used in the treatment of tension and anxiety, chronic fatigue states, insomnia, and paranoid tendencies. Several problems in using meditation are listed: refusal to learn how to meditate, resistance to regular meditation, and overmeditation. It is recommended that meditation be employed in therapy, and that psychiatrists first learn to use it themselves.

1413. Carrington, Patricia, and Harmon Ephron. "Meditation and Psychoanalysis." JOURNAL OF THE AMERICAN ACADEMY OF PSYCHOANALYSIS 3 (1975): 43-57.

Explores various ways in which psychoanalysis and Transcendental Meditation are related and may fruitfully interact. Seven effects of meditation on personality are listed: tension reduction, energy release, superego amelioration, mood stabilization, availability of affect, individuation, and anti-addictive properties. Meditation has both similarities and differences to the technique of systematic desensitization used in behavior therapy. It is similar to psychoanalysis in its use of free association, but differs in its lack of the rational and highly interpersonal elements so central in psychoanalysis. In spite of the positive effects of meditation, the authors do not think that it is a form of psychotherapy in its own right. It can, however, be an adjunct to psychoanalytic treatment. The benefits that an analyst can reap by meditation in his or her professional work are listed.

1414. Carruthers, Malcolm E. "Voluntary Control of the Involuntary Nervous System: Comparison of Autogenic Training and Siddha Meditation." EXPERIMENTAL AND CLINICAL PSYCHIATRY 6 (1981): 171-81.

Draws attention to the dangers of using drugs to control the nervous system when other, safer means, like those developed in the East, are available. Autogenic training, which is labeled "a Western form of meditation," is compared with the Buddhist Siddha Meditation, which has recently become better known in the West through Swami Muktananda Paramahamsa. Siddha meditation gives direct access to one's inner conscious energy which sets in motion a self-exploration process. This form of meditation is clinically applicable for physiological and emotional problems.

1415. Carsello, Carmen, and James W. Creaser. "Does Transcendental Meditation Affect Grades?" JOURNAL OF APPLIED PSYCHOLOGY 63 (1978): 527-28.

Reports on an experiment with 70 students at the University of Illinois to assess the impact of TM on their grades. The

results show clearly that TM had no effect on their exam
performance. The work of Orme-Johnson and others (item 1554),
which registered positive results, is criticized for relying
on selected samples. It is acknowledged that some students
might be helped by meditation, which is not, however, a cure
for all human problems, as it is sometimes said to be.

1416. Casper, Marvin. "Space Therapy and the Maitri Project."
        JOURNAL OF TRANSPERSONAL PSYCHOLOGY 6 (1974): 57-67.

        Describes the Maitri Project, an application of Tibetan
        Buddhist psychology and meditation practice to the problem of
        mental illness. The basic principles of Buddhist psychology
        are outlined and the goal of Maitri therapy is explained as
        an attempt to make the patient accept his or her neurotic
        ways. Various neurotic styles of relating to space and the
        Buddhist way to counteract them are discussed in detail.
        This Maitri technique was designed by Trungpa, a Tibetan
        Buddhist meditation master, to deal effectively with highly
        neurotic states. In this therapy, the patient, placed in a
        specially designed room, maintains, for a prescribed length
        of time, specific bodily postures designed to counteract the
        neurotic ways people relate to space.

1417. Cassel, Russel N. "Fundamentals Involved in the Scientific
        Process of Transcendental Meditation." JOURNAL OF INSTRUC-
        TIONAL PSYCHOLOGY 3 (1976): 2-11.

        Describes the practice of TM in four stages: orientation,
        relaxation, centering, and creating the retreat. Inner peace
        and harmony are the principal expected results in religiously
        oriented TM, while self-control, relaxation, freedom, and
        self-actualization are secondary. The latter effects, how-
        ever, become primary when TM is approached scientifically.

1418. Cassel, Russel N. "Fostering Transcendental Meditation
        Using Biofeedback Eliminates Hoax and Restores Credibility
        to Art." PSYCHOLOGY: A JOURNAL OF HUMAN BEHAVIOR 13.2
        (1976): 58-64.

        Surveys the outcomes which those practicing TM expect to
        receive: mind control, progressive relaxation, improved
        personal health, increased freedom, personal power, peak
        experiences, self-acutalization, and the development of a
        higher level of reality. The author thinks that biofeedback
        makes TM more effective and corroborates its claim to be a
        science rather than a religion.

1419. Cassel, Russel N. "Basic Fundamentals of Mind Control and
        Transcendental Meditation." PSYCHOLOGY: A JOURNAL OF
        HUMAN BEHAVIOR 11.2 (1974): 24-33.

        Relates TM to mind control, that is, to the mastery of
        one's own intellectual functions and of the involuntary
        aspects of the human organism. This type of self-control

can be developed in many stages, including relaxation,
breath control, and mental imagery. TM is viewed as a
useful therapy, especially in cases of drug abuse.

1420. Chang, Suk C. "The Psychology of Consciousness." AMERICAN
JOURNAL OF PSYCHOTHERAPY 32 (1978): 105-16.

Points out that psychology has neglected the faculty of
awareness, thus limiting our understanding of the human psyche.
Psychologists have concentrated their studies on sensations,
feelings, and thoughts, and this explains why they have not
been able to understand the psychology of meditation. The
author distinguishes between free meditation (as in the use
of a "koan" in Zen Buddhism, and as practiced in Morita
therapy), and concentration (where the stress is to focus on
one object). Meditation is the experimental examination of
the two selves, the changing and unchanging ones, and is,
therefore, a beneficial tool for self-growth.

1421. Chapman, A. H. WHAT TM CAN DO FOR YOU. New York: Berkeley
Publishing Corporation, 1976. ix, 208 pp.

Outlines the principles, history, and technique of TM, and
shows how it produces beneficial results. The following areas
of scientific and popular interest are discussed: the effects
of TM on intelligence, its impact on emotional functioning and
social adjustment, and its effects on alcohol consumption,
smoking, and drug use. The relationship between TM, psychiatry and psychosomatic medicine, and the possible use of
meditation for treating psychosomatic disorders are also dealt
with. Some of the interpersonal problems that can be compli-
cated by TM and the hallucinations and psychiatric disorders
which it can precipitate are surveyed and illustrated by
case examples. The author points out that a few people with
emotional problems have grown worse through the practice of TM.

1422. Cohen, Daniel. MEDITATION: WHAT IT CAN DO FOR YOU. New York:
Dodd, Mead, and Co., 1977. 144 pp.

Presents a panorama of meditation techniques, including:
1) Christian, Judaic, and Muslim practices; 2) Eastern methods
in the West, like Zen and TM; and 3) modern developments, such
as Gurdjieff, Arica, and Subud. Two chapters are dedicated
to TM, "the fastest-growing form of meditation in the West
today" (p. 37). TM promotes a helpful, healthy relaxation.
The book discusses the fears, fantasies, and dangers of meditation: the accusation that it is diabolical, a form of
brainwashing, or a panacea for all problems.

1423. Compton, William C. "Meditation and Self-Actualization: A
Cautionary Note on the Sallis Article." PSYCHOLOGIA 27
(1984): 125-27.

Criticizes Sallis's article (item 1579) in that it fails to
distinguish between the various levels of (Zen) Meditation
practice and consequently proposes apparently contradictory
aims or goals for meditation.

1424. Compton, William C., and Gordon M. Becher. "Self-Actualiza-
       tion and Experience with Zen Meditation: Is a Learning
       Period Necessary for Meditation?" JOURNAL OF INDIVIDUAL
       PSYCHOLOGY 39 (1983): 925-29.

       Argues that Zen meditation is primarily a method of self-
       actualization and not an exercise for relaxation and anxiety
       reduction. Research on the relationship between Zen and self-
       actualization has been inconsistent because most of the people
       tested had not been practicing meditation for a long time. The
       authors conducted their research with two groups of meditators,
       one of which had been meditating for over nine months. The
       results confirm the hypothesis that a learning period of about
       one year is required before any self-actualization takes place.

1425. Corby, James, Walton R. Roth, Vincent P. Zarcone, and Bert S.
       Kapell. "Psychophysiological Correlates of the Practice of
       Tantric Yoga Meditation." ARCHIVES OF GENERAL PSYCHIATRY
       35 (1978): 571-77.

       Reviews briefly some of the research on Yoga and meditation.
       The authors concentrate on one type of Yoga, namely Tantric,
       as practiced by the Ananda Marga Yoga Society, which clearly
       involves intense concentration of attention and a personal
       struggle towards achieving samadhi. The study compares three
       carefully balanced groups of subjects, including Ananda
       trainees and experienced meditators. The results indicate
       that meditators become physiologically activated during their
       meditation, while the control subjects achieved relaxation.
       The same results are compared with other experiments, par-
       ticularly on those who practice Transcendental Meditation.

1426. Coward, H. G. "Jung's Encounter with Yoga." JOURNAL OF
       ANALYTICAL PSYCHOLOGY 23 (1978): 339-57.

       Describes the place of Yoga in Jung's psychology. The
       attitudes which Jung brought to the study of Yoga and his
       analysis of the Easterner's experience of Yoga are outlined.
       It is shown how Jung's study of early Christian mysticism led
       him to the Eastern traditions, especially to Yoga. In his
       view, Yoga is both a religious path and a psychological dis-
       cipline through which the tensions of opposites could be
       overcome. The benefits and dangers of the Western encounter
       with Yoga are explained.

1427. Cowger, Ernest L., and E. Paul Torrence. "Further Examination
       of the Quality of Changes in Creative Functioning Resulting
       from Meditation (Zazen) Training." CREATIVE CHILD AND ADULT
       QUARTERLY 7 (1982): 211-17.

       Examines the effects of Zazen on creative test performances
       of 27 students who committed themselves to the practice of
       (Zen) meditation, and ten who had followed the relaxation-
       training program. Using the Torrence Test of Creative Think-
       ing, the authors explored the effects of meditation on

several creativity indicators, such as heightened consciousness, invention, sensory experience, humor, and fantasy.
They concluded that meditators attained statistically significant gains in most areas.

1428. Croake, James W., and Ronald Rusk. "The Theories of Adler
and Zen." JOURNAL OF INDIVIDUAL PSYCHOLOGY 36 (1980):
219-26.

Outlines briefly the principles of Adlerian psychology and
the practice and theory of Zen Buddhism. The similarities
between the two systems are discussed. Both are said to be
humanistic attempts to solve the frustration inherent in human
existence. Zen Buddhism, being a religion, does not directly
address psychological problems, nor does it offer any form
of psychotherapy. It can, however, contribute to the development and elaboration of Adlerian views through an alternative
but complementary view of human existence.

1429. Daniels, Lloyd K. "The Treatment of Psychophysiological Dis-
orders and Severe Anxiety by Behavior Therapy, Hypnosis, and
Transcendental Meditation." AMERICAN JOURNAL OF CLINICAL
HYPNOSIS 17 (1975): 267-70.

Gives a brief history of a patient who suffered from various
ailments, including anxiety and tension. The treatment in a
number of stages consisted of hypnosis, covert reinforcement,
and the practice of TM. Permanent recovery from acute situational anxiety resulted.

1430. Davidson, Richard J., and Daniel J. Goleman. "The Role of
Attention in Meditation and Hypnosis: A Psychobiological
Perspective of Transformation of Consciousness." INTER-
NATIONAL JOURNAL OF CLINICAL AND EXPERIMENTAL HYPNOSIS 25
(1977): 291-308.

Starts with the assumption that meditation, particularly
by its focus on attention, is one of the oldest techniques
for achieving some degree of self-regulation. A model for
understanding some fundamental principles in the self-
regulation of consciousness is outlined in three temporal
stages: before (the psychobiological patterns of a person
before an altered state of consciousness), during the state
(the effects of a particular method, such as meditation and
hypnosis), and after (the effects of a specific exercise).
The authors carefully describe these levels and compare them
to hypnosis, mentioning some of the good psychological results, like the reduction in anxiety.

1431. Davidson, Richard J., Daniel J. Goleman, and Gary E. Schwartz.
"Attentional and Affective Concomitants of Meditation: A
Cross-Sectional Study." JOURNAL OF ABNORMAL PSYCHOLOGY 85
(1976): 235-38.

Explores the difference in attentional absorption and trait
anxiety in 58 subjects (divided into control group, beginners,

and long-term meditators) by administering several psychological tests (e.g., the Tellegen Absorption Scale and the
Shor Personal Experiences Questionnaire Anxiety Inventory).
The results showed that long-term meditators developed an
increased absorption and a decreased anxiety trait. These
data correspond to physiological changes associated with
different forms of meditation (including Zen and TM).

1432. Deatherage, Gary. "The Clinical Use of 'Mindfulness' Medi-
       tation Techniques in Short-Term Psychotherapy." JOURNAL
       OF TRANSPERSONAL PSYCHOLOGY No. 2 (1975): 133-43.

       Discusses a Buddhist meditation method and its possible use
       with short-term psychiatric patients. The author holds that
       Buddhism is a highly systematic psychology and philosophy,
       and explains why the mindfulness technique (Satipatthana) is
       a client-oriented psychotherapeutic approach to human problems.
       Three objectives of this meditation are singled out: 1) knowl-
       edge of one's own mental processes; 2) power and control of
       them; and 3) freedom from those which are beyond one's control.
       The psychotherapeutic application of meditation is outlined
       and several case studies are given. The author is of the
       opinion that Buddhist meditation is more effective with
       patients who suffer from depression, anxiety, and many neurot-
       ic symptoms, than it is with hallucinations, illusions, and
       severe withdrawal. The therapist who plans to use this tech-
       nique should first of all explore them personally.

1433. De Grace, Gaston. "Effects of Meditation on Personality and
       Values." JOURNAL OF CLINICAL PSYCHOLOGY 32 (1976): 809-13.

       Reports on a five-month research on Zen meditators using
       the Californian Psychological Inventory (CPI) and several
       values tests (like the AVS). Meditators became less aggres-
       sive, less manipulative and verbal, less independent, less
       concerned with planning for their future, less ambitious, and
       less interested in some social activities than non-meditators.
       The results confirmed the author's hypothesis. He still has
       some reservations about those studies which conclude that the
       positive results of meditation can be achieved within a matter
       of weeks.

1434. Deikman, Arthur J. "The State of the Art of Meditation."
       MEDITATION: CLASSICAL AND CONTEMPORARY PERSPECTIVES (item
       45), pp. 679-80.

       Admits that meditation has the effects of increasing calm-
       ness, creativity, concentration, and endurance, and of curing
       stress-related illnesses. The author, however, complains
       about the acquisitiveness and self-centered attitude that lies
       behind the usage of meditation practices. It is alleged that
       the need to develop a selfless orientation and to follow the
       advice of a teacher are necessary adjuncts of meditation.

1435. Delmonte, M. M. "Meditation and Anxiety Reduction: A Litera-
       ture Review." CLINICAL PSYCHOLOGY REVIEW 5 (1985): 91-102.

Provides an extensive review of the research literature
which measures the effects of meditation on self-reported
anxiety levels. The evidence suggests that those who practice meditation regularly tend to show significant decreases
in anxiety. The author thinks, however, that meditation is
not more effective than comparative interventions. Hypnotizability and expectancy may be key factors in most cases of
anxiety reduction. Sixty-six references are included.

1436. Delmonte, M. M. "Response to Meditation of Physiological,
       Behavioral, and Self-Report Measures: A Brief Summary."
       PSYCHOLOGICAL REPORTS 56 (1985): 9-10.

Examines the reports of physiological and psychological
benefits of meditation, and suggests that some predisposing
factors may contribute to the outcome of meditation practices.
Prospective meditators tend to be more anxious, neurotic, and
dysthymic, and to have more drug-related problems. The contribution of expectancy and of increased hypnotic suggestibility during meditation should not be ignored. The clinical
value of meditation seems to be limited to patients suffering
from mild neurotic and psychosomatic disorders.

1437. Delmonte, M. M. "Psychosomatic Scores and Meditation Practice:
       A Literature Review." PERSONALITY AND INDIVIDUAL DIFFERENCES
       5 (1984): 559-63.

Examines psychosomatic profiles of whose who practice meditation (especially Transcendental Meditation and its non-
cultic or clinically standardized derivatives). The following
features are considered: self-esteem, depression, psychosomatic symptomology, self-actualization, locus of control, and
introversion/extraversion. Meditation may increase reported
levels of self-actualization, but its ability to reduce
depression has not been conclusively demonstrated. The
literature suggests that the value of meditation may lie in
its ability to reduce anxiety. Thirty-four references are
given.

1438. Delmonte, M. M. "Meditation: Similarities with Hypnoidal
       States and Hypnosis." INTERNATIONAL JOURNAL OF PSYCHO-
       SOMATICS 31.3 (1984): 24-34.

Draws attention to the numerous procedural, phenomenological, and psychological similarities between integrated
meditation (especially Zen and TM) and hypnosis. Both are
altered states of consciousness sharing introductory procedures and effects. The literature comparing some forms of
meditation with autohypnosis is surveyed. There is evidence
that hypnotic suggestibility may be increased by the practice
of meditation. The author thinks, however, that advanced
meditation may not be a form of autohypnosis.

1439. Delmonte, M. M. "Factors Influencing the Regularity of
       Meditation Practice in a Clinical Population." BRITISH
       JOURNAL OF MEDICAL PSYCHOLOGY 57 (1984): 275-78.

Reports on the results of tests administered to subjects who were instructed in a non-cultic technique of mantra meditation. The author concludes that meditation appears to be effective as a therapeutic adjunct with patients who have milder complaints.

1440. Delmonte, M. M. "Meditation Practice as Related to Occupational Stress, Health and Productivity." PERCEPTUAL AND MOTOR SKILLS 59 (1984): 581-82.

Reviews several studies (e.g., item 1411) on the effects of meditation on employees' health in the work setting. Though the evidence pointing to meditation as a way of reducing occupational stress is very promising, the author feels it is premature to conclude that meditation can be usefully introduced into the work environment.

1441. Delmonte, M. M. "Mantras and Meditation: A Literature Review." PERCEPTUAL AND MOTOR SKILLS 57 (1983): 64-66.

Examines the literature on the use of a mantra during meditation with the intention of exploring the claim that meditation works because mantras fit personality types. It is concluded that no correlation exists between mantra and personality, and that researchers have invented their own equally successful mantras.

1442. Delmonte, M. M. "Expectation and Meditation." PSYCHOLOGICAL REPORTS 49 (1981): 699-709.

Examines the often-repeated view, expressed in introductory talks on Transcendental Meditation, that expectation and placebo effects play no role in the effects of meditation. Tests which the author administered to over ninety prospective meditators showed that a positive self-image and high expectations were related to a high frequency of meditation practice. Noting that the large-scale interest in the practice of meditation is not without potential danger, the author suggests that in future research the element of "expectancy" be taken into consideration.

1443. Delmonte, M. M. "Personality Characteristics and Regularity of Meditation." PSYCHOLOGICAL REPORTS 46 (1980): 703-12.

Gives the results of a variety of personality tests, such as Eysenck's Personality Inventory, Byrne's Depression-Sensitization Scale, Rotter's Locus of Control, and Barber's Suggestibility Scale, on 55 prospective Transcendental Meditators. Regular meditation, it is concluded, appeared to be a rewarding experience to about 25 percent of those who took up the practice. Although it is difficult to predict which individuals will find meditation beneficial, there is a definite correlation between the maintenance of the practice of meditation and low scores on both sensitization and neuroticism.

1444. De Silva, Padmal. "Early Buddhist and Modern Behavioral
       Strategies for the Control of Unwanted Intrusive Cognition."
       PSYCHOLOGICAL RECORD 35 (1985): 437-43.

       Presents and analyzes the early Buddhist methods for con-
       trolling and eliminating undesirable thoughts, and compares
       them to modern techniques devised by behavioral psychologists.
       The methods used are listed as follows: 1) switch to opposite
       or incomparable thoughts; 2) ponder on harmful consequences;
       3) ignore or distract; 4) reflect on removal of causes; and
       5) control with forceful effort. These Buddhist methods are,
       in fact, similar to behavior modification techniques.

1445. Dilleck, Michael C. "The Effect of the Transcendental Medi-
       tation Technique on Anxiety Level." JOURNAL OF CLINICAL
       PSYCHOLOGY 33 (1977): 1076-78.

       Applies the State-Trait Anxiety Inventory to 33 graduate
       and undergraduate students who were randomly chosen to prac-
       tice TM or spend two sessions a day in passive relaxation.
       After two weeks, those who practiced meditation were more
       successful in reducing their anxiety. Further research, how-
       ever, is needed since the TM subjects' expectation may have
       contributed to the positive results.

1446. Dinklage, Helen A. "Personal Intervention: Meditation May Be
       the Answer." JOURNAL OF THE AMERICAN SOCIETY FOR PREVENTIVE
       DENTISTRY 5 (May/June 1975): 23.

       Suggests very briefly that meditation may be the answer to
       daily stressful states. Transcendental Meditation, Psycho-
       synthesis, and Anthroposophy are cited as examples of how a
       person may counteract tension.

1447. Domino, George. "Transcendental Meditation and Creativity:
       An Empirical Investigation." JOURNAL OF APPLIED PSYCHOLOGY
       62 (1977): 358-62.

       Examines the claim that TM increases the individual's
       creative powers. A battery of five creative measures was
       applied to five different groups of students before and after
       a six-month period of meditation. The result did not support
       the thesis that TM increases one's creativity.

1448. Ehrlich, Milton B. "Self-Acceptance and Meditation."
       JOURNAL OF PASTORAL COUNSELING 11 (Fall-Winter, 1976-77):
       37-41.

       Claims that the experience of meditation can provide an
       important contribution to therapy for both the patient and
       the therapist. The author's own experience is presented as
       a case history in which meditation added to awareness and
       perspective. Meditation leads to self-knowledge, reintegra-
       tion, and self-acceptance.

1449.   Ehrlich, Milton B. "Family Meditation." JOURNAL OF FAMILY
        THERAPY 4.2 (1976): 40-45.

        Describes the author's own quest for a meditation technique
        (including Zen and Yoga) and the problems encountered in
        accepting the direction of a guru. It is concluded that
        self-discovery was achieved through meditation as a shared
        experience.

1450.   Ellis, Albert. "The Place of Meditation in Cognitive-
        Behavior Therapy." MEDITATION: CLASSICAL AND CONTEMPORARY
        PERSPECTIVES (item 45), pp. 671-73.

        Maintains that meditation is a form of psychotherapy. The
        meditator employs a mode of cognitive distraction or diver-
        sion which not only temporarily frees one from anxiety, de-
        pression, or hostility, but also alters one's philosophical
        outlook. Meditation is a self-regulation strategy leading
        to self-actualization. The author is concerned that the
        practice of meditation, when used as a form of spiritual
        discipline, can easily be combined with mysticism and magic,
        and thus become dangerous and anti-therapeutic. Meditation
        is recommended as a palliative, a distraction technique, to
        be used with discretion and in conjunction with cognitive-
        behavior therapy.

1451.   Engelman, Suzanne R., Pauline R. Clance, and Suzanne Imes.
        "Self and Body-Cathexis Change in Therapy and Yoga Groups."
        JOURNAL OF THE AMERICAN SOCIETY OF PSYCHOSOMATIC DENTISTRY
        AND MEDICINE 29 (1982): 77-88.

        Attempts to answer the question whether group therapy, which
        stresses interaction and confrontation among the participants,
        and Yoga, which centers on silent, non-interactional states,
        calmness of mind, and relaxation of body, show comparable
        change in self-cathexis and body-cathexis. The Secord-Jourard
        scale was used to measure both cathexes on those in regular
        therapy, practitioners of Yoga, and a control group. Results
        show that, as opposed to the control group, both self- and
        body-cathexis improved for Yoga subjects, whereas only self-
        cathexis improved for therapy patients. Therapy and Yoga
        groups were not significantly different from each other either
        before or after treatment. The authors suggest that a form
        of therapy, which combines interaction and non-verbalization,
        body work, and cognition, would obtain the best results.

1452.   Engler, Jack. "Therapeutic Aims in Psychotherapy and Medita-
        tion: Developmental Stages in the Representations of Self."
        JOURNAL OF TRANSPERSONAL PSYCHOLOGY 16 (1984): 25-61.

        Discusses Buddhist Vissipana or Insight meditation, par-
        ticularly in relation to the development of a sense of self.
        The view of the ego in object-relations theory and in Buddhism
        is compared. Several clinical features of meditation practice
        are noted: slow progress of Western students; fixation on

psychodynamic levels; and strong transference to teachers.
The author rejects the reasons meditation teachers usually
give to account for these negative effects. He argues,
instead, that they are the result of vulnerability and disturbance in the meditators' sense of identity and self-esteem.
Buddhism attracts those whose view of the self is pathological.
Vissipana meditation presents serious risks to these people.

1453. Epstein, Mark D., and Jonathan D. Lieff. "Psychiatric Compli-
      cations of Meditation Practice." JOURNAL OF TRANSPERSONAL
      PSYCHOLOGY 13 (1981): 137-47.

      Discusses the negative side effects of meditation, namely,
depersonalization, anxiety, and tension, which depend to some
degree on the theoretical approach of the observer. The
stages of meditation, which include preliminary exercises,
concentration, samadhi, and insight, are described. The
authors raise the major questions: 1) whether the pathological
effects of Eastern meditation are limited to Western practitioners; and 2) how to distinguish innocuous from pathological
side effects.

1454. Eyerman, James. "Transcendental Meditation and Mental Retar-
      dation." JOURNAL OF CLINICAL PSYCHIATRY 42 (January 1981):
      35-36.

      Describes the effects of TM on a 26-year-old mentally re-
tarded woman. Spontaneous improvements on the intellectual,
physical, and psychological levels were recorded after two
months of practice. The author recommends the use of TM as
an adjunct to traditional rehabilitation programs.

1455. Ferguson, Phillip C. "The Psychobiology of Transcendental
      Meditation: A Review." JOURNAL OF ALTERED STATES OF
      CONSCIOUSNESS 2 (1975): 15-36.

      Presents a study of TM as one path to self-actualization
and self-integration. This unique form of meditation is
described, and the literature which records physiological,
psychological, and social changes produced by its practice
is reviewed. Its effects, according to the author, are seen
both during and after the meditation periods. The beneficial
results of TM extend to almost all areas of human behavior.
A reference list of 82 items is included.

1456. Ferguson, Phil, and John Gowan. "TM: Some Preliminary Find-
      ings." JOURNAL OF HUMANISTIC PSYCHOLOGY 16.3 (1976): 51-60.

      Describes the TM technique, and tests the hypothesis that
its regular practice reduces negative personality traits and
increases positive ones. The following tests were administered
to three groups of university students, two of which were made
up of recent and long-time TM practitioners, and one was the
control group: the Northridge Developmental Scale, the Cattell
Anxiety Scale, and the Spielberger State-Trait Anxiety Inven-

tory. The results showed that the meditators registered an
increase in self-actualization, experienced a reduction in
depression and neuroticism, and exhibited a significant
decrease in the level of anxiety. The regular use of TM has
positive psychological benefits.

1457. Feuerstein, George. THE ESSENCE OF YOGA: A CONTRIBUTION TO
        THE PSYCHOHISTORY OF INDIAN CIVILIZATION. London: Rider
        and Co., 1974. 224 pp.

        Points out the fundamental criteria which underlie the his-
        torical development of Yoga, and describes its philosophical
        and practical aspects. Two tendencies in Yoga are distin-
        guished: the magical, mythic structure of consciousness (as
        in classical Yoga) and the holistic approach (as in the
        Bhagavad-Gita). Yoga expresses the individual's struggle for
        self-integration in Indian culture. In discussing the signif-
        icance of Yoga for the West, the author contends that self-
        alienation or depersonalization cannot be cured by the adop-
        tion of Eastern practices, such as Yoga and Zen. Yoga is not
        a panacea for all human ills and problems, though it can make
        a substantial contribution to the mechanics of meditation.

1458. Finney, John R., and H. Newton Malony. "Contemplative Prayer
        and Its Use in Psychotherapy: A Theoretical Model." JOURNAL
        OF PSYCHOLOGY AND THEOLOGY 13 (1985): 172-81.

        Presents a model of contemplative prayer based on the lit-
        erature on prayer, mysticism, and meditation. Three major
        psychological processes can contribute to the effects of con-
        templative prayer, namely, hypnotic suggestion, non-directive
        trance, and decreased psychological arousal through periodic
        relaxation and desensitization. It is strongly recommended
        that contemplative prayer be employed therapeutically, though
        with caution in cases of psychosis, severe neurosis, and bor-
        derline personality disorder. Such prayer, however, should
        not be used simply to bring about beneficial, psychological
        results but, primarily among Christians, as a technique for
        spiritual development.

1459. Fling, Sheila, Anne Thomas, and Michael Gallaher. "Partic-
        ipant Characteristics and the Effects of Two Types of
        Meditation vs. Quiet Sitting." JOURNAL OF CLINICAL PSYCHOL-
        OGY 37 (1981): 784-90.

        Compares the effects of clinically standarized meditation
        and Open Focus meditation with quiet sitting on over eighty
        undergraduate students during a test period of eight weeks.
        Among the results was the observation that a significant de-
        crease of anxiety and an increase of intuitiveness became
        evident, especially in those pursuing the clinically stan-
        dardized meditation program.

1460. Frager, Robert, and James Fadiman. "Personal Growth in Yoga
        and Sufism." JOURNAL OF TRANSPERSONAL PSYCHOLOGY 1 (1975):
        66-80.

Holds that two popular spiritual disciplines, namely, Yoga and Sufism, provide models of human nature, human potential, and psychological functioning. The four stages of life, the goal of self-realization, and the obstacles to life according to the Yoga system of Pantajali, are described, and the different stages of personal development as propounded by Sufi teachers are briefly sketched. It seems to be implicitly maintained that, because Yoga and Sufism both propose alternative ways to personal growth, they can be applied to help people solve their personal problems.

1461. French, Alfred P., Albert Schmid, and Elizabeth Ingalls. "Transcendental Meditation, Altered Reality Testing, and Behavioral Change: A Case Report." JOURNAL OF NERVOUS AND MENTAL DISEASE 161 (1975): 55-58.

Presents a case of psychotic-like behavior which occurred in direct conjunction with TM practice, and discusses the theoretical and therapeutic implications. While not as dangerous as other forms of meditation (for example, Zen), TM, by decreasing repression, can bring about compelling fantasies which are harmful. The authors contend that this is not clinical psychosis, though it resembles it. They suggest that the persons involved in such meditation should interact with an experienced guide.

1462. Fritz, George, and John A. Mierzwa. "Meditation: A Review of Literature Relevant to Therapist Behavior and Personality." PSYCHOTHERAPY IN PRIVATE PRACTICE 1.3 (1983): 77-87.

Studies those informal reports that relate meditation to the capacity of therapists to treat patients. A definition of meditation and its typology are provided. Several beneficial effects which meditation can have on therapies are listed: 1) an enhanced awareness of one's own feelings; 2) an increase of empathy; and 3) an intensification of one's ability to interpret dreams with greater insight. Various tests on the effect of meditation on counselors register a greater aesthetic sensitivity, self-confidence, and emotional stability, as well as a reduced anxiety and a better organization of one's thought and behavior. The methodological issues in meditation research and its clinical applications are discussed.

1463. Galanter, Marc, and Peter Buckley. "Evangelical Religion and Meditation: Psychotherapeutic Findings." JOURNAL OF NERVOUS AND MENTAL DISEASE 166 (1978): 685-91.

Studies the psychotherapeutic effects of evangelical religious experience in members of the Divine Light Mission, particularly the claims that initiation into its meditation technique yielded relief from alcohol and drug abuse. Group functions, psychiatric symptoms, drug use, and meditation practices were recorded. A "decline in perceived psychiatric symptoms" (p. 687) was observed. Group cohesiveness, group

activities, and meditation point to the decline of pathological symptoms and of drug and alcohol abuse. Conversion
can in some cases be an alternative to "decompensation."
Parallels between certain religious practices of the Divine
Light Mission and traditional psychotherapy are drawn.

1464. Ganguli, H. C. "Meditation Subculture and Drug Abuse."
HUMAN RELATIONS 38 (1985): 953-62.

Seeks to determine the effect of meditation on the use of
drugs among members of an Eastern meditation group. The
training program these members took with their guru in India
is briefly described. The author admits that there is some
empirical evidence that meditation practice by itself leads
to a sense of peace and a reduction of anxiety. However, in
this particular study, the environment appeared to have been
a major reason why a substantial reduction of drug abuse took
place. The communal life, with its values, conduct norms,
and influential leader is more effective than the practice of
meditation in private.

1465. Ganguli, H. C. "Meditation Program and Modern Youth: Dynamics
of Initiation." HUMAN RELATIONS 35 (1982): 903-26.

Criticizes the many studies on the individual therapeutic
effects of meditation since they fail to take into account
that belonging to a group produces similar results. The
author also objects to the untested assumption that people
join cults only for therapeutic purposes. This study
explores the causes and motives for participating in meditation programs through data from 230 members of a Western
meditation school. The results suggest that many participate
in meditation groups to relieve stress, while many others
join such groups because they are seeking a more meaningful
level of existence or greater knowledge and happiness. The
underlying motives of those suffering from stress and anxiety
are pathological; the rest point to a healthy search for
growth and development.

1466. Gendlin, Eugene T. "The Newer Therapies." AMERICAN HANDBOOK
OF PSYCHIATRY. Edited by Silvano Arieti. New York: Basic
Books, second edition, 1974, vol. 5, pp. 269-89.

Gives an account of the new therapies, a kind of "third
force," which consists of many diverse methods and procedures.
A description of the attributes of these therapies, such as
direct experience, responsibility, trust in one's own body,
and interaction, is provided. Yoga and meditation are included with the Body Therapies, which give rise to psychological experiences and lower tension.

1467. Gergen, Kenneth J. "Zen Buddhism and Psychological Science."
PSYCHOLOGIA 26 (1983): 129-41.

Discusses the relationship between Zen and modern psychology. Several questions open to scientific analysis are

raised, such as: 1) the extent to which Zen practices actually
achieve their goals; 2) the effectiveness of Zen therapies,
like meditation, Morita, and Naikan, as compared with Western
treatments; and 3) the degree to which Zen can be applied
to the general population. It is explained that Zen brings
with it a radical change in our perception of psychological
knowledge. The author believes that Zen has made an important
contribution in probing the limitations of our conceptual and
verbal knowledge and in developing ways for acquiring non-
conceptual knowledge. Several benefits and problems involved
in non-conceptual or intuitive thinking are discussed.

1468. Gersten, Dennis J. "Meditation as an Adjunct to Medical and
       Psychiatric Treatment." AMERICAN JOURNAL OF PSYCHIATRY 135
       (1978): 598-99.

       Discusses the claim that meditation has therapeutic effects
       in the context of a patient who suffered from various physical
       and psychological problems. The author asserts that medita-
       tion was probably a significant factor in his cure.

1469. Girodo, Michael. "Yoga Meditation and Flooding in the Treat-
       ment of Anxiety Neurosis." JOURNAL OF BEHAVIOR THERAPY
       AND EXPERIMENTAL PSYCHIATRY 5 (1974): 157-60.

       Reports on an experiment on nine neurotic patients who began
       practicing Yoga meditation regularly. After four months, five
       improved significantly, while the rest showed no decline in
       anxiety symptoms. These latter then engaged themselves in
       imaginal flooding, and registered an improvement. The results
       indicate that Yoga meditation was beneficial with subjects
       with a short history of illness, and that flooding was effec-
       tive for those who had a long history of neurotic problems.

1470. Glueck, Bernard C., and Charles F. Stroebel. "Biofeedback
       and Meditation in the Treatment of Psychiatric Illness."
       CURRENT PSYCHIATRIC THERAPIES 15 (1975): 109-16.

       Maintains that for the treatment of anxiety one can effec-
       tively use, besides psychodynamic insight therapy and chemical
       intervention, biofeedback and Yogic meditation. Experimental
       results show that these latter can reduce stress and create
       relaxed, peaceful feelings which free one from worry. Clini-
       cal indications seem to favor the use of TM over biofeedback
       in most cases. The author is of the opinion that TM is the
       best form of meditation since it has been standardized, is
       simple to learn, and requires no special diet, exercise,
       drugs, or ascetic practices. Two possible negative results
       of TM are the appearance of primitive, distressing thoughts
       and the precipitation of overt, psychotic episodes. The need
       for adequate supervision in meditation is stressed.

1471. Goldberg, Philip. THE TM PROGRAM: THE WAY TO FULFILLMENT.
       New York: Holt, Rinehart and Winston, 1976. xiv, 178 pp.

Develops the argument that the TM program is a powerful
approach to full human potential. The author, himself a TM
teacher, shows how meditation helps a person reach self-
transcendence in the expansion of consciousness. Though not
proposed as a form of therapeutic treatment, TM can eliminate
stress and promote psychological well-being.

1472. Goldman, Barbara L., Paul J. Domitor, and Edward J. Murray.
       "Effects of Zen Meditation on Anxiety Reduction and Percep-
       tual Functioning." JOURNAL OF CONSULTING AND CLINICAL
       PSYCHOLOGY 47 (1979): 551-56.

       Maintains that early studies which concluded that meditation
       reduced anxiety were methodologically inadequate. More recent
       research, which either shows that meditation fosters personal
       growth, or concludes that it has no measurable beneficial
       effects, is hampered by theoretical and methodological limi-
       tations. The authors designed a laboratory test to evaluate
       the effects of Zen on several measures of anxiety and percep-
       tual functioning. Any favorable outcome, they concluded, must
       be accounted for by other variables, such as expectancy and
       personality.

1473. Goleman, Daniel. "The Buddha on Meditation and the States
       of Consciousness." TRANSPERSONAL PSYCHOLOGIES (item 1338),
       pp. 203-30.

       Summarizes some of the author's earlier work on Buddhist
       meditation (cf. items 1043 and 1475 for a fuller and more
       recent treatment of the topic).

1474. Goleman, Daniel. "A Taxonomy of Meditation--Specific
       Altered States." JOURNAL OF ALTERED STATES OF CONSCIOUS-
       NESS 4 (1978-79): 203-13.

       Attempts an "applied attentional typology" of meditation
       techniques, which are divided into three types: 1) concen-
       tration (Bhakti, Kabbalah, Sufi, Zen, and Kundalini Yoga);
       2) integrated (Tibetan Buddhism, Theravada Buddhism, and Zen);
       and 3) mindfulness (Gurdjieff and Krishnamurti). Each method
       allows the meditator to enter into a distinct altered state
       of awareness.

1475. Goleman, Daniel. THE VARIETIES OF MEDITATIVE EXPERIENCES.
       New York: Dutton, 1977. xxv, 130 pp.

       Surveys the various meditative principles and techniques
       in different religious traditions, including Transcendental
       Meditation, Sufism, Yoga, Buddhism, and Gurjieff's Fourth
       Way. The author contends that there is an essential unity
       underlying all these methods which aim at changing one's
       consciousness. Though the psychological impact of meditation
       is not discussed, it is assumed throughout that all forms of
       meditation and contemplation lead to personal growth and
       development.

1476. Goleman, Daniel. "Meditation Helps Break the Stress Spiral."
       PSYCHOLOGY TODAY 9 (May 1976): 82-86, 93.

       Suggests that there is strong evidence that the practice
       of meditation helps a person cope with the main stresses of
       life, and gives him or her the strength to withstand the
       life-changes with less turmoil. Though there seems to be
       little difference between the various meditation techniques,
       all seem able to promote physiological and psychological
       control.

1477. Goleman, Daniel. "Meditation and Consciousness: An Asian
       Approach to Mental Health." AMERICAN JOURNAL OF PSYCHO-
       THERAPY 30 (1975): 41-54.

       Examines the Buddhist psychological system known as Adhid-
       hamma which, stemming from the Buddha's original insights,
       has developed into a school of psychology. The Adhidhamma
       model of the mind and its method of dealing with mental ill-
       ness are briefly outlined. Fourteen unhealthy factors, such
       as delusion, greed, and envy, are compared and contrasted with
       their opposite healthy counterparts, like mindfulness, non-
       attachment, and impartiality. Healthy personality traits
       are developed and enhanced by meditation. According to the
       author, meditation is clinically useful because it can provide
       a psychological pattern of positive states, rather than a re-
       sponse to particular problems. The author proposes a neuro-
       physiological interpretation of meditation, and observes that
       modern therapies, like Gestalt in the United States and Morita
       in Japan, incorporate some aspects of meditation. He proposes
       its use as a complementary adjunct to psychotherapy.

1478. Goleman, Daniel. "Meditation as Meta-Therapy: Hypothesis
       Towards a Proposed Fifth State of Consciousness." JOURNAL
       OF TRANSPERSONAL PSYCHOLOGY 1 (1975): 1-25.

       Reflects on the author's own experience with meditation,
       particularly with Transcendental Meditation. This practice
       is viewed as a "meta-therapy," that is, a technique which
       brings about the major goals of conventional therapies plus
       an altered state of consciousness. Several hypotheses on
       meditation are drawn up. Its practice is said to reduce
       anxiety neurosis, to increase performance in learning and
       perceptual tasks, to enable a person to be more accurate in
       the perception of others, and to lead to a diminished discrep-
       ancy between the real and ideal self. The change brought
       about by meditation contributes to the mental health of the
       individual. The fifth state of consciousness (the other four
       being waking, sleeping, dreaming, and meditating) is described
       and identified with Maslow's peak experience. People in the
       fifth state would tend to have an absence of psychopathology.

1479. Goleman, Daniel, and Mark Epstein. "Meditation and Well-
       Being: An Eastern Model of Psychological Health." REVISION:
       A JOURNAL OF CONSCIOUSNESS AND CHANGE 3.2 (1980): 73-84.

Describes the main principles of Buddhist philosophy,
pointing out how in this philosophical system the healthy
and unhealthy mental features of human personality are seen
as a series of events, rather than as qualities of an "ego."
Meditation is a means to a healthy personality because it
aims to eradicate its unwholesome features. The Arhat is
viewed as the ideal type of healthy personality. The authors
think that Buddhist psychotherapy is complementary to Western
therapies.

1480. Goleman, Daniel J., and Gary E. Schwartz. "Meditation as an
      Intervention in Stress Reactivity." JOURNAL OF CONSULTING
      AND CLINICAL PSYCHOLOGY 44 (1976): 456-66.

Attempts to determine the efficacy of Transcendental Meditation in stress situations and its ability to transform the
meditators into less anxious and more actualizing individuals.
Sixty subjects, half of whom had been meditators for more than
two years, the other half being non-meditators, were tested.
The researchers' confirm their hypotheses that: 1) the condition of meditation led to less automatic arousal and less
subjective anxiety; and 2) experienced meditators tend to show
personality traits more consistent with the expected meditation
effects.

1481. Goodman, Guruneel Singh Khalsa. "The Effects of an Advanced
      Yoga Practice, the Doei Shabd Kriya, on States of Conscious-
      ness." JOURNAL OF ALTERED STATES OF CONSCIOUSNESS 4 (1978-
      79): 369-83.

Discusses the effects of the author's own practice of an
advanced form of Kundalini Yoga over a 40-year period. The
postures adopted and the mantra used are described. Several
conclusions are drawn regarding the kinds of experiences and
altered states of consciousness which can be achieved. Among
the results listed is an increased motivation which this Yoga
stimulates.

1482. Gowan, John Curtis. "The Facilitation of Creativity Through
      Meditation Procedure." JOURNAL OF CREATIVE BEHAVIOR 12
      (1978): 156-60.

Reviews some of the research which has been done on Transcendental Meditation and concludes that the claim that it
increases one's creative performance is justified. The author,
who practices TM, accounts for this creativity by the fact
that meditation brings about a quasi-hypnotic state, which
renders one more open to the pre-conscious elements in one's
psyche. One could, therefore, attribute to TM the useful
educational objective of helping children and young adults to
greater creativity.

1483. Goyeche, John. "Yoga as Therapy in Psychosomatic Medicine."
      PSYCHOTHERAPY AND PSYCHOSOMATICS 31 (1979): 373-81.

Tries to convey an understanding of Yoga philosophy and
practice and its implications for preventing and treating
psychosomatic illnesses. The author points out that in
spite of their philosophical differences, Yoga therapy and
some Western self-regulatory treatments, such as progressive
relaxation, biofeedback methods, and breathing therapy, have
much in common. The rationales for the use of Yoga therapy
and the evidence for its success are provided. It is asserted
that the effectiveness of Yoga can in part be understood in
terms of neurophysiological theory.

1484. Goyeche, John, and Yujiro Ikemi. "Yoga as Potential Psycho-
      somatic Therapy." ASIAN MEDICAL JOURNAL 20 (1977): 90-96.

Postulates that psychosomatic disorders are related to the
patient's egocentricity, which accounts for symptoms like
heightened self-consciousness, increased dependency-needs,
social-interaction difficulties, and lack of emotional
expressiveness. Yoga treats these problems by addressing
itself to their root, namely, egocentricity. Yoga therapy
tends to produce the same results as autogenic training,
systematic desensitization, progressive relaxation, and
biofeedback. Several case studies of the application of
integral Yoga therapy are presented, and the effectiveness
of Yoga for treating psychosomatic illness is corroborated.

1485. Griffith, Fred F. "Meditation Research: Its Personal and
      Social Implications." FRONTIERS OF CONSCIOUSNESS. Edited
      by John White. New York: Julian Press, 1974, pp. 119-38.

Examines the claims of various schools of meditation which
promise health, happiness, increased powers of concentration,
and spiritual development. The scientific data on meditation
is discussed in relation to established psychological mechanisms and therapeutic techniques. Research on Yoga, Zen, and
TM are overviewed in connection with systematic desensitization and deautomatization. The author thinks that the claims
of the powers of meditation to lead a person to a sense of
deep relaxation have been substantiated by evidence. This
relaxation in turn reduces stress and produces mental catharsis with consequent psychological growth. Meditation has
thus a place in both therapy and education.

1486. Grisell, Ronald D. "Kundalini Yoga as Healing Agent."
      DIMENSIONS IN HOLISTIC HEALING (item 1288), pp. 441-61.

Presents Kundalini Yoga as a physical-psychological method
of preventive medicine. The basic Yoga therapy--with its use
of mantras and sound, breath control, and meditation--is described. Several principles of this approach to therapy are
outlined. Yoga can be applied in the treatment of drug
problems, severe headache (including migraine), and hypertension. It would seem that Yoga is effective, especially
in psychosomatic illnesses.

1487. Haines, Norma. "Zen Buddhism and Psychoanalysis: A Biblio-
       graphic Essay." PSYCHOLOGIA 15 (1975): 22-30.

       Reviews some of the literature on the relationship between
       Buddhism and psychoanalysis, including works which express
       Western interest in Zen. Literature on Eastern philosophies
       is also included.

1488. Hanley, Charles P., and James L. Slates. "Transcendental
       Meditation and Social Psychological Attitudes." JOURNAL
       OF PSYCHOLOGY 99 (1978): 121-27.

       Explores whether there is a correlation between TM and
       social-psychological attitude changes. The following six
       attitudes were selected for examination among college
       students: 1) social withdrawal; 2) negative conception of
       human nature; 3) positive self-image; 4) level of tolerance;
       5) sociability; and 6) social inadequacy. In all but the
       last-mentioned factors, practitioners scored well, confirm-
       ing previous studies which indicated that meditators have
       more positive attitudes than the general population. The
       researchers found that exposure to the philosophy of TM was
       not the cause of these positive attitudes, and that longer
       meditation practice was related to healthy psychological
       attitudes. The technique itself, it is suggested, might
       bring about the beneficial changes which make TM therapeutic.

1489. Harvey, John. "Behavior Therapy and Yoga." PSYCHOLOGY:
       EAST AND WEST (item 1367), pp. 50-74.

       Argues that, although behavior therapy and Yoga seem at
       first sight to be quite different, closer analysis reveals
       many important similarities. The basic differences between
       the two on the nature of truth and reality and on ultimate
       goals are outlined. Desensitization in Yoga and behavior
       therapy are discussed. Because behavior therapy techniques
       are venturing into new areas, such as biofeedback and thought
       control, one can expect an increasing interaction between
       Yoga and behavior therapy. The author's view is that many
       spiritual techniques, like Yoga, are practical means of deal-
       ing with psychological problems encountered in daily life.

1490. Hearn, R. J. "Zen Buddhism." ENCYCLOPEDIA OF PSYCHOLOGY
       (item 12), vol. 3, pp. 485-86.

       Summarizes briefly the main principles of Zen Buddhism and
       the major psychological evaluations of its practice. The
       author's view is that Zen "potentially provides potent addi-
       tional means whereby contemporary psychologists may treat the
       troubled" (p. 486).

1491. Heide, Fredrick J., and T. D. Borkovec. "Relaxation-Induced
       Anxiety: Paradoxical Anxiety Enhancement Due to Relaxation
       Training." JOURNAL OF CONSULTING AND CLINICAL PSYCHOLOGY
       51 (1983): 177-82.

Tests the hypothesis that some relaxation methods actually induced anxiety. Fourteen subjects suffering from general tension were divided into two groups, and each group was given one session of training in progressive relaxation or mantra meditation. It was found that focused meditation was more likely to produce anxiety. Progressive relaxation resulted in a greater reduction of anxiety and tension.

1492. Helminiak, Daniel A. "Meditation--Psychologically and Theologically Considered." PASTORAL PSYCHOLOGY 30 (1981): 6-20.

Summarizes research on meditation under six headings: 1) relaxation, 2) systematic desensitization, 3) release of repressed psychic material, 4) unstressing, 5) dissolution of habitual patterns of perception, and 6) cosmic consciousness. The practice of meditation seems recommendable to those who have a stable personality and a supportive community, and should not be adopted as a cure for psychological problems.

1493. Hemingway, Patricia Drake. THE TRANSCENDENTAL MEDITATION
PRIMER: HOW TO REDUCE TENSION AND START LIVING. New York:
Dell, 1975. xviii, 264 pp.

Provides an outline of the introductory and advanced lectures on Transcendental Meditation and an account of the initiation ritual. The positive effects of TM on sleep, work, creativity, stress reduction, sex, learning, and relationships to other people are described. TM, according to the author, is only one of the many positive life-supporting techniques (which include prayer, Zen, self-hypnosis, religious conver-sion, and Sufi dancing).

1494. Hendricks, C. G. "Meditation as Discrimination Training:
A Theoretical Note." JOURNAL OF TRANSPERSONAL PSYCHOLOGY
7 (1975): 144-46.

Argues that meditation is a process by which one learns how to discriminate one's thoughts. The effects of this knowledge are beneficial to psychological growth and devel-opment.

1495. Hewitt, Jay, and Ralph Miller. "Relative Effects of Meditation vs. Other Activities on Rating of Relaxation and
Enjoyment of Others." PSYCHOLOGICAL REPORTS 48 (1981):
395-98.

Investigates whether meditation, compared with other methods of tension reduction, is more effective, and whether its effects improve other aspects of one's life. The authors conclude that meditation, while it does reduce tension, does not produce better results than other means of stress reduc-tion. They are, however, cautious of their conclusions because they believe that better control subjects were needed in their experiments.

1496. Hirai, Tomio. ZEN MEDITATION THERAPY. Tokyo: Japan Publica-
          tions Co., 1975. 103 pp.

       Proposes Zen as a method of physical and mental health,
       which is not necessarily connected to Buddhism or to its
       cultural background. Zen is a way to control one's posture
       and breath and to achieve stability of the mind. The result-
       ing ability to control one's mind leads to the resolution of
       personal problems and to the acquisition of several spiritual
       and psychological benefits, such as the skill to better live
       and work with others. Zen can be seen as a form of meditative
       contemplation which leads to self-examination and restores
       one's mental health.

1497. Hirai, Tomio. THE PSYCHOPHYSIOLOGY OF ZEN. Tokyo: Igaku
          Shoin, Ltd., 1974. vi, 147 pp.

       Investigates Zen meditation from two points of view, phys-
       iological and psychological. Two forms of Zen meditation
       practiced in the Soto and Rinzai sects are described. The
       implication of the psychological aspects of Zen are discussed
       with reference mainly to experimental work conducted by Japa-
       nese psychologists. In a chapter on Zen and psychotherapy,
       Zen meditation is linked with Morita therapy, autogenic train-
       ing, and self-control techniques.

1498. Hjelle, Larry A. "Transcendental Meditation and Psychological
          Health." PERCEPTUAL AND MOTOR SKILLS 39 (1974): 623-28.

       Reports on several tests, namely, Bendig's Anxiety Scale,
       Rotter's Locus of Control Scale, and Shostrom's Personality
       Orientation Inventory, administered to 15 experienced tran-
       scendental meditators and to 20 young adults who had recently
       been initiated into the practice. The results show that the
       former were less anxious, more internally controlled, and
       more self-actualized. The author suggests the use of TM for
       clients experiencing vocational, social, or personal problems,
       such as depression, suicidal thoughts, academic deficiencies,
       and sexual difficulties.

1499. Holmes, David S. "Self-Control of Somatic Arousal: An Ex-
          amination of the Effects of Meditation and Biofeedback."
          AMERICAN BEHAVIORAL SCIENTIST 28 (1985): 486-96.

       Contends that there is little or no support for the wide-
       spread opinion that meditation and biofeedback are effective
       ways of reducing somatic arousal or other symptoms. Simple
       rest can achieve just as much as these two techniques. The
       author reviews the methodological issues and related findings,
       and urges researchers to include appropriate controls in
       their investigations.

1500. Holmes, David S. "Meditation and Somatic Arousal Reduction:
          A Review of Experimental Evidence." AMERICAN PSYCHOLOGIST
          39 (1984): 1-10.

Reviews meditation research under four sections: 1) conceptual and methodological issues and problems; 2) evidence for lower somatic arousal for meditators and for subjects who are simply resting; 3) evidence for less somatic arousal in subjects who meditate; and 4) overall conclusions. The author concludes that there is no real evidence that the practice of meditation is more effective than simple rest periods. Over seventy references are provided, mostly to physiological studies on meditation.

1501. Holmes, David S., Sheldon Soloman, Bruce M. Cappo, and Jeffrey L. Greenberg. "Effects of Transcendental Meditation Versus Resting on Physiological and Subjective Arousal." JOURNAL OF PERSONALITY AND SOCIAL PSYCHOLOGY 44 (1983): 1245-52.

Gives the results of an experiment designed to correct the methodological and statistical weaknesses of earlier studies on Transcendental Meditation. The researchers observed both physical and subjective arousal in highly trained and experienced meditators, and compared the results to non-meditators while they rested. They also measured their subjects on four separate occasions. The results indicate that: 1) there is no evidence for the generalized effects of meditation on arousal; 2) meditation was linked with a decrease in physiological and subjective arousal; 3) the same lower levels of arousal were achieved by both meditators and non-meditators while resting; and 4) meditation was not more effective than resting for reducing subjective arousal. It is argued that these findings are relevant to those interested in personality functioning, stress management, and psychotherapy.

1502. Hoover, Thomas. "Zen Culture: 'Modern' and Mind-Manipulating." REVISION: A JOURNAL OF CONSCIOUSNESS AND CHANGE 2.1 (1979): 59-63.

Proposes the view that Zen cultural forms--in architecture, ink painting, ceramics, landscape gardening, and Haiku (literary form)--are designed to operate on the mind in a manipulative, non-Western fashion. The goal is to encourage people to be spontaneous and to elicit direct, intuitive experiences. This leads one to a better acquaintance with the non-rational mind and to a new view of the world. The underlying assumption seems to be that the individual's well-being is enhanced.

1503. Hopkins, J. Thomas, and Laura J. Hopkins. "A Study of Yoga and Concentration." ACADEMIC THERAPY 14 (1979): 341-49.

Reports on a modified Yoga program for young school children (between the ages of 6 and 12) to test the potential of Yoga in dissipating excessive energy and fostering concentration. The results support the view that physical education (such as Yoga and general psychomotor activity) should be an essential part of an elementary school program. There is no evidence, however, that Yoga significantly increased the performance of the students.

1504.   Ikemi, Yurijo. "Eastern and Western Approaches to Self-
        Regulation." CANADIAN JOURNAL OF PSYCHIATRY 24 (1979):
        471-80.

        Shows how different Eastern and Western therapeutic methods
        are applied in daily practice and explains their similarities
        and differences. Zen, Yoga, and Transcendental Meditation,
        by creating altered psychological states, help a person reach
        self-actualization. These autogenic, self-regulatory methods,
        however, have their limitations and, in serious cases, psycho-
        analytic or behavioral approaches should be used. Naikan,
        Morita, and Zen therapy should be reevaluated from the stand-
        point of behavior and existential therapy.

1505.   Ikemi, Yujiro, Hitoshi Ishihawa, J. R. M. Goyche, and Y.
        Sasaki. "'Positive' and 'Negative' Aspects of 'Altered
        States of Consciousness' Induced by Autogenic Training, Zen,
        and Yoga." PSYCHOTHERAPY AND PSYCHOSOMATICS 30 (1978):
        170-78.

        Observes that because altered states of consciousness have
        become widely used by psychotherapists, one must acknowledge
        both the positive and negative results which such states can
        produce. The most important contributions of religious
        practices, such as Yoga and Zen, to psychoanalysis may be a
        broadening and deepening of its horizons and the clarifica-
        tion of its major goals. Altered states of consciousness may
        force people to confront unconscious material when they are
        not prepared to deal with it. The authors think that one
        would expect less psychotic problems with classical Yoga than
        with Zen. The negative aspects of ASC can be controlled or
        prevented by, among other things, preparatory education and
        an evaluation of the person's personality.

1506.   Jedrczak, Andrew, and Geoffrey Clements. "The TM-Siddhi
        Programme and Motor Skills." PERCEPTUAL AND MOTOR SKILLS
        59 (1984): 999-1000.

        Reports briefly on several studies which confirm that the
        practice of TM-Siddhi meditation, as taught by Maharishi
        Mahesh Yogi, produces a positive effect on field independence.

1507.   Jichaku, Patrick, George Y. Fujita, and S. I. Shapiro. "The
        Double Bind and Koan Zen." JOURNAL OF MIND AND BEHAVIOR 5
        (1984): 211-21.

        Examines Zen Koan practice from the epistemological stand-
        point of double-bind theory, which has been linked with the
        context of evoking schizophrenia. The "koan," it is main-
        tained, creates a beneficial double-bind situation, and
        suggests ways in which pathogenic double-binds can be trans-
        formed into beneficial ones. The nature of the double-bind,
        which is basically a paradox with emotional and behavioral
        implications, is briefly explained, as is the way it operates
        in Zen. Several issues, such as whether beneficial double-
        binds are peculiar to Zen, are raised.

1508. Johnston, William. SILENT MUSIC: THE SCIENCE OF MEDITATION.
       New York: Harper and Row, 1974. 190 pp.

       Discusses the use and effects of meditation techniques in
       various religious traditions. The recent rise of interest
       in the practice of meditation and in the different levels of
       human consciousness is described. One section deals with
       healing and covers the effects of meditation on health.
       Meditational therapy is distinguished from religious medi-
       tation, the latter having the added quality of "grace." Some
       kinds of meditation are beneficial and therapeutic for cer-
       tain people. Scientific studies show that those who choose
       a meditative or contemplative life in a Carmelite monastery,
       Hindu ashram, or Zen temple are not seeking a refuge from the
       reality of everyday life.

1509. Kabar, Sudhir. "The Person in Tantra and Psychoanalysis."
       SAMIKSA 35 (1981): 85-104.

       Hints that there are parallels between psychoanalysis and
       Tantric Yoga, notwithstanding some major differences. Both
       recognize that the two great experiences of life, namely,
       separation from one's mother in the first three years of life
       and differentiation between the two sexes, are the major human
       traumas. Both consequently stress the sexual act and its
       influence on the psyche. Tantra should not be identified with
       exotic sexual behavior, but is rather considered as an ancient
       and arduous way to the pursuit of happiness.

1510. Kabar, Sudhir. "Relative Realities: Images of Adulthood in
       Psychoanalysis and the Yogas." SAMIKSA 31 (1977): 37-48.

       Explores the notions of psychological maturity in Western
       psychologies and in the various schools of Yoga. In psycho-
       analysis, maturity is linked with the humanistic ideals of
       moderation, control, and responsibility. From the Hindu point
       of view, there are two stages of adulthood: the first is one
       of psychic balance, instinctual restraint, and freedom from
       anxiety; in the second a higher order of knowledge is reached.
       This second stage involves a shift from outward to inward
       reflection, and contains a mystical element. The final goals
       offered by psychoanalysis and Yogic psychology are based on
       different visions of reality. These divergences should not
       be called pathological.

1511. Kabat-Zinn, Jon, Leslie Lipworth, and Robert Burney. "The
       Clinical Use of Mindfulness Meditation for the Self-Regula-
       tion of Chronic Pain." JOURNAL OF BEHAVIORAL MEDICINE 8
       (1985): 163-90.

       Reports on a ten-week experiment testing the effects
       of Buddhist mindfulness meditation on 90 chronically ill
       patients. Significant reductions were observed in negative
       body images, inhibition of activity by pain, mood distur-
       bances, and psychological symptoms, such as anxiety and

depression. This Eastern meditation has several unique features which recommend it as a reliable clinical method for
teaching self-regulation and as a psychological intervention in persistent pain. Besides being less expensive than
traditional methods, it stresses self-observation and responsibility. It is applicable, moreover, in several perceptual,
cognitive, and behavioral contexts, and facilitates deep
psychological relaxation.

1512. Kaplan, Stephen. "An Appraisal of a Psychological Approach
      to Meditation." ZYGON: A JOURNAL OF RELIGION AND SCIENCE
      13 (1978): 83-101.

      Examines some of the current psychological theories on the
      nature of meditation with the intention of discovering which
      functions it is suited to serve. Three areas are studied,
      namely, the mechanics of meditation, altered states of con-
      sciousness during meditation, and its psychological and physio-
      logical results. The author concludes that the experiences
      attained in meditation "are not those which can provide us
      with knowledge of the world beyond our own immediacy" (p. 94).

1513. Katz, Richard, and Edward Rolde. "Community Alternatives to
      Psychotherapy." PSYCHOTHERAPY: THEORY, RESEARCH, AND PRAC-
      TICE 18 (1981): 365-74.

      Maintains that there are important theoretical conflicts
      between dynamic therapy and alternative therapies, such as
      Alcoholics Anonymous, and alternatives to therapy, such as
      Transcendental Meditation, Zen, and the meditation taught by
      the Divine Life Mission. Among the major conflicts listed
      are: serious disagreements about the nature of reality, the
      existence and validity of the ego, and the functions the ego
      is meant to represent. Models for combining the different
      approaches are available, and two case studies are brought
      forth to illustrate how this combination is expected to work.
      In such consumer packages, however, the individual's conflicts
      are often ignored or deemphasized. It is admitted that some
      of the combinations could be therapeutically valuable, but
      further research is needed to determine which can be used in
      treatment.

1514. Keefe, Thomas. "Meditation and the Psychotherapist." AMERI-
      CAN JOURNAL OF ORTHOPSYCHIATRY 45 (1975): 484-89.

      Argues that meditation behavior and technique need not in-
      clude the suspension of rational thought, as it is required
      in religion and mysticism. Three areas are covered, namely:
      1) the identification of the barriers to meditation as a
      behavior-changing method; 2) the definition and description
      of meditation; and 3) the ways in which meditation can be
      helpful to both the patient and therapist. The author holds
      that the common technique of meditation, which strives for
      "the minimization of thought in the verbal, lineal, and
      analytic sense" (p. 486), need not be pursued in the context

of a particular spiritual discipline or community. Meditation can further enhance both interpersonal functioning and the therapist's effectiveness.

1515. Keefe, Thomas. "A Zen Perspective on Social Network." SOCIAL CASEWORK 56 (1975): 140-44.

Describes the Zen experience, and points out its relevancy for the social worker, the client, and their relationship. Because Zen stresses the here-and-now and the changing nature of all phenomena, clients will be able to accept the fact that change is part of life, become aware of their true desires, needs, and feelings, and succeed in living in the present moment without feeling guilty about the past and worrying about the future. Zen encourages the direct perception of reality, which enhances one's capacity for empathy and imbues the person with a sense of compassion, both of which are crucial in the relationship between social workers and their clients.

1516. Kennedy, Raymond B. "Self-Induced Depersonalization Syndrome." AMERICAN JOURNAL OF PSYCHIATRY 133 (1976): 1326-28.

Reports on two subjects who, after engaging in meditation techniques as recommended by a Yoga group and Arica respectively, experienced depersonalization and derealization. The author thinks that such casualties might increase, especially among those who seek to alter their consciousness outside a supportive group setting.

1517. Kindlon, Daniel J. "Comparison of Use of Meditation and Rest in Treatment of Test Anxiety." PSYCHOLOGICAL REPORTS 53 (1983): 931-38.

Seeks to determine the effects of meditation on the anxiety of college undergraduates brought about by exams. The conclusion reached was that meditation, or a rest/sleep period, could equally lower the level of test anxiety as measured by self-report, performance, and physiological indices. Teaching meditation is not a solution for psychological problems. Those who have practiced meditation for many years within a religious belief system have gone through some marked changes which have been registered on the EEG. The therapeutic significance of this is not discussed.

1518. Kirsh, Irving, and David Henry. "Self-Desensitization and Meditation in the Reduction of Public Speaking Anxiety." JOURNAL OF CONSULTING AND CLINICAL PSYCHOLOGY 47 (1979): 536-41.

Tests the effects which 1) systematic desensitization, 2) desensitization with meditation, and 3) meditation by itself might have on those students who are anxious when they speak in public. All the treatments were found to be equally effective in reducing this kind of anxiety.

1519. Klajner, Felix, Lorne M. Hartman, and Mark B. Sobell. "Treat-
       ment of Substance Abuse by Relaxation Training: A Review of
       Its Rationale, Efficacy, and Mechanisms." ADDICTIVE BEHAV-
       IORS 9 (1984): 41-55.

       Reviews the efficacy of relaxation training techniques (in-
       cluding progressive relaxation and meditation) as a treatment
       for anxiety and for alcohol and drug abuse. The conclusion
       drawn is that "the available evidence offers neither clear
       support nor clear disconfirmation of the efficacy of such
       techniques" (p. 50). The need for clinical research addres-
       sing the following issues is underscored: appropriate control
       groups; adequate follow up assessment; proper assessment
       measures; optimization of training; matching of client and
       treatment; and continuation of techniques after treatment.

1520. Kline, Kenneth S., Edward M. Doherty, and Frank H. Farley.
       "Transcendental Meditation, Self/Actualization, and Global
       Personality." JOURNAL OF GENERAL PSYCHOLOGY 106 (1982):
       3-8.

       Applies several psychological tests (MMPI and TSC) to a
       group of recovering alcoholics and of individuals with emo-
       tional problems who were taking part in a three-month TM
       program, and to a control group. No significant effects of
       the meditation were noticed. The authors discuss possible
       reasons why their results differ from most of the previous
       research on TM. The need for caution in conducting research
       on TM is underscored.

1521. Kohr, Richard L. "Changes in Subjective Meditation Experience
       During a Short Term Project." JOURNAL OF ALTERED STATES OF
       CONSCIOUSNESS 3 (1977-78): 221-34.

       Investigates the quality of meditation over a 28-day period
       by giving daily questions to over 140 participants. The
       results showed that low-anxiety subjects reported new, satis-
       fying experiences and a greater sense of mental alertness,
       while the low-problem group was less frustrated and more
       able to relax. Suggestions for future research are given.

1522. Kolsawalla, Maharukh B. "An Experimental Investigation into
       the Effectiveness of Some Yogic Variables as a Mechanism of
       Change in the Value-Attitude System." JOURNAL OF INDIAN
       PSYCHOLOGY 1.1 (1978): 59-68.

       Tests two hypotheses about Yogic meditation (similar to
       TM): 1) it changes a person from closed- to open-mindedness,
       leading to less dogmatic opinions; and 2) it reduces the level
       of tension, resulting in a more positive attitude to life.
       Three groups of subjects were tested on several personality
       scales, and both theories were confirmed. Other positive
       results were also recorded: an increase in emotional maturity,
       an urge to reach out to people, and a general sense of well-
       being. The study found no evidence that the use of a special
       mantra made any contribution to the good effects of meditation.

1523. Kopp, Sheldon B. "Tantric Therapy." JOURNAL OF CONTEMPORARY
        PSYCHOTHERAPY 9 (1978): 131-34.

        Maintains that the psychotherapeutic technique which, like
        Tantric Yoga, uses paradox, could transform and overcome the
        client's resistances. The author describes a few paradoxical
        instructions he gave his patients and shows how the seemingly-
        strange directives actually helped his clients.

1524. Krishna, Gopi. "Meditation: Is It Always Beneficial? Some
        Positive and Negative Views." JOURNAL OF ALTERED STATES
        OF CONSCIOUSNESS 2.1 (1975): 37-47.

        Reflects on the current wave of interest in higher states
        of consciousness in Western culture, and argues that it is
        not a fad, but rather a spiritual search which accompanies a
        certain level of civilization. There are three dangers to
        which the author draws attention, namely: 1) that of confus-
        ing mystical experience with biofeedback; 2) that of equating
        mystical consciousness with drug states; and 3) that of
        thinking that true illumination can be acquired by passive
        forms of meditative tricks. Enlightenment is the state of
        enhanced awareness which goes beyond the senses and the mind.
        There is an implicit criticism of many new religious practices
        in the West, which are neither genuinely religious nor psycho-
        logically healthy.

1525. Kroll, Una. THE HEALING POTENTIAL OF TRANSCENDENTAL MEDITA-
        TION. Atlanta: John Knox Press, 1974. 176 pp.

        Presents a study of TM aimed at making sure that it is not
        harmful to patients and at finding out how the technique works.
        It is concluded that TM is definitely effective in healing
        stress. The affinities between TM and Christianity are also
        explored. The author holds that while TM bridges the gap
        between scientific and religious experiences, there are cer-
        tain religious and medical difficulties which it cannot answer.
        Though TM has a valuable role to play in the healing process,
        it should not be used as a panacea for all stress conditions.

1526. Krynicki, Victor E. "The Double Orientation of the Ego in
        the Practice of Zen." AMERICAN JOURNAL OF PSYCHOANALYSIS
        40 (1980): 239-48.

        Maintains that there is a psychopathological regression in
        Zen practice, during which primordial states of a union of
        self with object can occur. To understand the conflict
        between union and separateness in Zen practice, the following
        areas are discussed: 1) the childhood and adolescence of Zen
        practitioners (especially traumatic and anxiety experiences);
        2) the reactivation of childhood memories; 3) the sense of
        timelessness and spacelessness; and 4) the appearance of
        symbolic imagery of separation and death. It is concluded
        that Zen meditators exhibit unresolved anxieties as well as
        deviation in self-development. Meditation produces both
        relaxation and ego-regression, while the state of enlighten-

ment is one of symbiotic union with others. Psychoanalysis
differs from meditation in that it rebuilds structures and,
therefore, does not need the experience of merging. It is
admitted that both meditation and psychoanalysis relieve
separation anxiety.

1527. Kubose, Sunnan K. "An Experimental Investigation of Psychological Aspects of Meditation." PSYCHOLOGIA 19 (1976):
1-10.

Categorizes meditation research under three headings,
namely, description, production, and utilization, and explores the variables in each of them. The following areas
are the focus of this study: 1) disruptive occurrences during
meditation; 2) exercises, such as sitting still and concentrating, which produce the meditation effects; and 3) the
actual results one obtains by practicing meditation. The
experiment was conducted on 27 introductory psychology
students at the University of North Carolina. The results
show that one of the effects of concentration on one's breathing is the improvement of control over one's thoughts. In
other areas, however, as in the 14 scales of the POI questionnaire, no statistically significant effects were revealed.
The author suggests that the individual's motivations and
expectations should be investigated carefully, since they
influence, in part, the effects of meditation practice.

1528. Kubose, Sunnan K., and Takao Umemoto. "Creativity and the
Zen Koan." PSYCHOLOGIA 23 (1980): 1-19.

Argues that creative problem solving and reflection on a
Zen "koan" share several things in common. Both involve, for
example, getting rid of prior influencing factors and the use
of common psychological processes. Further, both go through
four stages: those of preparation, incubation, illumination,
and evaluation.

1529. Kuna, Daniel. "Meditation and Work." VOCATIONAL GUIDANCE
QUARTERLY 23 (1975): 342-46.

Observes that meditation has become part of the American
scene, and that it is "part of a cultural and historical
movement as well as a stimulus for individual and social
change" (p. 342). Transcendental Meditation is briefly
described and some research findings summarized. The author
believes that meditation leads to physiological and psychological changes that are conducive to better work performance.
Rehabilitation, vocational and employment counselors as well
as work evaluators and adjustment specialists can perform
their respective tasks better if they practice meditation.

1530. Kutz, Ilan, Joan Z. Borysenko, and Herbert Benson. "Meditation and Psychotherapy: A Rationale For the Integration of
Dynamic Psychotherapy, the Relaxation Response, and Mindfulness Meditation." AMERICAN JOURNAL OF PSYCHIATRY 142
(1985): 1-8.

Presents a uniform theoretical model for incorporating the
practice of meditation in psychotherapy. Meditation can be
viewed apart from its cultural and religious trappings as a
set of mental exercises, which bring about psychological
changes called the relaxation response. Several psychological effects of Buddhist meditation are relevant to psychotherapy. The meditator starts by developing a detached
observation that is suitable for examining one's own ideas
and feelings. An intensification of perceptual awareness
and emotional receptivity, which allow for the emergence of
repressed material, follows. The therapeutic value of meditation lies in its potential for relabeling and restructuring
one's cognitive and mental state. Both psychotherapy and
meditation profit from their combination in a clinical setting.
The latter intensifies the healing process; the former provides
the theoretical grounding of meditation, which is detached
from its religious roots.

1531. Lazarus, Arnold A. "Psychiatric Problems Precipitated by
      Transcendental Meditation." PSYCHOLOGICAL REPORTS 39
      (1976): 601-2.

Argues against the promotion of TM as a solution for all
psychological ills. When properly applied to selected cases,
TM can be therapeutically beneficial in relieving stress,
tension, and anxiety. On the other hand, TM can have negative effects, such as increased depression, heightening of
tension and restlessness, depersonalization, and even mental
breakdown. Because of the many material benefits promised
to meditators, a strong sense of failure and ineptitude can
result when the benefits do not materialize. The author
thinks that TM is more effective with people who have moderate
levels of tension and anxiety.

1532. Lehrer, Paul M., Robert M. Woolfolk, Anthony J. Rooney,
      Barbara McCann, and Patricia Carrington. "Progressive
      Relaxation and Meditation: A Study of Psychophysiological
      and Therapeutic Differences Between the Two Techniques."
      BEHAVIOR RESEARCH AND THERAPY 21 (1983): 651-62.

Reports on a study of anxious patients to check the theory
that different relaxation procedures bring about specific
results. The authors discovered that most of these procedures
are noteworthy more for the similar, than for the diverse,
effects they produce. Meditation, unlike simple relaxation,
seemed to increase transient anxiety, but it also provided a
better motivation. It is theorized that meditation could be
more effective among young hyperactive children and psychotic
individuals, while relaxation might be more helpful for those
suffering from physical ailments.

1533. Lesh, Terry V. "Zen Meditation and the Development of Em-
      pathy in Counselors." JOURNAL OF HUMANISTIC PSYCHOLOGY
      10.1 (1974): 39-74.

Attempts to determine if a relationship exists between the
practice of Zazen and the development of empathy in counselors. After a description of empathy and Zen meditation,
the author formulates and tests the hypothesis that the two
are connected. Three groups of students participated in a
four-week long experiment. The results show that meditation,
which is positively related to openness to experience, significantly increased their empathetic ability, and that it led
to self-actualization which is itself related to the ability
to empathize.

*   Lesh, Terry V. "Zen and Psychotherapy: A Partially Annotated
         Bibliography." Cited above as item 32.

1534.   LeShan, Lawrence. HOW TO MEDITATE: A GUIDE TO SELF-DISCOVERY.
         Boston: Little, Brown, and Co., 1974. 161 pp.

         Presents a practical guide to various kinds of meditation
         techniques, including Zen, Yoga, Sufism, and Jewish and Chris-
         tian mysticism. Other topics dealt with are the psychological
         and physiological effects of meditation, the process of choos-
         ing a teacher, alluring traps in meditation and mysticism, and
         the role of meditation in psychotherapy. It is explained how
         meditation leads one to a higher state of consciousness and
         contributes to an increase in efficacy and enthusiasm in one's
         daily life. A set of guidelines for psychotherapists who
         might want to integrate psychotherapeutic and meditational
         procedures is presented.

1535.   Leslie, Robert C. "Yoga and the Fear of Death." JOURNAL OF
         TRANSPERSONAL PSYCHOLOGY 8 (1976): 128-32.

         Points out that, according to the Yoga Sutras of Pantajali,
         the fear of death is one of the five major obstacles to self-
         realization. Pantajali explains the fear of death as an
         attempt to deny its existence, rather than face the fact that
         one's personal life will come to an end. The theory and
         practice of Yoga can help the individual accept the reality
         of death.

1536.   Linden, William. "Practice of Meditation By School Children
         and Their Levels of Field Dependence-Independence, Test-
         Anxiety, and Reading Achievement." JOURNAL OF CONSULTING
         AND CLINICAL PSYCHOLOGY 41 (1973): 139-43.

         Gives the results of a study of 26 third-grade children who
         practiced meditation over an 18-week period. In relation to
         two control groups, the meditators became more independent and
         less anxious about exams. No differences in reading ability
         were apparent. Meditation seems to make a person more alert
         to certain environmental sensory data and more aware of one's
         own experiences. In general, meditation was judged to be
         psychologically advantageous because it reduced stress and
         anxiety. The author suggests the possible use of meditation
         as a "training method of self-discovery and self-mastery."

1537. Majumdar, Sachindra Kumar. INTRODUCTION TO YOGA PRINCIPLES
       AND PRACTICES. Secaucus, NJ: Citadel Press, 1976. pp. 318.
       First published in 1964.

       Provides the philosophical background to Yoga and describes
       two of its main practices: Hatha Yoga and meditation. The
       latter dissolves tensions, fears, and anxieties, and brings
       about many positive attitudes to life. Modern man is faced
       with the problem of meaning. The resulting neuroses cannot
       be addressed by Western psychotherapy which deals primarily
       with integration and individuation. Yoga provides the theory
       and practice to enable us to come to grips with the underlying
       spiritual problems of our age.

1538. McDonagh, John M. "The Double Mantra Technique." JOURNAL OF
       CONTEMPORARY PSYCHOTHERAPY 8 (1977): 109-11.

       Discusses the mind's tendency to be distracted from the
       mantra, and suggests the use of several mantras because they
       have definite calming effects. The method of "double mantra"
       is described. Besides having the same beneficial results on
       its practitioners, this method was found particularly helpful
       to those who had difficulty focusing on a single mantra.

1539. Meissner, John, and Michael Pirot. "Unbiasing the Brain: the
       Effects of Meditation on the Cerebral Hemisphere." SOCIAL
       BEHAVIOR AND PERSONALITY 11 (1983): 65-76.

       Assesses the effect of Transcendental Meditation on the
       cerebral hemisphere and discovers that it suppresses the
       left side and enhances the use of the right side. According
       to the authors, this explains, among other things, why medi-
       tators report phenomenological descriptions of altered states
       of consciousness, such as heightened clarity and greater
       ability to see hues and color richness. The clinical impli-
       cations of the results are discussed, and the authors think
       that more research is needed to determine what kinds of
       psychopathology can be treated by meditation.

1540. Meltzer, Gloria. "Some Applications of Yoga to the Treatment
       of Drug Addicts." YOGA RESEARCH 1 (978): 31-38.

       Describes her application of Yoga techniques to treat drug
       addicts. Yoga exercises, such as mantra chanting and pranayama
       (breathing), decrease impulsive behavior and reduce tensions
       and feelings of frustration. They also indirectly lead to
       more individual autonomy and strengthen one's self-acceptance
       and self-esteem. Yoga can further be of assistance in reduc-
       ing withdrawal symptoms. As patients respond to Yoga, they
       lose their defensiveness and begin to relate warmly to their
       peers and to authority figures.

1541. Mooney, Lucindi Francis. STORMING EASTERN TEMPLES: A PSYCHO-
       LOGICAL EXPLORATION OF YOGA. Wheaton, IL: Theosophical
       Publishing House, 1976. 207 pp.

Explores Yoga from the point of view of Jungian psychology,
which sees Yoga as a method of psychic hygiene for Western
users. Yoga can be highly therapeutic for those verging on
loss of ego and on identification with some contents of the
unconscious.

1542. Morse, Donald R., and M. Laurence Furst. "Meditation: An In-
       Depth Study." JOURNAL OF THE AMERICAN SOCIETY OF PSYCHO-
       SOMATIC DENTISTRY AND MEDICINE 29.5 (1982): 1-96.

Presents a comprehensive study of meditation with 72 subjects at Temple University School of Dentistry carried out
between 1978 and 1982. The following aspects of meditation
are considered: 1) the use of simple words for meditation;
2) its psychosomatic effects; 3) the physiological and psychological response to its practice; 4) personality differences,
which influence the effects of meditation; and 5) its stress-
reducing potential. The authors conclude that meditation can
actually be taught in one session, that simple meaningful words
are as effective as mantras, that proper use can result in
many benefits, and that regular use can reduce stress.

1543. Murray, John B. "What is Meditation? Does it Help?" GENETIC
       PSYCHOLOGY MONOGRAPHS 106 (1982): 86-115.

Surveys current research on meditation techniques, which
are being used by businessmen and women, college students,
and professional athletes to obtain relief from tension and
to acquire self-control, knowledge, and peace of mind. The
historical and cultural origins of meditation and its physiological and psychological correlates are briefly dealt with.
Experiments on Zen, Yoga, and TM are evaluated. The author
thinks that methodological limitations (such as small samples
and lack of control of important cognitive and social variables) prevent firm conclusions from being drawn on the
therapeutic effects of meditation.

1544. Naranjo, Claudio. "Meditation and Psychosomatic Health."
       DIMENSIONS IN WHOLISTIC HEALING (item 1288), pp. 253-65.

Argues that meditation is not only a way to enlightenment,
but also a practice beneficial to physical and mental health.
Four basic types and four dimensions of meditation are proposed, all of which converge in the meditator's final goal of
higher consciousness. The role of relaxation is discussed.
Meditation can be a therapeutic way to better psychological
health.

1545. Naug, R. N. "Yoga Therapy in Neurotic Disorders." INDIAN
       JOURNAL OF CLINICAL PSYCHOLOGY 2 (1975): 87-90.

Describes the use of Yoga in the treatment of 20 patients
who suffered from different kinds of neurotic problems. Most
of those treated registered at least some moderate improvement.

Although Yoga is recommended as an effective treatment, the author cautions that in certain types of neuroses harmful results may occur if the Yoga treatment is applied without proper supervsision.

1546. Nespor, Karel. "The Combination of Psychiatric Treatment and Yoga." INTERNATIONAL JOURNAL OF PSYCHOSOMATICS 32.2 (1985): 24-27.

Points out that Yoga appears to be helpful in preventing stress-related disorders and treating psychosomatic ones. The author, who has experimented with the use of Yoga in psychiatry for five years, examines the possibility of applying Yoga as a treatment for drug and alcohol addiction. The possible combination of medical drugs and Yoga, or psychotherapy and Yoga, or hypnosis and Yoga are discussed. Yoga seems to be a beneficial ingredient in any therapy which seeks to control human addictions.

1547. Nidich, Sanford, William Seeman, and Thomas Duskin. "Influence of Transcendental Meditation: A Replication." JOURNAL OF COUNSELING PSYCHOLOGY 20 (1973): 565-66.

Summarizes a successful repetition of an experiment which some of the authors had conducted on Transcendental Meditators (see item 594). The results confirm the positive influence of TM on self-actualization.

1548. Norberg, Robert B. "Meditation: Future Guidance for Career Exploration." VOCATIONAL GUIDANCE QUARTERLY 22 (1974): 267-71.

Recommends meditation and other forms of mystical practices as means of career exploration through heightened self-understanding and as a balance to the goals of the objective scientific approach. Meditation is, therefore, indirectly seen as a means for self-development and as a useful tool in the hands of vocational counselors.

1549. Norton, G. R., and Wendy E. Johnson. "A Comparison Between Two Relaxation Procedures For Reducing Cognitive and Somatic Anxiety." JOURNAL OF BEHAVIOR THERAPY AND EXPERIMENTAL PSYCHIATRY 14 (1983): 209-14.

Tests the hypothesis that those who experience cognitive anxiety might benefit more from Agni Yoga, while those who suffer from somatic anxiety are more likely to profit by using progressive relaxation techniques. Subjects who expressed a moderate fear of God were used in the experiment and the hypothesis was confirmed. The researchers think, however, that the effects of Yoga on cognitive anxiety are still far from clear.

1550. Nuernberger, Phil. "Yoga Encounter Groups." PSYCHOLOGY: EAST AND WEST (item 1367), pp. 75-101.

Describes the psychology of a Yoga encounter that is unique
in both its philosophy and techniques. In such an encounter
the focus is on self-awareness, which leads to a natural
transformation, including self-mastery and the development of
one's full potential. A Yoga encounter group can lead to a
better understanding of, and dealing with, one's emotion in the
process of growth. A case history of one person is presented
to show how a Yoga encounter works.

1551.   Nystul, Michael S., and Margaret Garde. "Comparison of Self
        Concepts of Transcendental Meditators and Non-Meditators."
        PSYCHOLOGICAL REPORTS 41 (1977): 303-6.

        Uses the Tennessee Self-Concept Scale to test 15 Australians,
        who had been practicing TM for a mean of three years, and an
        equal number of non-meditators. It was found that meditators
        project a consistently more positive image of themselves than
        those who did not meditate.

1552.   Onda, Akira. "Zen, Hypnosis, and Creativity." INTERPERSONAL
        DEVELOPMENT 5 (1974-75): 156-63.

        Focuses on several hypnotic elements in Zen, and describes
        the mental process during Zen meditation which encourages
        the development of creativity. The following areas are con-
        sidered: concentration, meditation, relaxation of body and
        mind, suggestion, separation from environment, tension reduc-
        tion, self-control, self-development, and contemplation. The
        author holds that autogenic training, counseling, sensitivity
        training, and various religious practices, such as Yoga, are
        comparable to Zen.

1553.   Orme-Johnson, David W. "Automatic Stability and Transcen-
        dental Meditation." PSYCHOSOMATIC MEDICINE 35 (1973):
        341-45.

        Conducts the Galvanic Skin Response Test on several medita-
        tors and on a control group. The results indicate that TM
        practitioners develop rapid GSR habituation and low levels of
        spontaneous GSR. These features are related to physiological
        and psychological features of good mental health, such as a
        strong ego, independence, an outgoing personality, and less
        susceptibility to stress. TM meditators were judged to be
        more stable than the control subjects.

1554.   Orme-Johnson, David W., and John T. Farrow, Editors. SCIEN-
        TIFIC RESEARCH ON THE TRANSCENDENTAL MEDITATION PROGRAMS.
        COLLECTED PAPERS, VOL. 1. Seelisberg, Switzerland: Maharishi
        European Research University Press, Second Edition, 1977.
        722 pp.

        Contains over 100 papers on TM, some of which had been
        previously published in scientific journals. This massive
        volume is divided into five parts: 1) the physiology of TM;
        2) its psychology; 3) its sociology; 4) theoretical papers;

and 5) the TM-Siddhi program. The articles depict TM as a means to physical, mental, and psychological health, a cure to many social ills, and a path to enlightenment. Among the many benefits of TM are listed an increase in intelligence and academic performance, development of one's personality, the rehabilitation of drug users, and an overall improvement in the quality of life.

Contains items 594, 1456, 1553, 1562.

1555. Otis, Leon S. "Adverse Effects of Transcendental Meditation." MEDITATION: CLASSICAL AND CONTEMPORARY PERSPECTIVES (item 45), pp. 201-8.

Concludes, from experiments conducted on Transcendental Meditators, that the longer a person practices TM and the more committed he or she becomes to TM as a way of life, the greater are the chances of experiencing adverse results like anxiety, confusion, depression, and frustration. Two hypotheses are offered to explain the data which contradicts promotional statements depicting TM as a simple, beneficial exercise. The first is that the practice of meditation makes a person more aware of his or her problems and/or more willing to talk about them. The second is that these adverse results are a manifestation of "unstressing," a term used in TM circles to refer to a transient process when one's problems are solved or normalized. The author argues, however, that the data collected raises serious doubts about the claimed innocuous nature of TM, and suggests instead that its practice may be "hazardous to mental health."

1556. Otis, Leon S. "The Facts On Transcendental Meditation, III: If Well-Integrated But Anxious Try TM." PSYCHOLOGY TODAY 7 (April 1974): 45-46.

Maintains that TM can probably benefit a large number of people, but it could also be, for some, a waste of time. The author observes that records are seldom kept for those who quit meditating. With the help of the Stanford Research Institute staff he conducted an experiment to test ex-meditators to determine what kind of personality is attracted to TM. It is suggested that there might be a predisposed personality which responds positively to TM. A person's motivation and commitment to the ideals of TM are probably the more important variables. TM provides rest for overworked people and gives them the opportunity to desensitize themselves at their own pace. Those who quit appear to be of two types: 1) those with serious problems that are not effected by the mild technique of TM; and 2) those who are already well-integrated.

1557. Pagano, Robert R., and Stephen Warrenburg. "Meditation: In Search of a Unique Effect." CONSCIOUSNESS AND SELF-REGULATION: ADVANCES IN RESEARCH AND THEORY. Edited by Richard J. Davidson, Gary E. Schwartz, and David Shapiro. New York: Plenum Press, 1983, vol. 3, pp. 153-210.

Reviews research on Transcendental Meditation over a six-
year period (1976-1982). Four areas are covered: 1) the
psychophysiological effects of TM; 2) hemispheric dominance;
3) personality tests; and 4) clinical outcome effects. It
is concluded that the practice of TM "promotes healthier
self-reports of lowered stress and anxiety on the one hand,
and increased well-being and self-actualization on the other"
(p. 193). These good effects, however, can be replicated by
other relaxation methods. Hence the unique, dramatic impact
that TM is supposed to have on one's personality was not
confirmed.

1558.   Patal, Chandra. "Yoga Therapy." PRINCIPLES AND PRACTICE OF
        STRESS MANAGEMENT. Edited by Robert L. Woolfolk and Paul
        M. Lehrer. New York: Guilford Press, 1984, pp. 70-107.

        Gives a short history of Yoga as a therapeutic treatment,
        and outlines the theoretical assumptions underlying the method.
        The various physiological and psychological illnesses which
        can be treated with Yoga are listed. The author believes that
        Yoga has its limitations, especially when it is used in its
        religious setting and not simply as a scientific relaxation
        technique. The Yoga method is described in some detail,
        stressing its introduction to the client, the physical equip-
        ment and environment, and the therapist-patient relationship.
        The resistance to, compliance with, and maintenance of behavior
        change brought about by Yoga are discussed. The efficacy of
        Yoga is corroborated by many scientific studies.

1559.   Pathak, M. P., and L. S. Mishra. "Rehabilitation of Mentally
        Retarded Through Yoga Therapy." CHILD PSYCHIATRY QUARTERLY
        17 (1984): 153-58.

        Maintains that Yoga therapy is more beneficial than medical
        approaches to cure and rehabilitate the mentally retarded.
        Several therapeutic Yoga methods, such as "kriyas," "asanas,"
        and "mudras," are useful tranquilizers which can be safely
        used in the treatment of mentally retarded children. The Yoga
        asanas improve memory, concentration, learning and thinking
        powers, and curiosity to learn.

1560.   Pelletier, Kenneth R. MIND AS HEALER, MIND AS SLAYER: A
        HOLISTIC APPROACH TO PREVENTING STRESS DISORDERS. New York:
        Dell Co., 1977. xv, 366 pp.

        Discusses the nature of stress and its relation to disease.
        Meditation is listed as one of the methods of controlling
        stress. The research on the role of meditation in reducing
        stress, its relationship to psychosomatic medicine, the three
        major types of meditation, namely, TM, Yoga, and Zen, and
        their effects on stress-related disease are among the topics
        covered.

1561.   Pelletier, Kenneth R., and Charles Garfield. CONSCIOUSNESS:
        EAST AND WEST. New York: Harper and Row, 1976. x, 307 pp.

Considers the nature of psychotic, psychoactive, and
meditative states of consciousness, as well as new systems of
psychological and psychosomatic therapy, such as meditation
and biofeedback. The various meditative states of awareness,
the relationship between schizophrenia and mystical experience,
and the psychology of meditative states are all discussed.
Various psychotherapeutic treatments, such as psychosynthesis,
Morita therapy, Zen, and meditation are described. The authors
think that a highly sophisticated form of Western Yoga, or
"meta-therapy," is evolving, capable of alleviating many
psychological and physiological disorders. A lengthy bibliography is included (pp. 275-307).

1562. Penner, Wes J., Harvey W. Zingle, et al. "Does an In-depth
Transcendental Meditation Course Effect Change in the Personalities of the Participants?" WESTERN PSYCHOLOGIST 4.4
(1973): 104-11.

Tests 100 Transcendental Meditation volunteers on the Omni-
bus Personality Inventory (OPI) and compares them to a control
sample. The results reveal several significant changes in
personality among those who practice TM, but they do not prove
that these changes were caused by the meditation experience.
The participants' attempts to justify their involvement and
to demonstrate the efficacy of TM may have drastically influenced the outcome of the experiment. The researchers state
that better controlled studies conducted over a longer period
of time are needed to assess TM's influence on personality.

1563. Persinger, Michael A. "Striking EEG Profiles From Single
Episodes of Glossolalia and Transcendental Meditation."
PERCEPTUAL AND MOTOR SKILLS 58 (1984): 127-33.

Reports on two cases where direct measurement of EEG showed
a relationship between religious experience and epileptic-like
electrical changes in the temporal lobe, which the author
calls "temporal lobe transients" (TLTs). The two incidents
occurred in a TM teacher during meditation and in a member of
a Pentecostal sect during glossolalic utterances. Neither
subject had any detectable epileptic condition or psychiatric
history. Most TLTs that are linked with religious experiences
usually remain within deep subcortical structures and can
never be observed in laboratory experiments.

1564. Persinger, Michael A., with Normand J. Carrey, and Lynn A.
Suess. TM AND CULT MANIA. North Quincy, MA: Christopher
Publishing House, 1980. 198 pp.

Investigates the precise psychological and sociological
procedures by which TM manipulates human behavior. Although
restricted to TM, this study clearly implies that other cultic
groups, such as Jim Jones's People's Temple and Rev. Moon's
Unification Church, have also developed into cult manias or
fads, while others, like the Baha'is, Jehovah's Witnesses,

and Christ Light, have espoused elements which could lead
them to tragic consequences. The authors evaluate many TM
experiments and find flaws in them. The alleged results of
meditation can be produced by hypnosis, suggestibility, or
the placebo effect. The neurotic dependency on TM and its
power to trigger psychotic behavior are among the major problems with this form of meditation. In conclusion, the
authors offer some guidelines for protecting oneself against
cult mania.

1565. Piggins, David, and Douglas Morgan. "Note Upon Steady Visual
      Fixation and Repeated Auditory Stimulation in Meditation
      and in the Laboratory." PERCEPTUAL AND MOTOR SKILLS 44
      (1977): 357-58.

      Observes that many religions, including new religious move-
      ments like Transcendental Meditation, use techniques of Yoga
      and/or meditation to help participants fix their attention
      and stimulate themselves by the repetition of mantras. The
      result of these practices appears "to waken phenomena and
      experiences related to reduced sensory input" (p. 358). The
      authors make no comment on the possible therapeutic value of
      this condition.

1566. Prince, Raymond. "Meditation: Some Psychological Specula-
      tions." PSYCHIATRIC JOURNAL OF THE UNIVERSITY OF OTTAWA
      3 (1978): 202-9.

      Contends that the neglect of meditation by such influential
      writers as Bucke and James was due to the Christian belief
      that mystical experiences should not be sought after. Several
      new typologies of meditation, especially those of Naranjo,
      Orstein, and Goleman, are described. So also are a number of
      techniques called "the repetition of the divine names," Zikr
      (in Sufism), the Jesus Prayer (in Christianity), and Japa
      (in Bhakti Yoga). The psychoanalytic theory that mystical
      states are a regression in the service of the ego, and that
      meditation is the tool used to bring about this regression,
      is refuted. The author proposes the view that the meditative
      state is related to different cerebral hemispheric functions.
      Meditation shifts the focus of consciousness to the right
      hemisphere of the brain, and this brings about an ineffable,
      timeless, and holistic experience.

1567. Prince, Raymond, Antoinette Goodwin, and Frank Engelsmann.
      "Transcendental Meditation and Stress: An Evaluative Study."
      R. M. BUCKE MEMORIAL SOCIETY NEWSLETTER-REVIEW 8 (1976):
      19-27.

      Studies the effects of TM practice upon stress and drug
      use by comparing three groups of subjects, one consisting of
      initiates in TM, another of dropouts, and one of people who
      had never practiced TM (controls). The results of the re-
      search, conducted by questionnaires and interviews, are
      presented under three areas, namely: 1) the kind of people

who enroll in the TM introductory classes; 2) the effects of meditation on stress reduction; and 3) the interview data. Various positive and negative experiences with TM are listed. The results indicate that meditators registered the greatest improvement in decrease of stress, increase in positive self-feelings, increase of energy and power to concentrate, decrease in the need for sleep, and relief from headaches and other nervous complaints. The author thinks that TM may be a safe procedure which may reduce stress and enhance personal effectiveness.

1568. Puryear, Herbert B., Charles T. Cayce, and Mark A. Thurston. "Anxiety Reduction Associated With Meditation: Home Study." PERCEPTUAL AND MOTOR SKILLS 43 (1976): 527-31.

Investigates the "anxiolytic efficacy" of a meditation technique first described by Edgar Cayce. This method involves some physical and mental preparation and a period of silent attention focused on one's ideal for spiritual growth. The Cayce technique, followed for several weeks, reduced anxiety as effectively as other methods of meditation, including Transcendental Meditation.

1569. Rachman, Arnold W. "Clinical Meditation in Groups." PSYCHOTHERAPY: THEORY, RESEARCH, AND PRACTICE 18 (1981): 252-58.

Describes Buddhist meditation as a tool for self-analysis and self-actualization, and "a gentle, positive, accepting approach to self-exploration" (p. 252). It reduces anxiety and emphasizes self-acceptance. The use of meditation as a clinical procedure is outlined, and the way it can be employed in groups is explained. Four phases of this approach are listed: 1) sharing meditation within a group; 2) group interaction and reaction to meditation; 3) the discovery of a "clinical mantra" for each individual; and 4) development of insight regarding the relationship between the clinical mantra and clinical practice. Several effects of group meditation, like anxiety reduction and the exploration of sensitive material with relative comfort, are listed.

1570. Radford, John. "What Can We Learn From Zen? A Review and Some Speculations." PSYCHOLOGIA 19 (1976): 57-66.

Reviews some attempts to use Zen Buddhist concepts within the framework of Western psychology. Zen Buddhism includes three groups of techniques, namely, meditation, mental exercises, and training in skills, all of which are intended to change behavior and experience. The author states that the literature fails to reveal any investigation of Zen as a therapeutic technique. Several areas of psychological interest, like creativity, might profit from a comparison with Zen. Psychologists should be interested in Zen because it is one kind of religious experience that has been neglected for a considerable time.

1571. Rama, Swami, Rudolph Ballentine, and Swami Ajaya. YOGA AND
       PSYCHOTHERAPY: THE EVOLUTION OF CONSCIOUSNESS. Glenview,
       IL: Himalayan Institute, 1976. 332 pp.

       Examines and explores five levels of being which unfold in
       meditation and Yoga. The body postures, breath and energy,
       the mind, altered states of consciousness, and the state of
       bliss are successively dealt with. The authors explain that,
       although there seems to be some similarity between certain
       euphoric states and the experience of higher consciousness,
       there is a radical difference between the mystic and the
       psychotic. The former's expanded awareness leads to the
       integration of diverse and contradictory aspects of life,
       while the latter's consciousness is fragmented, changing from
       moment to moment. Finally, the chakras, the seven centers of
       consciousness, are described. It is argued that proper medi-
       tation on each chakra results in a new level of integration,
       which includes the overcoming of primitive fear, the avoidance
       of aggression, the development of creativity, and the channel-
       ing of one's emotions. Meditational therapy, a branch of Yoga
       science, can be used to alter basic mental patterns and heal
       psychopathological disorders, which cannot be treated by
       modern therapeutic methods.

1572. Raskin, Marjorie, Lekh R. Bali, and Harmon V. Peeke. "Muscle
       Biofeedback and Transcendental Meditation." ARCHIVES OF
       GENERAL PSYCHIATRY 37 (1980): 93-97.

       Evaluates the efficacy of TM in reducing several kinds of
       anxieties as compared to other self-regulating therapies.
       The various groups of subjects taking part in the experiment
       were treated with electromagnetic biofeedback, relaxation
       training, or TM. It was concluded that all treatments had
       the effect of lowering anxiety levels but that none of them
       stood out as more effective than the rest. In more serious
       cases it seems that these ways of handling anxiety are, by
       themselves, insufficient to relieve the symptoms.

1573. Ravindra, R. "Is Religion Psychotherapy?: An Indian View."
       RELIGIOUS STUDIES 14 (1978): 389-97.

       Studies the relationship between religion and psychotherapy
       in the context of the Bhagavad Gita and the Yoga Sutras of
       Pantajali. The aims and method of Yoga are described. Since
       Yoga not only diagnoses the human condition, but also pre-
       scribes a remedy for healing the whole person, it can be seen
       as both "physio-psychology" and "physio-psychotherapy." Yoga
       differs from Western psychotherapy in the transcendence of its
       aims.

1574. Rawlinson, Andrew. "Yoga Psychology." INDIGENOUS PSYCHOL-
       OGIES (item 657), pp. 247-63.

       Outlines the nature and working of human consciousness
       according to the Yoga traditions of Pantajali, Buddhism, and
       the Advaita Vedanta. The author explains why Yoga places

great emphasis on altered states of consciousness, and how it
leads to personal transformation. Although the implications
on mental health are not explicitly discussed, the reader is
led to see that self-understanding as taught in Yoga is bound
to improve one's awareness and promote self-development.

1575. Rivers, Stephen M., and Nicholas P. Spanos. "Personal Vari-
      ables Predicting Voluntary Participation in and Attrition
      from a Meditation Program." PSYCHOLOGICAL REPORTS 49 (1981):
      795-801.

      Argues that many studies of the psychotherapeutic effects
      of meditation are unreliable, because they do not take into
      account the fact that psychological differences between medi-
      tators and non-meditators may reflect initial pre-meditation
      differences. To test this possibility the authors assessed
      college students on various measures, e.g., absorption, self-
      esteem, hypnotic suggestibility, and depression. They con-
      clude that previous tests, supporting differences between
      meditators and non-meditators, may have reflected selective
      volunteering rather than genuine effects of meditation.

1576. Rubin, Jeffery R. "Meditation and Psychoanalytic Listening."
      PSYCHOANALYTIC REVIEW 74 (1985): 599-613.

      Observes that, although the psychotherapeutic process depends
      on the therapists' ability to listen to their patients, very
      little is said in psychoanalysis as to how one develops this
      faculty. The meditation technique as taught in Theravada
      Buddhism is examined as a tool for developing the listening
      skills of the therapist. The author sees in this meditation
      a systematic and efficacious method of cultivating precisely
      that capacity and state of mind that Freud recommended for
      optimum listening. Meditation provides a remedy to some of
      the issues which Freud and subsequent clinicians ignored.
      Eastern meditation can make a major contribution to psycho-
      analytic listening.

1577. Russel, Peter. THE TM TECHNIQUE: AN INTRODUCTION TO TRAN-
      SCENDENTAL MEDITATION AND THE TEACHINGS OF MAHARISHI MAHESH
      YOGI. London: Routledge and Kegan Paul, 1976. xi, 195 pp.

      Offers a primer of TM describing its process and providing
      its historical and theoretical backgrounds. TM is presented
      as a way of overcoming stress, improving one's general health,
      and contributing to one's creativity and intelligence. Its
      regular practice is regarded as a step to higher mystical con-
      sciousness which transforms the individual into a whole, self-
      actualized person.

1578. Sabel, Bernhard A. "Transcendental Meditation and Concen-
      tration Ability." PERCEPTUAL AND MOTOR SKILLS 50 (1980):
      799-802.

      Assesses whether there is an immediate improvement in con-
      centration following a single meditation exercise, and whether

such concentration increases with the regular use of TM.
Sixty persons were tested before and after they started meditating and were randomly split in two groups, one instructed
to continue to meditate, the other to read quietly for a while.
Both groups registered an improvement but there was little
difference in the results. The need to apply appropriate
control procedures is discussed.

1579. Sallis, James F. "Meditation and Self-Actualization: A The-
       oretical Comparison." PSYCHOLOGIA 25 (1982): 59-64.

       Relates the theory and practice of meditation to the goals
       of humanistic psychotherapy, particularly to self-actualiza-
       tion as exemplified in the writings of Maslow. Meditation
       and humanistic psychology share the same view of human nature,
       which includes the possibility of actualizing many human
       potentialities. Maslow's characteristics of self-actualizers,
       or the requisite conditions for reaching self-actualization,
       are enumerated and matched with corresponding features in
       meditation. The author holds that the goals of humanistic
       psychology can be actively pursued by using meditation
       techniques.

1580. Schuster, Richard. "Empathy and Mindfulness." JOURNAL OF
       HUMANISTIC PSYCHOLOGY 19 (1979): 71-77.

       Explores the meaning of empathy in Western psychotherapies,
       and argues that it has mystical connotations. In spite of
       the general agreement that empathy is essential for effective
       psychotherapy, there is no training designed to teach thera-
       pists how to be empathetic in the clinical context. This kind
       of training has, however, been developed in the East. The
       Buddhist tradition proposes mindfulness meditation (Satipat-
       thana), which should become a routine habit in one's daily
       life. The author thinks that this meditation is the best way
       to develop the empathy needed in therapy. Therapists who
       practice this meditation should easily establish empathetic,
       moment-to-moment contact with their clients. Both their pro-
       fessional skills and their own personal growth will be
       enhanced by Buddhist meditation.

1581. Seiler, Gary. "A Comparison Between Yoga, Psychoanalysis,
       and Client Oriented Therapy." YOGA RESEARCH 1 (1978):
       21-30.

       Contends that the goals of Yoga, psychoanalysis, and client-
       oriented therapy are similar. All these techniques aim at
       integrating the human personality and at increasing one's
       rational consciousness. They agree that mental illness is a
       result of ignorance, repression, or lack of awareness. The
       author draws in schematic form the main similarities and
       differences among these therapies in the following areas:
       origins, the essential nature of a human being, focus, objec-
       tives, methods, nature of the therapeutic relationship, and
       basic concepts.

1582. Seth, B. B., J. K. Trivedi, and Rajiv Anand. "A Comparative
       Study of Relative Effectiveness of Biofeedback and Shavasana
       (Yoga) in Tension Headache." INDIAN JOURNAL OF PSYCHIATRY
       23 (1981): 109-14.

       Reports on a study to assess the efficacy of Yoga as com-
       pared to biofeedback in the reduction of tension headache.
       Both were found to be equally effective. It is suggested that
       further research might point to the beneficial results of the
       practice of Yoga in other psychophysiological disorders.

1583. Shafii, Muhammad. "Adaptive and Therapeutic Aspects of Medi-
       tation." INTERNATIONAL JOURNAL OF PSYCHOANALYTIC PSYCHO-
       THERAPY 2 (1973): 364-82.

       Observes that because Westerners are practising Eastern
       meditation, such as Yoga, Zen, and TM, psychoanalysts are
       bound to have contact with patients who have been exposed to
       these methods of psychoreligious growth and self-realization.
       The author argues that psychiatrists must be acquainted with
       these forms of meditation. He describes Western attitudes
       towards passivity and quiescence, defines meditation, and ex-
       plores its adaptive and therapeutic significance. Although
       Western culture has been heavily biased against meditation,
       it is emphasized that psychoanalytic principles could be
       applied to further our understanding of meditation and its
       psychotherapeutic applications. The similarities and dif-
       ferences between meditation, defined as "a psychophysiological
       state of activity and creative quiescence" (p. 369), and
       psychoanalysis are pointed out. During meditation, dehabit-
       uation or deautomization (see Deikman, item 124) takes
       place, and the individual develops a temporary, controlled
       regression, which in the end serves the ego.

1584. Shafii, Muhammad. "Silence in the Service of the Ego: Psycho-
       analytic Study of Meditation." INTERNATIONAL JOURNAL OF
       PSYCHOANALYSIS 54 (1973): 431-43.

       Argues that the silence in meditation, rather than being a
       form of inhibition, transference resistance, and severe ego
       regression, is a temporary and controlled regression in the
       service of the ego. During meditation, the individual re-
       experiences earlier traumas and deals with them. This leads
       to freedom from internal conflict and to the experience of
       internal peace and harmony. Meditation can, therefore, be
       conceptualized "as an integrative and adaptive phenomenon,
       rather than as a pathological experience" (p. 431). The
       author explores both the general human attitude and the
       psychoanalytical view of silence. After describing the
       practice of meditation from a psychoanalytic point of view
       and reviewing the psychological studies of it, the author
       concludes by speculating that the great Yogis, Sufis, and
       Zen masters experienced peace and tranquility because of the
       creative silence of meditation.

1585. Shafii, Muhammad, Richard Lavely, and Robert Jaffe. "Medi-
          tation and the Prevention of Alcohol Abuse." AMERICAN
          JOURNAL OF PSYCHIATRY 132 (1975): 942-45.

          Reports on their findings of the effects of TM on those
          who abuse alcohol. Meditators were divided into five groups,
          according to the length of time they had been practicing TM.
          The researchers are not certain whether meditation can have
          a significant therapeutic effect on the decrease and discon-
          tinuation of alcohol. It could, however, be used a tool to
          help a person become less dependent on alcohol. Meditation
          could also be used as a preventive method in potential alcohol
          abusers.

1586. Shafii, Muhammad, Richard Lavely, and Robert Jaffe. "Medita-
          tion and Marijuana." AMERICAN JOURNAL OF PSYCHIATRY 131
          (1974): 60-63.

          Reports on the effect of TM on marijuana users based on a
          survey administered to examine the impact of TM on alcohol
          and drug abuse. The conclusion reached is that TM can make a
          significant contribution to freedom from the use of marijuana
          and hashish.

1587. Shapiro, Dean H. "Meditation as an Altered State of Con-
          sciousness: Contributions to Western Behavioral Science."
          JOURNAL OF TRANSPERSONAL PSYCHOLOGY 15 (1983): 61-81.

          Reviews the literature which has concentrated on the study
          of meditation as an altered state of consciousness as opposed
          to a self-regulation technique. Several approaches to medi-
          tation and research findings are described and evaluated.
          The author thinks that "greater clarity and precision seem
          necessary in describing altered states" (p. 77). More precise
          information is required in order to determine whether medi-
          tation experiences are psychotic or truly enlightened and
          spiritual.

1588. Shapiro, Dean H. "Overview: Clinical and Physiological Com-
          parison of Meditation with Other Self-Control Strategies."
          AMERICAN JOURNAL OF PSYCHIATRY 139 (1982): 267-74.

          Reviews the literature on meditation as a way of achieving
          self-control. A non-cultic definition of meditation is
          proposed. Meditation is not a unique therapeutic method
          since its effectiveness in reducing anxiety, insomnia, and
          hypertension can be attained through other methods, such as
          progressive relaxation, desensitization, pseudo-medication
          treatment, and biofeedback. Several adverse effects of
          meditation, including increased anxiety, boredom, confusion,
          depression, restlessness, and withdrawal, have also been
          observed. The author thinks that, while meditation can help
          many patients, it may not be a useful therapeutic intervention
          for the chronically depressed individual. Several suggestions
          for conducting clinically-oriented research are offered.

1589.   Shapiro, Dean H. MEDITATION: SELF-REGULATION STRATEGY AND
        ALTERED STATES OF CONSCIOUSNESS. New York: Aldine, 1980.
        xxiii, 318 pp.

        Presents a comprehensive manual on meditation showing its
        clinical applications and combining the scientific approach
        with a personal one. Among the many areas covered are the
        various effects which meditation has and the reasons for
        its great success. Each chapter contains suggestions for
        further reading. A lengthy bibliography (pp. 281-306) is
        appended.

1590.   Shapiro, Dean H. PRECISION NIRVANA. Englewood Cliffs, NJ:
        Prentice-Hall, 1978. xxiii, 344 pp.

        Attempts to combine the best in Western psychology, which
        is rational and intellectual, with Zen psychology, which
        stresses egolessness, non-attachment, and altered states of
        consciousness. Both traditions can be profitably used in
        clinical practice, educational settings, and daily living.
        Different meditation techniques are discussed and specific
        instructions of how to use them are clearly given. The author
        argues in favor of developing a new awareness or state of
        consciousness by meditation and self-observation strategies.

1591.   Shapiro, Dean H. "Instructions for a Training Package Com-
        bining Formal and Informal Zen Meditation With Behavioral
        Self-Control Strategies." PSYCHOLOGIA 21 (1978): 70-76.

        Describes the essential techniques of Zen and behavioral
        control methods for clinical and research purposes. The
        setting, position, and process of meditation are outlined.
        Self-control strategies, which involve training in self-
        observation and functional analysis, including relaxation
        and thought-stopping, are combined with the practice of
        meditation. The author suggests that the above approach
        is a good way to handle tension, anger, and stress.

1592.   Shapiro, Dean H. "Zen Meditation and Behavioral Self-Control:
        Strategies Applied to a Case of Generalized Anxiety."
        PSYCHOLOGIA 19 (1976): 134-38.

        Reports on a treatment applied to a female undergraduate
        student who suffered from loss of self-control and anxiety.
        Zen meditation and behavioral self-management techniques were
        used, and a significant decrease in anxiety, stress, and
        tension was observed. The author holds that the combined
        use of Zen Buddhism and social learning theory can lead to
        more effective clinically-oriented self-control strategies.

1593.   Shapiro, Dean H., and David Gilber. "Meditation and Psycho-
        therapeutic Effects: Self-Regulation Strategy and Altered
        State of Consciousness." ARCHIVES OF GENERAL PSYCHIATRY
        35 (1975): 294-302.

Reviews research literature which deals with the psychotherapeutic effects of meditation used as a self-regulatory
process or as an altered state of consciousness. When used
to acquire self-control, meditation can serve as a form of
rehabilitation in drug and alcohol addictions, stress and
tension management, hypertension, fears, and insomnia. As
an altered state of consciousness, meditation can serve as
means of personality change, resulting in greater creativity,
heightened awareness, and self-actualization. Several methodological weaknesses with past studies are noted, and guidelines for future research suggested.

*   Shapiro, Dean H., and Roger N. Walsh, editors. MEDITATION:
         CLASSICAL AND CONTEMPORARY PERSPECTIVES. Cited above as
         item 45.

1594.   Shapiro, Dean H., and Steven M. Zifferblatt. "Zen Meditation
         and Behavioral Self-Control: Similarities, Differences, and
         Clinical Applications." AMERICAN PSYCHOLOGIST 31 (1976):
         519-23.

         Compares self-control techniques developed within Zen Bud-
         dhism and the social learning theory of Western psychologists.
         Although these methods came into being in different geograph-
         ical areas for different philosophical reasons, and with
         different assumptions about human nature, the authors think
         that a comparison is justified on behavioral grounds. Zen is
         thus removed from the realm of mysticism to rational technique,
         which can be understood and practiced by everybody. A five-
         stage conceptualization of Zen is proposed, and clear simi-
         larities and differences between Zen meditation and behavior
         therapy are drawn up. The conclusion reached is that both
         can be used in clinical contexts.

1595.   Shimano, Eito T., and Donald B. Douglas. "On Research in
         Zen." AMERICAN JOURNAL OF PSYCHIATRY 132 (1975): 1300-2.

         Describes the nature of Zen meditation and outlines the
         studies that could be undertaken to check its physiological
         and psychological effects. The need for researchers to be
         practitioners of meditation is underscored.

1596.   Simon, Jane. "Creativity and Altered States of Consciousness."
         AMERICAN JOURNAL OF PSYCHOANALYSIS 37 (1977): 3-12.

         Examines the claim that certain altered states of conscious-
         ness produced by Zen, Yoga, TM, and other methods contribute
         to increased creativity. Although classical psychoanalysis
         has considered ASC as a regressive phenomenon, sometimes in
         the service of the ego, the author holds that, today, these
         states can be regarded as a progression or integration, a
         means for personal growth. It is proposed that traditional
         analysis and ASC may not be far apart, since the latter occur
         within an analytic or therapeutic situation. It is confirmed
         that mystical experiences and psychological well-being often
         go together. Yoga is interpreted as containing a large
         measure of self-hypnosis.

1597. Singh, Ratan, and Irmgard Oberhummer. "Behavior Therapy
       Within a Setting of Karma Yoga." JOURNAL OF BEHAVIOR
       THERAPY AND EXPERIMENTAL PSYCHIATRY 11 (1980): 135-41.

       Maintains that therapy should be conducted within the
       framework of one's cultural norms and values. The therapist
       whose patients have been brought up in the Hindu religion
       should take into consideration the system of Karma Yoga which
       stresses inactivity, passivity, and being rather than action.
       Yoga can be very beneficial when one is applying behavior
       therapy in an Eastern culture. The way the authors treated
       a 43-year-old Hindu woman suffering from obsessive fantasies
       is described. Flooding, assertion training, correction of
       misconceptions, and Karma Yoga were combined to bring about
       an improvement in her condition.

1598. Smith, Jonathan C. "Meditation Research: Three Observations
       on the State-of-the-Art." MEDITATION: CLASSICAL AND CONTEM-
       PORARY PERSPECTIVES (item 45), pp. 677-78.

       Observes that: 1) meditation research has ceased to be
       conducted solely by meditators themselves with the intention
       of proving that their new discovery is a solution to all
       human ills; 2) meditation research has moved away from ties
       to philosophical and religious traditions; and 3) meditation
       itself seems to be a very complex phenomenon. The issues of
       its effectiveness as a therapeutic agent and its link to a
       religious or spiritual discipline remain unsolved.

1599. Smith, Jonathan C. "Yoga and Stress." MEDITATION THERAPY
       (item 1366), pp. 1-15.

       Reviews research on stress and points out that meditation
       can change the way a person reacts to stress situations.
       Hatha Yoga and meditation, combined with traditional psycho-
       therapy, may help individuals suffering from acute anxieties
       and phobias.

1600. Smith, Jonathan C. "Psychotherapeutic Effects of Transcen-
       dental Meditation with Controls for Expectation of Relief
       and Daily Sitting." JOURNAL OF CONSULTING AND CLINICAL
       PSYCHOLOGY 44 (1976): 630-37.

       Describes two experiments conducted to isolate the effects
       of TM from the expectation of relief. The first tried to
       compare the effects of TM with a control treatment, which
       matched TM in every respect that might foster expectation of
       relief, except the actual reciting of the mantra during
       meditation. The other consisted of contrasting TM with an
       exercise designed to be the antithesis of meditation. It
       was found that TM is not more effective in reducing stress
       and anxiety than just sitting in a relaxed posture. The TM
       exercise was not the "crucial therapeutic component."

*   Smith, Jonathan C. "Meditation as Psychotherapy." Cited
       above as item 47.

1601. Solomon, Earl G., and Ann K. Bumpus. "The Running Meditation
       Response: An Adjunct to Psychotherapy." AMERICAN JOURNAL
       OF PSYCHOTHERAPY 32 (1978): 583-92.

       Combines the physical technique of slow, long-distance
       running with the recitation of the mantra device of Tran-
       scendental Meditation to create a peak experience. Like TM,
       this technique is another method of achieving self-hypnosis
       and should not be taken as an alternative to professional
       psychotherapy, but rather as an adjunct to it. The results
       of this method can be influenced both by the patient's needs
       and by the psychotherapist's style and experience.

1602. Spanos, Nicholas P., Jack Gottlieb, and Stephen M. Rivers.
       "The Effects of Short-Term Meditation Practice on
       Hypnotic Responsivity." PSYCHOLOGICAL RECORD 30 (1980):
       343-48.

       Tests the hypnotic effect of meditation by experiments
       on three groups, one which practiced meditation for eight
       sessions, a second which listened to lectures on hypnosis
       for the same period of time, and a third control group
       which was subjected to no treatment. Over 80 students were
       pre-tested on several attitudinal and cognitive measures,
       including Tellegen and Atkinson's absorption questionnaire.
       The results showed that meditation and lectures did not
       enhance performance on the test. It is possible that sus-
       ceptible persons would be more open to modify their initial
       levels of nonanalytic attention. More tests are needed to
       determine the relationship between meditation and hypnosis.

1603. Spanos, Nicholas P., Henderikus J. Stamm, et al. "Meditation,
       Expectation and Performances on Indices of Nonanalytic
       Attending." INTERNATIONAL JOURNAL OF CLINICAL AND
       EXPERIMENTAL HYPNOSIS 28 (1980): 244-51.

       Investigates the theory that both meditation and hypnotic
       responsivity involve a faculty for sustaining attention in
       an nonanalytic manner. Over 30 introductory psychology
       students at Carleton University participated in an experiment
       lasting for four weeks. Meditation practice, it was con-
       cluded, failed to enhance hypnotic susceptibility because it
       did not succeed in increasing proficiency in nonanalytic
       attending. Some problems with this type of research are
       discussed, and it is suggested that future research take
       into account such variables as attitude, expectancy, and
       motivation.

1604. Stainbrook, Gene L., John W. Hoffman, and Herbert Benson.
       "Behavioral Therapies of Hypertension: Psychotherapy,
       Biofeedback, and Relaxation/Meditation." INTERNATIONAL
       REVIEW OF APPLIED PSYCHOLOGY 32 (1983): 119-35.

       Maintains that relaxation/meditation techniques are more
       clinically effective in reducing tension than supportive

psychotherapy or biofeedback. Further, meditation seems preferable in terms of treatment outcome, durability, and lasting effectiveness.

1605. Stewart, Robert. "States of Human Realization: Some Physiological and Psychological Correlates." PSYCHOLOGIA 17 (1974): 126-34.

Examines the research on the effects of Transcendental Meditation and other meditation techniques (such as Yoga and Zen), particularly on their contribution to human realization. Some of the earliest physiological and psychological studies on TM are briefly described.

1606. Strassman, Rick J., and Marc Galanter. "The Abhidhamma: A Cross-Cultural Model for the Psychiatric Application of Meditation." INTERNATIONAL JOURNAL OF SOCIAL PSYCHIATRY 26 (1980): 293-99.

Describes contemporary Western paradigms--psychophysiological, psychoanalytic, and systems-approach model--which have been employed to specify the subjective aspects of meditation phenomena. The authors find that these models are not useful for describing in detail the meditation experience. They suggest instead a model drawn from the Buddhist tradition, and argue that the Abhidhamma psychological system can help clarify, aid, and direct therapeutic endeavors.

1607. Thorpe, Timothy. "Effects of Hatha Yoga and Meditation on Anxiety and Body Image." MEDITATION THERAPY (item 1366), pp. 16-36.

Reports on significant positive changes brought about by Hatha Yoga and meditation on the way one experiences one's body and on the level of anxiety. The results of a questionnaire point not only to decreased anxiety and improved psychological health, but also to an increased vitality and an enhancement of one's spirituality. Yoga and meditation proved effective in drug rehabilitation. Their practice could serve as a powerful adjunct in the treatment of patients suffering from anxiety and/or depression. Both can be used to facilitate progress in self-actualization and in the experience of deeper humanistic values.

1608. Throll, D. A. "Transcendental Meditation and Progressive Relaxation: Their Psychological Effects." JOURNAL OF CLINICAL PSYCHOLOGY 37 (1981): 776-81.

Applies various tests (the Eysenck Personality Inventory and the State-Trait-Anxiety-Inventory) to find out whether TM differs from progressive relaxation in its effects, and discovers that the former led to more significant results, particularly in the decrease in neuroticism, anxiety, and drug use. No real differences were noted in the level of psychotic tendencies. The fact that those who practiced TM spent more time in meditation explained in part the favorable results.

*   Timmons, Beverly, and Demetri P. Kanellakos. "The Psychology
        and Physiology of Meditation and Related Phenomena: Bibliog-
        raphy II." Cited above as item 50.

*   Timmons, Beverly, and Joe Kamiya. "The Psychology and Physi-
        ology of Meditation and Related Phenomena: A Bibliography."
        Cited above as item 51.

1609.   Travis, Fredrick. "The Transcendental Meditation Technique
        and Creativity: A Longitudinal Study of Cornell University
        Students." JOURNAL OF CREATIVE BEHAVIOR 13 (179): 169-80.

        Reviews some of the studies on TM which strongly indicate
        that its practice brings about positive psychological changes,
        including a decrease in anxiety levels and a growth in self-
        actualization, the latter being a state which enhances one's
        creative powers. The relationship between TM and creativity
        is explored in 90 subjects who were given the Torrance Tests
        of Creative Thinking (TTCT), and it is concluded that five
        months of meditation improved one's "primary process creativ-
        ity," but had little impact on one's "secondary process
        creativity."

1610.   Tribbe, Frank C. "The Role of Meditation in Holistic Heal-
        ing." JOURNAL OF THE AMERICAN ACADEMY OF RELIGION AND
        PSYCHICAL RESEARCH 2 (1979): 17-21.

        Maintains that meditation has both prophylactic and thera-
        peutic uses. The author recommends that meditation practice
        should be guided by a therapist or a competent leader. Group
        meditation is favored and encouraged.

1611.   Vahia, N. S. "Yoga in Psychiatry." READINGS IN TRANSCULTURAL
        PSYCHIATRY. Edited by Ari Kiev and Venkoba Rao. Madras,
        India: Macmillan, 1982, pp. 11-19.

        Shows how Pantajali's view of mental health stands on the
        person's ability to control one's personal functions with
        less preoccupation in a constantly changing environment.
        Pantajali's eight steps of Astanga Yoga provide the essential
        principles of psychotherapy and lead the individual to com-
        plete internal harmony. The work of the author and his
        collaborators to test the efficacy of Pantajali's Yoga in
        hospital patients is described. The results are very encour-
        aging, and show that Yoga is comparable to conventional
        psychotherapy. Yoga is a treatment that can be applied to
        prevent and treat some psychiatric disorders in different
        cultures.

1612.   Vahia, N. S., D. R. Doongaji, and D. V. Jeste. "Value of
        Pantajali's Concepts in the Treatment of Psychoneurosis."
        NEW DIMENSIONS IN PSYCHIATRY: A WORLD VIEW. Edited by
        A. Arieti and G. Chrzanowski. New York: Wiley and Sons,
        1975, pp. 293-304.

Maintains that the therapeutic technique based on the Yoga of Pantajali (c. 400 B.C.) deserves consideration because of its novel approach and its holistic method. This Yoga system teaches the harmonious functioning of the personality by a gradual development of control over thought processes, bodily functions, and social relationships. The various concepts and techniques in Pantajali's system as well as the work carried out with patients are outlined. Several shortcomings in current psychotherapeutic treatment are listed. Yoga therapy is superior to internal influences, such as the placebo effect and suggestibility, and in many cases is better than Western techniques.

1613. Vahia, N. S., D. R. Doongaji, et al. "Psychophysiologic Therapy Based on the Concept of Pantajali: A New Approach to the Treatment of Neurotic and Psychosomatic Disorders." AMERICAN JOURNAL OF PSYCHOTHERAPY 27 (1973): 557-65.

Argues that the value of treating neurosis and psychosomatic disorders by psychotherapeutic techniques, behavior modification, and drugs has not been proven conclusively. It is suggested that Pantajali's principles of Yoga give a therapeutic system aimed at dealing with the preoccupation of human frustration, increasing self-awareness, and integrating one's personality. The theoretical concepts of Pantajali and the five steps in the therapy are described and contrasted to psychoanalytic psychotherapy. The authors used Pantajali's system on 250 patients in Bombay who suffered from various types of neurotic and psychosomatic problems. The results show definite improvement. The authors think that Pantajali's system should be tested in different cultural settings.

1614. Vahia, N. S., D. R. Doongaji, et al. "Further Experience with the Therapy Based Upon Concepts of Pantajali in the Treatment of Psychiatric Disorders." INDIAN JOURNAL OF PSYCHIATRY 15 (1973): 32-37.

Reviews briefly the literature which shows that psychiatric treatment of neurosis is unsatisfactory. The researchers then present the results of therapy based on Pantajali's Yoga. Since, according to the latter, preoccupation with environmental gratification and the consequent frustrations are at the root of many psychological disorders, the aim of therapy is to reduce this preoccupation. The objective of the treatment is not adjustment to society, but self-realization. The authors conclude that this therapy is of definite value in the treatment of psychoneurosis.

1615. Van Nuys, David. "Meditation, Attention, and Hypnotic Susceptibility: A Correctional Study." INTERNATIONAL JOURNAL OF CLINICAL AND EXPERIMENTAL HYPNOSIS 21 (1973): 59-69.

Concludes, after experiments with 49 male undergraduates, that there is a significant correlation between various levels of hypnotic suggestibility and the meditative measures of of attention. Concentration, which is central to meditation, seems to be a necessary, but not sufficient, condition for hypnosis. The author establishes a relationship between the development of attention and altered states of consciousness, such as hypnosis and meditation.

1616. Vasavada, Arwind. "The Development of Psychotherapy." PSYCHOLOGY: EAST AND WEST (item 1367), pp. 22-49.

Traces the development of psychoanalysis in the schools of Adler, Jung, Freud, and others, and maintains that these approaches are comparable to Yoga in three areas: 1) the method of free association; 2) the concept of the human psyche; and 3) the relationship between master and disciple, or therapist and patient. Western psychotherapies have moved towards a theoretical position and practical methods similar to those of Eastern spiritualities.

1617. Walsh, Roger. "Meditation Practice and Research." JOURNAL OF HUMANISTIC PSYCHOLOGY 23 (1984): 18-50.

Provides an introduction to, and review of, meditation theory, research, and practice. A brief sketch of the history of meditation over the last 3,000 years is given. Several models of meditation are examined. The theory that meditation is a better state of consciousness than normal awareness is usually rejected by Western psychologists as nonsensical or pathological. Several neurophysiological and Buddhist models are briefly reviewed. Finally, the practice of meditation is briefly described, and its possible application as a therapeutic treatment for psychological illnesses and as a method for training therapists in empathetic sensitivity, is considered. A lengthy bibliography is included.

1618. Walsh, Roger. "A Model for Viewing Meditation Research." JOURNAL OF TRANSPERSONAL PSYCHOLOGY 14 (1982): 69-84.

Provides an evolutionary model of meditation research. The aim of meditation is described as an attempt to enhance control of one's mind, and to develop levels of psychological well-being and states of consciousness not recognized by Western psychological models. The author favors a general stimulus-response model for studying meditation. He also thinks that the study of Asian meditation literature and of the personal meditative experiences of researchers is important.

1619. Walsh, Roger N. "Meditation." HANDBOOK FOR INNOVATIVE THERAPIES. Edited by Raymond Corsini. New York: Wiley and Sons, 1981, pp. 470-88.

Describes meditation as "probably the most widespread and popular of the 'innovative therapies'" (p. 471). A brief history of its use and its theoretical background is provided.

The meditation model of consciousness is described and compared with Western psychological models. The author discusses
the mechanisms that are possibly operative in the production
of the effects of meditation. It is maintained that, although
it has been clearly shown that meditation can be an effective
treatment for relaxation and stress management, little research
and few experiments have been undertaken to test the original
scope of its practice, namely, a deeper psychological insight
through an altered state of consciousness. The advantages
of meditation over other techniques are recorded.

1620. Walsh, Roger N. "Meditation Research: An Introduction and a
       Review." JOURNAL OF TRANSPERSONAL PSYCHOLOGY 11 (1979):
       161-74.

       Reviews the principles underlying meditation research in
       the last two decades (1960-1979). The psychological, physio-
       logical, and clinical response to meditation indicate that
       it has considerable therapeutic potential. Methodological
       research problems as well as studies showing that meditation
       is not necessarily more effective than other self-regulatory
       strategies, such as relaxation-training and self-hypnosis,
       have cast some doubts on its real effectiveness. The author
       believes that considerable work still has to be done to bridge
       the gap between Eastern meditation, where the goal is to
       shift consciousness and perception, and Western research,
       which looks for variables which can be measured empirically.

1621. Walsh, Roger. "Initial Meditation Experiences." JOURNAL OF
       TRANSPERSONAL PSYCHOLOGY 9 (1977): 151-92; 10 (1978): 1-28.

       Gives a reflective account of the author's two-year experi-
       ence with Vissipana (Buddhist Insight meditation). The
       process of meditation is described, and the emotional and
       psychological impact of its practice explored. The author
       suggests that meditation, which can be misused for egocentric
       purposes, is beneficial in that it reduces fantasy which
       plays a major role in pathology.

1622. Walsh, Roger, et al. "Meditation: Aspects of Research and
       Practice." JOURNAL OF TRANSPERSONAL PSYCHOLOGY 10 (1978):
       113-33.

       Presents an edited transcription of a discussion held at
       the Sixth Annual Conference of the Association for Trans-
       personal Psychology in September of 1978. Several positive
       and negative features of meditation are brought up with
       reference to some of the more influential literature on the
       subject.

1623. Walsh, Roger, and Lorin Roche. "Precipitation of Acute
       Psychotic Episodes by Intensive Meditation in Individuals
       With a History of Schizophrenia." AMERICAN JOURNAL OF
       PSYCHIATRY 136 (1979): 1085-86.

Admits that meditation is capable of producing a wide range
of psychotherapeutic benefits, but points also to several
reports where the practice of meditation led to depersonalization, the appearance of previously suppressed conflicts, and
other adverse effects. The authors report on three patients,
all of whom had a history of schizophrenia, in whom meditation
led directly to psychotic behavior. Although these are rare
cases, psychiatrists should be alerted to them.

1624.   Welwood, John. "Vulnerability and Power in the Therapeutic
        Process: Existential and Buddhist Perspectives." JOURNAL
        OF TRANSPERSONAL PSYCHOLOGY 14 (1982): 125-39.

        Compares the existential and Buddhist attempts to deal with
        ontological anxiety. Meditation provides some context for
        working with those "moments of world collapse." It develops
        gentleness, which helps people relate to their vulnerability.
        Meditation, according to the author, can be successfully used
        in therapy.

1625.   Welwood, John. "Reflections on Psychotherapy, Focusing, and
        Meditation." JOURNAL OF TRANSPERSONAL PSYCHOLOGY 12 (1980):
        127-41.

        Explains some of the similarities and differences between
        meditation and focusing, the latter consisting of "paying
        attention to an as yet unclear felt sense underlying all one's
        thoughts, emotions, and familiar feelings about a particular
        problem" (p. 128). Focusing can serve as a bridge to medi-
        tation, even though it helps an individual expand the sense
        of personhood, while meditation tends to question personal
        identity. Meditation points to a larger sanity, health,
        and wholeness which go beyond simply developing a strong
        functional ego in the therapeutic sense. The author, how-
        ever, prefers to maintain, in his work with clients, a
        distinction between psychotherapy and meditation. He thinks
        both are valuable, but in different ways.

1626.   Welwood, John. "Meditation and the Unconscious: A New Per-
        spective." JOURNAL OF TRANSPERSONAL PSYCHOLOGY 9 (1977):
        1-26.

        Argues that the depth-psychology model of the unconscious
        is dualistic and, therefore, inadequate for understanding
        meditation. An attempt is made to reformulate the uncon-
        scious process as part of a person's multi-leveled awareness.
        Meditation should not be viewed as another technique for
        self-improvement or mastery over the world or people, nor as
        a passive withdrawal from the world. It is rather a process
        of discovery of both the self and of the world.

1627.   Welwood, John, editor. AWAKENING THE HEART: EAST/WEST
        APPROACHES TO PSYCHOTHERAPY AND THE HEALING RELATIONSHIP.
        Boulder, CO: Shambala, 1983. xiv, 219 pp.

Presents a collection of essays describing new perspectives on health and healing relationships that have developed through contact with Eastern meditation disciplines. The papers, which are personal and practical rather than theoretical and technical, are divided into four areas: basic questions, psychotherapy and spirituality, working on oneself, and working with others. The volume's main concern is to explore how meditative and contemplative practices provide information and context for healing relationships. The therapeutic task and the contemplative path are distinguished and their limits delineated.

1628. West, Louis Jolyon. "Transcendental Meditation and Other Non-Professional Psychotherapies." COMPREHENSIVE TEXTBOOK OF PSYCHIATRY. Edited by A. M Freedman, H. I. Kaplan, and B. J. Sadock. Baltimore: Williams and Wilkins, second edition, 1975, vol. 2, pp. 2561-67.

Reflects on the merits and dangers of non-professional approaches to psychological healing and self-improvement. Non-professional healers tend to be, like cultists, "uncritically enthusiastic." A short history of faith-healing is given. Among the modern psychotherapies considered are Scientology and Transcendental Meditation. The latter is judged to be much less likely than other similar enterprises to cause any harm.

1629. West, Michael A. "The Psychosomatics of Meditation." JOURNAL OF PSYCHOSOMATIC RESEARCH 24 (1980): 265-73.

Gives the historical context of meditation, and asks whether its practice has anything to offer in the field of mental health. Results of the current research on the psychological effects of meditation, its influence on personality, and its place in therapy are surveyed. There is some evidence that meditation reduces one's level of anxiety and neuroticism and can, therefore, be used therapeutically in the treatment of stress-related disorders, such as insomnia. Those meditators who, according to several authors, had a recurrence of serious pathological symptoms, were actually overmeditating, and the problems they encountered are not to be generally applied to all meditators.

1630. West, Michael A. "Meditation and the Perception of Self." THEORIA TO THEORY 13 (1979): 243-48.

Comments on the view that meditation leads to personal growth, greater awareness, and mystical states of consciousness. The author endeavors to explore how the regular practice of meditation can lead an individual to change one's self-image and one's relationship with the environment.

1631. West, Michael A. "Meditation." BRITISH JOURNAL OF PSYCHIATRY 135 (1979): 457-67.

Considers various works on the nature of meditation and its
alleged effects. Studies on Transcendental Meditation and
the main problems involved in its research are reviewed.
Various psychophysiological correlates and the effects of
meditation practice on personality are considered. The
therapeutic potential of meditation is covered under four
main headings: 1) meditation and drug abuse; 2) meditation
in psychiatric practice; 3) meditation and insomnia; and
4) meditation and hypertension. Some of the dangers of meditation are listed. It is concluded that, though some evidence
exists to support the thesis that meditation reduces anxiety
and can be used in therapeutic settings, adequate and satisfactory tests to measure its effectiveness have still to be
designed. A lengthy bibliography is included.

1632. Williams, Paul, Anthony Francis, and Robert Durham. "Person-
        ality and Meditation." PERCEPTUAL AND MOTOR SKILLS 43
        (1976): 787-92.

        Studies the relationship between the practices of Tran-
        scendental Meditation and certain psychological and psycho-
        pathological states. The researchers attempted to answer
        the following questions: What is the personality profile of
        a meditator? Does the meditator experience any changes which
        can be related to the regularity of meditation? The following
        conclusions were reached: 1) there is a high dropout rate from
        the practice of meditation; 2) people who go into TM are less
        well-adjusted; 3) male meditators who practiced TM are also
        less well-adjusted; and 4) male meditators experienced a
        decrease in neuroticism. In general, regular practice of
        TM tended to lessen both psychotic and neurotic traits.

1633. Witmer, Neil. THE REDUCTION OF ENCODED STRESS THROUGH THE
        TRANSCENDENTAL MEDITATION PROGRAM. Washington, DC: American
        Psychological Association, 1980. Psychological Documents,
        MS 2290, 39 pp.

        Discusses the meaning of stress, the contingencies and
        mediators of the stress process, and the enduring effects of
        the stress response hindering the physiological adaptation
        abilities. TM is seen as an effective technique reducing
        physiological enthropy.

1634. Woolfolk, Robert L. "Self-Control Meditation and the Treat-
        ment of Chronic Anger." MEDITATION: CLASSICAL AND CONTEM-
        PORARY PERSPECTIVES (item 45), pp. 550-54.

        Applies meditation as a treatment for a subject suffering
        from chronic debilitating anger. The results show that,
        although the patient showed no improvement by meditating twice
        a day, substantial alterations in his anger were recorded when
        he combined this regular routine with self-control meditation,
        a contingent, informal meditation used to combat arousal
        states. Meditation by itself may not, therefore, be suffi-

cient to alleviate serious stress-related disorders. It is
suggested that brief meditation periods in conjunction with
a self-control strategy may be of greater clinical value.

1635. Woolfolk, Robert L. "Psychophysiological Correlates of Meditation." ARCHIVES OF GENERAL PSYCHIATRY 32 (1975): 1326-33.

Maintains that research results on Yoga, Zen, and Transcendental Meditation, which confirm their psychological benefits,
are suggestive, but leave unanswered the question about which
aspects of the practices are the active ingredients, and which
mechanisms underlie the alleged efficacy. The basic writings
are reviewed to clarify what exactly is known of the effects
of the various meditative techniques. Studies in Zen and TM
have produced the most consistent findings, but adequate
experimental controls, as well as testable hypotheses, are
still needed. Research has failed to demonstrate an integrated, clearly-defined set of responses common to all forms
of meditation.

1636. Woolfolk, Robert L., and Cyril M. Franks. "Meditation and
Behavior Therapy." MEDITATION: CLASSICAL AND CONTEMPORARY
PERSPECTIVES (item 45), pp. 674-76.

Discusses the degree to which meditation has employed or
could employ the methodological assumptions and practices
of behavior therapy, which involve a commitment to rigor,
objectivity, specificity, and testability. Behavior therapy
requires that both dependent and independent variables and
the relationship between them be clearly specified. The
authors insist upon the need to apply such specification to
meditation which, removed from the realm of the arcane, can
become an integral part of therapy.

1637. Wortz, Edward. "Applications of Awareness Methods in Psychotherapy." JOURNAL OF TRANSPERSONAL PSYCHOLOGY 14 (1982):
61-68.

Shows how two forms of meditation, namely, listening and
breathing, were used in therapy. A case study is presented
in which the subject was instructed to relax, to examine
negative self-statements, and to practice internal dialogue.
The mapping of one's feelings and the developing of control
over one's negative feelings are also part of the treatment.
Meditation assists a person in reducing labeling, achieving
some detachment from words and phrases, and refraining from
judgment of others. Another method used was to instruct
patients to "practice sufferings," that is, to bring discom-
fort into one's awareness. Exaggerating, producing, and
dissipating negative habits is part of a continuous healing
process. Borrowed from Buddhism, the above techniques lessen
psychological suffering.

1638. Yalom, Irvin D., Gary Bond, et al. "The Impact of a Weekend
Group Experience on Individual Therapy." ARCHIVES OF
GENERAL PSYCHIATRY 34 (1977): 399-415.

Examines the effects on 33 psychiatric patients who were
referred to one of three weekend groups, namely, affect-
arousing encounter, Gestalt therapy, and meditation Tai-Chi.
The method used to carry out the experiment and the different
techniques employed by these newer therapies are described.
It was found that an affect-arousing weekend group did exert
a beneficial influence on the subjects, but that it was rather
short-lived, lasting only about 12 weeks. The results thus
questioned the exaggerated claims of many of those who tried
the newer therapies. Marathon sessions in most weekend groups
are rather risky, and a small minority of the subjects were
emotionally hurt by the experience.

1639. Yuille, John C., and Lynn Sereda. "Positive Effects of
       Meditation: A Limited Generalization." JOURNAL OF APPLIED
       PSYCHOLOGY 65 (1980): 333-40.

Explores further the positive psychological effects of
Transcendental Meditation, such as improved retention of
paired associations and increase of intelligence. It is
argued that previous research on meditation has suffered
from procedural inadequacies, particularly the application
of inappropriate experimental controls. The Yoga technique
for relaxation (savasana, the corpse pose) was used as a
second technique. The results cast considerable doubt on
previous research findings. The promised positive effects
are not great enough to motivate people to continue to meditate, and many of the high percentage of dropouts were badly
affected by meditation. The cognitive abilities of the
meditators showed no signs of improvement. Improvements on
other levels were the same for TM as for a pseudo-meditation
group and for Yoga practitioners. It is concluded that, not-
withstanding the enthusiastic claims and encouraging adver-
tisements by the proponents of TM, meditation has no effect
on one's cognitive processes. The claims that TM is an
effective tool in the educational process could not be
substantiated.

1640. Zika, Bill. "Meditation and Altered States of Consciousness:
       A Psychodynamic Interpretation." JOURNAL OF PSYCHOLOGY AND
       CHRISTIANITY 3 (1984): 65-72.

Poses several questions regarding the use of meditation and
other altered states of consciousness techniques in psychotherapy. Can they be used to promote personal growth and
development from a secular point of view? Can they increase
a person's spiritual awareness? And can they be abused and
bring about detrimental effects? The author maintains that
the intention of the client is the main factor that determines whether the employment of these methods produces personal
growth, spiritual awareness, and the resolution of conflict.
The client may experience a "restructuring of images" which,
rather than solve problems and minimize conflicts, may lead
to the reinforcement of maladaptive behavior patterns.

2. Pentecostal and Charismatic Groups

The recent influx and appeal of many Eastern religions in the
West have been accompanied by a resurgence of Christian fundamentalism and Pentecostalism, which often pursue a militant form of evangelism. These Christian groups are of interest to psychologists and
psychiatrists for several reasons. Many of them practice healing
rituals in which both physical and psychological problems are
addressed. Some charismatic churches consciously practice a form
of psychotherapy and have devised a method of "charismatic counseling." Further, many of the beliefs and practices of Christians, who
join one of these new groups, have been linked in clinical practice
to various kinds of disorders. The dogmatic stance which tolerates
no variety, the narrow-mindedness and exclusiveness which are the
hallmark of membership, the authoritarian attitudes which often
dictate the lives of the members in both spiritual and material
matters, and the occasional refusal to take recourse in medical
doctors for what has become standard, routine treatment in Western
culture, have long been recognized as signs of mental illness by the
majority of psychiatrists. Finally, the phenomenon of speaking in
tongues, a common, if not universal, practice of the neo-pentecostal
or charismatic renewal, has been, for many decades, extensively examined with great interest by psychiatrists.

Although the number of psychiatric studies on the members of the
new Pentecostals is rather limited, the tendency to regard them as
suffering from some psychological weakness or mental disorder still
dominates psychiatric literature. Charismatic and evangelical movements are said to attract the emotionally disturbed and mentally ill
and do nothing to better their conditions. Similarly, the majority
of their enthusiastic leaders, such as Billy Graham and Ruth Carter
Stapleton, are judged to be emotionally unstable persons. Faith
healers have, moreover, been outrightly denounced as sheer psychopaths.

There is, however, another psychiatric opinion which seems to be
gaining momentum, namely, that many of these new movements may be
helping people in distress; that, in spite of the aberrant behavior
of both leaders and members, people are being cured of mild emotional
and functional disorders and helped to cope with the problems of
daily life. Consequently, the revival of Pentecostalism might have
some therapeutic value and should not, therefore, be easily dismissed
as a psychopathological phenomenon.

Studies of glossolalia among charismatics have generally followed
the same lines as previous work on the subject. There is still
disagreement as to whether speaking in tongues is a form of trance,
altered state of consciousness, a cathartic expression of one's
emotions, a sign of hysteria or neurosis, or just a form of impro-
vised religious language. One should note, however, that even those
who are positive in their evaluation of glossolalia, more often than
not point to some dangerous elements which might accompany it. The
more optimistic writers see it as a form of therapy because it tends
to relieve emotional stress and anxiety and caters to the need for
spiritual development.

Pentecostal belief in demon possession and the ritual practice
of exorcism, highlighted in many modern films beginning with THE
EXORCIST, have also been the subject of debate. The resurgence of
interest in occult matters and the revival of witchcraft, paganism,
and satanism have been vehemently condemned by Pentecostals as the
work of the devil. The common psychiatric opinion seems to be that
belief in demon possession is pathological. It may be an indication of hysterical or obsessive neurosis, or schizophrenia, since
it manifests all the signs of a psychotic flight from reality. Some
point out that for those who believe that they are really possessed
by the devil, the ritual of exorcism may actually perform a therapeutic service.

1641. Alsdurf, Jim M., and H. Newton Malony. "A Critique of Ruth
      Carter Stapleton's Ministry of 'Inner Healing.'" JOURNAL
      OF PSYCHOLOGY AND THEOLOGY 8 (1980): 173-84.

      Seeks to evaluate Stapleton's healing ministry through an
      analysis of her personal life, theological framework, psycho-
      logical dynamics theory, and the integration of theology and
      psychology into her dynamic life. She is criticized for using
      her own experience with her parents as a model for interpret-
      ing all psychological and spiritual disturbances, and for
      propounding an incoherent theological system which betrays,
      among other things, an inadequate understanding of Jesus, and
      a purely psychological view of evil as something in the per-
      ception of people. Her lack of sophistication about psycho-
      dynamics leads her to incorrect formulations about the role
      played by childhood experiences in later life. Her integra-
      tion of psychology and theology are found to be faulty and
      shallow. The authors conclude that her impact for good
      cannot, however, be questioned. Several reactions to this
      essay with a response from the authors are included to make
      for a lively debate.

1642. Archer, Anthony. "Teach Yourself Tongue-Speaking." NEW
      BLACKFRIARS 55 (1974): 357-64.

      Describes the essential features of glossolalia, and shows
      how people acquire the ability to speak in tongues under cer-
      tain conditions. The author favors the view that glossolalia
      which occurs in a religious context is a kind of improvised
      language, which is expected of those who join a Pentecostal
      group. The rise of both classical Pentecostals and contem-
      porary charismatics can be explained by the deprivation theory.
      Glossolalia confers a feeling of well-being and an effective
      problem-solving device. Like the Billy Graham Crusade and
      the Divine Light Mission, the phenomenon of glossolalia is
      "a middle class cop-out."

1643. Bach, Paul J. "Demon Possession and Psychopathology: A
      Theological Relationship." JOURNAL OF PSYCHOLOGY AND
      THEOLOGY 7 (1979): 22-26.

Responds to Sall's view (item 1689) which separates mental illness from demonic influence, and argues that his theory is not supported by biblical and clinical evidence. Demon possession and psychopathology are two separate phenomena with similar symptomatology and variant etiologies. Both exorcism and psychotherapy are, in the author's view, part of the church's ministry.

1644. Balter, Leon. "The Charismatically Led Group: The Mental Processes of Its Members." PSYCHOANALYTIC STUDY OF SOCIETY 11 (1985): 173-215.

Examines the psychology of group membership and formation in those movements led by charismatic figures. Several non-religious examples are given, and some generalizations are drawn up. Two mental processes are singled out: 1) the idealization of the leader which is a form of conflict resolution involving the adoption of a regressed, ambivalent relationship with the leader, and expressing clear, passive masochistic trends in the oedipal phase; and 2) a mutual, partial identification of the members, which is a resolution of the conflict about the leader, and which leads to the uniformity and equality of the members. To what extent this model can be applied to Pentecostal and charismatic groups is not discussed.

1645. Blank, Richard J. "The Charismatic Clergyman and Counseling." COUNSELING AND VALUES 21 (1977): 76-83.

Introduces the reader to charismatic counseling. The author describes his own Pentecostal experience, and how it affected him in helping others. He argues that a deep understanding of human nature, stressing the part played by the soul, is at the basis of the charismatic approach to counseling, which takes into account the Christian community. Examples show how the Pentecostal experience helps patients therapeutically.

1646. Brende, Joel O., and Donald B. Rinssley. "Borderline Disorder, Altered States of Consciousness, and Glossolalia." JOURNAL OF THE AMERICAN ACADEMY OF PSYCHOANALYSIS 7 (1979): 165-88.

Outlines the typical features of borderline psychosis, and comments on its relation to social trends, particularly those of the late 1960s, when many new Eastern mystical groups established a foothold in Western society. The authors relate altered states of consciousness to both the relaxation response and glossolalia, and discuss their alleged benefits on a person's physical and mental health. Glossolalia is also considered with reference to a case study, and although it seems related to infantile regression and psychosis, it does not connote major psychopathology. On the contrary, glosso-lalia has a possible role in the treatment of some cases of borderline psychotic behavior.

1647. Castelein, John Donald. "Glossolalia and the Psychology of the Self and Narcissism." JOURNAL OF RELIGION AND HEALTH 23 (1984): 47-62.

Surveys the many interpretations of the glossolalia phenomenon in the context of its increasing practice in the United States. The literature on glossolalia is divided into three sections: historical survey, early studies, and more recent works. The focus of the author is on the sociopsychological reasons for its manifestation. It is proposed that speaking in tongues "may be seen to function as a therapeutic practice for people who predominantly already have a conservative background, but suffer from narcissistic disorders" (p. 48). The person who approaches a tongue-speaking group is a "battered, enfeebled, dependent self." The receptive and supportive charismatic fellowship provides a narcissistic therapy to restore the fragmented seeker's sense of wholeness. The glossolalia experience functions as a transitional phenomenon which restores a sense of balance and acceptance to the modern believer who ends up reaffirming a personal relationship with the supernatural.

1648. Chordas, Thomas J., and Steven Jay Gross. "The Healing of Memories: Psychotherapeutic Ritual Among Catholic Pentecostals." JOURNAL OF PASTORAL CARE 30 (1976): 245-57.

Examines the various kinds of healing among Catholic Pentecostals and focuses on the "healing of memories," that is, inner healing or the removal of psychologically and emotionally harmful scars acquired over a period of one's life. The prayer for the healing of memories, which should preferably occur in the presence of a person who assumes the role of healer, is described. The authors see several similarities between this ritual and psychotherapy. The healer and the therapist have similar roles, and both are recognized for their healing power, reliance on which is part of the cure. Empathy, non-possessive warmth, and genuineness are therapeutic qualities used by Catholic Pentecostals. The healing of memories can be treated as a modern form of "folk psychiatry," which is similar in its major aspects to conventional psychotherapy.

1649. Christie-Murray, David. VOICES FROM THE GODS: SPEAKING WITH TONGUES. London: Routledge and Kegan Paul, 1979. xiii, 280 pp.

Contains a brief survey of glossolalia in non-Christian cultures and a history of speaking in tongues in Christianity from Pentecost to the charismatic movement of the twentieth century. Evidence from medical literature is brought forth to show that speaking in tongues can be caused by moments of crisis, physical injury, or mental disturbance. The psychological effects of tongues are discussed with reference to the various theories which have been advanced to explain the phenomenon. The author maintains that glossolalia can be dangerous to the neurotic or mentally unbalanced person, but it can also bring about emotional and spiritual fulfillment.

1650. Corcoran, Charles J. "Psychology of the Charismatic Renewal." LISTENING: JOURNAL OF RELIGION AND CULTURE 12 (1977): 59-68.

Argues that the people involved in the charismatic renewal
should not be judged by writings hostile to Pentecostalism.
Three areas of ambiguity in the movement are noted: 1) the
meaning of the phrase "charismatic renewal"; 2) the meaning
of the term "spirit"; and 3) the external phenomena, which
are often equivocal. A theological, rather than a psychological, evaluation seems to be the thrust of this article.

1651. Coulson, Jesse E., and Roy W. Johnson. "Glossolalia and
       Internal-External Locus of Control." JOURNAL OF PSYCHOLOGY
       AND THEOLOGY 5 (1977): 312-17.

       Evaluates some of the principal hypotheses which have been
       advanced to explain glossolalia, and reports on the results
       of Rotter's Internal-External Locus of Control Scale which was
       administered to 95 glossolaliacs from the Four-Square Gospel
       and Assembly of God churches and to 79 non-glossolaliacs from
       the Methodist church. The former tended to be more internal
       than the latter. The authors think that the behavior of some
       of the members of the Pentecostal holiness sects may be devi-
       ant, but when displayed within the context of their religion,
       it cannot be considered pathological.

1652. Csordas, Thomas J. "The Rhetoric of Transformation in Ritual
       Healing." CULTURE, MEDICINE, AND PSYCHIATRY 7 (1983): 333-75.

       Examines psychotherapeutic value of ritual among Catholic
       Pentecostals who practice four kinds of healing: 1) physical
       healing; 2) spiritual healing (the confession of sins);
       3) the healing of memories (inner healing from emotional scars);
       and 4) deliverance (from demons). Several case studies are
       presented, and the clinical, comparative, and methodological
       implications are discussed. "The net effect of therapy is
       to redirect the patient's attention to various aspects of
       his life in such a way as to create a new meaning for that
       life, and a transformed sense of himself as a whole and well
       person" (p. 360). How well ritual therapy works, and what
       disorders it can cure, are questions left unanswered.

1653. Devol, Thomas J. "Ecstatic Pentecostal Prayer and Medita-
       tion." JOURNAL OF RELIGION AND HEALTH 13 (1974): 285-88.

       Reflects on the recent resurgence of glossolalia and pro-
       poses that ecstatic Pentecostal prayer is a unique kind of
       altered state of consciousness. The author, himself a Pente-
       costal, holds that speaking in tongues can be induced at will
       without drugs, can be put into use by anyone without prior
       training, has socially redeeming overtones, and can be
       enjoyed frequently without inhibitive results. The mental
       health values of the Pentecostal experience are reaffirmed.

1654. Dominian, J. "A Psychological Evaluation of the Pentecostal
       Experience." EXPOSITORY TIMES 87 (July 1976): 292-97.

       Presents a generally favorable view of the charismatic
       renewal but with a warning about the spiritual and psycholog-

ical dangers of stressing some of its extreme manifestations.
Glossolalia can be an sign of hysterical mutism, expressing
individual and group stresses, fantasies, and distortions.
The social structure of the charismatic group encourages the
type of leader who is unconsciously a frightened but determined child who is plagued by doubt and uncertainty and who
could, thus, create the perfect climate for preoccupation with
the belief in demon possession, which is a sign of pathology.
The Pentecostal movement has an built-in attraction for the
emotionally disturbed or mentally ill person. Some psychological criteria for evaluating the movement are suggested.

1655. Ehrenwald, Jan. "Possession and Exorcism: Delusion Shared
      and Compounded." JOURNAL OF THE AMERICAN ACADEMY OF
      PSYCHOANALYSIS 3 (1975): 105-19.

      Distinguishes four major aspects or sources of the so-called
      possession syndrome: 1) the inner conflicts of the victim,
      whose possession occurs in a trance state; 2) the hallucina-
      tory, delusional changes brought about by drugs and/or the
      pathologically altered states of consciousness; 3) imitation
      and emotional contagion, such as a collective acting-out of
      sexual pathology; and 4) the religious or parapsychological
      elements. Several examples to show how possession is a
      "hysterical contagion originating from either primary or
      artificial, media-made sources of pathology" (p. 117). A few
      clinical ways of handling the problem are proposed.

1656. Favazza, Armando R. "Modern Christian Healing of Mental Ill-
      ness." AMERICAN JOURNAL OF PSYCHIATRY 139 (1982): 728-35.

      Points out that the increasing popularity of the practice
      of Christian healing of mental illness requires that psychi-
      atrists be informed of the phenomenon. The historical context
      and the rebirth of Christian healing in the modern Pentecostal
      movement are described. Faith healers are adopting a thera-
      peutic approach based on the theory of demon possession and
      on the need for prayer as a remedy. Besides prayer and
      psychological therapy, they offer a lifelong support system
      in a Christian community and in small faith-sharing groups.
      Therapists must endeavor to understand the beliefs of those
      who come for help. They must determine whether a patient's
      religious sentiments are healthy or pathological, which might
      not be easy when the subject belongs to a small sect. The
      author thinks that, at times, it might be advisable to include
      the minister as part of the therapeutic process.

1657. Favazza, Armando R., and Ahmed D. Faheen. "The Heavenly
      Vision of a Poor Woman: A Case Report with Commentary."
      JOURNAL OF OPERATIONAL PSYCHIATRY 10.2 (1979): 93-120.

      Discusses the case of a Pentecostal woman's vision from
      God, and reproduces a lengthy interview with her. The case
      is diagnosed as one of hysterical psychosis.

1658. Frazier, Claude A., editor. HEALING AND RELIGIOUS FAITH.
       Philadelphia: United Church Press, 1974. 190 pp.

       Gives a collection of essays covering various aspects of
       physical and psychological healing in the context of reli-
       gious belief. It is maintained that faith-healing can cure
       some emotional and functional disorders. Elimination of
       stress and coping with various problems are among the many
       benefits one can reap from religion.

1659. Garrison, Vivian. "Sectarianism and Psychosocial Adjustment:
       A Controlled Comparison of Puerto Rican Pentecostals and
       Catholics." RELIGIOUS MOVEMENTS IN CONTEMPORARY AMERICA
       (item 1360), pp. 298-329.

       Compares demographic features, socioeconomic variables,
       migration history, family organization, patterns of social
       participation, and several indices of mental health of Puerto
       Rican Pentecostals and Catholics in the South Bronx, New York
       City. The author's aim is to determine if there are any dif-
       ferences between mainline churches and sects, and what effects
       sect membership has on the daily life of its members. It was
       found that Pentecostals differed very little from the members
       of major churches, and exhibited no greater inadequate func-
       tioning and emotional disturbances. Pentecostalism can help
       individuals in times of acute distress. Some evidence was
       found for the hypothesis that economic crisis does play a
       part in the conversion of some individuals.

1660. Gibson, Dennis L. "The Obsessive Personality and the Evan-
       gelical." JOURNAL OF PSYCHOLOGY AND CHRISTIANITY 2 (1983):
       30-35.

       Discusses Saltzman's view of obsessive personality (see,
       for example, items 172-73), and shows how it relates to
       evangelicals. Three obsessive tactics are common among them:
       1) indecision (seen in their procrastination and doubt); 2)
       perfectionism (manifested in their tendency to be utterly
       precise); and 3) rituals (which are often used as a means of
       acquiring magical power). Evangelicals are also known for
       their repetitive, inflexible, and compulsive thinking. The
       author maintains that obsessive techniques give the individual
       a sense of security through "control over the verdicts of
       public opinion." Some curative antidotes to obsessive trends
       are recommended.

1661. Griffith, Ezra E. H., Thelouizs English, and Violet Mayfield.
       "Possession, Power and Testimony: Therapeutic Aspect of the
       Wednesday Night Meeting in a Black Church." PSYCHIATRY 43
       (1980): 120-28.

       Recognizes the fairly common view that prayer meetings
       contribute to the psychological health of impoverished and
       politically powerless people, and explores specific mechanisms
       which churches use to achieve this end. A Wednesday night

gathering at an independent black church is described, and
the structures of the service which facilitate mutual aid are
outlined. Various features of the meeting, like spirit possession, are seen as temporary pathological experiences, but
helpful to the participants in the long run. The mental
health needs of the congregation are served by the church
services, which form a support system for blacks in the midst
of urban depersonalization, alienation, and lack of status.

1662. Henderson, James. "Exorcism and Possession in Psychothera-
        peutic Practice." CANADIAN JOURNAL OF PSYCHIATRY 27 (1982):
        129-34.

        Outlines several stages in Western European history of the
        community's understanding of mental disorders. Besides the
        prominent medical and psychoanalytic model current today,
        two theories are gaining popularity: 1) the view that inter-
        personal, rather than intrapsychic, processes are the cause
        of mental illness; and 2) the belief that supernatural forces
        are responsible for psychological and mental disorders. An
        attempt is made to link both theories in an explanation of
        possession. The author thinks that the contribution of object-
        relations theory is especially relevant to a psychodynamic
        understanding of possession and exorcism.

1663. Hohn, Nils G. "Functions of Glossolalia in the Pentecostal
        Movement." PSYCHOLOGICAL STUDIES ON RELIGIOUS MAN (item
        1070), pp. 141-58.

        Comments briefly on studies made of the sound structure of
        glossolalia, and accepts the position that people may have a
        natural ability to speak in tongues. The Pentecostal view of
        speaking in tongues is described. The use of glossolalia in
        charismatic meetings suggests that it is a learned behavior,
        sanctioned and controlled by the group. Glossolalia performs
        the function of meaningful communication in a religious set-
        ting, transcending normal interaction between people. Though
        it is admitted that there are some elements of suggestion,
        communication theory is judged to be a better explanation of
        what goes on in those meetings where glossolalia occurs.

1664. Hutch, Richard A. "The Personal Ritual of Glossolalia."
        JOURNAL FOR THE SCIENTIFIC STUDY OF RELIGION 19 (1980):
        255-66.

        Reviews critically some major literature on the speaking in
        tongues, a phenomenon usually regarded as aberrant, extra-
        ordinary, and anomalous. The view that glossolalia is a form
        of religious ritual is then proposed. More specifically,
        speaking in tongues is a ritualized amalgamation of crying
        and laughing, which are two basic forms of human feeling and
        relating to the world. Its function is to activate a range
        of possible painful and pleasant conditions, which are part
        of human existence. It is a personal ritual which can deepen
        one's spiritual life.

*   Jones, Charles Edwin. A GUIDE TO THE STUDY OF THE PENTECOS-
        TAL MOVEMENT. Cited above as item 26.

*   Jones, Charles Edwin. A GUIDE TO THE STUDY OF THE HOLINESS
        MOVEMENT. Cited above as item 27.

1665.   Kane, Steven M. "Holiness Ritual Fire Handling: Ethnographic
        and Psychophysiological Considerations." ETHOS 10 (1982):
        369-84.

        Discusses the fire-handling performances of the Holiness
        snake-handlers in Southern Appalachia, and focuses on the
        psychophysiological factors that leave its practitioners
        unharmed. The beliefs associated with fire handling and
        the trance-like states associated with it are described.
        Evidence is put forward to show how the power of suggestion
        can explain why the persons involved experience no harm.

1666.   Kane, Steven M. "Holiness Fire Handling in Southern
        Appalachia: A Psychophysiological Analysis." RELIGION
        IN APPALACHIA. Edited by John D. Photiadis. Morgantown:
        West Virginia University Press, 1978, pp. 133-24.

        Aims at uncovering the specific psychophysiological factors
        and mechanism that make Pentecostal fire-handlers of the South
        immune from the injurious effects of torch flames. A general
        description of the church and the torches used is provided.
        The author holds that those who take part in the ritual are in
        an altered state of consciousness, or trance, which produces
        numbness in several parts of one's body. He explains the fact
        that the fire-handlers not only feel no pain, but also avoid
        tissue damage by the theory that the entranced fire-handler's
        belief in his or her own invulnerability sets into action a
        protective nervous system process, which prevents pain and
        damage.

1667.   Kane, Steven M. "Ritual Possession in a Southern Appala-
        chian Religious Sect." JOURNAL OF AMERICAN FOLKLORE 87
        (1974): 293-302.

        Describes the ritual of snake-handling and manipulation of
        oil torches among Holiness churches in Appalachia. The wor-
        shippers go into a possession trance, which is preeminently
        a social and collective phenomenon. The possession by the
        Holy Ghost is a good example of hysterical contagion. It is
        stressed that this type of trance is learned and triggered in
        the context of certain psychological variables and external
        clues. The theory that the Holy Ghost people suffer from
        schizophrenia or other nervous disorders is refuted. The
        author states that these people, far from being psychotics
        or neurotics, are normal, well-adjusted, and suitably adapted
        to their environment.

1668.   Kelsey, Morton T. TONGUE SPEAKING: THE HISTORY AND MEANING
        OF CHARISMATIC EXPERIENCE. New York: Crossroads, second
        edition, 1981. xvii, 252 pp.

Presents an account and interpretation of glossolalia in
the history of the Christian church. The following areas are
covered: 1) speaking in tongues in the Bible and in the early
church; 2) the Pentecostal churches (such as the Holiness
movement and the Full Gospel Businessmen's Fellowship); and
3) the recent charismatic renewal. Various theories of glossolalia are discussed. The author rejects the common link
made between tongue-speaking and schizophrenia, hysteria, or
some kind of suggestion. He holds instead that the dream
state is very similar to the condition of those speaking in
tongues. Glossolalia has both positive and negative aspects.
It can be especially dangerous if used outside the context
of the Christian community.

1669. Lantz, Cary E. "Strategies for Counseling Protestant Evan-
        gelical Families." INTERNATIONAL JOURNAL OF FAMILY THERAPY
        1 (1979): 169-83.

        Comments on the little work which has been done to guide
        therapists who counsel religious patients, particularly
        Christian evangelicals, and attempts to examine and offer
        suggestions in this unexplored area of psychotherapy. The
        main features of evangelical religion are drawn, and the
        issues which both evangelical and non-evangelical therapists
        face are delineated. Four stages of the therapeutic endeavor
        with evangelical families are discussed: entry, translation,
        mobilization, and exit. It is suggested that various natural
        (supportive church communities) and supernatural (prayer)
        mental health resources may be employed in therapy.

1670. Lindstrom, Lars G. "Religious Faith Healing and its Psycho-
        logical Conditions: A Methodological Study." PSYCHOLOGICAL
        STUDIES ON RELIGIOUS MAN (item 1070), pp. 219-41.

        Reflects on the increase in the practice of faith-healing
        from the end of the last century to the current charismatic
        renewal. Several explanatory models, physiological, psycho-
        analytic, and sociological, are considered. The author
        questions both the methods used and the conclusions reached.
        His main criticism is that most of the research has been
        carried out without serious consideration of its specific
        religious character.

1671. Lovekin, A. Adams, and H. Newton Malony. "Religious Glosso-
        lalia: A Longitudinal Study of Personality Changes."
        JOURNAL FOR THE SCIENTIFIC STUDY OF RELIGION 16 (1977):
        383-93.

        Assesses personality change over a period of time among
        a group of people, who had acquired "the gift of tongues"
        while participating in the "Life in the Spirit Seminar," a
        spiritual program run by the Catholic Pentecostals at Notre
        Dame, Indiana. A battery of psychological tests led the
        researchers to the conclusion that all those who took part
        in the program, whether they had become glossolalic or not,

changed in the direction of personal integration. It was the
attendance at the seminar, rather than the emotional experience of speaking in tongues, that was responsible for the
positive changes which the researchers recorded.

1672. Malony, H. Newton, and A. Adams Lovekin. GLOSSOLALIA: BEHAV-
IORAL SCIENCE PERSPECTIVES ON SPEAKING IN TONGUES. New
York: Oxford University Press, 1985. ix, 292 pp.

Offers a critical but sympathetic view of glossolalia
written by two psychologists and ordained ministers, one of
whom speaks in tongues. The glossolalia phenomenon is examined as anomalous, aberrant, and extraordinary behavior.
Various interpretations of glossolalia as hysteria, hypnosis,
or pathology are reviewed. Its physical, psychological,
behavioral, cognitive, and attitudinal effects as recorded
by the researchers are outlined. Finally, the authors
attempt an "integrated interpretation." They suggest that
glossolalia can be best understood as a "transcendency deprivation," a search for a more immediate religious experience.
Glossolalia is a form of mysticism and should not be mistaken
for a cultic quality or feature. A good lengthy bibliography
(pp. 263-79) is included.

*   Martin, Ira Jay. GLOSSOLALIA, THE GIFT OF TONGUES: A BIBLIOG-
RAPHY. Cited above as item 33.

1673. McDonnell, Kilian. CHARISMATIC RENEWAL IN THE CHURCHES. New
York: Seabury Press, 1976. x, 202 pp.

Examines the Pentecostal/charismatic movement with special
emphasis on the speaking in tongues. Sociological and psychological theories which see glossolalia as expressive of
economic, social, or ethical deprivation are outlined and
evaluated. The author divides these theories into two historical periods: 1) those propounded between 1911 and 1966; and
2) the more recent ones proposed between 1967 and 1975. The
early theories interpreted on glossolalia as a sign of the
abnormal psychological condition of marginal people. The
later theories indicate a movement to treat the phenomenon
of speaking in tongues as normal behavior not necessarily
linked to pathology.

1674. McGuire, Meredith B. PENTECOSTAL CATHOLICS: POWER, CHARISMA,
AND ORDER IN A RELIGIOUS MOVEMENT. Philadelphia: Temple
University Press, 1982. ix, 270 pp.

Presents a sociological study of the Catholic charismatic
renewal. The groups studied and the methods of research
used are described, and the central beliefs, values, and
meanings specified. The processes of conversion, commitment,
and socialization are traced, the ritual language analyzed,
and the views about illness, health, and healing expounded.
The author stresses that glossolalia, a species of religious
speaking, is not pathological when seen in its total setting.

Faith-healing is compared to psychotherapy and, together with
speaking in tongues and prophecy, fulfills many rich and
meaningful functions within the group.

1675. McNutt, Francis. HEALING. Notre Dame, IN: Ave Maria Press,
        1974. 333 pp.

        Offers a study of the Christian ministry of healing by one
        of the leaders of the Catholic charismatic renewal. After
        discussing the underlying meaning and importance of the heal-
        ing ministry in the church, the author explains four basic
        kinds of healing, namely, spiritual healing (from sin), inner
        healing (of memories), physical healing, and deliverance (from
        demons). Inner healing is a cure for one's emotional problems,
        anxiety, and depression, and consists of praying to God to
        remove the binding effects of hurtful incidents of the past.
        Such healing is, according to the author, therapeutic.

*   Mills, Watson E. CHARISMATIC RELIGION IN MODERN RESEARCH: A
        BIBLIOGRAPHY. Cited above as item 37.

1676. Mills, Watson E. "Literature on Glossolalia." JOURNAL OF
        THE AMERICAN SCIENTIFIC AFFILIATION 26 (December 1974):
        169-73.

        Surveys materials on glossolalia under the following head-
        ings: primary works; historical studies; tongues and other
        traditions; psychological, biblical, and theological studies;
        testimonials; and unpublished materials. Over 100 items are
        listed.

1677. Montgomery, John Warwick, editor. DEMON POSSESSION: A MEDI-
        CAL, HISTORICAL, ANTHROPOLOGICAL, AND THEOLOGICAL SYMPOSIUM.
        Minneapolis: Bethany Fellowship, 1976. 384 pp.

        Contains 24 essays on demon possession seen from different
        academic perspectives within a largely Christian fundamental-
        ist framework. Several essays approach the issue from a
        psychiatric point of view, and some link demon possession
        with hysteria, and demon oppression with depression. Guide-
        lines for Christian counselors are provided.

1678. Ness, Robert C., and Ronald M. Wintrob. "The Emotional Im-
        pact of Fundamentalist Religious Participation: An Empirical
        Study of Intragroup Variations." AMERICAN JOURNAL OF ORTHO-
        PSYCHIATRY 50 (1980): 302-15.

        Reviews some of the literature which shows that intense
        religious participation leads either to emotional integration
        and adaptive behavior or to psychological disintegration.
        A study of the relationship between religious participation
        and the emotional state of the members of a Pentecostal church
        in a small coastal village in Newfoundland is conducted to
        test the negative and positive effects on their mental health.
        Glossolalia, spirit possession, testimonials, ritual healing,

and consistent attendance were included in the study. There
is strong support for the view that people who take part in
non-medical healing are less likely to report symptoms of
psychological distress. The study found that glossolalia and
possession appear to lessen emotional distress and frequently
bring emotional well-being. Participation in fundamentalist
religious activities, plus the social support of the congregation, has a beneficial impact on demoralized individuals.
Minority religious groups (sects) may attract people who have
been emotionally harmed by regular religious participation.

1679. Niecz, Nancy L., and Earl J. Kronenberger. "Self-Actualiza-
       tion in Glossolalic and Non-Glossolalic Pentecostals."
       SOCIOLOGICAL ANALYSIS 39 (1978): 250-56.

       Studies self-actualization in Roman Catholic college
       students. Glossolalic neo-Pentecostals were compared with
       non-glossolalic neo-Pentecostals and a control group of non-
       Pentecostals. The only statistically significant difference
       among the groups was between those who spoke in tongues and
       non-Pentecostals. The former seem to have achieved a higher
       degree of self-actualization.

1680. Ormand, Donald. "Exorcism: An Adjunct to Christian Counsel-
       ing." COUNSELING AND VALUES 21 (1977): 84-88.

       Compares marriage counselors with exorcists in that they
       both aim to expel evil and disruptive influences, and to help
       people live peacefully together. There are three forms of
       illness, physical, mental and spiritual, and not all of them
       can be cured by psychiatrists. The author believes strongly
       in the possibility of demonic possession and maintains that
       psychologists, psychiatrists, medical doctors, and exorcists
       should be advisors to Christian counselors.

1681. Osser, H. A., P. F. Oswald, B. MacWhinney, and R. C. Casey.
       "Glossolalic Speech from a Psychotherapeutic Perspective."
       JOURNAL OF PSYCHOLINGUISTIC RESEARCH 2 (1973): 9-19.

       Studies glossolalia as a form of speech and distinguishes
       two basic styles, formalistic (stereotyped and repetitive)
       and innovative (varied and creative), which differ in their
       characterization, and in their syntactic, morphological, and
       intonational modes. Glossolalia differs also from non-
       sensical language and should be considered a unique phenom-
       enon. It is pathological only "when a patient seems to lack
       self-control, cannot limit his nonsensical behavior to move-
       ments when it is expected or tolerated by others, or speaks
       in this way for the sole purpose of annoying or confounding
       the listeners" (p. 11).

1682. Pattison, E. Mansell. "Ideological Support for the Marginal
       Middle Class: Faith Healing and Glossolalia." RELIGIOUS
       MOVEMENTS IN CONTEMPORARY AMERICA (item 1360), pp. 418-55.

Demonstrates how the belief and value system of Christian
fundamentalists is at variance with the mainstream of the
American middle class, thus creating major social and psychological problems and distortions in the lives of the former
group. Six typical personality traits of fundamentalists
are listed, namely, a marked degree of hostility, paranoia,
psychosomatic symptoms, masochism, depression, and conflicts
over sexual identity. Their value orientation is discussed,
and it is shown how it negatively influences the development
of personality. The cultural dissonance in which fundamentalists live is counteracted by ritual support of their ideology,
namely, glossolalia and faith-healing, which reduce both
cultural and psychological dissonance. Only a few members
actually engage in these relief-bringing rites.

1683.   Pattison, E. Mansell, Nikolajs A. Lapin, and Hans A. Doerr.
        "Faith Healing: A Study of Personality and Function."
        JOURNAL OF NERVOUS AND MENTAL DISEASE 157 (1973): 397-409.

        Discusses faith-healing as part of a continuum of magical
        belief systems ranging from witchcraft to Christian Science.
        This study concentrates on fundamentalist, Pentecostal sects
        (e.g., the Assemblies of God and the Churches of the Nazarene
        in Seattle), and attempts to determine: 1) whether there is a
        typical personality of those who claim faith-healing; 2) why
        people participate in these rituals; 3) whether faith-healing
        changes one's symptoms; and 4) whether involvement in these
        churches significantly alters one's life-style. From a
        clinical point of view, the adherents of these sects show no
        sign of gross pathology and any pathological disorder or
        illness is well within normal limits. They show a strong need
        for social acceptance and affiliation. Magical faith-healing
        itself does not represent psychopathology, but rather "an ego-
        integrative and socio-integrative mechanism." It is a coping
        mechanism for externalization and explanation when anxiety,
        misfortune, and illness occur. Hence, within the believer's
        frame of reference, faith-healing is not aberrant behavior.

1684.   Peacock, James. "Symbolic and Psychological Anthropology:
        The Case of Pentecostal Faith Healing." ETHOS 12 (1984):
        37-53.

        Discusses two different interpretations of faith-healing
        in American fundamentalist religion. The symbolic approach
        stresses the conscious expression of one's beliefs, while the
        psychological approach searches for unconscious pathological
        conditions. The author attempts a synthesis between the two
        approaches. He maintains that faith-healing is not a response
        to psychological problems, but rather an expression of a
        religious world view.

*   Persinger, Michael A. "Striking EEG Profiles from Single
        Episodes of Glossolalia and Transcendental Meditation."
        Cited above as item 1563.

1685.   Propst, L. Rebecca. "A Comparison of the Cognitive Re-
        structuring Psychotherapy Paradigm and Several Spiritual
        Approaches to Mental Health." JOURNAL OF PSYCHOLOGY AND
        THEOLOGY 8 (1980): 107-14.

        Maintains that some evangelical and charismatic modes of
        counseling are psychologically legitimate because of their
        similarity to cognitive therapy. The author draws parallels
        between the use of imagery in psychotherapeutic and in evan-
        gelical pastoral literature. The charismatic inner healing
        movement is seen as psychotherapeutic with a solid foundation
        in contemporary psychiatry.

1686.   Richardson, James T. "Psychological Interpretations of
        Glossolalia: A Reexamination of Research." JOURNAL FOR
        THE SCIENTIFIC STUDY OF RELIGION 12 (1973): 199-207.

        Surveys literature on speaking in tongues, particularly in
        the context of recent charismatic or neo-Pentecostal revival.
        Both earlier studies and more recent research on the psycho-
        logical aspects of glossolalia still link it with various
        forms of pathology. The author reexamines the theories which
        relate speaking in tongues with mental illness and finds
        that they are based on scanty information and too subjective
        in their approach. He suggests, among other procedures, that
        adequate instruments be developed for studying the phenomenon,
        that the sources of glossolalia be investigated, and that
        longitudinal research designs with follow-up processes be
        adopted.

1687.   Riscalla, Louis Mead. "A Study of Religious Healers and
        Healees." JOURNAL OF THE AMERICAN SOCIETY OF PSYCHOSOMATIC
        DENTISTRY AND MEDICINE 29 (1982): 97-103.

        Investigates religious healing, i.e., healing of the whole
        person through the use of prayer, anointing with oil, and/or
        the laying on of hands. The motivations of those individuals
        seeking this kind of healing in randomly selected Presbyterian,
        Episcopal, Catholic, and non-denominational churches are ex-
        plored using a participant-observation method. Those report-
        ing either complete healing or an improvement in their health
        condition came from lower occupational classes. Older people
        sought relief from physical conditions, while younger ones
        from emotional problems. The healing service itself created
        an atmosphere conducive to receptivity to healing. All
        healers claimed that God is the actual healer and that reli-
        gious and medical healing are complementary.

*   Rosten, Leo, editor. RELIGIONS IN AMERICA: FERVENT AND FAITH
        IN AN AGE OF CRISIS. Cited above as item 1303.

1688.   Sall, Millard J. "A Response to 'Demon Possession and Psy-
        chopathology: A Theological Relationship.'" JOURNAL OF
        PSYCHOLOGY AND THEOLOGY 7 (1979): 27-30.

Examines Bach's response (item 1643) to his position that
demon possession and psychopathology are distinct phenomena
(see item 1689). His original argument is clarified and more
biblical and clinical evidence is adduced to support it.

1689. Sall, Millard J. "Demon Possession or Psychopathology?: A
       Clinical Differentiation." JOURNAL OF PSYCHOLOGY AND
       THEOLOGY 4 (1976): 286-90.

Discusses, in the context of the contemporary interest in
witchcraft and the occult, the relationship between mental
illness and diabolical possession. The author maintains that
there is a clear distinction between those who suffer from
some kind of mental disease and those who are possessed.
Hallucinatory mental illness should, therefore, not be confused with the work of the devil. Most deviant behavior can
be explained by natural causes, although, in some cases, it
could be a sign of demon possession.

1690. Samarin, William J. "Glossolalia as Regressive Speech."
       LANGUAGE AND SPEECH 16 (1973): 77-89.

Contends that psychological or physiological theories of
glossolalia are inadequate because they do not take into
account all the relevant data. The thesis presented here is
that glossolalia is a linguistic anomaly (i.e., it cannot be
accounted for by the rules of ordinary language), similar to
other marginal linguistic phenomena. Glossolalia involves, to
some extent, a primitivization and simplification of language.
The author rejects the explanation that glossolalia is a product of trance, for this fails to account for 1) glossolalic
behavior that is patently not pathological and dissociative,
and 2) similar "meaningless" utterances in non-religious
contexts.

1691. Schwarz, Berthold E. "Ordeal by Serpents." THE WORLD'S
       WEIRDEST CULTS. Edited by Martin Ebon. New York: New
       American Library, 1979, pp. 49-61.

Describes a religious meeting in a Holiness church in
Tennessee where the ordeal by fire, the drinking of strych-
nine, and the handling of poisonous snakes are believed to be
signs of one's faith in God. Some of the members went into
"deep dissociated trances" that are interpreted as violent
upheavals of the unconscious. The author thinks that the
avoidance of being bitten is related to the magnitude of the
trance, in the sense that rhythmic stimulation brings about
inertia and drowsiness in the snakes. The Holiness people
act out in their strange rituals their conflicts and tragic
realities of life.

1692. Silverman, Gilbert, and William B. Oglesby. "The New Birth
       Phenomenon During Imprisonment: Corrective Emotional
       Experience or Flight Into Health?" PASTORAL PSYCHOLOGY
       31 (1983): 179-83.

Examines the social and psychological aspects of the born-
again experiences among prison inmates. The dehumanizing,
authoritarian, oppressive, bleak, and dangerous conditions
of a prison create and aggravate many psychological problems,
including loss of identity, alienation from society, sense of
failure, and fear of death. The inmate's experience makes
him or her open to receive the message of hope and good news
of the Gospel. The experience of conversion may be therapeutic or merely a temporary emotional high with a feeling
of well-being.

1693. Simson, Eve. THE FAITH HEALERS: DELIVERANCE EVANGELISM IN
      NORTH AMERICA. New York: Pyramid Books, 1977. 223 pp.

Covers the so-called deliverance evangelists, one type of
itinerant protestant preacher, who propound a fundamentalist
religion with belief in the gifts of the Holy Spirit and in
faith-healing. Roxanne Bryant, Kathryn Kuhlman, Oral Roberts,
Don Stewart and Aimee McPherson are taken as typical examples.
The author traces the way a person becomes a faith healer,
his/her occupational substructure, and family and societal
relationships. The social background of the followers are
also described. Some major personality traits of both the
evangelists and their followers are noted. The evangelists
tend to have been prone to periods of daydreaming and restlessness in their youth. They are, moreover, high-strung.
Some are emotionally unstable and susceptible to extrasensory
perception, for which reason they have been accused of being
psychotic. The followers have a sense of rejection and uncertainty, and demand clear-cut answers to their problems.
They are introverted, unpretentious, and credulous, and lean
to psychotic behavior, even though they do not appear to be
more psychologically maladjusted than the rest of society.
The author concedes that they might be able to deal successfully with such functional illnesses and personality disorders
as drug addiction and alcoholism. But their success in coping
with, and healing, organic ailments is doubtful, and their
methods in this area are likely to yield harmful effects.

1694. Smith, Daniel S., and J. Roland Fleck. "Personality Corre-
      lates of Conventional and Unconventional Glossolalia."
      JOURNAL OF SOCIAL PSYCHOLOGY 114 (1981): 209-17.

Reviews current theories on glossolalia, and tests several
hypotheses to determine whether glossolalia is pathologically
linked with recent trauma or whether it is therapeutic.
People who speak in tongues were found to display more overt
anxiety and more likely than non-glossolalics to discharge
their tension through verbal and physical behavior. Speaking
in tongues provides immediate release from anxiety and emotional stress and is thus therapeutic in nature. Glossolalics
are able to face life more easily and directly, to integrate
themselves more readily, and to achieve comfort and intra-
psychic relief. But compared to non-glossolalics, they are
less intelligent, come from a slightly lower socioeconomic

level, and have experienced more frequent and recent crises.
Glossolalia can be considered a regressive experience in the
service of the ego.

1695. Sneck, William J. CHARISMATIC SPIRITUAL GIFTS: A PHENOMENO-
        LOGICAL ANALYSIS. Washington, DC: University of America
        Press, 1981. xiii, 298 pp.

        Employs the phenomenological method to explain the meaning
        of the gifts of the Holy Spirit stressed in the modern Charis-
        matic movement, particularly in the Word of God community in
        Ann Arbor, Michigan. Attempts are made to discover the rele-
        vant psychological variables involved in acquiring these gifts.
        The author's method is mainly descriptive and emic, a method
        which he holds to be better than the traditional psychological
        approach to interpret religious experience. The book tends
        to focus on describing the charismatics and to report on their
        experiences of prophecy, healing, and deliverance. The author
        prefers to interpret the charismatic gifts, including glosso-
        lalia, as a visionary's interaction with the paranormal
        rather than an instance of abnormal schizophrenic behavior.

1696. Spanos, Nicholas P., and E. C. Hewitt. "Glossolalia: A Test
        of the 'Trance' and Psychopathology Hypothesis." JOURNAL
        OF SOCIAL PSYCHOLOGY 88 (1974): 427-34.

        Interprets glossolalia as a pattern of vocal behavior,
        which anyone who has the right motivation and exposes oneself
        frequently to the phenomenon can acquire. The authors find
        no support for the theory that glossolalia is a result of
        trance, a direct effect of hypnotic suggestibility, or a
        clear symptom of psychopathology.

1697. Stanley, Gordon, W. K. Bartlett, and Terri Moyle. "Some
        Characteristics of Charismatic Experience: Glossolalia in
        Australia." JOURNAL FOR THE SCIENTIFIC STUDY OF RELIGION
        17 (1978): 269-77.

        Considers the question whether the "charismatic experience
        is a unitary phenomenon by examining the written responses of
        a sample of Australian charismatics to a request for their
        views about the experience" (p. 270). The author concluded
        that four varieties of glossolalia experience can be distin-
        guished. Two features are common to all types: 1) the absence
        of the feeling of unity; and 2) the presence of the ability
        to control the production of glossolalia. Such qualities
        seem to indicate that speaking in tongues is not an altered
        state of consciousness. Samarin's view (item 585) that the
        glossolalia experience occurs in a fairly normal state of
        consciousness and functions primarily as a ritual which con-
        firms one's experience is supported by the author's research.

1698. Stanley, Gordon, and Peter Vagg. "Attitude and Personality
        Correlates of Australian Protestant Fundamentalists."
        JOURNAL OF SOCIAL PSYCHOLOGY 96 (1975): 291-92.

Compares the results of several personality tests conducted on students from an Australian Protestant Bible college and from the general population of the city of Melbourne. Though the fundamentalist students were found to be more conservative, they were also judged to be less neurotic than the rest of the population.

1699. Swanson, Guy E. "Trance and Possession: Studies of Charismatic Influence." REVIEW OF RELIGIOUS RESEARCH 19 (1978): 253-78.

Presents a study of the general sources and qualities of trance and possession when they arise in charismatic encounters, whether they occur spontaneously outside ritual practice or within the framework of established rite and worship. Both trance and possession are said to be common, but powerful, experiences which shape people's conduct from within. Active and passive modes of trance are distinguished, and daily trance experiences are related to hypnotizability. Those experiences of possession which are not under the subject's control can be brought about or heightened by social experiences, where decision making is in the hands of one or a few of the members, or where means of making collective decisions have not yet been developed.

1700. Tappeiner, Daniel A. "A Psychological Paradigm for the Interpretation of the Charismatic Phenomenon of Prophecy." JOURNAL OF PSYCHOLOGY AND THEOLOGY 5 (1977): 23-29.

Attempts to understand charismatic behavior from a scientific and psychological point of view, which sees it as a product of natural mechanisms and not as a manifestation of the Holy Spirit, even though the author admits that his theological framework leans towards accepting the validity of spiritual charisms in the Christian context. The focus is on the prophetic experience, which is a hypnogogic state, a state of consciousness that precedes sleep. Pentecostal baptism is explained as the opening of a channel between the conscious and the unconscious, glossolalia as a form of prayer which increases one's awareness and openness to the Spirit, and the revelatory or prophetic state as the expression of words and images similar to the creative imagery of the hypnogogic state.

1701. Taylor, Graeme. "Demonical Possession and Psychoanalytic Theory." BRITISH JOURNAL OF MEDICAL PSYCHOLOGY 51 (1978): 53-60.

Surveys some of the psychoanalytic writings on demonical possession, and discusses its relation to Freud's libido theory and to Fairbain's relations theory. A case example is presented to demonstrate that, while there is some value in both theories, they need to be integrated in clinical practice. The devil, according to the author, symbolizes repressed evil impulses and desires and becomes a scapegoat for unacceptable sexual impulses. Demonic possession is a sign of neurotic and psychotic flight from reality.

1702. Trethowan, W. H. "Exorcism: A Psychiatric Viewpoint."
       JOURNAL OF MEDICAL ETHICS 2 (1976): 127-37.

       Espouses the view that psychiatrists should interest them-
       selves in exorcism for several reasons: 1) it still takes
       place in modern times with tragic consequences; 2) there are
       cases of patients who suffer from the delusion of possession,
       a sign of an ongoing psychotic illness; and 3) the roots of
       modern psychopathology are to be found in medieval demonology,
       the concept of the devil being equivalent to the "id" in
       psychoanalysis. The exorcist's necessity for belief and the
       nature of the demoniacal possession syndrome are discussed.
       The signs and symbols expressed in the possession phenomenon
       are analyzed in some detail. The author proposes a Freudian
       psychodynamic theory, which interprets belief in possession
       by demons as a projection to relieve the individual from the
       responsibility for his or her behavior. Possession states
       are a form of hysterical neurosis which the exorcist, who
       shares in the belief system, encourages and supports. While
       the author is clear in his opinion that belief in demon
       possession is pathological, he seems to suggest that the ex-
       orcist might perform a function similar to that of a psychi-
       atrist. Two short commentaries debate some of the author's
       views and presuppositions.

1703. Virkler, Henry A., and Mary B. Virkler. "Demonic Involvement
       in Human Life and Illness." JOURNAL OF PSYCHOLOGY AND
       THEOLOGY 5 (1977): 95-102.

       Discusses the role of demons in the etiology of physical
       and psychological illness. Four major areas are explored:
       1) those illnesses which Scripture links with demonic posses-
       sion; 2) the general scriptural view of illness (mental and
       physical); 3) the scriptural position on psychological demons
       (so often spoken of today in some Christian groups and cults);
       4) the criteria which should be used to differentiate between
       demonic possession and mental illness. Several symptoms of
       possession, including occult manifestations such as polter-
       geists and mediumistic abilities, are listed.

1704. Whitlock, F. A. "The Psychiatry and Psychopathology of Para-
       normal Phenomena." AUSTRALIAN AND NEW ZEALAND JOURNAL OF
       PSYCHIATRY 12 (1978): 11-19.

       Examines certain classes of paranormal phenomena to see
       whether any of them can be understood in psychiatric or psy-
       chophysiological terms. Among the topics considered are faith-
       healing and religious stigmata. The author maintains that
       suggestion, faith in the healer, the placebo effect, and the
       reinforcement of social attitudes through charismatic sects
       are sufficient to explain the majority of the alleged mirac-
       ulous cures, while hysteria, or blood and skin diseases, can
       account for reported cases of stigmata. Further study of
       these manifestations are encouraged because of their possible
       contributions to psychotherapy.

1705. Whitwell, F. D., and M. G. Barker. "Possession in Psychiatric
       Patients in Britain." BRITISH JOURNAL OF MEDICAL PSYCHOLOGY
       53 (1980): 287-95.

       Attempts to understand those people whose abnormal mental
       states are often linked with possession by evil spirits. The
       symptoms of 16 patients who believed they were possessed by
       the devil or by a spirit, together with their family and
       religious backgrounds, are described. The author thinks that
       the subjects he examined are disturbed individuals who respond
       to the suggestion that they are possessed. It is stressed
       that knowledge of, and respect for, their religious beliefs
       are necessary, if the psychiatrist is to establish a thera-
       peutic relationship with these clients.

1706. Wikström, Owe. "Possession as a Clinical Phenomenon: A Cri-
       tique of the Medical Model." RELIGIOUS ECSTASY (item 1057),
       pp. 87-102.

       Deals with the experiences of those individuals who strongly
       believe they are possessed by the devil or by evil spirits.
       Four case studies of common possessional states found in
       clinical practice are presented. The neurophysiological and
       psychoanalytical theories of possession, as well as those
       which see it as a form of hypnosis or an interaction between
       language and emotion, are all discussed. The author equates
       possession with psychosis, schizophrenia, or obsessive
       neurosis. Possession is a process involving a dynamic rela-
       tionship between the verbal representation of evil and the
       intrapsychic, anxiety-filled emotive state.

1707. Williams, Cyril G. TONGUES OF FIRE: A STUDY OF PENTECOSTAL
       GLOSSOLALIA AND RELATED PHENOMENA. Cardiff: University of
       Wales Press, 1981. xiii, 276 pp.

       Compares ecstasy in Hebrew prophecy with the Christian
       phenomenon of glossolalia, especially in the New Testament
       and in the Pentecostal and neo-Pentecostal movements. Three
       areas of research on glossolalia are delved into: 1) the
       personality and (physical and mental) condition of those who
       speak in tongues; 2) the function of glossolalia; and 3) the
       form of glossolalia utterances. Explanations in terms of
       abnormal psychological states, social disorganization, eco-
       nomic deprivation, and cultural conditions are reviewed.
       Several purported functions of abreactive release or energy
       discharge, and of restoration of infantile megalomania are
       discussed. Glossolalia can function as a unifying element,
       strengthening the individual's group allegiance, and as a
       symbol of a break with the past. Xenoglossia, the speaking in
       a real language unknown to the speaker, as well as shamanism,
       Sufism, and the use of mantras are briefly looked into. It
       is concluded that glossolaliacs do not seem to be more dis-
       oriented or inadequate than those who do not speak in tongues.
       When abnormality is present in the individual, glossolalia is
       not the determining factor. The author speculates on some
       of the reasons which might explain its current resurgence.

1708. Wilson, Michael. "Exorcism: A Clinical/Pastoral Practice
       Which Raises Serious Questions." EXPOSITORY TIMES 86
       (July 1975): 292-95.

       Discusses several theological and psychological questions
       about belief in the devil and the practice of exorcism. He
       concludes that exorcism fits neatly into Western culture.
       "Our whole idea of health," he writes, "is clinical, and we
       believe that health is obtained by the diagnosis, prevention,
       and treatment of illness. Exorcism is a typically clinical
       approach to evil" (p. 295).

1709. Wimberley, Ronald, et al. "Conversion in a Billy Graham
       Crusade: Spontaneous Event or Ritual Performance." SOCIO-
       LOGICAL QUARTERLY 16 (1975): 162-70.

       Examines the nature of a religious revival or crusade, and
       finds evidence that the conversions that occur during such
       events are ritualistic, integrative occurrences. The Billy
       Graham organization structures revival meetings in such a way
       that many who attend are, through screening questions, reli-
       gious literature, church referrals, and counselors, led to
       the ritual of conversion. Because of the "integrative"
       results that such revivals have on one's personality, they
       can be considered therapeutic to many.

3. Eastern and Other Cultic Groups

    In-depth psychological or psychiatric studies on individual cults
and sects have tended to lag behind sociological research, which has
produced several monographs on the new religious movements. It is,
therefore, difficult to point to a single in-depth psychiatric work
which has concentrated on one religious cult over a relatively long
period of time. Psychiatric literature, moreover, leaves one with
the impression that members of Eastern religious groups, for example,
can be psychologically evaluated without much knowledge and understanding of their religious and philosophical backgrounds. Whether
and to what degree the available psychological tests are suitable
to determine the emotional and mental health of cult members is a
question which still has to be asked. Although psychological anthropology and, more recently, transcultural psychiatry have made significant progress in remedying this problem, many counselors and
psychiatrists, who are concerned with the ill effects the new cults
are having on their membership, pay little or no heed to the content
of Eastern traditions. One is not surprised to discover that those
cults which incorporate Eastern thought, values, and life-styles,
are invariably judged to be more pathological than the rest.

    The sweeping conclusion that involvement in cults is the cause of
major psychopathology is not supported by the research results of
several studies, particularly those of Galanter and his associates
on (items 1722, 1742 ff.) the Unification Church and the Divine Light
Mission, and by the less comprehensive work of Ross (items 1792-93)

on a group of Australian members of the Hare Krishna Movement. Two common conclusions can be drawn from studies of this type: 1) that those who join a new religious movement are going through some life-crisis which involves psychological weakness, but which is not the cause of serious pathological impairment of their judgment and freedom of decision; and 2) that membership in a cult has some positive results, in that it alleviates psychological stress and has adaptive outcomes. Cults address themselves to largely neglected and unsolved problems. Their appeal lies in the fact that they make apparently genuine and successful efforts to deal with them.

Cult and sect leaders have not fared that well in psychiatric examinations, even though some researchers have suggested that they play the role of folk psychiatrists. The tragedy of the People's Temple under Jim Jones seems to have confirmed, once and for all, that the gurus and self-styled prophets of our age are psychologically sick people who are not likely to be of much assistance to their devotees in their quest for peace and happiness. But once again, psychiatric research on contemporary cult leaders, which is admittedly somewhat difficult to pursue, is still in its infancy. There have been more studies published on Mary Eddy Baker than there have been on all the modern cult leaders combined.

Several studies on human potential groups, often accused of having cultic characteristics, have been, on the whole, favorable. The most comprehensive research spread over a period of five years seem to have been on Silva Mind Control conducted by McKenzie and his associates (items 1778-79). Est has also been subjected to several investigations and, although the reports indicate that its program is a kind of awareness training and resembles traditional therapy to some degree, there are a few reservations about its acclaimed beneficial effects. One is inclined to conclude that most of these human potential groups are not meant for persons with serious pathological problems.

The psychiatric literature on the new religious movements does not provide us with an unquestionable answer to the psychopathological or therapeutic nature of contemporary cultism. One is left with the weak solution that some cults may help some individuals, but may also cause serious psychological damage to others. As has been pointed out in the introduction, some theoretical and methodological issues have to be clarified and new directions followed if any progress in the psychology and psychiatry of the cults is to be achieved. One has to agree unconditionally with the often-repeated statement, in many of the studies quoted in this work, that more research is necessary and that the methods need to be refined.

1710. Angell, Donald L., and George T. Desau. "An Investigation of Silva Mind Control in Rehabilitation Counselor Education." COUNSELING AND VALUES 21 (1977): 229-36.

Observes that Western education has paid little attention to exploring and understanding inner subjective states which are ignored, if not completely rejected, in the training

PSYCHIATRY AND THE CULTS

programs of counselors and psychologists. Silva Mind Control, an alternative education system which emphasizes subjectivity and expanded awareness, was applied to a group of graduate students in rehabilitation counseling at the University of Scranton. Those who participated in the program, compared to a control group, acquired a greater maturity, increased their powers of relaxation, and developed more open attitudes towards subjective states. The authors contend that these qualities are certainly needed in counselors, and suggest that Silva Mind Control might play a part in the therapeutic process.

1711. Anthony, Dick, Thomas Robbins, Madeline Doucas, and Thomas E. Curtis. "Patients and Pilgrims: Changing Attitudes Towards Psychotherapy of Converts to Eastern Mysticism." AMERICAN BEHAVIORAL SCIENTIST 20 (1977): 861-85.

Describes the experiences with psychotherapy of converts to the Meyer Baba movement and the Divine Light Mission. Those converts who had tried traditional psychotherapy before conversion had found the experience unsatisfactory. There is a tendency among these cult members to harmonize their religious and psychotherapeutic involvements. These cult members go through three distinct stages: 1) pre-conversion experiment with psychotherapy; 2) spiritual awakening, "the Honeymoon period"; and 3) reentry into psychotherapy. The authors claim that the monistic view of the universe, common in Eastern mysticism, is in harmony with some of the assumptions of modern psychotherapy.

1712. Babbie, Earl, and Donald Stone. "An Evaluation of the Est Experience by a National Sample of Graduates." BIOSCIENCE COMMUNICATIONS 3 (1977): 123-40.

Surveys a probability sample of 2,000 graduates from a population of 12,000 Est graduates, and assesses the Est experience as conceived by the graduates themselves. Those who had taken the program report favorable benefits derived from the training as well as a wide variety of unexpected improvements in their lives, including better relationships with family members and friends, more productivity in school and job, more satisfaction in sexual relations, and an overall amelioration in mental health. These benefits do not seem to disappear or diminish over time. Several suggestions for further research are made.

1713. Baer, Donald M., and Stephanie B. Stolz. "A Description of the Erhard Seminary Training (Est) in the Terms of Behavior Analysis." BEHAVIORISM 6 (1978): 45-70.

Describes the procedures of the Est training, its probable or possible products, and explains them in terms of behavior analysis. Est's instruction control is compared and contrasted to brainwashing. It is concluded that in spite of the similarities, there are many differences in content. It

is maintained that Est may enable the trainees to gain better
control over their lives and to achieve better harmony with
their present condition. Increased satisfaction with life
is a common outcome. Some patterns, which the authors think
are Est failures, are considered, and the amenability of Est
to research is discussed at some length.

1714. Baer, Hans A. "Prophets and Advisors in Black Spiritualist
Churches: Therapy, Palliative, or Opiate?" CULTURE, MEDI-
CINE, AND PSYCHIATRY 5 (1981): 145-70.

Explores a variant of Black ethnomedicine in United States
urban areas, centering upon advisors and prophets in syncretistic sects known as "spiritual" churches. The classification
of illness, its diagnosis and treatment, the different kinds
of folk healers, and the client-practitioner relationship are
described. The author thinks that the spiritual advisor in
these churches is the "poor man's psychiatrist." He favors
the theory which regards spiritualist healing as an adaptive
mechanism which helps Blacks survive in a hostile environment.
These indigenous healers, however, may be deflecting attention
from the real problems of their clients, namely, their inferior
position in a stratified and racist society. For this reason
the author is skeptical of the therapeutic alliance between
traditional healer and Western therapist.

1715. Baer, Hans A. "An Anthropological View of Black Spiritual
Churches in Nashville, Tennessee." CENTRAL ISSUES IN
ANTHROPOLOGY 2.2 (1980): 52-68.

Offers a study of a somewhat neglected religious movement in
the United States, namely, the Black Spiritual Church, which
incorporates elements from Protestantism, Roman Catholicism,
Voodoo, and spiritualism. A brief history of the movement and
an outline of its beliefs and rituals are provided. Spiritual
churches "provide mechanisms of addressing the psychosocial
and socioeconomic problems" of black people and "serve to
alleviate their alienation from society by promising financial
success or the restoration of personal conflict in return for
carrying out certain magico-religious rituals" (p. 66). These
benefits, however, are not lasting since the problems can only
be eliminated by a radical change in the social structure of
American society.

1716. Bainbridge, William Sims. SATAN'S POWER: A DEVIANT PSYCHO-
THERAPY CULT. Berkeley: University of California Press,
1978. 312 pp.

Presents a vivid, ethnographic account of the rise of a
new religious movement in the early 1960s, of its internal,
political conflicts and social structure, and of its historical development until its wane in the mid-1970s. The Power,
a pseudonym of the author's choosing, came into being in
London as a therapy group, and then evolved into a center
for psychic, occult experimentation and stunning ritual per-

formances, which included the worship of the great gods of
the universe: Lucifer, Jehovah, Christ, and Satan. The author
maintains that the cult became more socially deviant with the
passage of time, and that those who joined it in the 1970s
were a "pathological majority."

1717. Beckford, James A. "Psychiatry and Sectarians." BRITISH
       JOURNAL OF PSYCHIATRY 127 (1975): 414.

       Criticizes Spencer's essay on the mental health of Jehovah's
       Witnesses (item 1808) for containing several factual errors
       and methodological flaws. The main thesis that members of
       this sect are paranoid-schizophrenics is found to be rather
       unlikely.

1718. Bloom, Christopher D. "'Space Brothers' Over Hollywood."
       THE WORLD'S WEIRDEST CULTS (item 1200), pp. 49-61.

       Gives a short description of the Aetherius Society, a UFO
       cult which still thrives in a scientific world. Membership,
       it is maintained, meets the psychological needs of its con-
       verts for a paternal space-figure, and helps them overcome
       their feelings of low self-esteem and uselessness. The author
       endorses the deprivation theory of cult formation.

1719. Brewer, Mark. "We're Going to Tear You Down and Put You Back
       Together." PSYCHOLOGY TODAY 9 (August 1975): 35-40, 80,
       88-89.

       Presents an account of the author's own experience with
       Erhard Seminar Training (Est). The common-sense psychology
       and the high-handed tactics used in one of the most popular
       pop-psychology programs are described. The general view ex-
       pressed in this essay is that brainwashing techniques are
       used ostensibly to enhance people's lives.

1720. Brink, T. L. "Joseph Smith: The Verdict of Depth Psychology."
       JOURNAL OF MORMON HISTORY 3 (1976): 73-84.

       Brushes aside the early psychological studies of Smith, and
       investigates the founder of Mormonism from the viewpoint of
       depth psychology. Freud's general tendency to depict reli-
       gious leaders as pathological is, according to the author,
       not applicable to Smith's life. Taking a Jungian approach,
       Smith's writings are seen as a creative relationship with
       unconscious forces. From the psychological perspective of
       Adler and Erikson, Smith appears to be a well-adjusted person.
       He may have effectively utilized adaptive regression prior to
       his transformation into a healthy, creative individual. There
       is no doubt that he was mentally healthy, and that religion
       played an important role in his personality development.

1721. Bry, Adelaide. EST: SIXTY HOURS THAT TRANSFORM YOUR LIFE.
       New York: Harper and Row, 1976. x, 181 pp.

Contains mainly testimonies of people pursuing different
careers in Western culture who took Erhard Seminar Training.
The main thrust of the book is to show that the program has
the potential of changing the participant's life for the
better, and of enabling people to cope with life. The success
which Est has achieved in a relatively short time indicates
that it is more effective than ordinary therapy.

1722. Buckley, Peter, and Marc Galanter. "Mystical Experiences,
        Spiritual Knowledge, and a Contemporary Ecstatic Religion."
        BRITISH JOURNAL OF MEDICAL PSYCHOLOGY 52 (1979): 281-89.

Studies members of the Divine Light Mission in order to
elucidate some of the psychological factors, in particular
its ecstatic quality, underlying its appeal. Questionnaires
were given to over one hundred members, several of whom were
interviewed. Their mystical experiences are described, and
it is suggested that the similarities to the effects of
hallucinogenic drugs may be explained in part by the members'
use of drugs before joining the movement. It is concluded
that initiation into the group, which is referred to as "the
receiving of knowledge," is, for at least some members, a
mystical experience, comparable to those of St. Augustine or
of the founder of Alcoholics Anonymous. The experience of
the members of the Divine Light Mission can be viewed as "a
regression in the service of the ego that resolved their
immediate intrapsychic and social conflicts" (p. 286). It
retains their sense of identity, and is not a return to the
symbiotic state, though it has similarities to it, especially
in its use of an affective ecstatic experience as a form of
knowing. The Divine Light Mission experience is compared
to that of the Quakers and of members of possession cults as
well as to the conversion of Christian saints like Ignatius
of Loyola.

1723. Chang, Stephen Thomas. THE COMPLETE BOOK OF ACUPUNCTURE.
        Millbrae, CA: Celestial Arts, 1976. xix, 244 pp.

Provides a history of acupuncture and a description of how
it diagnoses and heals illness. The acupuncture points are
outlined in great detail. Chinese medicine maintains that
excessive emotions are the cause of most diseases. Although
used mainly to cure physical illness, acupuncture can be
effective in the treatment of drug addiction.

1724. Cleveland, Sydney E. "Jehovah's Witnesses and Human Tissue
        Donation." JOURNAL OF CLINICAL PSYCHOLOGY 32 (1976):
        453-58.

Tries to determine whether personality patterns of the
people at large who do not donate human blood and tissue
are similar to those of Jehovah's Witnesses who refuse blood
transfusions on religious grounds. The author found that
although the latter vigorously oppose such donations, they
do not, unlike the other non-donors, possess a weak body

image, nor an anxiety about body integrity, nor an unusual
concern about personal death. It is held that the Jehovah's
Witnesses' stand on this matter is based on strong religious
faith. In refusing to give blood, members reaffirm their
religious allegiance and exercise some of their personality
needs. Tests indicate that they are emotionally constricted
and inhibited, suspicious and distrustful of secular authority,
and alienated from the world.

1725. Cohen, Jay, and Fredrick J. Smith. "Socially Reenforced
        Obsessing: Etiology of a Disorder in a Christian Scientist."
        JOURNAL OF CONSULTING AND CLINICAL PSYCHOLOGY 44 (1976):
        142-44.

        Reports on an ex-Christian Scientist who exhibited obsessive
        behavior and fears in connection with her previous religious
        affiliation. As a Christian Scientist for ten years, the
        subject had several experiences which either challenged or
        strengthened her beliefs in the validity of "prayer" as taught
        in Christian Science. Her irrational fears were instrumental
        in triggering her obsessive behavior. As her disavowal of
        the efficacy of Christian Science procedures increased during
        therapy, her obsessive thinking decreased.

1726. Cunningham, Raymond J. "Christian Science and Mind Cure in
        America: A Review Article." JOURNAL OF THE HISTORY OF
        BEHAVIOR SCIENCE 11 (1975): 299-305.

        Surveys some of the writings on Christian Science, a sect
        which is regularly included in works dealing with mental
        therapy.

1727. Dane, Leila. "Astral Travel: A Psychological Overview."
        JOURNAL OF ALTERED STATES OF CONSCIOUSNESS 2 (1975-76):
        249-57.

        Discusses the issue of out-of-body experiences, allegedly
        confirmed by Kirlian photography, and describes the feelings
        of those who have had such experiences and the paranormal
        abilities which one is said to acquire during such flights.
        Astral travel is viewed, from the standpoint of abnormal
        psychology, as an incidence of hallucinations and illusory
        visions. It seems to occur in connection with the mystic
        state, and reveals striking similarities with physiological
        changes that take place during Transcendental Meditation
        and isolation experiments. The author thinks that out-of-
        body experiences are related to those individuals who are
        psychically preparing for death.

1728. Deikman, Arthur J. "Sufism and Psychiatry." JOURNAL OF
        NERVOUS AND MENTAL DISEASE 165 (1977): 318-29.

        Argues that psychiatry has contributed to the healing of
        mental disease, but has paid less attention to how a healthy
        person functions. Modern scientific culture has created

"anomie," an illness of meaning which psychiatry is unable
to cope with, since it lacks a theoretical framework to come
to grips with the problem. Particularly when one approaches
the mid-life crisis, modern culture has no advice to give
except that a person should be stoical and accept with courage
the oncoming, inevitable end. In contrast, Eastern mystical
disciplines have provided methods which combine a focus and a
purpose to life. The author holds that such disciplines must
be adopted by the West, and then shows how Sufism, through
its stories, supplies answers to basic human existential
problems without being bogged down, as Western religion is,
in set rituals, dogmas, and organizations. Psychological
stress stems from three conflict levels: 1) those which arise
from one's wishes, fears, and fantasies; 2) those which come
from the absence of perceived meaning; and 3) those which
derive from frustration in making progress. Psychiatry deals
with the first kind of conflicts, Sufism with the other two.

1729.   Deutsch, Alexander. "Tenacity of Attachment to a Cult Leader:
        A Psychiatric Perspective." AMERICAN JOURNAL OF PSYCHIATRY
        137 (1980): 1569-73.

        Follows up on the author's previous study (item 1730) of a
        cult whose leader became cruel and increasingly bizarre in
        his behavior. The attitudes of those devotees who remained
        loyal to the guru, seeing him as a benevolent leader, a
        teacher, God's agent, a model of freedom, and a person who
        suffered vicariously for his followers, are described. His
        irrational behavior, when recognized, was explained as divine
        madness or as a way of teaching them a lesson. The group
        attracted alienated youths in search of guiding principles.
        Membership, however, brought with it a regression. The group,
        according to the author, "is somewhat reminiscent of Freud's
        primal horde" (p. 1572).

1730.   Deutsch, Alexander. "Observations on a Sidewalk Ashram."
        ARCHIVES OF GENERAL PSYCHIATRY 32 (1975): 166-75.

        Describes the meetings between an American guru and his
        disciples, and the author's interviews with 14 of them. The
        subjects are evaluated as unhappy and their relationships
        with their parents as unsatisfactory. Their new allegiance
        brought about happiness, a result of their relief from guilt,
        a sense of freedom, an acquiring of a new purpose, and a
        feeling of being accepted and loved. Various elements in
        their life-style, their sexuality, employment, ambition, and
        food habits are examined. The influence of psychedelic drugs
        is also considered. Mystical experience and conversion to a
        cult are given a psychoanalytic interpretation as a regression
        to the infant's experience of union with the mother and as a
        conflict resolution of oedipal expression, respectively.

1731.   Deutsch, Alexander, and Michael J. Miller. "A Clinical Study
        of Four Unification Church Members." AMERICAN JOURNAL OF
        PSYCHIATRY 146 (1983): 767-70.

Reports on the testing of four female Unification members
and ex-members. The results indicate that they had difficulties with heterosexual relationships, were idealistic in
their desire to serve or unify others, had a spiritual world
view with mystical overtones, and nurtured a tendency to deny
or wish away threatening perceptions. The authors think that
these features predisposed the subjects to the life-style and
doctrine of the Unification Church.

1732. Dressler, William W. "Stress and Sorcery in Three Social
       Groups." INTERNATIONAL JOURNAL OF SOCIAL PSYCHIATRY 31
       (1985): 275-81.

       Studies beliefs in witchcraft and sorcery among Afro-
       Americans in the West Indies, in the rural southern United
       States, and among Puerto Rican immigrants to the mainland
       USA. Such beliefs are linked to social stresses, especially
       those which accompany cultural changes. The formulation of
       these personalistic beliefs about witches and sorcerers is a
       "culturally constituted defense mechanism" which enables the
       individual to relieve distress by projecting it onto the
       supernatural world. The question of whether these beliefs
       are adaptive still needs further study.

1733. Dwyer, Philip M. "An Inquiry into the Psychological Dimension
       of Cult Suicide." SUICIDE AND LIFE-THREATENING BEHAVIOR 9
       (1979): 120-27.

       Examines the mass suicide at Jonestown (led by Jim Jones)
       and compares it to the suicide of nearly 1,000 Jews at the
       mountain fortress of Masada in 73 A.D. (led by Eleazar), and
       the account of the "Pequod" (led by Captain Ahab). The effec-
       tiveness of totalitarian control, isolation, and mystical
       manipulation are the psychological elements investigated. In
       spite of important differences, the author observes some
       similarities between the three cases in which the ultimate
       sacrifice leads to tragic results.

1734. Egeland, Janice A., Abram M. Hostetter, and S. Kendrick
       Eshleman. "Amish Study III: The Impact of Cultural Fac-
       tors on Diagnosis of Bipolar Illness." AMERICAN JOURNAL
       OF PSYCHIATRY 140 (1983): 67-71.

       Reviews some cultural factors encountered in diagnosing
       manic-depressive illness among the Amish. The researchers
       point out that the symptoms of grandiosity and excessivity
       are very prone to cultural conditioning, thus making it
       difficult to assess affective disorder in the Amish patient.
       The misdiagnosis of manic-depression for schizophrenia
       has been very common. It is suggested that a closer scrutiny
       of both the clinical and cultural factors which influence
       diagnosis is necessary.

1735. Erhard, Werner, and Victor Gioscia. "Est: Communication in
       a Context of Compassion." CURRENT PSYCHIATRIC THERAPIES
       18 (1978): 117-25.

Describes the format of the Est training program, giving detailed content of the four-day period in which four main topics, namely, belief, experience, reality, and self, are addressed in lectures, guided personal experiences, and sharing sessions. The goal of Est is to enable the participant to transform his or her ability to experience living fully with an emphasis on self-determination. Those who took the course succeeded in experiencing each other with "absolute compassion." The assumption throughout is that Est helps the individual grow and mature psychologically.

1736. Erhard, Werner, and Victor Gioscia. "The Est Standard Training." BIOSCIENCE COMMUNICATIONS 3 (1977): 104-22.

Examines Est as an example of an "awareness training" in relation to contemporary psychiatry. The format of the training is outlined with the three relationships which the participant develops, that is, to the training itself, to the group, and to the self. The "superrational epistemology" of Est is discussed. It is argued that Est is not therapy and it does not solve problems, but rather brings about those moments in life when people experience themselves as fully alive.

1737. Fenwick, Sheridan. GETTING IT: THE PSYCHOLOGY OF EST. Philadelphia: J. B. Lippincott, 1976. 191 pp.

Presents a description and evaluation of Est by a psychologist who participated in the training program. The total experience, from the pre-training to the post-graduate sessions, is covered, and the various activities, like "sharing," "sourcing," and "disappearing your problems," are treated in depth. Among the issues discussed is whether Est is a form of brainwashing or psychotherapy and whether it could be harmful to one's health. The author admits that there is some coercive persuasion in Est which is not, however, a brainwashing technique. Est has as many similarities to psychotherapy as the various psychotherapies have to each other. The Est experience is a stressful one, because it strips the participants of their psychological defenses and resistances and increases anxiety. It could be harmful, especially since the trainees do not take any precautions.

1738. Finkelstein, Peter, Brant Wenegrat, and Irvin Yalom. "Large Group Awareness Training." ANNUAL REVIEW OF PSYCHOLOGY 33 (1982): 515-39.

Reviews the literature on awareness training programs (such as Lifespring, Actualization, and Est), discusses the similarities between them and psychotherapy, and suggests directions for future research. A description of Est is given and its results, as recorded by graduates and by psychological tests, are outlined. It is concluded that surveys of Est graduates do establish their high satisfaction with their training, but methodological flaws make it

impossible to assess the program objectively. The literature
on casualties and psychiatric patients of Est is "largely
anecdotal and impressionistic" (p. 530). Est is finally
examined as behavior therapy, group psychotherapy, and
existential therapy in order to clarify some of its
possible psychotherapeutic content.

1739. Fishman, Robert G. "Transmigration, Liminality, and Spiri-
        tualist Healing." JOURNAL OF RELIGION AND HEALTH 19 (1980):
        217-25.

        Reports on an urban spiritualist organization in Western
        New York State. The church service is seen as the mechanism
        by which the medium creates a "spiritual liminality," that is,
        a transition period in which the healing of interpersonal
        relationships and the solution of daily problems takes place.
        It is concluded that "spiritualism functions to alleviate
        physical, psychological, and social disorders of church
        members" (p. 224).

1740. Fishman, Robert G. "Spiritualism in Western New York: A
        Study in Ritual Healing." MEDICAL ANTHROPOLOGY 3 (1979):
        1-22.

        Studies the spiritist beliefs and attitudes of members of
        a Unity Science Church in Western New York, and attempts to
        assess how they affect one's health. The major beliefs of
        the church, including psychic phenomena, mediumship, faith
        and prayer healings, and reincarnation, are briefly described.
        The healing rituals serve important therapeutic functions
        in that they generate hope, give rise to positive emotions,
        change attitudes, and finally lead to the relief of suffering.
        Many of the illnesses dealt with in these churches are caused
        by social conflicts that occur in daily affairs. The cure is
        an attempt to reintegrate the individual with society. It
        reduces the symptoms of illness, thus enabling people to cope
        more effectively with others and with their environment.

1741. Fransella, Paul R. "Mind Control: A Spiritual Bridge."
        COUNSELING AND VALUES 21 (1977): 247-52.

        Describes the author's own dramatic change after taking
        the Silva Mind Control course. His previous condition was
        "mentally and emotionally beaten" and physically unhealthy.
        After the program, he gave up smoking and drinking, acquired
        an inner peace and balance, and discontinued medication. He
        claims that his life and the lives of his family members
        became "full, meaningful, productive, and creatively
        positive" (pp. 251-52).

1742. Galanter, Marc. "Engaged Members of the Unification Church
        (Impact of a Charismatic Large Group on Adaptation and Be-
        havior)." ARCHIVES OF GENERAL PSYCHIATRY 40 (1983): 1197-
        1202.

Studies Unification Church members a year after they were assigned marriage partners in a engagement ceremony. Two questions were asked: how is such unusual behavior brought about in the group and how do these members respond to life-stresses? The questionnaire was aimed at recording information in the following areas: social cohesiveness, neurotic distress, religiosity, psychological traits, social adjustment in the year after the engagement, general well-being, and health problems. Two specific cases, one positive and one negative, are given to convey the nature of individual responses to the engagement. The author thinks that the research findings suggest that intense affiliation to the church lessened the impact of this radical behavioral change in engagement and marriage practices.

1743. Galanter, Marc. "Unification Church ('Moonie') Dropouts: Psychological Readjustment After Leaving a Charismatic Group." AMERICAN JOURNAL OF PSYCHIATRY 140 (1983): 984-89.

Investigates the nature of the influence which an intense group has on its members and the impact on the individual who leaves the Unification Church. Over one-third of ex-members of the UC experienced serious emotional problems and still felt the influence of their former associations. The large majority felt that they had gained some positive things during their membership, which they viewed as a developmental stage in their lives. Voluntary and coercive reasons for leaving are examined, and clinical implications are discussed. The author thinks that "social support networks, with a clear-cut cognitive framework, may be important contributors to individuals' psychological health" (p. 988).

1744. Galanter, Marc. "Sociobiology and Informal Social Controls of Drinking: Findings from Two Charismatic Sects." JOURNAL OF STUDIES ON ALCOHOL 42 (1981): 64-79.

Examines two religious groups, the Unification Church and the Divine Light Mission, on certain traits disposing individuals to accept their respective informal social controls with regard to drinking. The research recorded drinking habits, neurotic distress, and group cohesion in the Divine Light Mission, and the role of religious norms and induction procedures in the Unification Church. The author's view is that balance between neurotic distress and psychological well-being plays a role in the sociobiological regulation of conformity to a relatively large social group. The intensive large group experience, as in Alcoholics Anonymous, Recovery Inc., Est, and Gestalt, is a mental health paradigm which has gained widespread recognition. Membership in such groups reflects an innate inclination to experience a "relief effect."

1745. Galanter, Marc. "Psychological Induction into Large-Group: Findings from a Modern Religious Sect." AMERICAN JOURNAL OF PSYCHIATRY 137 (1980): 1574-79.

Explores the psychological aspects of conversion during
several 21-day workshops held for new recruits to the Unification Church in a number of major U. S. cities. Four areas
were the subject of tests given to these prospective members:
general well-being, cohesion level, creed, and sense of
purpose. By comparing these results with those acquired
from ex-members and current members, the author reached the
conclusion that weak ties to the family were an important
factor which led young adults to join the Unification Church.
Members of this religious sect do experience an amelioration
of their psychological state, but "considerable psychopathology unrelated to situational issues is common to sect members"
(p. 1579). It is pointed out that the lectures and discussion
in UC workshops have parallels in Alcoholics Anonymous and
in other Christian sects, such as the Anabaptists and the
Moravians.

1746. Galanter, Marc, and Luiza Cohen Diamond. "Relief of Psychi-
       atric Symptoms in Evangelical Sects." BRITISH JOURNAL OF
       HOSPITAL MEDICINE 26 (1981): 495-97.

       Questions whether religious conversion can lead to a relief
       of psychological distress in the context of two new religious
       movements, the Divine Light Mission and the Unification Church.
       Tests reveal that members of both sects had experienced psycho-
       logical difficulties prior to conversion, that many had been
       drug users, and that some had sought professional help.
       Several changes after conversion were evident: less neurotic
       stress, sharp decline in drug use, and improvement in tests
       evaluating one's general psychological health. The sense of
       affiliation to the group is held to be partly responsible for
       the improvements. The implications for psychotherapy are
       discussed. Certain parallels between religious cults and
       psychiatric treatment are noted.

1747. Galanter, Marc, Richard Rabkin, et al. "The 'Moonies': A
       Psychological Study of Conversion and Membership in a Con-
       temporary Religious Sect." AMERICAN JOURNAL OF PSYCHIATRY
       136 (1979): 165-70.

       Reports on a questionnaire given to members of the Unifica-
       tion Church to explore the nature of their conversion and
       continued membership in this new group. The tests, adminis-
       tered to a representative sample of full-time members in a
       large, unspecified, metropolitan area, and conducted with the
       cooperation of the church leaders, were intended to check the
       level of neurotic stress, religiosity, and general well-being.
       The replies showed that the members had experienced a signif-
       icant amount of psychological problems before joining the
       new religious movement. They reported no overt coersion or
       physical deprivation during the initial UC workshop. Their
       affiliation provided considerable and sustained relief from
       neurotic stress. The author thinks that the attribution
       theory provides a better model than that of brainwashing to
       account for conversion.

1748. Garvey, Kevin. "The Prophet from Palmyra: Joseph Smith and
       the Rise of Mormonism." PSYCHODYNAMIC PERSPECTIVES ON
       RELIGION, SECT, AND CULT (item 1226), pp. 59-72.

       Studies Mormonism in the context of the Second Great Awak-
       ening and the religious crisis of the nineteenth century.
       Some similarities are noted between Mormonism and Jim Jones's
       People's Temple. Attention is drawn to the dictatorial atti-
       tudes of both founders, who wanted to secure their prominent
       role and control the lives of their followers. Mormonism
       created an environment in which the powerless, the helpless,
       and the alienated found an escape.

1749. Geary, Thomas F., Marcia Rudin, and Michael W. Ross. "Prob-
       lems With Research on Hare Kirshna Devotees." AMERICAN
       JOURNAL OF PSYCHIATRY 141 (1984): 142-44.

       Contains two critical responses to Ross's study on Hare
       Krishna devotees in Australia (item 1792) and his rebuttal.
       Geary objects to some of Ross's comparisons; for example,
       that between the life-style of ISKCON and of some Catholic
       religious orders, and thinks that the input of parents and
       families should have been included in any research. Rudin
       reiterates her adamant position that cults are destructive
       organizations. Ross replies to both by confirming his
       statistical research method and by restating his results.

1750. Glass, Leonard L., Michael A. Kirsch, and Fredrick N. Parris.
       "Psychiatric Disturbances Associated With Erhard Seminar
       Training: I. A Report of Cases." AMERICAN JOURNAL OF
       PSYCHIATRY 134 (1977): 245-47.

       Presents five case-reports of people who enrolled in the
       Est program, which seems to attract clients who suffer from
       intrapsychic and interpersonal distress. The researchers
       speculate that an authoritarian, confrontational, and aggres-
       sive leadership may lead to fusion with leaders, ego fragmen-
       tation, and other psychotic problems in those who are psycho-
       logically deprived.

1751. Griffith, Ezra H., and Marie A. Mathewson. "Communitas and
       Charisma in a Black Church Service." JOURNAL OF THE NATION-
       AL MEDICAL ASSOCIATION 73 (1981): 1023-27.

       Describes a mid-week service in a black urban church which
       uses prayer, testimony, and spirit possession. This kind of
       church could be looked upon as a healing institution providing
       a therapeutic resource for its members. Their weekly service
       is a vehicle for closer human contacts and group involvement,
       and is a therapeutic asset in some black communities.

1752. Haaken, Janice, and Richard Adams. "Pathology as 'Personal
       Growth': A Participant-Observation Study of Lifespring
       Training." PSYCHIATRY 46 (1983): 270-80.

Investigates the structure and processes of one of the
most widely marketed human potential movements, Lifespring
Training. A description of the group, focusing on the role
the leaders play, the participants' behavior, and the activities and techniques employed, is given. The effects of
the program are explained from a psychoanalytic perspective.
It is contended that, although the participants often experience a sense of well-being, the training leads to pathology
in the sense that it undermines ego functioning and promotes
regression by stressing submission and surrender. It further
fosters magical thinking and stimulates early narcissistic
conflicts and defenses.

1753.   Halifax, Joan, and Hazel H. Weidman. "Religion as a Mediat-
        ing Institution in Acculturation: The Case of Santeria
        in Greater Miami." RELIGIOUS SYSTEMS OF PSYCHOTHERAPY
        (item 1021), pp. 319-31.

        Describes the way certain strategies within Santeria, a
        "crisis cult" among Cubans in Florida, helps resolve some
        of the adaptive problems these immigrants experience. The
        foundations and features of Santeria and the priestly role
        of the santero, or diviner, are outlined. Santeria is an
        institution that functions both as a "testing ground for the
        adoption of values and behaviors," and as "a mechanism of
        translating the threatening and potentially destructive into
        the meaningful and constructive" (p. 328).

1754.   Halleck, Seymour L. "Discussion of 'Socially Reinforced
        Obsessing.'" JOURNAL OF CONSULTING AND CLINICAL PSYCHOLOGY
        44 (1976): 146-47.

        Rebuts Cohen and Smith's study (item 1725) on a Christian
        Scientist whose faith was judged to be directly responsible
        for her obsessional and irrational fears. The author observes
        that changing one's religious ideology after therapy is not
        an unheard-of phenomenon, even though the therapist is careful
        not to lead patients to abandon their beliefs and practices.
        The ethical nature of the psychiatric treatment and the
        neutrality of the therapist are questioned. It is argued
        that the subject in question had already abandoned her Chris-
        tian Science faith, a change in ideology which led her to
        approach a psychotherapist for consultation.

1755.   Higgitt, A. C., and R. M. Murray. "A Psychotic Episode
        Following Erhard Seminar Training." ACTA PSYCHIATRICA
        SCANDINAVICA 6 (1983): 436-39.

        Reports on a case of a young man who experienced psychotic
        symptoms associated with his participation in the Est program.
        Grandiosity, paranoia, uncontrollable mood swings, and delu-
        sions observed in this patient were similar to those recorded
        by other scholars (see items 1750, 1763). The need to deter-
        mine what kind of personality is at risk when undergoing the
        Est training is emphasized. The precise factors in Est which
        caused the psychotic problems are not mentioned.

1756. Hosford, Ray E., C. Scott Moss, Helene Cavior, and Burton
       Kerish. RESEARCH ON ERHARD SEMINAR TRAINING IN A CORREC-
       TIONAL INSTITUTION. Washington, DC: American Psychological
       Association, 1982. Psychological Documents, MS 2419,
       123 pp.

       Reports on the effects of the Est training program on about
       one half of the 313 inmates in a California federal prison.
       The authors provide background information on the theory and
       practice of Est, and describe their experimental design and
       procedures as well as the characteristics of the subjects
       studied. The psychological, physiological, and behavioral
       results are recorded. The psychological changes did not
       manifest themselves in measurable changes of behavior. The
       high experience which the subjects reported at the end of
       the course did not influence their state of anxiety. Over
       60 references are given.

1757. Hume, Nicholas, and Gerald Goldstein, "Is There an Associa-
       tion Between Astrological Data and Personality?" JOURNAL
       OF CLINICAL PSYCHOLOGY 33 (1977): 711-13.

       Administers the Minnesota Multiphasic Personality Inventory
       (MMPI) and the Leary International Check List to nearly 200
       college students and relates the results to their astrolog-
       ical charts. The similarities that emerged did not exceed
       chance expectation. Although the link between natal astro-
       logical variables and personality features was not supported,
       the author thinks that astrological data could be used, in
       part, in a personality assessment conducted on an individual
       basis by an experienced clinician competent in astrology.

1758. Jaffe, Dennis T. "Therapy Types: Bureaucrats, Healers, and
       Communities." JOURNAL OF HUMANISTIC PSYCHOLOGY 16.3 (1976):
       15-28.

       Maintains that one can distinguish between three overlap-
       ping types of therapies, namely: 1) those which predominate
       in institutions, such as hospitals and prisons, which aim at
       compelling the patient to behave properly (the bureaucratic
       type); 2) those where healers or gurus help people to change
       by virtue of their authority that is based more on charisma
       than academic credentials; and 3) those where a community
       creates an environment which influences people to improve.
       The author's encounter with these therapies is sketched. He
       argues that the desire to help in a democratic, supportive,
       and expressive community setting seemed much more therapeutic
       than the bureaucratic efforts of psychiatrists and nurses with
       their traditional distance and detachment. He is still ambiv-
       alent with regard to the guru type, since personality cults
       have grown around such healers who have become as authoritarian
       as the bureaucrats. The kind of therapy that cult and ex-cult
       members are given is indirectly criticized and rejected as
       harmful.

1759. Johnson, Doyle Paul. "Dilemmas of Charismatic Leadership:
       The Case of the People's Temple." SOCIOLOGICAL ANALYSIS
       40 (1979): 315-23.

       Develops a theoretical model of charismatic leadership,
       which focuses on strategies employed by leaders themselves
       to strengthen their position and to overcome its precarious
       nature. Various ways are used by these leaders to consolidate
       their position: 1) recruiting from among deprived members of
       society; 2) requiring members to contribute all their resources
       to the group; 3) demanding that they sever their ties with the
       outside group; and 4) seeking an isolated environment for com-
       munal living. Jim Jones made efforts to use these strategies
       which, although they might have enhanced his powers, did not
       reduce the insecurity of his authority. The author points out
       that this approach avoids the common interpretation of Jim
       Jones as a psychopathological personality.

1760. Johnson, Roger A. "Discussion: Mary Baker Eddy as a Religious
       Leader." JOURNAL OF GERIATRIC PSYCHIATRY 12 (1979): 27-35.

       Comments on Silberger's study (item 1800) clarifying Eddy's
       distinctive message. Her early life history is related to
       that of shamans and situated within the framework of other
       psychological accounts of religious founders, particularly
       the study of Martin Luther by Erikson (item 230). The two
       major features of shamans--1) their trances, visions, and
       hallucinations; and 2) their illnesses and manifest patho-
       logical symptoms--were also characteristic of Mrs. Eddy,
       preparing her for the role of founder/leader of Christian
       Science.

1761. Kakar, Sudhir. "Psychoanalysis and Religious Healing:
       Siblings or Strangers?" JOURNAL OF THE AMERICAN ACADEMY
       OF RELIGION 53 (1985): 841-53.

       Explores why psychoanalysts have tended to link the reli-
       gious world with psychopathology. It is argued that religion
       and psychoanalysis are rivals rather than enemies, and that
       they both use the same processes and mechanisms of the psyche
       to heal hysterical and other neurotic disorders. The author
       illustrates this by examining the Radhasoami sect or cult.
       Initiation in this group's life restores a sense of well-
       being to some people who were depressed and emotionally
       unstable. The place of the guru in the devotee's life, how-
       ever, marks a sharp contrast with the psychoanalytical
       approach. The practice of darshan, the most important form
       of interaction between the guru and his/her disciple, is an
       effective therapeutic technique, for it creates a healing
       relationship with the guru.

1762. Kelly, I. W. "Studies in Astrology and Personality."
       PSYCHOLOGY: A JOURNAL OF HUMAN BEHAVIOR 16.4 (1979/80):
       25-32.

Reviews the behavioral evidence of studies which examine the possible relationship between the movement of the planets and personality variables. The material is divided into two parts, namely, traditional astrology and neo-astrology. Most studies have failed to substantiate the claims of astrologists. The hypothesis that there exists a relationship between introversion/extraversion factors and zodiacal signs appears to be the only area supported by research.

1763. Kirsch, Michael A., and Leonard L. Glass. "Psychiatric Disturbances Associated With Erhard Seminars Training: II. Additional Cases and Theoretical Considerations." AMERICAN JOURNAL OF PSYCHIATRY 134 (1977): 1254-58.

Reports on two more cases (see item 1750) of people who consulted the author after participating in an Est program. The material from all cases is discussed in terms of group and psychodynamic theories. Although insisting that one cannot make generalizations about the causality of the patients' disorders and about the rate of their occurrence, the authors think that the authoritarian and confrontational style of leadership fosters psychological harm. Further, Est training is structured to promote regression where the participants are infantilized and the leaders exalted to a state of omnipotence. Various mechanisms of defense by which the trainers try to cope with these problems are discussed.

1764. Klein, Mavis. "How Est Works." TRANSACTIONAL ANALYSIS JOURNAL 13 (1983): 178-80.

Reports on the author's experience with Est training, which consists of freeing the trainees from being an "adopted child" to the original free child. Est makes the individual less tensely defensive and imbues him or her with self-confidence and self-esteem. In relatively few trainees whose parent ego-states are not well-established and integrated in their personalities, the training may result in premature self-confidence. The Est training, according to the author, is a late twentieth-century substitute for religiously-imposed mortification of the flesh, and thus compensates for the handicaps of contemporary hedonism.

1765. Kriegman, Daniel, and Leonard Solomon. "Cult Groups and the Narcissistic Personality: The Offer to Heal Defects in the Self." INTERNATIONAL JOURNAL OF GROUP PSYCHOTHERAPY 35 (1985): 239-61.

Presents a clinical study on members of the Divine Light Mission, which tests the hypothesis that membership in a religious group may provide some relief from the disorder of a narcissistic personality. A religious group offers a substitute for those people who seek to heal defects in their self-development. The author holds that there is a "psychosocial fit" between what the narcissistic personality seeks and what the cult has to offer.

1766. Kroening, Richard J., Michael P. Volen, and David Bresler.
       "Acupuncture: Healing the Whole Person." DIMENSIONS IN
       WHOLISTIC HEALING (item 1288), pp. 427-39.

       Maintains that acupuncture is more than a technique for
       producing surgical analgesia. The theory and practice of
       acupuncture are described, and it is observed that many of
       its patients, who have their physical symptoms relieved,
       experience feelings of relaxation, well-being, and, at times,
       also a mild euphoria. Acupuncture as a therapy is advocated
       for use in the United States.

1767. Kroth, Jerry. "Recapitulating Jonestown." JOURNAL OF PSYCHO-
       HISTORY 11 (1984): 383-93.

       Approaches the phenomenon of Jonestown from the point of
       view of Jungian collective dream analysis. The settlement
       in Guyana is seen as "a condensed version and recapitulation
       of the American experience" (p. 384) in the composition of
       its members, in its reasons for existence, and in the gradual
       loss of faith in the adventure. Jones appeared to have re-
       gressed and developed megalomania and psychosis. Although
       the massacre has no precedent in American history, the sui-
       cide rehearsals have a parallel when military stategists draw
       doomsday scenarios. The author sees a connection between Jim
       Jones and General Sam Houston, a connection which goes beyond
       the symbolical raven which appears in the mythology surround-
       ing both figures.

1768. Kutty, I. N., Authur P. Froese, and O. Rae-Grant. "Hare
       Krishna Movement: What Attracts the Western Adolescent."
       CANADIAN JOURNAL OF PSYCHIATRY 24 (1979): 604-9.

       Gives a brief historical sketch of the Hare Krishna move-
       ment and reflects on its significance as a religion from a
       psychoanalytic point of view. The case of a 15-year-old
       male who joined the movement is explained by the theory that
       this Hindu group met his major needs. The author thinks that
       professional intervention often suppresses, rather than solves,
       the intense and painful conflicts of adolescent development--
       conflicts which may be solved by joining the movement.

1769. Lansky, David, and R. O. Phil. "Personality Correlates of
       Placebo Reciprocity and Religiosity." PSYCHOLOGICAL RE-
       PORTS 39 (1976): 975-82.

       Compares members of the Hare Krishna movement, Divine Light
       Mission "Premies," users of marijuana, and a sample of uni-
       versity students as regards their field independence, toler-
       ance of ambiguity, and automatic perception. The results
       indicate, among other things, that members of religious
       groups were less tolerant of ambiguity than members of the
       other groups, but that they had experiences similar, to some
       degree, to those of drug users. Cult members were also less

"automatially reactive," because they experienced less anxiety. Meditative experiences tend to eliminate ambiguity by teaching individuals to control their internal states.

1770. Leninger, Madaleine. "Witchcraft Practices and Psychocultural Therapy with Urban U. S. Families." HUMAN ORGANIZATION 32 (1973): 73-83.

Notes that because those people who believe they are bewitched are being admitted to mental clinics and hospitals in larger numbers, it is necessary for therapists to be aware of witchcraft behavior and its significance. A theoretical framework, based on empirical data collected from Spanish-speaking and Anglo-American families in the United States, is constructed. Three psychological stages are identified: 1) pre-witchcraft stress period; 2) displacement to the outgroup (consisting of witches); and 3) identification of the bewitched victim, the witch, and the witch medium. Witchcraft practices are important psychocultural and social mechanisms by which people cope with ingroup problems generated by external social concerns. Instead of treating the subjects as paranoid schizophrenics, the author developed a psychotherapeutic method in which cultural data, such as kinship ties, ethnohealth beliefs, and religious attitudes and values, were used to help subjects come to grips with their problems.

1771. Lilly, John C., and Joseph E. Hart. "The Arica Training." TRANSPERSONAL PSYCHOLOGIES (item 1338), pp. 331-51.

Explains the Arica theory of human personality, which is hampered by cultural and environmental factors. Practical exercises, offered by Arica, to counteract and overcome one's deviations are accounted for. Because the Arica training is given under tension and involves group interaction, it is not intended for those who are emotionally unstable. Arica does not cure psychosis. Its main aim is the improvement of one's personality.

1772. Littlewood, Roland. "The Antinomian Hasid." BRITISH JOURNAL OF MEDICAL PSYCHOLOGY 56 (1983): 67-78.

Endeavors, with reference to the Hasidic community, to understand how an abnormal individual reconstructs personal identity and social role by using ideas available in one's culture. The author briefly describes the Hasidic community, with its strict adherence to Jewish law and tradition, its cultivation of ecstasy, and the role of its male leader, the Zadik or Rebbe. A case study of a Jew, whose behavior was at variance with the external features of community life, is presented and interpreted in the context of both the Jewish mystical and messianic traditions and the various solutions to Jewish relationships with outsiders that were supported by rabbinical orthodoxy, Sabbatianism, Hasidism, and Zionism. Various ways of interpreting the patient's psychosis are given, and the author opts for explaining his problems as part of a culture-bound syndrome.

1773.   Livsey, Clara. THE MANSON WOMEN: A 'FAMILY' PORTRAIT. New
        York: Richard Marck Publishers, 1980. 244 pp.

        Studies the women who became part of the Manson family and
        who participated in the bizarre slayings that led to their
        prosecution and conviction. The question of psychiatry and
        the law is discussed, and it is maintained that, while Manson
        was the product of a troubled and deprived childhood, he still
        is--as are his weak, submissive women--responsible for his
        actions. The author, a family therapist, tries to explain how
        a group like Manson's, which started as a love-in experience,
        turned to violence, and lists several similarities among the
        many groups and cults whose leaders are charismatic. Their
        followers are megalomaniacs who suffer from narcissism and
        infantilism and who have developed a closed-system mentality.
        The author depicts a clear portrait of each of the Manson
        women and states that they all had the need to belong to a
        cultish, semi-religious, and semi-philosophical group.

1774.   London, Perry. "Psychotherapy for Religious Neurosis?:
        Comments on Cohen and Smith." JOURNAL OF CONSULTING AND
        CLINICAL PSYCHOLOGY 44 (1976): 145-46.

        Rebuts Cohen and Smith's view (item 1725) that Christian
        Science was responsible for the psychiatric disorders of one
        of their patients. The apparent assumption behind their
        study, namely, that sectarian religious attitudes are more
        harmful than secular ones, is rejected. The cause of this
        patient's neurosis could have been explained by the guilt
        feelings she might have had over matters not directly related
        to her faith. The ethical issue of the use of psychotherapy
        to undermine a client's religious beliefs is raised.

1775.   Macklin, June. "Belief, Ritual, and Healing: New England
        Spiritualism and Mexican-American Spiritism Compared."
        RELIGIOUS MOVEMENTS IN CONTEMPORARY AMERICA (item 1360),
        pp. 383-417.

        Argues that rituals of salvation in both groups heal the
        split between the temporary and eternal orders, and thus
        bring about personal wholeness and physical health to the
        participants. A short intellectual history of spiritualism
        and spiritism is outlined. The author maintains that both
        can be conceived as a response to the stresses brought about
        by the conflicts between science and religion and between
        the material and spiritual world views. The rituals of
        healing practiced by Mexican curanderos and by American
        mediums function positively in bringing healing to cultural
        and personal tensions.

1776.   Madsen, William. "Alcoholics Anonymous as a Crisis Cult."
        ALCOHOL HEALTH AND RESEARCH WORLD 1 (Spring 1974): 27-30.

        Sees parallels between Alcoholics Anonymous and other
        religiously-inspired minority movements, which include mes-
        sianic and nativistic groups like Cargo cults. The leaders

of AA went through a period of personal crisis before experiencing a spiritual awakening. Members of AA usually join
at a time of serious crisis in their lives. Their membership
becomes a source of comfort and relief. As in many other
cults, their change from alcoholics to abstainers is testi-
fied to in group meetings. A sponsor is assigned to new
members, who are indoctrinated into the group's value system.
The group becomes a refuge, especially when the members are
tempted to return to drink. AA is conceived of as a kind of
folk psychotherapy offering love, tension-relieving laughter,
prestige, and rewards to those who remain sober.

1777. McCarthy, Katherine. "Psychotherapy and Religion: The
      Emmanuel Movement." JOURNAL OF RELIGION AND HEALTH 23
      (1984): 92-105.

      Considers the significance of the Emmanuel Movement, a
      method of church-sponsored healing, founded by Elwood
      Worcester in 1906. The movement is seen as 1) a popular
      effort by the Protestant clergy to claim religious authority
      over psychological and psychosomatic disorders; 2) an effort
      to combat the scientific materialism of the time; and 3) an
      attempt to construct a non-reductionist view of the inter-
      action of body, mind, and spirit. The author thinks that
      the movement was a pre-Freudian psychotherapeutic system.

1778. McKenzie, Clancy D., and Larry Wright. "Mind Control and
      the Mental Patient." COUNSELING AND VALUES 21 (1977):
      237-46.

      Reports on an in-depth study, five years in duration, on
      the effects of Silva Mind Control on 75 highly disturbed
      mental patients. Contrary to hearsay, rumors, and specula-
      tions on the harm this method could bring to those who are
      emotionally ill, the researchers found that it was highly
      therapeutic. The study project is described, and the main
      features and benefits of the program are outlined. It is
      argued that the mobilization of energy, the generation of
      positive and optimistic attitudes, the diminishing of anxiety
      through relaxation, and the improvement of one's affective
      state are some of the reasons Silva Mind Control helps the
      mental patient. All but one of these subjects registered a
      marked improvement on reality tests. Although Silva Mind
      Control is not a psychotherapy, it can be used in any psycho-
      therapeutic treatment, especially if the therapist is familiar
      with its methods.

1779. McKnight, Alice A. "An Interview with José Silva." COUN-
      SELING AND VALUES 21 (1977): 208-18.

      Records the answers of José Silva, founder of Silva Mind
      Control, to several questions on the origins of his methods
      and goals. The aim of this training is "to educate the mind
      to function consciously within its own psychic dimensions"
      (p. 209). The contents of the Basic Lecture Series are

described, and some of the theory behind them is explained.
The founder believes that his method is the best system of
mental training available for developing inner awareness and
insists that it should not be confused with the occult.

1780. Montagu, Havor. "The Pessimistic Sect's Influence on the
       Mental Health of Its Members: The Case of Jehovah's
       Witnesses." SOCIAL COMPASS 24 (1977): 135-47.

       Reviews studies on Jehovah's Witnesses, and finds that the
       rate of mental illness among them by far surpasses that of
       the population as a whole. Various features are said to
       account for this: new recruits to the sect are often people
       with emotional problems; pressure to conform to the congre-
       gation; a belief structure which causes emotional turmoil;
       and a tendency to force out intelligent and more educated
       members. Members who have psychological difficulties are
       encouraged to shun secular advice and to seek counseling from
       church elders, who are not competent to handle even the most
       normal interpersonal friction. The elders' advice elicits
       guilt or a high level of aggression, which complicates,
       rather than solves, the initial problem.

1781. Moody, Edward J. "Magical Therapy: An Anthropological
       Investigation of Contemporary Satanism." RELIGIOUS MOVE-
       MENTS IN CONTEMPORARY AMERICA (item 1360), pp. 355-82.

       Attempts to answer the question of why the occult practices
       of witchcraft and satanism have experienced a resurgence in
       the 1970s. It is theorized that those who join such reli-
       gious groups are abnormal, in the sense that their behavior
       is sociologically incorrect. The roots of such abnormality
       are usually to be found in childhood experiences, which make
       youngsters anxious and socially inept. Would-be Satanists
       first get involved in occult rituals, seeking reassurance and
       relief from anxiety. The new Satanist goes through a person-
       ality transformation, "a modification of many formerly malad-
       aptive anxiety-producing behaviors" (p. 368). Satanic rituals,
       like the invocation of lust and the Shibboleth, help members
       of the Church of Trapezoid satisfy their desires, reach con-
       tentment, and achieve a more successful adaptation to life.

1782. Nudleman, Arthur E. "The Maintenance of Christian Science
       in Scientific Society." MARGINAL MEDICINE. Edited by Roy
       Wallis and Peter Morley. New York: Free Press, 1976, pp.
       42-59.

       Examines how Christian Science has managed to survive in
       an increasingly secular world. Four factors relevant to the
       sects' continued existence are dealt with: 1) the beneficial
       effects of the church; 2) the institutionalized concessions
       to reality; 3) individual behavior and belief; and 4) the
       behavior and belief of the larger society. The author thinks
       that Christian Science can definitely make an important con-
       tribution to physical and emotional health, because it cul-

tivates a relationship between clients and practitioners, it
employs to its advantage the placebo effect, and it offers a
satisfying philosophical system.

1783. Nurbakhsh, Djavad. "Sufism and Psychoanalysis: Part I: What
       Is Sufism?" INTERNATIONAL JOURNAL OF SOCIAL PSYCHIATRY 24
       (1978): 204-12.

       Describes Sufism with its goals and the aspirations of those
       who follow the path. The relationship between the spiritual
       master ("Murab") and the disciple ("Murid") is outlined. The
       conditions necessary to begin the training ("Tariqah") are
       listed. As one starts following the path, one gradually
       escapes from the pressure of psychic conflicts through dream-
       analysis done by the master, then strives to acquire spiritual
       virtues. The author calls the first stage a "spiritual
       psychotherapy."

1784. Nurbakhsh, Djavad. "Sufism and Psychoanalysis. Part II: A
       Comparison Between Sufism and Psychoanalysis." INTERNA-
       TIONAL JOURNAL OF SOCIAL PSYCHIATRY 24 (1978): 213-19.

       Discusses the Sufi view that the disciple is to prefer the
       will of the master to his or her own; the Sufi theory of two
       intellects, one particular and one universal; and the stress
       on love. The transference phenomenon in psychoanalysis be-
       tween the analyst and client is related to the exchange which
       takes place between Sufi master and disciple. This and other
       similarities are judged to be rather superficial. The aims
       of psychoanalysis and Sufism are profoundly different. The
       former treats an abnormal or sick person; the latter deals
       with a psychologically healthy one. The relationship between
       the Sufi master and his disciple, unlike that between the
       psychoanalyst and his or her client, is religious, divine,
       and spiritual.

1785. Olsson, Peter A. "The Psychology of a Modern Warlock: Rap-
       prochement in a Coven of White Witches." AMERICAN JOURNAL
       OF PSYCHOTHERAPY 39 (1985): 263-76.

       Describes a young man who became involved with white witch-
       craft and a coven of witches during crucial phases of psycho-
       therapy. In the course of his successful treatment, the coven
       served as a "transference-laden peer group" (p. 264). The
       group dynamics of the coven and the metaphors used in witch-
       craft helped the individual resolve childhood traumas and work
       through unresolved separation-individuation issues which were
       the cause of his psychological problems.

1786. Paul, Norman L., and Betty Byfield Paul. "The Use of Est
       as Adjunction to Family-Focused Treatment." JOURNAL OF
       MARRIAGE AND FAMILY COUNSELING 4 (1978): 51-61.

       Suggests the use of Est as an additional therapeutic compo-
       nent in family therapy. The authors, who are Est graduates,
       describe the program briefly, and suggest ways of applying it

in therapy sessions, illustrating their method by means of a
case study. Several goals of family therapy, like tolerance
of differences in perception, are reinforced by Est training.

1787.   Perry, Robert U. "ESP and Silva Mind Control: A Christian
        Perspective." COUNSELING AND VALUES 21 (1977): 219-28.

        Attempts mainly to evaluate Silva Mind Control from a
        Christian point of view. The author holds that Silva's
        method results in a release of ESP. The program is found
        faulty for its teaching of karma and reincarnation, its
        crusading spirit, and its apparent millennial views. Yet
        these deficiencies are minor compared to what it has to
        offer on the education level. The fruits of the method lie
        in its ability to teach others how to solve their problems.
        The author seems to imply that Silva Mind Control is thera-
        peutic, not only because it helps people overcome many of
        their psychological difficulties, but also because it en-
        hances the lives of those who are healthy.

*   Porterfield, Amanda. "Native American Shamanism and the
        American Mind-Cure Movement." Cited above as item 979.

1788.   Richard, Michel P., and Albert Adato. "The Medium and the
        Message: A Study of Spiritualism at Lily Dale, NY." REVIEW
        OF RELIGIOUS RESEARCH 22 (1980): 187-96.

        Studies of a Spiritualist summer camp. The role of the
        medium, the characteristics of the participants, and the
        implication for mental health are investigated. Two main
        questions are raised: whether the medium can treat some people
        more effectively than psychotherapists, and whether both types
        of healers can cooperate.

1789.   Riordan, Kathleen. "Gurdjieff." TRANSPERSONAL PSYCHOLOGIES
        (item 1338), pp. 283-332.

        Outlines briefly the philosophy and psychology of Gurdjieff,
        and describes the Fourth Way, that is, the method and stages
        of self-development and self-realization propounded in his
        teachings. Because Gurdjieff regarded the ordinary waking
        state as pathological, his method is directed to the solution
        of human personality problems and can, therefore, be said to
        be therapeutic.

1790.   Rochford, E. Burke. "Recruitment Strategies, Ideology, and
        Organization in the Hare Krishna Movement." SOCIAL PROBLEMS
        29 (1982): 399-410.

        Examines the interrelationships between the ideology,
        structure, recruitment tactics, and external social forces
        which might account for the growth of the Hare Krishna Move-
        ment in the United States. A survey of over 200 devotees led
        the author to conclude that the opportunistic exploitation
        of local conditions was the main factor in the success this

movement has had in recruiting young adults. Social networks, rather than the psychological state of individuals, seem to be the important element in the expansion of new religious groups.

1791. Rosén, Anne-Sofie, and Ted D. Nordquist. "Ego Developmental Levels and Values in a Yogic Community." JOURNAL OF SOCIAL PSYCHOLOGY 39 (1980): 1152-60.

Administers several personality tests (e.g., Rokeach's Value Survey and Musgrove's Counter-Cultural Attitude Test) to 28 residents of a collective ashram, which was founded on the principles laid down by Swami Paramahamsa Yogananda. Members of at least two years standing had typically experienced a period of frustration, anxiety, and meaninglessness, all of which decreased with the increasing familiarity with the new teachings. Conversion brought answers to existential problems and normative guidelines for everyday life. The authors accept the view that ashram life makes a synthesis of religion and psychotherapy.

1792. Ross, Michael W. "Clinical Profiles of Hare Krishna Devotees." AMERICAN JOURNAL OF PSYCHIATRY 140 (983): 416-20.

Reports on several psychological tests which were administered to Australian members of the Hare Krishna Movement. A short historical background of the movement, the characteristics of those who join, and a description of the research methods are provided. The results show that the members are within the normal range, although there seems to be some decline in mental health after 18 months of membership and an increase after three years. There is no evidence that membership in this Hindu group leads to psychopathology, or that the members have been brainwashed.

1793. Ross, Michael W. "Mental Health and Membership in the Hare Krishnas: A Case Study." AUSTRALIAN PSYCHOLOGIST 18 (1983): 128-29.

Argues that only longitudinal studies can test the mental health of cult members. A five-year case history of a member of the Hare Krishna Movement is presented. No evidence of thought disorder or instability was detected either on entering the group or after years of involvement. The author, however, is cautious about making generalizations from single cases, and thinks that more studies are needed before one can conclude that membership in a minority religion does not lead to the deterioration of the mental health of the devotees.

1794. Royster, James E. "Sufi Shaykh as Psychotherapist." PSYCHO-LOGIA 22 (1979): 225-35.

Presents the view that the Sufi path, though basically mystical in its goals, is also a therapeutic process. The shaykh's therapeutic skills are based on his qualities as an

integrated person--qualities such as acceptance (or resigna-
tion), non-attachment, and equilibrium. He acts as a catalyst
while maintaining his informal, open, flexible method in the
guidance he offers his disciples. He establishes a special
relationship with the murid (disciple) who is led to personal
integration and mystical union.

1795. Rush, John A. WITCHCRAFT AND SORCERY: AN ANTHROPOLOGICAL
       PERSPECTIVE OF THE OCCULT. Springfield, IL: Charles C.
       Thomas, 1974. 166 pp.

       Examines various anthropological theories of witchcraft and
       sorcery. Beliefs and practices concerning witchcraft in
       different parts of the world, including Italy, other European
       countries, Asia, Africa, and America are briefly outlined.
       In a short chapter on the occult and psychotherapy (pp. 123-
       27), the relation between magic, religion, and mental illness
       is explored. The author points out that the Western faith
       healer "may be more effective than the Western psychiatrist,
       because the 'patient' is a believer, feels that the healer
       is, indeed, a possessor of mystical powers, and the process is
       reenforced by the 'community' or group, who are also believers"
       (p. 127).

1796. Safier, J. C. "Hasidism, Faith, and the Therapeutic Paradox."
       MEDICS AND MYSTICS (item 1011), pp. 53-62.

       Points out that because the Rebbe's instructions and the
       relationship he offered helped guide the Hasid in the latter's
       search for meaning, the Rebbe can be seen as an existential-
       humanistic psychotherapist. The author illustrates the thera-
       peutic paradox that is apparent in Hasidism, which approaches
       the contradictions of life from a mystical point of view.
       "It is the sharing of the tales which makes Hasidic and
       therapeutic encounters interpersonal, intimate, and meaning-
       ful" (p. 62).

1797. Schwarz, Berthold E. "A Psychiatrist Looks at Flying Saucers."
       THE PSYCHIC SCENE. Edited by Martin Ebon. New York: New
       American Library, 1974, pp. 56-67.

       Reports on the mental state of two women who testified to
       UFO sightings, and observes that neither had a history of
       psychiatric disorder and both appeared to be stable, healthy
       people when they had their unusual experience. The author
       thinks that the UFO vision cannot be explained by the theory
       that the two subjects were in a state of heightened emotion.

1798. Scott, Edward M. "Witches: Wise, Weak or Wicked Women?"
       JOURNAL OF RELIGION AND HEALTH 15 (1976): 136-39.

       Presents a short background of the different categories of
       witches, and describes a few of his patients who claimed to
       be witches. Traditional therapy helped at least one to
       release her anger and hatred and to feel stronger. Witch-
       craft is treated as a kind of psychological illness.

1799. Sharma, Arvind. "Was Ramakrishna a Hypnotist?" JOURNAL OF
       PSYCHOLOGICAL RESEARCH 25 (1981): 105-7.

       Discusses whether Ramakrishna, who reportedly had the power
       to influence a person's thoughts or induce a trance by mere
       touch, was in fact a skilled hypnotist. A few typical exam-
       ples from his biography are brought forth to show that the
       state of awareness, which he transferred to some of his fol-
       lowers, was actually a sharing of a condition he himself was
       experiencing. The distinction between the mental condition
       of the hypnotist and that of the subject is central to the
       practice of hypnosis. Consequently, one cannot interpret
       Ramakrishna's actions as a form of hypnosis.

1800. Silberger, Julius. MARY BAKER EDDY: AN INTERPRETATIVE BIOG-
       RAPHY OF THE FOUNDER OF CHRISTIAN SCIENCE. Boston: Little
       Brown and Co., 1980. x, 274 pp.

       Gives a biographical account by a psychoanalyst, which con-
       siders four different influences on Mrs. Baker Eddy's life,
       namely, her natural talents, her psychological development,
       the environmental and social factors that influenced her, and
       her religious role. She is depicted as a woman who harnessed
       and integrated her conflicts and symptoms for the creation of
       her church. Although rather eccentric, she had great strength,
       determination, and ingenuity. In spite of her weakness she
       was a creative person who not only made sense out of her life,
       but also directed it to help others.

1801. Silberger, Julius. "Mourning and Transformation: How Mary
       Baker Eddy Found in Middle Age a Way of Making a New Life
       for Herself." JOURNAL OF GERIATRIC PSYCHIATRY 12 (1979):
       9-25.

       Provides a brief biography of the founder of Christian
       Science, and attempts to show the psychological forces that
       led to her unusual career. Mrs. Eddy's conflicts and symp-
       toms were harnessed and integrated in the creation of her
       church. Her bodily symptoms were explained either as a
       yearning for the healing of her disciples, or as an attack of
       her enemies--the latter being a mechanism labeled Malicious
       Animal Magnetism (MAM) in Christian Science theology. Her
       nightmares were also interpreted as the work of her enemies
       and, later on, used as intuitive guides to the solution of
       problems. Mrs. Eddy is seen as mastering and integrating
       her symptoms into a mechanism useful for her career.

1802. Silva, José, and Philip Miele. THE SILVA MIND CONTROL
       METHOD. New York: Simon and Schuster, 1977. 208 pp.

       Contains a description of the program by its founder, and
       some reflections by a psychiatrist who advocates its use.
       Silva Mind Control can have beneficial effects on people
       suffering from neurosis. It also strengthens one's self-
       esteem, which is necessary for fighting drug and alcohol

addiction, and for helping those struggling against poverty.
The program seems to have been especially successful in the
business world. Several appendices deal with the organization of the course, its use in psychiatry, and its effects on
EEG correlates of attention.

1803. Simon, Justin. "An Evaluation of Est as an Adjunct to Group
        Psychotherapy in the Treatment of Severe Alcoholism."
        BIOSCIENCE COMMUNICATIONS 3 (1977): 141-48.

        Makes an attempt to explore the possible psychiatric bene-
        fits of Est on alcoholics. Two groups of patients were
        chosen and given traditional therapy in conjunction with Est.
        The results indicate that, while Est did not seem to add any
        benefits to the treatment discernibly, it certainly did not
        produce any harmful clinical effects. Three conclusions are
        reached: 1) the benefits derived from Est are a function of
        ego strength, or positive mental health; 2) Est is not
        effective as an adjunct to psychotherapy for alcoholics; and
        3) the effectiveness of Est as an adjunct to therapy might
        be enhanced under certain conditions.

1804. Simon, Justin. "Observations on Sixty-Seven Patients Who
        Took Erhard Seminary Training." AMERICAN JOURNAL OF PSY-
        CHIATRY 135 (1978): 686-91.

        Discusses some of the powerful psychological effects of
        Est in patients suffering from various psychiatric problems.
        Several standard psychological tests were administered, and
        five cases are reported in some detail. Almost two thirds
        of those undergoing psychotherapy showed some positive re-
        sponse to the Est program, a response which is seen as a
        function of good ego strength. For those who are strongly
        motivated and ready for change, Est can be psychotherapeuti-
        cally beneficial.

1805. Singer, Merrill. "Christian Science Healing and Alcoholism:
        An Anthropological Perspective." JOURNAL OF OPERATIONAL
        PSYCHIATRY 13 (1982): 1-12.

        Explores the use of Christian Science healing as an alter-
        native therapy for alcohol addicts. The attitudes of the
        general practitioners towards alcohol, and the way they treat
        those who come for their assistance, are examined and com-
        pared to those of psychotherapists. The possible cooperation
        between various therapists is considered, since there are
        some basic similarities between the attitudes and rehabili-
        tation process of Christian Science, psychotherapy, and
        Alcoholics Anonymous. Some cooperation is favored, even
        though there are some major differences in their views on
        the very nature of the disease. Christian Science "provides
        a relatively inexpensive form of supportive interaction for
        recovering alcoholics" (p. 11).

1806. Skultans, Vieda. "Empathy and Healing: Aspects of Spiritual-
        ist Ritual." SOCIAL ANTHROPOLOGY AND MEDICINE. Edited by
        J. B. Loudon. New York: Academic Press, 1976, pp. 190-222.

Discusses healing in three spiritualist churches in Swansea,
England. It is pointed out that spiritualism makes a contribution to the management of all sickness, since it aims to
increase the persons' overall vitality and resistance to disease, and their strength to withstand the stresses of life.
The healing methods, especially those connected with the
spirit world, are described. Key spiritualist rituals are
considered, and the underlying attitudes toward pain are
inferred. Spiritualism encourages states of mind which traditional psychiatry sees as indicative of psychopathology.
The author, however, sees spiritualism in a more positive
light, and stresses its supportive and therapeutic functions.

1807. Skultans, Vieda. INTIMACY AND RITUAL: A STUDY OF SPIRITUAL-
ISM, MEDIUMS, AND GROUPS. London: Routledge and Kegan Paul,
1974. vii, 106 pp.

Studies spiritualism in south Wales. Several church rites
are described and the role of illness in spiritualist belief
and practice is sketched. The author sees spiritualism as a
coping mechanism designed to help women accept a traditional
feminine role, which they often find difficult and frustrating.
Spiritualism is, therefore, a response to conflict-ridden
situations. There is a strong similarity between spiritualist
circles and psychotherapeutic groups. They both have strong
healing properties.

1808. Spencer, John. "The Mental Health of Jehovah's Witnesses."
BRITISH JOURNAL OF PSYCHIATRY 126 (1975): 556-59.

Surveys briefly some of the more well-known studies on the
relationship between religion and mental illness, and reports
on the condition of 50 Jehovah's Witnesses who were admitted
to mental institutions in Western Australia. The aim of the
study was to determine whether extreme religiosity is a symptom of psychiatric disorder or a complex defense mechanism
dealing with an underlying problem. Jehovah's Witnesses are
overrepresented in mental hospitals, and the incidence of
schizophrenia among them is about three times as high as that
of the rest of the population, while the rate of paranoia is
four times higher. It is concluded that either the sect tends
to attract pre-psychotic individuals, or else being a member
of the sect creates a stressful condition leading to psychosis.

1809. Spero, Moshe H. "Discussion: On the Nature of the Therapeutic
Relationship Encounter Between Hasid and Master." MEDICS
AND MYSTICS (item 1011), pp. 63-74.

Compares the relationship between the Hasidi Rebbe and his
pupil with that of the psychoanalyst and his/her client. The
Hasidic-Rebbe relationship subscribes to the general psychotherapeutic goals, although it is not easily comparable to
psychoanalysis. The author points out that one area of
similarity between the two systems is the insistence on the
need for self-analysis. Unlike psychoanalyst-client interchange, the Hasid-Rebbe relationship has, however, no systematic psychology underlying its practice.

1810. Stones, Christopher P. "A Community of Jesus People in South
       Africa. Changes in Self-Actualization." SMALL GROUP BE-
       HAVIOR 13 (1982): 264-72.

       Reflects on the problem that while those who join the Jesus
       Movement should be self-actualizers because of their religious
       experiences, they still conform to such norms as Biblical funda-
       mentalism, which is inimical to self-actualization. Several
       psychological tests were administered to 22 Jesus People in
       Johannesburg. No significant differences were recorded in
       tests conducted before and after the conversion experience
       in the following areas: time-ratio, time-competence, self-
       actualizing values, self-regard, and capacity for intimate
       contact. The experience itself, however, seemed to inhibit,
       rather than promote, self-actualization.

1811. Stones, Christopher P. "A Jesus Community in South Africa:
       Self-Actualization or Need for Security." PSYCHOLOGICAL
       REPORTS 46 (1980): 287-90.

       Presents a study of 22 members of the Jesus Movement, who
       were tested on the Shostrom's Personal Orientation Inventory
       to "assess perceived change in self-actualization as a func-
       tion of their religious conversion." The author concludes
       that the Jesus Movement supplies its members with a feeling
       of belonging, which brings with it a sense of security, and
       that the members were more inner-directed and individualistic
       and, therefore, more self-actualizing before their conversion.
       Whether and to what degree this is a healthy improvement is
       not discussed.

1812. Stones, Christopher P. "The Jesus People: Changes in Security
       and Life-Style as a Function of Nonconformist Religious
       Influence." JOURNAL OF PSYCHOLOGY 97 (1977): 127-33.

       Reports on an experiment using various psychological tests
       on members of the Jesus Movement in Johannesburg, South
       Africa. Compared to members of mainline Christian churches,
       the Jesus People were more fundamentalist in their religious
       views and more secure psychologically, a direct result of
       their conversion experience. Jesus People underwent social
       and personal changes that are beneficial both to the indi-
       viduals themselves and to society at large. The author's
       position is that the Jesus Movement acts as a halfway house,
       helping people to be reintegrated into mainstream society
       and religion.

1813. Tan, Leong T., Margaret Y.-C. Tan, and Ilza Veith. ACUPUNC-
       TURE THERAPY: CURRENT CHINESE PRACTICE. Philadelphia:
       Temple University Press, 1973. xii, 159 pp.

       Provides the basics of acupuncture therapy and a descrip-
       tion of the most commonly used acupuncture points. Among
       the diseases and symptoms which can be treated are neuras-
       thenia, hysterical behavior, and schizophrenia.

1814. Wallis, Roy. "Dianetics: A Marginal Psychotherapy." MARGIN-
       AL MEDICINE. Edited by Roy Wallis and Peter Morley. New
       York: Free Press, 1976, pp. 77-109.

       Describes Ron Hubbard's theory and practice of Dianetics as
       a therapeutic system. The social organization and develop-
       ment of Dianetics in the early 1950s are briefly outlined.
       Its decline and internal crises, together with the societal
       reaction to it, are discussed. The author places this move-
       ment within the tradition of healing movements in the United
       States. Several reasons for its initial success are given.

1815. Wardwell, Walter I. "Christian Science and Spiritual Heal-
       ing." RELIGIOUS SYSTEMS OF PSYCHOTHERAPY (item 1021), pp.
       72-88.

       Describes the values and religious orientations of Christian
       Science and its explanation of mental illness. Various levels
       of its therapeutic treatment are outlined. Central to its
       theory is the denial of reality. The insistence on Malicious
       Animal Magnetism (MAM), with its obvious sexual symbolism, is
       the result of the denial and projection of hostile impulses,
       which were characteristic of Mrs. Baker Eddy. Christian
       Scientists are alienated from other human beings not only
       because sin and suffering are denied, but also because there
       is very little religious basis for concern for other people.

1816. Westley, Francis R. "Ritual as Psychic Bridge Building:
       Narcissism, Healing, and the Human Potential Movements."
       JOURNAL OF PSYCHOANALYTIC ANTHROPOLOGY 6 (1983): 179-200.

       Examines the ritual configuration of a human potential
       movement, namely, Silva Mind Control, in relation to psycho-
       analytical theory of the etiology and treatment of narcissis-
       tic personality disorders. Silva Mind Control techniques
       focus on narcissistic elements, and are just as likely to
       compensate for structural defects as they are to exacerbate
       them. Those who take the Silva Mind Control program, whether
       they have a personality disorder or not, are "unlikely to
       experience a cure in the psychoanalytic sense of the term"
       (p. 198). Silva Mind Control and other similar programs may
       offer some temporary relief by building the individual's
       self-worth and esteem.

1817. Whitlock, F. A. "The Psychiatry and Psychopathology of Para-
       normal Phenonema." AUSTRALIAN AND NEW ZEALAND JOURNAL OF
       PSYCHIATRY 12 (1978): 11-19.

       Discusses, from a psychiatric point of view, extrasensory
       phenomena, such as telepathy, out-of-body experiences, pre-
       cognition, faith-healing, religious stigmata, and psycho-
       kinesis. Most of the above phenomena are inexplicable. The
       author suggests that another look should be taken at these
       rather unusual claims, if for no other reason than because
       scientific determinism and mechanistic assumptions about
       mind-body relationship are not beyond question.

1818. Wilson, Stephen A. "Therapeutic Processes in a Yoga Ashram."
       AMERICAN JOURNAL OF PSYCHOTHERAPY 39 (1985): 253-62.

       Examines the life-style and social structures of a Kripalu
       Yoga Ashram in eastern Pennsylvania. The teachings of its
       founder, Yogi Desai, and the central place of the guru-
       disciple relationship in the yogic life-style are described.
       Ashram life contains "built-in" stressors, which exist to
       help residents learn to drop their usual defenses and escapes.
       Contact with the guru and ashram life leads to a "cathartic"
       experience, which then motivates the individual to become
       involved. Ashram life teaches the members to respond to the
       distressing elements of life. The author views the monastic
       practices of the ashram as healthy forms of behavior, rather
       than expressions of pathology.

1819. Wolf, Margaret S. "Witchcraft and Mass Hysteria in Terms of
       Current Psychological Theories." JOURNAL OF PSYCHIATRIC
       NURSING AND MENTAL HEALTH SERVICES 14 (March 1976): 23-38.

       Attempts to understand the individual and mass response to
       the occult by means of a study of the Salem witchcraft phe-
       nomenon in the seventeenth century. The existence of witch-
       craft, the fraudulent behavior of those afflicted, and the
       mass hysteria it gave rise to are usually explained by
       1) current psychological theories of sexual repression; or
       2) the influences of ecclesiastical and civil law; or 3) the
       expropriation of land. The author rejects these theories
       and, finding similarities between the affliction caused by
       the witches and pathological cases of hysteria in the early
       twentieth century, opts for the view that autosuggestion
       explains witchcraft phenomena.

1820. Worsley, J. R. IS ACUPUNCTURE FOR YOU? New York: Harper
       and Row, 1973. xiv, 81 pp.

       Describes the use of acupuncture and the way it can be
       used to diagnose disease. The rules to be observed before
       and after treatment are given. Several psychological and
       psychosomatic illnesses--including drug, alcohol and smoking
       addiction, mental disease, and some forms of depression--can
       be successfully treated by acupuncture treatment.

1821. Zee, Hugo J. "The Guyana Incident: Some Psychoanalytic Con-
       siderations." BULLETIN OF THE MENNINGER CLINIC 44 (1980):
       345-63.

       Outlines some of the basic dynamics of the Guyana incident,
       relying on data from popular media accounts. The author
       comments particularly on the lives of Jim Jones and his
       followers. The leader of this cult was a narcissistic person
       with great dependency needs and a paranoid personality, which
       thrived in a sadomasochistic family atmosphere. About one
       third of his followers were psychologically-distressed people
       who maintained the group's pathological momentum. The rest

may have been swept into his church just when they were going through a period of depression. In Jim Jones's People's Temple, the group's regression had reached psychopathological proportions and represents a cult at its worst.

D. STUDIES ON, AND RELATED TO, THE BRAINWASHING VERSUS CONVERSION
                              CONTROVERSY

The process of joining a cult and accepting its ideology and life-style is one of the most frequently debated issues in psychological and psychiatric literature. Speculations on the matter have centered around either 1) the possible qualities of young adults, which make them vulnerable to the new ideas and life-styles the cults offer, and/or 2) those cultic activities, which have been explicitly devised to attract idealistic people, to instruct them in a new system of religious and philosophical thinking, and to elicit their dedication and commitment. Is membership in a cult arrived at by a process of religious questioning and self-examination leading to conversion? Or are cult members lured into a cult by carefully-devised socio-psychological means and then indoctrinated into its belief system and trained in a new way of life? Do individuals freely decide to join a new religious movement, or are they forced by indirect, subtle, and unethical means to full commitment? Is cult membership a new form of mental and/or physical slavery?

The popular view that cult members have been brainwashed and, therefore, lost their freedom, has support in professional litera- ture, where comparison between the initiation and training into a cult and the indoctrination of prisoners-of-war is often made. Scholars who oppose this view have pointed out that cultic commit- ment is achieved in stages, and usually after a relatively long period of self-searching and reflection. An attempt has been made to combine both theories (item 1872), but the issue of whether a person's decision to join a cult can be labeled a genuine religious conversion remains unsolved.

It can be argued that because people seem to join a cult under psychological stress, their decision lacks that quality of freedom which makes their entry into a cult a religious conversion. But one must also bear in mind that very few serious steps are taken in life when there are no social and/or psychological influences. Moreover, all people are educated into a specific culture and brought up in a particular system of attitudes and values which guide them through- out life. To some extent, everybody is conditioned by culture. This process can hardly be called indoctrination or brainwashing. The fact that those joining a cult are in search of a fuller meaning to life and a more satisfying life-style suggests that their decision is relatively free, in spite of the many conditions which have direct impact on the often drastic move of becoming a member in a new reli- gious movement. People can still freely choose a more rigid and authoritarian life-style which, in spite of its limitations, cannot be compared and much less identified with the mental and physical states of those living in concentration camps or prisoner-of-war cells.

There is no doubt that cult members are, over a period of time, enculturated in a different world view and life-style which clash with those of their family members and mainstream society. To what extent this socialization process can be called brainwashing is a debatable issue. Because cult practices differ, it is not possible to make a general statement about the training techniques of cults. Those groups which require community living exercise more control on the behavior and intellectual training of their members than do others which, after initiation, leave their members to their own devices. Although one may grant that, in some cults at least, there is heavy indoctrination, the rate of voluntary defection suggests that people in cults do not become transformed into helpless robots or thoughtless zombies.

The brainwashing versus conversion debate has repercussions in various fields of study outside psychology and psychiatry. It raises, first of all, the question of the nature of religious conversion, which is not a phenomenon restricted to the new cults. It further challenges the Western assumption of human freedom upon which our court system is based. For counselors, religious or otherwise, the debate has practical applications. Although the majority of centers which offer counseling to cult and ex-cult members and their families seem to have accepted the brainwashing theory, the available literature seems to lean to a more moderate explanation of why young people join cults. While there is some form of pressure exerted on cult members, especially those who live a community life, the physical and mental conditions of those in a cult can hardly be equated with those of prisoners-of-war in Communist China. Even if religious conversion is not what takes place when young adults join a cult and change their values, world views and life-styles, it would appear that theories of socialization or enculturation can more suitably explain the transformation from conformity to deviancy.

The debate on whether cult members are brainwashed or converted penetrates a large section of the literature on the cults. The previous sections of this chapter contain many items which assume that there is some degree of brainwashing in the cults, and that extreme forms of counseling, like deprogramming, are needed if cult members are to be returned to their former states of mind. In this final section, we include recent material on the issue as well as some of the earlier, pre-1973 literature on brainwashing, such as Lifton's book (item 1865), which is adduced as evidence that the theory of brainwashing is applicable to the new cults.

1822.   Adler, Herbert M., and O. Hammet Van Buren. "Crisis, Conversion, and Cult Formation: An Examination of a Common Psychological Sequence." AMERICAN JOURNAL OF PSYCHIATRY 130 (1973): 861-64.

Argues that group and system formation are the mainstreams of human functioning, the former based on interpersonal relations, the latter on well-organized, cognitive structures concerning the total environment. The therapeutic community,

which deals with poor prognosis character disorders and which
uses a behaviorally-oriented group approach, is compared and
contrasted with psychoanalysis, which is insight-oriented, and
relies on the one-to-one relationship between the therapist and
the client. Therapeutic communities, such as Alcoholics Anon-
nymous, Synanon, and Weight Watchers, employ powerful forces,
including cognitive dissonance, social integration, and group
cohesiveness. The sequence of crisis, conversion, and cult
formation provides a rationale for understanding both psychoanalysis and therapeutic communities.

1823.   Anderson, Susan M., and Philip G. Zimbardo. "On Resisting
        Social Influences." CULTIC STUDIES JOURNAL 1 (1984): 196-
        219.

        Argues that effective mind control is exerted on all people
        in ordinary experiences and is caused by social influences
        which distort one's integrity and diminish one's freedom of
        choice. The question at issue is whether one can counteract
        these influences. Several techniques of how people are led
        to change by subtle influences are outlined, and suggestions
        for counteracting them are given. Among the advice given is
        to develop a healthy, critical attitude and to develop an
        awareness of the confident, self-assuring, and ingratiating
        forms of persuasion. The authors discuss the problems of
        resisting social and psychological pressures within the con-
        text of cult recruitment. No consideration is given to the
        possibility of religious conversion.

*   Baer, Donald M., and Stephanie Stolz. "A Description of the
        Erhard Seminary Training (EST) in the Terms of Behavior
        Analysis." Cited above as item 1713.

1824.   Baer, Hans A. "A Field Perspective of Religious Conversion:
        The Levites of Utah." REVIEW OF RELIGIOUS RESEARCH 19
        (1978): 279-94.

        Discusses conversion experiences of members of the Aaronic
        Order, a Mormon schismatic group founded in the late 1930s.
        The backgrounds and types of conversion are described. The
        role of relative deprivation in sociological, psychological,
        ethical, and economic perspectives is examined, and it is
        concluded that deprivation plays an important part in the
        emergence and continued recruitment to religious sects and
        cults. Other factors leading to conversion, such as previous
        religious affiliation and educational background, are also
        considered. The author thinks that in order to explain the
        process of conversion, one must take into account both the
        deprivation theory and other operating factors.

1825.   Bakken, Timothy. "Religious Conversion and Social Evolution
        Clarified: Similarities Between Traditional and Alterna-
        tive Groups." SMALL GROUP BEHAVIOR 16 (1985): 157-66.

        Discusses "whether conversion is simply a timely psycho-
        logical intervention by religious intermediaries, a deviant

experience, or a true reintegration of one's fundamental
beliefs that leads ultimately to behavioral changes" (p. 158).
The author's view is that religious conversion is a reaction
to self-doubt and insecurity, and results in decision making.
Conversion to Est and to alternate religious groups is caused
by psychological factors. Some conversion experiences have
deleterious effects.

1826. Balch, Robert W. "Looking Behind the Scene in a Religious
        Cult: Implications for the Study of Conversion." SOCIO-
        LOGICAL ANALYSIS 41 (1980): 137-43.

        Studies the conversion process to a millennial UFO cult.
        The author questions the brainwashing model, which is often
        used to account for the allegedly dramatic transformations
        in personality which those joining a new religious movement
        undergo. He argues that the first step to conversion is to
        learn to act like a convert by adopting a new role and con-
        forming to cultic behavior. Genuine conviction, involving a
        radical change in values, beliefs, and attitudes, takes place
        later.

1827. Barker, Eileen. THE MAKING OF A MOONIE: CHOICE OR BRAIN-
        WASHING? Oxford: Basil Blackwell, 1984. ix, 305 pp.

        Examines the historical background and the belief system of
        Rev. Moon's Unification Church, and explores its attraction
        to potential recruits. The contributions to the debate on
        brainwashing are discussed and the accusations of environ-
        mental control, deception, and "love-bombing" are considered.
        Although the author discovered no evidence of the use of
        physical coercion, control of diet, and training sessions to
        impair a person's biological functioning, she admits that
        "there is plenty of reason to believe that the Moonies will
        do their best to influence their guests' perception of the
        situation in which they now find themselves" (p. 233). But
        the Moonie environment is not irresistible, and their conver-
        sion is not the result of mass-induced hypnosis.

1828. Beck, James R. "Post-Conversion Regression." JOURNAL OF
        PSYCHOLOGY AND CHRISTIANITY 4 (1985): 19-21.

        Points out that in spite of the frequently positive results
        of religious conversion, there are cases where the converts
        experience a worsening of their symptoms or a regression to
        previous psychological problems. A case is presented to
        illustrate some of the essential features of the regression
        state. Ways of dealing with these patients are suggested.

1829. Biderman, Albert D. "The Image of 'Brainwashing.'" PUBLIC
        OPINION QUARTERLY 26 (1962): 547-63.

        Reviews several studies on brainwashing and discusses their
        implications. The author reflects on the mistaken image of
        brainwashing found both in popular literature and in scientif-
        ic writings, and suggests that the West might have developed

an exaggerated view of the scientific significance of brainwashing. The history of brainwashing in Eastern Europe, the
significance of behavioral influence, and the possibility of
resisting brainwashing are among the topics covered. There
are some useful references to standard literature on the
topic.

1830. Bjornstad, J. "The Deprogramming and Rehabilitation of Mod-
      ern Cult Members." JOURNAL OF PASTORAL PRACTICE 2 (1978):
      113-27.

      Argues that the new cults are using programming strategies
      to manipulate cult members. Factors like isolation, fatigue,
      tension, and fear are employed by carefully trained leaders
      to program susceptible young people. It is the author's view
      that indoctrination and Christian conversion are not the same
      as programming, which utilizes a controlled, social environ-
      ment to achieve assent. Christian conversion may include
      some indoctrination, but, unlike programming, always allows
      for a free personal decision. The author concedes that the
      deprogramming of cult members has at times been used unethi-
      cally, illegally, and forcibly both on cult members and on
      evangelical Christians.

1831. Bowart, Walter. OPERATION MIND CONTROL. New York: Dell,
      1978. 317 pp.

      Discusses the issue of brainwashing or mind control that
      has been employed both by the Chinese Communists and by
      various secret United States government agencies. Brain-
      washing is seen as the use of isolation, deprivation, torture,
      and indoctrination to break the human will. The author does
      not cover the current debate on the cults, but states in a
      footnote (p. 27) that meditation groups practice techniques
      of "mind self-control," which are harmless and may at times
      be beneficial.

1832. Bragan, K. "The Psychological Gains and Losses of Religious
      Conversion." BRITISH JOURNAL OF MEDICAL PSYCHOLOGY 50
      (1977): 177-80.

      Presents clinical evidence which shows that religious con-
      version, although it may lead to the resolution of conflict
      and to the formation of one's identity, can also result in
      the loss of personal relatedness and the consequent inability
      to adjust to the environment. A case study of a 25-year-old
      student-minister is presented, and the therapeutic treatment
      outlined. The patient's conversion involved rejection and
      repression of libidinal needs and, although he gained a firm
      control of his anger and hatred, he became incapable of love
      and never developed a sense of wholeness.

*   Brewer, Mark. "We're Going to Tear You Down and Put You Back
      Together." Cited above as item 1719.

1833. Bromley, David G., and James T. Richardson, editors. THE
       BRAINWASHING/DEPROGRAMMING CONTROVERSY: SOCIOLOGICAL, PSY-
       CHOLOGICAL, AND HISTORICAL PERSPECTIVES. New York: Edwin
       Mellen, 1983. 367 pp.

       Presents a collection of essays, some previously published,
       written "neither by apologists nor antagonists of the new
       religions" (p. 11). The argument runs generally against the
       brainwashing hypothesis, which is held to be a mystifying
       explanation of why people join cults. A lengthy bibliography
       is included.

       Contains items 1902, 1910.

1834. Brown, J. A. C. TECHNIQUES OF PERSUASION: FROM PROPAGANDA
       TO BRAINWASHING. Baltimore: Penguin Books, 1963. 325 pp.

       Discusses various ways by which human thinking can be
       influenced and manipulated. Besides chapters on confession,
       indoctrination, and brainwashing, there is a chapter on "The
       Nature of Religious Conversion" (pp. 223-43) which, the author
       thinks, is to some degree caused by mental conflict and feel-
       ings of inadequacy. Several forms of conversion methods,
       such as public confession, fasting, Yoga, drumming, dancing,
       and singing, are likened to brainwashing. The Christian
       evangelist rouses conflicting emotions--fear, anger, anxiety,
       and mental or physical exhaustion--to break down a person's
       pattern of behavior. Evangelical campaigns, which are of
       temporary duration, are examples of mass hysteria. It is
       argued, however, that those who convert are in search of a
       system of belief, which is not forced upon them.

1835. Brownfield, Charles A. THE BRAIN BENDERS: A STUDY OF THE
       EFFECTS OF ISOLATION. New York: Exposition Press, second
       edition, 1972. xii, 218 pp.

       Studies brainwashing techniques in China and Korea. Part
       One deals with the psychopathology of the solitary mind, while
       Part Two explores experimental isolation. In a chapter on
       anecdotal reports of isolation experiences, a short section
       entitled "Positive Features" includes references to religious
       examples of isolation and mentions Moses, John the Baptist,
       Jesus, Eastern Mystics, and Swedenborg as examples. The
       author thinks that many people who go through an isolation
       experience develop the symptoms of the mentally ill.

*   Campbell, Robert J. PSYCHIATRIC DICTIONARY. Cited above as
       item 9.

1836. Cavenar, Jesse O., and Jean G. Spaulding. "Depressive Dis-
       orders and Religious Conversions." JOURNAL OF NERVOUS AND
       MENTAL DISEASE 165 (1977): 209-12.

       Reflects on the scanty psychiatric literature on religious
       conversions even though these occur frequently. The negative
       view of Freud is outlined. The authors claim that they have

witnessed many patients who were relieved of their psychological stress through a religious experience. Four cases
are brought forth as examples. It is concluded that religious
conversion increased and strengthened regression in depressed
subjects, a regression which might resolve conflict in people
suffering from hysteria, and create hostility and rage in
those who had obsessive personalities.

1837. Cialdini, Robert B. INFLUENCE: HOW AND WHY PEOPLE AGREE TO
       THINGS. New York: William Morrow, 1984. 302 pp.

       Presents a study of the psychology of compliance. The
       techniques and strategies most commonly and effectively used
       by those who influence people are described. The author
       narrows down the tactics employed to six basic categories:
       consistency, reciprocation, social proof, authority, liking,
       and scarcity. Each of these methods is able to produce a
       kind of automatic, mindless submission from people, a willing-
       ness to say "Yes" without thinking first. A short section
       (pp. 120-28) shows how the tactic of social proof operates in
       millennial religious movements, whose promise of impending
       doom never seems to materialize.

1838. Clark, John G., Michael D. Langone, Robert E. Schacter, and
       Roger C. B. Daly. DESTRUCTIVE CULTISM: THEORY, RESEARCH,
       AND TREATMENT. Weston, MA: Center on Destructive Cultism,
       1981. 58 pp.

       Outlines the approach to cultism adopted by the American
       Family Foundation, which maintains that the new religious
       movements employ mind-control techniques and irresponsible
       forms of behavior modification to recruit members and to
       elicit their commitment. The authors present an overview of
       the problem of cultism, review the vast literature on cults,
       provide a theory to explain their emergence and success, and
       give guidelines for treating members. Fifty-eight references
       are included.

1839. Coleman, Lee. "New Religions and the Myth of Mind Control."
       AMERICAN JOURNAL OF ORTHOPSYCHIATRY 54 (1984): 322-25.

       Suggests that the theory that new religious movements use
       mind control or brainwashing to gain converts does not rest
       on sound evidence, but is rather a strategy for justifying
       the practice of deprogramming. The author states that "anti-
       cult mental health professionals have relied overwhelmingly
       on biased sampling methods" (p. 323). Cult members who con-
       form to behavioral expectations have chosen to do so. What
       the cults bring about is behavior control rather than mind
       control.

1840. Conn, Walter E., editor. CONVERSION: PERSPECTIVES ON PER-
       SONAL AND SOCIAL TRANSFORMATION. New York: Alba House,
       1978. xxvii, 330 pp.

PSYCHIATRY AND THE CULTS

Gives a collection of essays and selections from various
books on the theological, historical, biblical, and psychological dimensions of conversion. Included are chapters from
Thouless (item 95), Oates (item 1097), James (item 144), and
Johnson (item 75).

* Conway, Flo, and Jim Siegelman. SNAPPING: AMERICA'S EPIDEMIC
OF SUDDEN PERSONALITY CHANGE. Cited above as item 1188.

* Corsini, Robert J., editor. ENCYCLOPEDIA OF PSYCHOLOGY.
Cited above as item 12.

1841. Demos, George D., and William F. O'Neill. "'Groupthink': The
Study Groups in Thought Reform." ETC: A REVIEW OF GENERAL
SEMANTICS 41 (1984): 187-205.

Studies the techniques used by the Chinese to bring about
political conversion. Many of the common methods found in
group therapy, such as self-criticism and ideological reedu-
cation, were effectively employed. The authors describe the
various kinds of meetings, and examine the factors which lead
to coercive cooperation.

1842. Dolliver, Robert H. "Concerning Parallels Between Psychotherapy and Brainwashing." PSYCHOTHERAPY: THEORY, RESEARCH,
AND PRACTICE 8 (1971): 170-74.

Draws some similarities between the methods of psychotherapy
and brainwashing, focusing on the interaction between the
interrogator and prisoner on the one hand, and that between
the therapist and client on the other. It is suggested that
the interpersonal processes have some elements in common.
The use of direct and indirect reinforcement techniques and
of repetition are among the similarities pointed out. Some
guidelines for identifying differences between brainwashing
and therapy are set forth. The author seems to hold that
brainwashing, unlike therapy, controls and manipulates the
individual.

1843. Downton, James V. "An Evolutionary Theory of Spiritual
Conversion and Commitment: The Case of the Divine Light
Mission." JOURNAL FOR THE SCIENTIFIC STUDY OF RELIGION 19
(1980): 381-96.

Maintains that spiritual conversion and commitment are
usually very gradual in their development and that radical
personality changes are rare. The author bases his analysis
on intensive interviews with 18 members of the Divine Light
Mission, and carefully draws up an elaborate process of conversion with 10 stages and 27 steps. His findings agree in
many respects with the Lofland-Stark theory of conversion
(item 1870).

1844. Downton, James V. SACRED JOURNEYS: THE CONVERSION OF YOUNG
AMERICANS TO DIVINE LIGHT MISSION. New York: Colombia
University Press, 1979. 245 pp.

Attempts to understand the social and psychological processes of conversion to an Eastern religious movement led by
Guru Maharaj Ji. In Part One, the author presents four
individual case studies. In Part Two, he traces the conversion and commitment of young Americans, and then analyzes
the dynamics of religious change. Several areas receive considerable treatment: 1) the stages leading to contact with
the Divine Light Mission; 2) the encounter with the guru and
his message; 3) the changes in life-style and attitudes; and
4) social and intellectual defection from the movement. It
is the author's view that "premies," as initiates in the
Mission are called, have undergone a positive change. They
seem "less alienated, aimless, worried, afraid, and more
peaceful, loving, confident, and appreciative of life"
(p. 210). The author warns, however, that prolonged dependence on the guru creates psychological problems.

1845. Ellens, J. Harold. "The Psychodynamics of Christian Conversion." JOURNAL OF PSYCHOLOGY AND CHRISTIANITY 3 (1984):
29-36.

Argues that Christian conversion is an event in which
adults grow or change mainly through the impact of a significant emotional experience. Conversion can start in trauma
or with a new relationship or insight, and then mature to
personal integration. Some conversions, Christian or otherwise, may be healthy. Conversions which lead to dependency
on cultic authority figures are examples of unhealthy religious experiences.

1846. Etemand, Bijan. "Extrication from Cultism." CURRENT PSY-
CHIATRIC THERAPIES 18 (1978): 217-25.

Gives a general view of modern cults, including the Divine
Light Mission, the Unification Church, the Hare Krishna Movement, and the Children of God. The recruitment techniques
and cult life are briefly described. The author's view seems
to be that those who join the new cults are depressed people,
susceptible to conversion, and that their commitment to the
cult is sustained by indoctrination techniques. Although he
disavows the deprogrammers' methods, which he thinks violate
the principles of the health profession, he proposes a
rehabilitation program which is not much different.

1847. Faber, I. E., Harry F. Harlow, and Louis J. West. "Brainwashing, Conditioning, and DDD (Debility, Dependency, and
Dread)." SOCIOMETRY 20 (1957): 271-85.

Explores, in the context of prisoners-of-war in China, the
reasons why the techniques which brought about their collaboration, conversion, and self-denunciation were so successful.
The three elements of debility, dependency, and dread are
discussed and some of their effects outlined. The physical,
emotional, and social conditioning of the prisoners, together

with the total experience of incarceration, are the causes
of brainwashing. Resistance is possible, but much depends
on the prisoners' mental and physical states.

1848. Feinstein, Howard M. "The Prepared Heart: A Comparative Study
of Puritan Theology and Psychoanalysis." AMERICAN QUARTERLY
22 (1970): 166-76.

Tries to relate the seventeenth-century Puritan procedures
to prepare an individual for salvation with the techniques
of psychoanalysis. The author finds that self-scrutiny and
voluntary participation are central to both methods. Besides,
both initiate major shifts in personality "by forcing awareness of the tenuous nature of presently accepted necessity"
(pp. 173-74). Some serious differences, like the diversity
in goal and the doctrine of election, are noted.

*   Fenwick, Sheridan. GETTING IT: THE PSYCHOLOGY OF EST. Cited
above as item 1737.

*   Franck, Loren, Monty L. Lynn, Mark Mendenhall, and Gary R.
Oddous. SEVEN YEARS OF RELIGIOUS CONVERSION: A SELECTED
ANNOTATED BIBLIOGRAPHY. Cited above as item 20.

1849. Frank, K. THE ANTI-PSYCHIATRY BIBLIOGRAPHY AND RESOURCE
GUIDE. Vancouver, Canada: Press Gary Publishers, 1979.
160 pp.

Provides a handbook for those who, maintaining that the
current health system and programs have too many failings,
wish to explore alternatives. There is a section on mind
control technology, which includes some basic texts on mind
control and brainwashing.

1850. Furlong, F. W. "Determination and Free Will: Review of Literature." AMERICAN JOURNAL OF PSYCHIATRY 138 (1981): 435-
39.

Shows how, in the psychological disciplines, the theological
view of free will and the legal assumption of responsibility
have been abandoned and replaced by a purely deterministic
theory of human nature, a theory which denies genuine autonomy, inner direction, or free will as unscientific or illusory. The author maintains that there is still a need for
the concept of self-determination and behavioral self-control.
The existential view that stresses one's freedom to choose
values, to follow a personally-selected course of action, and
to make decisions seems to be supported by some studies. A
useful bibliography is added.

1851. Galanti, Geri-Ann. "Brainwashing and the Moonies." CULTIC
STUDIES JOURNAL 1 (1984): 27-36.

Questions the concept of brainwashing or mind control, even
though it is admitted that the Unification Church is guilty
of depriving its members of proper nutrition and of training

them to commit suicide. What occurs in the Church's training camps is socialization or enculturation after the candidates have become emotionally attached to their peers. The author maintains, however, that this socialization is harmful because it retrains people, brought up in a culture which stresses the importance of the self, to give up their identities for the sake of the group.

*   Gallanter, Marc, Richard Rabkin, et al. "The 'Moonies': A Psychological Study of Conversion and Membership in a Contemporary Religious Sect." Cited above as item 1747.

1852.   Gillespie, V. Bailey. RELIGIOUS CONVERSION AND PERSONAL EXPERIENCE. Birmingham, AL: Religious Education Press, 1979. xi, 246 pp.

Surveys several theories of religious conversion and maintains that such experiences, whether gradual or sudden, are a vital force in one's life. Conversion plays a role in the construction of a person's identity, in ordering one's life, and in giving it a meaningful purpose. The emotional, social, psychological, developmental, and experiential dimensions of religious conversion are examined. The author stresses the links between conversion, identity formation, and crisis. Conversion presents opportunities for growth. The counselor's task in understanding and integrating religious conversion is discussed.

1853.   Goldberg, Lorna, and William Goldberg. "Group Work With Former Cultists." SOCIAL WORK 27 (1982): 165-70.

Describes their clinical work with ex-cult members, who were forced to convert by means of sensory bombardment, sleep deprivation, and emotional manipulation. Cult members in the "post-mind-control" phase are helped by group therapy, which serves as a mechanism for bridging the gulf between cult life and the outside world. The assessment interview and the three-stage recovery process, which the author labels the post-mind-control syndrome, are explained.

*   Goldenson, Robert M. THE ENCYCLOPEDIA OF HUMAN BEHAVIOR. Cited above as item 22.

1854.   Harsch, O. Henry, and Herbert Zimmer. "An Experimental Approximation of Thought Reform." JOURNAL OF CONSULTING PSYCHOLOGY 29 (1965): 475-79.

Describes the method used to create, artificially in the laboratory, a thought reform process. The researchers claim to have succeeded in changing a basic behavior pattern and that the change persisted for about a week.

1855.   Heirich, Max. "Change of Heart: A Test of Some Widely Held Theories About Religious Conversion." AMERICAN JOURNAL OF SOCIOLOGY 83 (1977): 653-80.

Discusses scientific studies that usually explain religious conversion with reference to psychological stress, previous socialization, or various forms of direct social influence. Relying on data on Catholic Pentecostals, the author questions whether any of the major theories explain what lies behind the religious quest of the convert and the responses to it. It is suggested that researchers could, with profit, explore the circumstances and procedures by which a sense of "ultimate grounding" is affirmed or changed in the conversion process. Rather than start with the assumption that converts are deviants, one should see them "as offering a unique vantage point for examining the establishment and disestablishment of root senses of reality" (p. 677).

1856. Hochman, John. "Iatrogenic Symptoms Associated With a Therapy Cult: Examination of an Extinct 'New Psychotherapy' with Respect to Deterioration and 'Brainwashing.'" PSYCHIATRY 47 (1984): 366-77.

Focuses on a now-defunct school of psychotherapy, the Center for Feeling Therapy with its similarities and differences to psychotherapy cults (see item 1338). The nature of the Feeling Therapy is described and compared to Synanon. Four cases are presented to illustrate how treatment was applied. The author holds that new forms of therapy can deteriorate when they acquire religious endorsement, and they could lead to serious problems for their members. The "therapy" of some cults is compared to brainwashing in Communist China.

1857. Hyde, Margaret O. BRAINWASHING AND OTHER FORMS OF MIND CONTROL. New York: McGraw-Hill, 1977. 147 pp.

Discusses various ways, like behavior modification, biofeedback, and hypnosis, in which human beings can influence and control the mind. In a chapter on mind control and the cults, the issue is raised regarding the practices of some of the new religious movements, such as the Unification Church, the Children of God, and the Hare Krishna. Altered states of consciousness, achieved through meditation, are a form of mind control over one's body.

1858. Janis, Irving L. "Personality Correlates of Susceptibility To Persuasion." JOURNAL OF PERSONALITY 22 (1954): 504-18.

Starts from the common assumption that personality factors play an important role in determining a person's response to invitations to change one's beliefs and attitudes. Some people are more amenable to be influenced, others more predisposed to resist. Two types of personality disturbances among college students, namely, low self-esteem and acute neurotic anxiety, are explored in order to assess how they are affected by persuasive communications. It was found that marked personality differences existed between those who were highly influenced and those who were relatively untouched. The former had feelings of personal inadequacy, the latter acute psychoneurotic symptoms. Some useful references are appended.

1859. Johnson, B. Cedric, and H. Newton Malony. CHRISTIAN CONVER-
      SION: BIBLICAL AND PSYCHOLOGICAL PERSPECTIVES. Grand
      Rapids, MI: Zondervan, 1982. 192 pp.

      Aims at developing a healthy integration of psychological
      and theological perspectives on conversion. The volume is
      divided into four parts: 1) the psychological understanding
      of the conversion experience; 2) a Biblical view of conver-
      sion; 3) a consideration of various processes, such as
      behavior change, evangelism, and psychotherapy, in relation
      to conversion; and 4) an attempt to develop a psychology of
      conversion. Among the issues discussed is whether sudden
      conversion is an indication of a person's pathology or a help
      in the resolution of inner conflict. Sargant's view (item
      1894) is criticized for leaving out the intellectual and
      volitional components of the conversion experience. The
      authors believe that conversion and psychotherapy, in spite
      of their different understandings of the nature of the human
      person and of pathology, can be seen as complementary.

1860. Kilbourne, Brock K. "The Conway and Siegelman Claims Against
      Religious Cults: An Assessment of Their Data." JOURNAL
      FOR THE SCIENTIFIC STUDY OF RELIGION 22 (1983): 380-85.

      Challenges the theory of Conway and Siegelman (item 1188)
      that cults have a deleterious influence on their members. It
      is argued that their data do not support most of their corre-
      lations between cult involvement and psychological problems.
      Their data, rather than confirming their "information disease
      theory," suggest that chanting, ritual, and altered states of
      consciousness "may actually safeguard the cult convert from
      certain long-term mental and emotional effects" (p. 384).

1861. Kim, Byong-suh. "Religious Deprogramming and Subjective Re-
      ality." SOCIOLOGICAL ANALYSIS 40 (1979): 197-207.

      Examines the religious deprogramming of cult members who
      had been allegedly brainwashed. Religious deprogramming is
      seen as a process leading to the rejection of the attitudes,
      beliefs, and practices of the religious group, to which the
      individual had given loyal commitment. The author maintains
      that deprogramming has the latent function of religious
      deconversion and reconversion, a process of "social construc-
      tion of subjective reality." There are indirect hints that
      brainwashing and deprogramming are similar, but the author
      does not explore the question.

1862. Langone, Michael D. "Deprogramming: An Analysis of Parental
      Questionnaires." CULTIC STUDIES JOURNAL 1 (1984): 63-78.

      Summarizes the results of a survey that was conducted to
      explore the attitudes of parents whose children had joined a
      cult and undergone rapid personality changes due to brain-
      washing. The author insists that many cults sometimes cause
      physical, psychological, and economic harm on their members.

He concludes that, since many cult members freely reevaluate
their commitment and leave voluntarily, deprogramming is not
a panacea for getting people out of cults, but rather one of
several options.

1863. Levin, Theodore M., and Leonard S. Zegans. "Adolescent
       Identity Crisis and Religious Conversion: Implications For
       Psychotherapy." BRITISH JOURNAL OF MEDICAL PSYCHOLOGY 47
       (1974): 73-82.

       Discusses the problems which face psychiatrists who coun-
       sel those caught up in religious revivals, and presents a
       case of a schizophrenic who used religious beliefs and rituals
       to resolve the difficulties of an adolescent phase. Although
       the patient's reconversion to Judaism was adaptive in that
       it helped him deal with his psychotic panic, his behavior was
       rather bizarre and actually prevented successful adaptation
       and growth. Suggestions for handling such patients are given.

1864. Levine, Edward M. "Are Religious Cults Religious?" CULTIC
       STUDIES JOURNAL 1 (1984): 4-7.

       Contrasts the position of the "cultic defenders" with that
       of the "cult critics," and maintains that cults aim at mind
       control. Cult members are psychologically manipulated, some-
       times physically abused, and often forced into a servile
       state which seriously impairs their emotional stability.

1865. Lifton, Robert J. THOUGHT REFORM AND THE PSYCHOLOGY OF
       TOTALISM: A STUDY OF 'BRAINWASHING' IN CHINA. New York:
       Norton, 1961. x, 510 pp.

       Presents a thorough study of the Chinese practice of brain-
       washing, or thought reform, on Western prisoners-of-war and
       Chinese intellectuals. Several case studies are given to
       illustrate the process of inducing a change in ideology by
       means of two basic methods: 1) confession--the exposure and
       renunciation of past and present evil; and 2) re-education--
       the remaking of the individual in the communist image. The
       author points out that, contrary to what many people think,
       brainwashing is not an "all-powerful, irresistible, unfathom-
       able, and magical method of achieving thought control over
       the human mind" (p. 4). Although this study restricts itself
       to political thought, the author maintains that imposed
       dogmas, inquisitions, and mass conversion movements in dif-
       ferent cultures and historical eras are similar efforts aimed
       at manipulating human beings. This book is frequently quoted
       in support of the view that the new cults actually brainwash
       their members.

1866. Lifton, Robert J. "'Thought Reform' of Western Civilians in
       Chinese Communist Prisons." PSYCHIATRY 19 (1956): 173-95.

       Describes the author's work in Hong Kong with Westerners
       who had undergone a thought reform process in China. The
       penal reform scheme, with its method of arrest, the subsequent

emotional assaults on those incarcerated, and their final
confessions, is described. The impact and origin of thought
reform are discussed. The author describes the method as an
"agonizing drama of death and rebirth" (p. 188).

* Lockwood, George. "Rational-Emotive Therapy and Extremist
  Cults." Cited above as item 1271.

1867. Lofland, John. "'Becoming a World-Saver' Revisited." AMER-
      ICAN BEHAVIORAL SCIENTIST 20 (1977): 805-18.

      Updates and extends his previous work with Rodney Stark
      (item 1870). The promotion tactics, the training sessions,
      the loving attention showered on prospective members, and the
      steps leading to commitment are described. The author thinks
      that his original conversion model is still applicable to
      the more recent evangelizing efforts of cult members, whose
      efforts have become more refined and sophisticated.

1868. Lofland, John. DOOMSDAY CULT: A STUDY OF CONVERSION, PROSE-
      LYTIZATION, AND MAINTENANCE OF FAITH. Irvington, CA:
      Halsted Press, enlarged edition, 1977. xii, 362 pp.

      Studies a Korean cult, which the author calls by the pseudo-
      nym of "Divine Precepts," which began its missionary activi-
      ties in the United States in the 1960s. The following areas
      are discussed: 1) the process of conversion, especially the
      conditions under which a person is expected to take up a
      deviant role; 2) the proselytization or recruitment strate-
      gies, which attract young adults and turn them into zealous
      missionaries for the cause; and 3) the ways in which faith
      and hope in the movement are maintained.

1869. Lofland, John, and Norman Skonovd. "Conversion Motifs."
      JOURNAL FOR THE SCIENTIFIC STUDY OF RELIGION 20 (1981):
      373-85.

      Identifies and describes six conversion themes, namely,
      intellectual, mystical, experimental, affectional, revival-
      ist, and coercive, and correlates them with the degree of
      social pressure, temporal duration, level of affective
      arousal, affective content, and belief-participation se-
      quence. Coercive conversion, often referred to as brain-
      washing, thought reform, or mind-control, is very rare. It
      entails "an extremely high degree of external pressure over
      a relatively long period of time, during which there is
      intense arousal of fear and anxiety, culminating in empa-
      thetic identification and even love" (p. 383).

1870. Lofland, John, and Rodney Stark. "Becoming a World-Saver: A
      Theory of Conversion to a Deviant Perspective." AMERICAN
      SOCIOLOGICAL REVIEW 30 (1965): 862-75.

      Outlines one of the more popular theories of conversion
      based on the study of a millennial cult, which the authors
      refer to as D. P. (Divine Precepts) and which is generally

understood to be the Unification Church in its earliest
stages in the United States. In the authors' words, conversion implies that "a person must: 1) experience enduring,
acutely felt tensions, 2) within a religious, problem-solving
perspective, 3) which leads him to define himself as a religious seeker, 4) encountering the D. P. at a turning point
in his life, 5) wherein an affective bond is formed (or pre-
exists) with one or more converts, 6) where extra-cult attachments are absent or neutralized, and 7) and, where, if he is
to become a deployable agent, he is exposed to intensive
interaction" (p. 874).

1871.   Lombillo, Jose R. "The Soldier Saint: A Psychological Analy-
        sis of the Conversion of Ignatius of Loyola." PSYCHIATRIC
        QUARTERLY 47 (1973): 386-418.

        Presents historical data on Ignatius of Loyola and focuses
        on his conversion experience. The author thinks that the
        saint's conversion process was a search for identity, a move
        from the repressive and primitive phallic narcissism of mili-
        tary identity, to the more normal and healthy religious self-
        conception. Arguing that true religious conversion involves
        an identity crisis, the author states that Ignatius, through
        his conversion, achieved a personal synthesis. His unusual
        experiences, which included solitary confinement, trance, and
        hallucinations, are discussed in terms of de-automatization,
        a regressive adaptation which eventually leads to better
        psychological health.

1872.   Long, Theodore, and Jeffrey K. Haddon. "Religious Conversion
        and the Concept of Socialization: Integrating the Brain-
        washing and Drift Models." JOURNAL FOR THE SCIENTIFIC
        STUDY OF RELIGION 22 (1983): 1-14.

        Presents the two common theories which explain why people
        join cults, namely, the one claiming that cult members use
        coercive means to gain mind control over prospective new
        recruits (the brainwashing model), the other suggesting that
        people join cults gradually, through the influence of social
        relationships (the drift model). A theory of socialization,
        which relies on both models, is given and applied to the
        members of the Unification Church. The authors hold that the
        social system of this movement combines strong incorporation
        of converts with a rather weak new belief system, thus fos-
        tering initially strong, but short-term, commitment.

1873.   Lynch, Frederick R. "Toward a Theory of Conversion and Com-
        mitment to the Occult." AMERICAN BEHAVIORAL SCIENTIST 20
        (1977): 887-908.

        Constructs a descriptive framework for studying conversion
        and commitment to the occult based on his study of a witch-
        craft group which he calls "Church of the Sun." Conversion
        to this church is a complex process which takes place in a
        number of phases over several years. Individuals who, after

a period of search and trials, finally commit themselves to
the occult, usually start by reading on occult topics or
with a personal psychic event. Contacts with other people
involved in the occult are eventually made, often by accident.
This leads to an exposure to collective symbolic rituals and
to consequent involvement.

1874. Malony, H. Newton. "G. Stanley Hall's Theory of Conversion."
JOURNAL OF PSYCHOLOGY AND CHRISTIANITY 3 (1984): 2-8.

Provides a short, favorable account of the view that
altruism is at the core of religious conversion. The author
thinks such an approach deals with both the content and the
process of conversion and deserves reconsideration.

1875. Meerloo, Joost A. M. THE RAPE OF THE MIND: THE PSYCHOLOGY OF
THOUGHT CONTROL, MENTICIDE, AND BRAINWASHING. New York:
Grosset and Dunlap, 1961. 320 pp.

Attempts to show how the free human mind can be transformed
into an automatically-responding machine or robot. The techniques of mass submission, which include false confessions,
are described, and ways of defending oneself against brainwashing are discussed. The book restricts itself to those
cultural and political influences which can be employed in
thought control.

* Melton, J. Gordon, and Robert L. Moore. THE CULT EXPERIENCE.
Cited above as item 1279.

1876. Moore, Robert L. "Justification Without Joy: Psychohistori-
cal Reflections on John Wesley's Childhood and Conversion."
HISTORY OF CHILDHOOD QUARTERLY 2 (1974): 31-52.

Assesses the effects of Wesley's childhood on his conversion and confirmation as an evangelist. The author considers
Wesley's experience in the family circle and his failed experiment in the State of Georgia. The superstructures of
his soteriology are foreshadowed in the rigid moral behavior
imposed by his mother. His appeal to members of the lower
classes was likely due to the fact that they, like himself,
"had known the terror and uncertainty of childhoods spent
with not only harsh and distant, but capricious and ambivalent parental authority" (p. 50).

* Mosatche, Harriet S. SEARCHING: PRACTICES AND BELIEFS OF
THE RELIGIOUS CULTS AND HUMAN POTENTIAL GROUPS. Cited
above as item 1281.

1877. Murphey, Murray G. "The Psychodynamics of Puritan Conversion." AMERICAN QUARTERLY 31 (1979): 135-47.

Studies conversion experiences among the New England Puritans of the seventeenth and early eighteenth centuries. The
nature of this experience and its psychological features are

described. The author sees some analogies between the Puritan
conversion process and the resolution of the male oedipus
complex, as defined in Freudian psychoanalysis. Both involve
conflict situations "in which an individual confronts an
overwhelming antagonist who threatens condign punishment,"
and a resolution "by identification with the authority figure
and introjection of his standards which become embodied in
the superego" (p. 141). The Puritans are not autonomous,
self-directing, self-controlling individuals, free of the
domination of impulse and authority. Rather, they have weak
egos, which are manifested in doubt and distrust, self-deni-
gration, and the great importance they attach to rituals.

1878.   Newton, James W., and Leo Mann. "Crowd Size as a Factor in
the Persuasion Process: A Study of Religious Crusade Meetings." JOURNAL OF PERSONALITY AND SOCIAL PSYCHOLOGY 39
(1980): 874-83.

Suggests that when a large crowd voluntarily attends a
meeting to hear a speaker, the larger the crowd, the greater
proportion of those present will accept the speaker's viewpoint. The theory is tested with data from four separate
crusades led by Billy Graham and Leighton Ford in Australia.
A positive correlation was found between crowd size and number
of inquirers, who were more likely to be women or young adults.
The authors offer some speculations on why such crusades are
successful.

1879.   Pilarzyk, Thomas. "Conversion and Alternation Processes in
the Youth Culture: A Comparative Analysis of Religious
Transformation." PACIFIC SOCIOLOGICAL REVIEW 21 (1978):
379-409.

Explores, from a phenomenological perspective, the nature
of the resocialization process of young adults who joined
two religious movements, namely, the Divine Light Mission and
the Hare Krishna. It is maintained that knowledge of the
quality of the individual's prior experience is necessary for
understanding what takes place in conversion. Two distinctive processes of personal transformation are observed:
1) sectarian conversion (evident in the Hare Krishna devotees); and 2) cultic conversion (manifest in the members of
the Divine Light Mission). The latter is transitional and
implies only an extension of, or minor break with, the
convert's former identity.

1880.   Pines, Maya. THE BRAIN CHANGERS: SCIENTISTS AND THE NEW MIND
CONTROL. New York: Harcourt Brace Jovanovich, 1973.
248 pp.

Discusses ways of controlling human thought by behavior
modification techniques and by drugs. Though there is hardly
any reference to religion, except the statement that religious
experience can be induced by drugs, the book provides some of
the physiological background to understanding mind control.

The author thinks that the human brain can be effectively and
positively controlled, preventing a great deal of misery and
enhancing human life.

1881. Poythress, Norman G. "Behavior Modification, Brainwashing,
       Religion, and the Law." JOURNAL OF RELIGION AND HEALTH 17
       (1978): 238-43.

       Discusses: 1) the religious origin of free will in the
       Western legal system; 2) the responsiveness of the courts to
       psychiatric intervention challenging free will; and 3) the
       procedural similarity between behavior modification, brain-
       washing, and religious indoctrination. Various issues about
       the process of religious training and the problems facing
       religious professionals are raised.

1882. Price, Robert. "The Centrality and Scope of Conversion."
       JOURNAL OF PSYCHOLOGY AND THEOLOGY 9 (1981): 26-36.

       Argues that recent controversies over the alleged brain-
       washing and deprogramming of cult members have brought the
       question of conversion to the fore. The author reconsiders
       the meaning and role of conversion in Evangelical Christian-
       ity and argues that it should be understood primarily as
       a miraculous work of the Holy Spirit and not merely as an
       initiation rite. The naturalist interpretation of conversion,
       espoused by many psychologists, is refuted. Three aspects of
       the born-again experience--personality growth, witnessing,
       and apologetics--are considered. The author holds that, when
       conversion is understood simply as a resolution of personal
       crises, the result is to evaluate it negatively, as stereo-
       typed thinking and stunted personal growth.

1883. Ramage, Ian. BATTLE FOR THE MIND. London: Allen and Unwin,
       1967. 269 pp.

       A critical assessment of Sargant's views (item 1894) on
       evangelical revivals and Christian conversions. An explana-
       tion of the revival under Wesley in purely psychological
       terms is rejected, even though the author admits that his
       preaching is a good example of emotional abreaction. The
       conversions, which were brought about by Wesley's evangelical
       activities, were essentially a response "of joy and liberation
       of personality; a breaking down of inner checks and barriers
       to life's energies, a recovery from hopelessness, lethargy,
       and vice....Anything further away from 'brainwashing' and
       the like would be hard to imagine" (p. 242).

1884. Rambo, Lewis R. "Charisma and Conversion." PASTORAL PSYCHOL-
       OGY 31 (1982): 96-108.

       Examines the dynamic processes involved in the charisma of
       religious leaders, and the conversion of young adults to new
       religious movements. Following Murphey's analysis (item
       1877), the author sees conversion in terms of identification,

introjection, and displacement. The charismatic leader assumes
a central leadership role in a group that serves to relieve
anxiety and the sense of isolation. Charisma is an important
ingredient in the conversion process, because it provides
legitimization to the group. The charismatic figure becomes
an embodiment of faith, a teacher and model, a cause for improvement, and a public relations person. Conversion can be
understood as an interaction between the religious leader,
the group, and the potential recruit.

*   Rambo, Lewis. "Current Research on Religious Conversion."
         Cited above as item 42.

1885.   Reich, Walter. "Brainwashing, Psychiatry, and the Law."
        PSYCHIATRY 39 (1976): 400-3.

        Discusses the appeal of brainwashing, or coercive persua-
        sion, in legal cases, in the context of the trial of Patricia
        Hearst. The author maintains that insanity and external
        coercion are valid defenses, but that internalized coercion
        or brainwashing are not. To accept the latter as admissible
        psychiatric evidence would destroy the already weak founda-
        tion of our legal system, namely, free will. Besides, the
        author thinks that the alleged power of the brainwashing
        experience has not been subjected to scientific scrutiny.

1886.   Richardson, James T., editor. "Conversion and Commitment to
        Contemporary Religion." AMERICAN BEHAVIORAL SCIENTIST 20
        (1977): 799-860.

        Presents a collection of essays which focus on the socio-
        psychological dimensions of the new religious movements. The
        editor maintains that it is important to study the process of
        conversion and commitment to these movements because of the
        recruitment tactics allegedly employed by some of them, and
        because of the charge of brainwashing which has been leveled
        against them.

        Contains items 1867, 1873, 1888.

1887.   Richardson, James T., editor. CONVERSION CAREERS: IN AND OUT
        OF THE NEW RELIGIONS. Beverly Hills, CA: Sage Publications,
        1978. 160 pp.

        Contains the material previously published in a special
        issue of the AMERICAN BEHAVIORAL SCIENTIST (item 1886).

1888.   Richardson, James T., and Mary Stewart. "Conversion Process
        Models and the Jesus Movement." AMERICAN BEHAVIORAL SCIEN-
        TIST 20 (1977): 819-38.

        Gives a shortened version of the author's study on the Jesus
        People. A summary of Lofland and Stark's model of conversion
        (item 1870) is presented critically. Additional perspectives

and predispositions to conversion are offered. The authors hold that those studying conversion must pursue different levels of analysis besides the political and religious. In particular they single out the psychiatric, physiological, and conventional perspectives. The static versus the dynamic approaches to conversion are discussed, and the authors leave no doubt that they favor the latter.

1889. Robbins, Thomas, and Dick Anthony. "Deprogramming, Brainwashing, and the Medicalization of Deviant Religious Groups." SOCIAL PROBLEMS 29 (1982): 283-97.

Examines the claim that brainwashing techniques used by cults to win converts have pathological results. This medical model of cult membership has led to the use of forced deprogramming as a counter-medical solution. It is suggested that the medical profession has a vested interest in this approach to the cults. While the authors admit that several factors have encouraged the medicalization of the cults, they insist that the model not only does not conform to reality, but threatens the very concept of religious liberty.

1890. Robbins, Thomas, and Dick Anthony. "The Limits of 'Coercive Persuasion' as an Explanation For Conversion to Authoritarian Sects." POLITICAL PSYCHOLOGY 2.2 (1980): 22-37.

Criticizes the model of "coercive persuasion," or brainwashing, which has been used to explain conversion and commitment to new religious movements. The authors question both the theoretical assumptions and the methodological procedures of the exponents of the brainwashing theory. In particular, they raise the question of free will and mental illness and challenge the method which relies solely on testimonies given by ex-cult members. The implicit equation of religious movements with government-operated institutions employing physical and psychological constraints is rejected.

1891. Robbins, Thomas, and Dick Anthony. "Brainwashing and the Persecution of Cults." JOURNAL OF RELIGION AND HEALTH 19 (1980): 66-69.

Argues that the validity of brainwashing as a scientific concept is problematic. Brainwashing appears to be a subjective metaphor used to justify attacks against the cults and the deprogramming of their members. The concept of coercive persuasion is less occult and mystifying. While highly authoritarian groups may, in fact, be using methods of coercive persuasion, claims that the converts' free will is destroyed and that religious authoritarianism is a sign of mental pathology are unwarranted.

1892. Ross, Michael W. "Psychological Malpractice and the Anti-Cult Battle: The Brainwash." AUSTRALIAN JOURNAL OF SOCIAL ISSUES 14 (1979): 201-10.

Comments on the introduction of deprogramming of cult members in Australia and on its religious, psychological, and
legal implications. The procedures of deprogramming published
in Great Britain are outlined and judged to be a threat to
personal freedom and to the ethics of psychological practice.
The author observes that the accusation that cults brainwash
their members is unwarranted, and that some of the procedures
used by cults to induct new members can be also found in
well-established religions.

1893. Ryan, Barrie. "The Lost Self Changes: Gestalt and Christian
        Concepts of Rebirth." JOURNAL OF RELIGION AND HEALTH 15
        (1976): 247-70.

Relates the authors' own experience of change through
Gestalt therapy and religious rebirth, an experience which,
after a period of confusion and depression, leads to personal
reintegration. This transformation is discussed in the context of various theological and psychological theories. It
is concluded that both therapy and religious conversion can
contribute to one's well-being.

1894. Sargant, William. BATTLE FOR THE MIND: A PHYSIOLOGY OF CON-
        VERSION AND BRAINWASHING. Garden City, NY: Doubleday, 1957.
        263 pp.

Discusses at length the relationship between conversion and
brainwashing. This book has become one of the most often-
quoted books in the debate on brainwashing and the new cults.
The author analyzes some of the more important mechanistic and
physiological aspects of an abrupt political and religious
reorientation of a person's viewpoint, frequently brought
about by outside influences. The techniques of religious
conversion and of eliciting confessions, of brainwashing in
ancient times, and of mind control, in both religious and
political settings, are among the topics dealt with. One of
the author's main tenets is that beliefs can be implanted in
people's minds after their brain functions have been deliberately disturbed by induced fear, anger, or excitement. The
suggestibility, anxiety, sense of guilt, and conflict of
loyalities can be intentionally heightened and used to manipulate people to an emotional state leading to conversion.
Examples are provided from Christian revivals, such as Wesleyanism, and religious movements from different parts of the
world.

1895. Scheflin, Alan W., and Edward M. Opton. THE MIND MANIPULA-
        TORS: A NON-FICTIONAL ACCOUNT. New York: Paddington Press,
        1978. 539 pp.

Discusses the various forms of mind manipulation throughout
history. In the author's view, the manipulation of the human
mind occurs when the influence exerted is not free, but coercive, and when special techniques are employed to facilitate
consent. People who voluntarily allow themselves to be

influenced (as is the case, for example, of those who agree
to sign for the Est program) are not included. Revival movements use pre-modern methods of mass mind control. In a
section on "Religious Brainwashing" (pp. 52-63), the authors
state that brainwashing flourishes among numerous evangelical
sects and also among deprogrammers who are hired by the
relatives of cult members. In most cults, however, group
pressure and isolation--the two main reasons often adduced
as evidence of brainwashing--do not explain the success of
the cults. The authors think that the substitute-family
function of many charismatic cults is the most important
factor which attracts converts and keeps them from returning
to their previous life-style.

1896. Schein, Edgar H. COERCIVE PERSUASION: A SOCIO-PSYCHOLOGICAL
        ANALYSIS OF THE "BRAINWASHING" OF AMERICAN CIVILIAN PRISONERS
        BY THE CHINESE COMMUNISTS. New York: W. W. Norton, 1971.
        319 pp. First published in 1961.

        Studies a group of American and European students, doctors,
        businessmen, and missionaries who were imprisoned in China
        for three to five years after the outbreak of the Korean war.
        The aim of the study was to find out what happened to these
        people, what attitudinal changes they went through, and what
        long-term effects could be observed after their release. Four
        major areas are explored: 1) the context of coercive persua-
        sion; 2) its structure, effects, and determinants; 3) theories
        of coercive persuasion; and 4) implications for a theory of
        influence. The author holds that Chinese indoctrination or
        brainwashing was not very effective, but that their social
        control was extremely successful. In a chapter on coercive
        persuasion in a non-communist setting, the author sees the
        process used also in religious orders and revival meetings,
        in Alcoholics Anonymous, in initiation rites, and in hospi-
        tals, reformatories, and prisons. It is maintained that in
        a narrow religious context, the social pressures can be as
        coercive as the physical constraints operative in prisoner-
        of-war camps.

1897. Schein, Edgar H. "The Chinese Indoctrination Program for
        Prisoners of War." PSYCHIATRY 19 (1956): 147-72.

        Accounts for the typical experience of United Nations POWs
        in China, and gives it a socio-psychological interpretation.
        After describing the POW experience, the author outlines the
        indoctrination program. Three elements of the treatment are
        explained in some detail: 1) removal of supports to beliefs,
        attitudes, and values; 2) direct and indirect attacks on the
        same beliefs and values; and 3) eliciting of collaboration
        by a system of rewards and punishments. Some general prin-
        ciples behind all techniques, such as control of the environ-
        ment, repetition, and manipulation, are noted. The POWs'
        reactions to the indoctrination program and the effectiveness
        of the methods are also covered. The author's view is that
        indoctrination is successful in eliciting and controlling
        certain kinds of behavior, but that it is much less effective
        in changing beliefs and values.

1898. Schwartz, Lita L., and Jacqueline L. Zemel. "Religious Cults:
       Family Concerns and the Law." JOURNAL OF MARITAL AND FAMILY
       THERAPY 2 (1980): 301-8.

       Discusses the complaint of the families of cult members and
       of mental health practitioners that cults use elements of mind
       control. The authors hold that young people do not make a
       free choice to join one of the new cults, since their consent
       is not an informed one. Moreover, cult members are not free
       to leave, because they are restrained both by physical means
       and by brainwashing methods. Possible legal remedies are
       discussed.

1899. Sexton, Ray O., and Richard C. Maddock. "The Missionary Syn-
       drome." JOURNAL OF RELIGION AND HEALTH 19 (1980): 59-65.

       Shows by reference to several clinical case histories how
       guilt feelings, which usually result from repressed childhood
       incidents, may lead a patient to choose a religious vocation
       to sublimate one's guilt. The authors call this conversion
       a missionary syndrome, which could include rituals, phobias,
       compulsions, and the like. The nature of the treatment is
       briefly outlined. Although not applied to cult members, its
       applicability is obvious.

1900. Shaver, Philip, Michael Lenaur, and Susan Sadd. "Religious-
       ness, Conversion, and Subjective Well-Being: The 'Healthy-
       Minded' Religion of Modern American Women." AMERICAN
       JOURNAL OF PSYCHIATRY 137 (1980): 1563-68.

       Suggests that "modern converts to Christian sects and denom-
       inations are similar, in rough outline at least, to people
       who convert to cults" (p. 1563). In the context of the reli-
       gious revival of the 1970s, the authors polled 2,500 American
       women who read REDBOOK MAGAZINE to determine: 1) the nature
       of their religiousness; 2) the relationship of religion to
       mental health; and 3) the differences between converts and
       non-converts. Most of the women in the study appear to en-
       dorse a healthy-minded religion. Converts were more religious
       and appeared to have acquired health and happiness through
       their conversion, which may have solved personal conflicts.
       They were, however, more likely to have had disciplinary
       problems as children, and to have adopted an authoritarian
       attitude to religion after their conversion experience.

*   Shupe, Anson D. SIX PERSPECTIVES ON NEW RELIGIONS: A CASE
       STUDY APPROACH. Cited above as item 1322.

1901. Snow, David, and Cynthia L. Phillips. "The Lofland-Stark
       Conversion Model: A Critical Assessment." SOCIAL PROBLEMS
       27 (1980): 430-37.

       Questions most of the features of the conversion model for-
       mulated by Lofland and Stark (item 1870). The affective bonds
       and intensive interactions developed with a cult are still

deemed central to conversion. It is argued, however, that
tensions, cognitive states, and prior socialization are not
as important as most researchers think they are. The key to
understanding conversion, according to the authors, lies in
the interactive process between the members of a religious
group and the possible recruits.

1902. Solomon, Trudy. "Programming and Deprogramming the Moonies:
      Social Psychology in the Field." THE BRAINWASHING/DEPRO-
      GRAMMING CONTROVERSY (item 1833), pp. 163-82.

      Compares and contrasts the modern Russian and Chinese ways
      of brainwashing with the process of cult indoctrination, and
      concludes that the latter could be better labeled "religious
      training" or "religious instruction." Both social and
      psychological perspectives are used to understand programming
      and deprogramming which, unlike brainwashing, are testable
      and amenable to research and study. Isolation, group pressure,
      and coercion are discussed in the context of the practices
      of the Unification Church.

1903. Somit, Albert. "Brainwashing." INTERNATIONAL ENCYCLOPEDIA
      OF THE SOCIAL SCIENCES. Edited by David Sills. New York:
      Macmillan, 1968, vol. 2, pp. 138-43.

      Presents a brief account of the method of brainwashing and
      its development through history. Though there are differences
      between the Chinese and European practices, there are some
      common, standardized methods, namely: total control; isola-
      tion torture; physical debilitation and exhaustion; personal
      humiliation; and guilt. The author lists ten psychological
      mechanisms and dynamics which are operative in brainwashing:
      1) identification; 2) decrease of intellectual capacity;
      3) disorientation arising from solitary confinement; 4) sug-
      gestion; 5) repetition; 6) guilt feelings; 7) ego destruction;
      8) conditioned behavior; 9) non-rational behavior in the
      face of sudden stimulus; and 10) alternation of fear and hope.
      The political capabilities and limitations of brainwashing
      are finally discussed.

1904. Sorrel, William E. "Cults and Cult Suicide." INTERNATIONAL
      JOURNAL OF GROUP TENSIONS 8 (1978): 96-105.

      Starts by describing the suicidal finale of the People's
      Temple in Jonestown and relating it to 1) the Jews at the for-
      tress of Masada, who decided to die rather than surrender, and
      2) the Japanese soldiers and civilians who, faced with defeat,
      committed suicide rather than be dishonored by surrendering
      to the enemy. All cult members who live in communes are,
      according to the author, in concentration camp conditions.
      They are psychologically searching for the comfort of child-
      hood to escape responsibility and decision making. Cult
      members are reduced to robots, who are controlled by their
      psychotic leaders through coercive mind-control techniques
      (brainwashing) which impair their mental functioning. Cults
      are microcosms of the Nazi and Marxist totalitarian systems.

1905. Southard, Samuel. "The Christian Individual in a 'Program-
       med' World." RELIGIOUS EDUCATION 60 (1965): 209-214, 243.

       Discusses the use of the techniques of programmed learning
       based on the views of B. F. Skinner and other behaviorists.
       While agreeing that "Christian educators may use programmed
       learning to indoctrinate pupils without regard for individual
       freedom of choice..." (p. 213), the author proposes several
       Christian guidelines which safeguard, among other things,
       individual freedom. Although not written in the context of
       the current debate on brainwashing in the cults, the author
       discusses an issue which is common to all religions, and
       provides some principles which can be adapted to evaluate
       the ways in which cult members are indoctrinated into their
       respective religious groups.

1906. Spero, Moshe M. "Clinical Aspects of Religion as Neurosis."
       AMERICAN JOURNAL OF PSYCHOANALYSIS 36 (1976): 361-65.

       Discusses a clinical case involving some manifestations of
       neurosis in a client who experienced a religious conversion.
       The patient is diagnosed as "orally fixated." Brought up in
       a harsh, punitive, rejecting family, the patient's feelings
       were projected from the earthly to the heavenly father. In
       this particular case, conversion was a neurotic defense mech-
       anism. Penitence and conversion should not, according to
       the author, be employed as a substitute for psychotherapy.

1907. Stipes, Gregory P. "Principles of Religious Cult Indoctri-
       nation." JOURNAL OF PSYCHOLOGY AND CHRISTIANITY 4.3 (1985):
       64-72.

       Discusses the definition of a religious cult, the reasons
       for its growth (the dissolution of the family and the iden-
       tity confusion among young adults), and the two basic types
       of religious cults (charismatic and spontaneous). Several
       principles of the cult indoctrination process, including
       need-fulfillment and isolation, are described. Cult indoc-
       trination is compared to Chinese brainwashing and thought
       reform.

1908. Trossman, Harry. "After 'The Waste Land': Psychological Fac-
       tors in the Religious Conversion of T. S. Eliot." INTER-
       NATIONAL REVIEW OF PSYCHO-ANALYSIS 4 (1977): 295-304.

       Gives an account of Eliot's struggles leading to his con-
       version to "Anglo-Catholicism" and attempts to understand
       the psychological processes involved in his transition. The
       author thinks that conversion combines responses to conflict
       with satisfaction of archaic needs. Eliot's conversion is
       interpreted psychoanalytically as an attempt to build a psychic
       structure, as a reaction to the deterioration of his marriage
       and the increasing psychosis of his wife, and as a means of
       providing "narcissistic stabilization and reintegrative
       merger with an idealized self-object" (p. 304).

1909. Ungerleider, J. Thomas, and David K. Wellisch. "Coercive
      Persuasion (Brainwashing), Religious Cults, and Deprogram-
      ming." AMERICAN JOURNAL OF PSYCHIATRY 136 (1979): 279-82.

      Describes certain psychosocial characteristics of clients,
      who were members of diverse new religious movements, and com-
      ments on their ability to make sound legal decisions about
      their life-styles. The authors divide their patients into
      four groups: 1) cult members who feared deprogramming; 2)
      those who returned to the cult after an attempted deprogram-
      ming; 3) those who were successfully deprogrammed; and 4)
      those who left the cult without deprogramming. The results
      of the authors' investigation led to the conclusion that all
      the subjects were intellectually, mentally, and personally
      able to make up their own minds regarding cult involvement.
      Cult members manifested some superego deficits and hostility,
      both of which might have existed before they joined the cult.
      Ex-cult members were both socially and emotionally alienated
      and lacked ego-mastery. Cults appear to satisfy ideological
      needs and to relieve their members of ambivalence. No evi-
      dence of brainwashing was found.

1910. Ungerleider, J. Thomas, and David K. Wellisch. "The Program-
      ming (Brainwashing)/Deprogramming Religious Controversy."
      THE BRAINWASHING/DEPROGRAMMING CONTROVERSY (item 1833), pp.
      204-14.

      Reports on the psychological examination of members of
      several religious groups. The authors found that none of the
      subjects showed any intellectual, personality, or mental state
      which would make them unable to make legal judgments. Cults
      provide nourishment for ideological quests as well as relief
      from internal turmoil.

1911. Verdier, Paul A. BRAINWASHING AND THE CULTS: AN EXPOSE ON
      CAPTURING THE MIND. Hollywood, CA: Wilshire Book Co., 1977.
      117 pp.

      Maintains that many cults exploit the relaxation response
      and use mass hypnosis as a method for brainwashing and turning
      their recruits into "glassy-eyed zombies or human robots serv-
      ing selfish masters" (p. 102). Quasi-religious cults use only
      a mild form of brainwashing. The author believes that some
      forms of brainwashing, used in the rehabilitation of criminals,
      education, and psychotherapy, are beneficial.

1912. West, Louis J. "Brainwashing." THE ENCYCLOPEDIA OF MENTAL
      HEALTH. Edited by Albert Deutsch. New York: Franklin
      Watts, 1963, vol. 5, pp. 1748-59.

      Discusses brainwashing or thought reform as practiced by
      the Chinese and North Koreans on American prisoners-of-war.
      The author explains how brainwashing differs from propaganda,
      the ways it is effective, and how it can be resisted.

1913. White, James W. THE SOKAGAKKAI AND MASS SOCIETY. Stanford,
       CA: Stanford University Press, 1970. x, 375 pp.

       Presents a study of a new Japanese religious movement more
       commonly known in the United States as Nichren Shoshu. Part
       One outlines its origin, structure, and politics, and Part
       Two deals with it as a mass movement. Various types of
       structures--vertical lines, peer groups, and functional
       groups--which perform the task of socializing new members
       are described. The author observes that in spite of the
       "magnitude of the system, the member does not feel himself
       the prisoner of an oppressive, indoctrination apparatus.
       The society has managed to keep the apparatus humanized
       through the intimate links built into the vertical line
       substructures" (p. 106).

1914. Winn, Denise. THE MANIPULATED MIND: BRAINWASHING, CONDITION-
       ING, AND INDOCTRINATION. London: Octagon Press, 1983.
       217 pp.

       Looks at the brainwashing processes used by the Chinese on
       prisoners-of-war to determine how they can be used to influ-
       ence people in their daily lives, and to what degree indoctri-
       nation, conditioning, need for social approval, and emotional
       dependency prevent people from being self-directed. In exam-
       ining the Chinese brainwashing system on prisoners-of-war,
       the author shows how: 1) their certainty was undermined by
       forcing them to question beliefs they had taken for granted;
       2) their behavior was shaped by the use of rewards and
       punishments; 3) induced anxiety, guilt, fear, and insecurity
       led to suggestibility and the need to confess; and 4) their
       attitudes finally changed. A chapter on sudden conversion
       discusses cults with particular reference to the Unification
       Church, the Manson family, and Patty Hearst. The author favors
       the theory of cult indoctrination or brainwashing as proposed
       by Margaret Singer (item 1323) and Conway and Siegelman (item
       1188).

1915. Wright, Stuart A. "Post-Involvement Attitudes of Voluntary
       Defectors From Controversial New Religious Movements."
       JOURNAL FOR THE SCIENTIFIC STUDY OF RELIGION 23 (1984):
       172-82.

       Explores the response of voluntary defectors from new re-
       ligious movements. These ex-cult members, who left without
       the aid of deprogramming or therapeutic treatment, do not
       have a romantic idealism of the group they joined. They never
       accuse the cult they belonged to of brainwashing or mind-
       control. On the contrary, they maintain that they joined the
       movement of their own free will and that, sometime after they
       left, they assimilated their learning experience in a con-
       structive way.

1916. Zerin, Marjory Fisher. "The Pied Piper Phenomenon and the
       Processing of Victims: The Transactional Analysis Perspec-
       tive." TRANSACTIONAL ANALYSIS JOURNAL 13 (1983): 172-77.

Contends that the charismatic leaders of modern cult movements, which may have some temporary benign effects on their members, are actually challenging the fabric of society and the stability and continuity of the family. The author compares cult leaders, such as Jim Jones and Charles Manson, with Hitler. She believes that, like the Pied Piper of Hamelin, they are seducing youngsters away from their families and from society into totalistic and mind-controlling movements. Cult members are victims who are indoctrinated by sociological and psychological manipulation into the world view of the cults.

SUBJECT INDEX

(Numbers refer to bibliographical entries.)

Aberle's theory of deprivation,
896.
Abhidhamma, 1477, 1606.
Actualism, 420.
Actualization, 1738.
Acupuncture, 53, 472, 497, 562,
577, 712, 1232, 1723, 1766,
1813, 1820.
Adler and Buddhism, 1428.
Adler's theory of,
mental health, 387.
religion, 254, 1616.
Admiralty Island, New Guinea,
Cargo cult, 889.
Advaita Vedenta, 1574.
Adventist sects, 360.
Aetherius Society, 541, 1200,
1347, 1718.
Afghanistan,
shamanism, 926.
Sufism, 815.
Africa (see also Egypt, Ethio-
pia, Ghana, Liberia,
Nigeria, Tanzanian folk
healing, Yoruba, Zimbabwe),
!Kung healing, 830-31.
Nubian Zar cult, 835.
spirit possession and medium-
ship, 59, 769, 772, 902,
916.
Voodoo, 780, 804.
Xesibe of East Transkei, 867.
Zar cult (see Zar cult).
African indigenous healing,
625, 634-43, 637, 649, 660,
665, 671, 687, 691, 709,
711.
bibliographies, 642-43.
African shamanism (see also
shamanism), 982-83.
African therapists (see African
indigenous healing).
Afro-Americans,
folk healers, 738.

spirit possession and medium-
ship, 59, 902.
supernatural beliefs of, 749.
Afro-Cuban cults (see Santeria).
Aggression and mysticism, 1050.
Agni Yoga (see Yoga).
Ainu shamanism, 996.
Alamo Foundation, 1259, 1305.
Albigenses, 1226, 1321.
Alchemy, 420, 1193, 1346.
Alcoholics Anonymous, 184, 297,
451, 1011, 1209, 1513, 1722,
1744, 1776, 1805, 1822, 1896.
Alcoholism,
and the Native American
Church, 872.
and Transcendental Meditation,
1372-73, 1585.
and Christian Science, 1805.
and Yoga, 1546.
Allport's theory of,
religion, 189, 1141.
religious experience, 109.
religious maturity, 91, 1033.
Almedha, St., 636.
Aloysius Gonzaga, St., asceticism, 196.
Alpert, Richard, 466.
Altered States of Consciousness,
449, 706, 772, 1024, 1043,
1046, 1056, 1083, 1273,
1325, 1857.
bibliography, 59.
and glossalalia, 805-6, 809,
811, 1646.
and meditation, 1279, 1640.
and possession, 766.
and rites of passage, 706.
and shamanism, 997.
and trance, 706.
and Transcendental Meditation,
636, 1385, 1505, 1587, 1596.
and Yoga, 1571, 1596.
and Zen, 1596.

Glossolalia (cont.),
   cross-cultural studies of,
      810-11.
   Cutten's theory of, 501, 551.
   and dissociation, 809, 1690.
   Goodman's theory of, 522-24,
      805-12.
   in Haiti, 768.
   and hallucination, 808.
   history of, 1668.
   Lapsley's theory of, 551,
      558-59,
   in mainline churches, 809.
   and mediumship, 559.
   in non-Christian religions,
      860.
   Oates's theory of, 573, 551.
   Samarin's theory of, 575,
      583-87, 810, 1697.
   and suggestion, 580, 1696.
   and trance, 522-24, 810-11,
      1696.
Gnosticism, 355, 1352.
Golem legend, 1072.
Gourd dance, 668.
Grad's theory of the laying on
   of hands, 388-90.
Graham, Billy, 421, 574, 1642,
   1709, 1878.
Greece, cult of Asclepius, 636,
   708, 857.
Guardian Angels ceremonies
   among the Salish Indians,
   827.
Gurage of Ethiopia, spirit
   possession, 733.
Gurdjieff, 1422, 1474-75, 1789.
Guruism, 1170, 1213, 1334.
Gurus, 1187, 1449, 1958.
   as psychotherapists, 368.
   therapeutic relationship
      with disciples, 700, 1189,
      1239, 1283-84, 1794, 1796,
      1809.
Guyana,
   astrology, 788.
   folk healing in, 736.

Haile Selassie, Emperor of
   Ethiopia,
   and Ras Tafarian movement,
      841, 892.

Haiti,
   spirit possession in, 769,
      771, 911.
   Voodoo in, 636, 768, 836-40,
      877, 893, 1310.
Hallucination,
   and glossolalia, 808.
   and shamanism, 949.
Hamadsha, 644.
Hare Krishna Movement, 170,
      1040, 1188, 1229, 1231,
      1237, 1259, 1281, 1303,
      1305, 1748, 1768, 1790,
      1792-93, 1846, 1857, 1879.
Hasidism, 433, 520, 1011, 1316,
      1672, 1796.
Hasidic Rabbi as psychologist,
      520.
Hawaii,
   Dancing Religion, 853.
Healing (see also laying on of
      hands and therapeutic
      touch),
   history of, 1221.
   of memories, 1080, 1438,
      1652, 1675.
Hearst, Patty, 1914.
Hele tribe, native psychiatry of,
      649.
Hell Fire Culb, 1200.
Hero images, 432.
Herschel, Joshua, mysticism of,
      350.
Hex and possession, 881.
Himalayan International Insti-
      tute, 1281.
Himalayan shamanism, 968.
Hindu astrology, 869.
Hindu festivals in Malaysia, 748.
Hinduism (see also Bhagavad
      Gita), 56, 328.
   bibliography, 2.
Hindu mysticism, 1020.
Hindu psychology (see also
      Bhagavad Gita), 60, 335,
      395, 542.
Hippies and mysticism, 431.
Hitler cult, 1200.
Holiness movements, 348, 396,
      1665-67, 1691.
   bibliography, 27.
Holistic health (see also Holis-
      tic Movement), 1288, 1326,
      1353.